Ethnic Patriotism and the East African Revival

Ethnic Patriotism and the East African Revival shows how, in the era of African nationalism, Christian nonconformists contended with East Africa's patriots over the definition of political communities. The book traces the history of the East African Revival, an evangelical movement that spread through much of eastern and central Africa. Its converts created solidarities outside the framework of convention, disavowing their civic duties and disregarding their obligations to kin. They garnered the ire of East Africa's patriots, who worked to root people within disciplined ethnic cultures. This book casts religious conversion in a new light: not as a private reorientation of belief, but as an act of political criticism that unsettled the inventions of tradition.

Derek R. Peterson teaches African history at the University of Michigan. He is the author of *Creative Writing: Translation, Bookkeeping, and the Work of Imagination in Colonial Kenya* and the editor of several books, including *Recasting the Past: History Writing and Political Work in Modern Africa* and *Abolitionism and Imperialism in Britain, Africa, and the Atlantic*. Peterson is a recipient of the Philip Leverhulme Prize for Modern History and a Fellow of the Royal Historical Society.

African Studies

The African Studies series, founded in 1968, is a prestigious series of monographs, general surveys, and textbooks on Africa, covering history, political science, anthropology, economics, and ecological and environmental issues. The series seeks to publish work by senior scholars as well as the best new research.

A list of books in this series will be found at the end of this volume.

Ethnic Patriotism and the East African Revival

A History of Dissent, c. 1935–1972

DEREK R. PETERSON

University of Michigan, Ann Arbor

CAMBRIDGE
UNIVERSITY PRESS

CAMBRIDGE UNIVERSITY PRESS
Cambridge, New York, Melbourne, Madrid, Cape Town,
Singapore, São Paulo, Delhi, Mexico City

Cambridge University Press
32 Avenue of the Americas, New York, NY 10013-2473, USA

www.cambridge.org
Information on this title: www.cambridge.org/9781107021167

First published 2012

Printed in the United States of America

A catalog record for this publication is available from the British Library.

Library of Congress Cataloging in Publication data
Peterson, Derek R., 1971–
Ethnic patriotism and the East African Revival : a history of dissent,
c. 1935–1972 / Derek R. Peterson, University of Michigan, Ann Arbor.
pages cm. – (African studies series ; 122)
Includes bibliographical references and index.
ISBN 978-1-107-02116-7
1. Christianity and politics – Africa, East – History – 20th century.   2. East Africa
Revival – History.   3. Conversion – Christianity.   4. Christianity and culture – Africa,
East.   5. Africa, East – Church history – 20th century.   I. Title.
BR115.P7P445   2012
305.6′7676082–dc23   2012012618

ISBN 978-1-107-02116-7 Hardback

For Adeline Mbabazi

Contents

List of Figures

Archives Abbreviations

ACK	Anglican Church of Kenya archives
AIM	Africa Inland Mission archives
Bristol	Imperial and Commonwealth Museum
Churchill	Churchill College archives, University of Cambridge
CMS	Church Missionary Society archives, Birmingham
CMS Oxford	Church Missionary Society archives, Oxford
Cory	Hans Cory papers, University of Dar es Salaam
CoU	Church of Uganda Provincial Archives
DCT	Diocese of Central Tanganyika archives
ELCT	Evangelical Lutheran Church of Tanzania, Northwestern Diocese archives
EUL	Edinburgh University Library archives
GW	Gakaara wa Wanjau papers, Yale University Library
HDA	Hoima District Archives
HMC	Henry Martyn Centre archives
JML	Entebbe Secretariat Archives, notes in possession of Prof. John Lonsdale
KabDA	Kabarole District Archives
KabDio	Diocese of Kabarole archives
Kahigwa	George Kahigwa papers
Kakamega	Kenya National Archives, Kakamega Provincial Records Centre
KasDA	Kasese District Archives
KigDA	Kigezi District Archives
Kisumu	Kenya National Archives, Kisumu Provincial Records Centre
KNA	Kenya National Archives
KTA	Kikuyu Traders Association papers
LSE	London School of Economic archives
Makerere	Makerere University Library archives

MAM	Mid-Africa Ministry archives
Mbarara	Ankole District Archives
Muchwa	Toro Government archives
Murray papers	Jocelyn Murray papers, London Mennonite Centre
Murugwanza	Diocese of Ngara archives
Mwanza	Tanzania National Archives, Mwanza Regional Records Centre
NAB	National Archives of Britain
NLS	National Library of Scotland
NMK	National Museum of Kenya
PCEA	Presbyterian Church of East Africa archives
RH	Rhodes House Library, University of Oxford
Rubaga	Archdiocese of Kampala archives
Rwamishenye	Bukoba District Archives
SOAS	School of Oriental and African Studies archives
St. Peter's	Diocese of Kigezi archives
TNA	Tanzania National Archives
TT	Tumutumu Church archives
UNA	Uganda National Archives
Virika	Catholic Diocese of Fort Portal archives
WFM	White Fathers Mission archives

Preface and Acknowledgments

History is playing a leading role in eastern Africa's political theater. In Tanzania, Maasai pastoralists have adopted the grammar of the indigenous peoples' movement in order to claim recognition and resources from the state.[1] In Kenya, the Kalenjin – an ethnic group that did not exist prior to the 1950s – are identifying themselves as the natives of the Rift Valley. Their political leaders thereby establish their position on contested terrain, making Gikuyu immigrants into outsiders.[2] In Uganda, the kingdoms of Buganda, Bunyoro, Busoga, and Toro – banned since 1967 – have been officially reconstituted as 'cultural institutions.' The musty ceremony of royalism has found a central place in Uganda's public sphere, and there has been a flurry of publications – books of proverbs, folktales, and historical narratives – that look to the past for moral and political guidance.

Confronted with these opportunistic uses of the past, professional scholars have responded by showing how Africa's political entrepreneurs intentionally manipulate, homogenize, and invent their people's history. This book takes a different approach. It investigates political and cultural actions that neither conformed to the template of tradition nor settled into the position of indigeneity. The modern-day brokers of autochthony are absolutists about culture: they insist that dissidents must conform, that immigrants and other interlopers must assimilate, and that wives and daughters must unthinkingly accept their elders' guidance. East African politics needs alternatives. It needs historians of idealism, utopias imagined and realized. It also needs histories of nonconformism. This book is a history of a religious movement whose converts journeyed outside their native homelands. I take conversion to be a critical practice, an act that set people in motion and obliged them to live across borders. In their own time, converts unsettled the conventions

[1] Dorothy Hodgson, *Being Maasai, Becoming Indigenous: Postcolonial Politics in a Neoliberal World* (Bloomington, IN, 2011).
[2] Gabrielle Lynch, *I Say to You: Ethnic Politics and the Kalenjin of Kenya* (Chicago, 2011).

of tradition and unmasked the fictions of nativism. It is my hope that this book will help to advance a dissident politics of cultural criticism in eastern Africa today.

In the course of my research I worked in a great number of archives, and I am tremendously grateful to the archivists who offered me their help. I worked particularly closely with Mr. Okello Ajum Alex and Ms. Justine Nalwoga of the Uganda National Archives in Entebbe. They are currently cataloging the files in the archives' vault, making the UNA into a space that enables critical reflection on Uganda's history. Mrs. Christine Byaruhanga, the archivist of the newly renovated archive of the Church of Uganda, has become a valued friend and colleague. In Fort Portal, the Kabarole District Archives – formerly kept in a wasp-infested, leaky attic – have now been transferred to a storeroom at Mountains of the Moon University. It has been a great pleasure to work with Mr. Evarist Ngabirano, Prof. John Kasenene, and other colleagues to preserve this important collection. In Tanzania, I worked closely with Mr. Herman Rwechungura of the Mwanza Regional Archives Depot and the Right Rev. Mdimi Mhogolo, Bishop of the Diocese of Central Tanganyika, who kindly gave me access to the diocesan archives in Dodoma. In Nairobi, a dedicated team led by Mr. Peterson Kithuka and Mr. Richard Ambani have made the Kenya National Archives into a model of efficiency. Mr. Lukas Alube helped me use the diocesan archive of the Anglican Church of Kenya; and Ms. Immelda Kithuka guided me through the important collections in the National Museum of Kenya. Over several years I had the pleasure of working closely with colleagues at the Henry Martyn Centre in Cambridge, which has become a pivotally important collection for the study of worldwide Christian evangelicalism. I thank Prof. John Iliffe, who allowed me to read through his handwritten notes on files held in the Tanzania National Archives, and Prof. John Lonsdale, whose notes on the Entebbe Secretariat Archives – taken in the late 1960s – are an invaluable resource. Nick Godfrey conducted preliminary research on my behalf in the Belgian archives, Susan Tilby translated material from the archives of White Fathers Mission, and Beth Philips helped to organize my research notes and transcribe interviews. I am very thankful for their help.

My most profound debts are to the priests, historians, and activists who were my translators and guides during the course of this research. In Fort Portal, Rev. Richard Baguma – the Toro kingdom's leading historian – introduced me to a network of officials and activists. His insights into western Uganda's political history have vitally shaped my thinking. Rev. Canon John Basingwire was my guide during a period of interviewing in southern Uganda. He folded me into his pastoral itinerary, and in his lively presence my dry interview questions were transformed into vital conversations about life history. Rev. Fareth Sendegeya took time from his busy schedule to organize a program of interviews for me with converts in Ngara in northwestern Tanzania. In Hoima, David Kato introduced me to a large network of Nyoro revivalists; and in western Kenya, Mr. Henry Adera helped me conduct interviews with Luo patriots and converts. Mr. Ezron Muhumuza organized my research work in the remote parts of Uganda's Rwenzori Mountains, and it has been a pleasure to learn with him about the history of the Rwenzururu movement. Billington Mwangi Gituto and Joseph Kariuki Muriithi – formerly my research assistants – have become my valued friends and interlocutors. Marcy and Muhia Karianjahi, Kyama and Wambui Mugambi, Johanna and Judy Kishoiyian, Godfrey Asiimwe, John Basingwire, Arthur Syahuka-Muhindo, Andrew State, Christopher Muhoozi, and other friends and colleagues in Uganda, Kenya, and Tanzania have enlivened my research work with their hospitality and their ideas. This book bears their imprint.

My research for this book was supported by the Leverhulme Trust, whose Philip Leverhulme Prize gave me valuable time away from my duties at Cambridge. Further funding was provided by the British Academy, which financed several trips to eastern Africa; the American Philosophical Association, whose Franklin Research Grant financed my research in Tanzania; and the Smuts Fund for Commonwealth Studies at the University of Cambridge. The Uganda National Council of Science and Technology granted me permission to conduct research in Uganda, and I am grateful to Ms. Leah Nawegulo and her staff for their help. During my work in Uganda, I was made a research associate of the Makerere Institute for Social Research, and I thank MISR's former Director, Prof. Nakanyike Musisi, its former Research Secretary, Mr. Patrick Mulindwa, and its current Director, Prof. Mahmood Mamdani, for the kindnesses they extended to me. I thank also the staff and faculty in the Department of History at Makerere, who provided a welcoming base from which to work. In Tanzania, the Commission for Science and Technology authorized my research, and I thank Ms. Hulda Gideon and her staff for their assistance. The Department of History at the University of Dar es Salaam was my institutional home, and I thank its former chair, Prof. Bertram Mapunda, and my friend and mentor Prof. Fred Kaijage for their generosity.

This book was very largely composed during my time as lecturer at Cambridge University, and Cambridge's unique intellectual culture shaped both the writing and the argument. I had the distinct pleasure of working with three eminent Africanists – John Iliffe, Megan Vaughan, and John Lonsdale – in whose benevolent shade my ideas matured. John Iliffe's pioneering book on honor in African history helped me to see etiquette as a matter of political consequence, and Megan Vaughan's work on food and environmental change fertilized my analysis of family life in eastern Africa.

My most profound debt is to John Lonsdale. I came to know John during my first years in graduate school, and during the years I spent in Cambridge I greatly valued his companionship. This book is an extension of his vitally important work on the moral economy of ethnicity in eastern Africa. At the University of Michigan, my home since 2009, I have found a congenial and lively community of colleagues who have helped me broaden and refine my thinking. I particularly thank Rebecca Scott, Nancy Hunt, Gabrielle Hecht, Adam Ashforth, Kelly Askew, Kevin Gaines, Anne Pitcher, Martin Murray, and Butch Ware, with whom I look forward to working in the coming years.

A number of people read and commented on parts of this manuscript. I thank Jesse Bucher, John Iliffe, Emma Hunter, Jim Brennan, Nelson Kasfir, Michael Twaddle, Isabel Hofmeyr, Stephanie Newell, Matthew Carotenuto, Omedi Ochieng, Ezron Muhumuza, Chandra Mallampalli, Joel Cabrita, Julie MacArthur, Jon Earle, Shane Doyle, and Paul Bjerk. Darren Walhof has long been a source of ideas and insight. Kevin Ward helped me think through this project in its earliest stages. Tim Parsons was my first teacher in the method of historical research in Africa. He made extraordinarily helpful comments on this manuscript, challenging me to lift my eyes from the trees to see the forest. Allen Isaacman and Jean Allman, formerly my dissertation advisors, are now valued friends and mentors, and I continue to learn from their example. Chapters from this manuscript were presented at seminars at the University of Chicago, Washington University at St. Louis, the University of Minnesota, Westmont College, Emory University, the University of Basel, the University of Edinburgh, the School of Oriental and African Studies, Oxford University, Princeton University, and at several seminars in Cambridge and in Ann Arbor. I am grateful for the invigorating questions I was asked at each of these gatherings. Eric Crahan, Abigail Zorbaugh, and their colleagues at Cambridge University Press have been a pleasure to work with. Philip Stickler and his staff at the Cartography Unit at the University of Cambridge drew the maps. In a different form, Chapter 6 was first published in Emma Wild-Wood and Kevin Ward, eds., *The East African Revival: History and Legacies* (Kampala, 2010). A different version of Chapter 9 was previously published in *Research in African Literatures* 37 (2006), in a special issue on 'Creative Writing in African Languages' edited by Karin Barber and Graham Furniss. Part of Chapter 10 was published as 'The Intellectual Lives of Mau Mau Detainees,' in the *Journal of African History* 49 (2008), and part of Chapter 11 was published in Derek R. Peterson and Giacomo Macola, eds., *Recasting the Past: History Writing and Political Work in Modern Africa* (Athens, OH, 2009).

As I finished the first draft of this book, my wife and I welcomed our daughter Adeline Mbabazi Peterson into our family. Her middle name – Mbabazi – means 'mercy,' 'grace,' or 'wonderment' at a gift one is given. It is one among several names coined by Ugandan converts of the Revival. At a time when many parents gave their children names that reflected pessimism about their mortality, converts identified children as a gift from God.[3] I dedicate this book to Adeline Mbabazi, as a small acknowledgment of the great gift that I have been given.

Ann Arbor
May 2012

[3] Shane Doyle, '"The Child of Death": Personal Names and Parental Attitudes Towards Mortality in Bunyoro, Western Uganda,' *Journal of African History* 49 (3) (2008), 361–82.

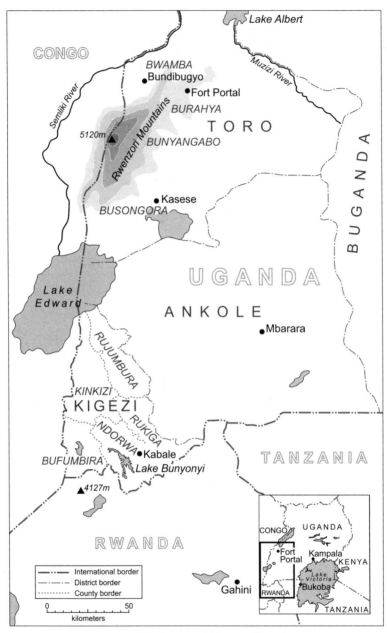

MAP I. Southern and Western Uganda.

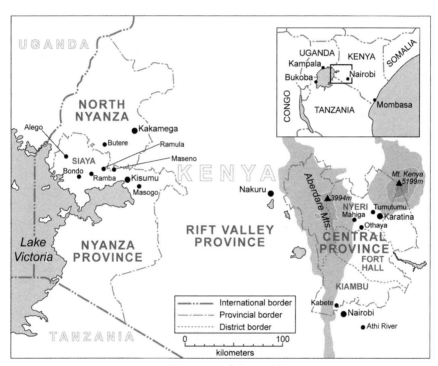

MAP 2. Western and Central Kenya.

MAP 3. Northwestern Tanganyika.

I

Introduction

The Pilgrims' Politics

It is August 1949, and several thousand people have gathered at Kabete, in central Kenya, to work on their autobiographies. They are converts of the East African Revival, a Christian conversion movement that began in northern Rwanda in the mid-1930s. The Kabete gathering is a cultural and linguistic hodge-podge: most in the congregation are Gikuyu people, but there are Luo men and women from western Kenya, Swahili speakers from the Indian Ocean coast, and a few Maasai women. A missionary takes a photograph. In blurred outline it shows people leaning forward, some on their knees. They think themselves to be on the cusp of a new life. 'Come, let us reason together,' reads the biblical text on the banner behind the speakers' platform. 'Though your sins be as scarlet, they shall be white as snow.'[1] These people are practicing forensics, contrasting the past with the future, and creating life histories. 'Imagine at the end of the day member after member of the audience coming forward, making confession of sin, and relating what Christ has done for him,' wrote a missionary observer.

Some of these, men and women known to be devout, are received quietly. The signature chorus of the revival is sung, and there is an occasional word or handshake from those nearby. Others known or felt to be insecure or partial in their witness are received in silence or by the singing of a hymn enjoining them to seek salvation. Still others, known to be careless or evil livers, whose witness rings true … are received in scenes of great enthusiasm. People start to their feet, singing. They throw their hands into the air and crowd round the person, all trying to shake his hand. His relatives and friends embrace him.[2]

The convention at Kabete was an arena where techniques of self-accounting could be practiced and a forum for the creation of autobiographical narratives. It was a court of judgment. It was also a point of departure. Converts' testimonies could propel them into a new life.

[1] PCEA II/C/22: Martin Capon to Philip Mitchell, September 1949.
[2] Robert MacPherson, 'The East African Revival,' *Kikuyu News* 193 (September 1950).

PHOTO 1. Kabete Convention, 1949. Photo by Gladys Beecher. Courtesy of the National Museum of Kenya.

Not everyone looked favorably on the revivalists and their self-propulsive testimonies. The British authorities who governed colonial Kenya worried about the aggressive character of revivalist preaching. Civil order seemed to be at risk. 'A stirring of souls is excellent,' wrote the District Commissioner shortly after the Kabete convention, 'but a stoking of fires hidden far below the smiling exterior of the African pagan can only lead to bloodshed and great bitterness.'[3] African political thinkers were likewise convinced that the Kabete autobiographers were troublemakers, undermining traditional standards of behavior. 'Christianity is love, compassion without end, great patience, and great civility,' wrote the newspaperman Henry Muoria in a Gikuyu-language pamphlet. 'But when it's taken to mean people confessing with their mouth, shouting loudly what they believe in and what others believe, such Christianity is what loud-mouthed and self-centered people conceive.'[4] Muoria and other Gikuyu thinkers thought revivalists were advancing themselves at other people's expense. 'Anyone who says that he is joyful when many of our people are oppressed slaves and left in landless poverty is deceiving himself in the hope of the good things he will get in heaven when he is dead,' wrote an editorialist shortly after the Kabete convention. 'Men who help themselves get justice.'[5] Patriotic men argued that Gikuyu people should work for the betterment of the commonwealth.

[3] KNA DC Fort Hall 1/26: Fort Hall District Annual Report, 1949.
[4] Henry Muoria, 'What Shall We Do, Our People?,' in Henry Muoria, *Writing for Kenya: The Life and Works of Henry Muoria*, eds. Wangari Muoria-Sal, Bodil Folke Fredericksen, John Lonsdale, and Derek R. Peterson (Leiden, 2009), 147.
[5] ACK 'North Highlands Rural Deanery' file: Extract from *Mumenyereri*, 9 December 1949.

They sought to build a community whose manners and comportment was evidence of their capacity for self-government. In their view, revivalists were delinquent in their civic duty: their never-ending sermons destroyed concord, undermined social discipline, and fractured community.

In this book, I use the controversy over the Revival as a lens through which to explore the social history of dissent in eastern Africa. Since the publication of Eric Hobsbawm and Terence Ranger's *The Invention of Tradition* in 1983, the Cambridge University Library has catalogued 223 books with titles beginning with 'The Invention of.'[6] A great variety of social formations – Somalia, Argentina, race, and religion, to name a few – have been shown to be constructs crafted by self-interested entrepreneurs, not holdovers from the distant past.[7] The book was particularly influential in shaping the method of African cultural history, and there are now a number of studies showing how tribes – previously thought to be organic to African political life – were conjured into being.[8] The constructivists have drawn the veil from the face of apparently timeless cultural practices, exposing their human origins and scrutinizing their claims to authenticity. But the constructivist literature makes it seem as though historical precedent was the only means by which cultural innovations could be authenticated. There is little space to consider how the inventors of tradition convinced doubting constituents to acknowledge a normative account of history as their own. Neither is there space to study interruptions in the onward march of historical time, eschatons, resurrections, or new eras. The 'invention of tradition' paradigm obliges scholars to focus on the small cadre of elites who identified ancestors, configured culture as heritage, and called new communities into being. It can do little to illuminate the logic of nonconformism.[9]

At Kabete, converts created solidarities outside the framework of cultural convention. Ethnicity in central Kenya, as elsewhere in eastern Africa, was a forum of argument, not an invented tradition to which people were obliged to conform.[10] Revivalists and their patriotic critics spoke the same

---

[6] Eric Hobsbawm and Terence Ranger, eds., *The Invention of Tradition* (Cambridge, 1983).

[7] Ali Ahmed, ed., *The Invention of Somalia* (Lawrenceville, NJ, 1995); Nicolas Shumway, *The Invention of Argentina* (Berkeley, 1991); Tommy Lott, *The Invention of Race: Black Culture and the Politics of Representation* (Malden, MA, 1999); A. A. Huemer, *The Invention of 'Race': the Columbian Turn in Modern Consciousness* (Lander, WY, 1998); Derek R. Peterson and Darren Walhof, eds., *The Invention of Religion: Rethinking Belief in Politics and History* (New Brunswick, 2002); Tomoko Masuzawa, *The Invention of World Religions* (Chicago, 2005).

[8] The key text was Leroy Vail, ed., *The Creation of Tribalism in Southern Africa* (Berkeley, 1989).

[9] Thomas Spear criticizes the constructivist literature on different grounds in 'Neo-Traditionalism and the Limits of Invention in British Colonial Africa,' *Journal of African History* 44 (1) (2003), 3–27.

[10] This is a thesis I derive from John Lonsdale, 'The Moral Economy of Mau Mau: Wealth, Poverty, and Civic Virtue in Kikuyu Political Thought,' in Lonsdale and Bruce Berman,

vernacular languages, but they constructed dramatically different accounts of history and positioned themselves differently in the social world. Morally conservative patriotisms were being formed all over postwar eastern Africa, as men came to feel themselves responsible for women to whom they were not directly related. Thousands of men were drawn to eastern Africa's cosmopolitan cities, where they were enclosed within a competitive, masculine world. Searching for means to generate social capital and prove their merit, men set to work creating institutions that would uphold social discipline and protect their reputations as Gikuyu, Luo, Haya, Toro, or Ganda people. They invented or refurbished customary legal codes, founded tribal welfare associations, wrote inspirational history, conducted anti-prostitution campaigns, and constituted nativisms. These self-interested activists constructed political community as a *patria*, a fatherland, rooting people in place as inheritors of their ancestors' instructive customs and traditions. Revivalists would not comport themselves as patriotic sons and daughters of the soil. Converts thought of themselves as pilgrims on the road toward another home. They were drawn together by their mastery over certain forms of self-presentation. In venues like the Kabete convention, they learned how to document their sins, describe their conversions, and chronicle their movements toward another life. Revivalists were inveterate travelers, avid users of the post office, and eager participants in the evangelical media. By attending cosmopolitan gatherings like the Kabete convention and through the exchange of autobiographical correspondence, revivalists came to see themselves as part of a large, transcontinental community of fellow travelers.

Seen through the eyes of eastern Africa's conservative reformers, converts were dangerous: they were displaced, unattached, and uncommitted to their natal communities. Revivalists willfully ignored the lessons that history taught about comportment, gentility, and respectability. Whereas patriotic organizers taught their constituents to behave with discipline and decorum, converts gossiped endlessly about their private lives. Patriotic organizers sought to impose discipline on troublesome converts. In northwestern Tanganyika, northern Rwanda, and southern Uganda, local government authorities barred converts from speaking or singing in public. In western Kenya, Luo patriots founded a church that they called the *Johera*, the 'People of Love,' as a rebuke to antisocial, aggressive revivalists. In central Kenya, the earnest patriots of the Mau Mau movement promised to fight for *wīathi*, for social discipline and self-mastery. Revivalists were their leading antagonists.

Scholars have said very little about the field of argument that revivalism generated. The historiography of the Revival has very largely been composed

Unhappy Valley: Conflict in Kenya and Africa (London, 1992), 315–504; and restated in Lonsdale, 'Moral and Political Argument in Kenya,' in Bruce Berman, Dickson Eyoh, and Will Kymlicka, eds., *Ethnicity and Democracy in Africa* (Oxford, 2004), 73–95.

as hagiography.[11] African converts were avid producers of autobiography (see Chapter 9), and some testimonies found their way into print in circular letters, newspapers, or books. There are now dozens of books published by evangelical presses that present revivalists' biographies as evidence of God's work in eastern Africa.[12] Bundled together between the covers of the book, it is easy to lift converts' earnest testimonies out of the polemical context in which they were composed. The back cover of one such collection invites readers to 'sense the freedom from bondage to heathen practices as [God's people] prove by their lives the God of the Bible to be the only true God.'[13] Packaged in this way, converts' autobiographies become inspirational literature, placeless, anodyne affirmations of the universal truths of Christianity.

In *Ethnic Patriotism and the East African Revival*, I disassemble the books published by evangelical presses, rip revivalists' testimonies out of their earnestly inspirational milieu and place them in the rhetorical context in which they were composed. Revivalists' autobiographies were subversive literature. Converts offered a contentious reading of their contemporary world: they sorted through cultures and traditions, identified their sins, disavowed their pagan contemporaries, and fashioned new lives for themselves. Their autobiographical work took place within a discursive field in which other entrepreneurs were also working over the past. In eastern Africa's several *patriae*, political entrepreneurs were identifying the historical grounds for moral discipline and creating ethnic homelands. On this political field converts acted as subversives, willfully upsetting the order of tradition. They were dissenters on the field of etiquette, manners, and social convention – a field that patriotic organizers sought by all means to regiment. Whereas patriotic men sought to confine constituents to a particular

---

[11] The most important exception is Catherine Robbins' excellent but unpublished dissertation '*Tukutendereza*: A Study of Social Change and Sectarian Withdrawal in the *Balokole* Revival of Uganda' (PhD dissertation, Columbia University, 1975).

[12] Herbert Osborn, *Pioneers in the East African Revival* (Eastbourne, 2000); Osborn, *Revival: A Precious Heritage* (Eastbourne, 1995); Osborn, *The Living Legacy of the East African Revival* (Eastbourne, 2006); Osborn, *Revival: God's Spotlight* (Crowborough, East Sussex, 1996); Festo Kivengere with Dorothy Smoker, *Revolutionary Love* (Fort Washington, PA, 1983); Edith Wiseman, *Kikuyu Martyrs* (London, 1958); Colin Reed, *Walking in the Light: Reflections on the East African Revival and its Link to Australia* (Victoria, 2007); Patricia St. John, *Breath of Life: The Story of the Ruanda Mission* (London, 1971); Bill Butler, *Hill Ablaze* (London, 1976); Mark Noll and Carolyn Nystrom, *Clouds of Witnesses: Christian Voices from Africa and Asia* (Downer's Grove, IL, 2011). African converts have published their own conversion stories: see Obadiah Kariuki, *A Bishop Facing Mount Kenya: An Autobiography, 1902–1978* (Nairobi, 1985); Festo Olang,' *Festo Olang': An Autobiography* (Nairobi, 1991); and John Gatu, *Joyfully Christian, Truly African* (Nairobi, 2006). Church historians are using this biographical literature to explain the changing demographic complexion of world Christianity: see, for example, Mark Noll, *The New Shape of World Christianity: How American Experience Reflects Global Faith* (Downers Grove, IL, 2007).

[13] Dorothy Smoker, *Ambushed by Love: God's Triumph in Kenya's Terror* (Fort Washington, PA, 1993).

homeland, converts lived on the road. Whereas patriots promoted vernacular languages as a mark of ethnic solidarity, converts were cosmopolitans, learning a variety of tongues. Whereas patriots sought to cultivate ties of love and affection among their ethnic confreres, converts composed their life stories in relation to an international ecumene. And whereas patriots shaped their constituents' manners to accord with traditional norms, converts comported themselves without reserve.

In the study of the Revival, we can see religious conversion in a different light: not as an inward reorientation in religious conviction, but as a political action that opens novel paths of self-narration, constitutes new ways of living, and unsettles the inventions of tradition. Conversion was a form of political and cultural criticism.

GENEALOGIES OF CONVERSION

The emphasis in scholarly writing about Christianity in Africa has been on continuity, on the underlying structure that guided Africans' engagements with 'world religions.' In theology, as in anthropology and history, the old religion is conceived as a foundation, establishing the symbolic and discursive categories through which Africans interpreted Christianity. As Joel Robbins has shown, the model is based on a homogenized conception of time in which change is conceived not as an event but as a perpetual process.[14] Even where converts describe the process of becoming Christian as a radical transformation in their lives, scholars see it as their task to uncover the continuities that link converts with their native religions and cultures.

This way of thinking about religious history is to a large extent derived from Protestant missionaries' evangelistic strategy. Missionaries sought to build on the old religion, not to supplant it.[15] Their model was the Apostle Paul's discourse at the Areopagus at Athens, described in Acts 17. In his homily, Paul offered a definition for the 'Unknown God,' a character who the Athenians had hitherto worshipped in ignorance. Paul gave this character a history (he 'made the world and all things therein') and an identity ('in him we live, and move, and have our being'), and then invited his listeners to repent of their sins. For the Anglican divine Christopher Wordsworth, whose 1857 commentary on Acts was read widely by his British contemporaries, Paul's speech at Athens was 'the model and pattern to all Christian missionaries for

---

[14] Joel Robbins, 'Continuity Thinking and the Problem of Christian Culture: Belief, Time, and the Anthropology of Christianity,' *Current Anthropology* 48 (1) (February 2007), 5–38.
[15] Argued in Lamin Sanneh, *Translating the Message: The Missionary Impact on Culture* (Maryknoll, NY, 1989); and in Andrew Walls, *The Missionary Movement in Christian History* (Maryknoll, NY, 1996). There were exceptions to this generalization: German Pietists, for example, thought the spirits of Ewe cosmology to be satanic. See Birgit Meyer, *Translating the Devil: Religion and Modernity among the Ewe in Ghana* (Trenton, NJ, 1999).

their addresses to the heathen world.'[16] With Paul's example before them, Protestant missionaries set out to identify, name, and preach about unknown Gods. Through this work they established the architecture of the old religion and related the new Christian religion to the vernacular vocabulary.

Christian missionaries in Africa were therefore the first systematic theologians of traditional religion.[17] The earliest missionaries in central Tanganyika lamented the poverty of the Gogo vernacular language. 'They have no idea of the purity of God or of that righteousness which is essential to a person becoming a member of his Kingdom,' wrote the Anglican missionary J. T. Last in March 1881. 'They have no literature, or any traditions likely to lead their minds to discover a higher state of righteousness.'[18] But in August of that same year, Last began to compose a dictionary. He ruled a notebook in parallel columns, with English at the left side and Gogo at the right. Then he 'wrote down what I thought were the most suitable [English] words from A to Z in their proper places, and then, as I found the native words I had only to put them down in the places allotted to them.'[19] In their dictionaries, missionary linguists imposed an order on the intransigent vernacular. Four handwritten English-Gogo dictionaries have survived in the archives.[20] On their pages, missionaries established correspondences between generic religious concepts and Gogo words. 'God' was *Mulungu*. 'Believe' was *-ihuwila*. 'Sacrifice' was *-ikumbiko*. With the vocabulary aligned on the page, missionaries found it easy to appreciate the Gogo religion. 'Their language is remarkably complete; their traditions are such as to amply repay the time and effort required to master them; while their parables and tribal laws are assets of no mean value,' wrote one missionary.[21] In 1902, the long-serving missionary Henry Cole published an essay on the Gogo in the *Journal of the Anthropological Institute*.[22] He was guided by the 'Ethnological Questions' that the Cambridge anthropologist J. G. Frazer had circulated in the course of his research for *The Golden Bough*.[23] 'Do

---

[16] Christopher Wordsworth, *The New Testament of our Lord and Saviour Jesus Christ: In the Original Greek* (London, 1857), 86.

[17] Argued in Paul Landau, '"Religion" and Christian Conversion in African History: A New Model,' *Journal of Religious History* 23 (1) (February 1999), 8–30; and in David Chidester, *Savage Systems: Colonialism and Comparative Religion in Southern Africa* (Charlottesville, 1996).

[18] CMS G3 A5 O: J. T. Last to Hutchinson, 18 March 1881.

[19] CMS G3 A5 O: J. T. Last to Whiting, 8 August 1881.

[20] DCT 'English Cigogo Dictionary,' n.d. (labeled 'Canon Hugh Prentice and Dr. Dorothy Prentice'); 'Cigogo Vocabulary,' n.d.; 'English-Cigogo Dictionary,' n.d.; 'Cigogo Dictionary,' n.d.

[21] T. Westgate, 'The Home of the Wagogo,' *Church Missionary Gleaner* XXXCI (1909).

[22] Henry Cole, 'Notes on the Wagogo of German East Africa,' *Journal of the Anthropological Institute of Great Britain and Ireland* 32 (1902), 305–38.

[23] Published in J. G. Frazer, 'Questions on the Manners, Customs, Religion, Superstitions &c. of Uncivilized or Semi-Civilized Peoples,' *Journal of the Royal Anthropological Institute* 18 (1889), 431–40. See J. G. Frazer, *The Golden Bough* (London, 1890), xxx.

they practice magic or witchcraft?,' asked Frazer. 'Do they think that human beings have souls?' 'Are sacrifices offered?' Henry Cole answered each question in turn by describing Gogo 'sacrifices,' documenting Gogo views on the 'soul,' and charting their conception of the afterlife.

Missionaries like Cole identified a terminology and a set of practices that could be named as an indigenous religion. Once the linguistic and theological foundation was in place, missionaries could compare the old religion with the new revelation. In 1886, while traveling through Gogo country, the missionary J. C. Price met with a group of elders who inquired after his purpose in visiting them.[24] 'I have come into Ugogo only to tell you something you do not know about the God who gives you food, rain, life and strength, for His Son came down from heaven,' Price declared. Price was taking a Gogo term – *Mulungu*, 'God' – and placing it within a Christian framework. When someone asked Price how to pray to God, Price told him to 'go and speak to God alone, away from everybody else.' Missionaries established a novel set of practices by which Gogo people could relate to a God whom they had hitherto known only distantly. The work of theological consolidation always involved a process of selection. When someone asked Price about *uganga* – which the dictionaries defined as 'witchcraft' – and *nkhumbiko* – the 'sacrifices' that Gogo people made to their ancestors – Price told him that 'they were all no use – he was simply to pray, to speak to, God.' Edited in this way, the old religion became a *preparatio evangeli*, setting up the vocabularic and intellectual structures with which the Christian gospel could be preached.

In the 1960s, the decade of Africa's political independence, a generation of African theologians returned to the dictionaries and anthropological studies that missionaries had composed, using them as evidence with which to reconstruct the logic and character of African Traditional Religion. They were driven by pressingly political concerns. African nation-builders were busily sorting out their cultural property, identifying legal codes, languages, musical genres, and styles of dress that were authentically African.[25] Theologians, too, worked to build the nation. The Kenyan theologian John Mbiti was appointed lecturer at Makerere University's Department of Religious Studies and Philosophy in 1964. As a matter of urgency, he established a new course on 'African Religions' and in 1969 published his lecture notes under the title *African Religions and Philosophies*.[26] He had

---

[24] The material in this paragraph comes from CMS G3 A5 O: J. C. Price to Lang, 1 February 1886.

[25] Kelly Askew, *Performing the Nation: Swahili Music and Cultural Politics in Tanzania* (Chicago, 2002); Andrew Ivaska, *Cultured States: Youth, Gender, and Modern Style in 1960s Dar es Salaam* (Durham, NC, 2011); Jean Allman, ed., *Fashioning Africa: Power and the Politics of Dress* (Bloomington, IN, 2004).

[26] John Mbiti, *African Religions and Philosophy* (New York, 1969). An assessment of Mbiti's work is in Jacob K. Olupona and Sulayman S. Nyang, eds., *Religious Plurality in Africa: Essays in Honour of John S. Mbiti* (Berlin, 1993).

missionaries' dictionaries open before him as he composed his lectures. Like Protestant missionaries, Mbiti sought to illuminate the logic of the old religion, casting African Traditional Religion as an integrated system of rituals and symbols that paralleled Christianity. With the vocabularic evidence before them, Mbiti and his contemporaries argued that, prior to Christian missionaries' arrival, Africans had already known God.[27] Their foreknowledge made it easy for Africans to fold their traditional ideas about divinity into missionaries' monotheism, making African Christianity an extension of the old religion. In Mbiti's 1975 *Introduction to African Religion*, 'conversion' does not even appear in the index.[28] Mbiti and his generation of religion scholars agreed that conversion was of little consequence. Africans, argued the Kenyan theologian J. N. K. Mugambi, 'do not have to choose between being Christian and being African. They can be both Christian and African at the same time.'[29]

The anthropological study of African religion developed alongside the enterprise of African theology, and, like the theologians, anthropologists emphasized the continuities joining old religions with new religions. Robin Horton's seminal essays on 'African conversion' set the agenda.[30] For Horton, conversion to a monotheistic religion, whether Christianity or Islam, was not a rupture between one way of life and another. Conversion was an organic social process through which Africans rearranged the elements of traditional cosmology. Africans had once lived in a microcosmic world, argued Horton, where religious practice focused on local tutelary spirits. Ideas about the macrocosmic, overarching Supreme Being were vague and unformed. With the advent of the modern world – the enlargement of scale, the improvement of communications, and the rise of nation-states – Africans were obliged to develop a code for the governance of wider life. They therefore clarified their hitherto unformed ideas about a Supreme Being, and some converted to one of the 'world religions.' Horton's thesis helpfully linked the study of religious change to the study of politics and economy. But like the theologians, Horton and those who followed him were disinterested in converts' consciousness. They preferred to focus on the material, political interests that prompted Africans to convert. For the anthropologist John Peel, the most pertinent questions were 'Why conversion occurred when it did (rather

---

[27] Mbiti's contemporaries included E. Bolaji Idowu, whose *Olodumare: God in Yoruba Belief* (London, 1962) and *African Traditional Religion: A Definition* (London, 1973) had a profound effect on the field.

[28] Mbiti, *Introduction to African Religion* (Portsmouth, NH, 1975).

[29] J. N. K. Mugambi, *African Heritage and Contemporary Christianity* (Nairobi, 1989), 22.

[30] Robin Horton, 'African Conversion,' *Africa: Journal of the International African Institute* 41 (2) (1971), 85–108. See also Robin Horton, 'On the Rationality of Conversion, Part I,' *Africa: Journal of the International African Institute* 45 (3) (1975), 219–35. For criticism, see Humphrey Fisher, 'Conversion Reconsidered,' *Africa: Journal of the International African Institute* 43 (1) (1973), 27–40.

than earlier or later) ... why it attracted the social categories that it did, why it moved through the society in the way that it did ... or why it created the disruption that it did (relative to comparable other places).'[31] In his foundational *Religious Encounter and the Making of the Yoruba*, Peel argued that converts' criteria of judgment were necessarily drawn from their 'prior cultural repertory.' Because these purposes had guided converts' decisions to convert, they were 'likely to continue as a substrate of the new beliefs and practices, whatever novelties may inhere in or follow from the fact of conversion itself.'[32] In Peel's view, the basic impulse guiding Yoruba people's engagements with the Christian religion was the search for power and prestige. 'To be really attractive, an identity must be such that people can see themselves adopting it without too much of a break with previous social commitments ... as well as one promising greater power,' he argued.[33]

The theologians' account of African Traditional Religion has been subjected to a welcome critique, first by the Ugandan intellectual Okot p'Bitek and later by John Peel, Paul Landau, and Rosalind Shaw.[34] But the emphasis on continuity persists in historical and anthropological writings about religious change in Africa. The project is to show how contemporary African Christianity grows out of older cultural forms, how Africans domesticated a religious import, as the title of a recent book puts it.[35] Religion scholars maintain that the things they study – symbols, logics, and power dynamics – are not readily subject to change. Culture, in this view, structures action and thought in such a way as to ensure that it will continually be passed on.[36] In Ogbu Kalu's recent textbook on African Christianity, there are twenty-five entries in the index under 'African theology' and none under 'conversion.' Even unorthodox revivalist movements, Kalu argues, embrace 'a certain sense of continuity with the traditional past, embedding African Christianity into the deep structure of all African traditional religions in spite of the varieties of names and symbols.'[37] Conversion does not appear as a subject of analysis in the long surveys on African Christianity authored by Adrian

---

[31] J. D. Y. Peel, 'Conversion and Tradition in Two African Societies: Ijebu and Buganda,' *Past and Present* 77 (November 1977), 108–41; quote at 110.

[32] J. D. Y. Peel, *Religious Encounter and the Making of the Yoruba* (Bloomington, IN, 2000), 216.

[33] Peel, 'Conversion and Tradition,' 132.

[34] Okot p'Bitek, *African Religions in Western Scholarship* (Nairobi, 1971); Peel, *Religious Encounter*, chapter 4; Rosalind Shaw, 'The Invention of "African Traditional Religion,"' *Religion* 20 (1990), 339–53; Landau, '"Religion" and Christian Conversion'; and Peterson and Walhof, eds., *The Invention of Religion*. Paul Landau has developed his insights in his remarkable *Popular Politics in the History of South Africa, 1400–1948* (Cambridge, 2010).

[35] Nicholas Creary, *Domesticating a Religious Import: The Jesuits and the Inculturation of the Catholic Church in Zimbabwe, 1879–1980* (New York, 2011).

[36] See Robbins, 'Continuity Thinking.'

[37] Ogbu Kalu, *African Christianity: An African Story* (Pretoria, 2005), 306.

Hastings and Elizabeth Isichei.[38] In a recent overview, Stephen Ellis and Gerrie ter Haar's 2004 book *Worlds of Power*, the focus is on Africans' collective *mentalité*, not on converts' creative thought.[39] Ellis and ter Haar take readers through the arenas of public life – there are chapters on politics, on economics, and on legal discourse – showing how at every turn Africans' essentially religious worldview informs their action in the material world. There is little space for the analysis of radical change, dissidence, or rupture in this account, for religion and the mundane are together naturalized, forming an integrated field of action.

The curious absence of discussion about conversion in scholarly writing on African religion is, in part, a consequence of the manner in which conversion has been conceived. Framed as a set of public rituals, 'religion' opens itself to the study of politics and social life, which is the substance of anthropological and historical study. Conversion, by contrast, seems to be an act of conscience, a private deal brokered between God and the individual, an analytical cul-de-sac for scholars studying human societies. It was William James, the American founder of the field of psychology, who in 1902 defined conversion as a subject of study.[40] For James, conversion was a psychological reconciliation, not a social event: it unified the divided self and assured the individual of his personal destiny. James deprived anthropologists and historians of a method by which to study the politics of conversion. Defined as a psychology, the study of conversion seems to offer scholars little purchase on the real world. In their important work on nineteenth-century missionary labors in South Africa, the anthropologists John and Jean Comaroff warn their readers about the 'analytic dangers [that] lurk behind the concept of conversion,' and brand the concept 'Eurocentric,' ineluctably wedded to a modern, liberal conception of subjectivity.[41] For the Comaroffs, the scholar's task is to look beyond believers' testimonies of conversion, ignore the 'spiritual and verbal battles' in which missionaries and heathen engaged, and focus instead on the material forms that structured colonial modernity. The priority is the study of hegemony, the 'order of signs and practices' that 'come to be taken-for-granted as the natural and received shape of the world.'[42]

[38] Adrian Hastings, *The Church in Africa, 1450–1950* (Oxford, 1994); Elizabeth Isichei, *A History of Christianity in Africa: From Antiquity to the Present* (Grand Rapids, MI, 1995).

[39] Stephen Ellis and Gerrie ter Haar, *Worlds of Power: Religious Thought and Political Practice in Africa* (London, 2004), 2.

[40] William James, *Varieties of Religious Experience* (New York, 2004 [1902]), 78–150.

[41] John and Jean Comaroff, *Of Revelation and Revolution*, vol. I: *Christianity, Colonialism, and Consciousness in South Africa* (Chicago, 1991), 250; for 'Eurocentric,' Comaroff and Comaroff, *Of Revelation and Revolution*, vol. II: *The Dialectics of Modernity on a South African Frontier* (Chicago, 1997), 117.

[42] Comaroff and Comaroff, *Revelation and Revolution*, vol. I, 23.

It has been hard to start a conversation about non-conformism in Africa. As scholars look for evidence of the continuities linking converts with their pre-Christian past, converts' radicalism – their epochal sense of time, their often-antagonistic relationship with contemporary culture-brokers, their rejection of social and familial obligations – is made to seem irrelevant. In a scholarship guided by the search for continuity, it was the sociologist Karen Fields who, in her 1985 study of the Watchtower movement in central Africa, brought the radically counter-cultural work of revivalism into view. Fields showed how Christian millennialism challenged the foundations of colonial governance. The whole structure of indirect rule in Northern Rhodesia and Nyasaland rested on a 'cushion of culture,' on the African chiefs' ability to command the 'routine ways of behaving and thinking that [gave] to social life [its] relative predictability.'[43] Watchtower partisans would not recognize the protocols that upheld the chiefs' authority. Convinced that the end of the world was soon at hand, they ignited a 'leaping fire of civil disobedience' that challenged missionaries, chiefs and colonial officials alike.[44] The Watchtower movement posed a threat to the discursive structures of colonial neo-traditionalism, argued Fields. In their anticipation of a quickly-coming millennium, Watchtower partisans rejected the hold that custom had on them, freeing themselves from the chiefs' power.

Fields' book helps us see how, in a context where culture defines majoritarian communities and upholds political hierarchy, religious nonconformism can be radical action.[45] Conversion is not only a change in religious identity, a statistic needing explanation. Neither is conversion only a strategy of political and social self-aggrandizement, a religious vehicle for the advancement of material self-interest. Conversion is a discursive act by which individuals take up a new position in the social world, reengineer time, and distance themselves from their native land. Converts are obliged to set themselves at variance from the dictates of cultural heritage. That is why they are so often offensive. In their movement from one life to another, they unsettle the convivial community that the architecture of culture upholds, opening avenues of action outside the containments of tradition.

East African revivalists did not share a theology with the Watchtower activists of central Africa. They were not anti-colonial radicals, and their conversion was not a willful act of disobedience. Neither did East African revivalists identify themselves as heroes, leading their people into a utopian future. Revivalists were engaged in a pilgrimage, not a rebellion. Their self-directed travel was modeled after *The Pilgrim's Progress*, the classic work

---

[43] Karen Fields, *Revival and Rebellion in Colonial Central Africa* (Princeton, 1985), 59.
[44] Fields, *Revival and Rebellion*, chapter 4.
[45] See Gauri Viswanathan, *Outside the Fold: Conversion, Modernity, and Belief* (Princeton, 1998).

of English nonconformism, which was generally the second book (after the New Testament) that missionary presses published in Africa's vernacular languages (see Chapter 2). Revivalists likened themselves to Bunyan's protagonist, Christian, who turned away from his kith and kin in order to follow the path toward the Heavenly City. Converts' nonconformity was articulated in the most intimate of settings: in their open and unbridled discourses about adultery and sexual deviance; in their refusal to live sociably with their kin; in their rejection of the dictates of custom and tradition. Only rarely did the Revival's controversies come to the notice of British officials. In Zambia – Karen Fields' area of study – worried British bureaucrats generated dozens of files about the Watchtower movement, material that is now deposited in the national archives. In Kenya, Uganda, and Tanzania, by contrast, the shelves in central government archives are largely empty of material on the Revival. The British officials who sat atop the colonial bureaucracies in Nairobi, Kampala and Dar es Salaam had little occasion to worry. It was in the mundane economy of conjugality, kinship, and ethnicity that the Revival generated controversy.

The intimacy of the controversies generated by the Revival did not make the movement less salient in eastern Africa's politics. To the contrary, controversies over the Revival were controversies over the definition of eastern Africa's public sphere. Even as revivalists rejected their cultural heritage and made themselves converts, other entrepreneurs were simultaneously working in the field of history. Men like Henry Muoria – the patriotic Gikuyu newspaperman who decried the noisy excesses of the Revival – were busily inventing traditions and consolidating ethnic identities. It was on the field of etiquette, manners, and comportment that ethnic patriots sought to regiment their constituents and produce a respectable people. Controversies over the Revival therefore give us access to the backstage of African political life, the arena where appearances are managed, political identities are debated and defined, and patriots are made.

THE CULTURAL WORK OF PATRIOTISM

In the 1960s, East Africa's nationalists set out to build independent states by dismantling tribes. At midnight on 9 October 1962, independent Uganda's flag was raised as a crowd at Nakivubo stadium sang the new national anthem. The lyrics, edited only a few weeks before by Prime Minister Milton Obote, went 'Oh Uganda, may God uphold thee/We lay our future in thy hands/United, free, for liberty/Together we'll always stand.'[46] Five years later, Obote abolished Uganda's kingdoms, declared Uganda to be a unitary state, and sent the army to destroy the palace of the king

---

[46] CoU 1 Abp 157/11: Milton Obote to Archbishop Erica Sabiti, 20 September 1962.

of Buganda.[47] 'We do not accept,' he announced in *The Common Man's Charter*, that 'feudalism ... is a way of life which must not be disturbed because it has been in practice for centuries.' The 'people of Uganda,' he proclaimed, must 'move away from the hold of tribal and other forms of factionalism ... and accept that the problems of poverty, development and nation-building can and must be tackled on the basis of one Country and one People.'[48]

Other unitary nations were similarly being summoned into being during the decade of African independence. The territory of Tanganyika achieved self-government in 1961 under the leadership of Julius Nyerere.[49] Nyerere's political aim was clear: he told an audience at the United Nations that he hoped to 'break up ... tribal consciousness and build up a national consciousness' among Tanganyika's people.[50] In 1967, the same year that Milton Obote abolished Uganda's kingdoms, President Nyerere announced a campaign to build a socialist state. The aim was both to ensure the country's economic self-reliance and to knit its people together as a national citizenry. 'All human beings are equal,' went the first clause of the Arusha Declaration. 'A truly socialist state is one in which all people are workers and in which neither capitalism nor feudalism exists.'[51] There followed the largest resettlement effort in the history of Africa: nearly 70 percent of Tanzania's rural people were uprooted and settled in collective villages. Kenya's nation-builders similarly argued that tribalism was a feudalist anachronism, inimical to political unity. During the run-up to independence, Kenya's minority ethnic groups insisted on a federal system of government, and the country's first constitution therefore established seven regional assemblies, each with its own police force and judiciary. After independence, however, the ruling Kenya African National Union argued that the federal constitution was both unworkable and unjust.[52] One official vowed that his party would not 'stand by and watch the country go to ruin because a few people want to carve out little kingdoms for themselves under the guise of protecting tribal interests.'[53]

[47] Described in vivid detail in Edward Mutesa, *The Desecration of my Kingdom* (London, 1967); in D. A. Low, *Buganda in Modern History* (London, 1971); and in Phares Mutibwa, *The Buganda Factor in Uganda Politics* (Kampala, 2008).

[48] Apollo Milton Obote, *The Common Man's Charter* (Entebbe, 1969), articles 7 and 19.

[49] Described in John Iliffe, 'Breaking the Chain at its Weakest Link: TANU and the Colonial Office,' in Gregory H. Maddox and James L. Giblin, eds., *In Search of a Nation: Histories of Authority and Dissidence in Tanzania* (Oxford, 2006), 168–97.

[50] Julius Nyerere, *Freedom and Unity* (London, 1967), 39.

[51] Printed in Julius Nyerere, *Ujamaa: Essays on Socialism* (Nairobi, 1968), 13, 15.

[52] Oginga Odinga, Kenya's first vice president, titled a chapter in his autobiography '*Majimbo* [Federalism] Gets in the Way of *Uhuru* [Freedom].' Oginga Odinga, *Not Yet Uhuru* (Nairobi, 1967), chapter 12.

[53] Joseph Murumbi in *Daily Nation*, 6 May 1963. Quoted in David M. Anderson, '"Yours in the Struggle for Majimbo": Nationalism and the Party Politics of Decolonization in Kenya, 1955–64,' *Journal of Contemporary History* 40 (3) (2005), 547–64.

Prime Minister Jomo Kenyatta refused to provide funds for the regional governments; and in 1964 the federal constitution was dissolved, the political opposition was disbanded, and Kenya became a centralized, one-party state.[54] Nationalism was *au courant* in 1960s Africa. Nationalist parties claimed to speak for a homogenous people whose historical destiny was to govern themselves. The tribes of Tanzania and Kenya, like the kingdoms of Uganda, were relics of an earlier age of inequality. They had to be extirpated through persuasion or crushed with military force.

The first scholars of African politics were seduced by the rhetoric and pageantry of nation-building. They thought national self-government to be the inevitable and necessary product of Africa's political evolution. The eminent political scientist James Coleman might have had Milton Obote's 'Common Man's Charter' before him when he defined the nation as 'a post-tribal, post-feudal community which has emerged from the shattering forces of disintegration that characterize modernity.'[55] He organized political history on a continuum, arguing that tribal society would naturally give way to nationalism as the 'end product of the profound and complex transformation' birthed by European imperialism. Writing about the kingdom of Buganda, historian Godfrey Uzoigwe blamed Ganda leaders for failing to acknowledge the changing times. He argued that they were

ethnic-minded politicians when broader nationalisms were the norm. They were conservative reactionaries when radicalism was abroad in the continent. They were unrepentant oligarchs at a time when socialism and progressive ideas were being adopted elsewhere. In short, they were hopelessly out of step with African history which … instead of leading them to victory, dragged them down to defeat.[56]

In evolutionary social science, tribes were out of time, and out of place, in independent Africa.[57]

---

[54] See Peter Anyang' Nyong'o, 'State and Society in Kenya: The Disintegration of the Nationalist Coalition and the Rise of Presidential Authoritarianism, 1963–78,' *African Affairs* 88 (351) (April 1989), 229–51; Keith Kyle, *The Politics of Independence in Kenya* (New York, 1999); and B. A. Ogot and W. R. Ochieng', eds., *Decolonization and Independence in Kenya, 1940–1963* (London, 1995).

[55] James S. Coleman, 'Nationalism in Tropical Africa,' *American Political Science Review* 48 (2) (1954), 404–26.

[56] G. N. Uzoigwe, 'Uganda and Parliamentary Government,' *Journal of Modern African Studies* 21 (2) (June 1983), 253–71.

[57] The liberal historiography of eastern Africa includes – pre-eminently – John Iliffe's *A Modern History of Tanganyika* (Cambridge, 1979). Other works include, for Uganda, Godfrey Uzoigwe, ed., *Uganda: The Dilemma of Nationhood* (New York, 1982); Kenneth Ingham, *The Making of Modern Uganda* (London, 1958); and Grace Ibingira, *The Forging of an African Nation: The Political and Constitutional Evolution of Uganda from Colonial Rule to Independence, 1894–1962* (New York, 1972). Kenya's liberal historiography includes Carl G. Rosberg and John Nottingham, *The Myth of Mau Mau: Nationalism in Kenya* (Stanford, CA, 1966); George Bennett, *Kenya, A Political History* (London, 1963); M. P. K.

But tribes were not passé during the decade of African independence, and neither were they holdovers from a former era.[58] Innovative cultural work was going on all over eastern Africa. Activists were conducting research on history, codifying customary law, standardizing vernacular languages, and constituting ethnic communities. There were no less than sixty ethnic welfare associations registered in Mombasa during the late 1950s.[59] The Luo schoolmaster Benaiah Ohanga conducted research in northern Uganda and southern Sudan and found evidence, he reported, that Alur, Acholi, and Lango were 'dialects of one original language.'[60] Ohanga's evidence helped political organizers conceive of the Luo as an international community (see Chapter 6). When the Luo Union published a five-year 'Plan of Work' in 1954, it proposed to build a museum in Kisumu containing 'all Luo past and present belongings[;]' to open offices in Mombasa, Kampala and Dar es Salaam; and to campaign against the prostitution of Luo women.[61]

The architects of eastern Africa's ethnic patriotisms were not involved in the anti-colonial struggle for political self-government. Neither were they engaged in the effort to build nations. They were driven by the urgent need to find institutions that could protect civic virtues and define honorable conduct. East Africa's nations – polyglot and culturally diverse – seemed to throw people together without discrimination, in a disorderly jumble. Ethnic patriots claimed to be defenders of particular fatherlands – of Gikuyuland, Nyanza, Buhaya, or Toro – whose future was endangered by cultural amnesia and demographic decline. They were not egalitarians, nor did they seek to defend personal freedoms. Writing from western Uganda, one of the architects of Konzo ethnic patriotism sketched a nightmare scenario, warning that the government of Milton Obote planned to 'apprehend girls and boys and detain them from their countries.' Once pried loose from their moorings, Konzo children would become amnesiacs. 'They are mixed and start breeding like animals. No doubt children bred in such mode will not know their language of origin,' he warned.[62] For East Africa's ethnic patriots, nation-building was a mortal challenge to moral order. It severed

---

Sorrenson, *Land Reform in the Kikuyu Country* (London, 1967); and John Spencer, *KAU: The Kenya African Union* (London, 1985). The Kenya historiography is reviewed in John Lonsdale, 'The Moral Economy of Mau Mau: The Problem,' in Bruce Berman and John Lonsdale, *Unhappy Valley: Conflict in Kenya and Africa* (London, 1992), 265–314.

[58] As shown for Ghana in Jean M. Allman, *The Quills of the Porcupine: Asante Nationalism in an Emergent Ghana* (Madison, 1993), and Richard Rathbone, *Nkrumah and the Chiefs: The Politics of Chieftaincy in Ghana, 1951–1960* (Athens, OH, 2000).

[59] KNA DC Mombasa 2/1/34: 'Associations, Unions, Societies and Clubs, 1955–1962.'

[60] KNA PC Nyanza 3/6/129: B.A. Ohanga, 'The Nilotic Peoples of Central Africa,' 1 May 1946.

[61] KNA DC Kakamega 2/1/99: Riwruok Luo, 'Plan of Work, January 1955–December 1960.'

[62] KabDA Box 102, 'Toro Intelligence Reports, 1968–71' file: Yolamu Mulima, circular letter, n.d. (but October 1970).

people from the taproot of culture. Ethnic patriots sought to define a community that could tutor the young and encourage social discipline.

East Africa's diverse peoples had long upheld different models of discipline, but everyone agreed that an honorable reputation was built at home. Honorable men needed to present a good face to the public, and in that endeavor they had to rely on the discretion of their wives.[63] In Rwanda, Tutsi aristocrats took care to wall their families off from outsiders' observation. Their homesteads were enclosed with thick hedges, some twenty or thirty feet in height.[64] Missionaries reported that, when a Tutsi woman wished to venture outside her home, 'everyone is chased out of the courtyard and a mat is held in front of the gateway, while another beautifully woven mat is held carefully round her so that she walks as if she were wrapped up from the outer gaze.'[65] These screens and fences organized human sociability, separating private life from the prying eyes of outsiders. When a curious missionary paid an unexpected visit to a chief's homestead in northern Rwanda in 1935, she surprised the lady of the house, who disconcertedly brushed past her visitor and hurriedly entered her compartment. Only there would she agree to greet her guests.[66] Respectable men were obliged to mask their interests and emotions, to cultivate, in the words of one anthropologist, 'the art of astutely disguising one's thoughts with consummate deception, of not seeing, not understanding, not reacting.'[67] The first Anglican missionaries in Rwanda – both of them graduates of the University of Cambridge – were impressed with the aura of civility that Tutsi elites managed to project. They were sure that Belgian Protestant missionaries – most of them artisans from lower-class families – had 'no human hope of touching the Batutsi aristocrats' because Rwandan elites demanded 'evangelization by *gentlemen* either black or white.'[68]

Luo people similarly built walls around their houses, but whereas the walls of the Rwandan elite were meant to guard their privacy, Luo householders seem to have welcomed newcomvers into the innermost parts of their homes.[69] The Luo were an acephalous society, not a centralized

---

[63] John Iliffe's *Honour in African History* (Cambridge, 2005) offers a full assessment of Africans' diverse theories of honor.

[64] CMS Annual Letters file: Dora Skipper, annual letter, 31 August 1930.

[65] Margaret Guillebaud, quoted in Meg Guillebaud, *Rwanda: The Land God Forgot? Revival, Genocide and Hope* (London, 2002), 41.

[66] CMS Oxford, Dora Skipper papers, folio 2: diary entry for 29 September 1935.

[67] F. M. Rodegem, *Anthologie Rundi* (Paris, 1973), 17–20. Quoted in Iliffe, *Honour in African History*, 163.

[68] CMS G3 A7 O: A. C. Stanley Smith to Ash, 22 September 1926. Emphasis in the original. See Nick Godfrey, 'Understanding Genocide: The Experience of Anglicans in Rwanda' (PhD dissertation, University of Cambridge, 2008).

[69] Joseph Thomson, *Through Masai Land* (London, 1895 [1885]), 282; C. Hobley, 'Nilotic Tribes of Kavirondo—Anthropological and Ethnological Notes,' in *Eastern Uganda: An Ethnological Survey* (London, 1902), 26–35.

kingdom, and they did not recognize an aristocracy. Prosperous men competed to attract loyal clients. Archaeological evidence suggests that ancient homesteads in Nyanza were culturally and linguistically diverse, full of people related through conjugal ties and other non-kin relationships.[70] What drew Luo people together was their dependence on a wealthy patron, and their shared commitment to sociable living. The verb *-sango* meant both to 'eat copiously' and also to 'form an alliance.'[71] Luo patrons and clients negotiated their social and economic relationships as they ate together. They scorned ill-mannered people: the verb *-chuto* meant both to 'eat raw flesh' and also 'to pick a quarrel'; while the verb *-ramo* meant to 'gobble the food' and to 'speak before one's time.' People who carefully observed the rules of etiquette earned other people's trust and affection. Living side-by-side in polyglot communities, Luo people cultivated sociable relationships through their deliberation and reserve (see Chapter 6).

Whereas Luo patrons expected politeness and circumspection from their clients, wealthy Gikuyu men were obliged to defend themselves against other people's intemperate accusations. Gikuyu people called themselves *mbarĩ ya atĩrĩrĩ*, the 'clan of I say to you,' and their vocabulary rings with the insults that the poor used to make demands of the wealthy.[72] What Gikuyu people shared with their Luo and Rwandan contemporaries was profound respect for a householder's managerial skill. As the historian John Lonsdale has shown, the Gikuyu made themselves a people through the hard work of clearing central Kenya's forests.[73] Sweating culture from nature, they came to regard the work of forest clearing as the surest proof of a man's integrity. Reputable men built fences of thorn trees around their homes, both to protect women and children from dangerous animals and also to keep their domestic affairs private. The noun *wĩkindĩru*, used by Bible translators for 'integrity,' also meant to 'ram down, pack tight (the earth around a newly erected post)' and to 'repress, restrain, keep a check on, moderate speech, feelings.'[74] People with integrity were restrained about what they said in public. The verb *-thinga* summarized what was needed. It meant 'to be honorable, live up to the commonly accepted standard of one's day,' and also 'to plaster the walls of a house.'[75] Fence-building was socially consequential work, for through it a householder presented a good face to the public.

[70] David William Cohen and E. S. Atieno Odhiambo, *Siaya: The Historical Anthropology of an African Landscape* (London, 1989), 13–15.
[71] Mill Hill Fathers, *Vocabulary Nilotic-English* (Nyeri, n.d. [but 1910?]).
[72] Described in Derek R. Peterson, *Creative Writing: Translation, Bookkeeping, and the Work of Imagination in Colonial Kenya* (Portsmouth, 2004), 10–14.
[73] Argued in John Lonsdale, 'The Moral Economy of Mau Mau: Wealth, Poverty, and Civic Virtue in Kikuyu Political Thought,' in Lonsdale and Bruce Berman, *Unhappy Valley: Conflict in Kenya and Africa* (London, 1992), 315–504.
[74] For *-kindĩra*, see T. G. Benson, *Kikuyu-English Dictionary* (Oxford: Clarendon Press, 1964), 218.
[75] Leonard and Gladys Beecher, 'A Kikuyu-English Dictionary' (Nairobi, 1938), 205.

Privacy-seeking Rwandan elites, living in splendid and unassailable isolation, were a world away from the scrappy, argumentative republicans of central Kenya. Their differences notwithstanding, Luo, Gikuyu, Tutsi, and other East African householders shared a fervent regard for social discipline. The fences they built around their homes – whether of mud, timber, or thorn bushes – were more than boundary markers. They advanced householders' efforts to screen their most intimate of social relationships from the public eye and to create a public persona. The demand that clients, wives, and children should act with discretion was articulated across eastern Africa. In Kigezi, in southern Uganda, Kiga wives were expected to defer to the interests of their husbands and fathers (see Chapter 3). This marital etiquette was widely observed, and Kiga marriages were extraordinarily long-lived: only 11 of the 3,972 cases (0.3 percent) that came before Kigezi's county courts in the 1930s concerned marriage.[76] Marital litigation was much more widely practiced in the kingdom of Buganda, in central Uganda. During the 1930s, 16 percent of the cases that came before Buganda's county courts concerned marital disputes. But as they confronted their argumentative wives, Ganda husbands also sought to uphold their dignity (see Chapter 4). A 1904 law made it a crime to 'publicly abuse any person in indecent words.'[77] The penalty was a year's imprisonment. Wives, children, and dependents were obliged to keep a careful check on their tongues, mind their manners, live behind screens, and keep secrets. Male householders had to hold back their words and manage their homes. Discretion was a civic virtue, for by it, people established their place within a civil society.

Revivalists made a point of living in the open. They would not stay behind the screens that respectable people erected. Mariya Kamondo, the aunt of Rwanda's king, was an early convert to the Revival. Like other elite women, she had spent much of her life out of the public view: when missionaries visited in 1937 they described her household as a 'complete maze,' with a 'huge hedge all round the outside, [and] when you get inside there are 9 or 10 other huts, all in their separate little hedges.'[78] But on the occasion of her conversion, Kamondo stood in a Revival meeting – with neither screen nor veil – and said that

she wanted all to know that the wrongs she had done to the various of her tenants … and in front of her children, servants and various Roman Catholics who were sitting round the door of the church she, the King's aunt, made a full confession of her past life, and finished up by saying, 'And everything else as God shows me I am going to speak of it.'

---

[76] Statistics from SOAS Melvin Perlman papers, Box 8, file 23: 'Buganda, Toro, Kigezi,' n.d.

[77] UNA A 46/618: 'Endagano zona Ezalaganibwa ne Gavumenti ya Bangereza na Baganda mu Buganda,' n.d. (but 1904).

[78] CMS Oxford, Dora Skipper papers, folio 2/2: diary entry for 22 May 1937.

PHOTO 2. 'Kamondo, a Chieftainess,' n.d. Photo by Dora Skipper. Courtesy of the Church Mission Society archives.

After her confession, Kamondo made a show of walking in revivalists' company as they set off on their homeward journey.

Converts like Mariya Kamondo were causing controversies all over eastern Africa. In their refusal to abide by socially validated standards of etiquette, they endangered civil order. Chiefs, elders, and other spokesmen for patriotic values regarded them with horror. Chief Edward Karegyesa, who ruled Rujumbura County in southern Uganda, was an early and effective critic. In the early 1940s, revivalists were gathering outside his home, giving their testimonies and condemning Karegyesa for his sexual profligacy. Female converts made a point of removing the veils that had customarily covered their faces. Karegyesa warned his nephew that '[t]his new kind of religion is dangerous. It invades your privacy. You have nothing left.'[79] In 1943, Chief Karegyesa prohibited revivalists from singing as they walked along the public roads; that same year he had a number of loudmouthed converts whipped and beaten (see Chapter 3).[80] Revivalists spoke openly about subjects that patriots like Chief Karegyesa sought to keep secret.

Revivalism was only one of several embarrassments that moralists like Chief Karegyesa had to face. East Africa's conservatives felt that the very fabric of social order was under attack from indiscipline and sexual deviancy. Thousands of men from Kenya, Uganda, and Tanganyika enlisted in

[79] Quoted in Festo Kivengere with Dorothy Smoker, *Revolutionary Love* (Fort Washington, 1983), 10.
[80] KigDA bundle 129, 'Church Missionary Society' file: Joe Church to DC Kigezi, 22 March 1943.

the colonial military during the Second World War.[81] Living in close quarters alongside men from other parts of eastern Africa, soldiers became ardent advocates for conservative reform. Writing from Dar es Salaam in June 1944, Private Abdullah Bikayuzi – from Buhaya, in northwestern Tanganyika – complained to the local government about the Haya women working as prostitutes in the city.[82] 'Our ladies are plenty in Dar es Salaam, but their activities here are so shameful,' he wrote. Haya women were practicing a novel form of prostitution in eastern Africa's cities, standing on the street corners and calling out their prices to men passing by.[83] Critics named them *wazi wazi*, from a Swahili word meaning 'open' or 'naked.' Like revivalists, prostitutes were open about the most intimate of acts. Haya soldiers found them to be extremely embarrassing. Corporal Arbor Godfred, stationed in Nairobi, could not conceive how anything would have 'power to wash away this shame of being called *dada* ['sister'], *kaka* ['elder brother'], *shemeji* ['countryman'] by every soldier, every civilian who knows me to be a Muhaya.'[84] Neither Corporal Godfred nor Private Bikayuzi were actually related to the women who frequented the street corners of wartime East Africa, but in the insults of other men they were lumped, willy-nilly, with their countrywomen. Army barracks, labor camps, and city street corners thereby became the recruiting sergeants for ethnic self-imagination.

In combating the menace of prostitution, men positioned themselves as patriots, upholding the virtues of a particular community endangered by social indiscipline. The anti-prostitution campaigners of the late 1940s and 1950s did not work on behalf of Kenyans, Ugandans, or East Africans. They claimed to be defenders of particular *patriae* – of Gikuyuland, Buhaya, or Toro – whose future was at risk. During and after the war, ethnic patriots created new institutions to police women's conduct. The most effective of these institutions was the Ramogi African Welfare Association, founded by Luo men in 1945 (see Chapter 6). In its constitution, the association vowed to 'prevent and prosecute all girls and women who are at the present time running away from their husbands ... and are engaged in the prostitution business.'[85] Luo women accused of practicing prostitution were stripped, clad in gunnysacks, and forcibly taken back to their rural homes. Other organizations learned from the Ramogi Association's example. In northwestern Tanganyika, the Haya Union adopted a system of pass control for

[81] Timothy Parsons, *The African Rank-and-File: Social Implications of Colonial Military Service in the King's African Rifles* (Portsmouth, NH, 1999).

[82] Rwamishenye archives, Box 18, 'Rwamishenye' file: Private Abdullah Bikayuzi to Rwamishenye Native Council, 16 June 1944.

[83] Luise White, *The Comforts of Home: Prostitution in Colonial Nairobi* (Chicago, 1990), chapter 5.

[84] Rwamishenye archives, Box 18, 'Rwamishenye' file: Arbor Godfred to DC Bukoba, 12 November 1945.

[85] KNA PC Nyanza 3/1/376: John Ogala to PC Nyanza, 19 October 1945.

Haya women in 1950, obliging women who wished to leave Bukoba to produce a pass signed by the chief of her location (see Chapter 7). Likewise in Uganda, the Kampala Batoro Association repatriated Toro women found living in the city of Kampala without the permission of their fathers (see Chapter 11).

The Kampala Batoro Association, the Ramogi African Welfare Association, and other patriotic organizations were the crucibles in which novel forms of discipline were defined and cultivated. Government chiefs – the official defenders of custom – were often their allies: in northwest Tanganyika, Haya chiefs sponsored the Haya Union's work, and the Ramogi African Welfare Association was likewise backed by Luo chiefs. But ethnic patriotism was more than an instrument of colonial indirect rule.[86] It was city men – labor migrants, soldiers, clerks, and artisans – who formed the membership of these welfare associations. Nairobi's African population grew from 41,000 in 1939 to more than 100,000 by 1952.[87] The African population of Dar es Salaam nearly tripled between 1940 and 1957.[88] These new city-dwellers were the most urgent campaigners against prostitution. Bundled into locations where they lived, cheek to jowl, with other men, city-dwellers had an urgent, pressing need for social capital. The Gikuyu ex-soldier Gakaara wa Wanjau felt himself to be particularly embattled (see Chapter 10). In 1948, Gakaara was living with several other men in tenement housing in the city of Nakuru, where he occasionally worked as a hawker of cigarettes. His wife was living in his father's house. 'The whole problem is that I don't have a permanent house for my own and I don't want to bring my wife to live in poverty,' he told his brother in an anguished letter.[89] He wrote in Gikuyu, but the phrase 'a permanent house of my own' was in English. The house, and the challenge it represented, seems to have haunted him. It was in these circumstances that he published the book *Wanawake ya Siku Hizi* ('Women of These Days'). He told prospective buyers how the book 'abhors the bad reputation brought up by lazy African women who roam about shamefully in town with nothing to do but prostitution.'[90] Like Corporal Arbor Godfred, who was offended by the Haya prostitutes crowding the street corners of wartime Nairobi, Gakaara wa Wanjau was convinced that delinquent women undermined his credibility.

[86] *Contra* Mahmood Mamdani, *Citizen and Subject: Contemporary Africa and the Legacy of Late Colonialism* (Princeton, 1996).

[87] David Throup, *Economic and Social Origins of Mau Mau* (London, 1988), chapter 8; Luise White, *The Comforts of Home: Prostitution in Colonial Nairobi* (Chicago, 1990), chapter 7.

[88] James Brennan, Andrew Burton, and Yusuf Lawi, eds., *Dar es Salaam: Histories from an Emerging Metropolis* (Dar es Salaam, 2007), 44.

[89] GW 'Correspondence, 1948–49' file: Gakaara wa Wanjau to 'My Brother,' 21 October 1948.

[90] GW 'Correspondence, 1948–49' file: Gakaara wa Wanjau to A Branch, East Africa Command, 5 January 1949.

Gakaara wa Wanjau was one of a great number of activists who were involved in the building of East Africa's ethnic *patriae* during the late 1940s and 1950s. Dozens of history books were composed. Jemusi Miti, founding father of the populist Bataka Union in Buganda, completed a multivolume, 400,000-word manuscript on the kingdom's history in 1946 (see Chapter 4).[91] He used the past as a resource with which to illuminate the corruption of the contemporary social order. In olden times, he wrote, Buganda's king, the Kabaka, had punished adulterers and upheld marriage.[92] But in contemporary times, Miti averred, 'it is not like that, because every women moves the way she wants and even boys and girls move the way they want.' Miti and other partisan historians used the past to cast light on the indiscipline of the present. Their command over history gave them the moral authority with which to establish normative standards of behavior, making deviancy look like a traitorous insult to their forefathers.

As a literary genre, the historical narratives that Jemusi Miti and other partisan historians produced were a novelty. Patriots sought to link a particular community to a particular history, to evaluate their contemporary world by comparing it to the past. For these partisan historians, narrative was the crucial literary form. They arranged historical time in a linear fashion, making the past into a fountainhead from which authentic morality and culture flowed. Oral literature had never before possessed this powerful motivational force. The meaning of the pithy riddles – called *ndaī* – that Gikuyu people told each other was never transparent, for riddlers played with figures of speech and took advantage of metaphors.[93] The answer to the riddle 'In your place there is a lily and a castor oil plant,' for example, was 'Boy and girl.' The lily – a deep-rooted plant – was like a boy, who stayed close to home upon his marriage; the girl, by contrast, was like a castor oil plant, a cash crop whose produce was to be traded away.[94] Gikuyu *ndaī* were addressed to people who had specific, particular knowledge, who knew about the properties of particular plants, or the value of certain commodities. Patriotic culture-builders took these locally meaningful puzzles and put them on the page, where they could be enumerated, standardized, and circulated to a wider audience. There was a sense of duty about their writing, an obligation to create useable knowledge. The first collection of Gikuyu proverbs, published in 1939, was created by a cadre of Gikuyu schoolteachers.[95] Each proverb was printed alongside an English-language analogue. In this and in other collections, the obscure *ndaī* were cast as moral admonitions or practical wisdom, bearing meanings that were transparently available

---

[91] The text is James Kibuka Miti, 'Buganda, 1875–1900: A Centenary Contribution,' trans. G. Rock (typescript, n.d. [but 1946]).

[92] CoU 02 Bp 184/20: Jemusi Miti et al. to the Kabaka, 22 July 1936.

[93] Vittorio Merlo Pick, *Ndaī na Gīcaandī: Kikuyu Enigmas* (Bologna, 1973), 26.

[94] Pick, *Ndaī na Gīcaandī*, 55, 57.

[95] G. Barra, *1000 Kikuyu Proverbs* (Nairobi, 1994 [1939]).

to readers. The Luo entrepreneur Paul Mboya published his *Luo Kitgi gi Timbegi* ('Luo Customs and Beliefs') in 1938.⁹⁶ He spent twenty-nine chapters describing Luo morality, marriage customs, and burial rights, and at the end of his book he printed 164 Luo proverbs in a numbered list. 'I have written this book to gather our traditions, customs and councils, so that they should not be lost to our children,' he wrote. Once proverbs had been put on the page, once all the riddles had been explained and edited, then books could be circulated to a wider readership that could – like biddable children – be chastened, guided, and inspired. In their textual work, patriots were creating a patrimony.

History writers like Paul Mboya were making the past accessible. Where proverbs and riddles had once been directed to communities with specific forms of knowledge, Mboya and his contemporaries sought to make proverbs' meanings generalizable. They were not simply scribes. They cleaned up the past, scrubbing out embarrassing customs and substituting creditable practices in their place. In his 1952 book on Luo customs, for example, Samuel Ayany faulted infirm people for consulting medicine men and opined against funerals, which bankrupted families. 'The kind of knowledge we should be seeking,' he argued, 'should be knowledge that enables us to love fellow men.'⁹⁷ As they edited aphorisms and riddles, as they translated *ndaī* and other literary forms into admonitory proverbs, homespun historians like Samuel Ayany composed a useable past that could call people, in the name of ethnic tradition, to loving obedience.⁹⁸

The organizers of eastern Africa's ethnic patriotisms aimed to define and protect a specific homeland. But they were by no means 'local historians.'⁹⁹ East Africa's ethnic patriots were cosmopolitan in their reading habits and in their frame of reference. Luo patriots looked with admiration on the Buganda kingdom's inspirational historiography. 'The Baganda have written their history fully,' Samuel Ayany noted. 'Thus, old practices are guaranteed longevity, with no fear of total loss at all.'¹⁰⁰ Haya patriots, confronting a crisis over prostitution and gender order, learned techniques of movement control by studying the Luo Union's anti-prostitution campaigns (see Chapter 7). They also looked to Buganda, which had adopted a draconian law against prostitution. 'This was one of the important means which

---

⁹⁶ Paul Mboya, *Luo Kitgi gi Timbegi* (Kisumu, 1983 [1938]).
⁹⁷ Samuel Ayany, *Kar Charuok Mar Luo* (Nairobi, 1952). Translated in E. S. Atieno Odhiambo, 'Luo Perspectives on Knowledge and Development: Samuel G. Ayany and Paul Mbuya,' in *African Philosophy as Cultural Inquiry*, eds. Ivan Karp and D. A. Masolo (Bloomington, 2000), 244–58.
⁹⁸ Karin Barber, *The Anthropology of Texts, Persons, and Publics: Oral and Written Culture in Africa and Beyond* (Cambridge, 2007), chapter 5.
⁹⁹ Compare Axel Harneit-Sievers, ed., *A Place in the World: New Local Historiographies from Africa and South Asia* (Leiden, 2002).
¹⁰⁰ Ayany, *Kar Charuok Mar Luo*, in Atieno Odhiambo, 'Luo Perspectives,' 249.

helped to return Hayas who were disgracing us in Uganda,' wrote a Haya activist.[101] In central Kenya, Gikuyu-language newspapers printed correspondence from Semakula Mulumba, the Ganda politician sent to represent the populist Bataka Union's interests in London. Ethnic patriots were participating in a trans-territorial discourse, a theater that spanned interlacustrine central Africa.[102]

Professional scholars have partitioned the whole field of discourse that patriotic activists created. Whereas men like the Luo historian Samuel Ayany were engaged in a transterritorial competition over moral authority, professional scholars almost always limit their work to the arena defined by the nation-state. The seminal book in Tanzania's scholarship is John Iliffe's *A Modern History of Tanganyika*.[103] Iliffe's account focused on the origins and growth of the Tanganyika African National Union (TANU), which he thought to be the cockpit of Tanganyika's nationalism. Later generations of scholars filled in Iliffe's cast of characters, bringing women, peasants, musicians, and other activists into a story about the making of the Tanzanian nation (see Chapter 7). In Uganda, historical scholarship is organized regionally: there are recent studies on demographic history in Bunyoro; agriculture in Kigezi; and politics in colonial Buganda.[104] Only a few works take 'Uganda' as a framework of analysis.[105] Kenya's scholars conventionally write about ethnic groups, about Christianity and gender in Masaailand, for example, or about widowhood among the Luhya.[106] The very considerable scholarship on central Kenya's history isolates the Mau Mau movement from its East African context, treating it alternately as a self-generated struggle originating from the Gikuyu people's unique historical experience or as an episode in British imperial history (see Chapter 10).[107]

---

[101] Mwanza archives, Bukoba acc., L5/II/B: Fr. Desire Kasangaki to Buhaya Council, 12 July 1961.

[102] This point is derived from John Lonsdale, 'Writing Competitive Patriotisms in Eastern Africa,' in *Recasting the Past: History Writing and Political Work in Modern Africa*, eds. Derek R. Peterson and Giacomo Macola (Athens, OH, 2009), 251–67.

[103] John Iliffe, *A Modern History of Tanganyika* (Cambridge, 1979).

[104] Shane Doyle, *Crisis and Decline in Bunyoro: Population and Environment in Western Uganda, 1860–1955* (Oxford, 2006); Grace Carswell, *Cultivating Success in Uganda: Kigezi Farmers and Colonial Policies* (Oxford, 2007); Holly Hanson, *Landed Obligation: The Practice of Power in Buganda* (Portsmouth, NH, 2003).

[105] See in particular Grace Bantebya Kyomuhendo and Marjorie Kenitson McIntosh, *Women, Work and Domestic Virtue in Uganda, 1900–2003* (Kampala, 2006).

[106] Dorothy L. Hodgson, *The Church of Women: Gendered Encounters Between Maasai and Missionaries* (Bloomington, 2005); Kenda Mutongi, *Worries of the Heart: Widows, Family, and Community in Kenya* (Chicago, 2007).

[107] The Mau Mau scholarship is too vast to list here. It includes work of great insight. Some of the key texts emphasizing the endogenous origins of Mau Mau are David Throup, *Economic and Social Origins of Mau Mau, 1945–53* (Nairobi, 1988); Tabitha Kanogo, *Squatters and the Roots of Mau Mau, 1905–63* (Nairobi, 1987); and Frank Furedi, *The Mau Mau War in Perspective* (Nairobi, 1989). Scholarship on the imperial politics of Mau

East Africa's historians have been seduced by the logic of the archivist, the administrator, and the census taker. The administrative grid structures the way we write history. *Ethnic Patriotism and the East African Revival* is organized according to a different logic. East Africa's ethnic patriots shared the same nightmares. With political independence on the horizon, they thought undisciplined women and talkative revivalists were an embarrassment, undermining their people's reputation. In addressing the challenges of their time, ethnic patriots learned from each other how to cultivate moral and social discipline. They read each other's history books, studied each other's customary legal codes, and modeled programs of social reform on each other's examples. Ethnic identity was not simply a heritage, a set of traditions handed down from the distant past to a particular set of people (though that was how its architects saw it). Neither was ethnicity a feudal anachronism, a residuum outmoded by the growth of national community (though that was how East Africa's nation-builders saw it), or an invention of colonial administration (though that is how many scholars see it today). Ethnic patriotism was a framework in which self-interested cultural entrepreneurs responded to the postwar crisis of social discipline. As patriots, activists cast themselves as inheritors of a fatherland. As patriots, activists identified a culture that needed preservation. As patriots, activists constituted communities that were linked not simply by a common purpose but by blood and history. The *patria* was the standard against which moral conservatives measured the debilitating effects of social change.

Seen through patriots' eyes, converts and prostitutes were alike in their displacement. Like prostitutes, revivalists were delinquents, willfully ignoring the lessons that history taught about comportment, gentility, and respectability. Like prostitutes, revivalists lived on the road, refusing to behave as natives. The history of gender relations in eastern Africa is nowhere separable from political history. Patriotic men sought to enter the political theater as credible husbands and fathers, as members of an upstanding moral community. That is why, on the eve of eastern Africa's independence, they were organizing anti-prostitution campaigns, reforming marriage, and silencing revivalists. These men were not interested in constructing an 'inner domain of sovereignty, far removed from the arena of political contest with the colonial state,' as the Indian historian Partha Chatterjee would have it.[108] To the contrary: patriotic men were establishing their political credentials. They thought national independence to be a moral test, an occasion that required them to prove their readiness to govern themselves by the evidence of their

---

Mau includes David Percox, *Britain, Kenya and the Cold War: Imperial Defence, Colonial Security and Decolonisation* (London, 2004); and Joanna Lewis, *Empire State-Building: War and Welfare in Kenya, 1925–52* (Oxford, 2000).

[108] Partha Chatterjee, *The Nation and its Fragments: Colonial and Postcolonial Histories* (Princeton, 1993), 133.

orderly households. The Revival challenged patriotic men's efforts to set their houses in order. In their lurid testimonies, converts opened up whole arenas of life to public view, undermining patriots' efforts to manage appearances. In their radical refusal to abide by traditional standards of etiquette, converts rejected the lessons that history had to teach them. Converts were subversives on the political and cultural landscape defined by the architects of eastern Africa's ethnic homelands. They dislodged the alignments that patriotic activists set in place.

ARCHIVE STORIES

Historians have come to recognize that archives are never simply sources of information, welling up with data about the past. Archives are dynamically related with the past and the present, and also with the fate of political regimes. Filing systems and other forms of bureaucratic organization enable specific methods of domination and produce particular forms of control.[109] 'The archive has neither status nor power without an architectural dimension,' writes Achille Mbembe. 'The physical space of the building, its motifs and columns, the arrangement of the rooms, the organization of the files, [and] the labyrinth of corridors' together regulate people's access to knowledge while simultaneously putting certain files – and certain forms of knowledge – out of reach.[110] Ann Laura Stoler comments on offices 'filled with directors, assistant directors, scribes, and clerks,' and on the 'massive buildings' that governments build to house their ever-proliferating papers.[111] For Stoler as for other scholars interested in the routines of official knowledge production, archives are 'an arsenal of sorts,' built to serve the purposes of government.[112]

The architecture of official knowledge production in eastern Africa is considerably less impressive than the archives about which Mbembe and Stoler write. There are two landmark buildings. The Kenya National Archives are kept in a glorious columned building, formerly occupied by the Bank of India, in downtown Nairobi. It is a thrillingly democratic place. Because Kenya does not require researchers to go through a lengthy process of government clearance, the search room is full of scholars, litigators, students, and activists arguing over the past.[113] The Tanzania National Archives,

---

[109] Ajay Skaria, 'Writing, Orality and Power in the Dangs, Western India, 1800s-1920s,' in *Subaltern Studies IX: Writings on South Asian History and Society*, eds. Shahid Amin and Dipesh Chakrabarty (Delhi, 1996), 13–58.

[110] Achille Mbembe, 'The Power of the Archive and its Limits,' in *Refiguring the Archive*, eds. Carolyn Hamilton et al. (Cape Town, 2002), 19.

[111] Ann Laura Stoler, *Along the Archival Grain: Epistemic Anxieties and Colonial Common Sense* (Princeton, 2009), 22.

[112] Stoler, *Along the Archival Grain*, 3.

[113] Matthew Carotenuto and Katherine Luongo, 'Navigating the Kenya National Archives: Research and its Role in Kenyan Society,' *History in Africa* 32 (2005), 445–55; Nathan

located in a leafy neighborhood in Dar es Salaam, is a comparatively quiet place, the preserve of professional historians.[114] Outside these two well-kept collections, archives in Kenya and Tanzania reside in the corners of old government buildings, and it is a challenge to locate them. Both countries have established regional depots where papers of a more contemporary provenance are deposited. The Tanzania National Archives' depot in Mwanza is located behind the weight room at the local football stadium. The district archive in Bukoba is kept in an odiferous room adjoining the water closet. In Kakamega, the local government archive is kept in an unmarked warehouse; and in Kisumu, the archive is located in a children's prison.

It is in Uganda that government archives have suffered the most undignified of fates. The archival landscape in Uganda is littered with endangered collections. The Uganda National Archives are held in a sub-basement below the National Agricultural Research Organization in Entebbe. There is no sign that marks the archive's location. Until very recently the catalogue covered only a fraction of the 1,200 boxes kept in the vault.[115] The situation in the provinces is particularly dire. At Hoima, in northwest Uganda, the oldest papers are kept in a mechanic's shed behind the offices of the Chief Administrative Officer. The files are piled high on shelves that overlook the workbench. In Fort Portal, the Kabarole District Archives were until recently kept in the attic above the Resident District Commissioner's offices. The roof was rotten, water leaked through broken windows when it rained, and the collection was infested with wasps. The Toro Kingdom's archives in Fort Portal are kept in a windowless sub-basement below the local government headquarters. The basement is a dumping ground for the government officers who occupy the building, and layers of outmoded bureaucratic machinery now cover the oldest files. At the upper strata are reams of dot-matrix printer paper; just below is a layer of typewriters, carbon paper and bicycles; then some cyclostyled paperwork; and at the bottom of the heap lie the files of the colonial kingdom of Toro.

In the eyes of most government officials, Uganda's archives are debris to be discarded. Uganda's post-colonial politics have been organized in jolting stages, and each successive regime sought to discredit its predecessor.[116]

Mjama, 'Archives and Records Management in Kenya: Problems and Prospects,' *Records Management Journal* 13 (2) (2003), 91–101.

[114] Leander Schneider, 'The Tanzania National Archives,' *History in Africa* 30 (2003), 447–54.

[115] For a description of early cataloguing efforts at the Uganda National Archives, see Patrick English, 'Archives of Uganda,' *American Archivist* 18 (3) (July 1955), 224–30.

[116] In summary: Milton Obote's first government ruled from 1962 to 1971; Idi Amin's regime lasted from 1971 to 1979; the Uganda National Liberation Front was in power from 1979 to 1980; Milton Obote returned to power from 1981 to 1985; and Tito Okello's government lasted from 1985 to 1986, when Yoweri Museveni's National Resistance Movement took power.

Officials of the *ancien régime* were turned out, new standards of weights and measures were established, official stamps were redrawn. Old files were likewise thrown away. It is ironic that the regime of Idi Amin – dysfunctional in so many ways – was the only Ugandan government to treat archiving as a priority. In a circular, Amin's Private Secretary proclaimed that archives were 'the instruments from which the present and future generations can learn about the history of this nation in its correct perspective.'[117] A consultant from UNESCO prepared a report recommending that Uganda should build a proper archive building equipped with a staff of sixty people.[118] Amin's government collapsed before this ambitious project could be launched. His successors sought to break with the past. In 1989, a few years after Yoweri Museveni's National Resistance Movement came to power, an official described the paradigmatic government bureaucrat as 'the model of the new man ... He is the individual who has moved beyond the classical solutions of human problems.' This new man had to be 'completely disencumbered of a shameful past, he must be free to think and act.'[119] Seen in the searching light of a new era, archives were not a resource to husband, organize, or protect. Like typewriters and other outmoded office equipment, like the outmoded philosophies of yesteryear, archives were trash to be cast aside.

Like Uganda's government officials, revivalists see the past as a burden. Their view of time teaches them to regard history not as a source of positive value but as an encumbrance to be discarded. The discipline of revivalism is grounded on the selective reading that converts do as they render their complicated, variegated life stories into testimonies of conversion. This forensic work goes on wherever revivalists gather, and it involves a great deal of selection and editing. I learned this in August 2006, while conducting research in Bugufi, on Tanzania's mountainous border with Burundi. In 1939 and 1940, thousands of Bugufi's people had spectacularly converted. Struck with guilt after hearing Ganda and Kiga revivalists preach, they fell to the ground, writhing in ecstasy and speaking in foreign tongues (see Chapter 5). I came to the parish church at Mubuhenge in hopes of meeting a few of these voluble converts. The priest ushered me into the building, where I found a large audience of people waiting for the interview to begin. As I began to talk with the oldest members of the congregation, a drunkard burst in, loudly proclaiming that he had once been converted. My interviewees insisted that the drunken revivalist should not talk with their foreign visitor, and so, over my protests, the man was ushered out of the building.

[117] KasDA 'Research Projects and Archives' file: A. Luziraa to Provincial Governors, 20 January 1977.

[118] J. M. Akita, 'Development of the National Archives and the National Documentation Centre' (Paris, 1979).

[119] KasDA 'Mr. Bonne Baluku-Nyondo' file: B. K. Stevens, General Secretary, Kasese District, 'Good Message to all R.C.s, Kasese District,' n.d. (but 1989).

In Bugufi as in other places where I conducted research, revivalists were actively engaged in compositional work. By circumscribing my list of interviewees, by configuring their life stories in accordance with a generic template, converts sought to make my program of interviews into a theater of evangelization, a vehicle by which their testimonies could be circulated to a wider audience. Their testimonial work was not only conducted for my benefit. Converts in Bugufi as elsewhere in eastern Africa have for more than seventy years been composing, editing, and circulating their autobiographies. Some of their testimonies became inspirational literature, part of an archive that the architects of the Revival used to compose a narrative about God's work in eastern Africa (see Chapter 2). The interviews that I conducted were not a means of accessing authentic African voices. Converts were speaking in genre, telling me stories they had practiced and polished over many years.[120]

But there are other frameworks in which revivalists' testimonies can be placed. It is the historian's vocation to disassemble the revivalist archive and reinsert converts' testimonies into the world of controversy and argument. I interviewed more than 170 people over the course of this project. My research was concentrated in seven regions: Kigezi, in southern Uganda, the engine of the Revival; Buganda, at the heart of East Africa's regional economy; western Uganda, where I focused on the intellectual history of the Rwenzururu movement; Bukoba, in northwestern Tanzania, the scene of urgent anti-prostitution campaigns; Bugufi, a labor reserve on Tanzania's border with Burundi; Nyanza, in western Kenya; and Gikuyuland, in central Kenya. In each region, I interviewed a wide variety of people: revivalists, ex-prostitutes, political entrepreneurs, ex-guerilla fighters, labor migrants, and local historians. I conducted interviews in Swahili or Gikuyu, and relied on translators when interviewing speakers of Lutoro, Lukonzo, Luamba, Lukiga, Lunyoro, Dholuo, or KiHangaza. In most of the interviews, I brought with me some of the partisan literature that I had culled from the local archives. I sought to bring interviewees back to a time when revivalists' testimonies aroused discord and dissension, to remind them of inconvenient facts, and to invite them to rearticulate discourses that now lie dormant. Archival material, in other words, was a prompt leading people to rehearse lines of thought that had been forgotten, overlaid, or actively discarded. By this means, I sought to unwind the editorial work that converts, patriots, and other partisans have done on the past.

In the course of this research, I have been obliged to engage in the creative, constitutive work of archives management. At the Uganda National Archives in Entebbe, I organized a team of students from the University of Michigan who, working with archives staff and colleagues from Makerere

---

[120] See Luise White, *Speaking with Vampires: Rumor and History in Colonial Africa* (Berkeley, 2000).

University, organized and catalogued the collection. In Fort Portal, I worked with colleagues at Mountains of the Moon University to remove the Kabarole District Archives from the leaky, wasp-infested attic where they were formerly kept. The files have now been cleaned, reboxed, and catalogued, and – using funds from the University of Michigan and the Center for Research Libraries – the collection is currently being digitized for preservation. I am involved in several projects to preserve and publish the private papers of African intellectuals.[121] Many African political actors kept their own archives, tucked away in tin trunks, suitcases, boxes, or cabinets.[122] The Gikuyu intellectual Gakaara wa Wanjau, for example, seems to have written on every scrap of paper that came to hand: there are hymns inscribed on the backs of receipts, pictures drawn on wedding invitations, and letters in the margins of cyclostyled forms. At the time of his death, there were more than 9,000 pages stored at his home in Karatina. In 2002, Gakaara's wife, Shifra Wairire, invited three of my colleagues to photocopy the whole collection; and in 2004 and 2005, I organized the papers, putting them into subject files and creating a catalogue for readers to use.[123] My colleagues and I hope to publish a selection of Gakaara's writings, bringing his creative work to a wider public.

This logistical and organizational work is essential to the historical method that underpins *Ethnic Patriotism and the East African Revival*. By cataloguing, organizing, and preserving archives, historians can reengineer the editorial work that government officials, patriotic entrepreneurs, and revivalists have done on the past. Disinterred from the accumulated strata of bureaucratic debris, archival material can bring people and discourses that have been edited out back into the story. Timosewo Bawalana, for example, has been resurrected out of the ongoing preservation work at the Kabarole District Archives. Bawalana was a Christian prophet who, in October 1970, announced that the Kingdom of God had come to earth. Western Uganda's people were at that time held in the grip of a long war fought between the Ugandan state and the Konzo ethnic minority (see Chapter 11). The prophet

---

[121] Charles Muhoro Kareri, *The Autobiography of Charles Muhoro*, ed. Derek R. Peterson, trans. Joseph Kariuki Muriithi (Madison, WI, 2000); Henry Muoria, *Writing for Kenya: The Life and Works of Henry Muoria*, eds. Wangari Muoria-Sal, Bodil Folke Frederiksen, John Lonsdale, and Derek Peterson (Leiden, 2009); Martin Shikuku 'The People's Watchman: The Life of Joseph Martin Shikuku,' ed. Derek R. Peterson (manuscript, n.d.).

[122] See Karin Barber, 'Introduction: Hidden Innovators in Africa,' in *Africa's Hidden Histories: Everyday Literacy and Making the Self*, ed. Karin Barber (Bloomington, IN, 2006), 1–24. One of Uganda's 'tin trunk' archives has recently been published in Andrea Stultiens, Kaddu Wasswa John, and Arthur C. Kisitu, *The Kaddu Wasswa Archive: A Visual Biography* (Rotterdam, 2010).

[123] Kimani wa Njogu coordinated the project, and Ann Biersteker and Dorothy Woodson photocopied the papers. The guide has been printed as Dorothy Woodson and Derek Peterson, 'A Guide to the Yale University Microfilm Collection of the Gakaara wa Wanjau Papers' (2007).

Bawalana announced that old antagonisms and enmities had come to an end. Hundreds of soldiers laid down their spears, and for a brief period, a peaceable era did in fact come to life in western Uganda. But in 1972, Konzo militants took up arms, drove out the prophet Bawalana, and restored their military campaign. Their long struggle bore fruit in 2009 when the Rwenzururu kingdom became one of several 'cultural institutions' recognized by Uganda's government (Chapter 12).

Timosewo Bawalana is not mentioned in the several published histories of Konzo ethnic separatism. His memory is an embarrassment to the architects of western Uganda's contemporary order, who work to project an image of unity and consistency into the past. But during his brief prophetic career, Bawalana made sure to copy his correspondence to an array of offices in the Uganda government. It is as though he knew that his paperwork would be preserved in the archives. In 2006, the Records Officer and I found his circular letters in the Kabarole District Archives, in files covered with mouse droppings and dampened with rain. I had never heard of Bawalana before, but I was immediately struck by the urgency of his political thought. In 2010 and again in 2011, I interviewed Timosewo Bawalana in Fort Portal. We spent hours going through his correspondence, line by line. I am now working with him to publish a short autobiography that will bring his prophetic career to the notice of a wider Ugandan public.

The work of archives management can revivify lines of discourse that find no place on the contemporary landscape. By preserving endangered papers, cataloguing archives, building repositories, and recovering files, historians can reopen questions that the architects of today's political order sought to close. That is where the work of archives management joins with the work of activism.

The chapters that follow explore how, in several of East Africa's *patrie*, pilgrims and patriots contended over etiquette, culture, and political duty. The book begins with a short chapter concerning the infrastructure of revivalism. Revivalists' self-conception was enabled by eastern Africa's developing technology of communication. They were avid users of the post office, dexterous riders of bicycles, and industrious readers of evangelical media. In their correspondence and through their reading habits, converts came to see themselves as cosmopolitans, sharing a trajectory and a set of disciplines with a widely dispersed community of co-travelers.

Converts' religious pilgrimage was only one of several paths that East Africa's people traveled in the twentieth century. Chapters 3, 4, and 5 together locate revivalists within the broader circulation of ideas and people in the region southwest of Lake Victoria. Chapter 3 concentrates on Kigezi, in southern Uganda, where the Revival originated. Kigezi's people were frontiersmen, independent pioneers who had fought off the autocratic kings of Rwanda in the nineteenth century. Their republican political culture was expressed in Nyabingi, a healing spirit who could not be pinned down to a particular locale. In 1935 and 1936, hundreds of Kigezi's people were seized with the conviction that the world was ending soon. These early revivalists acted in antisocial ways, speaking loudly about adultery and other topics that respectable people kept under wraps. Kigezi's chiefs, appointed by British rulers, thought converts were a threat to civil order. In Kigezi, the Revival was an episode in a long-running contest between political authorities, who sought to settle people down, and Kiga frontiersmen, who were always on the move.

Whereas Kigezi's politics were argumentative and egalitarian, in the kingdom of Buganda hierarchy was enacted in polite rituals and upheld by cultural tradition. Chapter 4 shows how, by managing their households, comporting themselves gracefully, and composing instructive history lessons, Ganda elites drew their clients – and their British rulers – into relationships of reciprocity and trust. In the 1940s, the angry populists of the Bataka Union challenged Buganda's mannered high politics. Claiming to represent the interests of Buganda's ancient landholders, Bataka partisans condemned Buganda's elites for their corruption and gave voice to a community of commoners. Both angry Bataka populists and polished political elites were terrified when, in the mid-1940s, Christian revivalists began to speak openly about their marital and sexual failings. In Buganda, as in Kigezi, revivalism threw conjugal life open to public examination, undermining reputations and publicizing the secrets that genteel Ganda men kept.

Chapter 5 explores the interlinked histories of property management and revivalism in northwestern Tanganyika. The focus is on Bugufi, a tiny chiefdom whose people were eastern Africa's most committed labor migrants. The Revival reached Bugufi with a clamor: its converts were Pentecostals, loudly speaking in tongues and prophesying about the end of the world. Like revivalists more generally, Bugufi's converts were also accountants. They engaged in forensic work, examining their deeds and identifying things that made them sinful. Revivalists owned up to their wrongdoings, even as they also claimed ownership over cattle, land, and other public goods. They moved laterally across different registers of accountancy, developing procedures and dispositions that they used to reconfigure Bugufi's moral economy.

Chapters 6, 7, and 8 are about the genealogy of patriotic thought in postwar East Africa. Labor migration was the drill sergeant for eastern Africa's ethnic patriotisms. Bereft of visible evidence with which to prove their masculine respectability, the thousands of men who migrated to eastern Africa's cities after the Second World War urgently needed social capital. They set about defining their people's customs, codifying their language, and reforming their manners. Chapter 6 focuses on Nyanza, in western Kenya. In the 1940s, Luo men began to represent women's conjugal independence as a traitorous corruption of traditional values. By composing instructive history lessons and by creating civic institutions that upheld patriarchal order, Luo men made urban women subject to discipline. It was on this terrain that the debate over the Revival was conducted. In their strident disavowals of polygamy and in their rigorous criticism of their kin, converts pulled social groups asunder and undermined the patriarchy that Luo men worked to create. When angry Luo churchmen founded a church called the *Johera*, the 'People of Love,' in 1957, they were acting as patriots, defending the convivial relationships that revivalists threatened.

Haya men lived alongside Luo men in eastern Africa's growing cities, and like their neighbors, they came to regard independent women as a threat to civil order. Chapter 7 shows how activists of the Haya Union created an institutional apparatus to manage public space. In a 1950 campaign against prostitution and again in 1961 on the eve of Tanganyika's national independence, Haya men worked out ways to identify, enumerate, and contain independent women. In their activism, they valorized rural life as the ground of virtue and assigned to local government the task of supervising women's conduct. In the late 1960s, the architects of Tanzanian socialism borrowed a set of administrative techniques from the Haya anti-prostitution campaigners. Tanzanian socialism pushed forward a moral and demographic project that Haya patriots had inaugurated.

Chapter 8 extends the argument of Chapter 7 by bringing the legal history of northwestern Tanganyika into sharper focus. For Haya converts, as for revivalists elsewhere in eastern Africa, legal discourse was a set of idioms and practices in which they could develop competence. Converts used the procedures of the courtroom – testimony, interrogation, and judgment – to organize their complicated autobiographies and chart a path out of the life of sin. Chapter 8 particularly focuses on the *Kanisa la Roho Mtakatifu*, the 'Church of the Holy Spirit,' an organization created by converts living on the desolate outskirts of civilized Bukoba. The church's members contrasted their ascetic self-discipline with the corruption and prolificacy of Bukoba's high society. The Haya debate over revivalism was conducted in the grammar of the law, as revivalists skilled in legal procedure sat in judgment on their neighbors.

Chapters 9 and 10 together focus on the moral economy of ethnicity in Gikuyuland, in central Kenya. The Revival was an engine for the production of autobiography. Chapter 9 focuses on two texts: the autobiography of Cecilia Muthoni Mugaki, an early convert to the Revival, and the life history of Charles Muhoro Kareri, a leading critic of revivalism. Literature scholars presume that African autobiographers will faithfully reproduce the values of their ethnic communities, but neither Charles Muhoro nor Cecilia Mugaki wrote ethnography. Their life writings were partisan interventions in a larger field of argument. Through his staid and rather boring book, Muhoro sought to coordinate his contemporaries' actions, rendering examples of self-sacrifice and discipline that his readers could emulate. Cecilia Mugaki's life story, by contrast, was a transcript of the lively testimony that she composed after her conversion in 1948. Where Muhoro wrote and acted as a patriot, Cecilia's text is the work of an agitator. For converts, as for patriots, autobiography was creative writing: it helped organize audiences and lay out paths of action for people to pursue.

Chapter 10 positions Mau Mau detention camps within the larger framework of East Africa's political and intellectual history. Like Luo and Haya men, Gikuyu men were worried about their marriages, about their rights to land, and about their children's prospects. In 1952, anguished Gikuyu men launched the Mau Mau war, fighting for *īthaka na wīathi*, a phrase often translated as 'land and freedom' but better rendered as 'property and moral agency.' Tens of thousands were detained by British officials. As detainees, Gikuyu men carried forward their struggle for moral agency. British officers working to 'rehabilitate' Mau Mau detainees borrowed techniques from Christian revivalists, forcing detainees to examine their deeds, identify their crimes, and confess in public assemblies. Like honorable men, Mau Mau detainees tried to keep their mouths closed, refusing to talk blithely about their private deeds and relationships. Detainees and their captors reenacted, in microcosm, an argument in which East Africans were more generally engaged. Mau Mau detainees endured awful trials, but their sufferings, their terrors, and their hopes were shared by patriotic men all over eastern Africa.

The book concludes in postcolonial Uganda. Like Mau Mau activists, partisans of western Uganda's Rwenzururu movement were convinced that their children's future was endangered by the corruption of their contemporary world. The Rwenzururu movement was conceived out of the historical research that intellectuals of the Konzo ethnic minority conducted during the 1950s. It taught them that their forefathers had once been sovereign, that they possessed an antique culture and a unique political trajectory. In 1962, Konzo activists declared independence and founded a kingdom, rejecting the authority of Uganda's African-run government. Like the men of the Haya Union and the Luo moral reformers, Rwenzururu's founders invented and defended an ethnic homeland; and like other patriotic entrepreneurs, Rwenzururu partisans thought the Revival to be a menace. Converts in Rwenzururu prophesized about the imminence of the eschaton, the moment when historical time would shatter and a peaceable millennium begin. Their radical view of history interrupted Rwenzururu's heritage lessons and undermined its nativism.

It is often said that contemporary Africa lacks a politically critical citizenry that can check rulers' power. Citizens and autocrats alike are said to be involved in a 'politics of the belly,' in the unmoderated consumption of public goods.[124] In Achille Mbembe's pessimistic view, the post-colonial

---

[124] Jean-François Bayart, *The State in Africa: The Politics of the Belly* (London, 1993). See also Basil Davidson, *The Black Man's Burden: Africa and the Curse of the Nation-State* (New York, 1993).

relationship between rulers and the ruled is an 'illicit cohabitation,' a logic that '[inscribes] the dominant and the dominated within the same episteme.'[125] Two recently published books about Kenya's post-colonial history both bear the title *Our Turn to Eat*.[126] It is as though there are no other options. But in fact there were, and are, a variety of epistemologies for East Africans to inhabit. Revivalists were never on convivial terms with the brokers of political and cultural power, and neither were they consumed by the hunger in their bellies. Converts were ascetics, laying down earthly attachments, moderating their appetites, and editing their possessions. Their pilgrimages took them outside the framework of culture and tradition, subverting the order that patriots sought to impose on them. In the study of the Revival, we can see dissent in a different way: not as an austere intellectual position but as a cultural practice, a bodily movement that leads toward another future.

---

[125] Achille Mbembe, *On the Postcolony* (Berkeley, 2001), 110. For criticism of Mbembe's view, see, among others, Mikael Karlström, 'On the Aesthetics and Dialogics of Power in the Postcolony,' *Africa* 73 (1) (2003), 57–76.

[126] Michela Wrong, *It's Our Turn to Eat: The Story of a Kenyan Whistle-Blower* (New York, 2009); and Daniel Branch, Nic Cheeseman, and Leigh Gardner, eds., *Our Turn to Eat: Politics in Kenya Since 1950* (Berlin, 2010).

2

The Infrastructure of Cosmopolitanism

Reacting to the contemporary crisis of multicultural politics in Europe and America, philosophers and political theorists have given the concept 'cosmopolitanism' a new life. In this new definition, cosmopolitanism is an ethical position, an openness to living in dialogue with others in a culturally variegated world.[1] In his 2007 book *Cosmopolitanism: Ethics in a World of Strangers*, Kwame Anthony Appiah argues that 'we have obligations to others, obligations that stretch beyond those to whom we are related by the ties of kith and kind, or even the more formal ties of a shared citizenship.'[2] When confronted by novel ideas and practices, Appiah argues, cosmopolitan individuals should not retreat to their cultural homelands: instead they ought to engage in vigorous conversation, working to understand others. Out of these dialogues, collective values will emerge. This is the foundation for a peaceable global community.

Whereas Appiah and other philosophers work to persuade their liberally minded readers to think and act as cosmopolitans, I am interested here in the technologies by which people are dislodged from their native provinces and propelled to live across linguistic and cultural frontiers. Cosmopolitanism is not only an ethical position. Cosmopolitans are produced within particular discursive regimes. East Africa's converts were formed by their engagements with a particular text – John Bunyan's 1678 *The Pilgrim's Progress*, the premier work of nonconformist Christianity. Modeling themselves after Bunyan's protagonist, African converts rejected the comforts of home and turned away from their obligations to kin. They engineered a cosmopolitan

---

[1] Paul Gilroy, *Postcolonial Melancholia* (New York, 2006); Andrew Dobson, 'Thick Cosmopolitanism,' *Political Studies* 54 (1) (2006), 165–84; Kwame Anthony Appiah, *Cosmopolitanism: Ethics in a World of Strangers* (New York, 2007); Ulrich Beck, *The Cosmopolitan Vision* (Cambridge, 2006). The political philosopher Seyla Benhabib harnesses 'cosmopolitanism' for different purposes in her *Another Cosmopolitanism* (Oxford, 2006). My thanks to Darren Walhof for his help in navigating this literature.

[2] Appiah, *Cosmopolitanism*, xv.

persona to inhabit, reworking their cuisine, stitching together new forms of clothing, and devising new domestic arrangements. Their social work distinguished them from their compatriots and made it possible for converts to see themselves as pilgrim sojourners. As they reworked their social lives, converts invested in eastern Africa's developing technology of communications. The proliferation of post offices, the widespread sales of bicycles, the circulation of newspapers, and the advancing road infrastructure made it possible for converts to travel across cultural and political frontiers, learn new languages, and read other people's autobiographies. Converts' cosmopolitanism was never simply an ethical commitment or a philosophical posture. Cosmopolitanism had a social and material history.

East Africa's ethnic patriots were no less involved in the modern world. Like revivalists, patriots were formed by their engagements with eastern Africa's communications network. Patriots read newspapers and traveled widely. The most ardent of these patriots dwelled in eastern Africa's multicultural cities. But while converts came to see themselves as cosmopolitan members of a multi-sited movement, patriots identified themselves as natives, defenders of a particular homeland. They thought the cosmopolitan urban world to be a competitive arena, in which they were obliged to contend with other men for honor and respect. In their search for social capital, urban-dwelling men worked to make their people's history into a heritage, the foundation for moral order and discipline. In earnestly instructive historical books, patriotic men contrasted the antique integrity of their people's culture with its contemporary degradation. Imagined as a *patria*, a fatherland, a patriot's native country was both a location and a set of duties and obligations (see Chapter 1).

Both cosmopolitan revivalists and ethnic patriots were configuring time and space. Geography was not simply the container for human action, and neither was time a measuring stick that indexed and sequenced events. Revivalists acted on a transcontinental scale, composing their lives in relation to people at a great distance. Patriots worked on a much smaller scale, anchoring people, both morally and politically, to a particular bordered homeland. Revivalists made a break in time, converting from one way of life to another. Patriots worked in linear time, making the ancestral past into a source of instruction and disciplinary authority. Revivalists modeled themselves after John Bunyan's pilgrim sojourner, laid down their attachments to kith and kin, and headed toward a distant horizon. Patriots read and wrote historical narrative and shaped their people's behavior in conformity with received wisdom. Revivalists and patriots lived on different scales. That is why their argument was so urgent. Revivalists were out of place, and out of time, in patriots' native land.

BUNYAN IN EASTERN AFRICA

Converts' travel was modeled on *The Pilgrim's Progress*, the foundational work of English nonconformism. The book is an allegory about the protagonist Christian, who, as the story opens, bears a heavy burden that 'lieth hard' upon his back.[3] Guided by the character Evangelist – who advises him to 'Fly from the Wrath to come' – Christian sets out on a long pilgrimage, blocking his ears to the entreaties of his wife and children. Along his way to the Celestial City, Christian reaches the 'place of deliverance,' where the straps that bind his burden to his back are broken and it rolls into an open sepulcher. For Protestant missionaries, Bunyan's book was both inspirational and useful. Even Anglican churchmen – historically antagonistic to Bunyan's nonconformist convictions – made haste to translate it. The first translation of *The Pilgrim's Progress* in eastern Africa was the Swahili edition, which appeared in 1888, only five years after the New Testament was published.[4] Uganda missionaries brought out a Luganda edition in 1900, only three years after the Luganda Bible was published.[5] The Kinyarwanda translation – published in 1933 – was partly composed by the cousin of the king of Rwanda (see Chapter 3).[6] A DhoLuo edition was published in 1943.[7] For missionaries and for African converts, translating Bunyan was an urgent matter. Perez Beyanga – one of the leaders of the Revival in southern Uganda – set to work translating *The Pilgrim's Progress* into his vernacular language, Lunyankole, in 1957. 'If a single day passes without writing something for the Saviour,' he told the Anglican bishop, 'I have a strong and strange sensation of not having done all that is required of me.'[8]

Rendered in DhoLuo, Swahili, Lunyankole, and Kinyarwanda by a cadre of earnest translators, Bunyan's text became standard reading material for students across eastern Africa. During the 1940s, it was one of three vernacular-language set texts for Luo-speaking students in western Kenya.[9] For Luo students, as for other East Africans, *The Pilgrim's Progress* was a resource: it gave them a commonly understood stock of characters and plotlines that could be meaningfully deployed to convince, chasten, or instruct.[10] But Bunyan's text was more than a reference book. It was a primer on ontology. The story invited revivalists to see sin in material form, as a weighty bundle of possessions, deeds, and dispositions that could – like the bundle on Christian's back – be separated from the whole fabric of their lives and disposed of. *The Pilgrim's Progress* thereby encouraged converts

[3] John Bunyan, *The Pilgrim's Progress from This World to That Which Is to Come* (Uhrichsville, Ohio, n.d. [1678]).

[4] *Msafiri: Kitabu Hiki Kimefasirika Katika Kitabu cha Kiingreza Kiitwacho* 'Pilgrim's Progress' (London, 1888).

[5] *Omutambuze* (London, 1900); *Omutambuze* (Kampala, 1927); 'Editorial Notes,' *Church Missionary Intelligencer* XXIII (1897).

[6] CMS G3 A11/O: Rwanda Council meeting, 29 May 1933.

[7] *Wuodh Jawuoth* (Nairobi, 1943).

[8] CoU 02 Bp 14/1: Perez Beyanga to Bishop, 27 December 1957.

[9] Kakamega NE 9/9: B. Ohanga to Senior Education Officer, 22 September 1947. The other books on the syllabus were titled 'Biographies of Luo Heroes' and 'Luo History and Customs.'

[10] Argued in Isabel Hofmeyr, *The Portable Bunyan: A Transnational History of* The Pilgrim's Progress (Princeton, 2004), chapter 5.

to practice the techniques of accountancy, to make lists and keep records, to document the provenance of their possessions (see Chapters 5 and 8). In 1936, Isaka – a cook in the employ of missionary Dora Skipper at Gahini, in northern Rwanda – confessed that 'I have stolen so much from you ever since I started that I don't know the value of it.'[11] The evening after Isaka made his confession, Skipper found him in the kitchen reading *The Pilgrim's Progress* aloud, while her garden boy looked up the biblical references. For Isaka as for other converts, even the smallest things had to be accounted for. Skipper could scarcely find time to rest when revivalist fervor became widespread at Gahini in 1937. 'Streams are still coming in,' she wrote, returning 'pencils, soap, francs and bits of cloth all stolen at some time or another.'[12] When a schoolgirl named Abisagi converted, she burned virtually all of her possessions – pillow, blanket, dresses, and photos – before an audience of her peers, explaining 'why each thing had to go.'[13] Converts like Abisagi were making an account of their lives and identifying articles that made them sinful.

Converts practiced the discipline of self-editing. They sought to open up a visible distance between themselves and their former lives. Like Bunyan's protagonist, African converts were on the move. The Gikuyu convert Bedan Ireri had a dream in 1945 that lasted two full weeks. The subject matter, he recalled, was of 'pilgrimage and the way to heaven.' 'It was like television,' Ireri remembered. 'I was walking, the time went on, and then I entered into Heaven.'[14] Like Bunyan's protagonist, revivalists thought they were traveling a perilous road. Heshbon Mwangi, a leading revivalist in central Kenya, issued a circular letter in 1950 titled 'Satan's attacks on the Kenya Revival.'[15] It likened Satan to Mr. Worldly Wiseman, the duplicitous character who lured Bunyan's protagonist off the straight and narrow way. Mwangi urged his readers to keep their feet on the highway to heaven. 'We need to watch this pilgrimage so that Satan may not kill some of us before we reach the heavenly city,' he wrote. 'This journey is not of a few days.'

When converts like Heshbon Mwangi represented themselves as pilgrims, they were not talking in metaphors. Converts conceived of themselves after the model of Bunyan's protagonist – as journeymen and journeywomen, leaving worldly attachments behind and moving unencumbered toward another home. In their careful editing of their possessions they cultivated a disposition to travel. Most of them traveled by bicycle, and it is not a coincidence that the history of the bicycle in eastern Africa overlaps with

[11] CMS Oxford, Dora Skipper papers, folio 2: diary entry for 7 May 1936.

[12] CMS Oxford, Dora Skipper papers, folio 2: diary entry for 19 April 1937.

[13] CMS Oxford, Dora Skipper papers, folio 2: diary entry for 18 April 1937; HMC JEC 3/4: Skipper to Church, 25 April 1937.

[14] Murray papers: interview, Bedan Ireri, Kabare, 26 May 1988.

[15] HMC JEC 5/4: Heshbon Mwangi, 'Satan's Attacks on the Kenyan Revival,' January 1950.

the trajectory of the Revival. Central Kenya's first African-owned bicycle shop was opened in 1926.[16] The Raleigh Company energetically marketed its bicycles in eastern Africa during the early 1930s. 'It has the strength of a lion! The lightness of a feather! It goes faster than the wind!' went one Swahili-language newspaper advertisement.[17] Demand during and after the war drove up the cost of bicycles: bicycle tires cost three shillings each in western Uganda in 1939; by 1947, they cost nine shillings forty pence.[18] For workmen earning an average of fifteen shillings per month, owning a bicycle required careful financial planning. There was a thriving black market in stolen bicycles in Buganda during the early 1950s: the Anglican bishop called the number of stolen machines 'stupendous.'[19] Uganda's government felt obliged to appoint a 'Bicycle Thefts Committee' to inquire into the problem.[20] But demand continued to rise, and the price of cycling correspondingly increased. In Bunyoro, in western Uganda, the political activist John Kakonge found it difficult to purchase a bicycle.[21] He wanted the government to set standard prices and punish shopkeepers who practiced price-gouging.

Revivalists thought bicycles to be essential to their religious vocation. One of my interviewees described how, after his conversion in February 1942, he used his savings to purchase a used bicycle. Every weekend, he told me, 'I went to the villages to go and preach the Gospel.'[22] On more than one occasion he cycled, in the company of dozens of converts, from his home in southern Uganda to Gahini, in northwestern Rwanda, to meet with other revivalists. Female converts rode on the backs of bicycles pedaled by their male colleagues. They were obliged to wear simple khaki clothing, called *ebikaru*, that was tailored to prevent the dress from tangling around the bicycles' wheels.[23] Their carefully contrived attire allowed converts to move with ease. Traders carrying salt from Lake Katwe, far in the west of Uganda, are said to have learned to ride bicycles with the help of dexterous

[16] NMK Dennis papers A/21: Charles Muhoro to Gordon Dennis, 30 March 1926.

[17] TNA Acc. J (450) 19153: *Mambo Leo* 90 (June 1930).

[18] KigDA Bundle 20, 'Labour, General' file: 'Western Province 1939 and 1947 Wage Rates,' 2 August 1947.

[19] CoU 02 Bp 205/24: Bishop to Controller of Supplies, 9 June 1951. In Nairobi, Ngugi wa Kabiro found a vocation as a retailer of stolen bicycles in 1953. He bought them from thieves at fifty shillings each, and, having altered the license number with the help of a corrupt clerk, he resold the same machines at 200 shillings each. Ngugi Kabiro, *Man in the Middle* (Richmond, British Columbia, 1973), 54.

[20] UNA Secretariat file 13635: J. W. Kyeyune to Secretary, Bicycle Thefts Committee, 6 March 1953.

[21] HDA 'Petitions, complaints, and enquiries, general' file: John Kakonge to District Commissioner, 29 September 1953.

[22] Interview: Enoch Lugimbirwa, Ruharo, Ankole, Uganda, 8 July 2004.

[23] John Muhanguzi, 'The Spread of the Revival Movement at Burunga in Nyabushozi County, East Ankole, Uganda' (Dip. Theo., Makerere University, 1985).

revivalists.[24] Evangelistic missions were bicycle-born: in 1957, a missionary observer counted twenty-six bicycles among a company of Ganda revivalists setting off to evangelize their district, and a revivalist in western Kenya remembered how he and other converts used to preach at 'two, three, or four places in one day,' moving from place to place 'in a great convoy' of bicycles.[25]

Whether on bicycles or (less commonly) on motorcycles or in automobiles, converts were crossing political frontiers to attend conventions, visit other converts, and conduct evangelism. The Revival's leading evangelists seem to have constantly been on the road. William Nagenda was the movement's most-traveled cosmopolitan. The son of a Ganda landholder, Nagenda converted in 1936, left his government position in Entebbe, and took up a post as an evangelist in the Anglican mission in northern Rwanda. In September 1938, Nagenda traveled to western Kenya, where he and other converts from Uganda and Rwanda preached at the region's first Revival convention (see Chapter 6).[26] In April 1941, Nagenda preached at a convention in Fort Portal, in western Uganda, and in June 1942, he spent a number of weeks in central Kenya.[27] By the 1950s, Nagenda was traveling constantly, usually in the company of missionary Joe Church. In 1951, Church and Nagenda conducted an evangelistic tour of Nyasaland; in 1952, they toured India; and in 1956, they managed to visit western Kenya, Angola, Nyasaland, and Tanganyika in the period of a few months.[28]

William Nagenda and Joe Church had unusually wide-ranging itineraries, but they were not unique in their propensity for travel. East Africans made the Revival a cosmopolitan network, opening a field of discourse that drew together people who were widely separated by language and geography. When revivalist enthusiasm gripped the schoolgirls in northern Rwanda in 1935, among the first converts was Margaret Chyambari from the kingdom of Toro in western Uganda. She became one of the region's first Revival evangelists, conducting preaching missions in Rwanda's southwest and in the southwest corner of Uganda.[29] The tiny chiefdom of Bugufi – away in the northwestern corner of Tanganyika – produced a great number of traveling evangelists. In 1939, a group of students and teachers from Bugufi set off for Kibondo, 120 miles to the south, to preach and make converts; in 1940, and again in 1945, Bugufi teachers led Revival conventions in central

[24] George Kafureeka, 'The Impact of the Revival Movement on the Church in East Ankole Diocese, with Particular Reference to Rushere Archdeaconry, Mbarara District, Uganda, 1965–75' (Dip. Theo., Uganda Christian University, 1999).

[25] CoU 02 Bp 192/83: J. Hodgkins, diary entry for 9 March 1957; George F. Pickens, *African Christian God-Talk: Matthew Ajuoga's Johera Narrative* (Dallas, 2004), 235–36.

[26] HMC JEC 1/2: Joe Church to Martin Capon, 30 June 1938. See J. Church, *Quest for the Highest: An Autobiographical Account of the East African Revival* (Exeter, 1981), 158–59.

[27] HMC JEC 5/1: William Nagenda to Joe Church, 15 June 1942.

[28] For the report, see HMC JEC 2/9: Church, 'Evangelistic Journeys, 1956.'

[29] Chyambari's travels are described in CMS Oxford, Dora Skipper papers, folio 2: diary entries for 2 July 1936 and 29 May 1937.

Tanganyika.[30] In 1956, Bugufi's chief traveled by car to western Kenya where he and William Nagenda preached at a convention attended by some 10,000 people (see Chapter 6).[31]

The Revival was a multilingual movement of people and ideas. It was punctuated by conventions where thousands of people gathered. At the 1956 convention in western Kenya there were attendees from central Kenya, coastal Kenya, Buganda, the Upper Nile, Rwanda, Tanganyika, Nairobi, and the Rift Valley.[32] Missionary Joe Church commented on the polyglot character of the proceedings: he met delegates who spoke Nandi, DhoLuo, Kikuyu, Luganda, Lunyoro, and Kinyarwanda.[33] English was never the Revival's lingua franca. Preachers relied on translators who rendered their words into the vernaculars of their audiences. Simeon Nsibambi – one of the Revival's founding architects – spoke both English and Swahili poorly. When he led a convention in central Kenya in 1937, he refused to allow his missionary host to translate his words into English. Nsibambi spoke Luganda to his Kenyan audience, relying on a traveling companion to translate his words directly into Swahili.[34]

Revivalists had to be cosmopolitans. They had to learn new languages, travel to conventions, and compose themselves in dialogue with people from distant corners of eastern Africa. In their polyglot gatherings, converts worked out novel techniques of self-presentation. The core discipline of the Revival was the testimony of conversion. Converts were obliged to describe their passage from one world to another, contrasting their former ways of sin with their new lifestyles. There was a specific set of criteria that revivalist audiences used in their evaluation of testimonies. Haya revivalists in northwestern Tanganyika were said to 'grade the testimonies given and to refuse to accept a conversion that does not follow the same pattern as their own. If one or more of the cardinal sins – adultery, drunkenness, theft or idolatry – is not mentioned, it is felt that something is missing.'[35] Converts needed to characterize themselves. The work of autobiographical self-positioning obliged converts to look for the smallest shred of material with which to dramatize their conversion. Missionaries worried that the first revivalists were 'wanting to sit and brood over themselves ... instead of feeding on the Promises.'[36] But converts were not passively brooding. They

[30] DCT loose papers: Central Tanganyika Diocesan Letter 38 (August 1939); HMC JEC 1/3: Lionell Bakewell to Joe Church, 22 March 1940; DCT Berega Log Book, entry for 7–11 May 1945.
[31] HMC JEC 2/9: Joe Church, 'Evangelistic Journeys,' 1956.
[32] ACK ACSO/CPN/1, 'Nyanza Chaplaincy, 1954–60' file: Festo Olang', et al., 'Maseno Convention,' n.d. (but 1956).
[33] HMC JEC 2/9: Church, 'Evangelistic Journeys, 1956.'
[34] CMS Annual Letters file: T. F. C. Bewes, 22 June 1937.
[35] ELCT Box BII: 1, 'Annual Reports, 1945–54' file: Bukoba area superintendent's report, 1952.
[36] CMS Oxford, Dora Skipper papers, folio 2: diary entry for 21 February 1937.

PHOTO 3. Kabale Convention, 1945. Photo by Joe Church. Courtesy of the Henry Martyn Centre, Cambridge.

were actively generating a narrative about themselves, a narrative that made them converts.[37] Testimonies were literary works: they had to be carefully composed, edited, and polished (see Chapter 9).

Some converts wrote their autobiographies in letters they posted to fellow-converts in other parts of eastern Africa. The development of the postal system in eastern Africa was uneven, overlapping with the region's political geography. The kingdom of Buganda – the jewel of Britain's East African crown – was favored with superior infrastructure, and as early as 1895 the British government organized a postal service there, using stamps printed on the Anglican mission's press.[38] The postal system was slower to arrive in regions outside Buganda. In Tanganyika – a British mandate after Germany's defeat in the First World War – a postal service was inaugurated in May 1917.[39] Much of the mail had to be transported on men's shoulders; in 1931, Tanganyika's government employed 148 runners to carry the post.[40] Everything sped up in 1937, when the Empire Air Mail Scheme was launched. It offered a thrice-weekly service between London and Kenya, Uganda, and Tanganyika.[41] By airmail it took only two weeks for a letter from Britain to reach the mission station at Gahini in northern Rwanda.[42]

[37] Bruce Hindmarsh shows that eighteenth-century English evangelicals were likewise engaged in a hermeneutical practice, reading a pattern into the details of past experience, and using the evidence they gathered to compose a testimony of conversion. See D. Bruce Hindmarsh, *The Evangelical Conversion Narrative: Spiritual Autobiography in Early Modern England* (Oxford, 2005).

[38] Edward Proud, *The Postal History of Uganda and Zanzibar* (Heathfield, East Sussex, 1993), 146–47.

[39] Edward Proud, *The Postal History of Tanganyika, 1915–1961* (Heathfield, East Sussex, 1989), 47.

[40] Proud, *Postal History of Tanganyika*, 63.

[41] Proud, *Postal History of Uganda*, 183.

[42] CMS Oxford, Dora Skipper papers, folio 2: diary entry for 21 March 1936.

Revivalists were early and enthusiastic users of eastern Africa's postal system. Letter-writing helped constitute the Revival as an imagined community. Through their correspondence, revivalists came to see themselves as part of a wider, intercommunicating movement. One of the earliest autobiographical letters came from Yosiya Kinuka. Kinuka put his testimony on paper in 1936, in a circular letter addressed to his 'Ruanda friends.'[43] With this letter, Kinuka got a wide readership: it was reprinted in the missionary journal *Ruanda Notes* and circulated in Britain, Kenya, and Tanzania.[44] In 1946, Kinuka's testimony was again reprinted in a book published by the Ruanda Mission.[45] Not all converts found such a large audience, but like Kinuka, they used letter-writing to communicate their life stories to a readership outside their immediate locale. In western Kenya, Luo revivalists sent a 'stream of letters' to a missionary schoolmaster in Nairobi, describing their evangelistic work and documenting the slow growth of the Revival community in Nyanza.[46] In Buganda, a student at the secondary school in Budo kept up a correspondence with William Nagenda's wife, announcing that she and other students had been converted.[47] In these and in many other letters, converts took up a place in a larger, multilingual sphere of exchange. The leading revivalists in Masaka in central Uganda were employees of the post office.[48] It was through the postal system that converts worked out their autobiographies.

As they put their life stories on paper, as they read other people's testimonies, and as they listened to the multilingual autobiographies at Revival conventions, revivalists came to see themselves as sharing a trajectory with people they had never met. This sense of simultaneity – the awareness that other people in distant parts of eastern Africa were likewise converting – was cultivated by the editorial work of missionary Joe Church, evangelist William Nagenda, and other architects of the Revival. Church had studied medicine at Emmanuel College, Cambridge, and went as a missionary to Rwanda in 1927, where he remained for more than forty years. When his private papers were brought for deposit at Cambridge in 2007, they filled eight footlockers and six suitcases.[49] Church was an avid and active archivist. He seems to have annotated virtually every piece of correspondence that passed into his hands, and with these annotations he created an index of the

[43] HMC JEC 6/3: Undated letter from Yosiya Kinuka to 'Ruanda friends,' n.d. (but 1936).
[44] MAM E/1 E: Yosea Kinuka, untitled essay, *Ruanda Notes* 51 (1936).
[45] A. Stanley-Smith, *Road to Revival: The Story of the Ruanda Mission* (London, 1946).
[46] HMC JEC 1/2: Martin Capon to Joe Church, 21 November 1939.
[47] HMC JEC 5/4: William Nagenda, circular letter, 1 July 1946.
[48] NAB CO 536/215/4: 'Activities of the Abalokole, Twice Born or Saved Ones,' part II, 30 April 1944; Bill Butler, *Hill Ablaze* (London, 1976), 113.
[49] Joe Church's papers are described in Terry Barringer, 'Recordings of the Work of the Holy Spirit": The Joe Church Archives,' in *The East African Revival: History and Legacies*, eds. Kevin Ward and Emma Wild-Wood (Kampala, 2010), 271–85.

Revival's onward course. In March 1937, for example, Church received a letter from the missionary Dora Skipper. Skipper described how, at an evening meeting in northern Rwanda, dozens of people prayed for salvation. 'It seemed something like the collapse of Jericho,' Skipper wrote.[50] Using a red pencil, Church wrote 'the collapse of Jericho' in the margins. Two weeks later he quoted Skipper's paragraph about 'the collapse of Jericho' in a letter he wrote to Uganda's bishop.[51] When he published *Quest for the Highest*, his 'autobiographical account of the East African Revival,' in 1981, Church once again cribbed from Dora Skipper's letter. At Gahini in 1937, he wrote, 'ten or more were praying with deeply convicted hearts … and the walls of Jericho came down.'[52] For Joe Church, the archive was never simply a repository. Church was practicing selective reading, looking for snippets of text that could illuminate God's work. His archive was a resource that had to be organized, edited, and presented.

This editorial work gave Church the evidence with which to compose a narrative about the Revival's trajectory. His favorite literary genre was undoubtedly biography. He kept files full of the correspondence he received from African converts, and he used this source material to compose a great number of biographies.[53] His first subject was Blasio Kigozi. Kigozi, an evangelist and schoolteacher in the employ of the Anglican mission in Rwanda, died in Kampala on 25 January 1936, after delivering a series of powerful sermons in southern and central Uganda (Chapter 3). Kigozi's body was scarcely in the grave when Church brought him back to life, on paper, as an advocate for the Revival. On 31 January, Joe Church sent his supporters in England a cyclostyled first draft of Blasio's biography. Titled 'Blasio, Friend of Ruanda,' the draft described his early life, his conversion, and his evangelistic labors on behalf of the Revival.[54] On 3 February, Church issued a second draft, titled 'Blasio Kigozi: An Appreciation.'[55] By April 1936, a scant three months after Kigozi's death, Church had prepared a book-length biography, in Luganda, entitled *Awake, Uganda!*[56] Church was convinced that 'Blasio's message must not be lost – it may have a very definite place in rousing the Baganda to think of Revival.'[57] It was Church's vocation to keep Kigozi in the public mind.

[50] HMC JEC 3/4: Dora Skipper to Decie and Joe Church, 31 March 1937.
[51] HMC JEC 3/1: Joe Church, untitled notes, 16 April 1937.
[52] Church, *Quest for the Highest*, 144.
[53] Church, *Forgive Them: The Story of an African Martyr* (London, 1966); Church, *William Nagenda: A Great Lover of Jesus* (London, 1974); HMC JEC 8/5: 'How are You Getting Along?,' n.d.
[54] MAM AC 4: Joe Church, 'Blasio, Friend of Ruanda,' 31 January 1936.
[55] CoU 02 Bp 223/28: Joe Church, 'Rev. Blasio Kigozi, Died 25 January 1936: An Appreciation,' 3 February 1936.
[56] Joe Church, *Awake, Uganda! The Story of Blasio Kigozi and his Vision of Revival* (Kampala, 1957 [1936]).
[57] CoU 02 Bp 223/28: Church to Bishop Stuart, 26 April 1936. Eighteenth-century evangelicals were likewise avid producers of biographies and autobiographies. In Edinburgh, William

Joe Church was not the only one organizing an archive. The Ganda evangelist William Nagenda also possessed a large mailing list. He composed lengthy circulars, duplicated with the aid of a cyclostyling machine, which quoted from the many letters he had received from other converts. Nagenda's circulars drew people widely separated by geography together on the page, attenuating distance and cultivating an intimate sense of shared purpose. A 1942 circular described how 'the work at Budo is still going ahead,' how 'at Gayaza, Ezra now is going on well in the light,' and how 'on Oct. 16th we are going to Hoima and Masindi; we hope for many blessings.'[58] These and other letters chronicled the spiritual condition of the far-flung people with whom Nagenda corresponded. Distributed through the post, the chronicles composed by Nagenda and Church helped revivalists see themselves as part of a larger community. The press gave revivalists an even wider readership for their chronicles. The Ruanda Mission – the Anglican organization to which a great number of missionary revivalists belonged – created a range of printed media to publicize its work. *Ruanda Notes* came out, on a quarterly basis, from 1924 until 1974.[59] From July 1944, the mission brought out a tabloid newspaper under the title *Front Line News*.[60] Edited by the indefatigable Joe Church, the newspaper carried reports on conventions, testimonies from African converts, and correspondence from Revival evangelists. The second issue of *Front Line News*, for example, contained an article titled 'The Conversion of M..., A Young Mututsi'; a letter from William Nagenda; and a report from Joe Church on 'The Revival at Shyira,' in Burundi.[61]

Through these media, the testimonies composed by Africans found an interested readership among English evangelicals. There was a particularly active readership at the University of Cambridge.[62] During the late 1930s and 1940s, a group of evangelical students met regularly to read missionary journals at Henry Martyn Hall, adjoining Holy Trinity Church. Joe Church – himself a graduate of Emmanuel College – thought Henry Martyn Hall to be the 'power house that had loosed God's movings in Ruanda and Uganda.'[63] Church's family house was in Little Shelford, near Cambridge,

McCulloch recorded the case histories of more than one hundred men and women who converted, noting their names, the location of their homes, and the 'time and manner of their being seiz'd.' See Hindmarsh, *Evangelical Conversion Narrative*, 197.

58 William Nagenda, circular letter, 14 October 1942. Quoted in NAB CO 536/215/4: 'Activities of the Abalokole, Twice Born, or Saved Ones,' 16 October 1943.

59 A complete run can be found in HMC JEC 20/1–9.

60 *Front Line News* was superseded in 1947 by *Revival News*, also under Church's editorship. These journals can be found in HMC JEC 25/6 and /9.

61 MAM E 1/7: *Front Line News* 2 (November 1944).

62 Cambridge had long been a center for Anglican evangelicalism. See Andrew Porter, 'Cambridge, Keswick, and Late Nineteenth-Century Attitudes to Africa,' *Journal of Imperial and Commonwealth History* 5 (1) (1976), 5–34.

63 Church, *Quest for the Highest*, 147.

and he and other revivalists made a habit of preaching at the university during their periodic visits to the United Kingdom. There was an international audience for African converts' life stories. When Joe Church and William Nagenda visited Lausanne in Switzerland in 1947, they spent most of their time describing the testimonies of African converts. The Swiss evangelicals who heard them were impressed: in a newspaper report, a group of pastors thought it 'amazing to see Africans of free and open face, who no longer blindly copy the Europeans.'[64] Carefully edited and polished, Africans' life stories were both inspirational and exemplary.

African converts organized their lives in dialogue with a far-flung fellowship. They addressed that larger community in their correspondence, in autobiographies, and through the evangelical media. In 1944, a Ruanda Mission newsletter carried a report on the convention at Kayero, in Burundi.[65] The congregation of 500 people had streamed from the church, 'carrying charms or even bits of the wrappings ... waving them over their heads and singing "Rejoice and be glad."' Penitent converts lined up some seventy charms on a table, and one of the converts told a missionary to select certain charms for display in Britain 'as a letter from us to show how God has set us free.' The remainder of the charms were burned in a huge bonfire, and 'an absolute shout of triumph went up as the flames rose.' Gathered round the bonfire, converts' dramatic self-representations were addressed to a proximal audience at Kayero. At the same time, converts also addressed a distant British audience that they knew through the post, through the media, and through Revival conventions. Converts composed their life histories at a frontier. They related their autobiographies to people who lived far away, people with whom they practiced techniques of self-representation.

The Lutheran bishop of northwestern Tanzania, Josiah Kibira, once argued that the Revival was best understood as a 'new clan,' a community with its own taboos and its own leadership.[66] But revivalism was never a comfortable affirmation of community. Revival meetings were judgmental occasions in which attendees formed relationships that were evaluative in character. With other people's eyes on them, converts had to engage in the work of making themselves converts. They did so through the composition and circulation of autobiographies. Converts were cosmopolitans, not clanspeople. They were living across the frontiers of their native communities. In this regard they were by no means alone: during the 1930s and 1940s, migrant laborers from Rwanda, northwest Tanganyika, and western

---

[64] HMC JEC 1/5: 'The Team of Ruanda among the Pastors of the Canton of Vaud,' *Semeur Vaudois*, March 1947. Vaud – the locality where Church and Nagenda preached – was a center of Swiss evangelicalism. See Patrick Harries, *Butterflies and Barbarians: Swiss Missionaries and Systems of Knowledge in South-East Africa* (Oxford, 2007).

[65] MAM E 1/5: Box Collectors Letter no. 1, January 1942.

[66] Josiah M. Kibira, *Church, Clan and the World* (Uppsala, 1974), 46–58.

Kenya were – like the revivalists – learning new languages, crossing borders, and living at a distance from their homes. Independent women were also on the move, settling in Nairobi, Kampala, and Dar es Salaam. But revivalists were unique in the cosmopolitanism of their self-conception. By reading other converts' correspondence and in their bicycle-born travels, converts came to see themselves as part of a large, multi-sited field of action. Through a set of generic practices – the confessional letter, the testimony, and the biography – converts learned how to contrast past with present, how to catalogue their sins and classify their possessions. In their letters and in their confessions of sin, they added to the archives kept by the architects of the Revival and made themselves nodes in an intercontinental network of intellectual and cultural exchange.

CONCLUSION

Revivalists posed a threat to eastern Africa's patriotic organizers because they would not organize their lives around the spatial coordinates of their fatherlands. Converts' cosmopolitanism was more than a principled embrace of multiculture, and more than a generous openness to others. Converts were not liberals, rejoicing in human variety. Converts became cosmopolitans as they uprooted themselves from their homes and set their feet on the pilgrim's path. By composing autobiographies, by carrying on postal correspondence with other converts, and by traveling to attend conventions, revivalists projected themselves out of their native territories and into a broader ecumene. The Revival was, among other things, a movement.

3

Religious Movements in Southern Uganda

In 1931 and 1932, the Anglican missionary Harold Guillebaud was work-ing to translate John Bunyan's *The Pilgrim's Progress* into Kinyarwanda. Guillebaud made a habit of reading each week's work aloud in the ser-mons he delivered at the Anglican church at Gahini in northeast Rwanda. 'It seems to live anew in its Ruandan dress,' he wrote, as 'phrase after phrase is matched by its corresponding idiom from the everyday speech of the people.'[1] Guillebaud used the passive voice when describing the work of translation, but it was, in fact, African actors who were bringing Bunyan to life. Convinced that the end of the world was at hand, people in southern Uganda and northern Rwanda were reworking their biographies to conform to Bunyan's template. On an evening in 1939, missionaries found 700 peo-ple gathered at a church compound, many of them crying uncontrollably. When they asked one woman to explain why she wept, she replied 'Because I am on the road to destruction.'[2] The woman knew herself to have strayed off the heavenward path that Bunyan's pilgrim had to follow. Converts in Burundi told missionaries that God had given them a 'new hymn about the way in which Christian came to the Cross and his burden of sin rolled away for ever.'[3] Their hymn referred to the culminating scene in Bunyan's book. The first Revival evangelists to preach in northern Kigezi arrived with the hymn 'Whither, Pilgrims, Are You Going?' on their lips.[4] The hymn went:

> 'Pilgrim, whither journey you along the path of life?
> What's the goal you have in view along the path of life?'

[1] MAM 1 E/1: Guillebaud, 'The Crowning Joy of Six Year's work,' *Ruanda Notes* 39 (January 1932).
[2] HMC JEC 3/4: Joe Church, circular letter, 13 March 1939.
[3] H. Osborn, *Revival: A Precious Heritage* (Winchester, 1995), 65.
[4] James Kyomukama, 'The Impact of the Balokole Movement on the Anglican Church in North Kigezi Diocese, with Particular Reference to Rubirizi Archdeaconry, Rukungiri District' (Dip. Theo. thesis, Bishop Tucker Theological College, 1995).

'Far beyond our vision, friend, is my journey's blessed end;
Heavenward my footsteps wend along the path of life.'

Revival converts thought themselves to be on a journey from one life to another. They were inveterate travelers. One of the first converts in southern Uganda was nicknamed 'the crane' because of his unending journeying. He told me how he had cycled to Ankole, Masaka, Rujumbura, Kinkizi, Bufumbira, and other places far distant from his home in order to preach.[5] At a 1939 Revival meeting in northeastern Rwanda, the preacher is reported to have addressed a crowd of some 1,500 people about 'frontiers and barriers broken down before Christ.'[6]

Boundaries in southern Uganda and northern Rwanda were notoriously difficult to establish. The region sits astride a crack in Africa's vast tectonic plate, and over hundreds of thousands of years the topography has been folded into steep ridges. State-builders, whether African or European, have always had difficulty in exerting their authority on this uneven terrain. In the late nineteenth century, Kiga highlanders repeatedly fought and defeated the invading armies of Rwanda's energetic king Rwabugiri.[7] The region was divided between British, German, and Belgian colonial powers in 1910, and in 1911 a team of surveyors set out to mark the boundary between Uganda and Rwanda.[8] One of the team, a sergeant in the King's African Rifles, was murdered when he stumbled upon a remote village deep in the hills. The murderers hoped to keep the survey party from discovering the path that ran through their village.[9] By 1914, the British officials of Kigezi District had marked the border with a series of telegraph poles, each one surrounded with a cairn of stones.[10] Even after the border had been set in stone, local people thought it to be of little consequence. The boundary cairns were often destroyed by elephants and by human agency. In any case, the people who lived in the highlands did not organize their lives into separate territorial spheres. In 1931, there were 47,500 Rwandans living in Kigezi District, most of them clustered in the southwest.[11] In 1936, 87,500 people, mostly from Rwanda, made their way north, through

---

[5] Interview: Amos Bitama, Kagarama, Ndorwa, Kigezi, 27 June 2004.

[6] HMC JEC 3/4: Joe Church to Lawrence Barham, 11 December 1939.

[7] Jan Vansina, *Antecedents to Modern Rwanda: the Nyiginya Kingdom* (Madison, 2004), 171–73.

[8] UNA A 46/1063: Kandt, 'Proposals for the Formalities to be Observed on the Anglo-German Border,' 9 October 1911. The 1910 boundary is described in Ian Brownlie, *African Boundaries: A Legal and Diplomatic Dictionary* (London, 1979), 991–93.

[9] JML Entebbe Secretariat archives, file 2196: Yonazani Basajabalaba, statement, 10 December 1911.

[10] UNA A 46/1063: Director of Public Works, minute, 2 May 1914.

[11] KigDA bundle 662, 'Native Affairs, Repatriation of Banyarwanda' file: DC Kigezi's note, 'Wanyaruanda,' 1931.

Kigezi and Ankole, to take up employment on the cotton farms of Buganda (see Chapter 4).[12]

The inhabitants of southern Uganda and northern Rwanda were frontiersmen.[13] British and African state-builders sought to erect their political communities on secure territorial foundations, but their constituents always seemed to slip out of their grasp. Political authorities' recurrent nightmare was expressed in the figure of Nyabingi, a spirit who repeatedly haunted the region's would-be rulers. The mediums of the Nyabingi spirit exercised a biological and social power that ran in parallel with political authority. The cult's lore described how her mediums outlasted even the most powerful of her opponents: one medium survived, unscathed, as her enemies burned her house around her; another bested a strongman who tested his spear against her power.[14] The Nyabingi cult expressed in religious form what governing authorities more generally knew: that Kigezi's people would not align themselves as natives of any territorial polity.

This chapter discusses the genesis of the East African Revival. It argues that the history of the Revival in Kigezi District can productively be seen as a chapter in a much longer argument over the exercise of territorial power. Kiga converts positioned themselves alongside Nyabingi devotees as antagonists of the settled hierarchies that British and African polity-builders sought to create. Converts followed John Bunyan's directions: they became pilgrims, set themselves on a narrow path, and moved away from their old lives of sin. Whereas Kiga chiefs sought to cultivate the habits of respect and obedience among their subjects, converts openly flouted chiefs' authority. Whereas cultural conservatives defended the sartorial and culinary practices that upheld social hierarchy, converts made a point of dressing and eating indiscriminately. In Kigezi, the pilgrims' progress was an engine for dissenting cultural politics.

TOPOGRAPHY AND POLITICAL CULTURE IN KIGEZI

Southern Uganda's political cultures were shaped by the region's uneven terrain (see Map 1). In Rujumbura, in the northern part of Kigezi, the rolling, grassy hills eased northward toward the plains of Ankole. Rujumbura's prosperous cattle-keepers had once been subjects of Ankole's kings, and from Ankole they inherited a hierarchical political structure. The first British officials thought the ruler of Rujumbura to be 'practically the only chief of

---

[12] KigDA bundle 171: Rhona Ross and Cyril Sofer, 'Survey of the Banyaruanda Complex,' 22 May 1950.

[13] I follow here John Iliffe, *Africans: A History of a Continent* (Cambridge, 2007), chapter 1.

[14] See discussion later in this chapter, and Steven Feierman, 'Colonizers, Scholars, and the Creation of Invisible Histories,' in *Beyond the Cultural Turn: New Directions in the Study of Society and Culture*, eds. Victoria Bonnell and Lynn Hunt (Berkeley, 1999), 182–216.

any real importance in the territory.'[15] By contrast, the southeastern part of Kigezi was full of steep hills and volcanic mountains. These highlands supported a variety of microclimates, ranging from the subtropical vegetation that grew along valley bottoms to the alpine forest that reached up to 12,000 feet.[16] When the first British political officer toured Kigezi in 1910, it took him five days to walk from one end of the highlands to the other. The country was composed of 'a mass of broken hills,' he reported, and the task of his porters was 'very arduous.'[17] For Kiga farmers, this topography was an agricultural opportunity. Kiga peasants generally built their houses along valley bottoms, and cultivated potatoes, corn, and beans in intercropped gardens stretching up the terraced hillsides.[18] Their agronomic industry made Kiga farmers prosperous: in the late nineteenth and early twentieth centuries, Kigezi was exporting food crops to trade in regional markets.[19] Missionaries were impressed with their self-sufficiency. 'Everyone grows their own food, makes their own mat, and baskets and cooking pots,' one missionary reported.[20]

Southern Kigezi's landscape gave farmers the material substance by which to maintain their economic independence. The broken terrain also allowed Kiga peasants to defend their political autonomy against outside rulers. The first British officer posted to Kigezi called Kiga territory a 'country of small independent clans': every hill supported an independent political community, and it was 'unheard of for a party of Bakiga to traverse the country in any direction.'[21] This political parochialism was articulated in the vernacular vocabulary. The first Bible translators were dismayed to find that 'one may greedily light on a new word only to find it contradicted the next minute by someone who says he has never heard of it.' Finding two people who agreed about a particular word's meaning, missionaries agreed, was 'quite a triumph.'[22] The earliest students of Kiga sociology were struck by their independence. May Edel, whose research on Kiga anthropology was conducted in the early 1930s, thought them to be a 'people united only in their common disunity.'[23] She could not identify a political unit larger than the patrilineage that drew Kiga people together. Neither were Kiga people united in their religion: they ignored their dead ancestors until they troubled

[15] UNA A 46/581: Capt. E. Reid, report for January 1912.
[16] J. D. Snowden, 'A Study of Altitudinal Zonation in South Kigezi and on Mounts Muhavura and Mgahinga, Uganda,' *The Journal of Ecology* 21 (1) (1933), 7–27.
[17] UNA A 46/579: Political Officer Kigezi to Chief Secretary, 6 September 1911.
[18] MAM E 1/1: *Ruanda Notes* 1 (7 May 1921); UNA A 46/581: Capt. E. Reid, report for February 1912.
[19] Grace Carswell, *Cultivating Success in Uganda: Kigezi Farmers and Colonial Policies* (London, 2007), chapter 2.
[20] MAM E/1E: Constance Hornby, 'GFS Corner,' *Ruanda Notes* 43 (January 1933).
[21] UNA A 46/581: Capt. E. Reid, report for February 1912.
[22] MAM E/1E: Miss Davis, 'Dispensing Under Difficulties,' *Ruanda Notes* 21 (July 1927).
[23] May Edel, *The Chiga of Uganda* (New Brunswick, 1996 [1957]), 28.

them, and made no attempt to establish a community between the living and the dead.[24] Anglican missionaries compared them with the lawless Israelites in the time of Judges. 'They have no King and everyone seems to do just as he pleases,' one missionary wrote.[25] Government officials concurred. 'Every man is his own master,' wrote an early district officer, and 'discipline and obedience among themselves are to them unknown quantities.'[26]

There was one authority to which independent Kiga peasants had to bend the knee. The Nyabingi cult first appears on the historical record in 1891, when the traveler Emin Pasha described a 'Queen Nyavingi' who governed the pastoralist state of Mpororo. She communicated with her subjects through a screen of bark cloth, and such was her mystique that she had 'never been seen by anyone, not even by her own subjects.' In Mpororo, as in the kingdoms of Ankole and Karagwe, she was said to be 'capable of bewitching people and also of benefitting them.'[27] Kiga highlanders found her to be a compelling figure. In the mid-nineteenth century they borrowed her cult from the Mpororo pastoralists and put her royal powers to their own purposes.[28] Nyabingi mediums lived in a manner styled after the Rwandan court: their houses and furniture were constructed on the model of Rwanda, while their insignia, a two-headed spear, was borrowed from Rwanda's royalty.[29] They made preemptory demands in their neighbors. Missionaries described how, in a village in northern Rwanda, Nyabingi's emissaries arrived very early one morning in 1933, carrying with them an iron staff. They demanded 'food here, a child there, and even the wife of an elderly man ... Whenever the wand is pointed at them by the servant of Nyabingi, people obey.'[30] Nyabingi's power was coercive, and her emissaries were arrogant. The medium Muhumusa was called *kabaka*, 'king' in Luganda, by her followers. She had six men in her retinue who carried her, shoulder-high, on a palanquin whenever she wished to travel.[31] In August 1911, at the height of her powers, there were

[24] Edel, *The Chiga*, 132.
[25] MAM E/1E: *Ruanda Notes* 1 (7 May 1921); MAM E/1E: David Strather Hunt, 'A Bird's Eye View of the Work at Kigezi,' *Ruanda Notes* 20 (April 1927). The scriptural reference is to Judges 17:6: 'In those days there was no king in Israel, but every man did that which was right in his own eyes.'
[26] UNA A 46/1085: Western Province Annual Report, 1913–14.
[27] Emin Pasha, *Emin Pasha: His Life and Work*, volume II (Westminster, 1898), 173.
[28] Jim Freedman, 'Three Muraris, Three Gahayas and the Four Phases of Nyabingi,' in *Chronology, Migration, and Drought in Interlacustrine Africa*, ed. J. B. Webster (Thetford, 1979), 175–87; Jim Freedman, 'Ritual and History: the Case of Nyabingi,' *Cahiers d'etudes Africaines* 14 (53) (1974), 170–80.
[29] Edel, *The Chiga*, chapter 7.
[30] MAM E/1E: 'Miss Skipper Explains One of Our Illustrations,' *Ruanda Notes* 49 (July 1934).
[31] JML Entebbe Secretariat Archives, file 2196: Statement of Yonazani Basajabalaba, 10 December 1911.

PHOTO 4. 'Nyabingi Agents,' n.d. Photo by Dora Skipper. Courtesy of the Church Mission Society archives.

some 3,000 people living around her fortified home in southern Kigezi. Her granaries bulged with produce, and there were great quantities of dried meat in her larders.

Nyabingi's mediums exerted a coercive authority over Kigezi's people, but the power that mediums exercised was not simply political in character. Stories about the origin of Nyabingi highlight the connection that Kiga people made between the medium's arrogant powers and human fertility.[32] One story linked Nyabingi with a breastless girl named Neeza, whose physical malformation embodied her antisocial character. Rivers in which she stepped dried up, and gardens in which she set foot caught fire. Her neighbors sent her into exile in a faraway forest. There she met a hunter, who built her a small house outside his home, and fed her with animals he killed. Neeza instructed the hunter to have sexual congress with his barren wife, and she brought forth twins, a boy and a girl. Before she died, Neeza gave the hunter's daughter Nyabingi, saying that all spirits would thereafter speak through her.[33] The story was about the transformation of antisocial power into a force that could be harnessed, tamed, and put to civil purposes. In the 1910s, the cult was sometimes called *Biheko*, derived from the verb *heka*,

---

[32] On Nyabingi and fertility, see Richard Vokes, *Ghosts of Kanungu: Fertility, Secrecy, and Exchange in the Great Lakes of East Africa* (Rochester, NY, 2009).

[33] Mafune, 'The Concept of Illness and Death in the Kiga Traditional Society,' in *Occasional Research Papers* vol. 12, ed. A. Byaruhanga Akiiki (Kampala, 1973).

to 'be with child' in Kinyarwanda.[34] Nyabingi's power, properly civilized, opened women's wombs. In amassing material wealth, in making demands on people, and in arrogating power, Nyabingi's mediums also enabled families to reproduce.[35]

The power that Nyabingi wielded ran alongside the constituted political authority. The kings of Rwanda found her to be a troublesome antagonist. Nyabingi lore is full of indestructible mediums that could not be touched by the political powers of their time. One song describes how the strong man Gakwaya went to visit Nyabingi, carrying with him two spears and two machetes. When various characters suggested he turn back, he confidently pointed to his weapons, saying 'I'll use them if I have to.' When he reached Nyabingi's compound, the spirit pinned his arms to his sides and killed him by throwing him against a rock.[36] Another story describes how Rwanda's seventeenth century king Ruganzu rejected his aunt, who had served as regent during his childhood. On her path to exile the woman had sex with an elderly man, and delivered a boy within a matter of hours. She sent him, unwashed and with his umbilical cord still attached, to Ruganzu's court, demanding a herd of cattle as a gift. Ruganzu attempted to murder the boy by setting his house alight, but the boy was unharmed as the building burned around him. When Ruganzu agreed to worship the boy, he disappeared into the wind.[37] The story highlighted Nyabingi's powers over human reproduction: she could attenuate biology, and bring forth children in haste. The story also highlighted the limits of political leaders' power. As the strong man Gakwaya discovered and as the king Ruganzu came to understand, Nyabingi could not be tamed by physical force. Her indestructible power was for Kiga people a bulwark against the autocratic kings of Rwanda. A favorite story described how King Rwabugiri, Rwanda's nineteenth-century state-builder, sought to bring southern Kigezi into his realm. Nyabingi is said to have lured Rwabugiri into a trap, only releasing him when he promised to leave the Kiga for her to govern.[38] In their devotion to Nyabingi, the proudly independent people of Kigezi affirmed their aversion to Rwanda's autocrats.

The first British official was posted to Kigezi in 1910. In Kigezi, as in other parts of Uganda, administrators sought to co-opt preexisting political hierarchies as instruments of colonial 'indirect rule.' They parceled out the district into counties and parishes, and identified chiefs to govern each

---

[34] RH Mss. Afr. s. 1384: J. E. T. Philipps, 'The Nabingi: A Mandwa Secret Society' (July 1919); Jim Freedman, *Nyabingi: The Social History of an African Divinity* (Tervuren, 1984), 79.

[35] My line of argument here is derived from Feierman, 'Colonizers, Scholars.'

[36] Freedman, *Nyabingi*, 44–45.

[37] B. Mugarura, 'The Nyabingi Cult in South Kigezi with Particular Reference to Ndorwa,' in *Occasional Research Papers in African Religions and Philosophies* (Kampala, 1974).

[38] Freedman, *Nyabingi*, 45, 95; see also Vansina, *Antecedents to Modern Rwanda*, 136–37.

tract of territory. In Rujumbura, where politics had long been centered on a royal court, British officials had no difficulty in naming a chief. But argument erupted when British officers sought to identify chiefs to govern the Rukiga highlands. One clan elder would not agree to be ruled by the leader of the Basigi clan who, he said, 'belonged to a different clan and had no authority over him.'[39] Kigezi's independent mountaineers would not submit to outside authorities. British officials were therefore compelled to appoint agents from the Buganda kingdom to govern the highlands of southern Kigezi.[40] The first Kiga chief in Kigezi was not named until 1922. This pioneer lacked substantial support: his qualifications were the several years that he had worked as an office boy in the District Commissioner's headquarters.[41]

British officials and their Ganda agents stood in a long line of political authorities who found an antagonist in Nyabingi. Like the kings of Rwanda, British administrators sought to exert their authority over Nyabingi's mediums, but Nyabingi seemed always to slip out of their grasp. As early as 1911, the British officer in Kigezi had determined that the Nyabingi cult was 'entirely subversive to all authority, whether local or European.'[42] His first antagonist was Muhumusa, a medium who claimed to be the mother of the Rwandan king Rwabugiri. Fleeing from imprisonment in the hands of the Germans, she had taken up residence in southern Kigezi where, according to the Ganda chief, she 'gave out that she had much power, and that if anyone would follow her, she would drive out the Europeans.'[43] The British officer and his Ganda allies attacked her compound in September 1911, killing forty people and wounding dozens.[44] Muhumusa was captured and sent into a long exile in Buganda, but military defeat did not put an end to her career. Within a few years, another medium living near Lake Bunyonyi was claiming to be Muhumusa.[45] In 1916, in 1917, and again in 1919, British forces confronted a Congolese medium named

---

[39] Described in Yowana Ssebalijja, 'Memories of Rukiga and Other Places,' in *A History of Kigezi in South-West Uganda*, ed. Donald Denoon (Kampala, 1972), 187–88.

[40] See A. D. Roberts, 'The Sub-Imperialism of the Baganda,' *Journal of African History* 3 (3) (1962), 435–50.

[41] KigDA Box 662, file 39: Western Province Annual Report, 1923.

[42] UNA A 46/579: Political Officer Kigezi to Chief Secretary, 6 September 1911.

[43] JML Entebbe Secretariat Archives, file 2196: Statement of Yonazani Basajabalaba, 10 December 1911. Muhumusa's career is described in Alison des Forges, *Defeat is the Only Bad News: Rwanda Under Musinga, 1896–1931*, ed. David Newbury (Madison, 2011), chapter 5.

[44] JML Entebbe Secretariat Archives, file 2196: Captain E. Reid to Chief Secretary, 30 September 1911. See M. J. Bessell, 'Nyabingi,' *Uganda Journal* 2 (2) (1938), 73–86; and Vokes, *Ghosts of Kanungu*, 35–36.

[45] UNA A 46/886: Western Province monthly report, August 1914; Western Province monthly report, November 1914; see Randall Packard, 'Cheifship and the History of Nyavingi Possession among the Bashu of Eastern Zaire,' *Africa* 52 (4) (1982), 67–90.

Ndochibiri, who mounted coordinated attacks on government agents.[46] British forces killed Ndochibiri in 1919, cut off his distinctive two-fingered right hand, dried it at the government prison, and then put it on display on the District Commissioner's verandah.[47] His head was cut off, displayed, and then sent to the British Museum. With these grisly artifacts, British officers sought to establish fleshly, corporeal evidence proving Ndochibiri's death. But within a few months another medium appeared, claiming to be Ndochibiri.[48] Like Rwanda's kings before them, British officials found it impossible to get control over Nyabingi's mediums. One frustrated official complained that 'it makes no difference to the Nyabingi or to the natives' when one of her mediums was killed: 'she simply nips off and inhabits someone else.'[49]

Scholars have organized the study of Kigezi's religious history on a chronological grid, identifying Christian revivalists as the lineal heirs to the agitators of the Nyabingi cult.[50] The anthropologist Elizabeth Hopkins, for example, argued that after the suppression of Nyabingi, it was the Revival that provided 'the subsequent matrix for political unrest' in the region. Hopkins thought that revivalists, like Nyabingi devotees, 'encouraged both a defiance of local administrative practices and open confrontation with local chiefs.'[51] The Ugandan scholar Murindwa Rutanga was likewise struck by the similarities between Nyabingi and revivalism. Though the Nyabingi movement had been effectively suppressed by the 1930s, he wrote, Kiga people's 'new resistance occurred in the form of the Revivalist movement.'[52] The historian Benoni Turyahikayo-Rugyema thought that the Revival was a 'religion of expression' that was 'consistent with the religious beliefs of the Bakiga' as expressed in the Nyabingi cult.[53]

[46] F. S. Brazier, 'The Nyabingi Cult: Religion and Political Scale in Kigezi, 1900–1930' (Kampala, 1968); Elizabeth Hopkins, 'The Nyabingi Cult of Southwestern Uganda,' in *Protest and Power in Black Africa*, eds. Robert Rotberg and Ali A. Mazrui (New York, 1970), 258–336.

[47] Ssebalijja, 'Memories of Rukiga,' 195; Philips, 'The Nabingi.'

[48] UNA A 46/887: Monthly report, July 1919.

[49] Major E. M. Jack, quoted in Brazier, 'The Nyabingi Cult.'

[50] But see Richard Vokes, who argues that it was the Catholic cult of the Virgin Mary – not the Protestant Revival – that inherited Nyabingi's logic and sociology. Vokes' thesis is in *Ghosts of Kanungu*, 77–87.

[51] Hopkins, 'The Nyabingi Cult,' 323.

[52] Murindwa Rutanga, 'People's Anti-Colonial Struggles in Kigezi Under the Nyabingi Movement, 1910–1930,' in *Uganda: Studies in Living Conditions, Population Movements, and Constitutionalism*, eds. Mahmood Mamdani and Joe Oloka-Onyango (Vienna, 1994), 229–71. See also Rutanga's *Politics, Religion and Power in the Great Lakes Region* (Kampala, 2011), which appeared as this book was going to press.

[53] Benoni Turyahikayo-Rugyema, 'The Impact of Christianity on the Bakiga of Southwest Uganda: The Revival Movement,' in *Occasional Research Papers* vol. 31, ed. Tom Tuma (Kampala, 1975).

In fact, converts were contemporaries of Nyabingi mediums, not their successors. Nyabingi remained a dynamic and attractive presence even as the Revival took shape. In the late 1920s, a clan leader named Bituura introduced a new form of Nyabingi called Kasenti, after the English word 'cents.' At Kasenti's shrine on Kagarama Hill, just outside Kabale town, devotees made offerings in cash money, not only in livestock or grain. Contemporary witnesses commented on the herds of cattle that filled the fields around Kasenti's shrine.[54] Bituura planned an assault on the British district headquarters at Kabale, allocating, on paper, the houses and contents of the government station to his followers.[55] In February 1928, the alarmed British administration attacked Bituura's residence and destroyed Kasenti's shrine. They found a water pot containing some 305 shillings, almost all of it in cents.[56] Missionaries were terrified by the spirit's power. In their melodramatic reports they imagined 'hundreds or thousands of devil inflamed Bakiga, armed with spears, sweeping down upon us and the Government station, believing that Nyabingi would make them proof against bullets!'[57] Even as colonial administrators were imposing a colonial order on Kigezi's people, Nyabingi's advocates found it possible to conjure up an alternative political hierarchy. Within a few years of the attack on Kasenti's shrine, another medium had erected a Nyabingi shrine in the Congo, two miles from the Kigezi border. Kiga devotees were the shine's most frequent visitors.[58] As late as 1944, a litigant could meaningfully tell a government court in Kigezi that another man had killed his daughter with the aid of Nyabingi. The court was obliged to inform the disbelieving litigant that 'there is no Nyabingi.'[59]

Nyabingi mediums and Christian converts inhabited the same time and place. Kigezi's religious world was a horizontal field, and people moved in and out of different therapeutic regimes. The anthropologist Derrick Stenning interviewed one woman who, after her husband's untimely demise, had suddenly begun to tremble and shake. She lived in the bush and, possessed by Nyabingi, traveled from house to house demanding cattle in payment for the divination she offered. Jailed at the command of the British

[54] JML Entebbe Secretariat Archives, file R. 127: A. Trewin, 'Inquiry into the Alleged Suppression of Evidence by Certain Members in Certain Areas in Rukiga and Bufumbira counties,' 1 May 1928.

[55] JML Entebbe Secretariat Archives, file 3173: PC Western to Chief Secretary, 29 March 1928. See Hopkins, 'The Nyabingi Cult,' 316–17.

[56] JML Entebbe Secretariat Archives, file R. 127: A. Trewin, 'Inquiry into the Alleged Suppression of Evidence by Certain Members in Certain Areas in Rukiga and Bufumbira counties,' 1 May 1928; see Hopkins, 'The Nyabingi Cult,' 316.

[57] MAM E 1/E: Leonard Sharp, in *Ruanda Notes* 25 (July 1928).

[58] KigDA bundle 662, 'Native Affairs: Correspondence with Biumba' file: DC Kigezi to Administrator, Biumba, 2 November 1931.

[59] KigDA bundle 258, 'Native Affairs' file: Rujumbura Lukiko minute, 26 October 1944.

officer, she married a Christian man, who convinced her that Nyabingi was a sin against God. She converted in 1936, and for several years she was an active evangelist for the Revival. But after her second husband died, the woman was again possessed by Nyabingi and traveled the country as a medium, preaching against adultery and stealing.[60] Women like her showed little regard for the conventions that guided ordinary behavior. In 1936, Karugaba, a schoolgirl at the Anglican mission in Gahini, was taken ill for more than a year. Her family thought Nyabingi had inhabited her body, and they planned to initiate her as a medium. Karugaba, however, chose to follow a different path: when Gahini's people were gripped by the Revival in 1936, she converted. But her conversion did not make her ordinary. Within a few weeks of her conversion she was destroying books, clothing, and other articles that came into her hand. Missionaries finally sent her home, where her relatives, terrified by her extraordinary strength and by her capacity for doing harm, bound her to a post.[61] The itinerate evangelist from Ankole and the unfortunate schoolgirl Karugaba lived in a world of open frontiers. As converts and as mediums, their movements placed them outside the fold of settled society.

Converts and mediums were alike in their resistance to the organizing conventions of territorial governance. Neither Rwanda's king Rwabugiri nor the British District Commissioner could pin their subjects in place. Political authorities struggled to close frontiers, elevate political authorities, and cultivate a biddable constituency. Nyabingi mediums were always slipping out of their grasp, and so were revivalists. The Revival opened a new chapter in Kigezi's longer history of argument over the politics of movement and the definition of political community.

ESCHATOLOGY AS LIVED EXPERIENCE

At the Anglican mission at Gahini in northern Rwanda, the Christmas celebrations of 1933 began on Christmas Eve, as missionaries stuffed their stockings while six schoolboys sang 'See Amid the Winter's Snow.' The following day, missionaries put on a sports program: schoolchildren and church members competed in spear-throwing and arrow-shooting, while other people, less athletic, entered the lime juice drinking competition. It was in this atmosphere of jollification that, on Boxing Day, a schoolteacher did something extraordinary. At a gathering of people connected with the mission, the teacher stood up and confessed a sin that he had committed. Following his revelation, reported a missionary chronicler, a 'wave of conviction' swept through the assembled crowd, and for two and a half

---

[60] Cambridge University Library Add. 7916, file B.5: Derrick Stenning, 'Persistence of Cult Elements in an East African Population' (Cambridge, April 1959).

[61] CMS Oxford, Dora Skipper papers, folio 2/2: letters for 12 and 16 July 1937.

hours the attendees confessed their sins. At times, three people were on their feet, trying to speak.[62] By January 1934, senior schoolboys at Gahini were confessing their sins and returning the paraffin, writing slates, salt, and other goods that they had stolen from the school's store.[63] The religious practices that the Gahini people pioneered were quickly taken up in other parts of Rwanda and in southern Uganda. In October 1935, a group of evangelists from Gahini visited the Anglican mission at Kabale in Kigezi District. Among them were the evangelists whose preaching and biographical writing would give form to the East African Revival: the Ganda landholder Simeon Nsibambi; the Hima hospital worker Yosea Kinuka; and the British medical doctor Joe Church. The most emphatic among them, the fiery Ganda evangelist Blasio Kigozi, focused his preaching on the themes of 'destruction' and 'the date of punishing.' 'Lots of people are simply doing nothing, they are perishing, but they don't know!' he wrote.[64] Missionaries at Kabale reported that the revivalists' preaching 'led to a great many confessions of money etc. stolen.'[65] Revivalism quickly outran missionaries' capacity to supervise it. Early one Sunday morning in July 1936, missionaries at Gahini were awakened by the shouts and screams at the girls' school. When they forced open the door to the dormitory, they were horrified at what they found:

The girls seemed to have gone mad and some were on the floor, they were all throwing themselves about, they were absolutely uncontrolled, some were laughing, some weeping, most were shaking very very much and they seemed to have supernatural strength. The powers of darkness seemed to be right on us, it felt like being in hell, as though Satan had loosed his armies.[66]

The missionaries dragged the noisy girls off to bed. The next day the girls arose at 3:30 in the morning to preach and pray. By the end of the month, women and men living in the hills around Gahini were having 'strange times.' Missionaries reported that in almost every village church people were gathering at nighttime to pray, with 'some shrieking to God to have mercy, others rolling about on the floor and tearing their clothes and foaming at the mouth in a regular fit.'[67] At Matana in Burundi, missionaries reported that there was an 'outbreak of wild singing and dancing.' The leaders were said to be the 'old hill women,' not mission school students. Even 'heathen' girls

---

[62] This paragraph is in summary of MAM E/1E: 'Dr. Church Reports on the African Convention,' *Ruanda Notes* 48 (April 1934).

[63] MAM E/1E: Joe Church, 'News of Gahini Hospital,' *Ruanda Notes* 47 (January 1934).

[64] CoU 02 Bp 224/28: Joe Church to Bishop Stuart, 5 January 1936; Joe Church, 'Rev. Blasio Kigozi, an Appreciation,' 3 February 1936; HMC JEC 17/2: Blasio Kigozi to Joe Church, 12 January 1936.

[65] CMS Annual Letters file: Rev. E.L. Barham, annual letter, 26 September 1936.

[66] CMS Oxford, Dora Skipper papers, folio 2: letter from Miss Gershom, 2 July 1936.

[67] CMS Oxford, Dora Skipper papers, folio 2: letter for 31 July 1936.

were said to be praying 'Oh Lord, teach us how we may sing and dance like these people and so please thee.'[68]

What inspired these and other early converts was their epochal view of time. In Kigezi, in Ankole, and in northern Rwanda, revivalists were sure that their contemporary world was coming to an end. They saw the evidence of an impending doom all around them. Joe Church, the most influential missionary advocate of the Revival, was convinced in 1938 that 'Armageddon is very near.'[69] With the evidence of the war in Europe before him, Church was sure that 'these are the last days. The Lord Jesus is calling us to a total war in this last battle before he returns.'[70] African converts did not need to look so far afield for evidence of the impending end of time. The evidence was all around them. 'I never cease to have sorrow for my friends who are still on the road that leads to destruction,' wrote the evangelist Yosiya Kinuka in 1938. 'I keep on telling them that they are in a land like the land of Sodom and they must come out of it and be born again.'[71] Kinuka thought his contemporary world was soon to be destroyed, just as God had destroyed the biblical town of Sodom. His conviction was widely shared. At Shyira in Burundi, Anglican missionaries reported that 'many people began to have dreams warning them of the nearness of the Second Coming, and of their unpreparedness for meeting Christ.'[72] One convert, a teacher from Gahini, dreamt that he was standing before God's throne in a long line of people. As their names were read out, some people passed upward to heaven, while others 'with terrible cries' fell into an abyss.[73] Another convert, from Ankole, dreamt of a scene where Jesus was sorting those who belonged to him from those who did not. Jesus spoke to him in an angry voice, saying 'I do not know you,' and he was cast into everlasting darkness.[74] These dreams were proleptic: they attenuated time, trimmed life's span, and brought dreamers face to face with a judgmental God.

For these converts, the eschaton – the end of time – was not an arid theological concept. They experienced the end of time as a visual, emotional, visceral encounter. The Revival in eastern Ankole is said to have begun when a visiting convert preached to an assembled group of women about Revelation 20:12–13, which depicts God's judgment. The preacher dramatized the text with illustrations of the fires of hell, and then called

---

[68] Murray papers: Mrs. Guillebaud to Bishop Stuart, 4 May 1942.

[69] HMC JEC 3/4: Church to Miss Hall, 29 December 1938.

[70] MAM A3: Joe Church, circular letter, 9 March 1942.

[71] HMC JEC 6/3: Yosiya Kinuka to 'Ruanda friends,' n.d. (but 1938).

[72] CMS Annual Letters file: Ms. L. Forbes, annual letter, 28 August 1936.

[73] MAM E 1/9: 'Reports of African Conventions,' *Revival News* 1 (2) (1950).

[74] George Kafureeka, 'The Impact of the Revival Movement on the Church in East Ankole Diocese with Particular Reference to Rushere Archdeaconry, Mbarara District, Uganda' (Dip. Theo. thesis, Uganda Christian University, 1999). The scriptural template for this dream is Matthew 25: 31–46.

for conversions. His message received a powerful reinforcement when a woman living an immoral life immolated herself in her house. Her body made an audible pop as it burst open, and on hearing the noise, people who previously had doubted revivalists' message were convinced of their impending doom.[75] People were prompted to think about the eschaton by the evidence around them. One woman converted in 1936 because 'she feared Hell which was waiting those who died before they repent and confess their sins.' Whenever a drop of hot water or a spark from the cooking fire touched her body, it reminded her of the 'horrible fire of Hell.'[76] Men also saw the fires of hell. One man was attending a marriage feast in central Ankole in 1937 when, at dusk, someone shouted 'Look at that fire over there, over the backs of the cattle!' The assembly was terrified at the vision, and hurried to the church to pray.[77] Men and women glimpsed a fiery doom in the ordinary course of their lives, in a cooking fire or in the midst of a herd of cattle.

For these first revivalists, God's judgment was a lived experience, woven into quotidian fabric. One of my interviewees, a man named Asanasiyo Rwandare, seems to have lived much of his life while standing in judgment. He has had dozens of visions over the course of his life, many of them summoning him to account for his sins.[78] In April 1936, Rwandare was lying in bed when he heard a voice telling him 'The end is at hand.' On opening his eyes Rwandare saw a man standing beside his bed, dressed in white robes and carrying a lamp. 'Why don't you allow me time to repent of my sins?' Rwandare cried. He was drawn to his feet, and just as he was leaving his family's compound, the man turned and said 'Go immediately and repent.' The following morning, Rwandare stood up in a church assembly and confessed his sins, but his dreams did not come to an end. Three years after his encounter with the white-robed man, Rwandare was again accosted. He was walking along a familiar path when, quite unexpectedly, he came upon a man leaning against a piece of wood. 'His hands were outstretched,' Rwandare remembered, 'and when I looked, there were nails in the hands, and even through the legs.' Crying, Rwandare followed the crucifix as he walked homeward. 'He went over the pieces of wood that had been used to close the gate,' Rwandare remembered. 'When I went into the enclosure, I found him standing right at the door of my mother's house.' The spectral

---

[75] John Muhanguzi, 'The Spread of the Revival Movement at Burunga in Nyabushozi County, East Ankole' (Dip. Theo. dissertation, Makerere University, 1985); E. Maari, 'The Balokole Movement in Nyabushozi County of Ankole,' in *Occasional Research Papers in African Religions and Philosophies, vol. 22*, ed. A. Byaruhanga-Akiiki (Kampala, 1974).

[76] N. Magambo, 'The Balokole Movement in Mitooma Parish' (Dip. Theo. thesis, Makerere University, 1974).

[77] HMC JEC 3/1: Joe Church, notes on Ankole, 16 April 1937.

[78] Interviews: Asanasiyo Rwandare, Rwenyunza, Rukiga, Kabale, 26 June 2004; and Kabale town, 21 August 2005.

Christ only disappeared when Rwandare 'realized what I had caused the Lord to go through.'

In visions like Rwandare's, southern Uganda's people came face to face with an impending judgment. Driven by the impending doom they witnessed, men and women made an inventory of their deeds and their goods. One man, a government chief, converted in 1936, confessing to a terrible temper. He made a list of his sins in columns on a piece of paper, and for each sin he promised to make restitution to those he had wronged.[79] A teacher at the Anglican school at Mbarara listed his sins in a letter to the school's governing board, describing how he had purchased two shirts with money that had been given him as a traveling allowance. He had forgotten about the incident, he wrote, 'but now the Holy Ghost revealed it to me, it was really a big sin which should throw me into Hell.'[80] Converts thought their eternal welfare was at stake in even the most inconsequential of things. One of my interviewees was lying in bed one evening in 1942 when a voice told him 'You stole your brother's handkerchief.' He had thoughtlessly put the handkerchief in his pocket while doing the family's washing.[81]

A stolen handkerchief. Two ill-gotten shirts. These are small things, and there is humor in the seriousness with which revivalists regard such trivialities. In 2005, I attended a Revival convention in Kabale, on the same ground where Blasio Kigozi, Joe Church, and other early converts had once preached. One of the speakers at the convention was Canon Mikekemo, by then ninety-two years old. Mikekemo had converted in 1935, in the first flush of revivalism in Kigezi. He told a crowd of some 3,000 people how as a boy he had stolen sweet potatoes from his neighbor's garden. The crowd tittered at his testimony. To people today, Canon Mikekemo's sin seems laughably inconsequential. But in the late 1930s and early 1940s, even the smallest of sins loomed large. The evidence that Kigezi people gathered in their forensic self-examinations was terrifying. In 1939, a missionary attending a service at Rujumbura found more than 100 men and women lying prostrate. 'In many places the floor was wet below their faces, and the bodies of many were convulsed with shaking which went on and on,' the missionary reported.[82] A service at Mbarara was interrupted when a man 'began to cry out, howling at the top of his voice.' When called to explain himself, he said he 'had seen a vision of Christ in the church and saw the awful state of the Lord, and he was overcome with grief.'[83] A missionary in Kabale reported that many people were having such powerful visions of doom that they 'have been in states of hysteria bordering on unconsciousness.'[84]

---

[79] CMS Annual Letters file: Butlin, annual letter, 1936–1937.
[80] CMS G3 A7/5: Master, CMS High School, Mbarara, to Clement Pain, 25 May 1942.
[81] Interview: Enoch Lugimbirwa, Ruharo, Kigezi, 8 July 2004.
[82] HMC JEC 3/4: Church, circular letter, 13 March 1939.
[83] HMC JEC 3/1: Joe Church, 'Diary Letter no. 12,' 12 July 1936.
[84] MAM E 1/E: 'The Rev. P.J. Brazier Calls for Prayer,' *Ruanda Notes* 58 (1936).

Their surety about the imminent end of the world drove some people to despair, and led others to act in a radical manner. Eschatology was the drill sergeant marshaling Kigezi's people to behave in antisocial ways. Wilson Komunda remembered that in 1935 he and other people in Kigezi began to 'hear voices in our minds about how God could kill us.'[85] On hearing the voice, he said, 'I would actually get out of bed, and ... I would raise my voice and tell them to run away from hell, because anyone who is not saved is bound for hell.' The favorite hymn which he sang during his night preaching sessions went:

> You people of this world which is being condemned,
> what are you thinking about the end?
> Why don't you think about what we have in store,
> to talk about the bad parts of our lives, thieving and other sins?
> We are going to leave you in your stupidity.

'There was something compelling us,' Komunda remembered, 'and whenever you got this vision and you saw people going into hell, all the other thoughts would disappear.' Some converts were so sure about the imminence of the second coming that they stopped cultivating, left their homes on the valley bottoms and went to live uphill, hoping to be the first to meet the Lord when he descended from the heavens.[86]

Kigezi's revivalists were disturbing the peace. I interviewed Julaina Mufuko in 2004 at her home in a remote part of Rukiga.[87] In answer to my first question – How were you converted? – she spoke, preached, and sang for more than thirty minutes. So deeply was she invested in her testimony that at certain points she began to cry, while at other times her conviction was so intense that my translator held up his hands, trying to cool her ardor. Julaina converted in 1936. She and a group of other girls had made a habit of playing sexually while herding the goats, but one morning, Julaina remembered, a voice told her 'That habit that you were in is sin.' The next day, Julaina stood up in a church assembly and confessed her sins, describing the deeds in which she had formerly been involved. In those days, Julaina remembered, she and other converts would sometimes see flames licking the tops of the hills, or the sun in the heavens shaking. And then, she remembered, they

used to shake, and there would be jumping and falling on the ground, and from that time we started cutting off the ornaments we used to wear, and we poured out the beer we were keeping at homes, and at night we went into churches, and we made

[85] Interview: Wilson Komunda, Bukinda, Rukiga, Kigezi, 25 June 2004.
[86] Ndambuki Peace, 'The Impact of the 1935–1937 Revival Movement on the Church of Uganda with Particular Reference to Kihanga Archdeaconry in Kigezi Diocese' (Dip. Theo. thesis, Makerere University, 1990).
[87] Interview: Julaina Mufuko, Kandago, 25 June 2004.

a lot of noise, both men and women ... So there would be screaming! People would climb to the tops of these mountains, and would begin exclaiming that the end of the world was coming!

Julaina did not stay on the hilltops. Her attention was particularly focused on Paulo Ngologoza, the county chief in Rukiga, in the heart of the Kiga highlands.[88] Ngologoza, a Catholic, thought Julaina to be a threat to public order. He summoned Julaina and three other girls to his headquarters, lined them up, and complained that 'everyone has been caught into this salvation, and women are disobeying husbands, and husbands are complaining everywhere.' He interrogated Julaina, whip in hand, asking 'How did you receive this Luther to come here?' For weeks his police often came to Julaina's home, summoning her to the county headquarters. Julaina tearfully told me how she and her friends were whipped on six separate occasions. One of their number was so badly hurt that she nearly died from her wounds. But Julaina would not close her mouth. 'They would beat me during the night, and that morning, I would be on top of the mountain, preaching,' she remembered. 'The Lord was forcing us to go and speak, speak, speak!' Her favorite song, which she made a habit of singing outside Chief Ngologoza's headquarters, went

> You are now beating us with wooden sticks,
> But when Jesus returns, he will whip you with iron sticks.
> You have beaten us with these wooden canes,
> But you will be beaten with iron canes.
> So why don't you think about what you are seeing?

How can we explain Chief Ngologoza's private war against Julaina Mufuko, who was at that time an unlettered girl barely into her teenage years? Chiefs in Kigezi were always in an insecure position, for independent Kiga highlanders had never before been governed by outsiders. Lacking indigenous authority, chiefs were obliged to be attentive to the slightest of infractions. In 1928, Kigezi's chiefs ordered the whipping of some 650 people. Many of the cases concerned minor offences: a man who sold butter adulterated with cow dung, for example, was punished with fourteen strokes and four months of jail; while a man who failed to report the birth of his child was punished with six strokes.[89] Even with their whips in hand, Kigezi's chiefs found it difficult to make their power felt. A visiting anthropologist found that the courts spent a great amount of their time trying litigants accused of disobedience. At a court in Rukiga county, for example, cases classified as 'disobeying chief' occupied from 22 to 26 percent of the annual caseload

---

[88] Chief Ngologoza's appointment is discussed in KigDA bundle 56, 'Native Affairs: Chiefs' Appointments and Dismissals' file: DC Kigezi to PC Western, 12 May 1936.

[89] KigDA bundle 146, file 160: Registrar to PC Western, 16 July 1929; DC Kigezi to PC Western, 9 October 1928.

between the years 1934 and 1939, far outstripping the volume of cases concerning assault, theft, tax evasion, and other infractions.[90] In a court in Ndorwa county, cases labeled 'disobeying chief' occupied between 26 and 30 percent of the caseload over the same period.[91]

Converts were the chiefs' leading antagonists. As a young man, Wilson Komunda sometimes joined Julaina outside Chief Ngologoza's door, preaching that 'if you don't get saved, you are going to hell.'[92] He was held in jail for nine full days. On his release, Chief Ngologoza warned him to 'Be sure to stop making that noise.' Komunda replied by saying 'If you want to kill me, I will accept it.' Rwandan converts were likewise making trouble for their chiefs. At Gahini, two converts camped outside the home of their chief, singing and preaching against his sins.[93] When the chief ordered them to desist, one of them replied 'We are not under the orders of the Government or you ... We are commanded by the Holy Spirit.'[94] The chief had the converts imprisoned, but neither Gahini's chief nor the embattled Paulo Ngolooza could get a grip on troublesome revivalists. Not even Rujumbura's formidable Chief Karegyesa – six feet nine inches tall – could put revivalists under his feet. During the late 1930s, several of Karegyesa's lovers converted, confessing in public to their liaisons with the chief. Converts stationed themselves outside his home, singing songs condemning his sexual prolificacy.[95] One of them, a schoolteacher, was so persistent that Karegyesa had him beaten, jailed, and exiled from the county. Other converts were arrested and made to walk fifty miles to the District Commissioner's headquarters in Kabale.[96] One of my interviewees thought that Chief Karegyesa doubted converts' sanity: he saw them as 'mad people. They were talking too much. They were not guided, they were just talking, and disturbing other people.'[97]

Offended chiefs sought to silence loudmouthed converts using the mechanisms of local government. In northern Rwanda, chiefs adopted by-laws mandating that church services were to end at nightfall.[98] In Rujumbura,

---

[90] The cases concerning 'disobeying chief' numbered 45 of 186 cases in 1934; 46 of 209 cases in 1935; 66 of 280 cases in 1936; 34 of 130 cases in 1937; and 78 of 326 cases in 1939. SOAS Melvin Perlman papers, Box 8, file 22: notes on Rwamucucu gombolola court.

[91] 'Disobeying chief' cases in Bubale numbered 38 of 143 cases in 1933; 43 of 157 cases in 1934; 34 of 118 cases in 1935; 43 of 122 cases in 1936; and 17 of 62 cases in 1937. SOAS Melvin Perlman papers, Box 8, file 22: notes on Bubale gombolola court.

[92] Interview: Wilson Komunda, Bukinda, Rukiga, Kigezi, 25 June 2004.

[93] CMS Oxford, Dora Skipper papers, folio 2/2: letter, 12 May 1937.

[94] CMS Oxford, Dora Skipper papers, folio 2/2: letter, 29 May 1937.

[95] Catherine Robins, 'Tukutendereza: A Study of Social Change and Sectarian Withdrawal in the Balokole Revival of Uganda' (PhD dissertation, Columbia University, 1975), 248–49.

[96] Paul Ngologoza, *Kigezi and Its People* (Kampala, 1998 [1967]), 116; Festo Kivengere with Dorothy Smoker, *Revolutionary Love* (Fort Washington, PA, 1983), 10–11.

[97] Interview: Phinhas Nyenda, Ruharo, Mbarara, 7 July 2004.

[98] CMS Oxford, Dora Skipper papers, folio 2/2: letter for 29 May 1937.

Chief Karegyesa barred noisy revivalists from gathering anywhere outside the precincts of the local church. Revivalists who sang as they walked along the road were liable to be fined.[99] In July 1942, the District Commissioner extended Chief Kargyesa's war against revivalists to the whole of Kigezi District: revivalists gathered in private homes were obliged to disband by 8:30 P.M., and singing was by government writ to cease by 9:30 P.M.[100] Eighteen Anglican teachers and forty unmarried girls were arrested in September for violating the curfew.[101] By October, the District Commissioner had made a district-wide law obliging unmarried girls to secure written permission from their parents if they wished to attend Revival meetings.[102] In May 1943, government authorities banned drum-beating in churches, made singing on the roadways illegal, and ruled that religious services could not be convened outside registered churches.[103] But even in the face of the District Commissioner's draconian rules, converts kept singing. The irrepressible Julaina Mufuko told me how, when passing a Catholic priest on the road, she and other converts would sing 'Hmm, hmm, hmm' to the tune of 'You have whipped us with wooden bars, but when the Lord returns he will whip you with iron bars.'[104]

British government officials were convinced that converts were subversives, willfully undermining chiefs' authority. Early in 1942, twenty-three converts were detained at the government jail in Ndorwa county. They had refused their chief's order that they should cultivate tobacco on their farms.[105] Kigezi's District Commissioner told Uganda's Governor that revivalists 'are unruly breakers of the peace and not controlled.' With Paulo Ngologoza's war with Julaina Mufuko in view, the District Commissioner described how revivalists 'engage in abusive attacks on chiefs and impugn their moral characters in public, in church and in law courts. Their attitude to authorities, even Europeans, is disrespectful and impertinent.'[106] The Governor of Uganda darkly worried that the

purely religious stage of the revival has practically passed, and a second and far more dangerous stage, in which violence between the balokole and non-balokole in the

---

[99] KigDA bundle 129, 'Church Missionary Society' file: Joe Church to DC Kigezi, 22 March 1943.

[100] KigDA bundle 129, 'Church Missionary Society' file: DC Kigezi to Joe Church, 13 July 1942.

[101] KigDA bundle 129, 'Church Missionary Society' file: DC Kigezi to Kabale missionaries, 28 September 1942.

[102] KigDA bundle 129, 'Church Missionary Society' file: DC Kigezi, circular letter, 28 October 1942.

[103] KigDA bundle 129, 'Church Missionary Society' file: DC Kigezi to Kabale missionaries, 4 May 1943.

[104] Interview: Julaina Mufuko, Kandago, Kigezi, 25 June 2004.

[105] CoU 02 Bp 227/28: Church to DC Kabale, 11 March 1942.

[106] DC Kigezi's report of May 1942, quoted in NAB CO 536/215/4: Governor of Uganda to Secretary of State for the Colonies, 4 May 1944.

name of religion may occur ... From the second stage to the third stage – violence against the state – is the logical sequence, and in fact we have already the beginnings in Kigezi.[107]

THE POLITICS OF ETIQUETTE

How did converts' loud songs and noisy sermons constitute a threat to the colonial state? It is tempting to follow the District Commissioner's lead and to treat converts as political agitators, stoking the fires of unrest against government chiefs. In fact, the threat that revivalists posed to public order was both more pervasive and more intimate than that. Kiga men expected their conjugal relationships to be decorous. When an anthropologist asked a Kiga schoolgirl to write an essay about her upbringing in 1956, she emphasized that Kiga girls were to keep their mouths closed. 'She was not to talk loudly or laugh loudly, for if a girl was like this, she was the one who would be called "The one without a heart", and she was not to enter into the men's conversation or sit with them around the fire,' wrote the schoolgirl.[108] This gendered form of respectability was called *etcitinisa*, meaning 'to cause fear.' One young woman told an anthropologist that a Kiga woman was to speak to her husband 'modestly, in a low voice. Do not attempt to outdo him in argument or contradict him. Speak only seriously. Never be frivolous or attempt to make jokes. Listen quietly when he speaks and agree with him.'[109] Kiga women were obliged to keep their husbands' names to themselves: flaunting one's husband's name in public was an act of defiance, and an invitation for divorce. A woman who mentioned the proper name of her father-in-law was doomed to suffer a difficult labor, for her child would have an overly large head.[110] Judging from the legal records, this economy of conjugal restraint seems to have been widely honored: of the 3,972 total cases filed in Kigezi's county courts before 1939, only 11 concerned marriage. From 1940 to 1949, only 20 of the 2,059 total cases concerned marriage.[111] Divorce rates were astonishingly low: in 1967, a scholar who interviewed 150 people about their marriages found only 2 who had been divorced.[112]

The values of probity and discretion were reinforced by the *emandwa* cult. *Emandwa* were tutelary spirits, heroic ancestors who possessed human mediums and, through them, offered advice and healing to supplicants. Where Nyabingi flitted from place to place, *emandwa* allied themselves

---

[107] NAB CO 536/215/4: Governor of Uganda to Secretary of State for the Colonies, 4 May 1944.

[108] LSE Audrey Richards papers 6/28: Ida Kenjokyi, untitled essay, March 1956.

[109] Edel, *The Chiga*, 32–33.

[110] Ngologoza, *Kigezi and Its People*, 41.

[111] SOAS Melvin Perlman papers, Box 8, file 23: notes on 'saza level' litigation.

[112] E. R. Yeld, 'Continuity and Change in Kiga Patterns of Marriage' (Kampala, January 1967).

with particular patrilineages. One priest in Ankole knew the names of his ancestors stretching forty-six generations into the past. His forefathers were buried in rows, three across, in his family's homestead.[113] British officers in Kigezi saw the *emandwa* cult as a potential ally: it was, wrote one officer, an 'established monotheistic faith traditionally allied and cooperative with the native government ... wielding a wholesome influence on tribal morality.'[114] The cult's initiation ceremonies affirmed its devotees' social discipline. Over the course of a twenty-four hour ritual, initiates performed a series of impossible actions.[115] They were obliged to carry water in a woven basket, dig up the soil with their teeth, and stand on the point of a spear. Initiates were also obliged to list the names of their relatives, names that should ordinarily never pass their lips, and to describe, in detail, the adulterous, incestuous, or bestial sexual relationships in which they had been involved. Once a whole series of infringements was thoroughly unearthed, once impossible feats had been attempted, and once all manner of scurrilous things had been sung and said, initiates were ritually brought back to life, taught new songs, and given new names. *Emandwa* rituals affirmed Kiga people's workaday discipline by caricaturing the dystopia of social anarchy, passing initiates through a disorderly, irrational, chaotic otherworld.[116]

In their testimonies of conversion, Christian revivalists brought the nightmarish indiscipline that *emandwa* initiates imagined into the light of day. Julaina Mufuko described how female converts would 'confess in public, right in front of the men they had committed adultery with!' Snapping her fingers to the rhythm of her words, Julaina described how the 'Holy Spirit would show you spontaneously, say this, say this, say this! If you have met Jesus, you have got to confess this!'[117] When the anthropologist Derrick Stenning attended a Revival meeting in Ankole, he listened as the parish chief's wife described how she had committed adultery with no less than fifty men.[118] It is not an accident that female converts were sometimes called

---

[113] CMS Annual Letters file: Brewer, annual letter, 1 September 1937.

[114] RH Mss. Afr. s. 1384: J. E. T. Philipps, 'The Nabingi: A Mandwa Secret Society' (July 1919). In another publication Philipps referred to the leading medium in the *emandwa* cult as the 'Pontiff,' and called the Nyabingi cult a 'protestant sect, an alien influence, popular and anarchic.' J. E. T. Philipps, 'Mufumbiro: The Birunga Volcanoes of Kigezi-Ruanda-Kivu,' *The Geographical Journal* 61 (4) (1923), 233–53.

[115] This paragraph summarizes Gershom Tumusiime, 'Impact of Bachwezi Bashomi on Christians: a Case Study of Kwamakanda Church in Uganda, Archdeaconry North-Kigezi Diocese' (Dip. Theo. thesis, Makerere University, 1990); Derrick Stenning, 'Persistence of Cult Elements in an East African Population' (Cambridge, April 1959); and Cambridge University Library Add. 7916.6: 'Okubandisa: Initiation into Embandwa,' typescript, n.d.

[116] But see Cecilia Pennacini, 'Religious Mobility and Body Language in Kubandwa Possession Cults,' *Journal of Eastern African Studies* 3 (2) (2009), 333–49.

[117] Interview: Julaina Mufuko, Kandago, Kigezi, 25 June 2004.

[118] Cambridge University Library Add. 7916, file B.5: notes on a service at Kiruhura, 20 October 1957.

prostitutes, or *katashwero*, 'one who will never marry' in Lukiga. In their loud confessions they threw their respectability to the winds. Many converts felt themselves acting immorally in their testimonies. Asanasiyo Rwandare, the convert who seems always to have been dreaming about an impending judgment, was terrified when in 1935 he stood to confess his sins. 'If I say all these things I have committed,' Rwandare worried, 'won't these people stone me to death? Because I had committed incest, I had intercourse with my close relatives, I used sometimes to destroy other people's gardens.'[119] Converts openly sullied other people's character. When Gersamu Ruhindi converted in 1941, he stood up in church and confessed to having written love letters to female friends. He read some of the letters aloud, even where the girl had no inkling of his affection. 'After the church services the girls would be embarrassed and run away,' Ruhindi remembered.[120]

Their open confessions of sin were in their critics' eyes a mark of converts' antisocial character. Converts' dining habits similarly undermined social discipline. In Chief Karegyesa's chiefdom in Rujumbura and in Ankole, the kingdom to the north of Kigezi, people made careful distinctions in their diet: women who ate goat meat or eggs, for example, were said to grow a beard or lay eggs like a hen.[121] Converts made a point of dining on taboo foods as a mark of their freedom from the strictures of traditional religion. When the cattle-keeper Kakoro converted in 1946, he pointedly took the milk that had been offered at a *mandwa* shrine, boiled it, and drank it.[122] His father, determined to punish him, burned Kakoro's house and forced his wife – also a convert – to drink beer and chew tobacco. 'We are Christians even if you have made us to drink,' she told him. In southern Uganda, debates over revivalism were often conducted as arguments over food. The leader of the Revival in the kingdom of Ankole, Erica Sabiti, was called before an assembly of government chiefs and accused both of 'allowing people to weep and confess their sins in churches' and of 'being a leader in eating and causing others to eat chicken.'[123] Other people were astonished at converts' indiscriminate willingness to eat whatever crossed their paths. In eastern Ankole, converts were called *abamwoyo*, 'those who eat the anus.' It was rumored that converts habitually ate ants, or supped from latrines.[124] Other rumors

[119] Interview: Asanasiyo Rwandare, Rwenyunza, Rukiga, Kigezi, 26 June 2004.
[120] Interview: Gersamu Ruhindi, Kabale town, 21 August 2005.
[121] Mariire Edward Kaborooga, 'The Impact of the Bakiga Immigration on the Religion of the Banyabutumbi of North Kigezi Diocese' (Dip. Theo. thesis, Makerere University, 1994).
[122] Muhanguzi, 'The Spread of the Revival Movement at Burunga.'
[123] HMC JEC 5/2: Sabiti to Joe Church, 21 October 1941; Sabiti to Church, 3 October 1941.
[124] John Ahimbisibwe-Katebaka, 'The Revival Movement and its Impact on the Church of Uganda in West Ankole diocese, with Particular Reference to Kabwohe Archdeaconry, 1935–1995' (Dip. Theo. thesis, Bishop Tucker Theological College, 1997); Muhanguzi, 'The Spread of the Revival Movement at Burunga'; Maari, 'The Balokole movement in Nyabushozi County.'

had it that converts ate placenta.[125] The rumors highlighted the indiscriminate character of converts' diets. Revivalists were as undisciplined in their dining habits as they were in their conversations.

Clothing and adornment constituted a further field of argument over revivalism. Converts made a point of shaving their hair, changing their attire, and removing the amulets that they wore. This bodily editing was meant to mark their passage from one life to another. When an *emandwa* medium in Ankole converted in 1937, revivalists arranged a meeting where his hair was publicly shaved. 'It was a wonderful head of hair,' reported an observer, 'a thick shaggy mass, which stripped off like the fleece of a sheep.'[126] Not everyone regarded converts' new style so favorably. When Asanasio Rwandare first heard Christian preaching, he removed the amulets he had tied around his neck and ankles and shaved off the hair that he had carefully styled into a three-fold pattern.[127] The following day, as he was herding his father's cattle, he met two women. 'As soon as they saw me, they gave way and went into the bush,' he remembered. 'They looked at me and said … "Do you mean that the converts are a bad omen to their parents when they are still alive?"' In his new hairstyle, Rwandare appeared to be in mourning, prematurely condemning his parents to death.

Rwandare's controversial haircut was part of a broader work of cultural editing in which Kigezi's people were engaged. The police had destroyed the Nyabingi shrine on Kagarama hill in 1928 (see above). It was rumored that the District Commissioner had decreed that all *emandwa* shrines, Nyabingi houses, talismans, and other religious objects were to be destroyed, and that Kigezi's people were to become Christians.[128] There is no evidence to show that British administrators actually ordered such wholesale repression: while they were implacable foes of Nyabingi, British officials encouraged *emandwa* cults, which they regarded as stabilizing presence in Kigezi's politics. Its truth notwithstanding, the rumor highlights the urgency with which Kiga people were reforming their religious practices. When an anthropologist conducted research in Kigezi in the early 1930s, she found very little physical evidence for Kiga religion: shrines had been hidden and diviners were reluctant to talk about their art.[129] Converts were the leading protagonists in this work of cultural engineering. One of my interviewees, Wilson Komunda, described how he destroyed the shrine where his father had offered beer to ancestral spirits. He brought the beer pots to the local church and smashed them to the ground in front of a revivalist

[125] Interview: Rwamangye Eliezar, Kabale, 20 August 2005.
[126] CMS Annual Letters file: Brewer, annual letter, 1 September 1937.
[127] Interview: Asanasiyo Rwandare, Rwenyunza, Rukiga, Kigezi, 26 June 2004.
[128] A. Karwemera, 'Christianity Comes to Nyakishenyi (1925–1935),' in *Occasional Research Papers*, vol. 31, ed. Tom Tuma (Department of Religious Studies and Philosophy, Makerere University, 1975).
[129] Edel, *The Chiga*, 157–58.

congregation.[130] The Ankole schoolteacher Samson Mbakiza converted in 1937. In the depths of the night, he had dipped his hand into a bowl of charms he kept beside his bed. His hand was so tightly gripped that he could not extricate it from the bowl, and for hours Mbakiza wept in fear. Finally he arose, walked through the night, and at daybreak he presented the charms to the Revival's leader in Ankole.[131]

Converts were cutting their hair, destroying their charms and shrines, and baring themselves for the general public to see. This practice of self-disclosure was particularly controversial for female converts in Ankole, just to the north of Kigezi. In Ankole, as in Rwanda, women's virtue was proven by their seclusion from men's eyes (see Chapter 1). Elite girls of a marriageable age were covered in a voluminous cloth and wore on their heads a grass mat, reaching from the back to the chest.[132] Wives of wealthy men stayed indoors, feeding on milk. One 25-year-old newcomer at the Anglican girls' school was so huge that she could barely walk.[133] Whereas elite women guarded their privacy, converts threw themselves open to the public view. Female converts marked their conversion by undressing: they took off their veils and put on simple cotton dresses.[134] In their critics' view, converts' openness was proof of their lack of discipline. Ankole's converts were rumored to sleep together, naked, as proof that they had conquered their fleshly desires.[135] The rumors highlighted converts' deviance; but more to the point, they cast light on their lack of discretion. One female convert was taken to court by her brother in law, who accused her of causing her husband's untimely death. After her conversion, she had shaved her hair and removed her veil, and her husband had died at that very hour.[136]

In their self-righteous denunciations of other people's behavior, in their clothing and adornment, and in their diets, converts laid down their responsibilities and cut themselves off from sociable communities. Critics were convinced that converts were consumed with self-interest. In Ankole, converts were known as *Abatarukukwatanisa*, 'Those who do not cooperate.'[137] In Kigezi, converts were known as *Binkwatiireki*, 'I am not concerned with whatever,' as *Tinfayo*, 'I am not bothered,' or as *Bafaki*, 'Don't worry about me.'[138] The nicknames were a form of criticism, given to converts by their offended neighbors. They showed converts to be both callous and

[130] Interview: Wilson Komunda, Bukinda, Rukiga, Kigezi, 25 June 2004.
[131] JEC 3/1: Joe Church, notes on Ankole, 16 April 1937.
[132] CMS G3 A7 O: Mbarara girls' boarding school, report, 30 June 1929.
[133] CMS Annual Letters file: Hogbin, annual letter, 23 August 1930.
[134] Interview: Zeb Kabaza, Kasanga, Kampala, 10 July 2004.
[135] Kafureeka, 'The Impact of the Revival Movement.'
[136] Muhanguzi, 'The Spread of the Revival Movement at Burunga.'
[137] Derrick Stenning, 'Preliminary Observations on the Balokoli Movement, Particularly Among Bahima in Ankole District' (Kampala, 1957).
[138] Ndambuki Peace, 'The Impact of the 1935–1937 Revival Movement.'

uncommitted. Converts would not comport themselves in a way that upheld sociable communities.

THE DISCIPLINE OF HISTORY

In the early 1940s, fathers, brothers, chiefs, and church authorities sought to restore social discipline by controlling troublesome converts. Georgina Kajagyi, who converted as a young girl in the late 1930s, remembered that her father punished her 'like beating a cow!' 'Why are you joining these mad people?,' her father asked.[139] Another interviewee described how husbands drove wives who converted from their homes, shouting 'I don't understand these things!'[140] Fathers and husbands were exerting their domestic authority. They found an ally in the Anglican bishop of Uganda, Cyril Stuart. While the evangelical missionaries in Rwanda and southern Uganda were generally eager participants in the Revival, Bishop Stuart and other churchmen in Uganda took a more critical view. Stuart was appalled when, early in 1942, he visited Kigezi to conduct confirmations. During the service, people were 'popping up all over the congregation to hold forth.'[141] 'I felt as if I was on the edge of a volcano,' he wrote. At the urging of Bishop Stuart, church authorities in Rwanda agreed in May 1942 to suppress both 'dancing under the impulse of the Spirit' and 'uncontrolled emotionalism in greetings, especially … between the sexes.'[142] Church authorities in Uganda were prepared to go further: they passed a rule that 'no interruption of divine service can be allowed by unauthorized speaking, singing, drumming etc.,' and that 'the public confession of shameful sins is not allowed' in church buildings.[143] Like Kigezi's District Commissioner, Bishop Stuart sought to restore order by closing converts' mouths.

Critics of the Revival found their most eloquent advocate in Chief Paulo Ngologoza. In the late 1930s and 1940s, Ngologoza had fought a private war against Julaina Mufuko, the irrepressible girl who seemed always to be preaching outside his door. In 1946, Ngologoza was made the first Secretary General of Kigezi District. With novel powers at his command, Ngologoza oversaw the resettlement of thousands of people from their homes in southern Kigezi to the sparsely inhabited plains of the north.[144] It was during this time that Paulo Ngologoza began to write history. In his writing, he found it possible to exercise an authority he had always sought in real life. His book *Kigezi and Its People*, published

[139] Interview: Georgina Kajagyi, Kabale, 18 August 2005.
[140] Interview: Robin Rwaminyinyo, Kabale, 18 August 2005.
[141] CMS G3 A7/1 Box 3: Stuart to Webster, 21 March 1942.
[142] HMC JEC 1/8: 'Text of an Understanding Arrived at Between the Missions Assembled at Muyebe, May 1942.'
[143] CMS G3 A11/1: Bishop Stuart to Webster, 18 January 1944.
[144] Carswell, *Cultivating Success*, chapters 3 through 5.

in the Kiga language in 1966, was a piece of creative writing.[145] In substance, the book testified to its author's efforts to create structures by which to govern Kigezi's disputatious people. Chief Ngologoza used his historical writing to identify the institutions that upheld discipline, and to elevate exemplary figures on whom readers could model themselves. The book's first chapters, on 'traditional government in Kigezi,' described how groups of Kiga elders adjudicated disputes among members of their lineages. They were like 'what the English would call a Standing Committee,' Ngologoza wrote.[146] He spent many pages detailing the biographies of eminent Kiga men. Magyengye, for example, occupied half a page: he was 'elder of Bakongwe at Mukyante' who 'killed many people in the neighborhood of Lake Bunyonyi' and was 'nicknamed Muyrima on account of his bravery.'[147] Among his descendants was the Catholic priest Pius Tibaanyendera. In his potted biographies Ngologoza was working to identify and elevate Kigezi's leading figures, anchor contemporary political and religious authorities within an inspiring past, and thereby impart to Kiga leadership both validity and authenticity.

The overriding theme of *Kigezi and Its People* is order. On the pages of his book, Paulo Ngologoza sought to conjure up the obedient, mannered people that he sought also to create in reality. In teaching his readers about self-discipline, Ngologoza relied on the validation that history could impart. Long ago, he wrote, 'people had good manners. A child gave its parents due respect and loved them very much. The young agreed to do all the work allotted to them.'[148] Parents likewise 'loved their daughters in law, and treated them tenderly as if they were their own children.'[149] Like generations of Rwandan and Ugandan polity-builders before him, Ngologoza sought to discredit Nyabingi's authority. In his partisan account, Nyabingi was a 'usurper woman' who had taken over a kingdom not her own. After her death, her servants had conspired to maintain their privileged position by deception, telling sick people that their diseases were caused by Nyabingi's avenging spirit. Thus, wrote Ngologoza, those who believed in Nyabingi 'fell into the flock of Satan.'[150]

Chief Ngologoza must have had the wraith of Julaina Mufuko at his elbow as he composed his paean to Kiga decorum.[151] In fact, she is more than a ghostly presence: the closing chapter of *Kigezi and Its People* is

---

[145] Paul Ngologoza, *Kigezi and its People* (Kampala, 1998 [1967]).
[146] Ibid., 21.
[147] Ibid., 24.
[148] Ibid., 33.
[149] Ibid., 35.
[150] Ibid., 48.
[151] Compare John Lonsdale, 'The Prayers of Waiyaki: Political Uses of the Kikuyu Past,' in *Revealing Prophets: Prophecy in Eastern African History*, eds. David M. Anderson and Douglas H. Johnson (London, 1995), 240–91.

Ngologoza's *apologia* for his treatment of revivalists. By the early 1960s, Ngologoza could be generous about Julaina. As a historian, Ngologoza described the whippings he had administered to Julaina and her friends as 'persecution,' and after several pages in which he documented how he, in Chief Karegyesa's company, had punished converts, Chief Ngologoza ended his book by pronouncing a benediction. 'May God have mercy on them' is the last sentence in *Kigezi and Its People*. It was a magnanimous ending. Ngologoza must have composed it with considerable relief. He was imagining a heavenly court where converts could, finally, be held to answer for their actions, where judgment could be executed and authority upheld. In God Chief Ngologoza found an authority that could get a hold on Julaina Mufuko.

CONCLUSION

Just as Rwanda's king Rwabugiri found an antagonist in Nyabingi, so did Chief Ngologoza find a foe in Julaina Mufuko and her talkative fellows. Nyabingi was a slippery presence in nineteenth and twentieth century Kigezi. In her travels from place to place and from person to person, the spirit evaded political authorities' efforts to bring her to heel. Julaina Mufuko was not a reincarnation of the queen Nyabingi, and neither was the Revival the Nyabingi cult dressed in new attire. Converts and Nyabingi mediums were co-travelers. The discourse and practice of revivalism took shape in a context where polity-builders were already at odds with their mobile constituents. Converts dreamt of an impending end of the world, reconfigured their biographies, and set themselves in motion. In their conversions they put distance between themselves and communities that claimed them in the name of ethnic identity. Revivalism was a form of dissent premised on movement, on the distance that self-directed people could put between themselves and their native communities. It expressed the indeterminances of territorial governance in a frontier zone.

In confronting this form of dissent Chief Ngologoza and other culture-builders in twentieth-century Africa possessed powers that Rwanda's kings could never match. The monarchs of precolonial Rwanda had enlarged their polity by the exchange of cattle, incorporating disparate people into vertical alliances as clients.[152] The culture-builders of colonial East Africa, by contrast, could count their people. They used bureaucratic techniques – the census, the identity card, the border, the court, the electoral roll, the history book – to link an identifiable people to a particular homeland. On the pages of their history books they marshaled up their constituents as sons of the

---

[152] See Catherine Newbury, *The Cohesion of Oppression: Clientship and Ethnicity in Rwanda, 1860–1960* (New York, 1988); Vansina, *Antecedents to Modern Rwanda*.

soil, and showed them how to act as patriots. As we shall see, the humble book that Paulo Ngologoza composed is one entry in a much larger library composed by patriotic entrepreneurs seeking to get a grip on their subjects. In Chief Ngologoza's legal efforts to bring Julaina Mufuko to heel, and in his authorial efforts to marshal up an obedient people, we can glimpse the origins of one of colonial Uganda's several patriotisms.

4

Civil Society in Buganda

In 1955, a sub-committee of the parliament of Buganda offered a visiting British commission a tutorial about the kingdom's history.[1] They began by quoting the explorer James A. Grant, who in 1864 expressed the view that Buganda's buildings were 'superior to any we have met with in Africa.'[2] The next quotation was from Sir Gerald Portal, who in 1894 averred that *Kabaka* [King] Mwanga's manners were 'a type of politeness itself' which 'would have fitted him for a post in any European court.' The parliamentarians were careful to quote Portal's conclusion: Buganda 'stands forth in strong contrast to all surrounding African nations.'[3] They closed their excursus on British travel writing by quoting Winston Churchill, then Britain's Prime Minister, who during his 1908 trip through Buganda was convinced that 'the scenery is different, the vegetation is different … and most of all, the people arc different from anything elsewhere to be seen in the whole range of Africa.'[4] The evidence, argued the Ganda parliamentarians, showed that the colonial relationship had in fact been a 'special friendship' between equals. Their historical lessons allowed Buganda's parliamentarians to speak as conservatives, not as radicals, when in December 1960 they declared the kingdom to be independent, both of Britain and of Uganda. 'Buganda was a real sovereign state before and at the time the British bestowed their protection,' the parliamentarians argued in their memorandum to the British Queen.[5]

---

[1] Churchill College archives DGFT 5/5: 'Report of the Sub-committee of the Lukiiko which was Elected to Examine the Recommendations made by the Hancock Committee,' n.d. (but 1955).

[2] James A. Grant, *A Walk across Africa, or, Domestic Scenes from my Nile Journal* (Edinburgh, 1864).

[3] Sir Gerald Portal, *The British Mission to Uganda in 1893* (London, 1894).

[4] Winston Churchill, *My African Journey* (London, 1908).

[5] RH Mss. Afr. s. 1483 (3): 'A Memorandum to Her Majesty Queen Elizabeth II,' n.d. (but 1960).

Buganda stood out in Britain's East African empire. No other polity possessed such an inspiring historiography. Buganda's intellectuals and political leaders were prolific writers of history. Apolo Kagwa, the Prime Minister whose military and political energy established Buganda's Protestant elite, wrote at least four historical works over the course of his long life. He began composing the first, *Ekitabo kye Basekabaka be Buganda* ('The Book of the Kings of Buganda') in 1892.[6] Radicals likewise wrote history: Jemusi Miti, the founder and chief organizer of the populist Bataka Party, had put 400,000 words on the page by 1946.[7] In historical works, in petitions, and in other media, Ganda elites established their kingdom's unique properties. Buganda's history was self-authored in these accounts, an achievement that set the kingdom apart from the rest of eastern Africa and entitled its leaders to play a preeminent role in the region's affairs.[8] Buganda's intellectuals were generating capital by writing history, turning the past into a political asset.

But the kingdom's history was never their exclusive property. Even as Ganda political organizers identified their distinctive inheritance, and even as they showed Buganda to be uniquely entitled to self-government, their constituency kept taking on new forms. The kingdom's culture and economy was from the early 1920s onward fed by a yearly flow of immigrants from Rwanda, Burundi, Kigezi, and northwestern Tanzania. Immigrants came to work for comparatively high wages on Buganda's cotton farms. Some of these immigrants made a home for themselves, and by 1948, 34 percent of the people living within the borders of the Buganda kingdom were immigrants, mostly from Rwanda and southern Uganda.[9] Many of them were tenants, living on farms owned by Ganda landowners. They adopted Ganda names – Kapere and Musoke were their favorites – and memorized the genealogies of Ganda clans in order to pass themselves off as

[6] Apolo Kagwa, *Ekitabo kye Basekabaka be Buganda* (Kampala, 1900). Historian Michael Twaddle identifies the other three texts as *Mpisa za Baganda* ('Customs of the Baganda,' 1907); Kagwa, *Ebika bya Buganda* ('Clans of the Baganda,' 1912); and Kagwa, *Ky'ekika kyw Nsenene* ('The Book of the Grasshopper Clan,' 1904). Michael Twaddle, 'On Ganda Historiography,' *History in Africa* 1 (1974), 85–100.

[7] Reported in CoU 02 Bp 184/20: Protectorate Agent to Robertson, 3 June 1946.

[8] The Luganda historiography is reviewed in John Rowe, 'Myth, Memoir, and Moral Admonition: Luganda Historical Writing, 1893–1969,' *Uganda Journal* 33 (1969), 17–40, 217–19; and in Twaddle, 'On Ganda Historiography.' Neil Kodesh's *Beyond the Royal Gaze: Clanship and Public Healing in Buganda* (Charlottesville and London, 2010) offers illuminating insights into the politics of Ganda historical writing in the twentieth century.

[9] J. M. Fortt, 'The Distribution of the Immigrant and Ganda Population within Buganda,' in *Economic Development and Tribal Change: A Study of Immigrant Labour in Buganda*, ed. Audrey Richards (Cambridge, 1954). See also Simon Rutabajuka, 'Migrant Labour in Masaka District, 1900–62: The Case of Coffee Shamba Labourers,' in *Uganda: Studies in Labour*, ed. Mahmood Mamdani (Dakar, 1996), 11–52.

clan members.[10] Ganda people looked on these ingratiating foreigners with scorn, but even they had difficulty telling newcomers from natives. When the government announced its plans to take a census in 1948, Ganda editorialists demanded that census-takers be careful in their work. 'Unless a proper census of pure bred Baganda be taken separately,' one editorialist worried, 'the Baganda will have totally disappeared among these foreigners in about ten years' time.'[11] The migration routes linking Buganda with Rwanda, Burundi, Kigezi, and Buhaya were conduits along which people and ideas flowed. Anthropologists reported that 'there is a constant traffic of relatives going to and fro in fulfillment of traditional kinship duties,' traveling with 'their pockets studded with scraps of paper and their heads with messages.'[12] Buganda's labor migrants were involved in a social network constituted by the movement of people and ideas from Kigezi and Rwanda and back again. Ganda politicians thought themselves a world apart from the rest of eastern Africa, but laborers, wives, messengers, and migrants knew differently. In their travels, they linked Buganda's economy and culture securely into the circuitry of a wider, East African world.

This chapter studies one form of discourse that traveled along the migration routes linking Buganda with Kigezi, Rwanda, and northwestern Tanganyika. Revivalists from Rwanda were preaching in Buganda in 1935. Gahini – the Anglican mission station where revivalism took form – was on the road linking Rwanda with Buganda. By the early 1940s there were nearly 1,000 converts in Buganda, many of them clustered in Mengo County at the kingdom's center. They took their place in a crowded political theater. Elite politics in Buganda were polite and well-mannered. In their comportment, powerful men upheld their kingdom's reputation for civility and positioned themselves alongside their British rulers as equal partners in the work of government. Not everyone conducted politics in such a polite fashion, however. In the 1940s, advocates of the populist Bataka party sought to open new channels of political activism. Bataka activists hoped to offend their antagonists, to clarify the interests that commoners shared, and to summon an egalitarian political community into being. Both the mannered men of Buganda's elite class and the radical populists of the Bataka party were horrified when revivalists began to preach openly about

[10] Audrey Richards, 'The Assimilation of the Immigrants,' in *Economic Development and Tribal Change: A Study of Immigrant Labour in Buganda*, ed. Audrey Richards (Cambridge, 1954). See also Shane Doyle, 'Immigrants and Indigenes: The Lost Counties Dispute and the Evolution of Ethnic Identity in Colonial Buganda,' *Journal of Eastern African Studies* 3 (2) (2009), 284–302.
[11] RH Mss. Afr. s. 951: Y. Nsigulamirambo, 'The Position of Doctors,' *Mugobansonga*, 18 November 1948.
[12] Audrey Richards, 'The Travel Routes and the Travelers,' in *Economic Development and Tribal Change: A Study of Immigrant Labour in Buganda*, ed. Audrey Richards (Cambridge, 1954), 71 and 74.

their sexual and moral failings. Whereas elites sought to polish over their private conjugal indiscretions, converts threw their honor to the winds and confessed their most embarrassing deeds in public. Whereas Bataka activists worked to lump their constituents together as partisan members of a community, converts insisted on standing apart. Buganda's politicians disagreed over the manner in which debate should be conducted and over the credentials leaders ought to possess. But polished elites and aggressive populists shared a profound respect for masculine honor and a firm conviction that wives, sons, and daughters should keep their mouths closed.

MANNERS AND AGENCY

Ganda people's estimation of good manners was modeled on the hierarchical relationship that joined generous patrons to respectful clients. Powerful men gathered communities of dependents around them, distributing food and land and demanding labor and produce from clients. When a group of British anthropologists conducted interviews in the early 1950s about Ganda people's expectations of political authority, their interviewees plied them with stories about food. One man recalled how 'in the past chiefs got rich through their people ... People would offer presents to chiefs e.g. bunches of plantains, hens, goats; and in return the chiefs would give them food and meat more than they could eat.'[13] Proverbs characterized greedy men as ungenerous hosts: 'he who intends to cheat ... cuts slantingly,' warned one proverb.[14] Honorable men sliced their meat generously, and drew people together around them. Men who aspired toward greater things made a point of joining their chiefs for meals. When the young civil servant Sepiria Kadumukasa sought to advance his career, he gave himself strict instructions in his diary. 'As I am a teetotaler, now try and make friends with the *saza* [county] chief,' he wrote. 'Never stay a long time without passing there. Make yourself at home. Dine and lunch with him. This is the most important thing to take in mind.'[15]

It was more than food that bound Ganda patrons and clients together. In their dinnertime conversations, Ganda people practiced the habits of polite speaking, deference, and civility. The Ganda word *obuntubulamu* captured what was required: it meant 'the possession of courtesy, compassion, good breeding, culture etc.'[16] Ganda language is rich in words describing different styles of talking. To *-gogomerera* is to 'speak languidly like a

[13] LSE Richards papers 7/2: Richards, interview with Noah Mubiazalwa, 19 June 1954. This paragraph is modeled after Carol Summers, 'Radical Rudeness: Ugandan Social Critiques in the 1940s,' *Journal of Social History* 39 (3) (2006), 741–70.
[14] Ferdinand Walser, *Luganda Proverbs* (Berlin, 1982), no. 507.
[15] Makerere archives AR KA 43/43 S. Kadumukasa papers: Kadumukasa, 'My Experiences and Hardship, 1943 Events.'
[16] John D. Murphy, *Luganda-English Dictionary* (Washington, D.C., 1972), 44.

sick person'; to -*gong'onta* is to 'be husky, talk through the nose'; while *buyabura* is the 'prattle of dementia.'[17] A compendium lists more than sixty proverbs that begin with the verb 'You are talking like.' One proverb compared a boring conversationalist to an empty packet of butter.[18] The 1904 'law of using indecent language' made it a crime to 'publicly abuse any person in indecent words' or to 'publicly do any indecent act or object.'[19] The penalty was a year's imprisonment. Ganda politicians thought the law to be a force for good. 'The Baganda were aware that a person had a right to respect of other people,' wrote a Ganda commentator in 1946, 'and that any infringement upon a person's good name ... would be a breach of the peace and punishable.'[20] Where undisciplined talkers felt the force of public disapproval, circumspect conversationalists earned a reputation and a following. 'Good conduct was a great demand of the community upon the individual,' wrote a Ganda commentator in 1945. 'Parents demand it from children; elders from their younger kinsmen; chiefs from their subjects; and needless to say, the Kabaka [king] from all.'[21] In their manners and in their eating, the Ganda people affirmed their position within a political and social hierarchy.

Ganda people's assessment of polite conduct overlapped with their British rulers' own models of propriety. Harry Johnston, who negotiated the charter that established Buganda's favored position in colonial Uganda, thought he had 'never encountered people of more delightful native politeness and tact than the Baganda.'[22] Trained in the polite rituals of Oxford and Cambridge, British officials in Buganda quickly found common ground with Buganda's mannered elite. In 1900, Buganda's prime minister, the historian Apolo Kagwa, organized a luncheon to mark the king's birthday. A company of Europeans and Ganda chiefs sat at a table set with knives, forks, and linen napkins, and dined on a meal of fish, soup, omelets, and lime juice.[23] By the 1930s, European officials and Ganda elites were involved in a regular round of dinner parties. Anthropologist Audrey Richards found the socializing to be so intense that she was constantly preoccupied with the condition of her

[17] Definitions from Albert Cook, *A Medical Dictionary and Phrase Book in Luganda* (Kampala, 1921).

[18] Walser, *Luganda Proverbs*, number 4639.

[19] UNA A 46/618: 'Endagano zona ezalaganibwa ne Gavumenti ya Bangereza na Baganda mu Buganda,' n.d. (but 1904).

[20] James Kibuka Miti, 'Buganda, 1875–1900: A Centenary Contribution,' trans. G. Rock (typescript, n.d. [but 1946]).

[21] E. M. K. Mulira, *Thoughts of a Young African* (London, 1945). Quoted in Summers, 'Radical Rudeness,' 746.

[22] Quoted in Audrey Richards, 'Traditional Values and Current Political Behaviour,' in *The King's Men: Leadership and Status on the Eve of Independence*, ed. Lloyd Fallers (London, 1964), 297.

[23] Described in Neil Kodesh, 'Renovating Tradition: The Discourse of Succession in Colonial Buganda,' *International Journal of African Historical Studies* 34 (3) (2001), 511–41.

dresses.[24] Some critics thought the social whirl to be too much to bear. Mabel Ensor, a missionary associated with the 'Mengo Gospel Church,' excoriated the Anglican bishop for his devotion to Buganda's polite society. 'Your presence at Saturday night dinners and dances in Kampala is frequently reported in the local Press,' she complained. 'The days of the Flood and of Sodom are literally upon us once more.'[25] But criticisms like Ensor's were rare. For Ganda elites as for British bishops, dinner parties were integral to the art of high politics.

Buganda's elite could come alongside their British rulers in polite society. In politics, too, Buganda's leaders positioned themselves beside Great Britain. Ganda socialites were outraged when, in 1928, Uganda's government mandated that primary schools should teach the Swahili language from Class II onward.[26] They interpreted Uganda's language policy as an act of enclosure. One critic termed Swahili a 'bulldozer language.' It flattened polite conversation, and made Buganda's people subject to Europeans' uninterrupted orders. 'Hear any European army officer addressing an African – the language should be Swahili,' this critic argued. 'But it is not the language for friendly talk. Who would drink pepper mixture if there is sugared tea?'[27] Swahili was a language for the regiment: it made it impossible for Africans to draw British officials into productive dialogue. Ganda intellectuals insisted that their children should learn English, the language of sugared tea and meaningful conversation, not Swahili. 'The native of Buganda wants to learn and there is no power on earth which could stop a British directed subject from going to England or anywhere for his education,' wrote a Ganda intellectual. 'We want to be lawyers, doctors, in fact everything the brain can master.'[28] Mastery over English was a critically important skill. Aspiring social climbers honed their rhetorical and political skills at schools like Erenesti Kalibala's, opened in 1934 in buildings owned by the Church Missionary Society. An advertisement promised that Kalibala's course would illuminate 'the secrets of the English language, how, why, and where to use it – develop your vocal power, persuasive personality and be your own master.'[29]

Tutored in English, confident Ganda elites took their places alongside British officials as co-participants in the work of government. The high

[24] LSE Richards papers 18/4: Richards to 'Dearie,' 6 August 1944. Cited in Carol Summers, 'Radical Rudeness,' 744.

[25] CMS Af 35/49 A7/1 Box 1: Mabel Ensor to Bishop, 16 December 1935.

[26] NAB CO 536/170/1: Director of Education to District Boards of Education, 15 August 1928.

[27] Makerere archives, Uganda Mission (unified) papers: Undated letter from Y. Okello, quoted in Dora Skipper, circular letter, 9 October 1926.

[28] Makerere archives, Yusufu Bamu'ta papers, Box B: 'Education,' n.d. (but late 1920s).

[29] The handbill advertising the course is in CMS G3 A7 O: Williams to Hooper, 18 October 1934.

politics of Buganda in the 1940s was driven by Ganda elites' efforts to hold on to their position alongside their British rulers. In 1947, a crisis developed in church politics when the Anglican bishop Cyril Stuart appointed as assistant bishop Aberi Balya, from the Toro kingdom in western Uganda. Buganda's ruling class was closely linked with the Anglican church: the kingdom's nineteenth-century wars of religion had been resolved in favor of the Protestant elite, and by 1935, 2 of the 3 ministers, 10 of the 18 county chiefs, and 92 of 153 sub-county chiefs were Anglicans.[30] Buganda's Anglican elite was terrified that Canon Balya's appointment would make a mockery of their religion. Balya had poor command over the English language, and he habitually walked barefoot as a symbol of simplicity. His chief critic was the Ganda churchman Timosewo Luule, who had a clear idea of the qualifications that a competent bishop ought to possess. He listed them in a 1947 petition:

A bishop must be a man of good faith who is well educated [and] who has attained some of these degrees:
M.A., B.A., D.D.
License in Theology
Scholar in Theology
Associate in Theology
Diploma in Theology[31]

For Luule and his colleagues, the bishop's curriculum vitae was a matter of vital consequence. When an African bishop was appointed, Luule wrote,

it will be he alone who will be invited to important episcopal councils … He should not be a mummy who will sit snug in the council and be told to sign things he has not understood. He should not be a dunce who will not be able to read for himself matters forwarded to him … Our church needs a native bishop – a true bishop to be relied upon, and who is equal to the other bishops.[32]

In a separate letter, Luule derided Canon Balya as the 'Cure d'Ars' of Uganda.[33] He was referring to the saint Jean-Marie-Baptiste Vianney, a priest who, because of his incapability in Latin, devoted himself to the service of the peasantry in post-revolutionary France. Canon Balya's appointment made Ugandans look like simpletons, country bumpkins who were unable to play a part in the intellectual commerce of church life.

The controversy over Bishop Balya's consecration lets us see, from Ganda elites' perspective, how high politics was supposed to work. In language

---

[30] Rubaga D.99 f.2: 'Synopsis of Comparative List of Catholic and Protestant Chiefs in Buganda,' 1935.
[31] CoU 02 Bp 16/1: Timosewo Luule to Synod of the Province of Uganda, 20 September 1947.
[32] TNA S4 36846: Luule to Church of Uganda Episcopal Council, 28 July 1947.
[33] CoU 02 Bp 184/20: Luule et al. to Lambeth Conference, 22 March 1948. See F. Trochu, *The Cure D'Ars: St. Jean-Marie-Baptiste Vianney* (Rockford, IL, 1977).

policy, in church life, in their manners and comportment, and in their historical research, Ganda politicians were identifying Buganda's distinct accomplishments, distinguishing the kingdom from the rest of eastern Africa. When the Colonial Office proposed to bring Uganda into a 'closer union' with the British territories of Kenya and Tanganyika, editorialists could argue that 'from the earliest years of European government, there was a marked difference between Uganda and the rest of East Africa ... God forbid that the Kingdom of Buganda should be pushed into that big huddle.'[34] Their historical argument was so convincing that the British felt obliged to acknowledge Buganda's distinctive trajectory. The anthropologist Cullen Young introduced a 1948 book on Ganda history by commenting that pre-colonial Buganda's attainments went 'far beyond what was expected out of Africa.' Once British administration was established, Young wrote, 'Buganda took its rightful place as by far the most developed African native state of pre-European origin.'[35]

Buganda's Protestant elite was claiming a place at the table where high politics were conducted. They learned English, polished their manners, and wrote partisan histories emphasizing Buganda's unique identity. Through their cultural and social work, they positioned themselves as a civilized elite, worthy of respect and attention from their British rulers.

OFFENSIVE POLITICS

Not every Ganda politician would conform to the comfortable rituals of high society. In the late 1940s, activists of the Bataka Union overturned Buganda's polite conventions and opened a new form of activism. Elite politics was conducted in a deferential fashion. Bataka activists set out to offend their enemies and clarify ideological differences. Elite politics were funneled through a small cadre of chiefs and powerful men. Bataka activists called Ganda commoners together as fellow citizens and as actors in a populist political movement. In large public meetings, in the press, and in their vitriolic petitions, they stirred people's emotions and created a new community of purpose.

The Bataka Union's genealogy can be traced to the early 1920s, when a cadre of activists – speaking as the *bataka*, the original landholders of Buganda – sought to defend their prerogatives against the overwhelming power of Buganda's chiefs. They marshaled history onto their side. Banana farmers had established permanent settlements on Lake Victoria's northwestern shores in the sixteenth century. On their productive gardens – called *butaka* – farmers buried their ancestors, establishing a lineal claim to the

---

[34] 'Uganda, not East Africa,' in *Gambuze*. Quoted in NAB CO 537/3600: Fortnightly review, 30 January 1948.
[35] Cullen Young, editorial note dated August 1948, in Miti, 'Buganda, 1875–1900.'

long-lived banana trees.[36] By the late nineteenth century, there were more than forty clans whose members venerated ancestors buried on ancient banana farms. It was these landholding clans that were disadvantaged by the 1900 Agreement, which settled Buganda's nineteenth-century wars of religion in favor of the Protestants and established a British protectorate over Buganda. Under the Agreement, the leading Christian chiefs in Buganda were awarded 8,000 square miles of the kingdom's most fertile land. In 1921, the clan leaders Joswa Kate and Jemusi Miti formed an organization called the Bataka Federation, arguing that *butaka* land should be removed from chiefs' control and restored to its original owners. 'From time immemorial all Baganda had their homeland, right from the time of King Kintu up to this year, 1900,' Jemusi Miti wrote in a 1922 petition.[37] Miti and other Bataka partisans sought to establish the landlords' presence at the beginnings of Buganda's political history. With their position in view, Miti and his colleagues could describe how the greedy Christian chiefs had seized the 'fertile homelands of the natives' and 'chased them from their lands.' Bataka activists conjured up a distant time when Buganda's citizenry had happily lived alongside their ancestors' graves. Their romantic self-portrayal made Protestant chiefs look like interlopers, and cast the 1900 Agreement as a betrayal of Buganda's founding principles.[38]

From the beginning, this argument over political power was conducted as a debate over history. The Bataka activists of the 1920s claimed a chronological and historical precedence over their antagonists. They made the Protestant elite look like *nouveau riche*, a recent addition grafted onto the bedrock foundations of Ganda polity. It is not a coincidence that one of leading figures in the Bataka party, Reuben Spartas Mukasa, was also the founder of the 'African Hellenic Catholic Orthodox Church.' Spartas had begun reading church history in the 1910s, trying to establish 'which is the true and real church that has stood loyally and uprightly up to date.'[39] He corresponded with the Garveyite bishop David William Alexander, who ordained several priests at Spartas's request, but in 1932 Spartas determined that Alexander's African Orthodox Church 'is not the real and true Orthodox Faith in Dogma, Doctrine, Culture and Principles.'[40] Spartas transferred his allegiance to the Greek Orthodox church, and sent three

---

[36] The history of banana cultivation is described in detail in Holly Hanson, *Landed Obligation: The Practice of Power in Buganda* (Portsmouth, 2003); David Schoenbrun, *A Green Place, a Good Place: The Social History of the Great Lakes Region, Earliest Times to the Fifteenth Century* (Portsmouth, 1997); and Neil Kodesh, 'Networks of Knowledge: Clanship and Collective Well-being in Buganda,' *Journal of African History* 49 (2008), 197–216.

[37] CoU 02 Bp 146/16: Jemusi Miti, Daudi Bassage and others to the bishops of Namirembe, Rubaga and Nsambya, 10 February 1922.

[38] See Hanson, *Landed Obligation*, for a full history of Bataka activism in the 1920s.

[39] CoU 02 Bp 8/1: Reuben Spartas to Archbishop of Canterbury, 26 September 1936.

[40] Makerere archives Ms. 276.762: Spartas Mukasa, 'History,' 1946.

Ganda students to Alexandria, in Egypt, where they were tutored in theology and the Greek language. Spartas identified himself and his followers with an antique church tradition, gaining rhetorical and theological leverage over the Anglican establishment in Buganda. He condescended to the Anglican bishop of Uganda, quoting Tertullian, Pope Gregory VII, and other ancient church fathers in long letters criticizing the modern innovations of Anglicanism.[41] In 1946, with the ancient character of his church established, Spartas could describe the Anglican church as 'only branches but not the real and actual foundation of Christianity ... not [the] True and exact Church founded, built, and established by Christ himself.'[42] In their Orthodoxy, Spartas and his compatriots made themselves into forebears of the Anglican church and ancestors of Buganda's Protestant establishment.[43]

Bataka activists were doing history on several fronts. In sacred time, they allied themselves with an ancient church tradition and identified themselves as advocates of a more authentic form of Christianity than the schismatic Protestants. In political history, they claimed a position as founders of Ganda polity. The Bataka organizer Jemusi Miti seems to have spent most of his life writing history. In the early 1920s, he helped to make the Bataka party's case against the kingdom's greedy Christian chiefs. By 1946, he had written a three-volume typescript on Buganda's history.[44] His *magnum opus* began by anchoring the *bataka* in Buganda's most distant beginnings. Before the mythical Kintu had founded his kingdom, Miti wrote, the Ganda people had lived in a republic, ruled by their elders. Kintu's good looks and superior fighting skills convinced these ancient elders to recognize him as their ruler. But they did not give up their hold over *butaka* lands: each clan retained its own property as 'an ancient right preceding the arrival of Kintu.' In Miti's view, the 1900 Agreement was a bargain among thieves. When British officials and Ganda elites signed the Agreement in 1900, the 'common people' 'expressed great dissatisfaction' with its terms. But their protests had been ignored, and Buganda's elite was free to '[grab] the best [of the land] for themselves and their relations and friends.'

Jemusi's Miti's book was never printed. The Anglican bishop thought it to be seditious. A British official who reviewed the text agreed: 90 percent of the third volume was unprintable, and 'even to publish a summary of the contents could have a subversive effect.'[45] But while it never appeared in print, Miti's historical work was put to good use. Bataka activists found a

[41] E.g. CoU 02 Bp 8/1: Spartas to Willis, 16 February 1931.
[42] Makerere archives Ms. 276.762: Spartas Mukasa, 'History,' 1946.
[43] Frederick Welbourn offers a biography of Spartas in his *East African Rebels: A Study of Some Independent Churches* (London, 1961), chapter 5.
[44] CoU 02 Bp 184/20: Bishop Stuart to Willis, 11 June 1946.
[45] CoU 02 Bp 184/20: Bere to Robertson, 3 June 1946.

distinctive role to play in Jemusi Miti's partisan history. The party's chief rhet-
orician, Semakula Mulumba, told Buganda's king in 1949 that the Bataka
were the 'children of the soil,' akin to the 'Britons, Saxons, Angles' and other
natives.[46] In another letter Mulumba called the Bataka 'our NATIONAL
GRANDPARENTS.'[47] The Bataka activists of the 1940s inherited both a
historical position and a political project from Jemusi Miti and Reuben
Spartas. Miti's historical writing made the Bataka spokesmen for traditional
values and allowed them to illuminate the corruptions and immorality that
Buganda's Protestant leaders had introduced.

A series of political crises in the 1940s lent credence to Bataka activists'
self-portrayal. In 1945, Buganda's king – the Kabaka – sought to force a
law through the kingdom's parliament allowing government to requisition
privately held land. Bataka critics argued that the land bill highlighted the
Kabaka's duplicitous relationship with his British overlords. 'The country
belongs to grandfathers and grandchildren,' wrote the author of the pamphlet *Buganda Nyafe* ('Buganda, Our Mother').[48] One editorialist darkly
worried that under the Kabaka's corrupt government Buganda's people
would be 'swept away, as the Romans were swept away.'[49] Like the elite of the
Roman empire, Buganda's leaders whiled away the hours in self-indulgence,
ignoring their responsibilities. The Kabaka's 1948 marriage to Damalie
Kisosonkole confirmed the critics' view. She was a member of a clan from
which Buganda's kings did not customarily choose their wives. For Bataka
partisans, the Kabaka's illicit romance was an occasion to speak as defenders of custom. In a public letter to the Kabaka, Semakula Mulumba argued
that the marriage would cause 'the rising tide of the evils of Western civilization [to] soon inundate the whole field of our national culture without a
single embankment to stem it.'[50] Mulumba compared the lovelorn Kabaka
with the deposed British king, Edward VIII. He had to 'choose either to
observe the national constitution on the throne, or embrace the bride off the
throne.' There could be no compromise.

In the controversy over the Kabaka's untimely marriage and in the debate
over the land bill, Bataka activists contrasted the popular interest with the
corruption of Buganda's elite. The problem they confronted was not simply
political. Buganda's elite had imposed a psychological tyranny over their
subjects. 'The people of Uganda are trained to prostrate, to go on all fours,
and worship the Kabaka,' complained Mulumba in a letter to the British
Resident.[51] Buganda's people, another editorialist observed, were obliged to
cloak even their most serious complaints in obsequious language, to write

[46] RH Mss. Afr. s. 951: Semakula Mulumba to the Kabaka, 21 February 1949.
[47] RH Mss. Afr. s. 951: Mulumba to Resident, 31 March 1949. Emphasis in the original.
[48] NAB CO 536/215: [Daudi Musoke], *Buganda Nyafe*, n.d. (but 1945).
[49] NAB CO 536/215: J. Kayembe in *Gambuze*, in Fortnightly review, 20 December 1945.
[50] RH Mss. Afr. s. 951: Mulumba to the Kabaka, 28 October 1948.
[51] RH Mss. Afr. s. 951: Mulumba to Resident, 31 March 1949.

'most humbly and respectfully sirs, we are requesting you to explain to us as regards the money you took from us.' Their deference made them 'downright slaves from the time when they are young until the time of their old age.'[52] 'Why is it that you should be so respectful?,' thundered Mulumba in a 1949 editorial. 'Why should you be so humble? You are trampled upon, you are plundered, you are despised because you are just there, swarming in humility, in obedience, in respectfulness.'[53]

Confronted with a tyranny of manners, Bataka activists vowed to misbehave. 'Let us run to our grandfathers, the Bataka, and there riot in pleasure,' Mulumba wrote. It was a relationship free of pretense:

Do not button your coats, but leave them hang freely; walk with airs ... Drive recklessly. Uganda is your country. Young men, leave your trousers hang down freely, walk as they flop about your feet. Feel confident as you walk about the roads. The nation, Uganda, is your country. Spinsters and girls, smarten yourselves up; walk with an affected gait; walk with airs, bubbling like beer; princesses of Uganda, the country is yours.[54]

Many Ganda people did feel free in their grandfathers' company. When anthropologists asked a group of eighteen schoolboys about their fathers in the early 1950s, sixteen said they felt fearful in their father's presence. 'The father? He is really like the Kabaka,' wrote one teacher in reply to the questionnaire. 'Whatever he does is right.'[55] Grandfathers, by contrast, were a benevolent presence in the lives of their grandchildren. Ganda children generally spent several years living in their grandparents' home, and there they felt liberated. 'In the home of the grandparents severity was not even theoretically expected,' an anthropologist observed. 'Here a child was free to behave exactly as it liked.'[56] As grandfathers and grandsons, Bataka activists were free to ignore the hierarchical conventions of Buganda's high society. In 1948 and 1949, as many as 10,000 people attended the meetings that the Bataka convened at the home of the long-lived historian Jemusi Miti. Under the direction of Reuben Spartas, attendees greeted each other with shouts of 'BU!,' an abbreviation of the initials of the Bataka Union.[57] This was a radical departure from Buganda's commonplace etiquette. Wives and children customarily knelt before their husbands and fathers, and clients who

---

[52] RH Mss. Afr. s. 951: Extract from *Munyonyozi*, 24 January 1949.

[53] RH Mss. Afr. s. 951: 'Semakula's Letter on Cotton,' *Mugobansonga*, 10 March 1949.

[54] RH Mss. Afr. s. 951: S. Mulumba, 'Uganda is a Nation,' May 1948.

[55] A. I. Richards, 'Authority Patterns in Traditional Buganda,' in *The King's Men: Leadership and Status on the Eve of Independence*, ed. Lloyd Fallers (London, 1964).

[56] Lucy Mair, *An African People in the Twentieth Century* (London, 1934), 60. My argument here follows Carol Summers, 'Grandfathers, Grandsons, Morality, and Radical Politics in Late Colonial Buganda,' *International Journal of African Historical Studies* 38 (3) (2005), 427–47.

[57] 'BU,' in *Gambuze*, February 1948; quoted in NAB CO 537/3600: Fortnightly review, 26 February 1948.

approached their landlords were obliged to sit quietly, on their knees, waiting for a reply.[58] Bataka activists greeted even the most distinguished of people with an egalitarian manner. In their assertive manner of greeting, Bataka activists were challenging the conventions that upheld Buganda's social hierarchy. 'We must simply squeeze and hold together like wax,' Mulumba wrote in 1948. 'We are one nation, there is no distinction ... We are all one lump. All are one in Uganda.'[59] Bataka leaders sought to form their constituents into an undifferentiated political community.

Lumped together, Bataka activists opened new channels of political action. Their chief political theorist was Mulumba, the nephew of Reuben Spartas, the Orthodox church's founder in Buganda. Bataka leaders sent Mulumba to London in 1947, and from his desk Mulumba kept up a steady stream of petitions and correspondence with the United Nations, the Secretary of State for the Colonies, the Anglican bishop, and the Governor of Uganda. He rarely got a reply to his missives. But that was not the point, for Mulumba's real audience was in Buganda, not in Britain. Mulumba's letters were reprinted, cyclostyled, published, and read aloud at the meetings convened by Bataka activists. He made careful plans for the distribution of his correspondence, listing the names and addresses of the authorities to whom he wanted copies of each letter sent. One of his distribution lists – intercepted by the Ugandan police – included 'Indians rich and poor,' the 'African clergy,' and 'the white professors at Makerere.'[60] Bataka activists found an even wider audience through the publishing industry. Buganda's vernacular press was well established by the 1940s. *Gambuze*, the longest-established newspaper, had a weekly circulation of 700 copies; *Munyonyozi*, the newspaper of the Bataka party, had a circulation of 975.[61] Newspapermen faithfully attended Bataka meetings, reporting on the speeches that activists made and printing the letters that Mulumba addressed to the Bishop, the British governor, and other authorities. Further afield, Mulumba found an audience in central Kenya, where newspapermen published, verbatim, his vitriolic correspondence with British authorities.[62] Gikuyu editorialists took inspiration from Mulumba's example. 'The Kikuyu must make known in Europe all that is done in their land,' the newspaperman Henry Muoria concluded (see Chapter 10).[63]

---

[58] Richards, 'Authority Patterns.'
[59] RH Mss. Afr. s. 951: S. Mulumba, 'Uganda is a Nation,' May 1948.
[60] RH Mss. Afr. s. 951: Mulumba to Om. Mponye Envumilo, 6 April 1949.
[61] NAB CO 536/215: Governor of Uganda to Secretary of State for the Colonies, 25 May 1945.
[62] E.g. the *Gikuyu Times*, 7 July 1949; quoted in KNA DC Kisumu 1/28/56: Kenya Information Office, 'Summary of Opinions on African Affairs Expressed in the Kenya Press,' 1 to 15 July 1949.
[63] *Mumenyereri*, 7 November 1949; quoted in KNA DC Kisumu 1/28/56: Kenya Information Office, 'Summary of Opinions on African Affairs Expressed in the Kenya Press,' 1 to 30 November 1949.

PHOTO 5. Semakula Mulumba at a rally in London protesting the abuse of Mau Mau detainees, n.d. Courtesy of Maurice P. K. Kiwanuka and the Benedicto K. M. Kiwanuka Family.

In his correspondence, Semakula Mulumba was generating evidence to show that commoners – and Africans more generally – could play a part in the theater of international politics. He was careful to advertise even the most formulaic aspects of his diplomatic work. In March 1948, Reuben Spartas proudly told an audience of some 3,000 Bataka party members that the United Nations had opened file number 1503/3/1 BA II to deal with

Mulumba's correspondence.[64] This was incremental progress in the world of diplomacy, but for Bataka activists, the file number was proof of the efficacy of populist politics. That same month, the newspaper *Gambuze* reported that Mulumba 'chose French when he was asked [with] what language he wishes to express himself to the International Council.'[65] Mulumba's practiced ease with the protocols of international diplomacy made an impression. 'Many people in Buganda seem to think that there are three important people in the world: the Prime Minister of England, the Secretary of State for the Colonies … and Ssemakula Mulumba,' wrote a contemporary observer, 'and they believe that … what the last man tells the other two becomes law.'[66] Bataka activists could see the evidence that their new form of activism was politically consequential. The crowds assembled at Bataka gatherings were given regular updates about the United Nations' meeting schedule, and circulars issued by the British Colonial Office were often read aloud and discussed by attendees. Their diplomatic work allowed a constituency of commoners to view themselves as actors in a global political theater.

The Bataka were a troublesome presence in the halls of diplomacy. Mulumba's capacious address list gave his petitions a wide audience, extending from the grounds where the Bataka Union assembled to the United Nations Trusteeship Council.[67] Bataka activists circumvented the normal procedures by which government authorities channeled and controlled political expression. In October 1948, activists instructed an audience of 3,000 people to write letters directly to the Kabaka.[68] The letter writers were given talking points: commerce should be in Africans' hands; educational opportunities should be increased; chiefs should be selected by the people. Ganda commoners had never before addressed themselves directly to their king. Convention dictated that commoners should appeal first to their chiefs, who would in turn present petitioners to the royal court. Bataka activists had no time for protocol. Semakula Mulumba's 1948 letter to the Anglican bishop of Uganda illuminates their strategy. In more than a dozen pages, Mulumba posed a series of rude, impolitic questions. 'Is not the land our mother?' he asked. 'Why should the British government and the missionaries steal our mother and remove her womb and cut off her breasts, so that she will neither be able to produce our fellow children, not suckle us?' Mulumba's grotesque questions amplified the stakes in land alienation. 'Is not Uganda a pigsty for white swine, wallowing and digging their snouts in the deep

---

[64] RH Mss. Afr. s. 951: Reports of Bataka Public Meetings in 1948 and 1949.

[65] Editorial in *Gambuze*, March 1948; quoted in NAB CO 537/3600: Fortnightly review, 25 March 1948.

[66] SOAS CBMS A/T 3/2 Box 281: Mulira, 'Background to the Troubles in Buganda,' n.d. (but 1949).

[67] See Ulrich Lohrmann, *Voices from Tanganyika: Great Britain, the United Nations, and the Decolonization of a Trust Territory, 1946–1961* (Berlin, 2007), 146–49.

[68] RH Mss. Afr. s. 951: Reports of Bataka public meetings in 1948 and 1949.

mire of ill-gotten African property?' he asked.[69] For Mulumba, the artifice of polite etiquette was stultifying, muffling real political expression. In his incendiary rhetoric, Mulumba sought to ignite the passions of his Ganda audience, molding them into a community driven by righteous indignation.

There was nothing conventional about this form of politicking. Bataka leaders bypassed the established hierarchy and invited commoners to engage directly in activism. In their historical research, they identified themselves as the national grandfathers, originators of Buganda's culture and guardians of custom. In their correspondence, they pushed Buganda's chiefs to the margins, speaking directly to local and international power brokers. In their rhetoric, they stripped away the discursive protocols that shrouded inequalities. Bataka activists were opening new ways of doing politics, summoning a constituency of commoners united not by genealogy but by their shared interests and commitments.

HONOR AND SHAME IN BUGANDA'S REVIVAL

In March 1936, William Nagenda – scion of a prominent Ganda family – came face to face with his sins. Nagenda, who worked as a government clerk in Entebbe, had borrowed money from the treasury. But on that fateful day,

> Jesus came and convicted me of all these things, of one thing after another. He said, 'That is stealing.' I said, 'Lord, I haven't stolen. I borrowed that money, hoping to pay it back.' Jesus said, 'That is stealing.' I had to bow my neck and acknowledge, 'Yes, Lord, I am a thief.' That is a very bad name to acknowledge, to be a thief ... He went on and on pointing out sin. In the end, I had to say, 'Yes.'[70]

Like his contemporaries in Kigezi, Nagenda sorted through his memories and identified otherwise forgettable actions as sins. He and nine other government clerks took a vow to 'resist sin' and began preaching in the countryside around Entebbe.[71] Later that year, Nagenda had a dream calling him to preach in Rwanda. He left his government post and became the head evangelist at the Anglican mission in Gahini, where Blasio Kigozi had formerly worked (see Chapter 3). In March 1937, with converts in northern Rwanda and Kigezi living in expectation of the end of the world, Nagenda preached a long sermon in which he listed dozens of sins on a blackboard, and then called for confessions. In the hours following, as many as 150 people confessed their sins.[72]

---

[69] CoU 02 Bp 184/20: Mulumba to Stuart, 26 July 1948.
[70] HMC JEC 17/1c: William Nagenda, 'The Lord is my Shepherd and That's All That I Want,' in *Living Water* III (January–March 1973).
[71] HMC JEC 3/1: Stuart to Joe Church, 3 March 1936.
[72] HMC JEC 3/4: Dora Skipper to Decie Church, 31 March 1937.

In 1939, Nagenda and two other leading revivalists were admitted to the Anglican theological school at Mukono, near Kampala, for ordination train-ing. At Mukono he and other converts made a habit of rising as early as 4 A.M. to preach and testify about their sins. When the warden insisted that the loudmouthed converts should stay in bed until 6 A.M., the converts refused, and Nagenda and twenty-five other students were expelled in punishment.[73] Even after their expulsion, the converts – scorned as 'rebels' by their crit-ics – would not close their mouths. One particularly noisy preacher was Dishon Mukasa, William Nagenda's elder brother. After his expulsion from Mukono, Mukasa was made an evangelist at the Anglican church at Gayaza, to the north of Kampala. By 1943, he had so offended his parishioners that they deserted the church in disgust. The Prime Minister of Buganda himself wrote to complain about Mukasa's preaching: he 'abuses and disgraces [the congregation] in the church,' the Prime Minister wrote, warning that the con-flict 'might cause the danger of fighting.'[74] At Ndeje, revivalists were likewise causing controversy. The leading evangelist was Benezeri Galiwango, for-merly a Mukono student, and the missionary in charge, Patty Drakeley, was herself a convert.[75] In 1942, parents withdrew three-quarters of the students from the girls' school, saying that they did not want their daughters to learn from the irresponsible converts. Miss Drakeley herself was renowned for her revealing sermons. Even the Governor complained when Miss Drakely and a group of revivalists from Ndeje visited Kings College Budo in October 1942 and 'confessed to all sorts of incredible evils and satanic temptations.'[76]

What was it about revivalists' sermons that so offended Buganda's par-ents and political leaders? Converts' testimonies seem to have been about their private sexual affairs. That was Dishon Mukasa's theme at Gayaza. A missionary critic reported in 1944 that Gayaza's revivalists had become 'violently coarse' in their sermons. Young male converts were confessing the most embarrassing sins 'without a spark of shame' before audiences of women and girls. 'Things I have never known or heard of are being broad-cast – appalling iniquity,' the missionary wrote. '"Confession is salvation, brings salvation, means salvation" is their theme, and you only have to wait three minutes before filth is introduced.'[77] Converts framed their theology

[73] The official report is in CMS G3 A7/5: College staff at Mukono to Bishop Stuart, 29 October 1941. See Kevin Ward, 'Obedient Rebels: The Relationship Between the Early "Balokole" and the Church of Uganda: The Mukono Crisis of 1941,' *Journal of Religion in Africa* 19 (3) (1989), 194–227.

[74] Katikiro to Bishop Stuart, 6 July 1943; quoted in NAB CO 536/215/4: 'Activities of the Abalokole, Twice Born, or Saved Ones,' 16 October 1943.

[75] See Bill Butler, *Hill Ablaze* (London, 1976), 52–53.

[76] NAB CO 536/215/4: Governor of Uganda to Secretary of State for the Colonies, 4 May 1944.

[77] Reported in NAB CO 536/215/4: 'Activities of the Abalokole, Twice Born, or Saved Ones,' part II, 30 April 1944.

in stark terms: they were said to preach that 'it is a choice between being a *mulokole* [saved person] and adultery.'[78] Bishop Stuart was convinced that 'the whole moral tone of the church has gone down because of the *balokole* [saved people], who by their quite revolting confessions and their constant reference to *obubaka* [adultery] cause people's minds to be fixed on *obubaka*.'[79] 'Because of their disgusting talk,' he argued, 'the whole atmosphere we breathe is defiled and they are putting thoughts into men's minds and causing them to sin.'[80]

Bishop Stuart's view of revivalists – as gossipmongers with dirty minds – seems to have been widely shared among Buganda's people. In their revealing sermons, revivalists shattered the commonsense bargain that husbands and wives made with each other. Ganda men and women had good reason to be circumspect about their conjugal relationships. Beginning in the late nineteenth century, British missionaries and government officials sought to make Ganda marriages into permanent, sexually exclusive, legally recognized unions. In 1893, the Anglican church council insisted that Christian women living as concubines in the households of elite men should leave their homes, requiring polygamous men to choose a single woman to name as wife.[81] Men who married in church and subsequently married other women were excommunicated.[82] The Buganda government adopted 'The Adultery and Fornication Law' in 1918. Under the law, a man who had sex with a married woman other than his wife could be jailed for up to a year.[83] In 1941, Buganda's parliament adopted 'The Law to Prevent Prostitution.' The law gave a remarkably capacious definition to the 'prostitute,' encompassing even a woman who 'persistently indulges in promiscuous intercourse with men even though she derives no gain or profit thereby.' Under the law, unmarried women under the age of twenty were forbidden to enter into employment or to live apart from their parents.[84] In the law and in the marriage register, missionaries and government officials were channeling Ganda people's sexual passions toward a single partner. Their legal innovations elevated monogamy over other conjugal forms.

Through these legal and social reforms, monogamous marriage became the foundation on which Buganda's Christian elite established their social

---

[78] MAM Y 4: Bishop Stuart, circular letter, 1 December 1941.

[79] CoU 02 Bp 226/28: Bishop Stuart to Stanley-Smith, 3 January 1944.

[80] HMC JEC 5/2: 'Bishop's Charge 1944.'

[81] E.g. Makerere archives AR N 3/2: Namirembe council minute book, entry for 18 January 1896.

[82] Makerere archives AR N 3/2: Namirembe council minute book, entry for 6 December 1893.

[83] LSE Richards papers 6/11: 'The Adultery and Fornication Law,' 15 June 1918.

[84] 'The Law to Prevent Prostitution,' 1 April 1941, in Kingdom of Buganda, *The Native Laws of Buganda* (Kampala, 1947), 6–8.

position.[85] In 1936, 240,000 of Buganda's 872,000 people were baptized Christians.[86] In Mengo, the kingdom's capital, a full half of the population was Christian.[87] For mannered Ganda elites, monogamy was an essential proof of their civility. 'Christianity is definitely the religion of the Baganda,' wrote the petitioner G. Kintu, and 'all her local as well as British laws are founded on the principles of Christendom.' He argued that it was England's 'duty of trusteeship' to 'put into force the English law for the African Christians. Christianity is the ruling religion of England and the British Empire. Polygamy is next to Bolshevism.'[88] Ganda elites modeled their marriages – and their religious lives – after a British template. Their social engineering made Ganda elites sensitive to even the slightest infractions against the rule of the law. When the Anglican bishop conducted the marriage of the illegitimate daughter of Buganda's king in 1937, churchmen loudly complained that 'it is a blow to family life.' The 'Buganda kingdom belongs to the people who went to the front of religious wars and bore the scars of those wars,' wrote one petitioner. 'The people's voice is that no state marriage should be done by the church for the illegitimate children of a Christian married king.'[89]

It was not only the mannered elite who were invested in monogamy. The radical populists of the Bataka Union were markedly conservative about gender relations. As Bataka partisans positioned themselves as spokesmen for an authentic culture, they found in the history of gender relations a useful means contrasting the antique integrity of Ganda culture with its contemporary degradation. In 1936, Jemusi Miti, the 'grandfather' of the Bataka party, told Buganda's king that 'Your country Buganda is becoming spoilt. Now there is the issue of sexual prolificacy that is rampant in the world which wasn't there before even at the time of the great-grandparents.'[90] In former times, government had upheld marriage: husbands could appeal to the Kabaka to punish their adulterous wives' lovers or to return runaway wives to their conjugal homes. Now, Miti wrote, 'it is not like that, because to day every woman moves the way she wants.' 'That's why diseases have become rampant in people,' he concluded, 'because there are no longer the good morals that our great-grandparents had that still are there in

---

[85] See Nakanyike Musisi, 'Morality as Identity: the Missionary Moral Agenda in Buganda, 1877–1945,' *Journal of Religious History* 23 (1) (February 1999), 51–74.
[86] 'The CMS in Buganda,' in *Uganda Church Review* 41 (January–March 1936).
[87] CoU 02 Bp 62/4: statistics for Mengo rural deanery, 1938.
[88] Rubaga D.32 f.6: G. Kintu, Makerere, to Resident of Uganda, 17 October 1938. In 1958, the missionary John Taylor noted that 'throughout Buganda, however critical men may be of the church's regulations in many respects, practically no-one suggests that the Christian ban on polygamy should be relaxed.' John Taylor, *The Growth of the Church in Buganda: An Attempt at Understanding* (London, 1958), 185.
[89] CoU 02 Bp 9/1: Yamasi Sempa to Stuart, 23 January 1937.
[90] CoU 02 Bp 184/20: Jemusi Miti et al. to Kabaka, 22 July 1936.

Buganda today.' Miti's historical research cast the contemporary hierarchy of Buganda in an unfavorable light, making the Kabaka and his chiefs look like corrupted libertines. By 1946, when he finished his magnum opus on Ganda political history, Miti had honed his account of gender relations to a fine point. 'Time was then a good reputation was the most highly prized gem of every Muganda girl,' he wrote. 'Let us revert to our old customs.'[91] Miti wanted new husbands to confirm their bride's virginity, and if fault was found, both the bride and her illicit lover were to be punished. Bataka activists were illuminating the immorality and corruption that Buganda's political establishment encouraged. Their political self-positioning obliged them to uphold a patriarchal model of gender order.

This political and rhetorical focus on monogamous sexual discipline was a convenient fiction. In fact, Ganda husbands and wives made practical, commonplace arrangements that circumvented the letter of the law. Catholic church authorities estimated that 24 percent of their parishioners were involved in 'irregular unions' outside their marriages.[92] Protestant missionaries thought the numbers were even higher: they lamented that Ganda husbands and wives very often separated without divorcing, with both parties drifting away to live with new partners.[93] Divorce was, in theory, available for any person whose marriage had been legally registered.[94] But divorce litigation could only be pursued through the High Court in Entebbe, not through Buganda's own court system. The anthropologist Audrey Richards, who conducted research in Buganda during the early 1950s, found 'the most common situation' was 'a man who has a main wife in one village and a permanent liaison with a woman in another village.'[95] These secretive conjugal arrangements demanded discretion and tact from both partners. In the 1930s, new brides were customarily instructed 'You are the mistress of your house and must cover up much in it.'[96] Proverbs advised a young bride to watch her mouth: 'A woman who talks about her marriage to outsiders, saying "What is wrong with my home is that and that" spoils the marriage,' went one proverb.[97] Wives who talked openly about their private marital disputes dishonored their husbands. Blasio Kibadawo and his wife, Dinah, had married in an Anglican ceremony in 1912, and she bore

---

[91] Miti, 'Buganda, 1875–1900,' Conclusion.

[92] Rubaga D 48 f.4: Vicarate apostolic of Uganda, annual report, 1946–47. See Melvin Perlman, 'Law and the Status of Women in Uganda: A Systematic Comparison Between the Ganda and the Toro' (Amsterdam, Summer 1969), 33.

[93] CoU 02 Bp 118/10: Conference of Missionary Societies in Great Britain and Ireland, 'Laws Governing the Marriage and Divorce of Native African Christians,' 1943.

[94] UNA A 46/618: 'The Divorce Ordinance, 1904,' in 'Endagano zona ezalaganibwa ne Gavumenti ya Bangereza na Baganda mu Buganda.'

[95] Cory file 373: Audrey Richards and Priscilla Reining, 'Report on Fertility Surveys in Buganda and Buhaya,' 1952.

[96] Mair, *An African People*, 97.

[97] Walser, *Luganda Proverbs*, 1347.

him seven children. They separated in 1941, and Dinah went to live with another man. He, meanwhile, married no less than three younger women. It was not until 1950, when Blasio insisted that Dinah return to their conjugal home, that their private arrangement came out into the open. When he confronted her, she 'talked ashaming words' at him and vowed 'Me I divorced you a long time ago.'[98] When Blasio insisted on pressing his case before the Anglican bishop, Dinah publicized his manifold sins: Blasio was a drunkard; he beat her and threatened her with a knife; and he had casual sex with schoolgirls.[99] Dinah had managed to practice the social discipline of discretion and secrecy for nine years. Only in the face of his pig-headed insistence that she should live with him did Dinah bring Blasio's dark misdeeds into the light of day.

Buganda's courts heard a great amount of salacious testimony in the 1930s and 1940s. An anthropologist who went through the kingdom's local court books found that a high percentage of the caseload concerned marriage disputes. In the years before 1939, some 16.3 percent of the caseload concerned marital disputes. Kigezi District's courts, by contrast, spent only 0.3 percent of their time on marriage litigation.[100] In conducting this litigation, husbands and wives were obliged to speak publicly about the private sexual and moral bargains that their spouses had made. The revelations that they made were shocking. The Anglican priest Fesito Luboyera had fathered two children out of wedlock. When his sin was revealed, his parishioners were astonished. 'A man who is like that is a killer,' they wrote.[101] The Luganda word they used to describe Luboyera was *mutemu*, the same word used for murderers or assassins.[102] As Rev. Luboyera discovered, as Blasio Kibadawo also knew, a testimony was never merely a dispassionate account of events. In opening men's private lives for inspection, wives were engaged in character assassination.

The Revival was controversial in Buganda because its converts publicized the private conjugal accommodations that Ganda husbands and wives had made.[103] Noisy converts brought the reputation-destroying testimonies that had been confined to the courtroom out into the open. By 1944, police observers estimated that there were some 500 revivalists in Mengo, at the center of the Buganda kingdom. In Masaka, converts numbered

---

[98] CoU 02 Bp 175/19: Blasio Kibadawo to Bishop Stuart, 24 March 1950.
[99] CoU 02 Bp 175/19: 'Issues that Confused Me and Caused Me to Divorce,' n.d. (but 1950).
[100] SOAS Melvin Perlman papers, Box 8, file 23: Perlman, statistics on litigation in Buganda and Kigezi.
[101] CoU 02 Bp 121/12: Mulago consistory court, minutes for 14 August and 10 September 1929.
[102] Murphy, *Luganda-English Dictionary*, 386.
[103] The public exposure of men's infidelity is no less controversial today. See Shanti Parikh, 'Going Public: Modern Wives, Men's Infidelity, and Marriage in East-Central Uganda,' in Jennifer S. Hirsch et al., *The Secret: Love, Marriage, and HIV* (Nashville, 2009), 168–96.

100 people.[104] Their constant theme, in the words of one of their leaders, was 'the terrifying condition of Christians in this country.'[105] In Masaka, a revivalist caused a sensation in 1945 when he confessed to murdering his child. The murder had taken place some years before his conversion.[106] One of the Revival's leaders composed a newspaper editorial identifying the first requirement of salvation as 'confession of sins to the very people whom we wronged.'[107] A missionary observer noted the variety of people who attended revivalist meetings in Buganda: there were university-trained teachers, migrant laborers from Tanganyika and Burundi, elderly women and young girls. They talked without compunction about their sins. 'This one could testify to having jealous thoughts,' the missionary wrote, 'this one to having been troubled with thoughts of impurity, this one to having quarreled with his wife, and so on.'[108] One convert, a man named Timosewo, wrote letters to several female missionaries, telling them that he had been tempted to commit adultery with them.[109] Missionaries opened up about their private lives, too: when Doris Hubbard converted in 1941, she told a crowd of Europeans and Africans that she would henceforth have 'no more sex relations with my husband.'[110] At Namutamba, where the planter Lea-Wilson had opened his farm to revivalists, a group of spinsters and widows became nudists in 1941 as evidence that they had tamed their sexual desires. They were inspired by the example of Adam and Eve, who in their prelapsarian innocence had likewise gone without clothing.[111]

Elites and radicals alike were horrified at converts' explicit testimonies. They were convinced that revivalists were undisciplined libertines. In a 1940 letter entitled 'The Church and the Sin of Committing Adultery,' the churchman Paul Balintuma reminded his readers about the scandal of Sodom and Gomorrah, where residents had openly lived in sin. He likened the story to contemporary 'Christians who have rumor mongering behaviours.' 'No one should just talk anyhowly because untrustworthiness with people is bad,' he wrote.[112] As evidence, Balintuma cited I Corinthians 10:10: 'Do not grumble, as some of them did – and were killed by the destroying angel.'

[104] NAB CO 536/215/4: 'Activities of the Abalokole, Twice Born, or Saved Ones,' Part II, 30 April 1944.
[105] CoU 02 Bp 186/21: L. Kafero to Bishop Stuart, 19 November 1941.
[106] NAB CO 536/215: African affairs fortnightly review, 10 May 1945.
[107] A. Binaisa, 'Anyone with Ears, Let Him Hear,' in *Ebifa mu Uganda* (June 1940). Quoted in C. Robbins, 'Tukutendereza: A Study of Social Change and Sectarian Withdrawal in the Balokole Revival' (PhD dissertation, Columbia University, 1975), 190.
[108] CMS Annual Letters file: Lionel Bakewell, annual letter, 30 June 1947.
[109] HMC JEC 3/5: Leslie Lea-Wilson to Joe Church, 29 November 1941.
[110] HMC JEC 3/5: Leslie Lea-Wilson to Joe Church, 29 November 1941.
[111] Interview: Zeb Kabaza, Kasanga, Kampala, 10 July 2004; CoU 02 Bp 226/28: Bishop Stuart to Webster, 7 January 1944.
[112] CoU 02 Bp 128/12: P. Balintuma, Haruni Sempala and L. Balintuma, 'The Church and the Sin of Committing Adultery,' n.d. (but 1940).

Balintuma wanted noisy converts to close their mouths and behave responsi-
bly. At Ndeje, parishioners were so infuriated at converts' aggressive preaching that they resolved to construct a separate church.[113] One of them wrote
an editorial to the *Uganda Star*, complaining that 'The church in Ndeje has
become as good as a husk, the self-styled saved ones abuse us that we have
sins.'[114] For people like the offended parishioners at Ndeje, converts were
slanderers, assassinating other peoples' good names. The missionary Mabel
Ensor excoriated converts for their 'rudeness, coarseness, barking outside
the place of worship, clawing one another as a sign of fellowship, [and] literally bellowing.'[115] Everyone, it seemed, was searching for ways to silence
the loudmouthed converts. Some critics adopted a direct course of action.
At Lea-Wilson's farm in Namutamba, the irate headman beat a particularly
loudmouthed revivalist with 'a big stick all over his head, till he knew no
more.'[116]

Converts' slanderous testimonies showed them to be delinquent in their
most basic responsibilities. For the populists of the Bataka party, converts
were agitators, diverting people's attention from the task at hand. 'They
behave as if they belong to no clan and are bound by no customs,' wrote an
editorialist in 1945, 'as though they were not Baganda before they became
balokole.'[117] 'Uganda is working toward unity, the [revivalists] are working toward disunity,' argued the labor leader Ignatius Musazi.[118] Semakula
Mulumba, the chief propagandist of the Bataka Union, thought revivalists
were traitors to their people. In a 1948 letter to Bishop Stuart, he asked 'Why
would you be so hard on the Africans who want to preserve their traditions
and customs while you wholeheartedly approve of the Abalokole Violent
Revival Movement which allows Caligula immorality? Do you not think
that the strict African moral code of Uganda should be preserved and trea-
sured in preference to your [Revival] movement?'[119] In fact, Bishop Stuart
was a critic of the Revival, not their supporter. It was he who offered the
most illuminating metaphor for their politics: he compared converts with
the Old Testament character Absalom, whose silver tongue had turned the
Israelites against King David.[120] Like Absalom, converts seduced otherwise

---

[113] CoU 02 Bp 187/21: Patty Drakely to Bishop, 31 August 1950.

[114] CoU 02 Bp 187/21: *Uganda Star*, 18 July 1950.

[115] Quoted in Samuel Ndahiro, 'The Impact of the Abalokole Revival on the Church of Uganda
with Particular Reference to the Diocese of Namirembe from 1940–1992' (BA thesis,
Association of Theological Institutions in Eastern Africa, 1992).

[116] HMC JEC 3/5: Leslie Lea-Wilson to Joe Church, 29 November 1941.

[117] N. Wampamba, 'Baganda and Their Customs,' *Ebifa mu Buganda* (May 1945). Quoted in
Robbins, 'Tukutendereza!,' 213.

[118] I. Musazi, in *Ebifa mu Buganda* (May 1952). Quoted in Robbins, *Tukutendereza!*, 213,
note 52.

[119] RH Mss. Afr. s. 951: Mulumba to Stuart, 26 July 1948.

[120] MAM Y 4: Stuart, 'Memorandum Regarding Dr. Stanley Smith's Survey of the Mission,'
1942. The biblical reference is to II Samuel 15.

disciplined people with their convincing speech. And like Absalom, who put the powerful King David to flight, converts undermined political authority.

Uganda's police were convinced that revivalists posed a threat to good government. Under wartime censorship regulations, the police Special Branch began opening revivalists' mail. Undercover agents attended Revival meetings and reported on the proceedings. The intelligence they produced was alarming. Uganda's Director of Intelligence and Security worried that the converts were 'openly attacking persons in authority in the established church, and the next step may easily be against the authority of the state.'[121] The Chief Secretary was concerned that 'the incitement of the African to indiscipline and contempt of authority is extremely dangerous in its potential repercussions,' while the Governor of Uganda thought that the 'unbridled ardour of African adherents' would outrun missionaries' ability to supervise the Revival.[122] The file they sent to the Colonial Office in London listed the names and addresses of all of Uganda's Revival leaders. The chief secretary in the Colonial Office thought it to be a 'tale of morbid religion and hysteria.' The Colonial Secretary himself felt moved to write to the Secretary of the Church Missionary Society, describing how the Revival had begun 'to manifest less agreeable symptoms: dissension ... accompanied by hysterical forms of public confession.' There was evidence, he warned, that the Revival had 'deteriorated to congregational rowdyism, indirect encouragement of immorality and an unwholesome atmosphere in certain Church schools.'[123]

Like Julaina Mufuko, the voluble woman who troubled Chief Paulo Ngologoza (see Chapter 3), Buganda's converts were agitators. Through their loud confessions of sin, they cast light on the dark corners of Ganda people's married lives, illuminating the private bargains that husbands and wives had made. Ganda husbands relied on the discretion and tact of their wives. They needed to project an image of marital harmony in order to establish themselves as reputable, upstanding, Christian citizens. Converts gossiped openly about their most private sexual and moral failings. Their testimonies destroyed reputations and set people at odds. Buganda's Revival was controversial because its converts published abroad the secrets that respectable men tried desperately to keep.

CONCLUSION

When Buganda's politics reached a crisis in 1949, it was the populists of the Bataka party who were behind it, not the meddlesome troublemakers of the Revival. On 25 April 1949, thousands of Bataka members

[121] KNA DC/Kisumu 1/36/88: Director of Intelligence and Security, 13 June 1944.
[122] NAB CO 536/215/4: Chief Secretary to Seel, 6 April 1944; Governor of Uganda to Secretary of State for the Colonies, 4 May 1944.
[123] NAB CO 536/215/4: Secretary of State for the Colonies to Hooper, June 1944.

gathered on the grounds of the Anglican cathedral, sang hymns, and then marched to the Kabaka's palace, demanding that the king should democratize Buganda's parliament.[124] In their assembly, they embodied the populist politics that Bataka activists had long sought to create. Commoners had always been obliged to approach the Kabaka through their chiefs. Bataka partisans made their own case before their king. Supporters sent lorries full of firewood and food to provision them. When the Kabaka finally summoned representatives to present their demands, they asked for the freedom to gin their own cotton and the right to elect their own chiefs.[125] The next morning, when a British police officer was reading out the Riot Act to the assembled crowd, an angry Bataka partisan knocked him to the ground. There followed several weeks of sporadic rioting. The Kabaka condemned the rioters as 'pests' and 'traitors,' while the governor was sure that rioters acted 'on communist inspiration.'[126] The protesters saw themselves as patriots, fighting for the commonwealth against the corrupted elite. Their violent acts were principled in character. Groups of up to 300 activists were carried by lorries to particular destinations, and of the 115 buildings that the rioters destroyed, 75 belonged to officials of the Buganda kingdom's government. Rioters also burned the houses of a profiteering butcher and the editor of a pro-government newspaper.[127] Not a single building owned by the Anglican church was burned.[128] The protests were only squelched when a King's African Rifles battalion was brought in from Kenya. In the police investigations that followed, at least 1,300 people were arrested, among them Reuben Spartas and Jemusi Miti. Both men were convicted of 'rebellion against the Kabaka,' and Spartas was sentenced to sixteen years in prison with hard labor. Miti was sentenced to fourteen years.[129]

Revivalists did not play a part in the disturbances of 1949. A year after the riots, in May 1950, a thousand revivalists gathered for a convention at Kako, in the southern part of Buganda. The convention's theme was 'He Sets the Prisoner Free.'[130] Among the leading speakers was Lady Irene Namaganda, the disgraced Queen Mother of Buganda. By custom,

---

[124] Described in CMS G3 A7/7: CMS Secretary Uganda to Hooper, 4 May 1949; UNA Secretariat file 1235/4/4: 'Kabaka's Message to Chiefs and People of Buganda,' n.d. (but April 1949); RH Mss. Afr. s. 1825/106: John Sibly, 'The April Riots of 1949,' n.d.

[125] 'Report of an Audience by Kataka Mutesa II to Eight People's Representatives,' in David Low, *The Mind of Buganda* (London, 1971), 136–41.

[126] CMS G3 A7/7: Communiqué by the Protectorate Government, 27 April 1949.

[127] RH Mss. Afr. s. 1825/106: John Sibly, 'Diary of the Riots in Uganda, April 26 to May 1 1949.'

[128] CoU 02 Bp 181/20: Bishop Stuart, circular letter, 17 May 1949.

[129] UNA Secretariat file 1235/4/4: *Uganda Herald*, 2 March 1950.

[130] Joe Church, *Quest for the Highest: An Autobiographical Account of the East African Revival* (Exeter, 1981), chapter 24.

Lady Irene was meant to remain an unmarried widow after her husband's death. But a young schoolteacher impregnated her, and in 1941 Bishop Stuart married the lovers.[131] Buganda's parliament barred the new couple from entering Mengo, the kingdom's central district, as punishment for the Queen Mother's uncustomary marriage.[132] The populists of the Bataka Union scorned Lady Irene for her immoral conduct, complaining that her marriage had substituted 'social confusion for the order established by our ancestors.'[133] In January 1949, just a few months before assertive Bataka activists confronted their king, Lady Irene converted. Her first public testimony was delivered at the 1950 convention in Kako. The archival record tells us nothing about what she said, and in an interview her husband, Peter Kigozi, was discrete about the character of her sins. But he was emphatic that 'Every saved person had to give a testimony!'[134] In the very midst of Buganda's political crisis, converts kept talking about their sins. They would not lump themselves together with Bataka activists as defenders of a national culture.[135]

These first revivalists from Buganda and Kigezi were inveterate travelers, and the Revival was the fruit of their organizational energy. William Nagenda, brother-in-law to the Revival's first martyr, Blasio Kigozi, was to become the leading evangelist; while Ernesti Nyabagabo, the Ganda headmaster of the high school in Kigezi, was one of the earliest preachers of revivalism in Kenya (see Chapter 6). Elisafati Matovu was another of Buganda's itinerate evangelists. Matovu had spent much of his life on the road: he owned a shop along the long road leading from Kigezi to the cotton farms of Buganda. His wife had once been a prostitute.[136] Matovu converted in 1937; in 1939 he preached at a convention at the Anglican school in Katoke in northwestern Tanganyika. He and other preachers spent a full day talking about sin, illustrating their sermons with an image of a bleeding Jesus.[137] Within a few weeks, students and teachers at Katoke were openly confessing their sins; and, for a brief period, revivalists in northwestern Tanganyika experimented with charismatic forms of repentance (see Chapter 5). In 1940, Matovu left his roadside shop and took a teaching post at Katoke from where he played an important role in linking Tanganyika's revivalists with their Ganda co-travelers.

[131] CoU 02 Bp 175/19: Bishop Stuart to Chancellor, 13 March 1941.
[132] CoU 02 Bp 58/4: Bishop Stuart to Cash, n.d. (but 1941).
[133] CoU 02 Bp 184/20: T. Luule to Lambeth conference, 23 March 1948.
[134] Interview: Peter Kigozi, Ntinda, Kampala, 13 July 2004.
[135] Nakanyike Musisi has given Lady Irene's biography in 'A Personal Journey into Custom, Identity, Power and Politics: Researching and Writing the Life and Times of Buganda's Queen Mother, Irene Drusilla Namaganda (1896–1957),' *History in Africa* 23 (1996), 369–85.
[136] CMS Annual Letters file: Lionel Bakewell, annual letter, 30 June 1947.
[137] HMC JEC 1/3: Bakewell, circular letter, 29 April 1939.

In history writing, in petitions, and in their manners, Buganda's political leaders were always working to establish their kingdom's unique identity. Revivalists undermined the political work of Ganda culture-builders. While Ganda elites sought to establish their reputations by their manners, converts gossiped openly about their private sexual misdeeds. While radical populists worked to lump Buganda's people together, converts set themselves apart from political and cultural community. Revivalists took their place alongside Kiga women, labor migrants, and other travelers along the migration routes that linked Buganda with Rwanda, southern Uganda, and northwestern Tanganyika. As people on the move, they would not settle in any civil society.

5

Taking Stock

Conversion and Accountancy in Bugufi

The rhetoric and practice of evangelical Christianity in eighteenth century England was conceived alongside the discipline of accountancy. In married life, in business, and in religion, English people developed mechanisms to hold each other accountable. This societal emphasis of accountability arose, argues historian Thomas Haskell, out of the organizational demands of commerce.[1] In an earlier time, promises exchanged between individuals were beneath the notice of the courts, but in the late eighteenth century, contract law emerged as a discrete field of litigation. English courts compelled parties involved in contracts, whether financial or conjugal in character, to keep their promises. Evangelical Christianity borrowed its theory of accountability from contract law. Evangelicals stigmatized external mechanisms of physical constraint and celebrated internal restraint and self-discipline. They sought to free individuals to make rational choices about God and about their personal vocations. Their agenda extended from the slave plantations of the West Indies to the urban slums of London. The abolitionist William Wilberforce was also the founder of the 'Society for the Suppression of Vice,' which campaigned against the moral decadence of London's lower classes. His contemporary Thomas Chalmers, a clergyman, abolitionist, and devotee of Malthus, argued that statutory poor relief should be abolished so that the poor could be responsible for themselves.[2] As they worked to free African slaves from their physical bondage, middle-class British reformers also sought to liberate working class people from moral bondage and financial dependency. In their philanthropic work,

---

[1] Thomas Haskell, 'Capitalism and the Origins of Humanitarian Sensibility,' *American Historical Review* 90 (2) (1985), 547–66. Haskell's work is debated in Thomas Bender, *The Anti-Slavery Debate: Capitalism and Abolitionism as a Problem in Historical Interpretation* (Berkeley, 1992).

[2] Patricia Hollis, 'Anti-Slavery and British Working Class Radicalism in the Years of Reform,' in *Anti-Slavery, Religion, and Reform: Essays in Memory of Roger Anstey*, ed. Christine Bolt and Seymour Drescher (Folkestone, 1980), 304.

as in their anti-slavery advocacy, reformers argued that people should be accountable for their actions and that social discipline should arise from an internalized moral order.[3]

This chapter discusses the interlinked disciplines of revivalism and accountancy in mid-twentieth century eastern Africa. It is not a coincidence that Kigezi, where the Revival first took its footing, was one of the first regions in eastern Africa to develop a market for land. Kigezi's farmers had been exporting food to neighboring communities since the nineteenth century, and by 1921 the District Commissioner could report that all the agricultural land in the district was 'intensively cultivated.'[4] In 1928, the government began to issue certificates verifying peasants' ownership of the gardens they cultivated. Within a month, more than 1,000 Kiga farmers had applied.[5] When the District Commissioner asked Kigezi's nineteen sub-county chiefs for information about land values in their locations in 1954, thirteen replied by listing the cash price per acre.[6] Kigezi's economic history was by no means unique. Throughout East Africa, farmers were turning away from older, more reciprocal patterns of landholding, assigning a monetary value to property, and asserting their property rights. In central Kenya, the wartime commodity boom encouraged Gikuyu landlords to increase the acreage they cultivated. Claiming that their farms were their personal possessions, rural capitalists expelled tenants and junior relatives from the land they had inhabited for generations.[7] The agonizing process of rural class formation was advanced after 1954, when, under the 'Swynnerton Plan,' government surveyors parceled out the landscape, assigning particular plots of land to particular people.[8] Surveyors were also at work in Nyanza province, in western Kenya, where in the mid-1950s government officials launched a program of land consolidation. Hoping to increase production, government-appointed committees assessed Luo farmers' property, reallocated land fragments, pushed tenants off their holdings, and created large farms for owners

---

[3] This paragraph summarizes David Brion Davis, *The Problem of Slavery in Western Culture* (Ithaca, 1966). See also Derek R. Peterson, 'Abolitionism and Political Thought in Britain and Africa,' in *Abolitionism and Imperialism in Britain, Africa and the Atlantic,* ed. Derek R. Peterson (Athens, OH, 2010), 1–37.

[4] KigDA Box 659, file 217: DC Kigezi to PC Western Province, 26 January 1921. See Grace Carswell, *Cultivating Success in Uganda: Kigezi Farmers and Colonial Policies* (London, 2007).

[5] KabDA 'Annual and Monthly Reports' file: PC Western, Half-Year Report, 30 June 1928.

[6] Replies are given in KigDA Box 659, file 1414: 'Land Policy, Natives in Kigezi.'

[7] Argued in John Lonsdale, 'The Moral Economy of Mau Mau: Wealth, Poverty, and Civic Virtue in Kikuyu Ethnic Thought,' in Lonsdale and Bruce Berman, *Unhappy Valley: Conflict in Kenya and Africa* (London, 1992), 315–504.

[8] For the policy, see J. Swynnerton, 'Kenya's Agricultural Planning,' *African Affairs* 56 (224) (1957), 209–15; for analysis, M. P. K. Sorrenson, *Land Reform in the Kikuyu Country* (Nairobi, 1967). For the Ugandan context for these reforms, see Carswell, *Cultivating Success.*

to cultivate (see Chapter 6). There was a booming market in barbed wire as Luo landowners fenced in their land.

As rural landholders were erecting wire fences and claiming land as their personal property, revivalists were cultivating new habits of accountability. First in Kigezi and later in Buganda and other parts of eastern Africa, converts sorted through their deeds and their possessions, looking for evidence that made them guilty. Even the smallest of things needed to be accounted for. Yudesi Mukakamare, a schoolteacher at Gahini, confessed to stealing two needles. She had thoughtlessly placed them in her Bible for safekeeping.[9] Other sins were more consequential: converts sometimes confessed to murder or adultery. Revivalism invited men and women to inventory their deeds and their possessions. As eastern Africa's capitalists were surveying land and claiming ownership of property, revivalists were learning to own up to their sins. The discipline of revivalism taught Africans to see their deeds and their possessions as a personal responsibility, and invited them to practice the forensic techniques of accountancy.

This chapter focuses on one node in the larger network of economic and religious interchange that drew Buganda together with Kigezi, Rwanda, and Burundi. The chiefdom of Bugufi, on Tanganyika's border with Burundi, was one of eastern Africa's most unequal societies (see Map 3). Beginning in the late 1920s, Bugufi's commoners, driven by the onerous demands of the chiefdom's ruling caste, began to travel northward to Buganda, where they worked short-term jobs for Ganda cotton farmers. Husbands' repeated absences from home left wives with heavy burdens, and Bugufi's courts were full of litigants arguing over their marital responsibilities. In 1939, Revival evangelists from Buganda and Kigezi preached in Bugufi. Inspired by their example, thousands of converts in Bugufi owned up to the dark deeds they had committed. The Revival taught converts to measure their biographies against the law, to take stock of their lives, and to evaluate their actions and their possessions. As they inventoried their sins, Bugufi's converts were also inventorying their cattle and their land and distinguishing their private property from common goods. From their critics' point of view, revivalists were self-promoters, turning their backs on older, more reciprocal standards of sociable interaction. As we shall see, Bugufi's debate over revivalism was conducted as an argument over property, ownership, and reciprocity.

This chapter brings two different archives into conversation. The papers of Hans Cory, held at the University of Dar es Salaam's library, are full of details about Bugufi's politics and economics. Cory – Tanganyika's government sociologist – was transferred to Bugufi in 1943. He spent much of his time making accounts. There is a survey of the conditions of local government, a report on Hangaza law and custom, a long analysis of Bugufi's

[9] CMS Oxford, Dora Skipper papers, folio 2/1: letter dated 14 March 1936.

system of land tenure, and a report on cattle-keeping.[10] In these and in other documents, Cory used bureaucratic procedures – the register, the list, and the rubber stamp – to label possessions and assign property to private individuals. He was not working alone. At his side was a cadre of young revivalists led by Bugufi's chief, Daudi Balamba. Balamba and his contemporaries also feature in the papers of Rev. Lionel Bakewell, the second archival collection on which this chapter is based. Bakewell was an Australian missionary and schoolteacher posted to the Anglican school at Katoke, near Bugufi. In his letters, preserved at the Henry Martyn Centre in Cambridge, Bakewell documented the long testimonies that Bugufi's people gave as they converted. In reading these two collections against each other, we can see how much revivalist discipline borrowed from the techniques of accountancy. Converts, like accountants, stood outside the dynamic social world, made a record of their personal property, and claimed certain goods and deeds as their responsibility. Revivalism was not capitalism in religious disguise, but the techniques of bureaucratic procedure gave converts the apparatus with which to take stock of their lives. In Bugufi's Revival, we can see modern subjectivity in a different light: not as a condition that was born, whole, from the colonial enterprise but as an ensemble of bureaucratic techniques that could be practiced, mastered, and deployed.

HUSBANDS, WIVES, AND WORK

Bugufi's political origins lie in the early nineteenth century, when Burundi's king Ntare II gave Balamba, one of his retainers, dominion over a desolate, sparsely inhabited region in the easternmost frontier of his kingdom.[11] Balamba's clan was called the *Abaswere*, the 'copulators,' by their Rundi detractors.[12] The name highlights the biological and sexual energy that it took to build up the human population. Many of the chiefdom's districts were founded by hunters, who drove off game, cleared the bush, and established settlements.[13] In the late 1930s, Bugufi was home to 28,500 people clustered on 170 square miles of cultivable land.[14] On some ridge tops, the population density approached 1,000 people per square mile. Bugufi was excised from the Belgian colony of Burundi in 1922 and made part of the British mandated territory of Tanganyika. Its rulers were related by

[10] Cory file 62: 'Survey of the Utwaliates of Bugufi,' 1944; file 98: 'Hangaza Law and Custom,' 1944; file 61: 'Bugufi Land Report,' 22 August 1944; file 170: 'Report on the Cattle Situation in Bugufi,' 1944.

[11] See David Newbury, 'Precolonial Burundi and Rwanda: Local Loyalties, Regional Loyalties,' *International Journal of African Historical Studies* 34 (2) (2001), 255–314.

[12] Cory file 350: 'Memorandum for Sir Alan Burns,' 1948.

[13] Cory file 62: Cory, 'Survey of the Utwaliates of Bugufi,' 1944.

[14] TNA Acc. 197 5/3: Assistant DO, 'Memorandum on Native Coffee Development,' n.d. (but late 1930s).

blood – three-quarters of Bugufi's villages were governed by relatives of the chief – and bound together with cattle, which Bugufi's chief loaned to his allies as an inducement to loyalty.[15]

The power of their alliances made Bugufi's ruling caste heedless of their subjects' welfare. Bugufi's chiefs made regular pilgrimages to Burundi, where they paid tribute to Ntare's successors.[16] Commoners benefited little from this royalist politicking. British officials estimated that more than 4,000 of the chiefdom's 13,000 taxpayers were tenants living on estates owned by other men.[17] They were obliged to perform menial tasks for the benefit of their landlords, and virtually the whole of their annual crop was taken from them in tribute payments.[18] Peasants farming their own land retained a greater percentage of their crops, but they had no security of land tenure. Customary law allowed headmen to dispossess them of their gardens and houses. The economic distance between the rulers and the ruled was reinforced by exclusionary social customs. Members of Bugufi's elite caste generally refused to dine with commoners.[19] Neither would women of the ruling caste marry male commoners – though court historians whispered that Balamba, the chiefdom's nineteenth century founder, was born of a noble mother and a common father.[20] It may be that their uncertain origins made the elite more protective of their prerogatives. By 1937, British officials had concluded that Bugufi's commoners were doomed to a life of subservience. 'They are simple folk who recognize appointed authority,' wrote the district officer, 'and have been accustomed to unquestioning acquiescence in the deeds and misdeeds of the royal house.'[21]

The heavy demands that their rulers placed on them made Bugufi's men into eastern Africa's most dedicated labor migrants. Beginning in the early 1920s, Bugufi men began to travel northward, seeking seasonal employment on the cotton farms of the Buganda kingdom. Some of them stopped along the road in Bukoba, on Tanganyika's northwestern border, where they took up employment on Haya coffee farms.[22] Others traveled via Rwanda and southern Uganda to Buganda, where they worked a series of short-term contracts for a fixed wage. Men bound for Buganda typically left their homes in January, during or just after the planting season, and returned in September or October. Catholic missionaries lamented how each year most of their congregations flitted away to Buganda like a 'nestful of sparrows,' leaving

[15] TNA Acc. 217 L5/XIII: PC Lake to Chief Secretary, 14 December 1948.

[16] Cory file 62: Cory to DO Ngara, 15 August 1944.

[17] TNA Acc. 217 L5/XIII: DC Ngara, 'Memorandum on the Bugufi Land Rules,' 1951.

[18] Cory file 61: Hans Cory, 'Bugufi Land Report,' 22 August 1944.

[19] Cory file 61: Hans Cory, 'Bugufi Land Report,' 22 August 1944.

[20] Cory file 350: 'Memorandum for Sir Alan Burns,' 1948.

[21] TNA Acc. 64 1737: Assistant DO Ngara to DO Biharamulo, 10 April 1937.

[22] TNA AB 40: Bukoba District Annual Report, 1925; TNA Acc. 215/77: Biharamulo Sub-District Annual Report, 1924.

women, children, and elderly people behind.[23] 'It is the modern Klondyke,' wrote one missionary.[24] Even church catechists laid down their responsibilities and followed the northward road.[25] By the late 1930s, 60 percent of Bugufi's men were migrating to Uganda each year for work.[26] The road that Bugufi's labor migrants traveled was strewn with hazards. Laden with cash and goods from Buganda, migrants returning to their homes were tempting prey for thieves. In the late 1920s, British officials arrested a witchdoctor for robbing Bugufi's migrants. He brandished a bunch of sisal leaves in front of his victims, and they, paralyzed with fear, gave him their earnings.[27] Thieves had developed more sophisticated techniques by the late 1930s: they manufactured a drug called *lukama*, made from the seeds of a bush mixed with creosote scraped off telegraph poles. They offered pots of beer mixed with *lukama* to unsuspecting migrants, and when their victims had been stupefied, they relieved them of their belongings. The police arrested several gangs of men who specialized in this drug-assisted robbery.[28] Other migrants were robbed in a more prosaic fashion: they were beaten until they gave up their money.[29]

Migrants who negotiated this perilous journey brought home a stock of cash, clothing, bicycles, and other consumer goods. Labor migrants pumped some 15,000 to 20,000 pounds per year into Bugufi's economy in the 1940s, far more than farmers earned from coffee or any other crop.[30] Migrants could earn up to 120 shillings per month by working for three or four Ganda employers simultaneously.[31] More than cash, migrants also earned social capital during their time on Ganda farms. Eliabu Ndimugwanko, whom I interviewed, made five trips to Buganda, each lasting less than a year. He thought going to Buganda was 'like attending school.' Ndimugwanko watched Ganda farmers tend their coffee, learned their techniques, and brought back coffee bushes, which he planted and cultivated on his own land.[32] Others among my interviewees described how they had learned the Ganda language and acquired Ganda clothing.[33] Men like these were enriching themselves, both materially and socially, by their cosmopolitan travels.

[23] WFM 'Diare de Buhororo, Bugufi,' entry for 15 June 1935.

[24] WFM 'Diare de Buhororo, Bugufi,' entry for 24 May 1935.

[25] WFM 'Diare de Buhororo, Bugufi,' entry for 25 January 1942.

[26] TNA Acc. 197 38: Handing over report, Ngara District, 11 March 1938.

[27] E. K. Lumley, *Forgotten Mandate: A British District Officer in Tanganyika* (London, 1976), 157.

[28] TNA Acc. 215 1158: Biharamulo District Annual Report, 1938; TNA Acc. 215 2070: Biharamulo District Annual Report, 1946.

[29] WFM 'Diare de Buhororo, Bugufi,' entry for 5 November 1939.

[30] Cory file 350: 'Memorandum for Sir Alan Burns on Petition of Mwami Mwambutsa of Urundi,' 1948.

[31] TNA Acc. 215 2510: Lake Province Annual Report, 1951.

[32] Interview: Eliabu Ndimugwanko, Murutabo, Ngara, 17 August 2006.

[33] Interview: Dario Bakundukize, Mugisagala, Ngara, 18 August 2006.

Their experience fortified labor migrants' masculine bravado. Bukoba's District Commissioner was struck by the 'virility and cheerfulness' of the migrants from Bugufi.[34] Migrants scorned men who did not make the dangerous trip: one of my male interviewees called them *watu fukara*, 'beggars,' layabouts lacking moral and economic substance.[35] The women I interviewed were less than admiring: one woman remembered that migrants returning from Uganda were 'coming with the *majivuno* [arrogance] and *dharau* [contempt]' for those they left at home.[36]

Bugufi's imperious labor migrants demanded that their wives practice a rigorous sexual discipline. Prior to the advent of British government in Bugufi, adulterers were customarily put to death. The penalties were so effective that the first British officer did not see a single case of venereal disease.[37] Even Catholic missionaries were impressed with Bugufi's stern rules: when one of their female converts was found to have committed adultery, her parents planned to drown her in a river. She entered the convent instead.[38] Among the 850 cases that the local courts in Bugufi tried between 1924 and 1930, only a single case mentioned adultery as grounds for divorce.[39] Bugufi's men and women are today unanimous in agreeing that wives were unfailingly faithful during their husbands' prolonged absences. 'The Hangaza think that the woman is the rib of the man,' one of my male interviewees told me. 'Therefore the man would know that woman wouldn't go round with other men.'[40] Customary penalties notwithstanding, it is clear that many wives did take up with other men. When government sociologist Hans Cory looked into labor migrants' domestic arrangements, he found that wives were generally free to live with other paramours during their husbands' protracted absences. After their return, husbands simply recalled their wives to their homes.[41] Returning migrants sometimes inquired after the paternity of their children: one interviewee recalled how jealous fathers asked their children '*Who* are you the child of?'[42] But these unwelcome questions must have been asked infrequently. Bugufi's courts granted remarkably few divorces.[43]

Wives were obliged to comport themselves honorably in the absence of their husbands. They, in turn, sought to exert control over the behavior of

[34] TNA AB 40: Bukoba District Annual Report, 1925.
[35] Interview: Wilson Nzobakenga, Mubuhenge, Ngara, 17 August 2006.
[36] Interview: Raymond Kagero, Mugisagala, Ngara, 18 August 2006.
[37] Lumley, *Forgotten Mandate*, 47.
[38] WFM 'Diare de Buhororo, Bugufi,' entry for 23 May 1937.
[39] R. de Z. Hall, 'A Study of Native Court Records as a Method of Ethnological Enquiry,' *Africa: Journal of the International African Institute* 11 (4) (1938), 412–27.
[40] Interview: Nathan Nzisehere, Muruvyagila, Ngara, 17 August 2006.
[41] Cory file 61: Hans Cory, 'Hangaza Law and Custom,' 1944.
[42] Interview: Mary Kagero, Mugisagala, Ngara, 18 August 2006.
[43] Hall, 'A Study of Native Court Records.'

their husbands. Mary and Raymond Kagero, for example, agreed on a set of priorities before Raymond's departure from home: if money was needed to improve the condition of their house, he stayed in Buganda for only a short time; but when they wished to purchase livestock, Raymond spent several months at work.[44] Women like Mary Kagero were able to bargain with their husbands, agreeing to shoulder a greater burden at home in the expectation that their husbands' cash earnings would help advance their collective welfare. More often women found themselves abandoned, obliged to care for farms and for children for months or years at a time. When the missionary Lionel Bakewell toured the area around Mabawe, he found several abandoned wives living within earshot of the local church. Two of them moaned piteously into the night, suffering both from overwork and from the open sores on their feet.[45] One of my interviewees, an elderly woman named Elina Kigabogabo, was married in 1943. A year later, her husband left for work in Uganda, leaving her pregnant with her first child. For 55 years she lived alone, waiting for her husband's return, until finally, in 1999, she remarried.[46] Her story is by no means unique: Bugufi's landscape is littered with wives and mothers abandoned by their husbands and sons.[47] Census figures illuminate the physical and emotional burdens that wives bore: whereas in 1931 men and women comprised an equal percentage of Bugufi's population, by 1948 there were 16,861 adult women and only 13,163 adult men.[48]

Bugufi's women were already hard at work when British agriculturalists first introduced coffee to the chiefdom's farmers in 1930. The government hoped that the profits to be earned from coffee would convince labor migrants to invest their time and energy in building up their homes. The plants were to be cultivated according to a strict regime: farmers were obliged first to dig contour terraces and then plant the bushes at a precise distance apart. Weeding, mulching, pruning and other work was to be performed according to a schedule set by the British agriculture officer.[49] By 1935, 75 percent of the taxpayers in the chiefdom possessed coffee plots.[50] The most

---

[44] Interview: Mary Kagero, Mugisagala, Ngara, 18 August 2006. Salmon Nzikobanyanka similarly described the agreements he struck with his wife before migrating (interview, Muruvyagila, Ngara, 17 August 2006).

[45] Bakewell to Bishop Chambers, 22 March 1933. Reproduced in Frances Dann, 'The Work of an Australian CMS Missionary in the Late Colonial Period in Tanganyika, 1929–1945' (B. Theo. thesis, Yarra Theological Union, 2002).

[46] Interview: Elina Kigabogabo, Murigina, Ngara, 19 August 2006.

[47] E.g., Apolonia Rugina, whose eldest son was lost to Buganda (interview, Mumahoro, Ngara, 19 August 2006); or Anastasia Sendegeya, whose husband left for Uganda in 1972 (interview, Burugina, Mabawe, Ngara, 19 August 2006).

[48] Mwanza archives, Acc. 1/2087: DO Ngara to PC Lake, 30 November 1948.

[49] TNA Acc. 217 2: Assistant Agriculture Officer, 'Memorandum on Programme of Coffee Work in Bugufi, Oct. 1936 to Ap. 1937.'

[50] TNA Acc. 215 193: DO Biharamulo to PC Lake, 13 December 1935.

successful farmers were landlords who could rely on their tenants' wives to do the hard work of cultivating coffee. In 1938, the brother of Bugufi's chief possessed a nursery with 24,810 bushes.[51] When agriculture officials asked the landholder Bakuru Sengirankobo about his coffee farm, he knew neither the number nor the location of the sixteen plots that he possessed: his tenants did all the work.[52] In 1935, British officials launched a campaign to eradicate couch grass from Bugufi farmers' plots. They were disturbed to find women uprooting the weed with their bare hands.[53] Coffee production peaked in 1942 when Bugufi's growers produced 222 tons of coffee beans.[54] The work was done largely by women. British officials congratulated them for their patriotism. 'Thirty percent of the adult males of Bugufi are away in Uganda,' wrote the chiefdom's agriculture officer, 'but their fathers, wives, and children are all playing their part in laying the foundation of Bugufi's future wealth.'[55]

Labor migration was an unequal bargain for Bugufi's women. Hans Cory, who studied Bugufi's labor system in 1944, thought the gender imbalance undermined both agricultural productivity and morality. During the growing season, grass stood high in the fields, and bananas remained untended. In many of Bugufi's houses, wrote Cory, 'one will find children under the age of ten years dirty and left with no care. Mothers cook food as they feel like it; they do not expect their husbands home in the evening and becoming furious if food is not cooked.'[56] Cory thought husbands' absences made wives undisciplined and irresponsible, but even the most energetic of women found it difficult to keep their houses in order. One of my interviewees described the burdens that women had to bear. 'Anger was there,' she remembered. 'If you finished a complete year [by yourself], you will be left with a small child … and if he returns, you get another child, and you have trouble … and so the mother was left without freedom.'[57] Husbands' absences condemned many Bugufi women to work like slaves.

The pressures that women faced came to a head in 1938. Early in the year, the government compelled women and elderly men to cultivate vegetables in the valley bottoms in order to increase the food supply.[58] At the same time,

---

[51] TNA Acc. 217 2: Assistant Agriculture Officer to Senior Agriculture Officer, Mwanza, 2 May 1938.

[52] TNA Acc. 217 2: Assistant Agriculture Officer to Senior Agriculture Officer, Ngara, 22 October 1947.

[53] Mwanza archives, Acc. 1 A3/57: 'A Brief History of Coffee Cultivation in Ngara District,' n.d. (but 1958).

[54] TNA Acc. 215 1898: Biharamulo District Annual Report, 1944.

[55] TNA Acc 215 193: Assistant District Officer Bugufi to District Officer Biharamulo, 14 July 1931.

[56] Cory file 61: Hans Cory, 'Bugufi Land Report,' 22 August 1944.

[57] Interview: Mary Kagero, Mugisagala, Ngara, 18 August 2006.

[58] TNA Acc. 215 1158: Biharamulo District Annual Report, 1938.

female workers on coffee farms were compelled to uproot banana trees and plant grass as an anti-erosion measure.[59] As they labored on farms that were not their own, Bugufi's women were unable to guarantee the welfare of their children. The rains had failed in 1937, and the shortage of staple crops left thousands of people in southeastern Bugufi confronting localized famine.[60] Overburdened women increasingly came to see their absentee husbands in an unfavorable light. Hundreds of them went to court, seeking to free themselves from their marriages. The volume of litigation conducted in Bugufi's courts expanded dramatically: whereas in 1936 the courts heard 231 cases, by 1940 there were 1,228 cases argued before the courts. A great amount of this litigation concerned marriage.[61] British officers complained that Bugufi's people were developing a 'litigious frame of mind.' But the crisis was more than a state of mind. Their overwork was for many women material proof of their husbands' delinquency.

Husbands and wives were arguing over their mutual obligations when Revival evangelists first preached in Bugufi early in 1939. Revivalism in Bugufi was more than a vent for women's disgust with their absentee husbands, and more than a convenient vehicle for protest against Bugufi's inhumane political economy. The Revival was one aspect of the larger process by which Bugufi's people took stock of their land, cattle, and social relations. As husbands and wives litigated about their hitherto private conjugal affairs, converts extended legal oversight to the mundane corners of their lives. In their rigorous self-examinations they owned up to the properties and dispositions that made them sinful. Conversion was a work of self-accounting.

THE EVIDENCE OF CONVERSION

British government kept Bugufi closed to European missionaries until 1932, but the chiefdom was not a religious backwater. The first Christian evangelist – a Ganda agent of the Anglicans' mission in Rwanda – was posted to Bugufi in 1923.[62] By 1929, there were seventy Christians in the chiefdom.[63] They were led by a medical worker from Nyasaland, who regularly led services in the dispensary.[64] Islamic evangelists were likewise hard at work. In Mabawe in the southeastern part of Bugufi, a Muslim entrepreneur named Ramazani had for several years operated a small school from his home.[65]

[59] TNA Acc. 215 2: Assistant Agriculture Officer to Senior Agriculture Officer, Mwanza, 2 May 1938.
[60] TNA Acc. 215 1158: Ngara Sub-Division Report, 1938.
[61] TNA Acc. 215 1158: Ngara Sub-Division Report, 1938; TNA Acc. 215/1650: Biharamulo District Annual Report, 1940.
[62] MAM E 1/1: Leonard Sharp, in *Ruanda Notes* 6 (February 1923).
[63] TNA Acc. 197 7 vol. 1: Acting DO to PC Bukoba, 1929.
[64] CMS Annual Letters file: Lionel Bakewell, 10 August 1932.
[65] TNA Acc. 197 7 vol. 1: Assistant DO Ngara to DO Biharamulo, 15 July 1932.

When European missionaries were given permission to enter Bugufi in 1932, Ramazani handed his students over to the Anglicans and gave the mission teachers the use of a room. During his first visit to Mabawe, the Australian missionary Lionel Bakewell found 'column after column of almost naked little boys marching out to meet me, singing "I will follow, I will follow Jesus."'[66] By 1933, there were 1,137 pupils attending the Anglicans' nine schools in Bugufi.[67] Several dozen boys from Bugufi attended the Anglicans' higher school at Katoke, several days' walk to the northwest.

In April 1939, a group of revivalists from Buganda and Kigezi spent six days preaching in Bugufi and at the Katoke school. Among the preachers were the Revival's leading evangelists: the Ganda landholder Simeon Nsibambi, the Kigezi schoolteacher Ezekieli Balaba, the Ganda shopkeeper Elisafati Matovu, and the missionary Joe Church. The Ten Commandments had been translated into LuHangaza, the language of Bugufi's people, in 1936.[68] The preachers spent their time going through them line by line. Their program focused consecutively on 'sin,' 'repentance,' 'the blood of Jesus,' 'the new birth,' and 'judgment.'[69] On the day the revivalists departed from Katoke, the schoolmaster Lionel Bakewell found a steady stream of students at his door, returning goods that they had pilfered from the school's store. Bakewell's own cook presented him with a gallon of oil and a cushion that he had stolen, and repaid a debt that he had forgotten he owed to the school. A schoolboy confessed to tearing a piece of paper out of a school exercise book.[70] By June, all the Katoke teachers, twenty-nine schoolboys from Bugufi, and many of the school's laborers had confessed to formerly hidden sins. Chapel services at Katoke ran into the early hours of the morning. 'Boys and teachers vie with one another to get up and make some confession or further confession,' Bakewell reported. One young man's confession lasted for a full fifty-five minutes.

Bugufi's converts were taking stock of their possessions. Following the example of their neighbors in Kigezi (see Chapter 3), Bugufi's revivalists learned to put a visual distance between themselves and their sins. Richard Bugwoya, who was at Katoke school in 1939, told me how revivalists preached that 'people must be shown their sins, so that the judgment can be seen clearly.' One evening, Bugwoya testified, 'I was shown by sins. I saw that I was a thief, I went into darkness, I told lies.'[71] Some converts saw their

---

[66] Lionel Bakewell, 'The Western Area of the Diocese of Central Tanganyika,' 1941. Typescript seen courtesy of Kathy Kozlowski, Rev. Bakewell's daughter.

[67] TNA Acc. 197 7 vol. II: Shaw to Assistant DO Ngara, 4 December 1933.

[68] DCT 'Mrs Dyson' file: 'Minutes of the First Conference of the Missionaries of the Western Mission of the Diocese of Katoke,' 6–11 January 1936.

[69] HMC JEC 1/3: Lionel Bakewell, circular letter, 29 April 1939.

[70] Lionel Bakewell, 'Revival in Tanganyika in East Africa,' n.d. Typescript seen courtesy of Kathy Kozlowski.

[71] Interview: Richard Bugwoya, Mubinyanganya, Ngara, 18 August 2006.

sin quite suddenly. One of my interviewees was brewing beer when, one evening, she recognized what she was doing was sinful. She gave the just-brewed beer to her neighbors, telling them 'I can't use it now.'[72] Converts saw their sins in the middle of lives that had formerly passed unexamined. The categories in which they placed their deeds sometimes surprised other people. One of my interviewees remembered how, as a young boy in 1942, he stood up in the midst of his classmates to confess his sins. His teachers mocked him: 'You! A little child like that! Ten years old! You are confessing sins, but what have you done?' My interviewee saw his actions in a different light than his teachers.

In their forensic work, converts generated a body of evidence and invited their audience to sit in judgment. It was the physical, corporeal quality of the evidence, its visibility, that made converts' testimonies convincing. One of my interviewees watched with wonderment as a man claiming to be a witch made a public confession of his sins. The man produced several articles – some leaves, some bones – named them as the root of his sin, and incinerated them in a fire lit for the purpose.[73] 'They were there, normal things only,' my interviewee remarked. What made them extraordinary was the meaning-making work of self-disclosure. Another of my interviewees described a man who stood up at a Revival meeting and testified 'I am a witch. I am killing people.' The man 'went to his place, and got out the head of a person. He also got the knife of killing people. He brought them all in front of the church, and said "I am not able to return again to witchcraft." We all said that truly he is now saved by God.'[74] Nathan Nzisehere described the form that a properly composed confession followed:

He who confesses truly truly is the one says, 'God has saved me, and this and this I give up in his name. These things of witchcraft, I have left them. I have been a thorn in other people's side, I have left it. These [pointing] are the things I was using for that sin.' That is how the converts will know if he is really saved. But the person who stands up and says [in a raised voice] 'Eeeh! God has helped me! Alleluia! Praise the Lord!' What has he done? He doesn't go through and say [gravely] 'I have stolen this oil, here, here, here,' all his deeds.[75]

Men like Nathan Nzisehere listened to other people testify and made judgments about their sincerity based on the evidence they presented. Converts had to dredge through their possessions and find the things that made them guilty.

Many people were emotionally overwhelmed by the evidence that they uncovered. At a chapel service early in 1940, Bakewell reported, the schoolteacher Denys Balonzi

---

[72] Interview: Apolonia Rugina, Mumahoro, 19 August 2006.
[73] Interview: Elias Bitambikwa, Muruvyagila, Ngara, 17 August 2006.
[74] Interview: Dani Nyanana, Muruvyagila, Ngara, 17 August 2006.
[75] Interview: Nathan Nzisehere, Muruvyagila, Ngara, 17 August 2006.

raised a scream of 'Dhambi, dhambi, dhambi' ['Sin, sin sin'], and rushed out of the church and went screaming among the trees 'Sin, sin has entered the church and is ruining it!' Later he came to our house and almost like one possessed preached to us for forty minutes, until I stopped him and insisted that we must have our meal.[76]

By February 1940, converts in Bugufi and at the Katoke school were gripped in what Joe Church later called an 'African Pentecost.'[77] Lionel Bakewell reported that some people were 'bowled over, almost as if they had fainted or had an electric shock or a fit.' They 'fell to the floor, often rolling about, sometimes calling out inarticulately, sometimes with words of praise to the Lord Jesus, sometimes laughing in what in other circumstances one would describe in a demented sort of way.'[78] A visiting missionary was disturbed to find that converts were 'falling to the ground, groaning and laughing accompanied by heavy breathing.'[79] Apolonia Rugina was one of the converts who missionary observers saw rolling about on the floor. She told me that she was feeling 'a lot of pressure from inside to vomit out my sins, to say everything publicly.' She confessed to stealing and to taking snuff, a habit that she had learned from her mother.[80] Rugina and other converts were overcome by the body of evidence that their self-examination revealed. Their ecstatic fits were paroxysms of despair.

Bugufi's converts were not alone in their despair about their sins, and neither was their Pentecostalism unique. In the earliest months of the Revival at Gahini in northern Rwanda, converts made a habit of 'shouting out [their] awful sins,' with 'some shrieking to God to have mercy, others rolling about on the floor and tearing their clothes.'[81] Worried missionaries and government officials adopted a series of rules to control the noisy revivalists (see Chapter 3). By September 1936, converts at church gatherings in Gahini were obliged to limit their testimonies to the simple phrase 'Once I was blind, but now I see.' If they began to preach or groan, missionaries intervened, instructing the speaker to keep to the script.[82] In Bugufi, by contrast, missionaries were supportive of converts' ecstatic practices. The schoolmaster Lionel Bakewell was seized by the Holy Spirit in October 1939, and for a time he joined his students and fellow-teachers, kneeling in their midst and speaking in tongues.[83] His missionary colleague defended the converts, likening the events of 1939–1940 to the biblical day of Pentecost.[84] Not

---

[76] HMC JEC 1/3: Lionel Bakewell to Joe Church, 22 March 1940.

[77] Joe Church, *Quest for the Highest: An Autobiographical Account of the East African Revival* (Exeter, 1981), 169.

[78] HMC JEC 1/3: Lionel Bakewell to Joe Church, 22 March 1940.

[79] HMC JEC 1/3: Bill Butler to Joe Church, 19 February 1940.

[80] Interview: Apolonia Rugina, Mumahoro, Ngara, 19 August 2006.

[81] CMS Oxford, Dora Skipper papers, folio 2/1: letter dated 31 July 1936.

[82] CMS Oxford, Dora Skipper papers, folio 2/1: letter dated 14 September 1936.

[83] HMC JEC 1/3: Lionel Bakewell to Joe Church, 28 October 1939.

[84] HMC JEC 1/3: Capt. W. McKee to Joe Church, 25 March 1940.

everyone was willing to accept Pentecostalism as evidence of divine providence. Catholic missionaries mocked the revivalists for their visions: 'One of these fine days half a dozen blacks will be taken up into heaven,' wrote a diarist at the Catholic mission.[85] Government officials worried over law and order, and cautioned missionaries when African converts were found 'continually throwing themselves on the ground and writhing, under the impression that they were possessed by the Holy Ghost.'[86] Even other revivalists thought Bugufi's Pentecostals were unbalanced. A group of African converts from Burundi visited Bugufi in February 1940. Their leader complained about Bugufi Pentecostals' odd standards of decorum:

They think that if a man has not fallen down and lost consciousness several times he is not born again ... They shouted and laughed until they were carried outside ... and when you meet him or her outside you find them taking off clothes or other things. Among the girls you see a girl just fallen and her friend trying to stop her crying like a baby.[87]

The two groups of converts were so distant from each other that the Bugufi revivalists would not even permit their Burundian colleagues to speak before the congregation.

In April 1940, George Chambers, the Anglican bishop of Tanganyika, traveled to Bugufi to investigate these troublesome converts. In a furious letter he wrote to Joe Church, Chambers called the evening service he attended 'pandemonium let loose.' He described how

As darkness drew near, the waving hands and arms increased to the rhythm of profane hymn tunes and choruses. The clapping of hands took place, people began to sing different hymns at the same time and persisted in doing so, some finished their hymn with a rocking laugh, and then followed cryings, screamings, shoutings, making noises like those of animals such as catcalls, the yelping of dogs and the snorting of wild beasts. Two women groveled and wailed on the grass floor of the church, another woman crawled on the floor like a [snake], a girl kept up an incessant shouting and crying for an hour, in a kneeling posture, with her face three inches from the wall ... There were loud utterances and unintelligible to others, mutterings and murmurings ... When exhausted and there was a lull in the noise, some one would rise to read the scripture. Immediately another would sing and drown the hearing of God's word or would pray aloud.[88]

Chambers was convinced that Bugufi's Pentecostals were on the edge of madness. He ordered missionaries to immediately 'cease such forms of devotion.' Lionel Bakewell initially refused to accept his bishop's instruction. But shortly after Bishop Chambers' departure, he consulted Ruddock's

---

[85] WFM 'Diare de Buhororo,' entry for 31 December 1939.
[86] TNA Acc. 215 1650: Annual Report, Biharamulo District, 1940.
[87] HMC JEC 1/3: J. Omusoke to Church, 19 February 1940.
[88] HMC JEC 1/3: Bishop Chambers to Joe Church, 5 April 1940.

Homeopathic Vade Mecum, and found that 'the descriptions given there fitted what was going on here almost exactly.'[89] The day after he completed his research, Bakewell told the Sunday congregation that their ecstatic experiences were in fact a 'pestilence,' *maradhi*, a wasting disease that was sucking out their lives.[90] He preached on I Corinthians 12, which described the fruits of the Holy Spirit as peace and self-control, and he instituted new rules to control converts' enthusiasm. Services at the school chapel were to be limited to one hour, and lights were to be out by nine o'clock in the evening. When a group of students gathered at one o'clock in the morning to preach and sing, Bakewell called them into his office and caned them, one by one. Like the embattled chiefs of Kigezi, like Buganda's embarrassed elites, Anglican churchmen sought to control revivalists by muffling their voices.

Bugufi's noisy converts would not assent to missionaries' rules. They practiced scriptural exegesis, looking for grounds on which to legitimate their Pentecostal practices. Revivalists at Katoke school spent long hours on the football field, loudly preaching against Bakewell. Bakewell described their invective in a letter to Joe Church: 'My name is mud, I'm unsaved, a blasphemer, quenching the spirit, seeking rank and position etc. etc.'[91] There was more to this debate than name-calling. Bugufi's Pentecostals were contending with their missionary critics over comportment. Bakewell told Joe Church that 'the Bible has been combed for texts about people falling down on their faces, and these have been used to justify rolling about when one receives the Holy Spirit, irrespective of whether it was angels in heaven who fell down or sinners like Saul or Balaam in Numbers 22:31.'[92] The teacher Denys Balonzi composed a ten-page epistle and read it aloud in the school's chapel. It condemned missionaries for 'daring to pass judgment on what was God's business alone.' He cited as a defense of Pentecostal practice Hebrews 2:4, which described how God ministered to people 'both by signs and wonders and by manifold powers and by the gifts of the Holy Ghost.'

It is tempting to regard this ecstatic period of revivalism in northwestern Tanganyika as politics in religious guise, as an expression of women's disgust with absentee husbands, or as lower-class people's protest against the inhumanity of their chiefdom's autocratic government. And there is evidence to show that converted women did, in fact, get leverage over their husbands. One of my interviewees described how female revivalists would

---

[89] E. Harris Ruddock, *The Homeopathic Vade Mecum of Modern Medicine and Surgery* (London, 1879 [9th edition]). For Bakewell's use of the book, see Murray papers: Christabel Bakewell, 'Brief Account of the Coming of Revival to Western Tanganyika in 1939,' n.d. (but 1980s).

[90] HMC JEC 1/3: Lionel Bakewell to Joe Church, 18 May 1940.

[91] HMC JEC 1/3: Lionel Bakewell to Joe Church, 15 May 1940.

[92] HMC JEC 1/3: Lionel Bakewell to Joe Church, 18 May 1940.

dictate to their husbands about marital affairs. 'This thing was so strong that [a husband] could not control [his wife],' my interviewee said. 'When the wife started to speak about Jesus, the husband would keep quiet.'[93] Conversion was a rhetorical bludgeon for wives to use. But it was more than that. What Bugufi's people gained in their conversion was a discursive and moral momentum that allowed them to put distance between themselves and their old lives. Converts likened themselves to labor migrants, traveling from their homes toward another place. Richard Bugwoya, who converted during the earliest years of the Revival, thought Christianity to be a 'life of traveling.' He remembered that the preachers he heard at Katoke school proclaimed that 'The Christian is traveling out of this country. He is at war with Satan and the world. So he doesn't sit as if he doesn't have anywhere to go.'[94] Converts learned poetry from the experience of labor migration, not politics. They were moving in parallel with the thousands of young men who annually traveled northward to Buganda for work. Bugwoya remembered that converts' favorite song went 'If you want to go to heaven, pass this road.' Several of my interviewees recounted how they traveled to hill-tops around Bugufi, singing antiphonal hymns with groups ascending the neighboring hills. One of my interviewees had already made three trips to Uganda before he converted in 1942. On that occasion he preached that the 'Word of God is a lamp unto my feet.'[95] Another interviewee noticed that preachers organized their itineraries in much the same way as labor migrants. After a week's stay near his home, they would 'go off to Burundi, they taught the children, then they went off to Murugwanza, they went for as much as a month ... They were going from here to there. They were people who didn't stay.'[96] Like labor migrants, revivalists were itinerates, making their lives on the move.

From their people's history of labor migration, revivalists learned to see movement as a productive, enabling endeavor. The lessons they learned about travel were discursive and metaphorical, not practical and factual. Labor migrants traveled in groups of three to four men and worked as a group for Ganda employers.[97] Converts were lonely pilgrims, reckoning with trials that were personal, not collective, in character. Labor migrants engaged strategically with Ganda patrons, learning skills and purchasing goods that gave them advantages at home. Converts conceived of the heavenly city as an otherworldly destination. Labor migrants brought home goods with which to establish marriages and build up their households. Converts anticipated a reward that would be for them alone. In their pilgrimage, converts

[93] Interview: Paulina Sendegeya, Murugina, Mabawe, 19 August 2006.
[94] Interview: Richard Bugwoya, Mubinyanganya, Ngara, 18 August 2006.
[95] Interview: Erasto Kigabogabo, Murugina, 19 August 2006.
[96] Interview: Salmon Nzikobanyanka et al., Muruvyagila, Ngara, 17 August 2006.
[97] Cory file 61: Hans Cory, 'Bugufi Land Report,' 22 August 1944.

were developing a novel way of being in the world, and a novel theory of property.

SELF-POSSESSION AND PROPERTY RIGHTS

Bugufi's leading convert was Daudi Balamba, the eldest son and heir to his father, Chief Kinyamazinge. He was a student at Katoke school in 1939, during the period of Pentecostal enthusiasm that unsettled Bishop Chambers. He converted that year and was received into the Anglican church, where he adopted the name 'Daudi' after David, the Old Testament's greatest king. Balamba was married at the Anglican mission in Burundi in 1942. His wedding was organized by two revivalists, both of them Bugufi men.[98] My interviewees remembered the wedding to be an austere occasion, with neither beer nor dancing.[99] Missionaries thought Daudi Balamba, like his Old Testament namesake, to be an instrument of divine providence. Balamba's father, Kinyamazinge, had been compelled to retire as chief in 1939, as British officials judged him to be incompetent.[100] In 1944, missionaries organized a grand coronation ceremony for Balamba, who wore a brass crown and carried a spear, a shield, and a small scepter. Bishop Chambers invested the chief with a purple robe, and the following day he baptized Chief Daudi's infant son. His name, inevitably, was Solomon.[101]

As a convert and as a pilgrim, Daudi Balamba was a more sober, self-possessed character than his father. Kinyamazinge had been made chief in 1922, the year Bugufi passed into British administration. Within a few years, British officials had determined that Kinyamazinge, then twenty-eight years old, was 'given over almost entirely to beer drinking and dancing.'[102] Government authorities appointed Swahili advisors to keep Kinyamazinge in hand. But by 1937, British officials had concluded that Kinyamazinge was an 'inveterate drunkard' with a 'deficient mentality amounting to irresponsibility.'[103] In British officials' view, Kinyamazinge's love for beer made him incapable of governing properly. Their view was too simple, for beer was more than a diversion from Kinyamazinge's real work. Brewed from red millet, beer lubricated an astonishing range of reciprocal relationships in Bugufi. Beer flowed particularly in the homes of chiefs and headmen,

[98] WFM 'Diare de Buhororo, Bugufi,' entry for 30 December 1942; Cory file 62: Hans Cory, 'Survey of the Utwaliates of Bugufi,' 1944.
[99] Interview: Richard Bugwoya, Mubinyanganya, Ngara, 18 August 2006.
[100] TNA Acc. 64 1737: PC Lake to Chief Secretary, 20 March 1939.
[101] CMS Annual Letters file: Lily Thrush, January 1944. Government officials and missionaries debated the form of this ceremony; the correspondence is in TNA Acc. 64/1737: McKee to Dobson, 23 December 1943; and DC Biharamulo to PC Mwanza, 27 December 1943.
[102] TNA AB 40: Bukoba District Annual Report, 1925.
[103] TNA Acc. 64/1737: DO Biharamulo to PC Lake, 6 February 1937.

who demanded a twice-yearly supply as tribute from their subjects. But beer payments could not be a one-way exchange, for it has a limited shelf life. It could not be stored up as capital. Wealthy men were obliged to share out the beer they collected. In the Hangaza language, 'to pay tribute' was a reciprocal verb: *kushikana*, 'to hold on to each other.'[104] Tenants often built houses on tiny gardens – as small as 400 square feet – close by their landlord's home, where they lived when beer was available to be drunk.[105] Wealthy chiefs' homes were beer fountains, drawing people together with sociable bonds. Bugufi's most popular headman in the early 1940s was a man named Bichinja. He was famous for the open house he kept, with beer always on tap.[106]

Bugufi's people knew sober men to be ungrateful, ungenerous, and out to advance themselves at other people's expense. When landlords began to ask for tribute in cash money in the early 1940s, tenants criticized them as misers, selfishly storing up their profits for their own benefit.[107] By claiming tribute in cash, sober landlords were transforming a public good into their private property. Chief Daudi Balamba was sober to a fault. He traveled widely with Revival evangelists, giving his testimony before conventions in Bugufi in 1946, at Kako in Buganda in 1950, and in western Kenya in 1956.[108] Missionaries were charmed at his biography, and they published pen portraits of the 'radiant faced young king' and his remote people.[109] Bugufi's people were less charmed by their chief's sobriety. Balamba appointed a cadre of revivalists as his chief advisors, displacing the authorities on whom Kinyamazinge had relied. One of them was Danieli Semiguruka, an immigrant from Burundi. Semiguruka had schooled with Balamba at Katoke, and like Balamba, he converted in 1939. Some said that the two young men were blood brothers.[110] In May 1943, shortly after his installation as chief, Balamba appointed Semiguruka as his deputy, and endowed him with a large, tenanted estate.[111] Joel Zinzabakwile was another of Balamba's chief advisors. Zinzabakwile had worked as a houseboy in several European homes during his youth. He converted and became a teetotaler in the early 1940s. Hans Cory, the government sociologist, thought Zinzabakwile to be the most unpopular chief in Bugufi. His men were said to 'dislike him because he is greedy and overbearing, at the

[104] TNA Acc. 217 L5/14: DC Ngara to PC Lake, 4 March 1954.
[105] Cory file 61: Cory, 'Bugufi Land Report,' 22 August 1944.
[106] Cory file 62: Cory, 'Survey of the Utwaliates of Bugufi,' 1944.
[107] Cory file 61: Cory, 'Bugufi Land Report,' 22 August 1944.
[108] Balamba's travel itinerary can be seen in TNA Acc. 64/1737: DC Ngara to PC Lake, 27 March 1950; and HMC JEC 2/9: 'Evangelistic Journeys, 1956.'
[109] MAM E 1/7: Esther Sharp, no title, in *Front Line News* 2 (November 1944).
[110] Cory file 62: Cory, 'Survey of the utwaliates of Bugufi,' 1944.
[111] TNA Acc. 64 1737: Assistant DO Ngara to DC Biharamulo, 15 May 1943.

same time he is cunning and clever.' Zinzabakwile was so unpopular that he was obliged to keep a bodyguard, as he feared that his own people would attack him.[112]

It was from their testimonies of conversion that Daudi Balamba and his colleagues learned about governance. Just as revivalists sorted through their possessions and made an account of their deeds, Chief Daudi was likewise extending the reach of the law and holding people accountable. Cattle-keeping was one area that Daudi Balamba sought to bring under legal oversight. Cattle, like beer, had in Kinyamazinge's time bound men together in reciprocal relationships. The chief had always been Bugufi's biggest cattle-keeper: in 1944, his herds were estimated at 1,500 head.[113] Bugufi's chiefs loaned out large numbers of cattle to their allies; the trustees used the milk from these cattle – called *inshumba* – for their own benefit, sending the offspring to the chief. Alternately, the chief might make a free gift of a small number of cattle to a favored client, which the client was free to slaughter or trade. Commoners also exchanged cattle, distributing their stock in order to minimize the risk of pestilence.[114] Cattle, then, were not property to be stored up as capital by a single owner. They were mobile assets, public goods, used to nourish alliances and cultivate ties between people. By the late 1930s, however, the British government was convinced that cattle in Bugufi and elsewhere in northern Tanganyika were damaging fragile soil.[115] The District Commissioner thought the chiefdom's large herds were a 'relic of autocracy,' and an 'anachronism in a country where democratic principles obtain.'[116] He wanted *inshumba* cattle to be assigned to particular owners, who would be responsible for their care and disposal. The district government appointed Hans Cory, Tanganyika's official sociologist, to sort out Bugufi's complicated stock market. In April 1943, with Chief Daudi at his side, Hans Cory summoned Bugufi's leading cattle-keepers and required each of them to sign a typewritten paper saying 'I possess __ number of *inshumba* cattle.'[117] Cory was inventorying cattle-keepers' herds and identifying government property.

Daudi Balamba was by no means a bystander in this exercise in property management. Like Hans Cory, he sought to make cattle into a possession, to transform a mobile asset into capital. He toured Bugufi in 1942

---

[112] Cory file 62: Cory, 'Survey of the Utwaliates of Bugufi,' 1944.

[113] Cory file 170: Cory, 'Report on the Cattle Situation in Bugufi,' 1944.

[114] Cory file 98: Cory, 'Hangaza Law and Custom,' 1944.

[115] TNA Acc. 197 23: PC Lake, circular to District Officers, 27 October 1937. More generally, see David Anderson, 'Depression, Dust Bowl, Demography, and Drought: The Colonial State and Soil Conservation in East Africa during the 1930s,' *African Affairs* 83 (1984), 321–43.

[116] TNA Acc. 214 E.1/II: DC Biharamulo to PC Lake, 21 September 1944.

[117] Cory file 170: Cory, 'Report on the Cattle Situation in Bugufi,' 1944.

in the company of his father, marking *inshumba* cattle; and in the months following his coronation, Balamba began collecting *inshumba* cattle from their trustees and giving them to Daniel Semiguruka, Joel Zinzabakwile, and others of his revivalist companions. When in July 1943 he heard that many cattle-keepers were sending their *inshumba* herds to Burundi, Balamba accused them of theft. He summoned Bugufi's sub-chiefs and headmen and locked them in the courthouse overnight; the following morning, Balamba and Danieli Semiguruka conducted the twenty-three men to a nearby riverbed, where they obliged to take up hoes and spend the day in punishing manual labor.[118] In November, Balamba demanded that all *inshumba* trustees should bring their cattle to his palace, where he carefully totaled them, comparing the numbers with the cattle register that Hans Cory had produced six months earlier. The *inshumba* trustees, for their part, tried to keep off Balamba's paper trail. One of the trustees, Semitende bin Rusengo, came before Balamba and Hans Cory and signed for eighty-four head of *inshumba* cattle. Within a matter of hours he reconsidered, asking for the return of the signed paper. Nearly a dozen other trustees likewise sought to renege on the account they had made. The controversy over Bugufi's stock exchange was only resolved late in 1944 when Cory and Balamba agreed that the trustees should each be given a certain number of cattle as their personal possession. The remaining *inshumba* cattle were carefully counted, and each trustee was obliged to sign a note agreeing that Balamba was entitled, at any time, to reclaim his herd.[119]

Daudi Balamba *the convert* was also Daudi Balamba *the accountant*. As Balamba and his revivalist lieutenants sorted through Bugufi's herds, as they identified cattle as their personal property, revivalists were also owning up to certain deeds and possessions as evidence of sinfulness. It is not a coincidence that in 1943, the same year that Balamba was made chief, he created three new courts at which Bugufi's people could conduct their litigation.[120] Revivalists were identifying bits of paper, articles of clothing, cash money, and other goods as evidence of their sins. Converts were also sorting out their characters, owning up to certain dispositions that they confessed. In their forensic work, converts gave their sins material form. Their lists of sins were like the typewritten lists of cattle that Balamba and Hans Cory produced. Converts were connecting individuals with their properties. Revivalists' bureaucratic and forensic work was a means of holding people accountable.

---

[118] Cory file 62: Cory to DO Ngara, 15 August 1944.
[119] This paragraph is largely in summary of Cory file 170: Hans Cory, 'Report on the Cattle Situation in Bugufi,' 1944.
[120] TNA Acc. 64 1737: Assistant DO Ngara to PC Lake, 8 June 1943.

Not everyone would agree to be accountable to Daudi Balamba's law books. Bugufi's people knew beer, cattle, and other goods to be liquid assets, circulating between people and binding them together in hierarchical relationships. Neither beer nor cattle were capital: they could not be stored up, banked, and credited to a particular individual. Beer had to be drunk, and patrons and clients together enjoyed consuming it. Cattle were not simply penned into a kraal: people related to cattle as drinkers of milk, as users of manure, or as sellers of beef. In their reluctance to list their stock in Daudi Balamba's account books, in their criticisms of teetotalling landlords' greed, Bugufi's cattle-keepers were defending an older, more fluid definition of property.

CONCLUSION

The Pentecostal Revival at Bugufi was short-lived. In August 1940, four months after Bishop Chambers' ill-tempered directive against Pentecostalism, missionary Lionel Bakewell was transferred to another station.[121] His replacement at Katoke school, a man named Charles Maling, could report that the 'excesses' of the Revival had fallen away by 1941.[122] Maling replaced converts' nighttime chapel services with a more sedate and ill-attended Bible study. In the absence of charismatic fervor, the missionary was struck by converts' probity and discretion. Where formerly 'lying, theft and laziness were prevalent,' he told Joe Church, 'honesty and hard work are now accepted principles.' The history of the Revival in Bugufi is the story of a road not taken. About Pentecostalism, at least, church authorities had the last word. Never again in the course of the 1940s and 1950s would revivalists in eastern Africa cultivate charisma as a sign of conversion. Where converts adopted Pentecostal forms of worship – as in Buhaya during the late 1950s – they were marginalized by the main body of revivalists (see Chapter 8).

The figure that emerged from Bugufi's noisy Revival was a self-possessed character, an individual who could stand at the middle of her social and material world and give an account of herself. Converts formed their self-assessments in their testimonies. In their forensic work they sorted out their sins, provided evidence of their iniquity, and owned up to their evil deeds. Their testimonies established the distance that they had traveled between the old life and the new, a movement that they mimicked in the real world as they traveled from place to place to preach. Their autobiographical practice was an intervention in Bugufi's political economy. In a time when wives were holding their footloose husbands to account, revivalism gave

[121] Bakewell, 'The Western Area of the Diocese of Central Tanganyika.'
[122] HMC JEC 1/3: Charles Maling to Joe Church, 12 June 1941.

converts a means of identifying their properties. At a time when absentee husbands were working to keep their wives faithful, converts made individuals accountable for their deeds. Revivalists extended legal oversight to new areas of social life – to the stock market, and to the economy of land. The history of the Revival in Bugufi helps us see accounting as a technique that people practiced as they moved between different theaters in the social world.

6

Patriotism and Dissent in Western Kenya

In November 1957, an indignant group of men from Akoko in western Kenya's Nyanza province announced their intention to secede from the Anglican church. Revivalists were haranguing the people of Akoko about their sins. They were notorious for the stark distinctions they made between the saved and the damned. Many Luo revivalists refused to lend clothing to other people, lest they use the clothing to commit sin. Neither would converts loan dishes or utensils to their relatives, even on the occasion of a funeral. And converts declined to travel in non-converts' company.[1] To the offended people of Akoko, revivalists seemed to be greedy self-promoters. They described the Anglican church, full of converts, as 'a refuge to witches,' and vowed to join a new organization, called the Church of Christ in Africa (CCA), known in DhoLuo as the *Johera*, the 'People of Love.'[2]

Revivalists were stirring up controversy all over East Africa. They refused to act as upstanding members of their political communities. In Kigezi, converts lived in anticipation of a radically new era. In their noisy songs and their lurid testimonies, they offended Kiga standards of etiquette (see Chapter 3). In Buganda, converts talked openly about adultery and other matters that respectable people urgently tried to keep secret. Their revelations undermined Ganda elites' reputations (see Chapter 4). In Bugufi, converts took account of their possessions, extricating their private property from public goods (see Chapter 5). Nyanza's converts likewise scorned the conventions that upheld human society. They seemed determined to put distance between themselves and their compatriots. At Akoko and elsewhere in Nyanza, indignant critics regarded converts as witches, self-regarding destroyers of civil communities. Like community-builders elsewhere in eastern Africa, the *Johera* – the 'People of Love' – sought to stitch society

---

[1] KNA DX 21/9/1: Special Branch to Superintendent of Police, 21 August 1956.
[2] NMK Leonard Beecher papers, file 2: Akoko meeting to Leonard Beecher, 15 November 1957.

together in hierarchical relationships of trust and dependence. They affirmed husbands' authority over their wives and advocated the civic virtue of circumspection in speech and conduct. Nyanza's debate over the Revival was conducted on the grounds of etiquette, because etiquette was the discipline on which civil society rested.

This chapter reconstructs the genealogy of Luo patriotism. Like John Lonsdale, I regard patriotism as 'pride in a specific local achievement of widely shared criteria of civility.'[3] Here I show here that the attainment of civil order in eastern Africa rested on a disciplinary apparatus: on the suppression of deviant forms of behavior; on the elevation of some forms of social life (but not others) as 'customary'; and on the routinization of hierarchy, especially in marriage. Luo patriotism was a means by which wage-working men, insecure in their rights over their wives, sought to reform their family lives. In Nyanza, as in Buganda (see Chapter 4), independent women negotiated with their husbands over the character of their conjugal relationships. In the 1940s and 1950s, Luo men began to represent the dynamics of conjugality in starkly absolute terms, contrasting the old order of custom with the immorality of their contemporary world. History-writing helped Luo men uncover the moral footings of their political community. It also helped them assert their rights over territory. Luo patriots defined their homeland and conjured up a constituency through the census, the electoral roll, and the identity card. By repatriating prostitutes and other urban-dwelling women, by enumerating, counting, and labeling their constituents, Nyanza's entrepreneurs built up a population and established their people's position in Kenya's political theater. The composition of a Luo civic culture involved a system of constraint that limited people's freedom of movement and made them natives.

Revivalists would not stand up and be counted. To their critics, converts were antisocial, undermining family life and setting people at odds with their incendiary testimonies. It was as defenders of their fatherland, and as advocates for decency and civility, that Luo patriots at Akoko and elsewhere in Nyanza worked to suppress the Revival.

CONJUGAL ARGUMENT AND CULTURAL INNOVATION

Nyanza's political culture was shaped by Luo people's distinctive pattern of conjugality (see Map 2). An anthropologist found that 30 percent of the adult men in one rural community spent the year working away from their homes in 1956.[4] They earned about 1,800 shillings per year, three times the

---

[3] John Lonsdale, 'Writing Competitive Patriotisms in Eastern Africa,' in *Recasting the Past: History Writing and Political Work in Modern Africa*, eds. Derek R. Peterson and Giacomo Macola (Athens, OH, 2009), 255.

[4] KNA DX 21/2/2: Gordon Wilson, 'The Land Tenure System in Winam,' 1956.

amount a subsistence farmer could make.[5] But Luo men were not committed, long-term urbanites. Many of them labored on the railway line, while others worked in detention camps, guarding the thousands of Gikuyu men and women detained during the Mau Mau war (see Chapter 10).[6] They resided in bachelor housing while maintaining their wives and children in their rural homes. The anthropologist found that the vast majority of migrants, nearly 70 percent, stayed away from their homes for less than one year. Only 13 percent stayed away for three years or more. Luo men were episodically involved with their families' lives.[7]

Their irregular attachment to their families made it difficult for Luo husbands to exercise influence over their wives. Husbands had to contend with fathers-in-law, brothers-in-law, and other suitors, all of whom made claims on women's loyalties. Soldiers, contract workers, and other husbands whose business kept them away from home for long periods were particularly imperiled. One husband, employed as a policeman in the city of Mombasa, was cuckolded when his wife went for a visit to her father's home in Nyanza. There she married another man.[8] Another man, a prisoner serving a six-year sentence in Kisumu prison, was cuckolded when his wife took up with her paramour, leaving a 4-year-old son in his mother's care.[9] Men like these were anchored to their posts in faraway places. They found it impossible to manage their marriages from a distance. In a competitive conjugal economy, husbands seeking to buttress their hold over their wives had to invest time and money in their rural homes, shuttling back and forth from town to countryside.

Luo men were obliged to engage in the social work of marriage-building because Luo wives were holding their husbands accountable. Women demanded that their husbands send home cash, clothing, and other provisions to outfit their families. In 1958, Grace Atieno told the sympathetic District Commissioner about her delinquent husband.[10] He was a wage worker living in Nairobi. He sent no money home to support her, and she lived in her father-in-law's house, because her husband had failed to build a home for her to live in. Moreover, she told the District Commissioner, her husband had failed to pay the bridewealth he had promised to her father. Atieno vowed therefore to marry another man. Women like Grace Atieno hoped to capitalize on the proceeds of their husbands' wage work. Wives

[5] Michael Whisson, 'The Journeys of the JoRamogi' (Kampala, July 1962).

[6] Over 40 percent of the East African Railways and Harbours labor force in Kampala in 1965 were from Kenya, most of them Luo. R. D. Grillo, *African Railwaymen: Solidarity and Opposition in an East African Labour Force* (Cambridge, 1973).

[7] David Parkin, *The Cultural Definition of Political Response: Lineal Destiny among the Luo* (London, 1978), 49.

[8] KNA DC Kisumu 1/21/11: Wilfred Otieno to DC Kisumu, 17 March 1955.

[9] KNA DC Kisumu 1/21/11: Ogendo Olwoch to DC Kisumu, 3 September 1955.

[10] KNA DC Kisumu 1/21/20: DO Maseno to DC Central Nyanza, 11 September 1958.

had several tactics they could employ in their negotiations over husbands' conjugal obligations. Some women formed strategic alliances with men as a route out of their unwanted marriages. A police officer based on Eldoret complained that a woman named Benta Obuar – married to a man working in Nairobi – had moved, uninvited, into his home. He asked the government to remove her.[11] Benta Obuar and other independent Luo women dragooned comparatively well-off men into conjugal relationships, and in this way they undermined their husbands' authority over them. Other women sought employment outside their homes, and used the wages they earned to put distance between themselves and their husbands. When Nereah Okech, married for a year to a Nairobi man, took up a post as nurse, her husband complained to the British medical officer: 'African women are never independent,' he wrote, 'they either depend on parents or husbands, and without approval of these guardians anyone keeping them is guilty of an offence.'[12] But Okech would not follow her husband's directions. She convinced the District Commissioner to intervene on her behalf, using her husband's refusal to provide financial support as evidence to attract his sympathy.[13]

Luo marriages were never fixed, stable, or finished. With their wives' loyalty in question, Luo men living in East Africa's cities cast about for means by which to exercise leverage over independent women. They filled government administrators' mailboxes with petitions, hoping to gain a legal advantage in their marital arguments. Some wage workers convinced their employers to write on their behalf.[14] Other petitioners relied on the strength of the evidence in making their case against their independent wives. In 1952, a railwayman complained that his wife had married another man. 'She is my wife as according to our African customs, I married her with heads of cattle and thirty shillings,' he told the District Commissioner.[15] Husbands represented their conjugal negotiations as commercial transactions, describing the bridewealth they offered to their wives' families as a fixed price that they had paid. In reality, paying bridewealth was always a lifelong undertaking. The *riso chege*, the 'bull of finality' that completed bridewealth transactions, was very often exchanged when husband and wife were quite elderly.[16] But

[11] KNA DC Kisumu 1/21/7: Dishon Ogutu to DC Central Nyanza, 14 October 1948.
[12] KNA DC Kisumu 1/1/181: S. Mitula to Medical Officer, Central Kavirondo, 2 January 1947.
[13] KNA DC Kisumu 1/1/181: DC Central Kavirondo to S. Mitula, 5 April 1947.
[14] KNA DC Kisumu 1/21/5: Borderland Syndicate to DC Central Kavirondo, 14 March 1946; KNA DC Kisumu 1/21/20: Officer in Charge, Lukenya Prison, to DC Kisumu, 26 March 1956; KNA DC Kisumu 1/1/181: Anglo-French Sisal Company to DC Kisumu, 28 January 1945.
[15] KNA DC Kisumu 1/21/11: Alfayo Indire to DC Kisumu, 2 September 1952.
[16] Gordon Wilson, *Luo Customary Law and Marriage Customs* (Nairobi, 1968). Anthropologist Parker Shipton titled a book chapter on marital practices in contemporary Nyanza 'Marriage

the husbands who in the 1950s filled government administrators' mailboxes with petitions could not afford to acknowledge the drawn-out, life-long work of conjugal negotiation. One complainant, employed in Dar es Salaam, sent the District Commissioner a stack of receipts showing the cash money he had paid to his wife during the years of their marriage. With this evidence he sought to indemnify his brother-in-law, who had sent his wife to live with another man.[17] Luo men represented dynamic relationships in simplified commercial terms. They hoped thereby to cement their claim on women's sexual and physical energies, attenuating their wives' freedom of action.

The redefinition of marriage – as a commercial transaction by which wives were made into husbands' property – was one aspect of a larger work of gender reform. Living as migrants in eastern Africa's cities, Luo men knew themselves to be in competition with other men for jobs and for honor. They thought assertive, independent Luo women were a danger to their reputation. In October 1948, a worried man wrote to the Luo-language newspaper *Ramogi* to complain about women who shopped in Nairobi's slaughterhouses. He had seen a pregnant Luo woman wrestling with a man over offal; the man had 'slapped her very frequently, but still she would not give up.' The editorialist thought the scene was an embarrassment to Luo people, and urged his readers to 'abolish such deeds of shame before other tribes.' 'No other tribes do this,' he noted.[18] He and other urban-dwelling men thought it imperative that Luo people should present a dignified, respectable face to the watching public. An editorialist argued that 'the Luo are letting themselves down when they send their wives to go and buy the heads and bones of fish from the European hotels,' for wives 'shame their husbands when going to buy waste from hidden corners.' He suggested that mothers should assign their children to this task, because children would be 'fit to stand in the cold and bear the shame of waiting for the fish to be skinned and sold to them.'[19]

With their reputations in danger, Luo men living in eastern Africa's cities sought to reform women's manners. They created a constellation of organizations that bridged town with countryside and gave them leverage over independent women. Founded in 1945, the Ramogi African Welfare Association's members were clerks, railway workers, and teachers, most of them employed in Kisumu town.[20] In its constitution, the association

on the Installment Plan.' Chapter 6 in Shipton, *The Nature of Entrustment: Intimacy, Exchange, and the Sacred in Africa* (New Haven, 2007).

[17] KNA DC Kisumu 1/21/20: Nelson Masure to DC Central Nyanza, 21 March 1956.

[18] *Ramogi*, 1 October 1948; in KNA DC Kisumu 1/28/154: Kenya Information Office, 'Summary of Opinions on African Affairs,' 1 to 15 October 1948.

[19] *Ramogi*, 15 April 1948; in KNA DC Kisumu 1/28/154: Kenya Information Office, 'Summary of Opinions on African Affairs,' 1 to 15 April 1948.

[20] KNA PC Nyanza 3/1/376: Special Branch to Police Superintendent, Kisumu, 30 November 1945.

vowed to 'prevent and prosecute all girls and women who are at the present time running away from their husbands … and are engaged in the prostitution business.'[21] Members pledged to uphold the institution of marriage, to 'fulfill the usual tribal obligations before the girl's or woman's parents,' and to place divorce cases before the association's leadership for arbitration.[22] Women found practicing prostitution in Kisumu were stripped, wrapped in gunnysacks, and forcibly taken back to their rural homes. The association's activists ran ten women out of Kisumu in this way in 1945.[23] Other organizations similarly sought to impose a patriarchal discipline on independent Luo women. The 'Bunyore Welfare Society,' formed in Central Nyanza in 1953, vowed to 'stop Banyore ladies or women to leave home to go to any town with a view to roam about and practice brothel.'[24] The Maragoli Association filled the District Commissioner's mailbox with letters naming women who were practicing prostitution in Kisumu town.[25] The best-organized of western Kenya's welfare organizations was the Luo Union.[26] The Union had it as a rule that Luo women should only take employment in Kenya's cities with the Union's approval.[27] The founders of the Dar es Salaam branch vowed to 'preserve and encourage the traditional Luo customs and culture, so that no Luo fools shall remain loitering about in this town and leading an immoral life.'[28] Union members kept a careful eye on city women. In 1961, the Union's secretary wrote to the District Commissioner listing the names of several dozen Luo prostitutes working out of two Kisumu hotels.[29] One of the women I interviewed remembered that when she went to Nairobi for the first time, she was visited at her home by a committee from the Luo Union.[30] They examined her marriage certificate, questioned her and her husband about their wedding, and finally took her photograph. Unionists were thorough, and their program of social reform was comprehensive. They

---

[21] KNA PC Nyanza 3/1/376: John Ogala to PC Nyanza, 19 October 1945.

[22] KNA DC Kakamega 2/1/99: Ramogi Welfare Association to PC Nyanza, 16 June 1947.

[23] KNA PC Nyanza 3/1/376: Special Branch to Police Superintendent, Kisumu, 30 November 1945.

[24] KNA DC Kakamega 1/1/153: General Secretary, Bunyore Welfare Society, to Locational Council, n.d. (but 1953).

[25] KNA HT 1/6: A. Malango to DO Vihiga, 2 November 1960; A. Malango, minutes of meeting with DC, 22 October 1960; A. Malango to DC, 23 December 1960. Kenda Mutongi offers a full analysis of the Maragoli Association in *Worries of the Heart: Widows, Family, and Community in Kenya* (Chicago, 2007), chapter 12.

[26] The history of the Luo Union is given in Matthew Carotenuto, 'Cultivating an African Community: the Luo Union in 20th Century East Africa' (PhD dissertation, Indiana University, 2006). Carotenuto's findings are published as '*Riwruok E Teko*: Cultivating Identity in Colonial and Postcolonial Kenya,' *African Affairs* 53 (2) (2006), 53–73.

[27] KNA PC Nyanza 3/1/316: DC Central Nyanza to Secretary, Luo Union, 6 May 1955.

[28] TNA Acc. 540/3/32: President Luo Union to Municipal African Affairs Officer, 20 August 1952.

[29] KNA HT 1/6: Luo Union to DC Central Nyanza, 12 January 1961.

[30] Interview: Naomi Olweny, Nyayiera, Bondo, 23 November 2007.

vowed to punish women who smoked cigarettes, wore pins in their hair, or bought bones from fishmongers. Delinquent men were likewise under examination: unionists disciplined men who played guitars in brothels, seduced other men's wives, or talked to each other in the Kikuyu language.[31]

Luo men knew themselves to be under examination. They conceived of East Africa's urban environment as a competitive theater in which men and women alike were obliged to behave with creditable decorum. In their campaign against the sexual and social corruptions of city life, the Ramogi African Welfare Association, the Luo Union, and other welfare organizations were obliged to represent independent women as deviants. For how else than by contrasting delinquency with accepted behavior could moral reformers put independent women on the margins, outside the fold of the Luo commonwealth? Conservative reformers had to speak as defenders of custom, righteously defending the majority's interests against a destructive minority. The anti-prostitution campaign thereby invited partisans to imagine a Luo polity.

British government had until the 1940s named Nyanza's linguistically and culturally diverse people with the collective ethnonym 'Kavirondo.' The first African welfare societies had not been organized on ethnic or linguistic lines. As late as 1938, the organization that later became the Luo Union had a chairman who did not speak the Luo language.[32] Over the course of the 1940s, a range of social institutions invited the people living in southern and central Nyanza to see themselves as 'Luo.' The Luo Language Committee was one such engine of cultural innovation. Formed in 1944, the committee was charged with the work of standardizing the Luo language and orthography.[33] By 1947, there were nearly a dozen Luo language books in print. Authors were inspired in part by the Luo Union, which encouraged its members to 'study and select the Luo customs which are decent and compatible with progress.'[34] Among the books composed in this era were a history of Kano location, a history of Asembo location, and J. Okinda's *History mar Luo*.[35] The author of the latter book proudly claimed to have traced the history of the Luo people 'as far back as 9,000 BC or thereabout.'[36] Historical research was a consequential endeavor in Nyanza, a work for

---

[31] *Ramogi*, 1 September 1949; in KNA DC Kisumu 1/28/56: Kenya Information Office, 'Summary of Opinions on African Affairs,' 1 to 15 September 1949. See Luise White, *The Comforts of Home: Prostitution in Colonial Nairobi* (Chicago, 1990), chapter 7.

[32] KNA PC Nyanza 2/1/8: DC Central Kavirondo to Minister of Native Affairs, 29 March 1938. The chair was Cleophas Sigge, a 'Bantu' (i.e., 'Luyia') speaker from Samia, who for a time changed the name of the association from the 'Luo Union' to the 'Central Kavirondo Union.'

[33] KNA DC Kisumu 1/10/60: Luo Language Committee, minutes, 11 August 1944.

[34] KNA DC Kakamega 2/1/99: F. Odede and N. Amura to PC Nyanza, 29 March 1945.

[35] Kakamega archives NE 9/9: Luo Language Committee secretary to Senior Education Officer, 12 July 1950.

[36] Kakamega archives NE 9/9: Director East African Literature Bureau to Senior Education Officer, 20 February 1951.

which dedicated people sacrificed both time and money. Joseph Ochieng, a bus driver working in Nairobi, did field research on the history of Alego location during his holidays. He and two colleagues toured Alego, using a two-page questionnaire to guide their interviews. The first question that Ochieng asked his respondents to answer was 'When did the Alego people arrive?'[37]

Students of Luo history were making inquiries into the distant past. They found therein models by which to orient their contemporaries' conduct. Paul Mboya's *Luo Kitgi gi Timbegi* ('The Luo, Their Cultures and Traditions'), published in 1938, established the template on which later historians worked.[38] Educated at a Seventh Day Adventist school, Mboya had helped missionaries translate parts of the Old Testament into the Luo language.[39] He must have had the lessons of the Babylonian captivity of Israel on his mind when in he told his readers of his history book that 'A nation that is mindful of its good customs and practices grows strong, and earns the respect of foreigners.' Mboya warned that 'People who had no respect for their society's customs and practices … are scattered all over the earth, and people refer to them as *jodak* [tenants, vagrants].' Luo people needed to defend themselves against the rootlessness of ignorance. Mboya – learning from Moses, the giver of the Ten Commandments – knew that the law was the surest guard against social amnesia. 'God did not leave a nation without providing it with laws,' he wrote, 'which acted as a shield for protecting its communities, villages and homes.' His book's first chapter listed the political and religious offices that leaders of the Luo community occupied, while the second chapter outlined the rules by which refractory people were disciplined. Mboya described, for example, the 'law regarding theft,' the 'law regarding herdboys' and other rules. Mboya defined a political community characterized by its obedience to legal writ.[40]

Mboya's work found a large readership in western Kenya. *Luo Kitgi gi Timbegi* was a required text in the primary school curriculum, and it is now in its eighth print run. In its focus on legal history Mboya's book set the agenda for later researchers to pursue. Shadrack Malo, a senior appeals court judge, began doing fieldwork on Luo history in the late 1940s. He followed

[37] KNA DC Kisumu 1/10/60: Joseph Ochieng, David Siganda and Lucas Ayugi to DC Nyanza, 3 August 1954.

[38] Paul Mboya, *Luo Kitgi gi Timbegi* (Kisumu, 1983 [1938]). In reading this work I have relied on Jane Achieng, *Paul Mboya's Luo Kitgi gi Timbegi* (Nairobi, 2001), and on Jim Harries's 2002 typescript translation, held in the library of the School of Oriental and African Studies.

[39] BSA E3/3/320/2: Minute, 5 November 1930.

[40] In 1978, Mboya published his *Richo ema Kelo Chira*, which argued that 'God gave the Luo FOURTEEN commandments.' The translation is in E. S. Atieno Odhiambo, 'Luo Perspectives on Knowledge and Development: Samuel G. Ayany and Paul Mbuya,' in *African Philosophy as Cultural Inquiry*, eds, Ivan Karp and D. A. Masolo (Bloomington, 2000). The text was published as Paul Mbuya (Mboya), *Richo ema Kelo Chira* (Nairobi, 1978).

the same itinerary in each location: he began by interviewing elders chosen for him by the chief, and after he had typed up their testimonies, Malo sent the transcript back to the chief for discussion at the local council. Once the councilors had given their approval, Malo added the transcript to his book.[41] He published his work in 1953 under the title *Dhoudi mar Central Nyanza* ('Clans of Central Nyanza').[42] His fieldwork gave him a source base from which to practice law. By 1962, Malo was a key member of the 'Luo Law Panel,' chosen by the Kenya government to consolidate and standardize Luo customary law.[43] Under Malo's direction, the panel established the procedure for traditional marriage, set the value of bridewealth, and defined the code that today guides 'customary' legal practice in Nyanza.[44]

Literate historians like Mboya and Malo claimed to be speaking for traditional values, but their antique chronology disguised their culturally innovative work. The architects of Luo tradition were filtering out local variety and setting standards by which to govern human conduct. At a time when wives and daughters seemed dangerously undisciplined, historical works like Mboya's and Malo's gave Luo entrepreneurs a baseline with which to measure the corruptions of modern life. With their history books in hand, Luo intellectuals could define customary practice, reify 'precolonial' Luo virtues, and contrast modern women's iniquities with their forebears' discretion. 'There was no prostitution taking place between the [Luo] women and other tribes' before colonial conquest, wrote the Ramogi Association's secretary in 1946. 'It originated in the European and Asian settlement in the colony.'[45] From this historical position, Luo patriots concluded that independent women were traitors to their people. When in 1951 British officials objected on the grounds of human rights to the Ramogi Association's maltreatment of Luo women, the Association's officials fulminated against the libertine policies of colonial government. 'There should be power to [an] Association such as this of ours ... to lead their own members of the community in the best way, instead of trying to confuse and discourage them from all their initiation and responsibility they owe to their tribe,' they wrote.[46] Their overwhelming sense of duty made disagreement seem traitorous.

---

[41] This procedure is described in KNA DC Kisumu 1/28/8: S. Malo to PC Nyanza, 22 November 1949.

[42] S. Malo, *Dhoudi mar Central Nyanza* (Nairobi, 1953). See David William Cohen and E. S. Atieno Odhiambo, *Siaya: The Historical Anthropology of an African Landscape* (Nairobi, 1989), 36.

[43] Cory file 324: Minutes of the Luo Law Panel, 2 to 4 April, 1962.

[44] For discussion, see E. S. Atieno Odhiambo and David William Cohen, *Burying S.M.: The Politics of Knowledge and the Sociology of Power in Africa* (Portsmouth: Heinemann, 1992).

[45] KNA PC Nyanza 3/1/376: Ramogi Association secretary to PC Nyanza, 11 January 1946.

[46] KNA MAA 2/5/155: Ramogi African Welfare Association to DC Central Nyanza, 29 May 1951.

When the Kisumu Debating Society invited the Ramogi Association's president to participate in a debate over the Association's policies in 1946, he refused to attend, calling the Debating Society's leaders 'clerks ... who think themselves too civilized to fall in with the masses.'[47]

The anti-prostitution campaigns of the 1940s and 1950s invited Luo thinkers to define their political community as a *patria*, a fatherland. At a time when husbands could not keep hold over their wives, Luo men found in patriotism a means by which to discipline women's behavior. The Luo *patria* imagined by the Ramogi African Welfare Association and the Luo Union was grounded in historical research. The customary virtues uncovered by the historians of the 1940s and 1950s gave Luo thinkers the means to show independent women to be unpatriotic. 'The Young Luo of today lacks the proper discipline which was exercised by our forefathers,' Oginga Odinga told a meeting of the Luo Union in 1955. 'If we do not think seriously now of uniting together as a tribe our children will have no discipline.'[48] The call for political unity, the work of historical research, and the demand for sexual discipline went hand in hand.

LAND TENURE AND HISTORICAL THOUGHT

The absentee husbands of the 1950s were also absentee landlords. Just as suitors contended with husbands for wives' loyalty, so did neighbors, tenants, and other claimants compete with city-dwelling men for control over property. Government policy made disagreements over land tenure more intense. In 1957, the district government inaugurated a program of land consolidation for parts of Nyanza province.[49] Their model was central Kenya where, under the 'Swynnerton Plan,' thousands of acres of land were being consolidated under the control of politically loyal Gikuyu farmers (see Chapter 10).[50] Government officials in Nyanza took notes on central Kenya's land consolidation program, and they brought groups of Luo chiefs to tour prosperous Gikuyu farms in 1956 and 1957.[51] Agriculture officials encouraged Luo farmers holding several small fragments of land to strike

[47] KNA PC Nyanza 3/1/376: Odele to Kisumu Debating Society, 11 March 1946.
[48] KNA DC Kakamega 2/1/99: General Secretary, Luo Union, to Superintendent of Police, 9 September 1955.
[49] See Parker Shipton, 'The Kenyan Land Tenure Reform: Misunderstandings in the Public Creation of Private Property,' in *Land and Society in Contemporary Africa*, eds. R. E. Downs and S. P. Reyna (Hanover, N. H., 1988), 91–135. Shipton has written more generally about land titling in Nyanza in his engaging *Mortgaging the Ancestors: Ideologies of Attachment in Africa* (New Haven, 2009), especially chapter 7.
[50] For the policy, see J. Swynnerton, 'Kenya's Agricultural Planning,' *African Affairs* 56 (224) (1957), 209–15.
[51] KNA DX 21/10/4: Assistant Agriculture Officer, 'Some First Impressions of Vihiga Division, North Nyanza,' 31 January 1957.

deals with their neighbors, trading blocks of land to create a contiguous farm. Teams of elders were appointed to survey boundaries and check the fences erected by landholders. The aim, in the words of one British official, was to create a class of politically conservative peasants who would become 'the anchor of the tribe, the solid yeoman farmer, the land owner who knows that he has too much to lose if he flirts, however lightly, with the passions of his nationalistic friends.'[52] By 1960, twenty-eight square miles of farmland in Nyanza had been consolidated, and 2,803 farms had been fenced in.[53]

Luo men living in Nairobi and other faraway cities were horrified at the land consolidation scheme. They were convinced that the government's surveyors were endangering their rights. Land consolidation reduced the ecological diversity of farmers' holdings, heightening the risks that farmers faced.[54] But it was more than agronomy that made Luo men worry over the land consolidation program. Living at a distance from their rural homes, migrant laborers exercised little influence over government surveyors. There were rumors among Luo farm workers in the Rift Valley that government planned to confiscate their homesteads.[55] In Mombasa, Luo migrants were sure that the government would seize land belonging to men who failed to return home to plead their case.[56] In Nyanza, elderly men were fearful that the government would bar them from passing their land on to their sons.[57] These and other worries terrified people and roused them to action. In June 1956 there was a riot in Kaloleni, the Luo suburb outside Nairobi. Rioters threatened to kill chiefs who supported land consolidation.[58] The Special Branch reported that Luo men in Nairobi were writing to their parents at home, telling them to keep the government's surveyors off their land. Writing from Tabora in Tanganyika, one man petitioned the District Commissioner to complain that the sub-headman in Gem had seized part of his farm.[59] His mother, left at home alone, was unable to defend her son's property. Another petitioner, a railwayman based in Mombasa, learned that his neighbor had fenced in a garden that belonged to his mother. The greedy neighbor had gone so far as to break up his mother's home.[60] Another petition came from a student at

[52] KNA VQ 1/51: PC Central, 'The Civil Problem of Mau Mau,' 14 January 1954. Quoted in Daniel Branch, *Defeating Mau Mau, Creating Kenya: Counterinsurgency, Civil War, and Decolonization* (Cambridge, 2009), 120.

[53] KNA HT 11/15: Director of Surveys to DC Central Nyanza, 5 May 1960.

[54] Shipton, *Mortgaging the Ancestors*, 149–50.

[55] KNA DX 21/10/4: African Land Officer, 'Notes on a Tour,' June 1956; DC Kitale to DC North Nyanza, 5 June 1956.

[56] Kakamega archives DA 14/18: Derrick to DC Kisumu, 21 May 1956.

[57] KNA DC Kisumu 1/28/81: Assistant Agriculture Officer to District Agriculture Officer, 4 June 1956.

[58] KNA DX 21/10/4: DO Kamba Centre, Nairobi to Special Branch, 10 June 1956.

[59] KNA DC Kisumu 1/18/19: Petro Jum to DC Kisumu, 13 September 1959.

[60] KNA DC Kisumu 1/18/19: Henry Oyange to DO Central Nyanza, 16 November 1959.

Manhattan College in faraway New York. He had learned that a neighbor had taken one of the pieces of land left to him by his father.[61]

With their land rights under attack from greedy neighbors, Luo land-holders searched for a secure platform on which to argue their cases. Here an essentialized view of the past proved useful. In establishing their claims, all the participants in the land consolidation controversy sought to show that they had been there first. The land crisis, in other words, encouraged Nyanza's people to elaborate a discourse of indigeneity. Writing from Busia, Funyula Buskeske protested against the seizure of his farm by a neighbor. Buskeske argued that his father had first cleared the disputed land in the early twentieth century. It 'bothers our souls very much indeed [that] we [are] to be called foreigners and we are the origin of that land,' he wrote.[62] Men like Buskeske identified themselves as autochthons, whose forefathers had established their prior claim to land. They sometimes went to extraordinary lengths to make their case. One man deserted his wife and children and moved to distant Samia, where his father had – fifty years before – occupied a plot of land.[63] He hoped to convince government surveyors to recognize his title. Another man petitioned Kenya's governor for land that his father had once cultivated in Buholo. His father had vacated the plot in question in 1919, forty years earlier.[64] Government officials worried that surveyors would be drawn into endless arguments over the distant past, and they sought to paper over these historical claims. 'If we tried to give everyone back the land of his forefathers we should probably have to move the whole population around,' the District Commissioner told a public meeting in 1960.[65] But how else could litigants establish their claim than by proving themselves to be indigenes?

Luo people were distinguishing natives from newcomers. In arguing over land tenure, Nyanza's people elaborated competing histories of land acquisition, making their claims by establishing the longevity of their families' tenures. This discourse of indigeneity was so pervasive that by 1968 anthropologist Gordon Wilson could begin his study of Luo customary law by asserting, prima facie, that 'the basis of right ownership to land in all of the Luo tribes is the fact that one's ancestor fought for the land and that it was acquired by conquest. There is no stronger claim to land in Luo.'[66] Through their investigations into the distant past, some people became landlords, with their rights securely anchored in a body of evidence about the past. Other people became tenants, newcomers, whose forefathers had settled on land that was not their own.

[61] KNA DC Kisumu 1/18/19: Boniface Nyimbi to DC Central Nyanza, 6 February 1960.
[62] KNA DC Kisumu 1/19/6: Funyula Buskeske to DC Central Nyanza, 4 June 1958.
[63] KNA DC Kisumu 1/19/6: David Majele Okelo to DO Kisumu, 17 June 1959.
[64] Kakamega archives DA 14/18: Ongor Awuor to Governor, 2 December 1958.
[65] KNA DC Kisumu 1/18/19: DC Central Nyanza to PC Nyanza, 23 June 1941.
[66] Wilson, *Luo Customary Law*, 18.

These arguments over indigeneity were especially urgent in the district of North Nyanza, where Luo people lived cheek to jowl with Wanga, Maragoli, and other Bantu groups that were collectively coming to know themselves as a 'Luyia' people. In this cosmopolitan, multilinguistic region, Luo and Luyia partisans worked for political leverage by identifying their people as firstcomers. The 'Luyia' had been so named in 1935, when North Nyanza's diverse inhabitants were summarily titled 'Abaluhia,' 'citizens,' by what missionaries termed a 'representative group of people' at a mission station in Bunyore.[67] By 1949, a petitioner could argue that 'the people of Northern Nyanza are not distinct tribes. These tribes have been living together for such a long time ... that we can no longer speak of them as tribes, but sections of a larger tribe, the Abaluyia.'[68] That same year, the British administration gazetted the name 'Abaluyia' as the 'comprehensive term to describe those who live in the North Nyanza District.'[69] Luyia political identity was thereby constituted spatially, encompassing the disparate people who lived within a particular, bounded territory. With their homeland defined, Luyia petitioners could distinguish their people from their Luo competitors. A petitioner from the Wanga people – a 'Luyia' subgroup – gave the Chief Native Commissioner a tour through the British government archives, highlighting two government reports that identified North Nyanza as Luyia territory. Luo immigrants, he argued, had settled on 'typical Wanga land.' This petitioner wanted Luo settlers to be expelled from their homes.[70] Later that same year, a half dozen Luo men living in North Nyanza were forcibly circumcised by their Luyia neighbors.[71] By these violent acts, Luyia circumcisers made uncircumcised Luo men into circumcised Luyia, and coerced them – unwillingly – into Luyia community.

On the other side of this ethnic boundary, Luo petitioners established their presence in North Nyanza by emphasizing the cultural differences between themselves and their Luyia neighbors. In 1946, three Luo petitioners wrote to the District Commissioner to complain that their Luyia chiefs discriminated against them. 'We want all Luo speaking people in North [Nyanza] to be under one chief,' they wrote. 'Why should we be separated from other Luo speaking people?'[72] These and other Luo petitioners were irredentists. They argued that people sharing a common language should also share a government and a homeland. Another petitioner compared the situation of

[67] KNA DC Kakamega 2/1/80: Ludwig to DC Kakamega, 5 June 1935. The social history of Luyia self-constitution is given in Julie MacArthur's 'Mapping Political Community Among the Luyia of Western Kenya, 1930–63' (PhD dissertation, University of Cambridge, 2010).

[68] KNA DC Kakamega 2/1/131: F. Ingutia to PC Nyanza, 23 July 1949.

[69] KNA DC Kakamega 2/1/131: PC Nyanza, general notice, n.d. (but 1949).

[70] KNA DC Kakamega 2/1/56: Moses Nanzai to Chief Native Commissioner, 26 February 1962.

[71] Kakamega archives DX 1/6: J. Ohanga to DC North Nyanza, 6 September 1962.

[72] KNA PC Nyanza 3/14/16: Niklolau Onyango, Antipa Ngutu and Daniel Musiogo to DC North Kavirondo, n.d. (but 1946).

the Luo living in North Nyanza with Quebecois living in Canada. 'Canada was divided into two, upper and lower Canada,' he wrote. 'We would like to receive the same treatment.'[73] This petitioner wanted the border between North and Central Nyanza to be redrawn, joining Luo people together under a Luo chief. Luo irredentists linked their people with an extensive territory. The president of the 'Ugenya Congress,' a Luo organization, wrote the governor's office to identify the territory that his clan had controlled in North Nyanza prior to British conquest. 'The boundary which enclosed nearly all our castles stretch from the Lusumu Bridge to Mureko passing through Butere Township to Regea in central Nyanza,' he wrote. 'Therefore any land which lies [within the boundary] belongs to the Luo by conquest.'[74] Luo thinkers were researching history, drawing boundaries, and establishing their rights to identifiable tracts of territory.

On both sides of this argument over territory and identity, activists were simplifying history, consolidating diverse cultural practices, and identifying a particular people with a particular homeland. Through this cultural work, they built up political communities. The Luo Union commissioned a census in 1954 to 'find out and record statistics on the total population of the [Luo people], with figures for those in towns and at the farms, those in business, and those loafing in towns.' The Union also wanted information on infant mortality, planning to establish maternity homes in Kenya's cities and in the Nyanza countryside.[75] Oginga Odinga, the Luo Union's leader, had even more expansive plans for the Union's census takers: he wanted statistics for the number of young Luo men attending school, and figures for mortality rates among Luo adults.[76] The Union's rules, adopted in 1955, stipulated that it was 'contrary to custom' for a Luo to marry a European, Asiatic, Arab, or Somali.[77] Luo activists used demographic techniques to organize a constituency. Their work generated statistical evidence with which to establish the Luo in western Kenya's political landscape.

Demography was more than an academic project in western Kenya. Partisans of both 'Luo' and 'Luyia' political communities needed evidence with which to claim a place in Nyanza's geography. They needed, that is, a citizenry that could be affixed to a particular territory and counted. Paul Mboya, the men of the Luo Union, and other culture-builders therefore sought to reign in prostitutes and other footloose vagrants, dragging independent women off East Africa's city streets and shipping them back to their homelands. Theirs was a moral project, meant to reinforce customary

[73] ACK ACSO/CPN/2 'Nyanza Chaplaincy minutes' file: Secretary for Ugenya Community Development to Education Officer, North Nyanza, 15 August 1951.
[74] KNA DC Kakamega 2/1/32: President, Ugenya Congress, to cabinet officer, 10 May 1962.
[75] KNA DC Kakamega 2/1/99: Riwruok Luo, 'Five Year Plan of Work, January 1955–December 1960,' 27 May 1954.
[76] KNA PC Nyanza 3/1/316: Oginga Odinga to PC Kisumu, 29 April 1954.
[77] KNA PC Nyanza 3/1/316: DC Central Nyanza to Secretary, Luo Union, 6 May 1955.

values. It was also a population-building exercise. By limiting prostitutes' intercourse with men from other places, political entrepreneurs generated the demographic and statistical evidence that they needed to gain leverage, and attention, in Kenya's political theater. Western Kenya's entrepreneurs were lining people up and pinning them in place. By these means, they created a community for which to speak.

REVIVALISM AND DISSENT IN NYANZA

It is in this rhetorical and intellectual context that Luo patriots' fury over the East African Revival can be understood. At a time when activists were organizing the cultural and social foundations for a political community, Revivalists set people against one another. At a time when patriotic census takers were establishing their constituency, revivalists would not stand up and be counted.

Nyanza's people first heard revivalists preach in September 1938 when Anglican missionaries organized a convention at the school in Maseno. Among the speakers was the widely-traveled Ganda evangelist William Nagenda, the Kigezi schoolteacher Ezekieri Balaba, and the Rwandan hospital worker Yosiya Kinuka.[78] Nagenda preached the opening sermon on the theme 'the wages of sin is death.' At the end of the week the head student converted, confessing to fornication, stealing money from his father, and to his abiding anger against the school's matron.[79] By 1944, there were 2,000 revivalists in Nyanza led by a schoolteacher named Ishmael Noo. Even today, elderly men and women remember their manners with astonishment. One of my interviewees described how converts refused to lend cups or plates to non-converts. Their belongings were said to be as 'saved' as their owners, and converts feared that non-converts would use them for sinful purposes. When non-converts visited a convert's home, the homeowner would cleanse the chairs in which his visitors had sat by passing a burning brand over them.[80] Converts refused to hang pictures on their walls, as they were thought to lead people into sin.[81] They refused to take part in funerals, even for their own fathers or mothers. They called the dead 'dry wood,' brushing off their obligations with the saying 'let the dead bury their own dead.'[82] Revivalists preached against polygamy:

---

[78] HMC JEC 1/2: Joe Church to Martin Capon, 30 June 1938. See J. Church, *Quest for the Highest* (Exeter, 1981), 158–9.

[79] HMC JEC 1/2: Joe Church, circular letter, 22 September 1938; Martin Capon to Cecil Bewes, 9 October 1938.

[80] KNA DX 21/9/1: Special Branch to Superintendent of Police, 21 August 1956; interview: Habakuk Abogno, Kisumu town, 20 November 2007.

[81] Interview: Naomi Olweny, Nyayiera, Bondo, 23 November 2007.

[82] Interview: Julia Okumu Mubiri, with Helen Anyang'o, Preska Sewe, and Preska Wajewa, Kisumu town, 24 November 2007.

one of my interviewees remembered how as a child she heard converts parading with trumpets around her home, singing *Nyachira wangdhiyo e mach*, 'The second wife is going to hell.'[83] Other interviewees recounted converts' insulting songs with a dramatic flair: one elderly woman held her hands to her mouth, as if shouting to a megaphone, while singing *Jodoho idong', nyachira idong'* ('The polygamist, you are left behind, the second wife, you are left behind') in imitation of the converts she had heard as a child.[84]

All of this was deeply offensive. But what particularly astounded Nyanza's people was converts' open talk about sex. A missionary was appalled when she attended a service where a revivalist was preaching.[85] He 'tended to dwell on old customs, particularly the immoral ones,' reported the missionary, 'and in the process of condemning them [he] recount[ed] unsavory details.' The sermon reached its climax when the preacher invited the congregation to shout the words 'fornication' and 'brothel' repeatedly. When revivalists held a convention in Nyanza in 1947, two Rwandan evangelists gave testimonies that were 'a bit lurid' in the view of an observer. One of the chief preachers was Lionel Bakewell, the missionary evangelist who had been at the center of the Pentecostal Revival in Bugufi (see Chapter 5). He was said to have 'dwelt rather unnecessarily on the details of his old thought life,' and Kenya's officials talked about expelling Bakewell from the colony for 'lowering European prestige.'[86] A petitioner from Nyanza wrote to the bishop of the Anglican church complaining about a Revival preacher who had used 'rude language during the preaching in the church and upon the inhabitants of the location.' This petitioner worried that the 'ears of the Church attendants could be filled up with unnecessary boastings.'[87]

Revivalists' habits led many people in Nyanza to doubt their moral fiber. Luo people knew that honorable people should build up human communities, not tear them down. Prosperous men lived in mud-walled compounds with their wives and offspring. They could be relied on to distribute food during the periods of famine that periodically gripped Nyanza. The word *duong*, 'greatness, majesty, power, glory,' also meant 'a very big basket'; while the word *luor*, 'honor' and 'glory,' also meant 'to surround.'[88] By their generosity prosperous men drew people together, socially and politically, and earned a favorable reputation. In the 1970s, the anthropologist Ralph Grillo found that the manner in which a Luo man received guests at his city

---

[83] Interview: Lois Achieng' Juma, Tieng're, 22 November 2007.
[84] Interview: Helen Anyang'o, Kisumu, 24 November 2007.
[85] ACK ACSO/CPN/1 'North Nyanza Rural Deanery' file: C. Appleby to Leonard Beecher, 9 March 1952.
[86] MAM AC/2: P. J. Brazier to R. Webster, 4 November 1947.
[87] Kakamega archives DX 8/1: Musumba Ahura to Leonard Beecher, 26 January 1950.
[88] Mill Hill Fathers, *Vocabulary Nilotic-English* (Nyeri, n.d. [1920]).

home was a matter for discussion in the Nyanza countryside.[89] Their generosity was not indiscriminate. Luo people were always careful about who they ate with. When the Luo Thrift and Trading Company opened one of Kisumu's first public restaurants in 1950, it had trouble finding a clientele.[90] The historian Paul Mboya instructed his readers never to dine with criminals or witches. Antisocial men and women were not only bad dining companions, they were morally suspect. The extraordinarily capacious verb *-bodho* meant to 'pick, as in chickens picking at their food,' and to 'scrape with fingers the food out of a pot and lick them.' *Bodho* also meant to 'mispronounce a word'; and in noun form the word meant 'prostitute, adulteress.'[91] An individual's undisciplined eating habits made other people doubt her moral integrity. Luo made themselves into social beings through their eating. They established and sustained their relationships, and their capacity for social agency, around the cooking pot.

Eating together did not in itself create sociable communities. Luo men and women needed to talk, to discourse effectively, in order to work out their relationships. Greedy, self-interested men scraped at the bottom of pots with their fingers. Their locution, like their manners, was undisciplined. The verb *-bomo* meant to 'sputter, speak indistinctly'; it meant also to 'do poorly, to scamp.'[92] Luo people had to be careful about their diction. Anthropologists founds that Luo parents generally did not address garbled baby talk to their youngest babies. They spoke forthrightly to children.[93] Respectable people were artful in their speech, careful of their pronunciation, and effective in what they said. The verb *-riwo* shows what was required. It meant to 'delay, detain,' and to 'tell something with reservation.' In a different form, it also meant to 'be united,' to 'be married,' and to 'merge into each other.'[94] Honorable people held back their words, measured their speech, and minded their manners. By their discretion they allayed petty conflicts and bound communities together.

Revivalists' unrestrained testimonies threw their characters in question. Whereas reputable men and women bound themselves to their relatives around the hearth, converts refused even to share their chairs or teacups with their kin. Whereas honorable men built up communities of wives and children around them, converts insisted on antisocial monogamy.

---

[89] Grillo, *African Railwaymen*, 55.

[90] Oginga Odinga, *Not Yet Uhuru: An Autobiography* (Nairobi, 1967), 86.

[91] Definitions from Mill Hill Fathers, *Vocabulary Nilotic-English*. A recent dictionary offers a similarly capacious definition for *bodho*: in verb form it is to 'scrape food with finger and eat' and 'of a hen pecking at food'; while in adjectival form it is 'an over-sexed person.' Asenath Bole Odaga, *Dholuo-English dictionary* (Kisumu, 2005), 54.

[92] Mill Hill Fathers, *Vocabulary Nilotic-English*.

[93] Ben G. Blount, 'Aspects of Luo Socialization,' *Language in Society* 1 (2) (October 1972), 235–48.

[94] Definitions of *-riwo* and *-riwore* in Mill Hill Fathers, *Vocabulary Nilotic-English*.

Whereas honorable people measured their speech, converts made incendiary accusations about other people. An observer described how at a 1957 convention 'one of the church teachers burst out in the middle of the morning service, walked up to the altar and declared at he was a sinner … Even children from the ages of eight upwards denounced their sins.'[95] One of my interviewees remembered that converts filled their testimonies with trivial details like 'My cat has spilt my milk, but now I have come to the Lord. I saw that woman, and I lusted after that woman, but now the Lord has washed me with the blood.'[96] Naomi Olweny told me how, while living in Nairobi during the mid-1940s, she had been embarrassed by a group of Luo converts.[97] 'They used to walk around in rags,' she remembered, 'and the testimonies they were giving were not pleasant.' There was one man who seemed always to be in her ear. He made a habit of testifying how he formerly frequented prostitutes' lairs. Naomi was so disturbed by the converts' pestering that she left Nairobi and returned to her rural home.

In 1956, revivalists organized a convention in Maseno with 10,000 people in attendance. The leading preacher was Daudi Balamba, the chief of Bugufi (see Chapter 5).[98] Observers reported that at the convention 'there was weeping, and some where physically shaking for their sins.' The most momentous conversion was of the schoolmaster Samuel Ayany. Ayany was one of the architects of Luo patriotism. In 1953, three years before the Maseno convention, he had published the book *Kar Charuok Mar Luo* ('On the Origins of the Luo'), which began by lamenting that 'New ideas are proving very attractive to ordinary folks, forcing them into forgetting totally the culture of their ancestors.'[99] As a historian, Ayany helped to establish the mechanism by which Luo people living at a distance from their rural homeland could learn about traditions, culture, and social discipline (see Chapter 1). But after his conversion, Ayany came to see the past as darkness, not as a source of inspiration. 'I knew that I was walking only by the light of tiny lamps I had made for myself,' he testified at the convention, 'but then came the message "I am the light of the world."'[100] Ayany described how 'The words of the old hymn became very true: "At the Cross … where I first saw the light, and the burden of my heart rolled away."' Like Daudi Balamba, like William Nagenda and other revivalists, the convert Samuel Ayany was modeling his life after *The Pilgrim's Progress*. He was leaving

[95] ACK ACSO/CPN/2 'North Nyanza Rural Deanery, 1952–1960' file: Daudi Udali, 'The North Nyanza Rural Deanery Mission,' 24 October to 17 November 1957.
[96] Interview: Matthew Ajuoga, Kisumu town, 24 November 2007.
[97] Interview: Naomi Monica Olweny, Nyayiera, Bondo, 23 November 2007.
[98] HMC JEC 2/9: Joe Church, 'Evangelistic Journeys, 1956.'
[99] Samuel Ayany, *Kar Charuok Mar Luo* (Nairobi, 1952). The translation is in E. S. Atieno Odhiambo, 'Luo Perspectives on Knowledge and Development.'
[100] HMC JEC 13/4: No author, 'Portraits of People,' 1956.

his benighted homeland, rolling the burden from his back, and traveling a pilgrim's path toward a brighter future.

To many Luo people, revivalists like Samuel Ayany seemed to be advancing themselves at the expense of other people. Converts' words tumbled on top of each other, like a *bodho*, an inarticulate talker, a picky eater, or a prostitute. They showed no discrimination in what they said. At the 1956 convention where Samuel Ayany converted, two laymen testified about the sins that their pastors had committed. Critics accused them of character assassination. 'It appears as though [they] are some CID from the Head Office,' the critics complained.[101] Other critics complained that converts 'cause ill humour and trouble between Christians,' that they 'always keep their collections very secretly to feed their leaders and build their houses,' and that they were 'always judging and forcing out troubled people by themselves.'[102] Converts were hoarding resources for themselves and undermining other people's reputations. Their self-centered immaturity made many Luo people doubt their integrity. Converts in central Nyanza were known collectively as *Jo-Par*, the 'people of the mat.'[103] The name referred to the woven mats, *par*, on which male and female converts were rumored to sleep, naked, while on preaching missions. There were accusations in North Nyanza that revivalist preachers were making other men's wives pregnant.[104] The District Officer reported that revivalists 'have dreams in which they commit adultery with some other person, and then according to the custom of the sect they do so in reality.'[105]

More than sexual deviance was at stake here. The rumors about revivalists' libertine behavior showed them to be antagonists of civil order. In 1955, the District Commissioner interviewed three Luyia elders, who told him that revivalists' 'hand was against all men.'[106] They went on to warn that 'if Government did not crush [the Revival] quickly there was a probability of serious trouble, and a possibility of civil disturbance and violence.' Luyia chiefs were convinced that revivalists were subversives. Chief Osundwa, who governed the Wanga, a Luyia group, concluded that the Revival was 'not compatible with the ethics of the Wanga people.'[107] The Luo chief Paul Mboya agreed about revivalists' unpatriotic character. Mboya was one of the

[101] ACK ACSO/CPN/2 'North Nyanza Rural Deanery' file: Caleb Migele and Alfayo Owiny to Beecher, 12 December 1956.
[102] NMK Leonard Beecher Papers, file 2: J. Ndisi, Rev. J. Nyende, and Rev. S. Okoth et al. to Beecher, 18 July 1957.
[103] Interviews: Fanuel Aguoko Agong'a, Rabuor, 21 November 2007; Habakuk Onyang'o Abogno, Kisumu town, 20 November 2007.
[104] KNA DX 21/9/1: Assistant DC, 'Report of the Committee on African Religious Bodies,' 20 January 1951.
[105] KNA DC Kakamega 1/17/3: DO to DC North Nyanza, 1 November 1954.
[106] KNA DX 21/9/1: DC Mumias, intelligence reports on 'Jolendo,' n.d. (but 1955).
[107] KNA DC Kakamega 1/17/3: Chief Osundwa to DC North Nyanza, 25 October 1954.

architects of Luo culture. In his 1938 history book, Mboya had instructed Luo people about the dangers of amnesia, warning that a forgetful people were doomed to live as vagabonds. A decade later, as government chief in South Nyanza, Mboya convened a public meeting where he condemned revivalists as the 'Anti-Christ,' warning his people not to fall into converts' traps.[108]

It was as defenders of their fatherland that in 1957 the leading critics of the Revival broke away from the Anglican church and established a new organization, called the 'Church of Christ in Africa.'[109] One of the priests who led the secession compared the new church to a 'break to stop the children of God from going astray,' and with 'the immune Dressers whose work is to vaccinate those who are suffering from Small-pox.'[110] Like hospital workers, the leaders of the Church of Christ in Africa were protecting human communities against their mortal enemies. In DhoLuo, members of the church called themselves *Johera*, the 'People of Love.' In a 1957 manifesto, their founder described how revivalists 'soil the church and … inflict ruin upon the souls of Christians.'[111] *Johera* leaders went on a speaking tour throughout Nyanza, comparing the Revival with the corrupted biblical cities of Sodom and Gomorrah.[112] *Johera* clerics highlighted how the revivalists believed 'that the only way to heaven … is by continual confession of sins.'[113] Whereas revivalists peppered their testimonies with trivial details about their private lives, the *Johera* – 'the People of Love' – were circumspect in what they said. One of the leaders of the church, Joshua Gawo, described how *Johera* people would quietly confess their wrongs. 'If you have sinned,' said Gawo, 'you stood and say [gravely] "I have seen on my side that I have done this sin and that sin. And I now pray that God will forgive me."'[114] Like honorable men, the 'People of Love' measured their speech. By their circumspection they joined people together.

Missionaries thought the *Johera* to be a 'cloak concealing an aggressive Luo nationalism,' and termed the church's members 'disrespectable malcontents.'[115] Leading revivalists thought the *Johera* to be akin to 'communism.' 'They are a stiff necked people who can never forgive,' wrote the

[108] Interview: Truphena Obisa Abayo, Masogo, 20 November 2007.
[109] The church's origins are described in detail in F. Welbourn and B. A. Ogot, *A Place to Feel at Home: A Study of Two Independent Churches in Western Kenya* (London, 1966).
[110] NMK Leonard Beecher papers, file 2: Rev. Meshak Owira to Hawse, 27 June 1957.
[111] NMK Leonard Beecher papers, file 2: J. Ndisi, 'Evangelical Revival Movement in the Church,' 18 July 1957.
[112] NMK Leonard Beecher papers, file 2: E. Agola to Beecher, 2 September 1957.
[113] CMS Acc. 392: 'Report of a Meeting Between the Anglican Church and the Christian Church in Africa, held on 15 August 1962.'
[114] Interview: Joshua Aluoch Gawo, Maseno, 23 November 2007.
[115] The first accusation is in NMK Leonard Beecher papers, file 2: Leonard Beecher to Governor of Kenya, 24 January 1958; the second comes from RH Micr. Af. 592: Ralph Leech, circular letter, April 1958.

revivalist Shadrack Osewe in 1957. 'They have sewn the seeds of obstinacy and hatred.'[116] Luo politicians adopted the critics' analysis of the *Johera* but reversed their value judgments. In a 1961 speech delivered before an assembly of Protestant churchmen, Oginga Odinga lauded the *Johera*, arguing that it was a 'significant sign of progress that Africans now had their own church.'[117] The first historians of Kenyan Christianity followed Odinga's lead. Writing in the shade of Kenya's national independence, Frederick Welbourn and Bethwell Ogot argued that the *Johera* represented an indigenization of Christian theology, a 'place to feel at home' for Kenya's people.[118]

In fact, neither theology nor nationalism drove the schism of 1957. The founders of the Christian Church in Africa regarded themselves as more fully Anglican than the Anglicans. In 1958, Matthew Ajuoga, the *Johera*'s leading priest, wrote three times to the Archbishop of Canterbury, asking him to consecrate a bishop to serve the church's members. 'We consider you as an elderly brother in that part of the Church of Christ on earth,' he wrote.[119] The 'People of Love' represented themselves as defenders of Anglican church order, and complained to the archbishop about revivalists' embrace of 'wrong doctrines which were entirely unscriptural.' When the *Johera* applied for membership on Kenya's national council of Protestant churches in 1962, an investigating committee could conclude that the applicants had 'no doctrinal differences' with the Anglicans.[120]

The 'People of Love' did not dispute theology with Anglican missionaries, and neither were they inspired by anti-colonial politics. The new church's energy was derived from the anxiety that Luo landholders felt over their property and their progeny. It was in 1957 – the year that the new church was founded – that the government launched its land consolidation scheme in Nyanza. With surveyors measuring boundaries and inquiring into the ownership of particular tracts of land, Luo landholders found themselves subjected to the arbitrary tyranny of outsiders. Masogo, east of Kisumu, was one of the first regions to be involved in the government's land consolidation program. The chief surveyor was Nathaniel Muga. Not coincidentally, Muga was also a leading revivalist. Like Chief Daudi Balamba of Bugufi, Nathaniel Muga moved fluidly between two registers of accountancy, pioneering new forms of property ownership while also encouraging people to own up to their sins (see Chapter 5). Muga toured the region, adjudicating boundaries and compelling Masogo's people to consolidate their holdings. In ecclesiastical life, too, Muga dictated to other people:

---

[116] NMK Leonard Beecher papers, file 2: S. Osewe to Leonard Beecher, 21 September 1957.

[117] *Taifa Leo*, 10 June 1960. Quoted in Welbourn and Ogot, *A Place to Feel at Home*, 68.

[118] Welbourn and Ogot, *A Place to Feel at Home*.

[119] NMK Leonard Beecher papers, file 2: Matthew Ajuoga to Archbishop of Canterbury, n.d. (but April 1958); Ajuoga to Archbishop of Canterbury, 31 July 1958.

[120] CMS Acc. 392: Standing Committee, Diocese of Maseno, 18 October 1962.

he and other revivalists refused to allow church members who were not converted to take Holy Communion.[121] In his critics' view, Muga was a tyrant. A fistfight broke out when a revivalist insisted the entire congregation at Masogo should sing a Revival hymn.[122] At another Sunday service a junior relative of Nathaniel Muga's interrupted him during the reading of scripture, shouting 'You are spoiling the children.' An angry churchman threatened to beat revivalists with a school form, saying that 'They will not rest until blood is shed.'[123] At the conclusion of the service, a junior relative demanded that Muga should hand over the church offering. In 1957, Masogo became one of many churches that broke away from the Anglican church and declared themselves allied to the *Johera*, the 'People of Love.'[124]

For the angry men of Masogo, as for Luo patriots more generally, revivalists like Nathaniel Muga posed a threat to social reproduction. Like surveyors, revivalists intruded into other people's intimate lives. Like surveyors, revivalists were dictators, whose selfish ambition was to advance themselves at other people's expense. Like surveyors, revivalists tore sociable communities apart. Luo people joined the Church of Christ in Africa to protect their households against outsiders' arbitrary and unanswerable dictates. At Ramula in Central Nyanza, revivalists were largely members of one clan, the Ulolo. Their number included the District Officer and the local chief.[125] One of my interviewees remembered Ramula revivalists' extraordinary exclusivity: they greeted other converts with an embrace, but to non-converts they would not even deign to offer a handshake.[126] To many Ramula people, the Ulolo revivalists seemed to be advancing their clannish interests at other people's expense. In November 1957, Jeremiah Otiende – the landlord on whose property the Anglican church was built – announced that Ramula church would join the *Johera*.[127] He barred revivalists and other Anglicans from attending services at the church building. When the Anglican bishop visited Ramula to conduct a service in 1958, he found that Otiende and his supporters had removed the chairs, the priestly vestments, the vessels of Holy Communion, and the marriage registers. After the service, the bishop was surrounded by what he called a 'hooligan mob' and was compelled

[121] ACK ACSO/CPN/2 'North Nyanza Rural Deanery' file: A. Owinyi and C. Migele to Leonard Beecher, 3 September 1956.
[122] ACK ACSO/CPN/2 'North Nyanza Rural Deanery' file: Secretary Masogo Pastorate to Beecher, 3 July 1956.
[123] NMK Leonard Beecher papers, file 2: H. Rachier to police, 24 October 1957.
[124] NMK Leonard Beecher papers, file 2: E. Agola to Leonard Beecher, 30 October 1957.
[125] KNA DC Kisumu 1/1/23: R. Anjer to DO Ramula, 9 July 1957.
[126] Interview: Habakuk Onyango Abogno, Kisumu town, 20 November 2007.
[127] NMK Leonard Beecher papers, file 2: Ramula Pastorate to Rural Dean, Central Nyanza, 12 November 1957.

to make a hasty escape.[128] At a time when Luo landholders were identifying themselves as indigenes, Jeremiah Otiende was reminding his revivalist tenants of his rights. In 1959 and again in 1960, Otiende tore up the fence surrounding the church plot and planted maize right up to the building's walls.[129] He and other partisans beat the Anglicans who attended the church, blocked the doors, and destroyed the road leading to the churchyard.[130] The District Officer was obliged to post a police guard to protect the Anglican congregation.

The 'People of Love' affirmed Luo householders' authority over their land, their property, and their progeny. At a time when the government's surveyors were obliging Luo people to argue about their rights over land, joining the *Johera* gave landlords like Jeremiah Otiende the authority with which to defend their property against expropriation. At a time when revivalists seemed bent on advancing themselves at other people's expense, the *Johera* affirmed the self-effacing virtues of probity and generosity. The 'People of Love' knit families and communities together in sociable relationships. *Johera* priests made a point of admitting polygamous men and their wives to full church membership. They answered revivalists' insulting hymns with a favorite recruiting song, which went 'The Anglicans take the first wife, but the *Johera* take the second, third and fourth wives.'[131] Whereas converts like Nathaniel Muga seemed to be tearing sociable communities apart, the 'People of Love' built them up. Several of the elderly wives of polygamists I interviewed remembered that *Johera* priests came to their homesteads during the late 1950s, baptizing women and children for fifty cents each.[132] Polygamous men financed the construction of church buildings and paid priests' salaries. The *Johera* church at Nyayiera, in Siaya, was built in 1958 by a man married to eight women.[133]

In their alliances with polygamous men, and in the probity and discretion of their sermons, the 'People of Love' upheld a particular model of conduct. They measured men's and women's maturity by their willingness to defer. Learning from their past, the 'People of Love' regarded kin collectivities as the foundation of moral order. They modeled sociable conduct after the *jaduon'g*, the 'big man,' whose generosity with food and diplomatic abilities knit dependents together in relationships of trust and obligation. Good etiquette was more than an affectation in this moral economy: it was a

---

[128] NMK Leonard Beecher papers, file 2: Leonard Beecher to PC Nyanza, 24 January 1958.
[129] KNA DC Kisumu 1/36/63: D.O. Maseno to DC Kisumu, 17 August 1960.
[130] KNA DC Kisumu 1/36/63: Hezron Rachier to G. Hawes, 22 June 1959; Rachier to DO Maseno, 29 October 1959.
[131] Interview: Eusto Ndege, Masogo, 20 November 2007.
[132] Interview: Preska Wajewa, Preska Sewe, Julia Okumu Mubiri, and Helen Anyang'o, Kisumu, 24 November 2007.
[133] Interview: Naomi Olweny, Nyayiera, 23 November 2007.

critical mark of civic virtue. The 'People of Love' fought against the Revival as defenders of their moral community and as critics of the self-promoting ethos that converts advocated.

The *Johera* vision of sociability proved both attractive and durable. The president of the Ramogi African Welfare Association joined the church, as did the president of the Luo Union.[134] By late 1958, virtually every Luo chief in Nyanza had joined the *Johera*.[135] In that year, the church's leaders controlled some 130 different congregations, with 16,000 members in total. In 1963, the year of Kenya's independence, the CCA counted 50,000 people as members. The church's archbishop, the Rev. Matthew Ajuoga, was president of the Nairobi-based Organization of African Instituted Churches in the 1980s, and in that capacity he played an important role in the enterprise of African theology.[136]

CONCLUSION

Luo patriotism was defined in opposition to the cosmopolitan, mobile world that revivalists, independent women, and other entrepreneurs created. Patriots had to be nativists. They had, that is, to identify their people with a particular tract of territory and convince them to uphold the traditions of their forefathers. There were two engines driving Nyanza's entrepreneurs to define Luo political community in this way. Luo migrants living in eastern Africa's cities knew themselves to be in a contest over moral authority with other men. They burnished their reputations by clarifying traditional values, chastening independent women, and creating welfare associations that upheld discipline. Luo patriotism was powered by male urbanites' politically creative worries over their conjugal lives. Land politics was a second engine for cultural innovation. Luo entrepreneurs represented themselves as autochthons because they needed the means to establish themselves on the landscape. As landholders and as moral reformers, Luo patriots had to name a geographic, cultural, and human patrimony that was identifiably theirs. They had, that is, to curb constituents' appetites, limit their movements, discipline their passions, and put them into alignment. Their research into history helped them define patriotic behavior and gave them the grounds on which to create a political community.

Luo converts were subversives because they would not stay in place. By hoarding their possessions, by their embarrassing testimonies, and by their

[134] Interview: Doris Achola Nyawara, Tieng're, 22 November 2007.

[135] ACK ACSO/CPN/2 'South Nyanza Rural Deanery' file: Bostock to Minister of African Affairs, 16 September 1958.

[136] See George F. Pickens, *African Christian God-Talk: Matthew Ajuoga's Johera Narrative* (Dallas, 2004). More generally, see Paul Gifford, *Christianity, Politics, and Public Life in Kenya* (London, 2009).

self-righteous denunciations of other people, they put distance between themselves and their kin. Whereas patriots were rooting their people in hierarchical, loving communities, converts propelled themselves forward toward another world. The Revival was controversial because its converts would not make their homes in a Luo *patria*.

7

The Cultural Work of Moral Reform in Northwestern Tanganyika

In 1950, two angry men from the Nairobi offices of the Haya Union wrote to the District Commissioner complaining about the Haya women who worked as prostitutes in their city. Women from Bukoba, in Tanganyika's northwestern corner, were postwar eastern Africa's most visible sex workers, practicing their trade in a manner that was both aggressive and profitable.[1] The assertive women scorned the men of the Haya Union, calling them *Bajubi*, 'fishermen,' country bumpkins.[2] The men of the Haya Union replied by castigating sex workers for their unpatriotic behavior. 'All prostitutes are against their parents as well as our home Government,' the petitioners wrote. 'We find them as abusers, shamers, scorners, blamers, uprooters of our nation Buhaya.' Another memoirist, writing from Tanganyika, agreed that sex workers shamed Haya polity. 'Prostitutes bring dangers to our country of Beauty, Land of Sunshine,' he wrote. He hoped that the local government would join the fight against the 'communism' of prostitution, 'before the whole world falls into the danger of starvation, Horrible Crime and even more spreading of every kind of infectious disease.'[3] For the patriots of the Haya Union, prostitution was more than an individual's moral failing. It was a political problem, a treasonous threat to the Haya community.

In no other state in Africa has nationalism exercised a stronger hold on historians' minds than in Tanzania. Published in 1979, John Iliffe's *A Modern History of Tanganyika* was the foundational book, 616 pages in all.[4] Working from research conducted shortly after the opening of the Tanzania National Archives, Iliffe described how new educational opportunities and new

---

[1] Luise White, *The Comforts of Home: Prostitution in Colonial Nairobi* (Chicago, 1990), chapter 5.

[2] TNA Acc. 71 790B: Burchard Kagaro and Sirdion Ndyeshobora to DC Bukoba, 8 September 1950.

[3] TNA Acc. 71 790B: A. J. Kweigira to Bakama of Buhaya, 1 August 1950.

[4] John Iliffe, *A Modern History of Tanganyika* (Cambridge, 1979).

economic realities obliged Africans to create a new, larger-scale political community. The protagonist in Iliffe's book was the Tanganyika African National Union (TANU), the political party that defined Tanganyika's nationalism. Subsequent generations of historians have expanded John Iliffe's storyline. Whereas Iliffe focused on male activists, *TANU Women* highlighted the role that female activists played in the articulation of Tanzanian nationalism.[5] Whereas Iliffe thought nationalism to be a project that welded Tanganyika's disparate people together, *A History of the Excluded* showed how people living in Tanzania's southern highlands defended the 'private sphere' of family life against nationalists' oversight.[6] Whereas Iliffe thought Tanganyika's liberal politics had reached their apotheosis with national independence in 1961, *In Search of a Nation* showed how the colonial state imparted its authoritarian tendencies to its post-colonial successor.[7] The revisionists largely worked on John Iliffe's terrain, coordinating their analyses around the geographical boundaries of Tanganyika Territory. Their aim was to show how women, peasants, and other marginal groups experienced and participated in the making of Tanganyika's nationalism.

But not everyone in Tanganyika was acting in the same theater. Even as Julius Nyerere and other organizers marshaled the diverse people living in Tanganyika, even as TANU activists argued with British administrators over the prospect of majority rule, Haya thinkers were looking across political boundaries and engaging in a regional debate about independent women. Many of their conversation partners lived outside Tanganyika. In western Kenya, Luo patriots were configuring their history and their culture in a patriarchal fashion. Through their cultural and political work they clamped down on independent women, and formed their people into an effective political constituency (see Chapter 6). Haya men studied the Luo Union's methods. They also learned from the Buganda kingdom's parliament, which in 1941 had adopted the draconian 'Law to Prevent Prostitution' (see Chapter 4).[8] Haya men's sources of reference and inspiration were not defined by Tanganyika's borders. These men were positioning themselves in a discourse about patriotism and women's morality that spanned eastern and central Africa.

Neither were Haya patriots' ambitions solely focused on the liberal goal of national self-government. Haya men knew themselves to be in a contest not only for electoral representation but also for moral authority. The men of the Haya Union were terrified about women's sexual independence

[5] Susan Geiger, *TANU Women: Gender and Culture in the Making of Tanganyikan Nationalism* (Portsmouth, NH, 1997), 15.
[6] James Giblin, *A History of the Excluded: Making Family a Refuge from State in Twentieth Century Tanzania* (Oxford, 2005).
[7] Gregory H. Maddox and James L. Giblin, eds., *In Search of a Nation: Histories of Authority and Dissidence in Tanzania* (Oxford, 2006).
[8] Kingdom of Buganda, *The Native Laws of Buganda* (Kampala, 1947), 6, 8.

because – like their Luo contemporaries – they regarded eastern Africa's political space as a theater of examination, where other men sat in judgment on their virility and respectability. The public sphere in which Haya moralists sought a voice was an arena of masculine self-assertion, a place where husbands and fathers needed first to take hold over their families before they could earn a hearing from other men. In Bukoba, as in other parts of interlacustrine central Africa, the history of gender relations must be studied alongside political history. For Haya patriots, the reform of conjugality, sexuality, and manners was never a diversion from the real work of politics. Like the men of the Luo Union, Haya patriots sought to enter into the public sphere as members of a credible moral community.

This chapter offers a genealogy of Haya men's discourse about prostitution. The focus is not on the history of sex work itself, but on Haya patriots' political thought. Male city-dwellers were embarrassed by Haya sex workers' loud business. In petitions, correspondence, and other media, they contrasted Haya people's traditional virtues with prostitutes' unpatriotic behavior. By this means, men positioned themselves as spokesmen for an offended Haya polity. Although patriots cast themselves as defenders of a traditional way of life, their social and political program was in fact quite novel. Conservative reformers created new institutions and brought new measures of human identity into being. They sought to fix mobile women in place, using bureaucratic procedures to transform assertive, independent women into hard working, upstanding wives. Their reformist activity shaped the conduct of government and established techniques of population control for the post-colonial Tanzanian state to adopt.

SHAME AND CONSERVATIVE REFORM IN BUKOBA

Haya people's political culture was formed by agronomy, by the claustrophobia-inducing density of human population supported on their rich banana gardens (see Map 3). The sandstone ridges lying to the southwest of Lake Victoria yield a difficult soil, deficient in plant nutrients.[9] Left in its natural state, the land can support harvests once every few years. In the late seventeenth and eighteenth centuries, Haya farmers began to build up fertile gardens by scouring the scrubland for mulch.[10] Even when fortified with

[9] G. Milne, 'Bukoba: High and Low Fertility on a Laterized Soil,' *East African Agricultural Journal* 4 (1938), 13–24; D. N. McMaster, 'Change of Regional Balance in the Bukoba District of Tanganyika,' *Geographical Review* 50 (1960), 73–88.

[10] Cory file 19: A. Culwick, 'Land Tenure in the Bukoba District,' 14 March 1939; Peter Schmidt, 'Archaeological Views on a History of Landscape Change in East Africa,' *Journal of African History* 38 (3) (1997), 393–421. The history of banana farming beside Lake Victoria over the *longue durée* is given in David Schoenbrun, *A Green Place, a Good Place: Agrarian Change, Gender, and Social Identity in the Great Lakes Region to the 15th Century* (Portsmouth, 1998), 172–84.

manure provided by cattle-keepers, it took as long as seven years to estab-lish the soil's fertility. On the productive islands they created, Haya farmers planted bananas, a calorie-rich perennial crop. The nutritional momentum that banana cultivation gave to Buhaya's population allowed its people to sustain an extraordinarily dense pattern of settlement. In some localities farmers were able to support themselves with as little as three-quarters of an acre of farming land.[11] By 1957, the banana-rich land near the lake shore supported as many as 1,250 people per square mile.[12]

Living cheek to jowl on islands of fertile soil, Haya farmers had to guard their privacy against neighbors' prying eyes. Haya people were by no means unique in their concern over privacy: in Buganda, elites desperately sought to keep their embarrassing affairs secret, and in Kigezi, women refused even to mention their husbands' names in public (see Chapters 3 and 4). Eastern Africa's people valued the discipline of discretion. Haya farms were partic-ularly claustrophobic, and with their neighbors breathing down their necks, householders came to regard decorum in spatial terms. In the Haya lan-guage, 'private matters' were called *eby'omunda*, literally 'inside matters,' while public affairs were called *eby'aheru*, 'matters of outside.'[13] Haya peo-ple habitually ate meals with the doors and windows of their houses care-fully closed, sometimes erecting large screens around the house itself.[14] Kings dined entirely alone.[15] Sexual life, like eating, was kept from public view. A newly married woman was sequestered in the back rooms of her house for as long as six months, hidden from outsiders' gaze by a wicker screen.[16] Noble women closeted themselves for most of their lives.[17] Respectable peo-ple in Buhaya fenced their private affairs off from the public eye. In the Haya language, a 'prostitute' was a *nyailya*, someone who 'eats here and there.'[18] Prostitutes were indiscriminate about their dining habits and about their sexual lives. Their prolificacy contrasted with the decorum with which respectable people ordered their surroundings.

To be visible was to be available, subject to other people's oversight. In the eighteenth century, Haya farmers had been made subjects of an immigrant nobility. They called themselves *Bahinda*, after their legend-ary forefather Ruhinda, a son of the ancient *Cwezi* kings of western

[11] TNA Acc. 289 14/2 vol. IV: Agriculture Officer, monthly report, 31 July 1946.
[12] Priscilla Reining, 'Haya Land Tenure: Landholding and Tenancy,' *Anthropological Quarterly* 35 (1962), 58–73.
[13] Peter Seitel, 'Blocking the Wind: A Haya Folktale and an Interpretation,' *Western Folklore* 26 (3) (1977), 199.
[14] Brad Weiss, *The Making and Unmaking of the Haya Lived World: Consumption, Commodification, and Everyday Practice* (Durham, 1996), 107.
[15] E. K. Lumley, *Forgotten Mandate: A British District Officer in Tanganyika* (London, 1976), 144.
[16] Seitel, 'Blocking the wind,' 190–91.
[17] ELCT Box E 1 a:2, file a: Superintendent Bethel Mission to DO Bukoba, 12 July 1940.
[18] Cory file 284: Haya glossary, n.d. (ca. 1946).

Uganda.[19] German and, later, British colonizers recognized eight Haya king-doms and made their rulers into functionaries of the colonial state, paid out of the tax that subjects were obliged to render.[20] In 1925, farmers in pros-perous Kianja paid their ruler 54,000 shillings per annum, more than the British Senior Commissioner's salary.[21] It was more than taxes that upheld kings' authority. Haya kings' power was articulated, and felt, through the medium of visuality. Kings masked their eyes with strings of pearls sus-pended from their foreheads, as their gaze was thought to be overpow-eringly dangerous. In Karagwe, the westernmost of Buhaya's kingdoms, Lutheran missionaries reported that every month, at the dying of the moon, the king went into hiding. Fires were extinguished, work ceased, and people spent three days in mourning. When the sickle of the new moon appeared, the king reemerged, and Haya people gathered to welcome him, bathed in moonlight and visible to his eye.[22] To *habuka* was to 'welcome' or venerate a king; it was also to 'appear,' to make oneself see-able.[23] When greeting their kings, Haya men called out *Kaboneka waitu!*, 'Visible our lord!,' or 'At your disposal!.'[24] European observers sometimes mocked Haya sub-jects for their obeisance. The anthropologist Arthur Culwick described how crowds would wait outside beer shops for their king to make his public appearance.

When at length the great man comes forth – he wishes to expectorate – shouts of Abuka! Abuka! go up. He is given fantastic titles: his decrepit body is likened to a lion, his sour expression to the moon, and he is thanked by his kneeling people for having favoured them with his bleary look. He takes no notice whatsoever, and goes inside again for another drink.[25]

Culwick thought public assemblies like these highlighted Haya people's thralldom to unworthy men. But the people who knelt before their kings were not helots, and neither were they deluded. In their gatherings before their kings, Haya people were opening themselves up to political authorities. They were stepping out from behind the screens that separated them from their neighbors, and constituting themselves as a public. Haya political com-munity was made through its visibility.

---

[19] The history of the Bahinda is discussed in Jean-Pierre Chrétien, *The Great Lakes of Africa: Two Thousand Years of History* (New York, 2003), 108–11.

[20] For which, see Ralph Austen, *Northwest Tanzania under German and British Rule: Colonial Policy and Tribal Politics, 1889–1939* (New Haven, 1968); Israel Katoke, *The Making of the Karagwe Kingdom* (Dar es Salaam, 1970); and Iliffe, *Modern History*, 24–25.

[21] TNA AB/40: Bukoba District Annual Report, 1925.

[22] Described in Finn Allan Ellerbek, *Karagwe Diocese: A Lutheran Church History, As Seen and Studied by a Missionary* (Copenhagen, 1992), 20–22.

[23] Cory file 12: Paul Betbeder and John Jones, 'A Handbook of the Haya Language' (Bukoba, 1949).

[24] Weiss, *Making and Unmaking*, 122.

[25] Cory file 239: Arthur Culwick, 'The Population Problem in Bukoba District,' 1938.

Haya householders learned a stern personal discipline from the partitions that they erected between cloistered private space and the open, light-filled public sphere. Householders sought to keep family affairs quiet, closing their mouths in public and keeping their voices low. The verb -*okwekomya* was both 'well-being' and 'to make one's self bound.'[26] Healthy people contained themselves. The inspector at Buhaya's girls' school noted that the chief challenge that his teachers faced was to convince students to speak with sufficient volume as to be audible.[27] When a British official interviewed a new bride in his office in the 1940s, he was obliged to communicate through the woman's sister-in-law. The bride kept her head averted throughout the interview, never allowing her interviewer to see her face.[28] Proverbs reminded Haya about the need to keep their affairs to themselves. 'When you have a load you should never try to unload it onto another person,' one proverb advised.[29] Respectable people kept their private lives under wraps.

In the late 1930s, Haya women began to travel to the cities of Nairobi, Dar es Salaam, and Kampala to become sex workers. They had little time for polite convention. Haya women pioneered a new form of sex work, called *wazi wazi*, that was bold and aggressive in character: they worked in public, calling out to prospective johns and haggling over a price.[30] In the Swahili language *wazi* means 'bare,' 'naked,' or 'open,' available for other people's disposal. Their contemporaries commented on the voluble nature of their work. Tabitha Waweru, a Gikuyu woman who worked as a prostitute in Nairobi during the 1930s, remembered that Haya women 'used to call out to men walking by … They used to call out "Come here, come here!" and some of them became very rich.'[31] While conducting research on urban life in Kampala during the 1950s, the sociologists Aidan Southall and Peter Gutkind were impressed at Haya women's volubility. Whereas Ganda women refused to discuss their prices or their biographies, Haya sex workers talked at great length about the most intimate aspects of their business.[32]

Noisy *wazi wazi* prostitutes were absolutely open about their trade. To horrified Haya men, they seemed to be everywhere. In 1945, a Haya soldier based in Nairobi reported that he had seen Haya prostitutes 'on every corner of a station, in every bed place near soldiers' camp.'[33] The prostitutes were

---

[26] Weiss, *Making and Unmaking*, 184.
[27] Cited in Birgitta Larsson, *Conversion to Greater Freedom? Women, Church and Social Change in North-Western Tanzania under Colonial Rule* (Stockholm, 1991), 190.
[28] Lumley, *Forgotten Mandate*, 161.
[29] Hellen Byera Nestor, *500 Haya Proverbs* (Mwanza, 1978), 6, 57.
[30] Described in White, *Comforts of Home*, chapter 5.
[31] Quoted in White, *Comforts of Home*, 117.
[32] A. W. Southall and P. Gutkind, *Townsmen in the Making: Kampala and its Suburbs* (Kampala, 1957), 86.
[33] Rwamishenye archives, Box 18, 'Rwamishenye' file: A. Godfred to District Commissioner, 12 November 1945.

so numerous that this petitioner thought Nairobi to be 'the Headquarters of Buhaya.' In Mombasa, on the Kenyan coast, Haya sex workers far out-numbered Haya men. Their contributions underwrote the budget for the 'Waziba Union,' a welfare organization for men and women from northwest Tanganyika.[34] In Dar es Salaam, missionaries estimated that 70 to 80 percent of the city's sex workers were from Haya country.[35] In Kisumu, in western Kenya, an observer reported that Haya sex workers had opened houses that operated according to a strict schedule.[36] One shift attended to customers from morning to afternoon, and another shift worked from afternoon into the night. Each shift had a clerk who recorded the number of customers that each woman served. The women were paid a commission based on their rate of work. In Kampala, by contrast, Haya prostitutes worked on their own, renting private rooms where they conducted their trade. Prostitutes saved considerable sums. One 20-year-old woman claimed to save thirty shillings per month, at a time when the average laborer earned from ten to fourteen shillings.[37]

How did Haya women come to dominate postwar eastern Africa's sex trade? In its own time, the cause of Haya prostitution was a subject of argument. Haya politicians blamed the problem on British men's promiscuity. 'Its source is attached to the coming of the European, and particularly the British rule,' wrote members of the Haya Union in a 1951 petition to the British government. Under cover of their 'assumed high morals,' British men had lured Haya women into their homes, fathered children with them, and then abandoned them. Cast out on their own resources, women had no choice but to become prostitutes.[38] This partisan version of history was meant to make British officials feel responsible for ending the prostitution problem. Other commentators blamed prostitution on Haya men's greed. Lutheran missionary Bengt Sundkler argued that the worldwide collapse of coffee prices in the 1930s had made Haya husbands desperate for cash. With creditors at the door, husbands divorced their wives and reclaimed the bridewealth they had paid to their fathers in law. Facing ruin, fathers invited their divorced daughters to take up the business of prostitution in order to refinance their failing coffee farms. Thus, argued Sundkler, Haya prostitutes were in fact dutiful daughters, willingly following their fathers' directions.[39]

---

[34] TNA Acc. 71 790B: Municipal African Affairs Officer to PC Mombasa, 3 October 1951.

[35] Holger Benettsson, 'Från Polygami till Prostitution,' *Nordisk Missionstidskrift* 1 (1953), 2–32. Quoted in Larsson, *Conversion to Greater Freedom?*, 132.

[36] Mwanza archives, Bukoba acc., L5/II/B: Bigirwa Komwiyangiro to Secretary, Buhaya Council, 3 July 1961.

[37] Southall and Gutkind, *Townsmen in the Making*, 81. The average wage rate is given in CoU 02 Bp 58/4: Bishop of Uganda, 'The Atlantic Charter and Uganda,' n.d.

[38] Mwanza archives, Acc. 1 A9/4: Haya Union to Secretary of State for the Colonies, 12 August 1951.

[39] CoU 'Marriage, 1931–45' file: Bengt Sundkler, 'Marriage Problems in the Church in Tanganyika,' July 1944. Luise White adopts Sundkler's line of interpretation in her *Comforts of Home*, 112–13.

Their differences notwithstanding, the missionary Sundkler and the men of the Haya Union agreed that prostitution was an extremity that degraded women reached through men's connivance. Because they thought prostitution to be a social pathology, Sunkler and the Haya patriots made it hard to see how sex work related to the broader dynamics of Haya conjugality. Sexual entrepreneurship was one of several routes by which Haya wives could find their way out of unwanted marriages. Haya people's marriages were short-term and sequential in character: one survey found that only 40 percent of women aged thirty to thirty-nine years were still married to their first husband.[40] The 1945 code of customary law was capacious in the provisions it made for divorce. Husbands could divorce wives who neglected their conjugal duties; women descended from spirit mediums could apply for a divorce in order to pursue their hereditary profession.[41] The Lutheran church's marriage committee similarly recognized a wide range of reasons for divorce. In the 1940s, 60 to 70 percent of the cases brought before the Lutheran church council were appeals for divorce.[42] One woman ran away from her husband's home on three occasions and was found to have committed adultery twice. The committee instructed the husband to divorce his wife.[43] The schoolteacher Joel Lutatelemuka obtained a divorce when his wife 'changed her behaviour, and now she is lazy and doesn't want to cultivate.' Lutatelemuka further complained that his wife was an adulteress, who 'walks with men who are without honour.'[44] Haya women took sexual liberties, formed alliances with other men, and put distance between themselves and their husbands. These exit strategies were endorsed by Bukoba's courts, which were quick to grant divorces, even to Christian couples.

Marriage in Buhaya was not a stable relationship. Haya women asserted themselves through their sexual labor. Their independence became a political controversy when, in the 1940s, Haya men began to travel to eastern Africa's cities to serve in the army. Across eastern Africa, conservatives in the 1940s were writing editorials, reformulating legal codes, and founding political associations that curbed independent women's behavior (see Chapters 1 and 6). The newspapers of Nairobi and Dar es Salaam were full of editorials decrying prostitutes' indiscriminate promiscuity.[45] But Haya soldiers did not

---

[40] W. Laurie and H. Trant, 'A Health Survey of Bukoba District,' *East African Medical Survey Monograph* 2 (Nairobi, 1954), cited in Larsson, *Conversion to Greater Freedom*, 104. The anthropologist Priscilla Reining found that some 60 percent of the men she interviewed in the early 1950s had been married more than once. For which, see Cory file 373: Audrey Richards and Priscilla Reining, 'Report on Fertility Surveys in Buganda and Buhaya,' 1952.

[41] Cory file 100: Hans Cory, 'Haya Customary Law' (1945), chapter 3.

[42] CoU 'Marriage, 1931–45' file: Bengt Sundkler, 'Marriage Problems in the Church in Tanganyika,' July 1944.

[43] ELCT Box AX 1: Marriage Committee minutes, 30 December 1953.

[44] ELCT Box E II f:1: John Lutatelemuka to Chair, Marriage Committee, 4 March 1967.

[45] James Brennan, 'Realizing Civilization Through Patrilineal Descent: The Intellectual Making of an African Racial Nationalism in Tanzania, 1920–50,' *Social Identities* 12 (4) (2006), 405–23.

need to read the newspapers to recognize prostitution as a pressing problem. In their densely packed barracks and on the streets of eastern Africa's cities, Haya men found themselves enclosed in a competitive masculine world. The shame they felt at Haya women's conduct was immediate and visceral. Corporal Arbor Godfred, posted to Nairobi with the King's African Rifles, described his embarrassment in a woeful letter to Buhaya's local government. 'I often die when hearing *Wasibota tata?* [How are you, brother?] which word is from time to time repeated by soldiers who by the means of Haya harlots have been familiar with us,' he wrote.[46] Haya soldiers were offended at their neighbors' jibes. Private Muhamed Bugoya described how Haya girls stood on Nairobi's street corners, soliciting soldiers for sex. 'I am very sorry when I hear my fellow soldiers insulting Haya, they say *Bahaya hawana haya* [Haya people don't feel shame],' he wrote.[47] His persecutors boasted of how their own wives had remained at home, faithfully caring for their families. Haya husbands, by contrast, could not rely on their wives. Their inability to control their women made it easy for other men to mock their virility. 'They laugh at us and joke that we can't play with women, we can't enter their vaginas,' wrote Bugoya.

Ironically, Private Bugoya's adversaries were probably Luo men from western Kenya. Luo laborers were Haya prostitutes' most frequent customers, because sex workers from other parts of eastern Africa were disinclined to cultivate an uncircumcised clientele.[48] Even as Luo husbands fretted over the loyalties of their own wives and daughters, even as the Luo Union and the Ramogi African Welfare Association conducted their war against female delinquency (see Chapter 6), boisterous Luo men were loudly insulting their Haya contemporaries. Their offensive jokes embarrassed men like Private Bugoya, making him feel complicit in the degradation of Haya womanhood. Regardless of their moral stature, notwithstanding their sexual potency, Haya men found themselves to be the objects of other men's humor. This ribaldry compelled Haya men to defend their ethnic community. One petitioner complained how, when riding in public transportation, Luo men 'call us brothers-in-law and impotent.'[49] Another petitioner described how, when drinking in bars, 'we normally heard other men talk to each other, one would say "Let me drink a lot so that I can screw them hard." When we feel such statements we feel ashamed.'[50] In buses and in

---

[46] Rwamishenye archives, Box 18, 'Rwamishenye' file: A. Godfred to District Commissioner, 12 November 1945.

[47] Rwamishenye archives, Box 18, 'Rwamishenye' file: Pvt. Muhamed Bugoya to DC Buhaya, 12 April 1944.

[48] White, *Comforts of Home*, 109.

[49] Mwanza archives, Bukoba acc., L5/II/B: Paul Lwejuna to Secretary, Buhaya Council, n.d. (but 1961).

[50] Mwanza archives, Bukoba acc., L5/II/B: Bigira Komwiyangiro to Secretary, Buhaya Council, 3 July 1961.

bars Haya men endured other men's scorn, and found themselves lumped, willy-nilly, into a Haya collectivity. A schoolteacher in Kampala described how a certain Haya woman had agreed to act as a white photographer's pornographic model. 'This shame penetrated to every Haya,' he wrote.[51] Another correspondent was ashamed at a newspaper report that described 'the way those prostitutes undress and disgrace themselves in bars in Dar es Salaam.'[52] Neither the newspaper reader nor the schoolteacher had actually met the women whose behavior embarrassed them. What aroused their shame, and fueled their indignation, was the sense of responsibility they bore. 'We Haya have to unite so as to fight against this problem,' wrote a petitioner.[53] Haya patriots were created out of their shared experience of shame. The embarrassment they felt was the drill sergeant driving Haya men to join a political project.

Their patriotism was fueled by what Haya people thought to be an impending demographic crisis. The Oxford-trained anthropologist Arthur Culwick published his essay on the 'Population Problem in Bukoba District' in 1938.[54] Culwick reported that the Haya population was not reproducing itself: the reproduction rate was 81.5 percent, meaning that population was decreasing each year. Culwick blamed the problem on venereal disease, which made it hard for Haya women to bear children in sufficient numbers. He was sure that Haya women's loose morals were primarily to blame, because 'almost all Haya women can be induced by the payment of sixpence to sleep with almost any man.' Culwick's gloomy predictions were soon proven to be baseless. In 1951, another anthropologist found that Buhaya's population had for many years increased by 0.9 percent annually.[55] But whether or not they were correct, Culwick's statistics played an important role in shaping Haya people's assessment of their collective future. His gloomy analysis became the subject of innumerable sermons about the need for moral reform in Buhaya. The District Agriculture Officer toured the district 'banging the big drum of falling fertility,' telling his audiences about 'human population halved in 25 years; cattle dropped from 300,000 to 60,000; bananas yielding only 30 percent of previous production.'[56] Haya memoirists wrote to the Secretary of State for the Colonies claiming that prostitution 'has a direct danger on reducing the population of the country in a very short time, and in the long

---

[51] Mwanza archives, Bukoba acc., L5/II/B: Yusto Balubuka to Secretary, Buhaya Council, n.d. (but 1961).

[52] Mwanza archives, Bukoba acc., L5/II/B: Ernest Ndyetukiba to Secretary, Buhaya Council, 25 June 1961.

[53] Mwanza archives, Bukoba acc., L5/II/B: Yunus Sulemami to Secretary, 7 July 1961.

[54] Cory file 239: Arthur Culwick, 'The Population Problem in the Bukoba District,' 1938.

[55] Cory file 373: Audrey Richards and Priscilla Reining, 'Report on Fertility Surveys in Buganda and Buhaya,' 1952; see also Mwanza archives, Acc. 1 2937: Bukoba District Annual Report, 1954.

[56] TNA Acc. 289 14/2 Vol. VI: District Agriculture Officer safari diary, February 1950.

run it will exterminate the tribe.'[57] The memoirists compared themselves with the 'poor Black fellows of Australia and the Red Indians of America who, under natural ignorance, could not realize their fate,' and with 'the late Paleolithic and Neolithic sub-men who were wiped out by the bitter cold of the Ice Age and completely disappeared.' Like aborigines, Native Americans, and the Neanderthals, Haya people seemed doomed to disappear.

Haya patriots worried that they were an endangered people. Prostitution was in their view the leading threat to Haya people's progeny. One petitioner decried the fact that

Many women throw away their children, others do abortions so as to be free to continue with prostitution, for this they cause the lowering of the number of citizens shamefully. Prostitution minimizes generations ... Prostitutes don't engage in any economic activity when they get back home. They like to go for a walk, drink, and enjoy but they eat what they did not produce, they don't produce food to cover what is already used. Buhaya society feeds people who sit idle and don't work, so prostitutes cause hunger in our societies.[58]

Other correspondents similarly cast the prostitution problem in a Malthusian light. One man lamented how prostitutes 'like to eat other people's calories. They don't think of farming and add to the stock of food which is the foundation of good health.'[59] Haya conservatives valorized rural life, contrasting prostitutes' turpitude with the productive labor that men and women did on the land.

In 1950, the Haya Union put forward a program of rules that inhibited women's freedom of movement. They argued that they were defending the Haya commonwealth. The Union had been created in 1924. Clerks and school teachers dominated its membership rolls.[60] Much of the organizational work was done by coffee traders whose wide-ranging networks gave the Union a base from which to draw support.[61] Under the rules the Union adopted in 1950, any woman who wished to leave Bukoba had to produce a certificate of marriage signed and stamped by the chief of her location.[62] Union representatives set up tables at the dock at Lake Victoria, where they checked the papers of women who wished to board the lake steamer. The Union had no legal authority to enforce these movement

[57] Mwanza archives, Acc. 1 A9/4: Haya Union to Secretary of State for the Colonies, 12 August 1951.

[58] Mwanza archives, Bukoba acc., L5/II/B: Yusto Balubuka to Secretary, Buhaya Council, n.d. (but 1961).

[59] Mwanza archives, Bukoba acc., L5/II/B: Ayub Said to Secretary, Buhaya Council, 19 July 1961.

[60] TNA Acc. 215 21: Senior Commissioner Bukoba to Chief Secretary, 18 August 1924.

[61] Ali Migeyo, a dealer in meat and in coffee, was the Union's chief organizer in Kiziba kingdom. The Union's president in the 1930s, Clement Kiiza, was one of Bukoba's chief coffee marketers. See G. Mutabaha, *Portrait of a Nationalist: the Life of Ali Migeyo* (Nairobi, 1969).

[62] TNA Acc. 71 790B: 'Utaratibu wa Kuzuia Utoro wa Wanawake wa Kihaya,' 6 June 1950.

restrictions.[63] But for almost a year, the District Commissioner required African women to submit their travel plans to the Union for approval. If a woman managed to leave Bukoba without the Union's permission, her family was punished.[64] Even local government authorities were subjected to the Unionists' discipline. When a young woman left for Dar es Salaam against her father's wishes in 1950, angry Unionists assembled outside the sub-chief's residence, accusing him of abetting prostitution. The terrified chief fled to the District Commissioner, pleading for police protection against his accusers.[65] By April 1951, ten months after the start of the program, Unionists had issued passes to 466 women for travel outside Bukoba.[66] They were convinced that their initiative had strengthened 'family peace and marriage ties respectively.' The kings of Bukoba agreed, describing how, under the new regime, 'a person believes that if he goes out for work or travel he will meet with his wife [when he returns].'[67]

Not everyone agreed that the Haya Union's rules were in the public interest. In a series of petitions, Haya women argued that profligate, self-indulgent husbands, not independent women, were endangering Haya people's collective future. 'It is difficult to talk about our lives together with men,' Geraldina Lutaibuza told the District Officer in a 1950 petition. Lutaibuza scorned men for their moral lassitude. The 'drunkards don't know how to take care of the plantations they have got from their fathers,' she wrote. 'When he sells coffee he divides up the shillings into two parts – to get drunk and to give to someone ... for fornication.' With the evidence of men's many failings in view, Lutaibuza argued that it was female sex workers, not lazy, good-for-nothing men, who had their people's best interests in mind. Sex workers used their cash earnings for public-spirited purposes. 'When we return home,' she wrote, 'we buy the plantations' that men had ignored. Without women's money, the plantations 'would otherwise have been taken by foreigners and tribes outside Bukoba.' Lutaibuza was arguing that sex work was a patriotic public service, a means by which women protected Haya farms from outsiders' clutches. 'Our fathers and our husbands ought to thank us' for these investments, Lutaibuza concluded.[68]

Lutaibuza's defense of prostitution was by no means idiosyncratic. It reflected a larger, controversial consensus in Buhaya. Sex work was a lucrative business: considerably more money came into Buhaya from prostitution

[63] TNA Acc. 71 790B: PC Lake to DC Bukoba, 3 June 1950.
[64] TNA Acc. 71 790B: Nestor Kabengula to DC Bukoba, 27 December 1950.
[65] Described in Tim Harris, *Donkey's Gratitude: Twenty Two Years in the Growth of a New African Nation—Tanzania* (Edinburgh, 1992), 262–63.
[66] TNA Acc. 71 790B: Bakama Office to Secretariat, 2 April 1951.
[67] TNA Acc. 71 790B: Bwogi III, Ruhinda, and several others to the Haya Union, 25 July 1950.
[68] TNA Acc. 71 790B: Geraldina Lutaibuza et al. to District Officer, Bukoba, 30 November 1950.

than from cash crops.[69] A missionary described the Haya sex worker as 'a respected person in society. When she returns from the city, feasts are arranged in her honour.' These celebrations, the missionary averred, were for a person of consequence, 'who is dressed according to the latest fashion and has got money in her bank account.'[70] Haya conservatives castigated prostitutes as antagonists of social order, but they also recognized how many people profited from their work. M. Mujwahuzi's work titled 'To Put Buhaya on the Right Path' ridiculed fathers who knowingly profited from the labors of their daughters in Nairobi and Dar es Salaam:

When she comes from Nairobi she finds you at the pier together with your wife and in laws waiting for her, and you say 'Welcome my dear daughter.' You go the whole way dancing while you personally carry some of her belongings on your head, while she walks boisterously brandishing her shoes. Who has ever seen a daughter making her sisters-in-law, mothers and fathers carry her things![71]

Many parents must have welcomed their daughters back from the city. One critic described how when parents 'hear that their children are about to come they prepare the local brew to welcome them happily,' and carried their baggage from the port.[72] Some parents provisioned their daughters with beans, groundnuts, and maize flour when they left for the city.[73] Angry critics maintained that 'parents should not be proud of the coins they get from their prostitute daughters, instead they should be ashamed at this.'[74] It is clear that many parents did not share the critics' indignation.

Geraldina Lutaibuza's petition highlighted what many Haya people seemed to believe: that prostitutes' work was a contribution toward the common good. Her line of argument did little to impress British officials. It was, instead, a narrower, legalistic critique that forced the district government to withdraw its support for the Haya Union's anti-prostitution campaign. In June 1950, a woman named Ernestina Mukakinanila wrote to the District Officer in Bukoba to complain against the restrictions that the government's headman had imposed on the women living in Buyanga, her village. Ernestina, who had returned to Buyanga after living for years in faraway Mombasa, found that her headman refused to allow women to ride motorcycles or wear fancy clothing. Ernestina professed herself to be 'amazed to see that the government of England has become like that of the

---

[69] TNA Acc. 215 2237: Bukoba District Annual Report, 14 January 1949.

[70] Benettsson, 'Från polygami till prostitution.'

[71] M. Mujwahuzi, *Obogorozi bwa Buhaya* (Ishozi, n.d.). Quoted in Larsson, *Conversion to Greater Freedom*, 133.

[72] Mwanza archives, Bukoba acc., L5/II/B: Stanislas Rwenyama to Buhaya Council, 26 June 1961.

[73] Rwamishenye archives, Box 18, 'Rwamishenye' file: A. Godfred to District Commissioner, 12 November 1945.

[74] Mwanza archives, Bukoba acc., L5/II/B: Edward Singini to Secretary, 28 June 1961.

Russians.'[75] Tanganyika was a United Nations mandated territory, not a colony, and the British government could not legally inhibit Africans' freedom of movement. Neither could Tanganyika appear to be like Stalinist Russia. In August 1950, under the orders of the District Commissioner, a policeman escorted Ernestina to the dock in Bukoba, past the outraged men of the Haya Union, and placed her on board the steamer bound for Mwanza town.[76] Later that same year, Ernestina and several other women living in Nairobi, Dar es Salaam, and Mombasa filed a case against the Union.[77] When the courts convicted the president of the Haya Union for hindering women's freedom of movement, the District Commissioner was obliged to withdraw his support for the anti-prostitution campaign. From March 1951, the district government allowed Haya women to travel without the Union's imprimatur.[78]

Unionists felt betrayed by namby-pamby British libertines. In the petitions and correspondence they addressed to officials in London and Geneva, they contrasted what they called 'traditional' Haya values with the corrupted colonial world, accusing the British of cultural imperialism. 'Yes, we now begin to feel the Partition of Africa and all its bad effects in Africa,' lamented the Union's Mwanza branch in a petition to the Secretary of State for the Colonies. 'No African community could succeed to remain independent and keep some of its good customary laws, such as the refusal to allow the practice of prostitution.'[79] The concept 'individual liberty,' fumed the Union's Geita branch in a 1951 memorandum to the United Nations:

means retrogression, disorganization, the breaking up of families, villages, and tribes. You can steal a girl and run off with her as you want. You can raise a family of half castes over which nobody has any control. You can seduce a dozen married women and drive away with them for good. Serious venereal diseases have spread beyond all available means to eradicate them. Are these the fruits to reap out of the slogan individual liberty?[80]

The controversy over women's freedom of movement led Haya patriots to romanticize traditional values and contrast old-time discipline with their people's contemporary degradation and immorality. Their cultural nationalism was an affirmation of a particular kind of political community. Haya patriotism was generated out of the inter-ethnic conversations that men had about sexual potency and women's virtue. In East Africa's cosmopolitan

75 TNA Acc. 71 790B: Ernestina Mukakinanila to District Officer, 12 June 1950.
76 TNA Acc. 71 790B: Lukiko Maruku to Bahaya Union, 28 August 1950.
77 TNA Acc. 71 790B: Vorha and Vorha to DC Bukoba, 20 February 1951; Dharsee and McRoberts to DC Bukoba, 20 November 1950.
78 TNA Acc. 71 790B: 'Office Minute,' 7 March 1951.
79 Mwanza archives, Acc. 1 A9/4: Haya Union Mwanza branch to Secretary of State for the Colonies, 12 August 1951.
80 Mwanza archives, Acc. 1 A9/4: Geita Bahaya Union to United Nations, 13 August 1951.

urban centers, Haya men confronted mirthful antagonists who lumped them together with the prostitutes who openly plied their trade. The shame that Haya men felt was politically productive. Other men's humor compelled them to see themselves as members of a community, sharing an interest in transforming women's behavior. Haya patriotism was conceived as a program of conservative reform, an effort to chasten refractory women by reinforcing the hold of traditional values.

MAKING SOCIETY CIVIL

The electoral ritual came to Tanganyika after the Second World War, as the British administration found itself under pressure from international diplomats to promote institutions of representative government. Local authorities throughout Tanganyika were obliged to prepare answers to a questionnaire, circulated by the United Nations Organization (UNO), asking how far 'native government representatives, councils, judicial organizations and other measures' had been introduced to help Tanganyika's people 'advance materially and culturally towards self-government and independence.'[81] British administrators often responded to these queries by reminding their questioners about the triumphs of Britain's civilizing mission.[82] But historical precedent would not in itself convince UNO observers of the educative qualities of British administration. Government authorities had to create bureaucratic institutions that would illuminate Tanganyika's steady progress toward self-government. 'The key to success,' averred the Secretary of State for the Colonies, lay in the 'development of an efficient and democratic system of local government.'[83]

With UNO diplomats looking over their shoulders, British authorities in Tanganyika set about organizing local councils and coordinating elections.[84] The earliest and most far-reaching program of political reform was in Sukumaland in northern Tanganyika, where British administrators created an astonishing number of village councils – more than 600.[85]

[81] TNA Acc. 215 2154/A: Provincial Office, Mwanza to District Commissioners, Lake Province, 19 November 1947.
[82] The Member for Local Government told an audience in 1952 that 'the United Kingdom has been administering colonies now for about four hundred years,' and trumpeted the fact that 'all the countries concerned are free and governing themselves.' TNA Acc. 71 280 v. IV: Conference in Malya, 24 October 1952.
[83] Arthur Creech-Jones, February 1947, quoted in Ronald Hyam, ed., *The Labour Government and the End of Empire, Part I* (London, 1992), 120.
[84] The history of political reform in Tanganyika is given in Andreas Eckert, 'Useful Instruments of Participation? Local Government and Co-operative Societies in Tanzania, 1940s to 1970s,' *International Journal of African Historical Studies* 40 (1) (2007), 97–118; and in Michael Jennings, '"A Very Real War": Popular Participation in Development in Tanzania During the 1950s and 1960s,' *International Journal of African Historical Studies* 40 (1) (2007), 71–95.
[85] See G. MacGuire, *Toward 'Uhuru' in Tanzania: The Politics of Participation* (Cambridge, 1969), 24–25.

Administrators in Bukoba were similarly energetic. Parish councils were set on a legal basis in 1952.[86] That same year, Bukoba's kings were made subject to election. These elections were carefully stage-managed affairs.[87] Candidates were selected from among each kingdom's ruling family. Voters assembled on election day and were divided into three groups: commoners, native authority officials, and the elderly courtiers who had traditionally selected kings. Each of these three groups chose a small number of delegates, who entered the courthouse one by one and whispered the name of their preferred candidate in the ear of the District Commissioner.[88] This and other electoral rituals allowed British administrators to generate evidence charting Tanganyika's progress toward self-government. A district-wide Buhaya Council was inaugurated, with appointed representatives from each of Bukoba's eight kingdoms.[89] The Council's chairman was Sylvester Ntare of Ihangiro, a leading figure in the Haya Union and the first elected king in Bukoba. The secretary was Sospeter Zahoro, the education secretary of the Haya Union.[90] His wife, Margaret Zahoro, was a leading advocate of Bukoba's women's clubs, which aimed to combat the lure of prostitution by teaching women sewing and handcrafts.[91]

The chairmen of Bukoba's local government councils were obliged to announce at the beginning of every meeting that 'The establishment of councils is the gift of government to its people,' but in fact, local democracy was more than a gift handed by generous colonial administration to a grateful public.[92] Haya intellectuals were deeply invested in the project of self-government. They understood political self-determination to be a moral challenge that made demands on them. In 1955, a group of Haya politicians applied to register a branch of the Tanganyika African National Union in Bukoba.[93] Their first president was Herbert Rugizibwa. As a younger man, Rugizibwa had worked as a part-time researcher, helping to compose histories of five Haya kingdoms.[94] As TANU president, Rugizibwa toured

---

[86] Cory file 160: Hans Cory, 'Procedures for Setting Up Parish Councils, with Particular Reference to Lake Province,' 1952.

[87] See Justin Willis, '"A Model of its Kind": Representation and Performance in the Sudan Self-Government Election of 1953,' *Journal of Imperial and Commonwealth History* 35 (3) (2007), 485–502.

[88] Cory file 156: 'Procedure for the Election of a Chief,' 2 December 1952.

[89] Mwanza archives, Bukoba acc., C 5/1: Buhaya District Council, 8 August 1951. See Harris, *Donkey's Gratitude*, 251.

[90] Rwamishenye archives, Box 17, 'Bahaya Union School Rubare' file: Meeting of the Bahaya School Committee, 22 December 1955.

[91] TNA Acc. 71 11/9: 'Gera Mashindano,' 29 October 1955.

[92] Cory file 160: 'Rules for Councilors,' n.d. (but 1952).

[93] TNA Acc. 71 A6/16: Mkutano wa Tanganyika ANU, Bukoba, 10 March 1955.

[94] The work in question was Francis Lwamugira's 'History of Buhaya,' which was later published, in a different form, as *Amakuru ga Kiziba: The History of Kiziba and its Kings*, trans. E. Kamuhangire (Makerere University Department of History, 1969). Rugizibwa

Bukoba constantly, corresponding with British authorities about the conduct of Haya chiefs. 'We are writing to our government to give some help to our Local Administration towards further advancement in our country,' he explained.[95] By early 1957, TANU authorities claimed a total membership of 7,462 people in Bukoba.[96] The District Commissioner thought it to be 'a force in the land, indeed the only organized political force.'[97] When a commission from the United Nations visited Bukoba in August 1957, TANU members raised banners reminding the delegates – in English – that 'our branch has registered membership of well over 15,000 members.'[98]

Rugizibwa and his contemporaries were claiming a place in Tanganyika's public sphere. As they positioned themselves in the political world, they also sought to reform Haya people's manners. In 1956, Rugizibwa wrote to local government authorities about the 'shocking subject of the Haya women intoxicating in bars.'[99] He described how during his military service in Nairobi 'I saw European gentlemen going with their ladies to cinemas, to dances and some other public places, [and] I did not see any European woman drunk and staggering in public roads.' European women, he knew, sometimes worked as prostitutes, 'but they know how to keep their morals.' From this exercise in comparison, Rugizibwa drew important lessons about Haya self-discipline. 'The woman must appear before the public as an image of decency and respect of a civilized Nation,' he wrote, 'and not a monster of immorality bringing down her nation.' He wanted local bars closed down and curfews established for Haya women.

Herbert Rugizibwa was not alone in his concern over Buhaya's public image. With the political future on their minds, Haya political thinkers were contrasting other people's virtuous self-control with Haya people's dissipation. Their comparative work fed the impulse toward reform. One petitioner noted that in 'countries like Germany, France, Egypt, and England you cannot see such behavior like in Buhaya.' From this comparison the petitioner concluded that Haya people should 'rule ourselves and live like the developed countries and there won't be shame like there is today.'[100] Their case studies were not always in faraway Europe. Haya moralists' favorite point of comparison was western Kenya, where the men of the Luo Union were leading a campaign to suppress Luo women's prostitution (see Chapter 6).

    was Lwamugira's research assistant. For which, see Mwanza archives, Bukoba acc., S 1/6: Lwamugira to Executive Committee, Rwamishenye, 14 September 1957.
[95] TNA Acc. 71 A6/16: H. Rugizibwa to DC Biharamulo, 21 May 1957.
[96] TNA Acc. 71 A6/16: H. Rugizibwa to PC Lake, 2 February 1957.
[97] TNA Acc. 215 2449: Bukoba District Annual Report, 1957.
[98] TNA Acc. 71 A6/16: Superintendent of Police to Provincial Secretary, TANU, 15 August 1957.
[99] Mwanza archives, Bukoba acc., A 6/B: Rugizibwa to Secretary of the Bakama, 23 May 1957.
[100] Mwanza archives, Bukoba acc., L5/II/B: Ahmada Musa to Secretary, 13 July 1961.

Haya conservatives studied how Luo men reformed women's manners, using their example to orient their own project. The Lutheran church leader Paul Lwejuna described how 'every Luo was given authority to return back home any Luo's wife who participated in prostitution.' They 'made her a laughing stock and sometimes they beat her, and she was not allowed to talk to any man.'[101] Another observer noted that Luo men 'allow their brothers to search for their sisters and send them back to their homes,' and if the women returned to her evil ways, 'they would face shameful punishment which involves wearing of sack bags in public.'[102] Haya men collected intelligence on other people's campaigns against moral and sexual delinquency, and from their research they derived lessons about how to reorganize their family lives.

By the early 1960s, Tanganyika's African leaders were constituting the legal and moral foundations of a sovereign state. The Tanganyika African National Union's victory in the Legislative Council election of 1959 compelled British administrators to agree to Tanganyika's independence, which was set for December 1961.[103] TANU won all of the seats in the Buhaya Council in the 1960 local government elections. The new chairman of the Council, Samuel Luangisa, was also TANU's local leader.[104] As its first order of business the Council adopted the 'Buhaya Prevention of Prostitution Laws,' which made provision for the arrest of any woman 'reasonably suspected of being a prostitute.' Under the law, the courts could send any woman who 'is or is likely to become a prostitute' to the home of her husband or guardian. Women convicted of prostitution were fined 100 shillings on their first offence, and 400 shillings or three months in prison on their second offence.[105] But even these stringent rules seemed inadequate to the task. In February 1961, Tanganyika's premier, Julius Nyerere, wrote to the district councils to advise them of the 'importance of a unified customary code of law to the building of a nation in Tanganyika.'[106] Each district was to nominate delegates to consult with sociologist Hans Cory, who was seventy-one years old, to work out a unified code of customary law.[107]

[101] Mwanza archives, Bukoba acc., L5/II/B: Paul Lwejuna to Secretary, n.d. (but 1961).
[102] Mwanza archives, Bukoba acc., L5/II/B: Felician Cyprian to Secretary, n.d. (but 1961). Other petitioners likewise noted the Luo Union's use of sackcloth as a punishment for refractory women. See, for example, Mwanza archives, Bukoba acc., L5/II/B: Ernest Ndyetukiba and Pastori Mpikile to Secretary, 25 June 1961.
[103] John Iliffe, 'Breaking the Chain at its Weakest Link: TANU and the Colonial Office,' in *In Search of a Nation: Histories of Authority and Dissidence in Tanzania*, eds. Gregory Maddox and James Giblin (Oxford, 2006), 168–97.
[104] Goran Hyden, *Political Development in Rural Tanzania: A West Lake Study* (Nairobi, 1969), chapter 7.
[105] Mwanza archives, Bukoba acc., L5/II/B: 'Sheria za Buhaya Kuzuia Umalaya,' 1960.
[106] TNA Acc. 64 WL/A2/15: Nyerere to members of Legislative Council and district councils, 8 February 1961.
[107] TNA Acc. 64 WL/A2/15: Hans Cory to PC Lake, 4 April 1961.

It was in a context of legal reform that the Buhaya Council circulated a survey in May 1961 titled 'How to Stop Prostitution.'[108] The survey was distributed widely: copies were sent to parish councils, churches, and mosques, and Bukoba's local trading cooperatives, and advertisements were placed in several of East Africa's Swahili-language newspapers. The survey itself was a didactic instrument. It began by asking correspondents 'Can prostitution be stopped?,' and went on to ask 'What are the bad outcomes associated with prostitution in towns, and in Bukoba itself?' Respondents were asked for suggestions on laws that could be used to inhibit prostitution. 'Are the customary laws dealing with marriages, child rearing and family life the main cause of prostitution? Can they be used to eliminate prostitution in Buhaya?,' asked the survey. And finally, the questionnaire asked for 'vivid examples from other tribes or nations which have managed to combat prostitution.'

The Council received more than seventy replies to its questionnaire, all but one completed by men. All the respondents in the 1961 survey agreed that the first step in any program to suppress prostitution was to bring Haya women back to Bukoba. Six years before the Arusha Declaration, Haya patriots had already come to see rural life as more moral, and more productive, than city living. Prostitutes and other jobless city dwellers 'should be sent back to their homes to engage themselves in productive activities such as agriculture,' wrote a church pastor in his reply to the questionnaire. 'This rule should be mandatory. People should not stay idle.'[109] Lutheran church teacher Paul Lwejuna wanted village headmen to search Bukoba's back alleys, gathering up young girls and returning them to their parents.[110] Lwejuna had himself spent nine long years looking for his wife, who had absconded from his home. He sent emissaries as far away as Tabora in search of her.[111] Respondents were confident that the discipline of rural living and hard work would chasten Haya women. One writer suggested that returning sex workers should be issued hoes and food provisions sufficient for six months. 'They should do heavy works every day,' he suggested, 'and on Saturdays they should be beaten with six strokes.'[112] Respondent Yusto Balubuka was very specific about how prostitutes should start their work. 'They should be forced to open farms of cassava, potatoes, tomatoes, and onions,' he wrote.[113] Balubuka was consigning Haya women to do extremely hard work: vegetable crops like these had to be grown on scrubland, not in the fertile banana gardens that men tended. Everyone was agreed that the reformed women would be cultivating more than vegetables. 'Nowadays

[108] Mwanza archives, Bukoba acc., L5/II/B: Komiti ya Kuzuia Umalaya, 19 May 1961.
[109] Mwanza archives, Bukoba acc., L5/II/B: Pastor Ch. Mugea to Secretary, 3 July 1961.
[110] Mwanza archives, Bukoba acc., L5/II/B: Paul Lwejuna to Secretary, n.d. (but 1961)
[111] ELCT Box AX: 1: Marriage Committee minutes, 24 October 1958.
[112] Mwanza archives, Bukoba acc., L5/II/B: Aloya Baterakki to Secretary, 5 July 1961.
[113] Mwanza archives, Bukoba acc., L5/II/B: Yusto Balubuka to Secretary, n.d. (but 1961).

in Tanganyika we have a slogan Freedom and Work,' wrote a respondent. 'Life is through farming. Prostitutes are not angels, [they] are human beings, and they should farm like other people do.'[114] In this partisan view, farming made immoral, dissipated prostitutes into virtuous human agents.

Respondents agreed that once Haya prostitutes had been removed from eastern Africa's cities and deposited in rural farms, their movements would have to be carefully controlled. One respondent suggested that the local government should build a special prison catering to Haya prostitutes.[115] Other respondents thought parents or husbands should act as women's jailors. A respondent named G. Bazila suggested that single women should be confined to their parents' homes. 'They should not go out at night,' he wrote. 'Men who would like to marry them should seek the approval of their parents.'[116] Respondents devoted dozens of pages deliberating over the mechanism by which women's movements should be controlled. A schoolteacher from southern Buhaya wanted female travelers to carry passports signed by the village council, the Buhaya Council, the District Commissioner, and a notional 'Special Committee for Preventing Prostitution.'[117] If the girl was a student, this respondent wanted the Provincial Education Officer and her parents also to sign. Local councilors at one village in Kiziba recommended that women who wished to travel should have passes signed by their mothers- and fathers-in-law, and by the headman of their village.[118] One respondent thought every woman proposing to travel outside her sub-county should carry a letter bearing the 'official rubber stamp or seal' of the sub-county council, listing the number of days she was permitted to travel.[119] Another respondent thought that local authorities' rubber stamps should be standardized to guard against forgery.[120]

The Haya men who filled up their questionnaires with long discourses about rubber stamps and identity cards were learning how to control women's movements from their neighbors. In the late 1940s, Luo women living in Nairobi were subjected to an interrogation by members of the Luo Union, who demanded that they produce marriage certificates and proof of respectable employment before granting them leave to stay in town. At this same time in central Kenya, the Gikuyu language press was full of letters deliberating over whether repatriated prostitutes ought to be returned to their families or housed in a purpose-built prison (see Chapter 10). Haya men studied

[114] Mwanza archives, Bukoba acc., L5/II/B: Ernest Ndyetukiba and Pastor Mpikile to Secretary, 25 June 1961.

[115] Mwanza archives, Bukoba acc., L5/II/B: Edward Singini to Secretary, 28 June 1961.

[116] Mwanza archives, Bukoba acc., L5/II/B: G. Bazila to Secretary, 13 July 1961.

[117] Mwanza archives, Bukoba acc., L5/II/B: No author to Secretary, 13 July 1961.

[118] Mwanza archives, Bukoba acc., L5/II/B: Bushasha Village Council to Secretary, 11 July 1961.

[119] Mwanza archives, Bukoba acc., L5/II/B: Damian Michael to Secretary, 12 July 1961.

[120] Mwanza archives, Bukoba acc., L5/II/B: B.A. Ziwane to Secretary, 13 July 1961.

the techniques employed by other East African reformers, but they had their own reasons for focusing on the bureaucratic minutiae of movement control. The patriots of northwestern Tanganyika knew that parents could not be made responsible for their daughters' moral conduct. Too many parents were complicit in the prostitution trade. Conservatives therefore sought to widen the circle of people and institutions that could be held accountable. The long lists of signatories required on women's travel documents was a way of relativizing parents' authority, of bringing outside authorities to bear in regulating women's conduct. Conservatives were creating procedures, in other words, by which women's conduct could be subjected to government surveillance.

No person bears outward, physical evidence of their moral conduct, of their marital status, or even of their name. Like the architects of modern systems of biometric identification, Haya reformers needed to find ways to decode humanity's intrinsic anonymity.[121] If government was to hold runaway wives or delinquent daughters responsible for their actions, they had first to be identified. One respondent to the 1961 survey thought that Haya women of doubtful morals should be labeled with numbers, to make it easier for government to trace their whereabouts.[122] Another respondent thought that the names of prostitutes should be put up on notice boards throughout Bukoba, so that 'we know them and keep apart from them.'[123] Throughout the 1950s and 1960s, Haya urbanites kept a close eye on city street corners, and sent reports naming the delinquent women they had found. A man living in Dar es Salaam wrote to the Buhaya Council naming four Haya girls who had resorted to prostitution.[124] The Council's secretary forwarded the report to the girls' fathers, telling them to fetch their daughters from the city.[125] A Mombasa resident wrote to the local government listing the names of four Haya women whose 'behavior is not in good conduct with our nation.'[126] Patriots also had their eyes open in rural areas. The sole female respondent to the 1961 survey suggested that village and county councilors should 'watch down streets and villages, to see men who are with ladies who are not their wives.'[127] Haya patriots were collecting intelligence, identifying culprits, and opening paths for legal and moral action.

---

[121] Keith Breckenridge, 'Verwoerd's Bureau of Proof: Total Information in the Making of Apartheid,' *History Workshop Journal* 59 (2005), 83–108.

[122] Mwanza archives, Bukoba acc., L5/II/B: Emmanuel Mutoka to Secretary, 12 July 1961.

[123] Mwanza archives, Bukoba acc., L5/II/B: Thomas Lwenyagira to Secretary, 8 July 1961.

[124] Bukoba Council chamber archives: Minutes of the Executive Committee, 4 May 1956.

[125] Rwamishenye archives, Box 35, 'Communicable Diseases' file: Zahoro to Lukikos at Rubungo and Kanazi, 6 June 1956.

[126] Mwanza archives, Bukoba acc.. L5/II/B: Peter Kafunga to Secretary, 21 May 1964.

[127] Mwanza archives, Bukoba acc.. L5/II/B: Scolastica d/o Dyonisia to Secretary, 23 June 1961.

Reformers knew that their effort to identify, enumerate, and contain prostitutes had to involve the reform of marriage. If they were to empower husbands to control women's conduct, the patriots of northwestern Tanganyika needed to know precisely who was married to whom. They thought marriage to be the duty of any patriotic person. 'Haya women have got some duties to perform at home as members of their households,' wrote a Unionist in 1952. 'These include inter alia, drawing water, cleaning the houses and looking after babies and gardens for their men, as theirs is mostly a sedentary life.'[128] One respondent to the 1961 survey suggested that all prostitutes, regardless of their religious allegiance, should be forced into marriages. Women who insisted on spinsterhood should be sent to jail. 'We are protecting and defending the Nation of God,' he wrote. 'What matters here is to build our nation.'[129] Respondent Swalehe Balelao suggested that local government should build ten houses in Bukoba to house women who had been arrested for practicing prostitution. Any man who wished to take one of them as wife should pay a very low bridewealth – twenty-five shillings only – to the government.[130] 'As God says in his books, a man has to get married,' wrote Balelao, 'and when it is done, angels celebrate in heaven, and God opens the seven doors of his blessings.' Another respondent to the 1961 survey outlined a complex system of marriage registration, arguing that local government should keep records on wives who had separated from their husbands.[131]

Haya patriots were bringing government bureaucracy to bear on dating, marriage, and other aspects of conjugality.[132] Parents could not be relied on. Wives were quick to desert their marital homes. Marriages were easily broken. Patriots thought government bureaucracy was the surest guarantor of marital stability and sexual order. One respondent to the 1961 survey even wanted government to regulate adultery: husbands were to be allowed to meet with their girlfriends only after working hours or on Sundays. Men who indiscriminately consorted with their paramours were to be fined.[133] Haya reformers sought to give local government oversight over the most intimate corners of married people's lives. They hoped thereby to make deviants visible as errant wives, calculating prostitutes, or delinquent husbands.

---

128 Mwanza archives Acc. 1 V 2/15: Secretary Haya Union Mwanza to Governor, 26 January 1952.

129 Mwanza archives, Bukoba acc., L5/II/B: G. Kilibwa to Secretary, 30 July 1961.

130 Mwanza archives, Bukoba acc., L5/II/B: Swalehe Balelao to Secretary, 11 July 1961.

131 Mwanza archives, Bukoba acc., L5/II/B: Jasoni Lwezaula to Secretary, 1 July 1961.

132 In southern and southeast Asia, British bureaucrats had similarly used the law to control and supervise the prostitution of European women. Like Haya patriots, British officials feared that women's indiscriminate sexuality would compromise their social and political standing. See Philippa Levine, *Prostitution, Race and Politics: Policing Venereal Disease in the British Empire* (New York, 2003).

133 Mwanza archives, Bukoba acc., L5/II/B: Samuel Samson to Secretary, 23 July 1961.

CONCLUSION

The respondents to the 1961 survey did not make policy, but the reforms they proposed shaped postcolonial Tanganyika's political culture. After independence in December 1961, Tanganyika's African leaders set about defining their nation's cultural and intellectual patrimony, seeking to create a dignified, cultured state.[134] In his inaugural address as president of Tanganyika, Julius Nyerere announced the formation of a 'Ministry for National Culture and Youth' by proclaiming 'I want it to seek out the best of the traditions and customs of all the tribes and make them part of our national culture.'[135] In the legal arena, Tanganyika's rulers sought to standardize local practices, eliminating inconsistencies and creating a unitary form. The goal, as the chairman of the Buhaya Council told his colleagues, was to 'write the laws which arise from the customs and practices of the tribes of the people of Tanganyika,' and to 'develop the law so that in future days it ... will be obeyed by all Tanganyikans like the law of the English.'[136] For several months prior to his death in April 1962, sociologist Hans Cory consulted with groups of delegates from Bukoba and other parts of northern Tanganyika. His chief conversation partners were Samuel Luangisa, the chairman of the Buhaya Council; Sylvester Ntare, king of Ihangiro and a former leader of the Haya Union; and Edward Barongo, who in the mid-1950s had been the secretary to TANU leader Herbert Rugizibwa.[137] They must have had the 1961 survey open before them as they worked. The legal code that Cory and his colleagues composed made government bureaucrats the arbiters of Haya conjugality. Under the 1962 rules, the payment of bridewealth from a husband to his parents-in-law played no role in determining the legal validity of marriage.[138] What mattered was registration: marriages that were not registered with local government authorities were regarded as invalid in the eyes of the law. Marriage and divorce registers were to be kept in all local courts, and certificates were to be issued to all newly married couples. The new law code made marriage into a bureaucratic institution, authorized by government and validated on paper. Legal reformers sought to clarify conjugal relationships, making it possible for government to identify and discipline recalcitrant husbands and wives.[139]

---

[134] See Andrew Ivaska, *Cultured States: Youth, Gender, and Modern Style in 1960s Dar es Salaam* (Durham, NC, 2011).

[135] Julius Nyerere, *Freedom and Unity* (London, 1967), 186.

[136] Rwamishenye archives, Buhaya District Council minutes, 9–10 January 1963.

[137] TNA Acc. 64 WL/A2/15: PC Lake to Cory, 21 April 1961.

[138] TNA Acc. 64 WL/A2/15: Mifsud to Regional Commissioner, Lake Province, 16 July 1962.

[139] This project reached its fruition in Tanzania's 1971 law of marriage and divorce. See James S. Read, 'A Milestone in the Integration of Personal Laws: The New Law of Marriage and Divorce in Tanzania,' *Journal of African Law* 16 (1) (1972), 19–39.

In economic and social life, the officials of the Tanzanian state made people subject to discipline. In 1967, as president of the new nation of Tanzania, Julius Nyerere inaugurated the reform program that he called *ujamaa*, 'familyhood.' He contrasted the corruption of urban life with the discipline of family living. The 'traditional African family,' Nyerere wrote in 1967, was 'an almost self-contained economic and social unit ... there was an attitude of mutual respect and obligation which bound the members together.'[140] In this traditional society, 'everybody was a worker,' contributing his efforts toward the good of the commonwealth. 'We did not have that other form of modern parasite,' wrote Nyerere, 'the loiterer, or idler, who accepts the hospitality of society as his right but gives nothing in return!'[141] Like the indignant men of the Haya Union, like the respondents to the Buhaya Council's 1961 prostitution survey, President Nyerere valorized the traditional past, contrasting modern people's dissipation with their forebears' discipline. Like Haya moralists, Nyerere sought to stiffen the backs of delinquent people by compelling them to engage in hard agricultural labor. In 1968, officials began inviting people to voluntarily move to new collective villages. Government made villagization compulsory in 1973. Between September 1973 and the end of 1976, 11,000,000 people were moved to the new villages – about 70 percent of Tanzania's population.[142] It was the largest resettlement effort in the history of Africa.[143]

In Bukoba, local officials generally declined to uproot prosperous farmers, whose coffee upheld Tanzania's export economy. The people who consented to move to the new villages were the landless poor.[144] Villagization was guided by bureaucrats' vision, not by local people's needs. New villages were sited in empty areas of the map, without regard to soil quality or local patterns of land use. In one case, a village was placed on land traditionally used for executions.[145] The new villages were laid out according to a singular plan. Each village was centered on the TANU headquarters, a dispensary, and other communal buildings. Each farmer was to possess half a hectare of private farming land, and a plot on which to build his house. Houses were laid out in straight lines. Villages were positioned along roadways, where they could easily be reached by visiting administrators.[146] By 1978, the architects of Tanzania's five-year plan could claim that the 'party has had

[140] Nyerere, *Freedom and Unity*, 8–9.
[141] '*Ujamaa*: The Basis of African Socialism,' in Nyerere, *Freedom and Unity*, 164–65.
[142] Julius Nyerere, *The Arusha Declaration, Ten Years Later* (Dar es Salaam, 1977), 41–42.
[143] Goran Hyden, *Beyond Ujamaa in Tanzania: Underdevelopment and the Uncaptured Peasantry* (Berkeley, 1980), 130.
[144] Jannik Boesen, Birgit Madsen, and Tony Moody, *Ujamaa: Socialism From Above* (Uppsala, 1977), 104, 110.
[145] Boesen et al., *Ujamaa*, 98.
[146] Henry Bernstein, 'Notes on State and the Peasantry: the Tanzanian Case,' *Review of African Political Economy* 8 (21) (1981), 57.

great success in resettling the rural people in villages where it is now possible to identify individuals able to work.'[147] Bureaucrats were regimenting rural people's lives. They were organizing domestic relations, and in so doing they made people subject to supervision.[148]

The architects of socialism in northwestern Tanzania were the same people who had conducted the anti-prostitution campaign of the 1950s. Herbert Rugizibwa, one of the founders of the Haya Union, was TANU's district chairman in Bukoba until 1958. His successor in the chairmanship was Ali Migeyo, another founder of the Haya Union. Migeyo was elected to TANU's National Executive Committee in 1958, and he served as a nominated member of Tanzania's parliament from 1965.[149] Samuel Luangisa, who as chairman of the Bukoba District Council had commissioned the 1961 anti-prostitution survey, was the Commissioner of West Lake Region from 1962. Edward Barongo, who began his career as Herbert Rugizibwa's secretary, was the national Deputy Secretary General of TANU from 1962.[150] When Barongo spoke at a TANU executive meeting in Dar es Salaam shortly after his election, an unnamed questioner told him that 'in Bukoba the prostitutes wear clothing that dishonours them and the nation at large.' Embarrassed, Barongo wrote to the Bukoba local government, instructing them to stop women from wearing 'a very shameful clothing which is cha cha cha.'[151] Barongo and other Haya politicians had buttressed their reputations by disciplining independent women in the 1950s. It was as husbands and fathers, as architects of a moral community, that Barongo, Luangisa, and their colleagues took their place in the public sphere. After Tanzania's independence, they used the instruments of government to advance their moral project. In 1967, government officials in Missenyi, Bukoba's northernmost chiefdom, ordered that women working in bars and hotels should be medically examined twice per month. Women without formal employment were arrested and sent back to their homes. The campaign was, in the words of a district official, a way of 'fulfilling our politics of *ujamaa* and self-independence.'[152] Late in 1968, the TANU Youth League launched

---

[147] Quoted in James Scott, *Seeing Like a State: How Certain Schemes to Improve the Human Condition have Failed* (New Haven, 1998), 241.

[148] But see Leander Schneider, 'Colonial Legacies and Postcolonial Authoritarianism in Tanzania: Connects and Disconnects,' *African Studies Review* 49 (1) (2006), 93–118; and Schneider, 'Freedom and Unfreedom in Rural Development: Julius Nyerere, Ujamaa Vijijini, and Villagization,' *Canadian Journal of African Studies* 38 (2) (2004), 344–92.

[149] See Mutabaha, *Portrait of a Nationalist*.

[150] Barongo's autobiography is given in Edward Barongo, *Mkiki Mkiki wa Siasa Tanganyika* (Nairobi, 1966).

[151] Mwanza archives, Bukoba acc., L5/II/B: E. Barongo to Chairman of the National Council, 12 January 1962.

[152] Mwanza archives, F37/54: Divisional Executive Officer to all Assistant Divisional Officers, Missenyi, 2 March 1967; Mwanza archives, M1/188: Sublocation Executive Officer to all bar and hotel owners, 12 April 1967. Cited in Shane Doyle, *Before HIV: Sexuality, Fertility and Mortality in East Africa, 1900–1980* (London, forthcoming).

'Operation Vijana,' a nationwide campaign aiming to eliminate the wearing and consumption of Western fashions and beauty products. In Dar es Salaam police and members of the Youth League rounded up hundreds of women wearing miniskirts, makeup, or wigs.[153] Contemporary press reports describe how offending women were pulled from buses, chased down city streets, and stripped by groups of angry young men.[154]

President Nyerere and his Haya compatriots were working together to create a civil society. In their outrage over independent women's conduct, Haya conservatives had valorized the traditional past and represented rural living as a virtue-building undertaking. In their effort to corral refractory women, Haya patriots worked out bureaucratic techniques that the postcolonial state could adopt. The architects of Tanzanian socialism borrowed a theory of citizenship and a set of bureaucratic practices from the Haya patriots of the 1950s. *Ujamaa* was more than one man's political vision.[155] It was – in part – an outworking of Haya patriotism.

---

[153] Described in Andrew Ivaska, 'In the "Age of Minis": Women, Work and Masculinity Downtown,' in *Dar es Salaam: Histories from an Emerging African Metropolis*, eds. James R. Brennan, Andrew Burton, and Yusuf Lawi (Dar es Salaam, 2007), 213–31; and in Ivaska, *Cultured States*, chapter 2.

[154] Ivaska, *Cultured States*, 99.

[155] Argued in James Brennan, 'Blood Enemies: Exploitation and Urban Citizenship in the Nationalist Political Thought of Tanzania, 1958–75,' *Journal of African History* 47 (2006), 389–413.

8

Conversion and Court Procedure

I interviewed Christian Mushumbuzi at his home on the outskirts of Bukoba town in 2006. As a younger man, he and his classmates at the Lutheran teacher training school had made a habit of heckling revivalist preachers, deriding them as 'prophets of evil.' But one afternoon in 1943, Mushumbuzi said, he was 'seized' by the Holy Spirit, and 'I saw my sins. And I said in astonishment, "Even I am in sins?" Because I had not seen it.'[1] Later that day, Mushumbuzi confessed his sins in a public assembly at the school, and, as he told me, 'I began a new life. The matter of beer, I left it. I was stealing things in school. The Spirit told me that if you don't return them, you will enter the fire ... The matter of adultery, I left it.' Upon his conversion Mushumbuzi returned several stolen articles to the school's storekeeper, and thereafter he refused to brew beer for his father's consumption.

Legal history in Africa has too often been conceived as a clash between the textualized, bureaucratic practice of modern governance and the oral, flexible *mentalité*.[2] Sean Hawkins's recent book, for example, studies the 'encounter between the LoDagaa and "the world on paper."'[3] Before colonial conquest, says Hawkins, LoDagaa social order was flexible and negotiable: conjugal relationships, social order, and ethnic identity were crafted out of the back-and-forth of human interaction. Colonial rule worked to 'subjugate and regulate [this] oral culture and force it within the conceptual framework of a literate society.'[4] In legal writs, in ethnographic writing, and

[1] Interview: Christian Mushumbuzi, Kibeeta, Bukoba District, 11 August 2006.
[2] The scholarship I have in mind here includes Martin Chanock, *Law, Custom, and Social Order: The Colonial Experience in Malawi and Zambia* (Portsmouth, NH., 1998); Diana Jeater, *Marriage, Perversion, and Power: The Construction of Moral Discourse in Southern Rhodesia, 1894–1930* (Oxford, 1993); and Peter Pels, *A Politics of Presence: Contacts Between Missionaries and Waluguru in Late Colonial Tanganyika* (Amsterdam, 1999).
[3] Sean Hawkins, *Writing and Colonialism in Northern Ghana: The Encounter between the LoDagaa and 'the World on Paper'* (Toronto, 2002).
[4] Hawkins, *Writing and Colonialism*, 32.

through map-making, colonial officials used foreign categories to gain a hold over the changeable LoDagaa world. This 'world on paper,' Hawkins argues, was divorced from the real world: it was an artifice created by British administrators and their African successors.

Converts like Christian Mushumbuzi did not inhabit a real world that was distant from the courtroom. Mushumbuzi used legal procedure to organize his life story. He was engaged in forensic work: he reviewed the events of his life, measured them against a code, and identified certain forms of behavior as sin. Mushumbuzi was shocked at the result of his analysis: with the evidence spread before him, he exclaimed that 'Even I am in sins?' Christian Mushumbuzi composed his life story as though he was being arraigned before a court of law. His reconstruction of his autobiography convicted him of his wrongdoing, and propelled him to act as a penitent.

Haya converts were by no means unique in their practice of self-interrogation, but they seem to have been particularly invested in legal practice. In no other part of eastern Africa was court procedure so enthusiastically studied and avidly pursued. In 1939, the same year that the Revival found its footing in northwestern Tanganyika, the sociologist Hans Cory was reading through the records of Buhaya's appeals court, comparing the decisions that court elders had made and developing a unified code of customary law for judges in Bukoba to use.[5] He sent the draft – written in Swahili – to each of the district's chiefs for comment, and met with fifteen specially chosen delegates for further advice. His leading interlocutor was Francis Lwamugira, the secretary of Bukoba's local government and an avid researcher into the history of the Haya kingdoms. In 1945, the legal code that Cory, Lwamugira, and other Haya jurists had worked out was published as *The Customary Law of the Haya Tribe.*[6] It became standard reading material for eastern Africa's legal reformers. Kenya's government circulated the study to district officers in western and central Kenya, hoping to give them 'an idea of the possibilities of recording native law.'[7] Cory's book was the definitive code for Haya customary law until the early 1960s.[8]

The care with which government authorities in Buhaya deliberated over the customary legal code reflected a larger societal engagement with legal practice. Haya people were eager and committed litigants: from the mid-1920s until Tanganyika's independence, a quarter of all Haya men were

[5] Mwanza archives, Bukoba acc., S 1/6: Hans Koritshoner to DO Bukoba, 2 October 1939.
[6] Hans Cory and M. M. Hartnoll, *Customary Law of the Haya Tribe, Tanganyika Territory* (London, 1945).
[7] KNA MAA 7/725: Arthur Phillips to Chief Native Commissioner, 20 July 1946; quoted in Brett Shadle, '"Changing Traditions to Meet Current Altering Conditions": Customary Law, African Courts, and the Rejection of Codification in Kenya, 1930–60,' *Journal of African History* 40 (3) (1999), 422–23.
[8] Mwanza archives, Bukoba acc., S 1/6: DC Bukoba to PC West Lake, 23 May 1960.

involved in a legal case in any given year.[9] Litigants were rarely satisfied with the decisions that lower courts handed down. In 1948, 66 percent of Bukoba's litigants appealed against lower courts' rulings, a percentage that British officials found 'staggering.'[10] 'In almost every case the loser would be waving a roll of notes to me to pay further appeal fees before I had even finished giving judgment,' remembered the District Commissioner.[11] Officials worried that the 'unhealthy national sport of arguing in court ... has a strong hold on the people,' and they lamented the 'unremitting tension' that the 'volume of work and the long hours of argument' produced.[12] One government officer felt himself driven to a state of 'near paranoia' by court work. But officials could do little to stem the flood of litigation: between 1953 and 1957 the volume of civil cases expanded by 28 percent, while the volume of criminal cases increased by 12 percent.[13] In 1957, the appeals court in Dar es Salaam heard more appeals from Bukoba than from all the other districts in Tanganyika Territory combined.[14] Haya people knew the law. Their command over court procedure made them Tanganyika's most avid litigants.

Even as jurists were standardizing the legal code and litigants were filling the dockets, revivalists were also investing themselves in court procedure. As defendants, converts like Christian Mushumbuzi could remove themselves from the fabric of their lives, pour over the evidence, and pick out possessions and deeds that made them sinful. As defendants, converts found a particular literary form – the confession – into which their complicated life stories could be cast. The procedures of litigation gave converts a forum wherein their past could be assessed and judgment could be rendered. Instead of seeing legal history as a straightforward contest between the 'world on paper' and the negotiated world of real life, we might better see the law as a set of generic practices in which Africans developed competence. Interrogation, confession, and judgment: these were standard elements of court procedure. Haya people practiced these forms in the law courts, and the competences they developed helped shape their actions in Revival meetings. Legal bureaucracy was never a separate arena from Haya people's ordinary lives. Haya people moved laterally through different theaters of social life, honing their characters, practicing their testimonies, and representing themselves.

---

[9] See Shane Doyle, *Before HIV: Sexuality, Fertility and Mortality in East Africa, 1900–1980* (London, forthcoming), chapter 5.

[10] TNA Acc. 215 2237: PC Lake to DC Bukoba, 4 January 1949.

[11] Tim Harris, *Donkey's Gratitude: Twenty Two Years in the Growth of a New African Nation—Tanzania* (Edinburgh, 1992), 266.

[12] TNA Acc. 215 2237: Bukoba District Annual Report, 1948; Harris, *Donkey's Gratitude*, 266.

[13] Mwanza archives Acc. 1 2937: Bukoba District Annual Report, 1954; TNA Acc. 215 2449: Bukoba District Annual Report, 1957.

[14] TNA Acc. 215 2449: Lake Province Annual Report, 1957.

This chapter begins by studying the history of the Revival in Bukoba. Evangelists from Rwanda and Uganda were preaching in northwestern Tanganyika in the late 1930s, and, from them, Haya converts learned how to take account of their lives. Conversion in Buhaya was an intersubjective event, not a decision brokered privately between God and penitent. Converts needed to expose themselves and open up about their dark deeds in order to narrate their passage into a new life. Their critics thought converts' testimonies to be a threat to Haya people's welfare. In their confessions of sin, converts violated Haya standards of decorum and damaged other people's reputations. Even as they used government bureaucracy to chastise independent women and reform marriage, Haya patriots also sought to bring noisy revivalists to heel. Spurned by the Haya establishment, converts broke away from the Lutheran church and formed a new organization, which they called *Kanisa la Roho Mtakatifu*, the 'Church of the Holy Spirit.' The church was headquartered on the desolate outskirts of Bukoba, and from this geography the church's leaders developed a muscular theology. Revivalists compared cultured Buhaya with Sodom and Gomorrah, contrasting their pioneering self-discipline with the corruption and decadence of the old world. In Buhaya, the pilgrims' progress became an exodus.

CONVERSION AND LEGAL PRACTICE

Bukoba was part of the larger network of economic and intellectual exchange that linked the cotton farmers of Buganda with the migrant laborers of Rwanda and Bugufi (see Chapters 3, 4, and 5). Bukoba stood astride one of the main routes that labor migrants followed, and, in 1930, government officials counted 15,944 men and women passing through the region bound for Uganda.[15] By the late 1930s, many of these migrants were making a home for themselves on the outer fringes of Haya country. Observers reported that hundreds of immigrants from Rwanda and Bugufi had established settlements in western Kianja, where they set to work clearing the scrubland and developing farms.[16] Immigrants also settled in Ihangiro, the southernmost kingdom in Buhaya, and in Karagwe to the west (see Map 3).[17]

These migrant laborers were the first emissaries of revivalism in Bukoba. As early as 1937, only a year after the Revival's conception, converts from Rwanda were traveling the long road to Buhaya, where they returned goods that they had stolen from their former employers.[18] A group of revivalists

---

[15] KigDA bundle 171, 'Survey of the Banyaruanda Complex' file: Rhona Ross and Cyril Sofer, 'Survey of the Banyaruanda Complex,' 22 May 1950. See John Iliffe, *A Modern History of Tanganyika* (Cambridge, 1979), 282.

[16] Cory file 19: A. Culwick, 'Land Tenure in the Bukoba District,' 14 March 1939.

[17] Mwanza archives Acc. 1 2937: Bukoba District Annual Report, 1954.

[18] ELCT Box E 1 a:2 file a: Cecil Verity at Kabale to Scholten, 25 August 1937.

from Katoke conducted a preaching tour through the central kingdoms of
Bukoba in 1939. At one of these occasions, a government clerk confessed
to immorality, homosexuality, drunkenness, thievery, pride, and other sins.[19]
Some of the Rwandan converts made a show of returning goods they had sto-
len from their employers. Ernest Lutashobya attended a Revival meeting in
Bukoba as a schoolboy, and watched in amazement as a Rwandan who had
worked as a missionary's houseboy returned stolen utensils to his employer.
He 'brought these spoons and forks and other things and confessed. Therefore
it was something new! People were shocked! And the Revival started there,'
Lutashobya remembered.[20] Other converts were similarly astonished by the
Rwandans' penitential acts. One of my interviewees remembered that 'the
thing that astonished many people, the thing that was really amazing, was
that the people of Rwanda normally came here to do work, they stole things,
and then they returned home ... But the people who came that time, they said
"I stole this, here it is, and I pray you will forgive me."'[21]

In their penitential acts, Rwandan and other early converts classified
otherwise inconsequential actions as sin. Their definitional work impressed
Haya people and drove them to make an inventory of their own lives. In
August 1936, as an ecstatic fervor gripped students in northern Rwanda (see
Chapter 3), the missionary Dora Skipper was visited by a Haya man who
had walked to Gahini from faraway Bukoba. He had been 'troubled at his
weakness and the desire to live a bad life,' he told her, and 'hearing that there
was teaching at Gahini that gave hope of victory over the old Adam,' he had
come for counsel. Skipper commented that she had 'never seen a man with
such sorrow in his face over the things of his soul.'[22] People like Skipper's
penitent visitor were convinced that their actions and deeds had eternal consequences. They felt themselves confronted with a straightforward choice
between two paths in life. One woman, named Justina, described how, in a
dream, she 'saw the two roads I like. I like my church, I give my offerings ...
but when I leave the church, I go to drink beer, I go with other men. Am I not
going to die? Will I really be able to go to heaven? I had better decide to take
one road.'[23] Other Haya converts likewise thought themselves at a turning
point. In his autobiography, the evangelist Jonathon Karoma described how
in a dream he saw two parties fighting over him. On one side were arrayed
the 'old ones,' and on the other were foreigners, dressed in white clothing.
The two groups took hold of his hands and pulled in opposite directions.
After he had awakened, Karoma told himself that 'This is a dream about the

---

[19] CMS Annual Letters file: Lionel Bakewell, annual letter, 19 September 1939.

[20] Murray papers: interview, Rev. Ernest Lutashobya, Bukoba, 30 July 1988.

[21] Interview: Jafeth Kabyemera, Bukoba town, 8 August 2006.

[22] CMS Oxford, Dora Skipper papers, folio 2: letter for 28 August 1936.

[23] Interview: Justina, no date, quoted in Birgitta Larsson, *Conversion to Greater Freedom:
Women, Church and Social Change in North-Western Tanzania under Colonial Rule*
(Uppsala, 1991), 155.

gang of Satan and the Knights of Jesus.'[24] Revivalists were pulled between one life and another.

Converts drew lines through the whole spectrum of human activity, distinguishing right conduct from wrongdoing. With new criteria in place, they sorted through half-forgotten deeds to find evidence of sinful conduct. Their forensic work helped Haya converts characterize themselves as sinners, and set them on a different course in life. Yonathoni Bengesi, a missionary's houseboy, heard revivalists preaching in 1939. Later that evening, after several hours spent in prayer, Bengesi

> saw his saviour stretched out on the cross for his sins. He saw the blood dripping down from the nail prints ... if he looked at the wall, he saw only this. If he tried to read a book, he saw only this ... He had pilfered salt, sugar, firewood etc. from the house, and had never realized that every sin he did was another nail fastening his saviour more tightly to the cross. He said he knew he had other sins, which he did not now remember, but the Lord would remind him later.[25]

Bengesi and other converts were looking at their actions from a novel angle. Many Haya revivalists describe the moment of awareness in which they came, for the first time, to see their sins. Martha Kibira, who converted as a schoolgirl in 1948, described how after hearing revivalists preach 'I came to see my sins. There were boys who were writing letters to me. I didn't obey the school's rules.' After her conversion, Kibira confessed her newfound sins to her father, telling him that 'The other day I told you that I was with my aunt, but I was walking with a boy and making friendship. Therefore forgive me.' Her father mocked her, saying that she was too young to have sinned.[26] Kibira saw her actions in a different light than her father. One of my interviewees described how, as a young boy, 'I used to take some things from mother, maybe small small things from the home. We would take a little food, and mother was not able to know.'[27] When later in life he heard the Ganda evangelist Samweli Matovu preaching, however, he came to see such actions as sin. Matovu, he remembered, 'was like a dictionary for us.' His preaching defined certain previously uncontroversial actions as sins. With Matovu's sermons in his ears, my interviewee confessed his youthful thefts of food to his mother.

Converts were generating hard evidence of their iniquity in the inventories they made of their lives. Through their testimonies, they were making visible actions and relationships that they defined as sin, and in so doing, they rendered their lives up for outsiders to examine. Felix Kabunga dreamt of a man in white robes, telling him to 'confess your sins and those of your

---

[24] Quoted in Bengt Sundkler, *Bara Bukoba: Church and Community in Tanzania* (London, 1980), 87.

[25] HMC JEC I/3: Lionel Bakewell, circular letter, 29 April 1939.

[26] Interview: Martha Kibira, Kibeeta, Bukoba, 22 August 2006.

[27] Interview: Herman Kataraia, Bukoba town, 11 August 2006.

own people.' For eight days, he remembered, 'I felt as though I was being judged. I cannot describe how terrible it was.'[28] Other converts similarly found themselves called to the docket. Ernest Lutashobya converted in 1938 while a student in Bukoba's teacher training college. In a dream he saw 'my whole sins come ... I didn't see the grass, or the stones, because it was foggy.' With his sins laid out, Lutashobya saw the Lord judging the world, and heard a voice saying that 'Ernest Lutashobya must not be included among those who commit sins of fornication.'[29] In their dreams Kabunga, Lutashobya, and other converts were being made to answer for their sins. With the evidence laid out before them, with their conviction assured, they knew what to do. Titus Lwebandiza had a vivid dream in which he saw himself burning in eternal fire. He arose at midnight and for four hours he walked through his village, stopping at each house to confess his sins.[30]

Haya converts were not actually arraigned in a court of law, but the process that converts followed was structured on the model of the courts. Conversion in Buhaya was a social event, an intersubjective occasion, in which other people were invited to act as judges. The confessions that converts produced were called *mashuhuda* in Swahili, 'testimonies,' the same name given to the evidence that witnesses produced in a court of law. These testimonies were a genre, patterned by a set of conventions. Revivalists had to configure their life stories to a template, and their listeners made judgments about the reality of their conversion based on the character of the testimony they gave. The Lutheran churchman Richard Mutembei described how in the 1940s and 1950s 'It was mandatory to use a lexicon ... the usage was *ndugu* ['brother'], *kuweka nuruni* or *kutembea nuruni* [to 'put at the cross' or to 'walk in the cross'], *kusikia rohoni* [to 'feel in the heart'], *kufunu-liwa* [to 'be opened'], *kuungama dhambi* [to 'confess sins'], *timu* ['team'], *kovensheni* ['convention'].'[31] Critics like Mutembei thought the predictable, patterned character of revivalists' testimonies was evidence of the insincerity of their faith. For Haya converts, however, the generic form was a useful means of self-presentation. They found in the testimonial genre a way of reordering their lives, of distilling a complicated, interrupted, circuitous life story into a straightforward narrative. There was a pedagogical process by which converts practiced and learned the technique of testimony-giving. In 1938, Jonathon Karoma began to feel hands pressing on his head while he was praying. On occasion, the pressure was enough to make him cry out in pain. To his relief, Karoma learned from a group of revivalists 'a good route

---

[28] Sundkler, *Bara Bukoba*, 202.

[29] Murray papers: Interview with Rev. Ernest Lutashobya, Bukoba, 30 July 1988; Sundkler, *Bara Bukoba*, 97.

[30] Described in Sundkler, *Bara Bukoba*, 120–21.

[31] Richard Mutembei, *Kristo au Wamara? Historia ya Dayosisi ya Kaskazini Magharibi ya Kanisa la Kiinjili la Kilutheri Tanzania, 1890–1985* (Mwanza, 1993), 116.

of confessing sins.' As he followed converts' examples, Karoma testified, 'I felt my voice loosened, and I began to pray.'[32] Other converts similarly described the sense of release that came with learning how to testify. One of my interviewees described how preachers came to his school and gave him, as he put it, 'directions.' 'If you have a sin with your family,' they told him, 'you put it right, you confess your sins, and you will get a new life. If you have carried someone else's things, return it.'[33]

Haya converts were putting their private lives on display. Learning from evangelists from Rwanda and Uganda, learning also from the litigants who filled up the court dockets, Haya men and women sorted through the past, dredged up previously uncontroversial deeds, and found evidence of sin. Through this forensic work Haya people generated the narrative they needed to make themselves converts. Their self-interrogation was critically important work. It helped them to chart a course from one life to another.

REVIVALISM ON THE FRONTIER

Critics thought that talkative revivalists were incontinent. Haya people knew that respectable people kept their private lives under wraps. They carefully guarded the most intimate aspects of their lives, erecting screens that shielded the procreative actions of eating and sex from outsiders' gaze (see Chapter 7). Revivalists would not keep their mouths closed. One interviewee remembered that converts made a habit of confessing their sins 'openly.' He used the term *wazi*, the same term by which the loud, aggressive prostitutes of Buhaya were known. My interviewee remembered that revivalists' chief critic, the Lutheran pastor Paulo Kanywa,

didn't like the practice of confessing sins in front of people. He thought it was something for a *mshenzi* [uncultured person] ... When [critics] heard that people were confessing their sins in church, they said [in a strangled voice] 'Aaah! What are they doing here?' They didn't want to hear it ... If someone has committed adultery, [and confesses] in front of other people? Eee![34]

In Paulo Kanywa's partisan view, converts who publically confessed their sins lacked discipline. In their testimonies, they sullied the minds of those people who were obliged to listen to them. Converts very often implicated other people in their autobiographies, dragging them, willy-nilly, into their embarrassing testimonies. The Lutheran schoolteacher Marko Kaizilege complained to his missionary supervisors when, in 1949, one of his colleagues began to 'proclaim bad news about me.'[35] Kaizilege accused the convert of 'dirtying my name before the people of the fellowship,' so that 'the

---

[32] Mutembei, *Kristo au Wamara?*, 41–49.
[33] Interview: Herman Kataraia, Bukoba town, 11 August 2006.
[34] Interview: Ernest Lutashobya, Dar es Salaam, 25 August 2006.
[35] ELCT Box E VI B:2: Marko Kaizilege to Education Secretary, 24 July 1949.

hearts of the people are getting doubts about me.' There was more than his good name at stake. Kaizilege was convinced that his family's future was endangered by his colleague's slander. His banana trees had begun to wither, and his wife suffered from a lingering but untreatable illness. Through their slanderous preaching, converts had damaged the welfare of his household.

In many parts of Bukoba, revivalists were thought to be a threat to the commonwealth. One of the most contentious arenas of argument over revivalism was the kingdom of Kiziba in the northern part of Buhaya. Kiziba was a stronghold of the Haya Union, the organization that conducted the campaign against Haya prostitution in the 1950s (see Chapter 7). Kiziba's men kept a close eye on their wives and daughters. The king of Kiziba, Nestor Lutinwa, set the tone: his ancestor Mutahembwa, who had ruled Kiziba for more than thirty years, had fifty wives and sixty daughters at the time of his death.[36] From his ancestor's example Lutinwa learned that a king's reputation depended on his female relatives' honor. When Lutinwa's wives and daughters went to the government dispensary for treatment, he routinely sent his soldiers to keep watch over the medical orderlies who attended them.[37] In 1950 and 1951, Lutinwa was one of the key personalities behind the Haya Union's effort to rein in independent women's movements. He helped to organize the 'Bahaya Control Union of Prostitution,' which had its headquarters in Buyango, at the center of the kingdom. It cooperated with the Haya Union in setting up checkpoints to keep women from boarding the ferry at Bukoba.[38] Lutinwa used the powers of his office to return refractory women to their husbands. In 1951, several Kiziba women living in Nairobi complained that Lutinwa was forcing them to live with men whom they had divorced long ago.[39]

In the severe discipline with which he governed his wives' behavior, and in his personal war against prostitution, Lutinwa upheld a particular model of masculine honor. He and other Haya patriots thought revivalists were disturbing the peace. In 1948, the District Commissioner reported that a 'large section of the population' was aggrieved by the fluorescence of the Revival in Kiziba.[40] That year, the Lutheran pastor, an ally of Lutinwa, forcibly drove a large group of converts out of the church in Kiziba.[41] In 1952, Lutinwa accused two revivalists of burning his royal drum.[42] He complained that the revivalists had 'broken completely the custom of the country,' and

[36] Cory file 100: Hans Cory, 'Haya Customary Law,' 1945.
[37] Mwanza archives, Bukoba acc., L 5/22: S. Rwezura at Gera dispensary to DC Bukoba, 16 February 1949.
[38] TNA Acc. 71 790 B: Bahaya Union and Bahaya Control Union of Prostitution, 'The System of Suppressing the Prostitution of Haya Women,' 6 June 1950.
[39] TNA Acc. 71 790 B: Vorha and Vorha to DC Bukoba, 20 February 1951.
[40] TNA Acc. 215 2237: Bukoba District Annual Report, 1948.
[41] ELCT Box A IV: 1 'Minutes, Pastors conference, 1941–75' file: 'Habari ya Mkutano wa Wachungaji,' n.d. (but May 1948).
[42] Nestor Lutinwa to DC Bukoba, 9 May 1952, quoted in Mutembei, *Kristo au Wamara?*, 37–38.

asked the British District Commissioner for help in guarding the 'wealth of the country' against malevolent converts. In Kiziba, as in other Haya kingdoms, the beating of royal drums was an expression of a king's coordinating power. Royal drums were beaten at the celebrations marking the new moon, where Haya people made themselves visible before their king.[43] Shouting *Habuka* ('Visible, my Lord!') and dancing to the drum's rhythm, they made themselves open to the king's authority (see Chapter 7). By destroying Lutinwa's drum, the revivalists threw the social order upheld by the king into disarray.

Revivalists burned a great number of drums during the late 1940s and 1950s. The chronicler Richard Mutembei remembered it as a time of *chomachoma*, of 'burning,' when converts searched out amulets, shrines, and drums to incinerate.[44] Many people objected to converts' arson campaign. In the tiny kingdom of Bugabo, Lutherans forcibly drove revivalists away from their churches.[45] John Kasimbazi, a revivalist who was preaching in Bugabo, remembered that he and his colleagues were expelled from the church by cudgel-wielding congregants and ordered not to return.[46] He and his colleagues carried on with their preaching, traveling throughout Kiziba, Bugabo, Karagwe, and Kianja, often without food or money.

With the doors of the Lutheran church shut against them, Haya revivalists formed a new organization in 1952, which they called *Kanisa la Roho Mtakatifu*, the 'Church of the Holy Spirit.'[47] It was, for a time, the largest African-run church in Tanganyika. The church's main bases of support were in the westernmost kingdom of Karagwe and in Ihangiro, to the south. In Karagwe, the church was led by Felix Kabunga. Some years before his conversion, Kabunga – then in training for ordination in the Lutheran church – had divorced his wife. He was barred from the church's ministry as punishment. When he met a group of revivalists from Bugufi in 1940, he asked them 'What does it mean to confess sin?.' They answered 'We confess everything.' The following Sunday, Kabunga confessed his sins before a Lutheran congregation in Karagwe. In the very next breath, he preached a sermon on Matthew 23, in which Jesus condemned Jewish leaders for their hardness of heart.[48] As a convert, Kabunga took a new position in the social world. By his confession, he was transformed from a wayward delinquent

[43] Sundkler, *Bara Bukoba*, 55. See Steven Feierman, 'On Socially Composed Knowledge: Reconstructing a Shambaa Royal Ritual,' in *In Search of a Nation: Histories of Authority and Dissidence in Tanzania*, eds. Gregory Maddox and James Giblin (Oxford, 2005), 14–32.

[44] Mutembei, *Kristo au Wamara?*, 38.

[45] ELCT Box A IV: 1 'Minutes, Pastors' Conference, 1941–75' file: 'Mkutano wa Wachungaji,' Kanyangegereko, 22 February 1949.

[46] John Kasimbazi, 'Historia ya Uamsho wa Afrika ya Mashariki,' n.d. (but 2005). Manuscript in possession of Rev. Samuel Habimana.

[47] Rwamishenye archives, Box 21, 'Church of the Holy Spirit' file: Church of the Holy Spirit, Ibwera, to DC Bukoba, n.d. (but November 1952).

[48] Kabunga's autobiography is given in Sundkler, *Bara Bukoba*, 200–203.

into a moral authority who commanded attention. Church elders, finding themselves the unwilling subjects of Kabunga's sermons against ecclesiastical hierarchy, put him in prison for two weeks. Missionaries were likewise offended: they thought him to be 'the most powerful and colorful personality' in Karagwe, 'feared alike for his cunning strategy and his trickery.'[49] Kabunga's colleague in Ihangiro, to the south, was Sylvester Machumu. Machumu's father had been an *emandwa* priest, and, after his father's death, Machumu had inherited his vocation.[50] In 1937, Machumu watched as a group of Rwandan converts tearfully confessed their sins. Their example led him to see his life in a new way, for, as he later wrote, 'I began to see all my sins.' He confessed before a group of revivalists, then returned to his home and burned the shrines of his ancestors, as his mother lamented that 'he is destroying our defence and our shield.'[51]

The theology of the church that Felix Kabunga and Sylvester Machumu founded was composed on a frontier that was both political and geographic. Haya people had always distinguished their civilized, green homeland from the uncultivated hinterland to the west and the south. The Karagwe kingdom, Felix Kabunga's home, was Buhaya's least populated region. Whereas banana and coffee cultivation sustained flourishing human populations in the core Haya kingdoms, Karagwe's barren soil limited crop yields and made human settlement difficult. The population density per square mile was estimated at twenty people, as compared with the central kingdoms, where there were as many as 1,250 people per square mile.[52] Karagwe's people were the poorest in Buhaya, with an average cash income of twenty-eight shillings per taxpayer in the late 1940s, compared to an average income of eighty-one shillings in the rest of Bukoba.[53] These demographic and economic realities invited Haya people to scorn Karagwe's frontiersmen. When a sorcerer was driven out of a Haya settlement, he was told to go *omu iragwe*, to the deserts of Karagwe.[54] Even churchmen practiced this geographic chauvinism: in a sermon a Lutheran pastor once described how, when a Christian was baptized, 'the ancestor spirit leaves that person and makes his abode on the plain ... toward Karagwe, where no people live.'[55]

Ihangiro, the second base of support for the Church of the Holy Spirit, was likewise a world apart from the hierarchically organized kingdoms of central Buhaya. Like Karagwe, Ihangiro was thinly populated.[56] From

---

[49] ELCT Box F II C:1: Finn Peterson, 'Progress Report on Union between ECNWT and CHS Karagwe,' April 1963.

[50] Machumu's autobiography is given in Mutembei, *Kristo au Wamara?*, 50–52.

[51] Described in Sundkler, *Bara Bukoba*, 74.

[52] Cory file 19: Arthur Culwick, 'Land Tenure in the Bukoba District,' 14 March 1939.

[53] TNA Acc. 215 2237: Bukoba District Annual Report, 1948.

[54] Cory file 284: Haya glossary, n.d. (but after 1946).

[55] Quoted in Sundkler, *Bara Bukoba*, 72.

[56] In 1939, Ihangiro was estimated to support some 90 people per square mile. Cory file 19: Arthur Culwick, 'Land Tenure in the Bukoba District,' 14 March 1939.

the geography of their homeland Ihangiro's people developed a distinctive brand of political thought. Ihangiro's people were republicans. With open land around them, they could afford to reject their king's onerous demands. When Ihangiro's king demanded rent from his subjects in the late 1930s, they enlisted *en masse* in the African Association, a political organization that promised to represent their interests in Dar es Salaam.[57] In 1939, Ihangiro's activists were accused of burning down the king's house.[58] It is not by coincidence that, in 1952, the district government chose Ihangiro to be the first kingdom in Buhaya to elect its king. Ihangiro's republicans would not bend the knee to royalty.

The Church of the Holy Spirit's theology grew out of the distinctions that people in Karagwe and Ihangiro made between the pioneering, independent lifestyle of their homelands and the corrupted decadence of Buhaya's polite society. In their hymnody, in their testimonies, and in their manner of living, Kabunga and Machumu transformed geography into theology, setting their people apart from Buhaya's mannered citizenry. The hymns composed by Machumu during the 1930s and 1940s were meant for a pilgrim people, journeying toward another land:

> You friends of the Lord Jesus,
> behind us is darkness,
> and in front the Red Sea.
>
> *Chorus: Have you forgotten, have you forgotten,*
> *from whence you came?*
> *Gird up your loins, that you may not be lost.*
>
> You forgot that the journey
> is towards Heaven,
> and forgot to be amazed.
> Therefore you will have to repent.
>
> The enemies are encircling you,
> dogs are barking, devils are beating
> triumphantly on the drum.
> 'We have caught them now.'
>
> The one who looks back
> has lost the battle.
> He does not fear the Word of God,
> and is therefore marked by death.
>
> So let us give ourselves to Jesus
> and not look back.
> Behind us burns the fire
> from which we have been saved.[59]

[57] TNA Acc. 571 25: General Secretary to L. Ludovic, Bukoba, 21 February 1938.
[58] TNA Acc. 571 25: Rwangisa to P.C. Mwanza, 19 June 1939.
[59] Sundkler, *Bara Bukoba*, 198.

In Machumu's hymnody, converts were reenacting the Israelites' long sojourn through the Sinai wilderness. Like the Israelites, who spurned the allures of Pharaoh's Egypt in search of the Promised Land, and like Lot, who fled from the corrupted cities of Sodom and Gomorrah, converts were fleeing an evil, corrupted society. Like Lot and like Moses, converts had to keep their faces resolutely forward. Machumu was translating the moral geography of Genesis 18–19 into northwestern Tanganyika. In his hymnody, he gave church members an identity as purposeful pilgrims leaving behind a world of sin, and placed them on a narrow path leading toward another world.

The pilgrimage on which Machumu and his co-travelers embarked was also an exodus. The distance that pioneering converts put between themselves and the rest of Buhaya was sometimes expressed in a polemical form, as they contrasted their people's self-discipline with the corruption of Buhaya's political hierarchy. In the early 1950s, Machumu composed a manifesto against the tyranny that men from the kingdom of Kiziba exercised over the rest of Buhaya.[60] Kiziba's king, Nestor Lutiinwa, coordinated the Haya Union's campaign against prostitution in the early 1950s (see Chapter 7). At the same time, he and other Haya patriots campaigned against revivalists, who they accused of fomenting discord (see discussion earlier in this chapter). Machumu argued that Kiziba's leaders were tyrants, unjustly discriminating against Ihangiro's pioneers. Addressing himself to the 'honorable men and women of Ihangiro,' he complained that clergyman from Kiziba had 'driven us away from all our churches here in our own Ihangiro.' 'We worked with them,' Machumu complained, 'but they despised us; they abused us, [saying] "In Ihangiro only groundnuts grow, but no men!"' Ihangiro people's diet was in fact unique: whereas the prosperous farmers of lakeside Kiziba grew fat on bananas, pioneers in Ihangiro and Karagwe had to subsist on beans and groundnuts. Corpulent Haya farmers mocked Ihangiro's impoverished farmers for the thinness of their soil and for the weakness of their masculinity. 'They said that Ihangiro people eat dung and urine,' Machumu complained. 'They say that the Ihangiro people are backward.' Self-satisfied Haya farmers made disparaging comparisons across the agronomic frontier. Machumu, Kabunga and their co-travelers felt this comparative ethnography as an insult, and from their sense of injury they developed a theology of difference.

Living across the frontier, the converts of the Church of the Holy Spirit could vividly contrast their aesthetic lifestyle with the decadence of the old world. Their co-travelers in western Kenya similarly set themselves apart: they refused to dine with non-converted people and declined even to loan their utensils to their relatives (see Chapter 6). Converts in Kigezi distinguished themselves by their characteristic manner of dress, by their hairstyles, and by their cuisine (see Chapter 3). Such contrasts were central to

---

[60] Quoted in Sundkler, *Bara Bukoba*, 197–98.

the discipline of revivalism, for by them, East Africans created visible evidence of their new lives. Haya converts made particularly vivid distinctions. The very geography of Buhaya reinforced their sense of difference. Living across the banana frontier, the men and women of Ihangiro and Karagwe ate differently, cultivated differently, and lived differently than the wealthy farmers of the central kingdoms. These differences invited the converts of the Church of the Holy Spirit to pursue a distinctive vocation, to travel in a direction that led them away from the manners and culture of Haya society. Missionaries reported that Machumu and Kabunga's followers 'drew the frontier very distinctly between the saved and not saved ... When they have met someone who had not grown as much as they have themselves, they have refused to greet him as a brother.'[61] Sylvester Machumu listed the behavioral reforms that converts had to make:

We returned stolen things to the owners, broke the wooden tools for brewing local beer, and [we] burned the shrines in [our] homes. Concubines divorced their illegitimate husbands. Men divorced second wives. Christians refrained from trusting charms that were considered as their god. They repented of those they committed adultery with and stopped that sinful relationship ... Many were abandoned by their parents or divorced by their husbands. Others were beaten. However, Christians continued to confess their sins and give their testimonies, and many were saved.[62]

Members of the Church of the Holy Spirit were barred from wearing a tie or shoes, using a walking stick, combing their hair, wearing ornaments in their hair, chewing raw coffee beans, or rubbing themselves with oil.[63] Those who did not abide by these rules were expunged from the church's membership rolls.[64] Even the British District Commissioner heard of their rigor, commenting that church members 'insist on a more austere mode of life on earth.'[65] Converts of the Church of the Holy Spirit organized their lives around a set of contrasts. As pilgrims along the way, they tracked their progress by putting distance between themselves and the proud Haya elite.

Converts also put distance between themselves and their former lives through their public speaking. Whereas cultured men comported themselves with reserve and discretion, members of the Church of the Holy Spirit were known throughout Buhaya for their loquaciousness. When Sylvester Machumu visited missionary Bengt Sundkler's home for lunch in 1964, he talked for two hours, 'gesticulating with both hands and talking about his

[61] ELCT Box B II: 1 'Annual Reports, 1945–54' file: Annual Report of the Lutheran Missions, Tanganyika Territory, 1955.
[62] ELCT Box F II C:1 'History and Progress Report' file: Sylvester Machumu, 'Histori ya Kanisa ya Roho Mtakatifu,' 9 May 1966.
[63] ELCT Box B II: 1 'Annual reports, 1945–54' file: Sven Nasmark, Bukoba Superintendent's report, 1953; Sundkler, *Bara Bukoba*, 197.
[64] ELCT Box F II C:1: Finn Peterson, 'Progress Report on Union between ECNWT and CHS Karagwe,' April 1963.
[65] Mwanza archives, Acc. 1 2937: Bukoba District Annual Report, 1954.

experience.'[66] One of my interviewees remembered that members of the Church of the Holy Spirit 'used to just say words that were not in the language, even if they didn't understand them. They just said words ... you have to shout, you must be healed! You make a lot of noise and say that the Holy Spirit led you.' My interviewee attended a service where Felix Kabunga prayed for 'five minutes, ten minutes, fifteen minutes, twenty minutes. He was saying "Wow, woo, wee!" Thirty, thirty five. They were making noise, they were doing this and that.'[67] Critics found this type of preaching too much to bear. When Sylvester Machumu conducted a preaching tour in Karagwe, a Lutheran pastor attacked him, asking 'Why do you keep hurting people with these words?'[68] Machumu replied by asking 'What's the use of their being Christians ... if they do not keep the Commandments of God?' In their testimonies and in their manner of living, Machumu and his colleagues were marking their progress away from the polite conventions of Buhaya. Critics called Machumu and Kabunga's followers *abahabe*, the 'lost ones,' journeying down the wrong path. For his part, Machumu called the Lutheran church councils the 'Sanhedrin.'[69] In his partisan view, church elders were false judges, corrupted by their moral indolence and unable to distinguish right behavior from sin.

The Church of the Holy Spirit fractured in 1960. Machumu's group, based in Ihangiro, accused the Karagwe leader Felix Kabunga of monopolizing the church's resources, of claiming ownership of church buildings for himself, and of prohibiting Ihangiro evangelists from preaching to congregations in Karagwe.[70] By 1963, the Church of the Holy Spirit's congregations in Ihangiro had rejoined the Lutheran church.[71] But the Karagwe pilgrims would not agree to leave the path they were following. In 1963, Lutheran missionaries visited Kabunga's cathedral in Karagwe to discuss reunification. When they proposed that Kabunga's people should attend the Lutheran church for Easter services, there followed a 'ten minute hurricane, in which four to six women sitting on a bench near Rev. Kabunga acted as if they were mad.' The loudest among them, who was Kabunga's daughter, said that she would die before she rejoined the Lutheran church.[72]

---

[66] The lunch is described in Bengt Sundkler's diary, entry for 1 February 1964. Summarized in Marja Lisa Swantz, *Beyond the Forest Line: the Life and Letters of Bengt Sundkler* (Herefordshire, 2002), 188.

[67] Interview: Johanssen Rutabingwa, Bukoba town, 14 August 2006.

[68] Sundkler, *Bara Bukoba*, 196.

[69] Sundkler, *Bara Bukoba*, 191.

[70] Rwamishenye archives, Box 21, 'Church of the Holy Spirit' file: Central Committee meeting, 11 June 1960; Central Meeting of the Church of the Holy Spirit to DC Bukoba, 30 July 1960.

[71] ELCT Box A IV: 1 file B II: 6: Ihangiro District Annual Report, 1963.

[72] ELCT Box F II c:1: Finn Peterson, 'Progress Report on Union between ECNWT and CHS Karagwe,' April 1963.

The Karagwe branch of the Church of the Holy Spirit survived into the late 1970s.[73]

CONCLUSION

Pastor Christopher Mugoa, leader of the Church of the Holy Spirit in the Kianja kingdom, responded to the Bukoba District Council's anti-prostitution survey by identifying the 'origin of prostitution' as 'disobedience against God.'[74] Prostitution 'is a breach of God's law "You shall not commit adultery,"' he wrote. 'If people disobey God, they put themselves in trouble and in the end they will be destroyed.' Mugoa thought the answer to the prostitution problem lay in Christian conversion. He called on prostitutes to 'think of her acts and confess her sins before God.' But Mugoa was not a prophet, calling down the vengeance of God on a corrupt world. He trusted the apparatus of the law to control and discipline refractory women. Mugoa filled the anti-prostitution questionnaire with helpful suggestions for government officials, suggesting that professional prostitutes should be made to pay tax, that roadside bars should be closed, that jobless men and women should be compelled to devote their energies to agriculture, and that prostitutes should not be allowed to travel outside Bukoba. In his concluding paragraph, Mugoa cited Ephesians 6:10–11, 'Put on the whole armor of God, that ye may be able to stand against the wiles of the devil.' Mugoa sought to outfit government officials for an ongoing bureaucratic war against deviant women.

A variety of legal projects were under way in postwar Bukoba. There was never a straightforward contest between the 'world on paper' and the mobile, dynamic world of real life. Neither was the legal bureaucracy solely an instrument of governmental administration. Haya Unionists used the law to advance their moral reforms. The bureaucratic institutions they created took hold over independent women, confining them to particular social roles as obedient wives and daughters. Like Haya patriots, converts of the East African Revival thought prostitutes to be morally delinquent. And like the men of the Haya Union, revivalists trusted legal bureaucracy to control women's behavior. But converts were never allies of the Haya Union. The same men who regarded prostitutes with horror also looked on revivalists as antisocial antagonists of order. Whereas patriots carefully managed their public appearance, converts paraded their private deeds for other people to examine. Whereas patriots edited their private lives, converts made a point of opening up about their sins. Whereas patriots sought to fix people

---

[73] Finn Allan Ellerbek, *Karagwe Diocese: a Lutheran Church History* (Copenhagen, 1992), 51.

[74] Mwanza archives, Bukoba acc., L5/II/B: Christopher Mugoa to Secretary of the Bukoba Council, 3 July 1961.

in place, converts were pilgrims, journeying metaphorically and physically toward the outskirts of Haya society.

It was their legal work that propelled converts on their journey toward a new life. Revivalists behaved as though they had never left the courtroom. Standing at a crossroads, converts shuffled through their memories and their contemporary relationships. The investigative work they performed generated evidence of sinful conduct. Revivalists used the practices of the law to organize their autobiographies, to evaluate their conduct, to generate evidence of guilt, and to present themselves as redeemed. Converts practiced the techniques of legal procedure, developed competences in its generic elements, and created a theater for self-representation. The Revival in Bukoba, as elsewhere in eastern Africa, was a chapter in the social history of the law.

9

The Politics of Autobiography in Central Kenya

Literary critics have spilt a great amount of ink over Africa's novelists. The Cambridge University Library holds no less than thirty books of literary criticism concerning the Kenyan writer Ngũgĩ wa Thiong'o. This outpouring of scholarly attention is entirely out of proportion with the novel's place in the larger field of creative writing from Africa. It is autobiography – not the novel – that is eastern Africa's most widely practiced literary genre. Autobiographers worked within particular discursive regimens that encouraged the production of life histories. Christian missionary organizations were engines for autobiographical writing. African school goers composed their life stories in classroom essays assigned by missionaries to encourage self-examination and teach compositional skills. Some converts and clerics published their autobiographies, in English, on missionary presses.[1] Others wrote their autobiographies in the vernacular and stored them away for their children and grandchildren to read. Nationalist movements were likewise crucibles for the writing of life histories. Central Kenya's Mau Mau guerrillas seem to have spent as much time composing their autobiographies as fighting the British. More than a dozen Mau Mau memoirs have been published.[2] Parliamentarians and political party leaders drew from their

---

[1] For Kenya, the list includes Obadiah Kariuki, *A Bishop Facing Mount Kenya: An Autobiography, 1902–1978* (Nairobi, 1985); E. N. Wanyoike, *An African Pastor: The Life and Work of the Rev. Wanyoike Kamawe, 1888–1970* (Nairobi, 1974); Festo Olang', *Festo Olang': An Autobiography* (Nairobi, 1991); John Gatu, *Joyfully Christian, Truly African* (Nairobi, 2006); and, most recently, Teresia Wairimu, *A Cactus in the Desert: An Autobiography*, with Anne Jackson (Nairobi, 2011).

[2] See, among many others, Waruhiu Itote, *'Mau Mau' General* (Nairobi, 1967); Mohammed Mathu, *The Urban Guerilla: The Story of Mohammed Mathu*, ed. Donald Barnett (Richmond, British Columbia, 1974); and Wambui Otieno, *Mau Mau's Daughter: A Life History* (Boulder, CO, 1998). For a review of this literature, see Marshall Clough, *Mau Mau Memoirs: History, Memory, and Politics* (Boulder, CO, 1998). This material is analyzed in Derek R. Peterson, *Creative Writing: Translation, Bookkeeping, and the Work of Imagination in Colonial Kenya* (Portsmouth, NH, 2004), chapter 8.

speeches and their diaries, composing autobiography as they defended the positions they had adopted.[3] Life history writing finds a wide and interested audience: East African Educational Publishers and other publishing houses are producing compact, inexpensive biographies and autobiographies for sale on the school market.[4]

Scholars are only now coming to recognize how widely spread the practice of life history writing actually was. Africa's autobiographers were not professional writers; they rarely had their work published on international presses. They squeezed their writing into time that was full of other pursuits.[5] Many autobiographies are therefore multi-generic, cribbed from the sermons, petitions, and diaries that their authors also composed. In Ibadan, Akinpelu Obisesan kept a diary detailing the most intimate aspects of his life. His diaries constitute eight of the seventy-two boxes of paper that he filled before his death in 1963.[6] The Nyasaland clerk Kenneth Mdala wrote dozens of autobiographical letters to senior administrators during the 1930s and 1940s, offering his opinions on local government and commenting on the political issues of the day.[7] The Kenyan writer Gakaara wa Wanjau was detained for eight years by British security forces during the Mau Mau emergency. He filled his time with writing, composing several plays and hymns, conducting ethnographic research, carrying on a long correspondence with his wife, and keeping a diary.[8] There are, in all, several thousand pages of material, created by a man who found it difficult to lay hands on pencil and paper (see Chapter 10).

---

[3] Oginga Odinga, *Not Yet Uhuru: An Autobiography* (Nairobi, 1967); Tom Mboya, *Freedom and After* (Nairobi, 1986 [1963]); Harry Thuku, *An Autobiography* (Nairobi, 1970); Bildad Kaggia, *Roots of Freedom, 1921–1963: The Autobiography of Bildad Kaggia* (Nairobi, 1975); Kenneth Matiba, *Aiming High: The Story of my Life* (Nairobi, 2000); Wangari Maathai, *Unbowed: A Memoir* (London, 2007); and Koigi wa Wamwere, *I Refuse to Die: My Journey for Freedom* (New York, 2002). See also Muthoni Likimani, *Fighting Without Ceasing* (Nairobi, 2005). The Luyia politician Martin Shikuku's autobiography is currently in draft: Martin Shikuku, 'The People's Watchman: The Life and Work of Martin Shikuku,' ed. Derek R. Peterson (manuscript, n.d.).

[4] Tabitha Kanogo, *Dedan Kimathi: A Biography* (Nairobi, 1992); Simiyu Wandiiba, *Masinde Muliro: A Biography* (Nairobi, 1996); Peter Wanyande, *Joseph Daniel Otiende* (Nairobi, 2002); Peter Ndege, *Olonana Ole Mbatian* (Nairobi, 2003).

[5] Karin Barber, 'Introduction,' in *Africa's Hidden Histories: Everyday Literacy and Making the Self*, ed. Karin Barber (Bloomington, 2006).

[6] Ruth Watson, '"What is Our Intelligence, Our School Going and Our Reading of Books Without Getting Money?" Akinpelu Obisesan and His Diary,' in *Africa's Hidden Histories*, 52–77.

[7] Megan Vaughan, 'Mr. Mdala Writes to the Governor: Negotiating Colonial Rule in Nyasaland,' *History Workshop Journal* 60 (2005), 171–88.

[8] The diary was published, in English, as Gakaara wa Wanjau, *Mau Mau Author in Detention* (Nairobi, 1986). The larger body of Gakaara's compositions is discussed in Cristiana Pugliese, *Author, Publisher and Gikuyu Nationalist: The Life and Writings of Gakaara wa Wanjau* (Bayreuth, 1995).

Contemporary scholarship on autobiography has been shaped by the French philosopher Georges Gusdorf's 1956 essay on the 'Conditions and Limits of Autobiography.'[9] Gusdorf showed that autobiographers consciously imposed an order on their narratives, lending direction and coherence to events that were in fact disconnected. By highlighting the creativity of autobiographers' works, Gusdorf made it possible to conceive of the genre as literature, not simply a transcription of past events. He was convinced that autobiographical writing was preeminently the work of white men.[10] Autobiography 'is not to be found outside our cultural area,' he wrote; 'one would say it expresses a concern peculiar to Western man.'[11] For Gusdorf, the appearance of autobiographical writing heralded the dawning of a new era of self-conscious individualism, a project realized primarily in modern Europe.

Gusdorf's essay shaped the scholarship on autobiography in at least two ways. First, Gusdorf's preoccupation with the subjectivity of the autobiographer put psychology squarely at the center of literary scholarship. Whereas Gusdorf claimed that autobiographical writing heralded the birth of the modern, self-conscious individual, literary critics have illuminated the variety of selves that autobiographers composed.[12] Diane Bjorklund's *Interpreting the Self* is emblematic of this body of scholarship. Arguing that autobiographies are 'a good source for investigating changing ideas about the self,' Bjorklund organized more than 100 American autobiographies in chronological order, showing how, over the course of two centuries, Americans' conceptions of themselves have changed.[13] Each of Bjorklund's chapters follows the same structure: there is a section on 'historical background'; another on 'components of the self'; then evidence of 'changes in self'; and a consideration of 'the role of society and significant others.' With this grid, Bjorklund puts American autobiographers on the psychiatrist's couch and uses autobiographical writing to unpack their mental constitution.

A second body of scholarship set out to relativize Gusdorf's claims about the Western provenance of autobiographical writing. Whereas Gusdorf argued that autobiography was preeminently the fruit of the Western *mentalité*, contemporary scholars have democratized the study of

---

[9] Georges Gusdorf, 'Conditions and Limits of Autobiography,' in *Autobiography: Essays Theoretical and Critical*, ed. James Olney (Princeton, 1980), 28–48.

[10] Argued in Olney, 'Autobiography and the Cultural Moment: A Thematic, Historical, and Biographical Introduction,' in Olney, ed., *Autobiography*, 3–27.

[11] Gusdorf, 'Conditions and Limits,' 29.

[12] James Goodwin, *Autobiography: The Self Made Text* (New York, 1993); Paul John Eakin, *How Our Lives Become Stories: Making Selves* (Ithaca, 1999); Michael Mascuch, *Origins of the Individualist Self: Autobiography and Self-Identity in England, 1591–1791* (Cambridge, 1997).

[13] Diane Bjorklund, *Interpreting the Self: Two Hundred Years of American Autobiography* (Chicago, 1998), xi.

autobiography by showing how, in a variety of cultural and political land-scapes, writers composed their life stories.[14] While this body of scholarship usefully challenges Gusdorf's ethnocentrism, scholars working in this area too often treat autobiographers as spokesmen for cultural blocs. In his foun-dational book *Tell Me Africa*, for example, James Olney argues that auto-biographies offer a unique means of accessing an African *mentalité*. The African writer's vocation, Olney writes, is to 'merge individual identity with group identity so that the part represents the whole, the whole is embodied and personified in the part, and the linear immortality of either is assured in the birth, reincarnation, and perpetuation of the common spirit.'[15] In a chapter on autobiographies from central Kenya, Olney claims that Gikuyu authors 'all seem to write the same autobiography: for them there is one archetypal Gikuyu life lived in turn by each successive embodiment of the Gikuyu spirit.'[16] For Olney, Africa's autobiographers are representatives of culturally homogenous collectivities.[17]

This chapter compares two very different autobiographies, both written in the Gikuyu language. The first, typed by Rev. Charles Muhoro Kareri dur-ing the 1970s, has almost nothing to say about the intimacies of the author's private life.[18] Born in Nyeri District, in northern central Kenya, Muhoro was one of the earliest students at the Church of Scotland's Tumutumu mis-sion; later, he became the first African moderator of the Presbyterian Church of East Africa. His autobiography poaches shamelessly from missionaries' archive. He rewrites missionary-authored biographies, clips pages from church minute books, and fills several chapters with lists of churchmen's duties. The second autobiography was handwritten by Cecilia Muthoni Mugaki, who grew up with Charles Muhoro in the classrooms of Tumutumu mission. Cecilia shared an education, a language, and a circle of acquain-tances with Charles Muhoro, but her life story followed a very different plotline. Cecilia was an early convert to the East African Revival, whose emissaries reached Tumutumu from faraway Rwanda in the late 1940s. The autobiography is her testimony of conversion. Both Cecilia Muthoni and Charles Muhoro composed their life histories with particular ends in view. Muhoro hoped that his readers would invest themselves in the text. His collection of lists and pithy biographies worked like a casting call: the book

---

[14] Pei-Yu Wu, *The Confucian's Progress: Autobiographical Writings in Traditional China* (Princeton, 1990); Noboru Tomonari, *Constructing Subjectivities: Autobiographies in Modern Japan* (Plymouth, U.K., 2008); Mariam Lichtheim, *Ancient Egyptian Autobiographies Chiefly of the Middle Kingdom: a Study and an Anthology* (Göttingen, 1988).

[15] James Olney, *Tell Me Africa: An Approach to African Literature* (Princeton, 1973), 67.

[16] Olney, *Tell Me Africa*, 248.

[17] See Carol Neubauer, 'One Voice Speaking for Many: The Mau Mau Movement and Kenyan Autobiography,' *Journal of Modern African Studies* 21 (1) (1983), 113–31.

[18] Published as Charles Muhoro Kareri, *The Life of Charles Muhoro Kareri*, ed. Derek Peterson, trans. Joseph Kariuki Muriithi (Madison, 2003).

opened itself out to its readers, summoning them to act as dedicated members of the church. Cecilia's autobiography is a transcript of a testimony she practiced and rehearsed over several decades. Whereas Muhoro's book invited his readers to act in faithful service to the church, Cecilia's testimony laid bare the private arguments that set her at odds with Tumutumu's bureaucrats.

Neither Cecilia Muthoni Mugaki nor Charles Muhoro Kareri can easily be fitted on the psychologist's couch. There is no autobiographical pact between writer and reader, no guarantee that the content of the book will faithfully articulate the author's life story, or disclose evidence about his or her psyche.[19] Cecilia Mugaki and Charles Muhoro composed their life stories within particular institutional settings and in the midst of specific discursive routines.[20] They folded texts composed by other writers – lists, meeting notes, and testimonies – into books that were ostensibly their own. Cecilia Mugaki and Charles Muhoro were writing motivational literature. They laid claim over the literary genres and bureaucratic disciplines that converts, church leaders, and politicians also practiced, and used them to shape their readers' agendas.

Neither do these autobiographies reflect an underlying, homogeneous Gikuyu *mentalité*. Cecilia and Muhoro were partisans, intervening in the debates in which Gikuyu people more generally were engaged. In central Kenya, as elsewhere in eastern Africa, revivalists and polity-builders disagreed over where to place private life in the public sphere. These autobiographies illuminate how far East Africans' arguments over the Revival were, also, debates over the politics and practice of life history work.

TEXTUAL WORK AND POLITICAL IMAGINATION

Charles Muhoro Kareri's autobiography is a collection of texts that other people composed. He shoehorns vampire stories, church council minutes, anthropology, adventure tales, and biblical exegesis into his book. This easy intertextuality is central to Muhoro's purpose. Like the missionaries and African thinkers whose strategies he emulates, Muhoro works to direct his readers' actions in the world.

The history of Muhoro's autobiography begins in the library and archive at Tumutumu mission, where Muhoro attended school (see Map 2). Tumutumu was established in 1908, when Church of Scotland missionaries secured a five-acre freehold plot from Gikuyu landholders.[21] Presbyterian missionaries

---

[19] This *contra* Philippe Lejeune, 'The Autobiographical Pact,' in Lejeune, *On Autobiography* (Minneapolis, 1989), 3–30.

[20] Sidonie Smith and Julia Watson, 'Introduction,' in *Getting a Life: Everyday Uses of Autobiography*, ed. Sidonie Smith and Julia Watson (Minneapolis, 1996), 10–11.

[21] PCEA I/A/1: Land Office to H. E. Scott, 15 October 1908. See Peterson, *Creative Writing*, chapter 2.

knew the power of biographical literature. Their religious tradition taught
them to regard biography as evangelistic pedagogy. The *Abridgement of
Mr. Baxter's History of His Life and Times*, published in 1702, contained
the life stories of some 2,435 persons, mostly Presbyterian divines, who had
suffered for the cause of nonconformity.[22] Baxter's writings were reprinted
in 1830, and excerpts from his collection of biographies were published in
several editions over the course of the nineteenth century.[23] The Presbyterian
missionaries who built the Tumutumu mission had a whole library of inspirational biographies at their disposal. In their hands, biographies became
classroom lessons. The earliest catechism course at Tumutumu concentrated
on 'The Lives of Extraordinary People.'[24] From 1909 on, the standard reading primer for was *Mohoro ma Tene Tene* ('Stories of Long Ago'). It featured
the story of Nebuchadezzar, the proud king humbled by God, and the story
of Samson, the strong man whose weakness was his pride. Missionaries told
stories like these to induce readers to reflect on their own lives and measure themselves against the characters in the story. As missionary Marion
Stevenson explained in 1910,

[The stories] can be used as a help to raise their ideas. I remember the almost amused
surprise with which tales of self-sacrifice used to be received; the other day the story
of the Roman soldier at the gates of Pompeii roused a very different emotion. They
are being helped to realize that a man's greatness is not always and everywhere measured by the number of wives he possesses.[25]

Biographies were the means by which missionaries modeled morality, good
conduct, and self-sacrifice for their students. As they advanced through the
upper standards of Tumutumu's schools, students were expected to master
the biographical genre for themselves. In 1930, prospective school teachers at Tumutumu had to write a series of short biographical essays in their
qualifying examinations. Their subjects, chosen by the headmaster, were
Dr. Krapf, Mr. Wakefield, Sultan Barghash, Sir William McKinnon, Carl
Peters, and David Livingstone.[26] In the early days of their work, Tumutumu
missionaries established a library for use by ex-students who wished to
continue their education. There were no geography books, nor were there
history books.[27] The Tumutumu library's shelves were crowded with biographies. It contained English-language biographies of the missionary David

[22] Edmund Calamy, ed., *Abridgement of Mr. Baxter's History of His Life and Times* (London, 1713 [1702]).
[23] Rev. William Orme, ed., *Practical Works of the Rev. Richard Baxter*, vols. 1 to 23 (London, 1830). See Ian Green, *Print and Protestantism in Early Modern England* (New York, 2000); Mascuch, *Origins of the Individualist Self*, 143.
[24] PCEA I/A/19: Marion Stevenson to Arthur Barlow, 2 February 1915.
[25] Marion Stevenson, 'Widening Horizons,' *Kikuyu News* 21 (July 1910).
[26] PCEA II/E/6–8: Headmaster at Tumutumu to Director of Education, 2 July 1930.
[27] PCEA I/C/7: George Grieve to Watson, 22 February 1922.

Hill in China, King Khama of South Africa, the ill-fated Anglican bishop James Hannington, the Scots missionary Mary Slessor, the West African educationalist James Aggrey, and Apollo Kivebulaya, the Ganda apostle to the Congolese pygmies.[28] It also held John Bunyan's *The Pilgrim's Progress*, both in Swahili and in English. By 1943, 200 ex-students at Tumutumu were members of the library, having paid a small fee for borrowing privileges.[29] Success in Tumutumu's schools meant mastering the biographical genre. Missionaries hoped Gikuyu readers would come alongside the characters portrayed in these stories, using their examples to chart the course of their own lives.

But it was more than missionaries' prompting that fed Gikuyu students' interest in biography. Tumutumu's students adopted exemplary biographies to orient their own life courses. Catechumens in search of baptismal names ransacked Tumutumu's library, dug through the Bible, and read biographies voraciously. One of my interviewees, a man named Arthur Kihumba, read English history for his baptismal name, choosing Arthur 'because it was the name of king.' Jedidah Kirigu, baptized in 1934, similarly named herself after royalty. She chose the name Jedidah – the mother of the Old Testament King Josiah – from a list prepared by a friend.[30] Their baptismal names positioned Gikuyu converts in the political world. In 1938, Kimamo, a squatter living on a white settler's farm in the Rift Valley, was baptized with his wife and children. He took the name Ibrahim; his son was Isaaka. They were the names of the founding family of Israel, to whom God had once promised the land of Canaan. By adopting their baptismal names, Ibrahim and Isaaka looked forward to a day when they would take possession of the land possessed by their white taskmasters.[31]

In writing his autobiography, Charles Muhoro elaborated on a literary genre in which missionaries and Gikuyu converts had invested themselves for nearly a century. His autobiography was a book of names, meant to introduce new role models to inquiring Gikuyu readers. Toward the beginning of his autobiography, for example, Muhoro reflected on the life of his missionary teacher Marion Stevenson. Stevenson was an accomplished woman: trained in language and music at the University of Edinburgh, she served as a missionary at Tumutumu for nearly thirty years. After her death, she became the subject of an English-language biography titled *A Saint in Kenya*, written by fellow missionary Mrs. Henry Scott and published in Scotland in 1932. It is clear that the autobiographer Charles Muhoro had Mrs. Scott's

---

[28] TT Presbytery of Tumutumu file: 'Mbuku Maria ma Library ya Kanitha Tumutumu,' November 1941.

[29] PCEA I/B/7: Tumutumu Annual Report, 1943.

[30] Interviews: Arthur Kihumba, Othaya town, Nyeri, 7 July and 16 September 1998; and Jedidah Kirigu, Magutu, Nyeri, 12 August 1998.

[31] PCEA I/A/40: Arthur Barlow to PC Central Province, 2 August 1938. See Peterson, *Creative Writing*, chapter 1.

book at his elbow as he composed his own biography of Marion Stevenson. This intertextuality is most obvious in his analysis of Stevenson's Gikuyu nickname, *Nyamacaki*. Mrs. Scott had explained the name by describing how Stevenson had once been robbed of a checkbook.

Her houseboy might have been involved in the inquiry, but she refused to give evidence or to implicate anyone. This boy, who is now one of the ordained ministers, says that she called him 'son.' It was the turning point of his life. From the incident of the cheque-book came her native name Namachecki, or One-who-possesses-many-cheques.[32]

There are other ways in which Mrs. Scott might have translated *Nyamacaki*. Several of my interviewees at Tumutumu thought the name meant 'the thin animal.' Their explanation made *Nyamacaki* into a comment on Marion Stevenson's dining habits. Stevenson was rumored to have eaten Chief Kariuki, who died in 1915 while under treatment in Tumutumu hospital.[33] She and the other missionaries were widely said to eat human flesh and to drink from human skulls.[34] At one of the small outschools near Tumutumu, students ran away in fright when one morning Stevenson appeared in the schoolyard. Only six of the thirty-three students were willing to sit for the examination she administered.[35] Jeremiah Waita, one of Tumutumu's earliest catechumens, remembered that on the first occasion he met Stevenson, 'my eyes found that she had bad teeth.'[36] Tumutumu people had their eye on *Nyamacaki*'s mouth, and her nickname reflected their unease with her dining habits.

Charles Muhoro was undoubtedly aware of the rumors regarding *Nyamacaki*'s dining habits, and he sought to clear her name. His account of Marion Stevenson's life story was modeled on the hagiography that Mrs. Henry Scott had published. Writing in Gikuyu, he explained that

She was given the name Nyamacaki after she refused to report a situation in which her checkbook and other things had been stolen. According to a book on her life, if she had reported the case, her houseboy would have been incarcerated. This man later became a student and one of the very first church ministers ... He said that Nyamacaki called him her son.[37]

Muhoro similarly borrowed from Mrs. Scott's biography when describing *Nyamacaki*'s personal discipline, her liberal politics, and her love for

---

[32] Mrs. Henry Scott, *A Saint in Kenya: A Life of Marion Scott Stevenson* (London, 1932), 125.

[33] Scott, *Saint in Kenya*, 207.

[34] Interviews: William Mwangi, Ruare, Nyeri, 3 April 1998; Elijah Kiruthi, Mahiga, Nyeri, 15 June and 16 September 1998; Gerard Gachau King'ori, Gitugi, Nyeri, 19 June and 8 July 1998; and Ngunu wa Huthu, Magutu, Nyeri, 12 August 1998.

[35] PCEA I/E/10: Marion Stevenson, 'Elementary Education,' July 1922.

[36] PCEA I/C/47: Jeremiah Waita, memorial to Miss Stevenson, n.d.

[37] Kareri, *Life*, 15.

students. Her life, he wrote, 'should challenge many women to offer themselves for the service of this country.' He invited his readers to measure themselves against *Nyamacaki*, to take her moral character on themselves. 'Many women named their baby girls Nyamacaki,' wrote Muhoro. 'The nickname stuck, because when the baby girls named Nyamacaki grew up and got married, their children were given the name Nyamacaki.'[38]

Charles Muhoro was a moralist. He needed to model behavior, shape readers' ambitions, and open grooves of social action that others could pursue. In his effort to model morality, Muhoro built on a textual strategy that Gikuyu Christians and Scots Presbyterians had been practicing for more than eighty years. Missionaries asked their charges to read biographies in order to impress them with the values of self-sacrifice, honor, and discipline. Gikuyu Christians read biography strategically, to tap into the political and moral resources of the British and Christian histories. Charles Muhoro invited his readers to invest themselves in other people's lives. He used missionaries' hagiography to clean up Miss Stevenson's reputation, suppressing Gikuyu rumors about her deviant eating habits. His sanitized sketches of Stevenson and other characters led readers to cast themselves in her character.

As a biographer, Muhoro laid out paths of action and imagination for his readers to follow. As an archivist, too, Muhoro gave his readers directions. Muhoro became Tumutumu's part-time archivist in 1936. 'I began by writing church registers, transferring the names of the people who had been baptized from the old record books to new ones,' wrote Muhoro. 'Anybody interested in seeing them can find them today at the Presbyterian church office at Tumutumu.'[39] Muhoro's autobiography is a digest of the archives he knew so well. The book is packed with lists: lists of first baptisms, lists of ordination dates, and lists of church members. Muhoro also gave his readers clippings from Kirk Session minute books, church constitutions, reports, and sermon notes. And, in the penultimate chapter to the book, he reconstructed the hierarchy of the Presbyterian Church of East Africa, listing the duties of church officials and admonishing them to perform their tasks properly.

For Presbyterian churchmen of the 1920s and 1930s, making lists was more than a bureaucratic formality. Record books constituted the membership of the church. Children or adults who passed through the catechumens' class had their names entered into a 'book of the sacrament.' This entitled them to take communion, to have a church wedding, and to participate on church committees. Any member who transgressed church law was banned from communion. In the record book, the word *githengio* (expelled) was carefully written against the sinner's name. Keeping these record books updated was a vitally important business. In 1933, missionaries drew up a

[38] Kareri, *Life*, 10–11.
[39] Kareri, *Life*, 61.

list of responsibilities for Tumutumu's Gikuyu pastors.[40] The first item on the list, before preaching, Bible study, or any other religious vocation, was 'Carefully entering up all church rolls, and seeing that those in the central station are also kept up to date.' The second item was 'Keeping a diary or a log book.' Bookkeeping was a preeminent pastoral duty.

These books did not record already-existing loyalties among Gikuyu people. Keeping records was a way for church organizers to create a political community. In 1929, Presbyterian missionaries toured churches in central Kenya asking members to sign a pledge promising to forgo circumcision for their daughters. John Arthur, head of the Scots' Kenya mission, began the campaign in the northernmost Presbyterian station at Chogoria. One of my interviewees remembered what happened in this way:

> At Chogoria there was a doctor called Dr. Arthur. He was very tough, that guy. Very authoritarian. He went and got a book, and put it in front of the church, and said 'From today in Chogoria there will be no-one circumcised, and that is an order, and anyone who agrees with that order come and write here.' And the ones who were refusing were saying, 'We do not want our girls circumcised because the Europeans want to marry our daughters.' After a while Jonathan Muriithi went and signed, and after that ten people signed.[41]

Dr. Arthur's record book constituted a political division among Gikuyu people. Those who signed the books, at Chogoria and elsewhere, came to be called *īrore*. The term means 'thumb-marks,' the mark that Jonathan Muriithi and others put on Arthur's book. Those who rejected the anti-circumcision program were called the 'refusers.' At Mahiga, one of Tumutumu's several outstations, a great number of church members refused to sign Dr. Arthur's pledge. In April 1930, the Tumutumu Kirk Session ruled that the names of two hundred 'refusers' at Mahiga should be removed from the communion rolls.[42] Three months later, it established the policy whereby excommunicated members could be returned to the communion list. The procedure went as follows:

a. If a person requests readmission, he should first rectify his sins and other non-Christian activities. He must show repentance.
b. Upon attending the elders' court, he is given time to confess his misdeeds and to repent. After this, the minister will tell him that he is readmitted. His name is then reentered in the baptism book.
c. The person is kept on probation for a period of not less than a month, during which time he learns the sacramental lessons again.

[40] TT 'Ministers' file: 'Pastoral Work,' 1933.
[41] Interview: Cecilia Muthoni Mugaki, Tumutumu, Nyeri, 25 July 1996 and 16 September 1998.
[42] PCEA I/Z/6: Tumutumu log book, 19 April 1930.

d. After the probation ends, his name is entered in the book of the sacrament.[43]

Record books were more than a formality. These books were the pivot around which contending Gikuyu political communities formed. Who signed what, whose name was written where, who refused to sign – these were the questions around which this political controversy was mobilized.

With their names excised from Tumutumu's communion register, the 'refusers' at Mahiga created their own roll books. They founded an independent church just down the hill from the Presbyterian congregation, at a place called Kagere. By October 1931, Kagere's church roll listed 465 members.[44] Some of those who enrolled were shop owners at a nearby trading center. Others were part-time wage earners, working as clerks for European planters in the Rift Valley. In 1931, this group of entrepreneurs banded together to form the Kikuyu Traders Association (KTA) to raise funds for a proper school building at Kagere. Fifty-eight men joined the KTA at its inception. Their names were carefully arrayed in columns in the association's books, noting the amount they had donated beside the name.[45] The association's 'Rules to Members,' penned in the midst of the fundraising campaign, went like this:

1. Anyone who wishes to join the school should put a signature that he is willing to assist with its work and abide by its rules.
2. He should agree to be like a firm soldier prepared to develop the country, willing to agree with what has been agreed upon. Whomever agrees can sign voluntarily, and those against will not be forced. Every signature is one shilling.
3. All deliberations by members should be put into writing. All agendas should arrive at the secretary's office prior to meetings and any agenda that does not arrive will not be discussed.[46]

In its lists and roll books, the KTA identified contributors and, in so doing, created a purposeful community. Members who refused to contribute funds had their name cancelled from the books. Those who contributed became 'firm soldiers,' partisan actors joined in their shared pursuit of education. Like Dr. Arthur and the note-takers at Tumutumu, the bookkeepers of the KTA used lists to define and solidify changeable human loyalties.[47]

---

[43] TT Kirk Session minutes for 8 June 1930.
[44] KTA 'Mariitwa ma Athomi a Mahiga: New Promise,' 26 October 1931.
[45] KTA 'Members, Kikuyu Traders Association, Kamakwa,' n.d.
[46] KTA 'Rules to Members,' Mahiga, 1932.
[47] For further discussion of the Kikuyu Traders Association, see Peterson, *Creative Writing*, chapter 6; and Derek R. Peterson, '"Be like Firm Soldiers to Develop the Country": Political Imagination and the Geography of Gikuyuland,' *International Journal of African Historical Studies* 37 (1) (2004), 71–101.

Presbyterian missionaries and the 'refusers' of the KTA differed in their evaluation of female circumcision, but they similarly recognized how record
books could help purposeful human communities cohere.

Charles Muhoro borrowed his motivational techniques from this wider
field of archival practice. In the thirteenth chapter of his autobiography,
Muhoro described the 'Matters of the Church and How it Conducts its
Affairs,' enumerating the duties of church elders, deacons, and ordinary
church members. Elders' duties are listed under five headings, which include
visiting the sick, administering Holy Communion, and shepherding the
Christian flock. Deacons, Muhoro warned, should not underestimate their
role. Like Stephen, who was stoned for being a follower of Jesus, deacons
should 'accept the work, performing it with humility and dedication.'[48]
Muhoro also gave directions to church ministers, listing the 'factors that
may hinder a minister from performing his duties.' These included laziness,
'desire for fame,' 'speaking with bad jokes,' and indebtedness. Muhoro the
church organizer was borrowing the motivational strategies that missionaries and Gikuyu political organizers had also pursued. In the 1930s, Dr.
Arthur and his antagonists in the female circumcision controversy had used
record books to hold their constituents to account. Charles Muhoro's memoir built on this strategy of mobilization. His lists of duties and responsibilities invited deacons, ministers, and other church officials to identify
themselves with their role, to play the part they had been assigned.

Muhoro's autobiography is a script through which readers were invited
to characterize themselves. Muhoro *the biographer* asked readers to invest
themselves in exemplary life stories. Muhoro *the archivist* reminded church
members of their duties and, in so doing, held them responsible for their
actions. His autobiography is populated with characters on which readers
were invited to model themselves. As a means of configuring human action,
the autobiography builds on the motivational literature that Gikuyu people
had already been composing.

CONVERSION AND AUTOBIOGRAPHY

Converts like Cecilia Muthoni Mugaki would not act out the roles that
Muhoro and his colleagues gave them. Baptized at Tumutumu and trained
as a teacher, Cecilia was Muhoro's neighbor, and served with him on several church committees during the 1940s and 1950s. While Cecilia Mugaki
lived her life alongside Charles Muhoro, their life stories take very different
forms. Muhoro wrote a staid and boring book, full of moralizing advice for
his readers but lacking any detail about his own private life. Cecilia's autobiography, by contrast, is full of intimacy. At its center is her testimony of
conversion.

[48] Kareri, *Life*, 90.

Gikuyu revivalists learned how to shape their life stories to conform to the discursive practices that converts in Uganda and Rwanda pioneered. In April 1937, a group of Ugandan and Rwandan preachers visited central Kenya. Their leader was Simeon Nsibambi, the brother of the fiery Ganda preacher Blasio Kigozi; among the company were the missionary Joe Church and the Kiga schoolteacher Ernesti Nyabagabo.[49] In June 1942, the voluble Ganda evangelist William Nagenda spent a number of weeks in central Kenya, preaching in several Anglican churches.[50] Gikuyu converts were so closely identified with the converts of central Africa that the Revival in Gikuyuland was known as *Dini ya Ruanda*, the 'religion of Rwanda.' A convention held in Fort Hall District in 1947 drew at least 3,000 attendees. One member of the congregation was Doris Nyambura, the sewing instructor for the Tumutumu Women's Guild. She became the first evangelist for the Revival in Nyeri District. By 1950, Nyeri's churches were filled with revivalists, many of them women.

Gikuyu people made themselves converts by constructing narratives about their past. Within a few months of the Ugandan evangelists' first visit to central Kenya, converts were bringing their gourds, sugar cane scrapers, straws, and other beer-brewing implements to church, vowing never again to drink.[51] At a 1944 convention, converts filled a table with clothing and other goods they had obtained dishonestly.[52] Like their co-travelers elsewhere in eastern Africa, Gikuyu revivalists sorted through their possessions and their relationships to find evidence of sin (see Chapters 5 and 8). Bedan Ireri heard a Revival preacher tell his audience 'Pray to God so that he may give you a mirror, so that you may know what you are.' Later that evening, Ireri was lying in bed after an intimate encounter with a young man when he 'saw a big light, and a cloud. Then the Voice spoke to me and said, "You commit fornication," and I said Yes. "You are a liar" ... Yes ... "You are a thief."'[53] The following morning, Ireri repented of his sins in a public assembly. Converts were prompted to see themselves in a new light. Geoffrey Ngare converted after hearing Willian Nagenda preach at a Revival convention in 1948. With Nagenda's voice in his ears, Ngare could visualize his sins:

I saw that there were times when I was with my wife and she faced one way and I faced the other, we were too angry to speak to one another, perhaps because of something a child had done. Then if we heard someone knocking at the door, immediately we began to smile and talk normally ... When I was angry I would beat her with angry words, I threw them at her violently until she cried bitterly.

[49] CMS Annual Letters file: T.F.C. Bewes, annual letter, 22 June 1937.
[50] HMC JEC 5/1: William Nagenda to Joe Church, 15 June 1942.
[51] CMS Annual letters file: Leonard Beecher, annual letter, October 1938.
[52] HMC JEC 1/2: Howard Church, 'Movement of the Spirit in East Africa,' 2 May 1944.
[53] Murray papers: interview, Canon Bedan Ireri, 26 May 1988.

But I was content, because if anyone heard her or saw her, I could say, I don't beat her.[54]

Converts like Geoffrey Ngare and Bedan Ireri were looking at their lives from a different vantage point. They found material proof of their sins in their most intimate relationships.

Converts used the evidence they created to plot a passage to a new life. After George Kimani Kirebu converted in January 1940, he asked his wife's forgiveness for all the wrongs he had done, naming each one by name. It was a long list: Kirebu later described how 'I had told her some lies, I had ill treated her, I'm sorry to say that I had even beaten her not once nor twice.' As part of his stock-taking he paid over the poll tax he had for several years withheld from government collectors.[55] Missionaries worried when converts engaged in 'competitive confessing, sometimes of sins which are better not mentioned in front of large mixed audiences containing a fair proportion of children.'[56] The popularity of the testimony of conversion highlights its power. To be converted, revivalists had to illuminate the distance they had traveled between the old life and the new. Revivalist preachers often illustrated their sermons using posters of life's travelers on two ways, one to destruction and the other to the Eternal City.[57] Central Kenya's earliest Revival leader was converted after hearing a sermon on Hebrews 11:24, which asked him to come from the kingdom of Satan into the kingdom of Christ.[58] In their conversions, revivalists contrasted their old lives with their new, redeemed lifestyles. Through this classification, they took up a new position in the social world.

At conventions, in fellowship meetings, and in private conversations, revivalists made a practice of narrating how God had saved them from sin.[59] An effective testimony was not an unrehearsed inventory of private life. Testimonies were a carefully practiced form, a genre in which converts had to develop competence. The revivalist leader Heshbon Mwangi warned converts to be careful about their testimonies. 'We must not joke or talk lightly of sin or play with it,' he wrote. 'Worldly people speak soft words like butter and those who have not wisdom to discern what they are after, are deceived and fall.'[60] Speaking well was a spiritual virtue. Revivalists punctuated their loud testimonies with catch phrases learned from the Ganda evangelists who first preached revivalism in Gikuyuland.

54 Murray papers: interview, Geoffrey Ngare, n.d.
55 Murray papers: 'Personal Testimony of George Kimani Kirebu,' n.d.
56 CMS Annual Letters file: O. Wigram, annual letter, July 1944.
57 PCEA II/BA/10: Irvine, Chogoria Annual Report, 1949.
58 Dorothy Smoker, *Ambushed by Love: God's Triumph in Kenya's Terror* (Fort Washington, 1994), 87.
59 Smoker, *Ambushed*; Edith Wiseman, *Kikuyu Martyrs* (London, 1958); Kariuki, *African Bishop*; Olang', *Festo Olang'*; Wanyoike, *African Pastor*.
60 PCEA II/D/30–34: Heshbon Mwangi to revivalists, 1949.

The first line in the Luganda hymn *Tukutendereza Jesu* ('Let Us Praise Jesus') became a password for the group. Gikuyu revivalists greeted one another by calling out 'Tukutendereza Jesu,' and identified other converts based on their reply.[61] They also salted their language with the phrase *Mwathani arogocwo*, 'Praise the Lord' in Gikuyu. Their uncomprehending critics complained that converts spoke in a 'foreign dialect,' and that they 'speak a new language to deceive people into thinking it is the language of the Spirit.'[62] The critics' complaints illuminate the distinctive character of converts' discourses. Revivalists had to compose their life stories according to the linguistic formulas of a particular genre.

Cecilia Muthoni Mugaki wrote 'History ya Eustace Mugaki na Cecilia Muthoni Mugaki' in the Gikuyu language in 1982. It is a transcript of a testimony she composed, practiced, and polished in dozens of public gatherings. The manuscript begins with a confession of sin. Cecilia focused on her unhappy marriage with schoolteacher Eustace Mugaki in 1937:

> The devil became jealous of us on 11 September 1937, when we got married. The happiness which we had enjoyed was destroyed by the devil and we became a couple of fighting people, complaining again and again, until I declared that the devil had come into our prayers, that this was not my real choice ... We spent ten years with domestic problems which were uncalled for such that love and joy between us ended completely.

The archival record shows that in June 1938, the Tumutumu Kirk Session heard evidence that Cecilia had married Eustace while pregnant by another man.[63] She denied the accusation, and the Session admonished the couple to live together in peace. But Cecilia could find no satisfaction in marriage. Her only pleasure, she wrote, was in procreation: 'there was nothing in our home that attracted me apart from getting a child which I could not get on my own.'

In January 1948, Cecilia met the evangelist Doris Nyambura, who was returning from a Revival convention. It was the turning point in her life. At an evening meeting with Nyambura and three other revivalists, Cecilia was discomfited when she was asked 'Teacher, how is your relationship with Jesus?' When she half-heartedly confessed to having lost her passion for Bible-reading, the revivalists sprang to their feet, singing the Revival anthem 'Tukutendereza' and rubbing her head until, as Cecilia remembered, 'the headscarf came untied and the hair which had been plaited was left uncovered.' 'I was so afraid that I kept silent,' she wrote. That night, though, Cecilia's mind moved to her prospects for life after death. 'I started

---

[61] Smoker, *Ambushed*, 161.

[62] PCEA II/D/30–34: Charles Muhoro, 'Memorandum on the Matters of the PCEA Church: Confusion of Teaching,' March 1950; AIM 'Papers on Isms' file: Harrison Kariuki, 'Some Errors of Ruandaism,' November 1957.

[63] TT 'Committee of Presbytery' file: minutes for 27 June 1938.

understanding what the whole thing was about,' she wrote. 'It's me who woke them up at 6:00 am to pray. I told the Lord to forgive me for I was a sinner. Tears poured out.' It was then that Cecilia began practicing her testimony:

From there I got a testimony which I never knew I would have. I told them how I feared for myself when thoughts of death visited me, when my name had not been written in the book of life ... I confessed how I fought with my husband for thinking that he is stupid and I was clever. I thought he was not clever because he had come from school much later than me, and he had not traveled as much as me. He would then think I was belittling him, that I did not think he was supposed to be the head. I confessed all this, and the fruits of pride. As I said all this they would praise.

Her husband was suspicious when Cecilia asked for his forgiveness. In November 1948, though, Eustace himself converted. Cecilia's autobiography draws a stark contrast with her former life of sin. 'With both of us being converts, our work for the Lord became lighter and lighter with time,' wrote Cecilia. 'Now it is very light and I praise the Lord when I see in retrospect my foolish attitude to issues. I used to say that it was devils who had invaded our home, yet it was me who failed to commit everything to the Lord.'

Charles Muhoro and other Tumutumu elders would have heard this testimony a great many times. Eustace and Cecilia were leaders of the Revival at Kiriko, a church/school under supervision from Tumutumu. They and other converts organized day-long preaching sessions, often without the pastor's permission.[64] Missionaries worried that the Kiriko revivalists were causing trouble for church leaders. 'Unsaved teachers [are] held in contempt by children,' one missionary wrote. 'A little child of Standard One will tell a Form One (unsaved) where he gets off. In short, very fractious.'[65] At a church/school near Kiriko, pastor Johanna Wanjau locked the door against the noisy revivalists and forbade them from using the church's building. Angry converts broke the lock, and, during their testimonies, they likened Wanjau to the devil (see Chapter 10).[66] At Tumutumu church, some revivalists compared Presbytery moderator Charles Muhoro with the walls of Jericho, doomed to fall at the sound of revivalists' trumpet.[67] Others scorned Muhoro's faith as 'salvage Christianity,' dredged up from the wreck of the real religion.[68] Muhoro, in reply, ordered church leaders to 'beat them, excommunicate them, and imprison them.'[69]

---

[64] TT 'Correspondence with Kikuyu' file: R. G. M. Calderwood to Charles Muhoro, 17 April 1951.
[65] PCEA II/C/22: Donald Lamont to R. G. M. Calderwood, 27 May 1953.
[66] PCEA II/C/25: Charles Muhoro to R. G. M. Calderwood, 9 April 1952.
[67] TT 'Correspondence with Chogoria' file: Charles Muhoro to Clive Irvine, 19 April 1952.
[68] TT Marua Makonii Synod file: Charles Muhoro to Geoffrey Ngare, 1 June 1950.
[69] PCEA II/C/25: Clive Irvine to Donald Lamont, 25 April 1952.

There was more than personal animosity at stake in church leaders' confrontations with revivalists. Revivalists were contemptuous of church bureaucracy and of the records that Charles Muhoro and other bureaucrats carefully kept. In January 1948, six months after her conversion, Cecilia publicly accused Charles Muhoro and church authorities of mishandling their duties.[70] No receipts were issued for money collected in church, she complained, and leaders were involved in business ventures, making some people wonder whether their offerings to the church were being used as start-up capital for greedy clerics. Moreover, church laws about marriage, female circumcision, and beer drinking were being ignored with ministers' connivance. When Charles Muhoro spoke to a group of revivalists in 1949 about the church's position on the Revival, converts would not consent to hear him, arguing that 'He must not speak as he is full of sin.'[71] Revivalists refused to take communion from the hand of Muhoro or any other of Tumutumu's pastors.

Church leaders were appalled at revivalists' incendiary talk. A deacon at Tumutumu remembered that the revivalists 'recited Bible verses like poetry but they were empty in [their] hearts.'[72] One of my interviewees recalled that revivalists were called *Ndukananderehere* ('You will not bring it to me') by their detractors.

We would tell them 'We are not interested in what is coming from Ruanda.' We hated them because of the way they used to jump and some other funny things. It was funny because it appeared like child's play. You know preaching in that time was cool. We were used to the Scottish way – the Europeans had come in a cool and decent manner. They would not speak harshly to people. They preached slowly and in an orderly manner – also in a mature manner and they would not cheat you. The revival was disruptive.[73]

Revivalists' many words ignited private vendettas. Charles Muhoro condemned the revivalists for 'preaching because of existing disagreements.' Other Gikuyu critics complained that revivalists 'have filthy conversation in their meetings in secret.'[74] American missionaries complained that 'sins of adultery, of lustful thought and desire (even towards those present in the gathering) are frequently confessed ... There are things of which it is a shame to speak, and surely these are among them.'[75] At some point during

---

[70] TT 'Presbytery of Tumutumu' file: 'Issues Addressed at Tumutumu Meeting,' 25 July 1948.
[71] PCEA II/D/30–34: Robert Philp, notes on conversation with revivalists at Tumutumu, 1949.
[72] Interview: Muriuki Kiuria, Magutu, Nyeri, 13 May 1998.
[73] Interview: Daudi Gachonde, Tumutumu, 22 February 1998.
[74] PCEA II/D/30–34: Charles Muhoro, 'Memorandum on the Matters of the PCEA church'; AIM 'Papers on Isms' file: Harrison Kariuki, 'Some Errors of Ruandaism,' November 1957.
[75] HMC JEC 5/4: Africa Inland Mission, 'Report of the Committee Appointed by the Field Council under minute 36 of January 1952.'

the 1940s, Gikuyu people began using the verb *-goco*, the root of the revivalists' oft-repeated phrase *Mwathani arogocwo* ('Praise the Lord'), to mean 'purposeless, idle talk; disturbing chatter causing disorder or discord.'[76]

Why were Charles Muhoro and other Gikuyu churchmen so alarmed by Cecilia Mugaki and her talkative companions? Gikuyu people derived their theory of social order from their remembered history of forest clearing (see Chapter 1). Pioneering immigrants had first settled in the highland forests of central Kenya in the late seventeenth century. Using iron crowbars and axes, it had taken 500 days to clear three acres of forest land.[77] As a society of forest clearers, Gikuyu thought about civility in spatial terms. Responsible men separated the productive space of human habitation from the threatening forest. The verb *-gita* identified the work of fencing as the foundation of human communities: it connoted both to 'flourish, prosper' and to 'grow too thick to be seen through (as in a hedge).'[78] Prosperous people were careful about their fences. They kept their private affairs separate from public life. 'Home affairs must not go into the open' advised one proverb.[79] Soft words proverbially made homes cool and prosperous.[80] Loud arguments between husbands and wives spilled out into the open, and destroyed families. 'Too much talk breaks marriage,' warned another proverb.[81]

Revivalists' testimonies were controversial because they threw people's domestic affairs open to public examination. Whereas Gikuyu homesteaders proved their virtue by building up fences and minding their tongues, revivalists talked transparently about their innermost sins. There were rumors that traveling evangelists had sexual rights to female converts.[82] A Presbyterian committee appointed to investigate the revivalists condemned the group for 'their manner of greeting which involves kissing and hugging and ecstatic jumping.'[83] Moreover, revivalists called each other by intimate names reserved for the closest of kin. As a result, the committee maintained, they broke up marriages, 'creating strife instead of harmony between husband and wife.' The committee also criticized revivalists for their failure to respect church order. Converts were said to 'cause confusion in the church … as they are in the habit of rising up and staggering (in the fashion of drunks) when prayer is in session.' To church elders, revivalists were subversives. Gikuyu

---

[76] EUL Gen. 1785/1: Arthur Barlow, notes on *–goco*.

[77] Louis Leakey, *The Southern Kikuyu before 1903* (London: Academic Press, 1977), 168–69; see John Lonsdale, 'The Moral Economy of Mau Mau,' in Lonsdale and Bruce Berman, *Unhappy Valley* (London, 1992).

[78] EUL Gen. 1785/1: Arthur Barlow, entry on *-gita*.

[79] G. Barra, *1000 Kikuyu Proverbs* (Nairobi, 1994 [1939]), 4.

[80] EUL Gen. 1786/6: Arthur Barlow, 'Kikuyu Linguistics.'

[81] Barra, *1000 Kikuyu Proverbs*, 6.

[82] AIM 'Papers on Isms' file: 'Report on Ruanda Activities,' 10 August 1950.

[83] PCEA II/G/2: 'Report of the Subcommittee Investigating Persons Associated with the "Ruanda" Revival,' 28–29 October 1949.

political leaders similarly doubted revivalists' integrity. In his 1948 pamphlet entitled 'What Should We Do, Our People?', newspaperman Henry Muoria urged his readers 'Don't spend time praying at home without doing anything, only crying on account of your sins, as some people do these days.' He urged Gikuyu people to 'pray for good thoughts so that they undertake good actions,' and the 'strength to work so that what they conceived will be done.'[84] Hard-working patriots like Muoria scorned gossiping converts for their lack of discipline. They refused to put their hands to work, spending their time in idle, antisocial gossip. In 1946, it was rumored that Revival evangelists traveling through southern Gikuyuland were marking Africans' farms for expropriation by white settlers.[85] In their irresponsible wordiness, revivalists looked like traitors.

In central Kenya, as in southern Uganda, political authorities sought to discipline revivalists by shutting their mouths (see Chapter 3). Early in 1948, the Tumutumu Kirk Session ruled that the revivalists would not be allowed to speak in church gatherings. The Session went further later in 1948, when it ruled that revivalists should not meet even in private homes for prayer.[86] The church's ban on revivalism was called the *mūhingo*, the 'closed door.' By closing converts' mouths, church leaders hoped to re-erect the barriers that screened private affairs from the public ear. But revivalists would not shut up. '[In the church] I could not even greet people, or even tell them what I was doing,' remembered the revivalist Peterson Muchangi. 'But when we walked out we built our church outside under the trees, and we started singing, and giving testimonies. So outside we took advantage.'[87] The Tumutumu parish voted to renew the ban on revivalist preaching in 1952. When the pastor at Kiriko church announced the decision, Cecilia Muthoni Mugaki and her husband rose to their feet and sang the Revival anthem 'Tukutendereza Jesu.'[88]

The guerrillas of central Kenya's 'Mau Mau' movement were protagonists in this war against sexual and social indiscipline. Mau Mau was, in one aspect, a nationalist struggle against British colonialism. It was also a morally conservative struggle against the social irresponsibility that Cecilia Mugaki and other delinquents seemed to promote (see Chapter 10). Men of the Kikuyu Central Association began administering oaths against the Revival in 1948. Oath-takers promised that those who revealed secrets would have their tongues pierced with a red-hot iron, their eyes plucked out, and their hands cut off.[89] When Mau Mau partisans demanded that the

[84] Henry Muoria, *Writing for Kenya: Henry Muoria's Life and Works*, eds. Wangari Muoria-Sal, Bodil Folke Fredericksen, John Lonsdale and Derek Peterson (Leiden, 2009), 147.
[85] NLS Acc 7548/B/270: R. G. M. Calderwood to Beattie, 30 November 1946.
[86] KNA MSS Bible Society 1/8: Robert Philp to Arthur Barlow, 1948.
[87] Interview: Peterson Muchangi, Tumutumu, 15 September 1998.
[88] PCEA II/B/5: Donald Lamont to R. G. M. Calderwood, 23 April 1952.
[89] ACK 'Mau Mau I' file: Pittway, letter to prayer partners, 23 January 1954.

convert Edmund Gikonyo should take the oath in 1953, he refused, saying that 'Every man has to choose which world he wants. You have chosen this world, but I have chosen the world of Jesus and his kingdom.'[90] Revivalists were Mau Mau partisans' chief antagonists. They refused to bear arms during the war, either on behalf of Mau Mau or for the British. In their endless talk about their private lives, they undermined the discipline that Mau Mau promoted. Mau Mau activists printed notices saying 'Everyone should listen [and] curb your tongue seven times before you say a word.' The notices, one of my interviewees noted, 'taught us not to be a loud-mouthed person.'[91] For Mau Mau partisans, curbing their tongues was an act of civic responsibility. Mau Mau organizers used violence to silence revivalists who talked too much. The Revival preacher Ephantus Ngugi was slashed on the mouth and had his front teeth knocked out by forest fighters. They also smashed his megaphone, saying that 'This will never speak again.'[92] James Karanja was waylaid by Mau Mau partisans after he had attended a Revival meeting. They told him that his head would be severed from his shoulders should he speak about the oath he had taken.[93] Converts who kept silent were generally left to live in peace. One of my interviewees explained that 'Mau Mau hated being talked about. If you were talking about them too much, then they would fight you. If you kept silent, they wouldn't touch you.'[94]

Mau Mau rebels' distrust of voluble converts illuminates how much its partisans shared with church elders. Like the Presbyterian bureaucrat Charles Muhoro, Mau Mau's organizers sought to turn divided people into partisans serving a common cause. Converts could not march lockstep with the constituencies that Charles Muhoro and the organizers of Mau Mau sought to create. Whereas Tumutumu churchmen and Mau Mau rebels sought to reform constituents' morals and curb their tongues, converts kept talking. Whereas political organizers assigned partisans a role to play, converts were actors in a different drama.

CONCLUSION

In his recent review of *The Life of Charles Muhoro Kareri*, historian Wunyabari Maloba complains that Muhoro 'does not succeed in helping us explore the interior lives of African individuals and communities.' Muhoro is evasive about key historical controversies. He makes no mention of the 'cultural and political divide that haunted Gikuyuland' during the 1929–30 circumcision controversy, and deals with the Mau Mau rebellion

[90] ACK 'Mau Mau I' file: Carey Francis to CMS missionaries, 30 April 1953.
[91] Interview: Peter Munene, Iruri, Nyeri, 12 May and 9 August 1998.
[92] Smoker, *Ambushed*, 111.
[93] PCEA II/G/4: James Karanja to church elders, 22 December 1954.
[94] Interview: Timothy Gathu Njoroge, Kangema, 29 June 1994.

in a few short pages. Moreover, Maloba suggests, Muhoro is derivative. He makes 'very minimal deviation ... from the details, examples, and emphasis already set by white missionaries in their accounts.' About his private life, too, Muhoro is silent: save a short description of a railway-station parting with his wife, Muhoro has virtually nothing to say about his thoughts or feelings.[95]

Muhoro's reticence about his personal life makes his autobiography boring, but his reticence has a history. Muhoro has little to say about a divisive, contentious past because he and other organizers were committed to papering over the disputes that divided Gikuyu people. Like missionaries, like the organizers of Mau Mau, Muhoro sought to turn people into activists. He and other activists used record books and biographical writing to convince people to overlook the personal, private issues that set them at odds with each other. Revivalism attacked this discipline by opening up sexual and marital disputes for public discussion. Whereas Charles Muhoro invited his readers to be single mindedly devoted to a cause, revivalists' testimonies made long-kept secrets public, dividing families and destroying concord. Muhoro's autobiography had to be tedious and uncontroversial because the author was furiously working to keep his readers on the same page, committed to a singular vision of the future. His boring, unilluminating biography was supposed to paper over the internecine controversies that divided Gikuyu people.

The interpretation of vernacular literature in Africa and elsewhere has been clouded by assumptions about the organic connection between authors and their communities. The autobiographies of Cecilia Muthoni and Charles Muhoro do not reveal an underlying consensus. Gikuyu were never of one mind about their politics. Once we dispense with the notion that vernacular literature must faithfully reproduce the values of African communities, we can begin to glimpse the wider field of action in which these texts took their place. The Gikuyu public sphere was a forum for argument, not an arena of consensus. The plot lines that Cecilia Mugaki and Charles Muhoro composed were radically different. The bureaucrat Muhoro offered carefully drawn roles that his readers would, he hoped, take up as their own. Cecilia's autobiography, by contrast, invited readers to set their feet on a pilgrim's way, to engage in ongoing acts of self-narration. These two autobiographies were partisan interventions in a wider field of argument over the future of Gikuyu political community.

As partisans, neither Cecilia nor Muhoro had time to write about themselves. Their autobiographies were part of a frame up: they were shaped by discursive procedures that led people to behave in particular ways.[96] Both authors poached from literature composed in institutional settings. As

---

[95] Wunyabari Maloba, 'Christianity in Colonial Kenya,' *Journal of African History* 45 (2) (July 2004), 343–44.

[96] Smith and Watson, *Getting a Life*, 11.

biographers, archivists, list-makers, or converts, Cecilia and Muhoro were borrowing the organizational practices of the institutions of which they were a part. These autobiographies laid out roles into which other people could cast themselves. As authors, Cecilia Mugaki and Charles Muhoro remind us that a *persona* is a character to be played.

10

Confession, Slander, and Civic Virtue in Mau Mau Detention Camps

Gakaara wa Wanjau was born in 1921 in Nyeri District in central Kenya. His father, the Rev. Johanna Wanjau, and his mother, Raheli Warigia, were among the earliest students at the Presbyterian mission at Tumutumu and friends of the reticent autobiographer Charles Muhoro (see Chapter 9). The elder Wanjau was Muhoro's chief ally in his struggle against troublesome revivalists: he locked the doors of his church against noisy converts, and in 1952 he physically assaulted a revivalist preacher.[1] Gakaara's mother similarly possessed a formidable character. Her first teacher was Marion Stevenson, the Tumutumu missionary whom the biographer Muhoro chose as his model of self-discipline.[2] As a young woman, Warigia was one of a small group of Tumutumu women who formed an organization called *Ngo ya Tũirĩtu* (the 'Shield of Young Girls') to oppose the Gikuyu practice of female circumcision. Its members sheltered runaway daughters whose fathers compelled them to be circumcised. Warigia and her colleagues offered an unapologetic defense of their actions. 'People are being caught like sheep,' they wrote. 'One should be allowed to follow her own way of either agreeing to be circumcised or not without being dictated on one's body.'[3]

Gakaara learned a stern, straight-backed moral philosophy from his parents. Like Johanna Wanjau and Raheli Warigia, like the autobiographer Charles Muhoro, Gakaara knew that a good reputation had to be earned through rigorous self-discipline and protected against other people's insults. In 1948, he was working for low wages in the Rift Valley town of Nakuru,

---

[1] TT 'Marua Makonii Synod' file: Executive Committee of Tumutumu Presbytery, 8 April 1952; PCEA II/C/25: Clive Irvine to Donald Lamont, 25 April 1952.

[2] GW 'Biographical Writing' file: Gakaara wa Wanjau, 'The Life History of Raheli Warigia,' n.d.

[3] PCEA I/C/12 and 13: Nyambura wa Kihurani, Raheli Warigia et al. to South Nyeri Local Native Council, 25 December 1931. Published in *Women Writing Africa: The Eastern Region*, eds. Amandina Lihamba, Fulata L. Moyo, M. M. Mulokozi, Naomi L. Shitemi, and Saida Yahya-Othman (New York, 2007), 118–20.

living in a rented room crowded with other men. It was then that he became the chairman of the 'Rift Valley Agikuyu Union,' an organization that aimed to 'do away with prostitution.'[4] He wrote no less than three books that year. The first, a Gikuyu-language text on the 'Manners of Children,' aimed to 'pull the minds of Kikuyu children to education and to be of good behaviour'; the second, a pamphlet entitled 'Women of These Days,' was full of invective against prostitution.[5] Gakaara's moralistic writing was crowned with the Swahili-language book 'The Spirit of Manhood and Perseverance for the African.'[6] The book argued that white settlers had masked their dependence on black laborers by humiliating them. For their part, blacks colluded in their own emasculation by debasing themselves in prostitution, thievery, and other corruptions. As a writer and as an activist, Gakaara sought to stiffen his readers' backs and teach them discipline. He took a Mau Mau oath in July 1952.[7] Like other oath-takers, Gakaara committed himself to work for the common good, to stay away from prostitutes, and to fight for *īthaka na wīathi*, for 'property and self-mastery,' the right to social respect.[8] On 20 October, Gakaara was arrested and accused of fomenting Mau Mau ideology. He was held in British-run detention camps for eight long years.

Gakaara spent much of his time in detention engaged in writing. By October 1953, a year after his arrest, he had written a book manuscript entitled (in Gikuyu) 'The Mysteries of the Kikuyu Witchdoctor' and a pamphlet called 'Spit Out What You Have Taken.'[9] In 1955, Gakaara was conducting ethnographic research with other detainees at Manda Island camp. He wrote up his research, in pencil, in six exercise books under the title 'Which Clan do You Belong To?' The following year, Gakaara confessed before British officers to his involvement with Mau Mau. He was employed as a staff member as a reward for his cooperation. Under the eye of the British commandant, Gakaara composed at least five plays for detainees to perform. He also edited the detention camp newspaper.[10] During his eight years

---

[4] KNA JZ 7/6: Sydney Fazan, 'Petition no. 632: J. J. Gakaara Wanjau,' 12 July 1954.

[5] Described in GW 'Correspondence, 1948–49' file: Gakaara wa Wanjau to A Branch, East African Command, n.d.; Gakaara to Secretary, District School Committee, PCEA Rift Valley, n.d.

[6] See Cristiana Pugliese, *Author, Publisher, and Gikuyu Nationalist: The Life and Writings of Gakaara wa Wanjau* (Bayreuth, 1994), 40–41.

[7] GW 'Detention' file: No title, confession notes, 8 May 1956.

[8] PCEA II/G/4: Mau Mau oath confession forms, 1955–1956; see John Lonsdale, 'The Moral Economy of Mau Mau: Wealth, Poverty, and Civic Virtue in Kikuyu Political Thought,' in Lonsdale and Bruce Berman, *Unhappy valley: Conflict in Kenya and Africa* (London, 1992), 315–504; and Derek R. Peterson, *Creative Writing: Translation, Bookkeeping, and the Work of Imagination in Colonial Kenya* (Portsmouth, NH 2004), chapter 6.

[9] These two manuscripts have not survived. GW Detention file: Gakaara wa Wanjau to Gordon Dennis, 18 December 1953.

[10] KNA AB 11/61: Gakaara wa Wanjau to Community Development Officer, 27 July 1957.

in detention, Gakaara composed dozens of songs, carried on an extensive correspondence with his wife, negotiated through the postal system over his sister's remarriage, directed litigation over land he had inherited from his father, and kept a diary. The diary, carefully edited, was published in 1983 as *Mwandīki wa Mau Mau Ithamīrio-inī* (*Mau Mau Author in Detention*).[11] It won the 1984 Noma Award for publishing in Africa.

In her Pulitzer Prize-winning book *Imperial Reckoning*, historian Caroline Elkins inducted Kenya's detention camps into the world history of state-sponsored genocide.[12] For Elkins, the Mau Mau war was a straightforward struggle between two sides. Gikuyu were either part of a 'Mau Mau population' or British loyalists, moving in 'lockstep with the British to ensure their common collective interests.'[13] This two-sided political struggle was carried forward in detention camps, as tens of thousands of Gikuyu people were interrogated and tortured by African loyalists and British officers. Elkins argues that long-term detainees were made 'socially dead' through violence, humiliation, and isolation.[14] Some detainees nonetheless forged a will to resist, defending their commitment to Mau Mau by convening secret prayer sessions and by administering new oaths to waverers. Other detainees, who could not withstand the physical and psychological pressure that British officers applied, 'broke.' Elkins argues that those who confessed to their involvement with Mau Mau were motivated by a desire to save themselves from torture, abuse, and hard work.[15]

Elkins' book illuminates an awful history, but her simplified analysis straightjackets the interpretation of detention camp culture, making it hard to see the range of intellectual and moral projects in which detainees were involved. Detainees like Gakaara wa Wanjau were not simply defending their loyalty to a Mau Mau movement. Their intellectual world was not defined by the stereotyped political choices that Elkins sees. Gakaara and the many other Gikuyu men and women who took an oath in the late 1940s and 1950s were involved in a moral project, not a straightforward political war. They were worried over women's sexual conduct, over their own reputations, and over the future of the Gikuyu commonwealth. After they were detained by the British, Gakaara and other entrepreneurs carried these discourses about family life and political self-mastery forward. The 'world behind the wire,' as Elkins calls it, was not a world of the socially dead.

[11] Gakaara wa Wanjau, *Mwandīki wa Mau Mau Ithamīrio-inī* (Nairobi, 1983); Gakaara wa Wanjau, *Mau Mau Author in Detention* (Nairobi, 1988).

[12] Caroline Elkins, 'Detention, Rehabilitation, and the Destruction of Kikuyu Society,' in *Mau Mau and Nationhood: Arms, Authority, and Narration*, eds. John Lonsdale and E. S. Atieno Odhiambo (London, 2003), 191–226; and Elkins, *Imperial Reckoning: the Untold Story of Britain's Gulag in Kenya* (New York, 2005).

[13] Elkins, *Imperial Reckoning*, 60.

[14] Elkins, *Imperial Reckoning*, 156.

[15] Elkins, *Imperial Reckoning*, 179, 186–87.

Detainees did cultural work to ensure their wives' fidelity, to get leverage over brothers and clansmen, and uphold their own reputations.

Central Kenya's detention camps have to be studied within a regional frame. The men behind the wire did not inhabit a world that was separable from the rest of eastern Africa. Gikuyu detainees were, like Luo migrant laborers, terrified that their prolonged absence would cause their wives to seek out other suitors and encourage malicious neighbors to steal their land (Chapter 6). Like the members of the Haya Union, Mau Mau activists were convinced that prostitutes were destroying their people's political and demographic future (Chapter 7). And like patriots in Buganda and Kigezi, Gikuyu patriots were horrified at the indiscipline that the Revival seemed to promote (Chapters 3 and 4). Mau Mau guerrillas fought against social maladies that East Africa's conservatives more generally feared. As detainees, Mau Mau partisans carried their war against indiscipline forward behind the wire. Athi River, Manyani, and the rest of Kenya's detention camps were not simply analogues for Auschwitz or Treblinka. Neither were detainees martyrs, laying down their lives for an otherwise quiescent East African public. Mau Mau detainees suffered more than most people, but their nightmares, their political visions, and their trials were shared by people in Nyanza, Bukoba, and Buganda.

This chapter begins by briefly exploring the intellectual history of the Mau Mau war. In the 1940s, rural class formation left tenants and smallholders without land, making it difficult for husbands and fathers to hold their families together. Mau Mau grew out of a wider concern over moral order. Its advocates fought to ensure that Gikuyu posterity would enjoy a brighter future. The second section documents Mau Mau detainees' cultural and political work. Confronted with a Hobbesian world in which kinspeople seemed dangerously unaccountable, detainees composed ethnography and wrote letters. In their correspondence, they exercised leverage over their families and upheld their reputations. Detention camps were crucibles where innovative cultural work took place. Camps were also engines of autobiographical production. As the third section shows, British interrogators insisted that detainees make an inventory of the work they had done for Mau Mau. The demand that detainees should confess was a police intelligence-gathering procedure, but it was also a technique of self-presentation that Christian revivalists had pioneered. Dozens of revivalists worked alongside detention camp 'screeners.' Confronted with the demand that they confess, many 'hard core' detainees resolved to keep their mouths closed. The battle behind the wire was a further iteration in a much longer East African debate over conversion, confession, and self-discipline.

MAU MAU AND MORAL DISCIPLINE

In the 1940s, East Africa's patriots were engaged in a regional discourse about the demographic and epidemiological perils of prostitution. In

Nyanza, Luo patriots founded the Ramogi African Welfare Association, aiming to 'prevent and prosecute all girls and women who are at the present time running away from their husbands ... and are engaged in the prostitution business.'[16] Its agents kept watch over Luo women living in Nairobi and Kisumu, and repatriated prostitutes back to their rural homes (see Chapter 6). In Bukoba, the Haya Union imposed movement restrictions on traveling women, requiring them to seek permission from their husbands and fathers before they could travel to East Africa's cities (see Chapter 7). And in Kampala, members of the Kampala Batoro Association conducted house-to-house searches through urban neighborhoods, looking for Toro women who were living in sin (see Chapter 11). There was a wider context in which central Kenya's moral reformers conceived their anti-prostitution campaign, but there were specific reasons why central Kenya's husbands and fathers were particularly worried over women's morality. During and immediately after the war, rural class formation left some men without land, endangering their marriages. Wartime profits drove Gikuyu farmers to expand their holdings, forcing tenants and junior men off the gardens they had long cultivated. Native tribunals in Nyeri District, in northern Gikuyuland, had to institute double panels to deal with the backlog of land cases (see Map 2).[17] Nearly 40 percent of the land in Nyeri was held by smallholders owning from 2 1/2 to 5 acres, much less than the 12 acres needed to sustain a family.[18] Lacking enough land for subsistence and facing pressure from landlords, smallholders became proletarians in increasing numbers. In 1943 and again in 1947, Nyeri District produced the most migrant workers per capita of all districts in Kenya colony.[19] People living in southern Gikuyuland were likewise divided by class: 40 percent of Kiambu District's population lived below the poverty line.[20] Farmers, traders, and educated men climbed the ladder to wealth during the war, while migrant workers and smallholding peasants trod the road downward to poverty.

Their poverty in land and cash was an ontological problem for Gikuyu working men. We can hear land-poor men's terror in Vincent Mwaniki's plea to the Nyeri District Commissioner for the grant of a plot of land:

I am in severe trouble due to lack of residence and food for the family, as I am landless even a small piece of ground on which to farm would enable me to fight for them. The family is ever miserable ... My father was a poor man, [he] has

[16] KNA PC Nyanza 3/1/376: John Ogala to PC Nyanza, 19 October 1945.
[17] KNA PC Central 4/4/2: Nyeri District Annual Report, 1946.
[18] Kenya Colony and Protectorate, *Kenya African Agricultural Sample Census, 1960–61* (Nairobi, 1961), 20–21.
[19] KNA PC Central 4/4/2: Nyeri District Annual Report, 1943; KNA PC/CP/4/4/3: Nyeri District Annual Report, 1947.
[20] Greet Kershaw, *Mau Mau from Below* (Oxford, 1997), 165–67.

suddenly died and left my mother with my young brother being 14 years old, now however that I have got a wife with one boy being 12 years old, really I am awfully worried about them, surely they cry, and their condition proves to be unhealthy. I try hard to work, but without land I cannot do more than just keep the wolf from the door.[21]

Gikuyu farmers had always worked hard to keep wild animals away from homesteads. They built thick hedges around their homesteads, walling out the wilderness and protecting children and women (see Chapter 9). Whereas prosperity built up respectable men and established households, poverty tore them down. The verb *-hungura* meant both to 'render destitute' and 'exhaust, drain of vitality.' Poor, exhausted men were compelled to keep silent in elders' meetings, sitting with women while eavesdropping on the deliberations of their social betters. They were sometimes dismissed as *atereki*, 'beggars' but also 'timid, silent people.'[22] 'A poor man's tongue is always wrinkled,' went one proverb.[23] Poverty shut men's mouths, making them socially inconsequential. By denying family juniors and tenants like Victor Mwaniki access to cultivable land, rural capitalism attacked the material basis of Gikuyu masculinity. Without sufficient land with which to support their families, impoverished men found it impossible to claim other people's attention or respect.[24]

Domestic harmony was increasingly a privilege of the wealthy. Commodity farmers used wartime profits to monopolize marriageable women, stifling young suitors' hopes. They and other wealthy men drove up brideprice. After the war, parents were asking for ninety goats and four rams, totaling 1,190 shillings in cash, for the right to marry their daughters.[25] Earning 180 shillings per year as wage workers, laborers had little hope of meeting such a price. The frequency of church marriages throughout Gikuyuland dropped precipitously.[26] Formal marriage was too expensive for the poor, who saw their path to adulthood closed off. Even married men had reason to worry. In Nairobi and throughout rural Gikuyuland, female entrepreneurs took advantage of the postwar economic boom and set themselves up in business.[27] The profits they earned allowed some Gikuyu women to put distance between themselves and their

[21] KNA VP 1/27: Vincent Mwaniki to DC South Nyeri, 21 July 1947.
[22] EUL Gen. 1786/6: Merlo Pick, notes on *mutereki*.
[23] G. Barra, *1000 Kikuyu Proverbs* (Nairobi, 1994 [1939]), 98.
[24] This paragraph is derived from Lonsdale, 'Moral Economy of Mau Mau,' 339–40.
[25] AIM 'Problems, Dowry etc.' file: AIM Women's Committee, untitled memorandum, 1946.
[26] TT 'Correspondence with Chogoria' file: Robert Philp to Clive Irvine, 24 July 1942.
[27] Clare Robertson, *Trouble Showed the Way: Women, Men and Trade in the Nairobi Area, 1890–1990* (Bloomington, 1997); Luise White, *The Comforts of Home: Prostitution in Colonial Nairobi* (Chicago, 1990), chapter 8.

husbands. Clement Kiamiru, married for several years to Jelious, reported on his wife's failings before the church council at Tumutumu:

She went to Nairobi having been urged otherwise. She went to a wedding even when Clement urged against it. Someone told Clement he had found her inside a wattle forest with someone else. She even refuses to give him food or water ... When Jelious sold milk or even dresses, Clement could not get any of the proceeds. Clement had gone to take some fermented porridge and when he came back he found she had escorted someone else.[28]

Their control over cash gave working wives like Jelious both material and moral leverage over their husbands. Another complainant, a man named Duncan Thinji, told the Tumutumu church council that his wife, a market trader, had made him sexually impotent. He called a traditional diviner to his house and asked him to determine if his wife had laid a curse on him.[29] Thinji received no reprimand from the church council for his dalliance with the pagan diviner. Regardless of their religious convictions, worried husbands and fathers could agree that independent women were dangerous.[30]

Gakaara wa Wanjau was one among a larger cohort of downwardly mobile young men from Nyeri. After his discharge from the King's African Rifles, Gakaara lived for two years in Nairobi, where he and his Tumutumu classmate Mwaniki Mugweru opened East Africa's first African-run publishing house: the African Book Writers Ltd.[31] By 1948, his failing finances had compelled Gakaara to move to Nakuru, where he worked for the municipal council. In a newspaper editorial, he complained at the poor quality of municipal housing, and of its high cost.[32] 'You would find an African employee, a driver, mechanic, clerk etc. wandering about during the night suffering for somewhere to sleep,' he wrote. 'It is even shameful to state how these people sleep in one small room.' Gakaara himself was living in a single room, together with other council employees. His constrained circumstances compelled him to live apart from his wife, who stayed with his parents at Tumutumu. Early in 1949, Gakaara, desperate for money, was compelled to hawk cigarettes and foodstuffs in Nakuru's African township.[33] It was during this dark time that he filled in an application for a correspondence course at the 'British Institute of Practical Psychology.' The

---

[28] TT 'Coci ya Tumutumu' file: minutes for 21 April 1945.

[29] TT Mbuku ya Maciira, Kiama gia Tumutumu: minutes for 5 August 1940. Twelve years later, Thinji took a 'Mau Mau' oath (TT Kirk Session: minutes for 12 November 1955).

[30] Lonsdale, 'Moral Economy of Mau Mau,' 386–87.

[31] Described in Pugliese, *Author, Publisher, and Gikuyu Nationalist*, chapter 4.

[32] GW 'Correspondence, 1948–49' file: Gakaara wa Wanjau to Editor, *Baraza*, 3 March 1948.

[33] GW 'Correspondence, 1948–49' file: DC Nakuru to Gakaara wa Wanjau, 2 March 1949.

application illuminates how far his poverty endangered Gakaara's sense of self-mastery. 'I have much propaganda to make me a big man,' he wrote, 'whereas I have no ways.' When asked 'Do you feel your life lacks purpose?' he replied 'Yes, because of poverty.' And when asked 'Are you inclined to turn your eyes away when people look straight at you?,' he replied 'Big people, more educated and very rich.'[34]

Gakaara joined the Rift Valley Agikuyu Union in 1948. The Union was reported to have expelled a number of prostitutes from the township; those who refused to leave had been imprisoned.[35] The Union also had its eye on men: members were resolved that 'men who live on women's earnings should be prosecuted.'[36] It was at this time that Gakaara published his pamphlet *Wanawake wa Siku Hizi* ('Women of These Days'). Its aim, Gakaara explained, was to '[abhor] the bad reputation brought up by lazy African women who roam about shamefully in town with nothing to do but prostitution,' while also 'urging African women and men in general to cooperate together ... [in] minimizing prostitution in the country which ruins the progress of Africans.'[37] The booklet was one of a series of pamphlets about marriage and family life that Gakaara composed during the late 1940s. His first book, *Ũhoro Wa Ũgũrani* ('Marriage Procedures'), was published in 1946, while the pamphlet *Kĩguni gĩa Twana* ('Manners of Children') listed 'some usual good manners which are common to Kikuyu children' and encouraged them to 'respect their superiors and parents etc.'[38]

Spurred by the insecurity he felt over his own conjugal life, Gakaara wa Wanjau was creating a textual architecture to uphold a conservative social order. His literary and political work was part of a larger field of patriotic thought and action. A newspaper editorialist complained that many Gikuyu girls, 'beautiful, strong, very fit for mothers at home still loiter on Nairobi streets disguised as Alimas and Fatumas.'[39] Another editorialist wanted Gikuyu prostitutes to remember that 'The result of the havoc they are doing will be to bring into existence a new tribe of half-castes and bastards.' 'Their fiendish game is one of the best ways of exterminating a

---

[34] GW 'Correspondence, 1948–49' file: Enrollment form, British Institute of Practical Psychology, n.d. (but 1949).

[35] *Mumenyereri*, 6 June 1949; quoted in KNA DC Kisumu 1/28/56: Kenya Information Office, 'Summary of Opinions Expressed in the Kenya Press,' 6 June 1949.

[36] *Mumenyereri*, 27 June 1949; quoted in quoted in KNA DC Kisumu 1/28/56: Kenya Information Office, 'Summary of Opinions Expressed in the Kenya Press,' 1 to 15 June 1949.

[37] GW 'Correspondence, 1948–49' file: Gakaara wa Wanjau to East Africa Command, n.d. (but 1948).

[38] GW 'Correspondence, 1948–49' file: Gakaara wa Wanjau to Secretary, District School Committee, n.d. (but 1949).

[39] *Gikuyu Times*, 27 January 1948; quoted in KNA DC Kisumu 1/28/56: Kenya Information Office, 'Summary of Opinions Expressed in the Kenya Press,' 15 to 31 January 1948.

tribe,' the editorialist averred.[40] With their demographic future in mind, Gikuyu reformers debated the mechanisms by which refractory women could be brought into line. One editorialist invited readers to subscribe money toward the building of a jail where prostitutes could be confined.[41] Another, with the example of the Luo Union in view, proposed that Gikuyu women living in Nairobi should be required to carry a pass from their husbands.[42] During and immediately after the war, the patriotic men of the 'Kikuyu General Union' were interrogating Gikuyu women who lived in Nairobi, and repatriating unmarried girls to their fathers' homes.[43] In 1943, Nyeri District's local government ruled that a man who impregnated a woman out of wedlock should pay a bullock and a sheep to government elders and ten goats and ten shillings to the woman's father.[44] The price of sexual indiscretion had increased by 1949: under a new law, men who eloped with women were criminals to be punished with jail time.[45]

Gakaara wa Wanjau took a Mau Mau oath in July 1952. He and other oath-takers promised that 'I shall not walk with harlots,' 'I shall not lay with woman in the bush,' 'I should not fight with another member of Mau Mau,' and 'I shall not disclose Mau Mau secrets.'[46] Gakaara was inspired by these promises. In August, he called his two business partners to his Nairobi office, where he had arranged to give them the oath.[47] Gakaara paid the forty shilling fee on their behalf.[48] When Gakaara saw one of his colleagues drinking beer at a Nairobi bar, he reported him to Mau Mau authorities. Gakaara's thirsty colleague was fined 100 shillings for his tipple. Mau Mau's partisans practiced a stern morality. Men who took the oath were barred from consorting with prostitutes.[49] Karari Njama, who took the oath in 1952, promised that he would never make a girl pregnant and leave her unmarried.[50] Taking the oath made men responsible. Women, too, were obliged to discipline themselves. Ruth Wambuku, who took the oath in 1952, promised that

I will not do sorcery against Gikuyu. I will not make trouble if my husband buys another wife. I will not go into prostitution leaving my children impoverished. I will

[40] *Mucemanio*, 14 August 1948; quoted in KNA DC Kisumu 1/28/154: Kenya Information Office, 'Summary of Opinions Expressed in the Kenya Press,' 1 to 15 August 1948.

[41] *Mumenyereri*, 5 July 1948; quoted in KNA DC Kisumu 1/28/154: Kenya Information Office, 'Summary of Opinions Expressed in the Kenya Press,' 1 to 15 July 1948.

[42] *Baraza*, 30 October 1948; quoted in KNA DC Kisumu 1/28/154: Kenya Information Office, 'Summary of Opinions Expressed in the Kenya Press,' 15 to 30 October 1948.

[43] Described in White, *Comforts of Home*, 191–93.

[44] PCEA II/A/4: Nyeri Local Native Council meeting, 13–14 December 1943.

[45] TT 'Nyeri District Law Panel' file: minutes for 30 November 1949.

[46] KNA AB 1/83: Officer in Charge, Manyani, to Minister of Defence, 6 April 1956.

[47] KNA JZ 7/45: Confession report, AWC 1209: Stephen Wangara, 23 September 1955.

[48] GW 'Detention Correspondence' file: Note with no title, 8 June 1956.

[49] M. Mathu, *The Urban Guerrilla* (Richmond, 1974), 13–14.

[50] Karari Njama and Donald Barnett, *Mau Mau from Within: An Analysis of Kenya's Peasant Revolt* (New York, 1966), 118.

not put sorcery on the child of my husband. I will give thanks for the land. I will not go with men of other tribes.[51]

Mau Mau oaths demanded that young women like Wambuku commit themselves to their marriages. Just as the men of the Haya Union were campaigning against the moral degeneracy of Haya womanhood (see Chapter 7), Mau Mau partisans were likewise reengineering conjugal relations. One father living in Nyeri town was fined thirty shillings for betrothing his daughter to a Somali man.[52] Mau Mau's partisans thought conjugality to be an estate that needed defending.[53] The thousands of young men who went into the forest as Mau Mau guerrilla fighters in 1953 and 1954 were protagonists in this battle against sexual and social indiscipline. Forest fighters made a point of provisioning their families. One of my interviewees, who joined the guerrillas in the Aberdares forest, received a letter from home telling him to 'help his wife as he was in the bush.' He sent her forty-five shillings.[54] The forest leader Dedan Kimathi ran a welfare system for deserted wives of Mau Mau guerrillas, sending them money in installments of twenty shillings.[55] Rape was a capital offense for some forest fighters. When the autobiographer Gucu wa Gikoyo came upon a Mau Mau fighter raping a woman during a raid, he and others hacked the man to pieces.[56] General Mwariama carried an abandoned baby for three full weeks, feeding it with food from his own mouth.[57] Mau Mau supporters living on the Gikuyu reserves adopted abandoned children for the duration of the war.[58] In a war animated as much by fears over their uncertain demographic future as by anti-British sentiment, Mau Mau's partisans protected posterity from danger.

The Mau Mau war began as a socially conservative struggle against sexual promiscuity and moral laxity. Until the war became violent in mid-1953, many Christians saw the Mau Mau movement as a commendably Christian undertaking.[59] The Nyeri District Commissioner wanted all Presbyterian schools in Mathira Division closed: teachers and students

---

[51] PCEA II/G/4: Ruth Wambuku, 'Second Oath Confession Form,' 7 April 1955.

[52] KNA JZ 7/40: Confession report, AWC 869: Joseph Kahiga, 28 July 1955.

[53] Luise White, 'Matrimony and Rebellion: Masculinity in Mau Mau,' in *Men and Masculinities in Modern Africa*, eds. Lisa Lindsay and Stephan Miescher (Portsmouth, NH, 2003), 177–91.

[54] KNA JZ 7/46: Confession report, AWC 2081: Arthur Kihumba, 23 November 1956; interview: Arthur Kihumba, Othaya town, Nyeri, 7 July and 16 September 1998.

[55] KNA JZ 7/45: Confession report, AWC 1213: Karioki Muchemi, 19 November. 1955.

[56] Gucu wa Gikoyo, *We Fought for Freedom* (Nairobi, 1979), 149.

[57] David Njagi, *The Last Mau Mau Field Marshals* (Meru, 1993), 56.

[58] Ngugi Kabiro, *Man in the Middle* (Richmond, CA, 1973), 53.

[59] Daniel Branch, *Defeating Mau Mau, Creating Kenya: Counterinsurgency, Civil War, and Decolonization* (Cambridge, 2009), 76–77; Peterson, *Creative Writing*, chapter 8; Lonsdale, 'Moral Economy of Mau Mau,' 452–54.

thought Mau Mau was a just cause.[60] Missionaries thought Christians' embrace of Mau Mau was an abdication of their religious duty, but most people did not make distinctions between the goals of Christianity and Mau Mau. Theirs was a theologically pragmatic world. Oaths helped redress moral indiscipline. Grace Gathoni, a Presbyterian communicant, returned from work in Nairobi early in 1952. Her parents, worried about her virtue, compelled her to be circumcised. She was given a Mau Mau oath at the same time.[61] Both circumcision and oaths were means of securing girls' virtue. Anglican missionaries thought that more than 80 percent of their teachers had taken the Mau Mau oath.[62] The number was probably higher for Presbyterian schoolteachers: missionaries thought it was impossible to discipline all of them.[63] Even Christian clergymen took oaths: Jeremiah Waita, a colleague of Charles Muhoro at Tumutumu church, took three.[64] These Christians were not being disloyal to their religion. They took oaths because they thought Mau Mau's call for social discipline was a Christian project.

Guerrilla fighters built up an astonishingly wide network of support among Nyeri's people. British police called them the 'passive wing,' but there was nothing passive about Nyeri people's commitment to Mau Mau. Dedicated men and women, many of them Presbyterians, put themselves in danger to provision the young men of the forest. The 300 guerrilla fighters camped at Ngorano in mid-1953 got their food from friends in the local Presbyterian church.[65] One of my interviewees remembered that villagers slaughtered goats when Mau Mau men visited; female cooks smothered the smoke with blankets to avoid questions from the chief.[66] Neighbors provisioned the houses where Mau Mau men came to stay. One man gave his neighbor a tin of coffee, four pounds of sugar, and five pounds of flour to feed his houseguests.[67] Nyeri's people also contributed cash. Kariuki Waiganjo of Othaya town gave Mau Mau's collectors a series of small sums to pay for particular items: three shillings to buy ammunition; five shillings to buy food; twenty-five for a watch.[68] These small contributions added up to a considerable sum. In 1952, Mau Mau's treasurer in one location in Nyeri had collected as much as 12,000 shillings.[69] Other people donated

---

[60] KNA VP/2/1: Nyeri Education Officer to Director of Education, 10 October 1953.
[61] TT Kirk Session minutes for 20 June 1953.
[62] KNA DC Murang'a 3/4/21: Cyril Hooper to CMS teachers, January 1953.
[63] TT 'Fort Hall Supervisor' file: Kingston to Cyril Hooper, 19 July 1955.
[64] TT 'Ministers' file: Dr. Brown to Charles Muhoro, 23 November 1954.
[65] Interview: John Muriuki, Ngorano, Nyeri, 14 May and 6 August 1998; Kiboi Muriithi, *War in the Forest* (Nairobi, 1971), 18.
[66] Interview: Liliani Gachigua, Kiamariga, Nyeri, 9 and 10 August 1998.
[67] KNA JZ 7/40: Confession report, AWC 847: Muragura Karianjahi, 25 July 1955.
[68] KNA JZ 7/42: Confession report, AWC 980: Kariuki Waiganjo, 22 July 1955.
[69] KNA JZ 7/46: Confession report, AWC 2086: Wathuta Mbache, 22 September 1956.

their time to uphold the patriots of the forest. A repairman living in Othaya town fixed several wristwatches for forest fighters, earning the rank of captain as recognition of his services.[70] The government detained five staff at Tumutumu hospital for treating Mau Mau in their homes. Among them was the head Hospital Assistant.[71] Some Tumutumu medical attendants went into the forest, inoculating fighters against typhoid and administering penicillin to treat wounds.[72] Christian charity, and a deep sense of duty, led Nyeri's Presbyterians to protect the young men of the forest from the dangers of war.

Missionary Neville Langford Smith lamented the Gikuyu Christians' close embrace with Mau Mau. 'The tone of various letters written by Mau Mau adherents is that they are enduring hardships and danger to fight for the freedom of *ciana cia Mumbi* [the 'children of Mumbi'],' Langford Smith wrote. 'Women tend to regard them as their warriors; educated girls sew them embroidered badges.'[73] The Mau Mau war was never a straightforward battle between British loyalists and Mau Mau nationalists. Mau Mau fought on behalf of Gikuyu posterity. Its advocates sought to restore moral order, refurbish standards of sexual discipline, and bring a new generation to life. Theirs was a project in which a wide range of people invested themselves.

CULTURAL WORK IN MAU MAU DETENTION CAMPS

On 20 October 1952, Gakaara wa Wanjau was arrested and accused of fomenting Mau Mau ideology. The state's evidence against him was the 'Creed of Gikuyu and Muumbi,' which Gakaara had published in 1952. It was a rewriting of the Apostles' Creed, which Gakaara had learned during the years he spent in the classrooms of the Tumutumu mission. When Gakaara appealed against his detention in 1954, the British officers who reviewed his file concluded that he was 'probably a sincere fanatic of unstable mental balance. If set at large he might be very dangerous.'[74] Gakaara was detained for eight years: first at Kajiado; then at Manda Island and Takwa camps, on the Indian Ocean coast; at Athi River camp; and finally at Hola Open Camp, in Kenya's arid east. He was one of the tens of thousands of people, most of them men, who by 1956 were crowded into Kenya's 176 camps, prisons, and detention centers.[75] In that year, Kenya's prison

---

[70] KNA JZ 7/40: Confession report, AWC 854: Wachira Karuri, 27 June 1955 and 4 August 1955.
[71] PCEA II/D/17: Tumutumu Hospital Annual Report, 1954.
[72] PCEA II/A/1: John Wilkinson, 'The Mau Mau Movement,' n.d.
[73] ACK 'Mau Mau I' file: Langford Smith, 'Report on the Church in Embu District,' 1954.
[74] KNA JZ 7/26: Fazan, comments on appendix LXXI: Petition no. 632, Gakaara Wanjau, 12 July 1954.
[75] An official report puts the daily average in Mau Mau detention camps at 86,634 in 1956. See SOAS CBMS A/T 2/5 Box 278, 'Letter from Prison' file: G. Heaton, 'Report on the

population was nearly ten times greater than Great Britain's.[76] In all, more than 150,000 Gikuyu men and women spent some time in detention camps during the course of the rebellion.[77]

As they languished in detention, men like Gakaara sought to advance their war against social indiscipline. They shared a philosophy with the moral reformers of the late 1940s and early 1950s. As younger men, Gakaara and his compatriots had worked to control women's sexual conduct. As detainees, they upheld a strict discipline, conforming their behavior to a markedly conservative standard. As younger men, Gakaara and his companions had established legal and social institutions with which to reform Gikuyu family life. As detainees, they created committees, did ethnography, and wrote letters. Their intellectual and organizational work extended their influence outside the wire, and gave them a role to play in their families' lives. As younger men, Gakaara and his compatriots had struggled against the social indiscipline and political duplicity that the Revival promoted. As detainees, they kept their mouths closed, rejecting their jailors' demand that they confess.

Detention camps were brutal, brutalizing places.[78] In 1954, Manyani camp was home to more than 15,000 men crammed into aluminum-sided barracks housing sixty each.[79] Sewage from the latrines pooled near the kitchens. Ninety-seven detainees died of typhoid in October 1954.[80] But more than physical indignity, detainees at Manyani and elsewhere felt themselves imperiled by other detainees' immorality. In February 1957, two detainees at Embakasi Quarry Farm wrote to the governor to complain against a group of convicts brought in from a Nairobi prison. 'We have many young boys of our own which they like to do them as women,' they wrote.[81] They asked to be separated from 'those [who] like to do shameful and wily deeds.' Other detainees were alarmed at the petty parochialism of detention camp politics. Writing from Manyani camp, a complainant reported that Special Branch officers were inflaming detainees' prejudices.

General Administration of Prisons and Detention Camps in Kenya' (Nairobi, 1956). David Anderson gives the daily average of Mau Mau detainees as 71,346 in December 1954, in *Histories of the Hanged: The Dirty War in Kenya and the End of Empire* (New York, 2005), 313.

[76] KNA JZ 8/1: No author, 'Medicine for Mau Mau,' n.d. (but 1956).

[77] This figure is from Anderson, *Histories of the Hanged*, 5. Caroline Elkins puts the number of people who passed through detention camps, prisons and enclosed villages at 1.5 million. Elkins, *Imperial Reckoning*, xiv.

[78] Described in Anderson, *Histories of the Hanged*, chapter 7; and Elkins, *Imperial Reckoning*, chapter 6.

[79] KNA AH 9/5: Assistant Director of Medical Services to Commandant, Manyani, May 1954.

[80] KNA AH 9/5: Legislative Council minutes, 9 December 1954; Elkins, *Imperial Reckoning*, 138–41.

[81] KNA JZ 7/4: Mbugwa Boro and Kimani Njoroge to Governor, 11 February 1957.

'They say that Nyeri people were cheated by Kiambu people and their young men and girls were killed,' he wrote.[82] 'They should not teach bad manners to foolish people.'

Confronted with these and other forms of immorality, detainees imposed a strict discipline on themselves. At Takwa camp, detainees made a point of honoring the wives of their warders. 'We always tried to behave respectfully, and there wasn't a detainee who would not try to help a woman on the path,' remembered Gakaara wa Wanjau. Their self-discipline earned them the respect of their jailors. Detainees habitually drank tea in their warders' homes, and 'even we loved their children; they greeted us with pleasure when they saw us.'[83] At Yatta camp, in eastern Kenya, detainees punished any among their compatriots who drank alcohol, took bhang, or consorted with loose women. Even 'talking words of love to a girl' was punishable, and offenders were compelled to crawl, on their knees, back and forth on a concrete floor.[84] Not everyone observed this strict morality. At Hola camp, detainees stood in queues up to twenty deep, awaiting the attention of a prostitute named Maya.[85] But detainees were not libertines. At Perkerra camp in 1957, where detainees lived in semi-supervised open villages, the detainees' committee resolved that inhabitants should be 'men of strong character, and able to control their desires, which often led them into ruin.'[86] The committee barred women from the surrounding Tugen and Njemps communities from entering the village at nighttime.[87]

Detainees imposed impressively strict standards of discipline on themselves, but they could not be sure that their wives were doing the same. Detainees had alarmingly little influence outside the wire. They were terrified that their wives, left to fend for themselves, would forfeit their fidelity. They had good reason to worry. In the mid-1950s, the ratio of women to men in Nyeri District was seven to one.[88] In the absence of husbands and brothers, women had to do hard work to care for children and elderly relatives. Gakaara's wife Shifra Wairire, released from Kamiti prison in April 1957, cared for half a dozen children while also building a new house and participating in government-mandated communal labor. 'We were left as people whose kin had all died,' she wrote to Gakaara. 'I know that if you

[82] KNA AH 9/37: Gitui to Governor, 20 February 1954.
[83] GW 'Detention Diary Ms.' file: entry for February 1956.
[84] J. M. Kariuki, *'Mau Mau' Detainee: The Account by a Kenya African of his Experiences in Detention Camps, 1953–1960* (Nairobi, 1963), 83.
[85] Kahinga Wachanga, *The Swords of Kirinyaga: The Fight for Land and Freedom* (Nairobi, 1975), 155.
[86] KNA AB 18/30: Village Committee meeting, 5 October 1957.
[87] KNA AB 18/30: Senior Rehabilitation Assistant, Perkerra, to DO Marigat, 10 December 1957.
[88] Dr. Shannon, 'The Changing Face of Kenya,' *Kikuyu News* 210 (October 1955); Branch, *Defeating Mau Mau*, 112.

were present, we would not be undergoing what we are experiencing now.'[89] Some abandoned wives, desperate for support, found it impossible to resist the advances of opportunistic suitors. The detainee Samuel Muiruri learned through the post that his wife, Wambui, had married another man.[90] When her brother was offered dowry by a neighbor, Wambui found it unprofitable to refuse the man's proposition. Detainees worried that the men with resources at their disposal would take advantage of lonely wives. 'I know that any man cannot play around with you and convince you to offer them your body recklessly,' Gakaara wrote in a nervous letter to his wife.[91] 'Never agree to such a thing as offering your body to anyone who comes with the lies that he will help you. These are all lies.'

Worried over their wives' fidelity, detainees also worried over their male relatives' greed. Many detainees were junior members of their families, with older brothers who stood to inherit the bulk of their father's property.[92] Detainees' property was particularly imperiled after 1954, when, under the Swynnerton Plan, government surveyors set out to consolidate Gikuyu landholders' scattered gardens into larger, more economic units.[93] The scheme was part of the Kenya government's larger effort to encourage the growth of a landed African peasantry (see Chapter 6). Gikuyu detainees, like their contemporaries in Nairobi's Luo community, regarded the plan with trepidation. The government planned to confiscate land owned by recalcitrant Mau Mau detainees, allocating it instead to faithful Gikuyu loyalists.[94] An editorialist for the detention camp newspaper warned readers that their property was in danger. 'Land is being consolidated and it is only the owner of the land who may know everything concerning his land,' he wrote. 'If you are in a camp far from home this will be difficult.'[95] Detainees had to rely on wives, brothers, or cousins to represent them before government surveyors. They worried that their greedy relatives would take advantage of the situation. In 1957, detainee Anderson Mureithi was refused parole by his village chief. His brother, Mureithi learned, did not want him to receive land from their father, and so had objected to his release.[96] Mureithi was not alone in his worries over his relatives' honesty. Gakaara wa Wanjau was involved in

[89] GW 'Detention' file: Shifra Wairire to Gakaara wa Wanjau, 4 July 1957.
[90] KNA AB 18/2: Community Development Officer, Perkerra camp, to Probation Officer, Kiambu, 19 December 1956.
[91] GW 'Detention' file: Gakaara wa Wanjau to Shifra Wairire, n.d. (mid-1957).
[92] See KNA AB 18/10: Community Development Officer to DC Nakuru, 15 December 1956.
[93] For the Swynnerton Plan, see Christopher Leo, *Land and Class in Kenya* (Toronto, 1984); Gavin Kitching, *Class and Economic Change in Kenya* (New Haven, 1980); and particularly M. P. K. Sorrenson, *Land Reform in the Kikuyu Country: A Study in Government Policy* (Nairobi, 1967).
[94] Branch, *Defeating Mau Mau*, 123–25.
[95] KNA AB 11/61: Editorial in *Atĩrĩrĩ* 1 (51) 21 September 1957.
[96] KNA AB 1/94: Anderson Mureithi at Hola Camp to Community Development Officer, Saiyusi, 29 May 1957.

protracted litigation with members of his clan over land he had inherited from his father. 'I have heard a lot of complaints here in detention from the detainees because they are shortchanged on land ... even from people from the same clan,' he wrote in a 1957 letter to his wife.[97] But Gakaara had also heard 'many women praised because of how strongly they defended their family's land.' He instructed his wife and mother that 'this is the time when one is called upon to open her eyes wide open and be extremely crafty in inquiring on these matters.'

In 1960, just after his release, Gakaara published his pamphlet *Mĩhĩrĩga ya Agĩkũyũ* ('Clans of the Gikuyu').[98] The book is a window into detainees' constructive cultural work. It was composed, with a pencil, in six exercise books during Gakaara's detention.[99] The detention camps had been an invaluable opportunity to conduct ethnographic research for Gakaara. 'I had all of these ten clans [in detention],' he said in an interview. 'Their characteristics are quite different ... One person whose clan is Anjiru may come from Nyeri, another from Kiambu or Murang'a, and they happen to meet in detention camp.'[100] Drawn together from distant corners of central Kenya, detainees compared their customs and developed a comprehensive picture of each clan's character. Gakaara's book lists ten different clans, identifying each clan's 'behavior,' its 'manners,' 'statesmanship and courage,' 'wealth,' 'witchcraft,' and 'attraction to women.' Detainees must have spent long hours in conversation before agreeing, for example, that the Mbui clan 'love fighting' and that they 'speak openly and hate interruption.' Detention camp ethnographers offered proverbs and stories as evidence to support these judgements. Concerning the Ceera clan, for example, the book describes how a Ceera man, traveling with a friend to look at a piece of property, crossed a river on a log, then turned and removed the log before his companion could cross. The Ceera man then raced ahead and claimed the land as his own. The story gave detention-camp ethnographers source material with which to evaluate Ceera men's character. Hasty and acquisitive Ceera men 'are not good friends of the poor,' says the book, and they are 'impatient before they understand a matter.' But, as a salve to Ceera men's dignity, the book assures the reader that Ceera men are 'liked by women because of the way they decorate themselves.'

These ethnographic stereotypes were a novelty. Never before had the Gikuyu clans been sorted with such care and precision. The earliest ethnographers in central Kenya, Scoresby and Katherine Routledge, thought that the Gikuyu people were divided into thirteen clans, not ten.[101] In 1911, the

---

[97] GW Detention file: Gakaara wa Wanjau to Raheli Warigia, 8 July 1957.
[98] Gakaara wa Wanjau, *Mĩhĩrĩga ya Agĩkũyũ* (Karatina, 1998 [1960]).
[99] GW 'Detention' file: Gakaara to Shifra, 12 July 1958.
[100] Cited in John Lonsdale and Caroline Elkins, 'Memories of Mau Mau in Kenya,' unpublished conference paper, n.d.
[101] W. Scoresby and Katherine Routledge, *With a Prehistoric People* (London, 1968), 20.

District Commissioner in Nyeri counted nine Gikuyu clans; and in 1921, the District Commissioner in Fort Hall thought there to be twelve clans in all.[102] Not until 1933, with the publication of Stanley Kiama Gathigira's *Mīikarīre ya Agīkūyū* ('The Ways of Staying of the Gikuyu People') did Gikuyu ethnographers begin to sort out their clans.[103] Gathigira, a schoolmaster at the Tumutumu mission, told his readers that there were ten Gikuyu clans. He said nothing about each clan's personality, or about its members' character. In documenting the personalities of central Kenya's several clans, Gakaara and other detention camp ethnographers were doing something new in Gikuyu intellectual history. Their ethnographic work was part of a wider effort to create crosscutting institutions that could impose order on the inhabitants of central Kenya's detention camps. At Manda Island, where Gakaara was held for a time, detainees created bureaucracies to foster clan allegiances. Each clan had a chairman and a membership roll, so that 'each member of the clan should know each other.'[104] At Embakasi camp, detainees created two organizations to keep discipline: a 'house committee' punished people who fought, stole from their compatriots, or disrespected their elders, while a 'parliament' discussed policy.[105] Organizations like these upheld strict standards of conduct. At MacKinnon Road camp, detainees who stole from their comrades were made to kneel on the hard earth for several hours.[106] At Mara River camp, the Mau Mau committee punished with twelve strokes of a cane anyone who smoked European cigarettes, and fined offenders a ram and a cow to be collected after their release.[107] Gakaara's ethnographic book was part of a larger effort to create cultural and political institutions that would hold divided detainees accountable. Its depiction of the character of each Gikuyu clan illuminates detainees' urgent search for cultural footings on which to organize themselves.

If *Mīhīrīga ya Agīkūyū* was an effort to codify men's loyalties, it was also a guide to the feminine psyche. Desperate detainees, cut off from their families, were casting about for intellectual and rhetorical leverage over their wives. Gakaara's book offered insight on how to tame wives' eccentricities. The book listed the tendencies of each clan's women. Ceera women, for example, were said to 'love their homes and work hard to help husbands get rich.' Moreover, the Ceera wife 'does not fail to report to her husband any time the boundaries are distorted by neighbors.' Detainees

---

[102] KNA DC Nyeri 1/6/1: McClure, January 1911; KNA PC Central 6/4/3: DC Fort Hall, 19 May 1921.

[103] S. K. Gathigira, *Mīikarīre ya Agīkūyū* (Nairobi, 1986 [1933]).

[104] Bristol Breckenridge papers, file with no cover: John Michael Mungai, confession report, 21 to 28 September 1956.

[105] KNA JZ 7/46: AWC 2010, Damiano Ndiritu, 13 September 1956; see Mohammed Mathu, *The Urban Guerrilla* (Richmond, British Columbia, 1974), 68.

[106] KNA JZ 7/46: Confession report, AWC 2002: William Ndiritu, 11 September 1956.

[107] KNA JZ 7/40: Confession report, AWC 812: Pio Kahiga, 3 August 1955.

needed to know whether their wives would guard their interests. Many of them were depending on their wives to protect their land from greedy surveyors. *Mīhīrīga ya Agīkūyū* is a window into the anxious conversations that detainees at Manda Island and elsewhere were having about women's behavior.

Guided by their insights into women's character, detainees used the postal service to supervise their families. In March 1956, 5,786 incoming and outgoing letters passed through the censors' hands at Kamiti prison.[108] Anxious husbands authored a great volume of this correspondence. Detainees used their letters to project their interests into a domestic arena in which they otherwise had little leverage. 'Inquire and know those who support me and those who say I do not have a right to a piece of land,' Gakaara told his wife. 'This way, I will secretly write to those who support me to thank them.'[109] He sent his wife a copy of the government newspaper *Tazama*, calling her attention to a feature story about how to welcome visitors. 'I would very much like you to read the story keenly,' wrote Gakaara. 'I have marked with pen all the area I think are important.'[110] In the same package he sent his wife a set of teacups. 'Keep them from children and maybe you should be using them only when you have visitors,' he advised his wife. Gakaara was managing appearances from afar.

This correspondence was, in one way, surveillance. It helped reassure Gakaara of his family's single-minded fidelity. In July 1957, after waiting for two weeks for a letter from his wife, Gakaara exploded with frustration. 'Why have you shamed me that way, Wairire?,' he asked. 'Surely, you can never fail to have nothing to tell me ... Is it stamps you don't have, or is it fatigue from communal work, or have you been taken ill?'[111] Gakaara similarly complained over Shifra's silence in June 1958. 'Why have you done this to me?' he asked. 'Why have you shamed me this way and the way I love you, dear?'[112] Shifra sometimes found Gakaara's injured pride too much to bear. In a harried letter of August 1958, she asked Gakaara 'When will you stop the noise over letters? The younger aunt to my mother died ... Also, the elder called Mbarithi has succumbed to disease. Wanjau Githaiga stabbed Mucoki Kagera to death. Wanjau [Gakaara's son] has been arrested ... For that reason, if you find an incomplete letter do not ask why.'[113]

Letter writing, like ethnography, was a means by which detainees sought to gain traction in the social world outside the wire. To Gakaara, as to other detainees, wives and kinsmen seemed dangerously unaccountable. In his

[108] KNA AB 1/92: Kamiti Rehabilitation Officer to Commissioner for Community Development, 25 March 1956.
[109] GW 'Detention' file: Gakaara wa Wanjau to Shifra Wairire, 4 November 1957.
[110] GW 'Detention' file: Gakaara wa Wanjau to Shifra Wairire, 2 July 1957.
[111] GW 'Detention' file: Gakaara wa Wanjau to Shifra Wairire, 28 July 1957.
[112] GW 'Detention' file: Gakaara wa Wanjau to Shifra Wairire, 18 June 1958.
[113] GW 'Detention' file: Shifra Wairire to Gakaara wa Wanjau, 13 August 1958.

stream of exhortation, and in his outrage over his wife's late-arriving letters, Gakaara was working to sway the behavior of his kin. His correspondence was also a way of creating a respectable persona in his own, immediate world. In one of his letters, Gakaara told Shifra to organize a family photograph, giving her specific advice on where his grandmother, mother and children were to position themselves.[114] When the photos reached him later in the month, Gakaara displayed them to his detention-camp compatriots. They caused quite a stir, as he told his wife:

> When people see Wanjau sitting alone, they say 'See how he has portrayed himself as brave,' and another is saying, 'He is intelligent as his father, just look at those eyes' ... They are saying that Muturi has closed his eyes in shrewdness, that he is furious and that he is more clever than Wanjau. I have heard all these things as I sit in silence as people here scramble to see the photos.[115]

By giving him an identifiable progeny, Gakaara's photo album earned him the respect of other detainees. Gakaara's virtual family took on flesh and blood in mid-1958, when his wife and children joined him on a four-acre homestead in Hola Open Camp. Gakaara wrote lengthy screeds instructing Shifra on how, exactly, to prepare for life in camp. 'Where it not for my inabilities, I would like you to be neat and clean thus becoming a true wife of Gakaara's,' he wrote in June.[116] He sent Shifra money to buy cloth for two dresses, and gave her specific instructions on the pattern she was to use. Gakaara the fashion designer was crafting a presentable wife. He also instructed Shifra also on the social grace of good conversation. 'You should update yourself on public issues so that you will be able to narrate to them well, for instance what is happening in Karatina,' he wrote.[117] In his letters home, Gakaara was stage-managing Shifra's appearance and giving her lines of conversation. He hoped to impress his detention-camp colleagues with his social attainments.

Men like Gakaara wa Wanjau were pursuing social and political projects that could not be defined by barbed wire. Detainees were also fathers, husbands, landholders, and kinsmen. In the 1940s and early 1950s, they had struggled to hold their families together, founding ethnic welfare organizations, repatriating prostitutes, and taking oaths that upheld discipline. As detainees in British-run camps, patriotic men carried this moral war forward. Detainees were not simply defending their commitment to a Mau Mau movement. They were doing ethnography, writing letters, and creating or renovating institutions that promoted social order. Their literary and intellectual work was a means of holding their families accountable.

[114] GW 'Detention' file: Gakaara wa Wanjau to Shifra Wairire, 8 July 1957.
[115] GW 'Detention' file: Gakaara wa Wanjau to Shifra Wairire, 29 July 1957.
[116] GW 'Detention' file: Gakaara wa Wanjau to Shifra Wairire, 21 June 1958.
[117] GW 'Detention' file: Gakaara wa Wanjau to Shifra Wairire, 8 August 1958.

CONFESSION, CONVERSION, AND HONOR

British and African officers perpetrated awful acts of violence against Gikuyu detainees, but detention camps could not be only places of punishment.[118] British officers needed means to reorient detainees' loyalties and reconfigure their sense of purpose. Detention camps were arenas where Gikuyu men and women were obliged to recompose their life stories. They were led, often by force, to take an inventory of their lives, to identify the work they had done on behalf of Mau Mau, and to make a confession. Detention camps were engines for the production of autobiographical testimonies. Many detainees refused to represent themselves in this way. They would not agree to open their private lives to public examination, and neither would they slander other people. Like Charles Muhoro, detainees made determined efforts to keep their private lives private (see Chapter 9).

The insistence that detainees should confess to their crimes was, of course, standard police procedure. Detainees' confessions were useful intelligence. By 1955, detention camp commandants were sending the information they gathered to the police Special Branch, where it was assembled in a numbered card index system.[119] One commandant found that, with a dossier in hand, 'It became almost possible to know a man's whole Mau Mau past before he confessed.'[120] But there was more than the desire for intelligence behind British officers' insistence that detainees should confess. British officers thought confession would work a psychological transformation in penitent detainees. In his 1954 book *Defeating Mau Mau*, Louis Leakey outlined the benefits that followed from a 'full and free confession,' arguing that the power of a Mau Mau oath could be removed if the partaker confessed to taking it.[121] In Leakey's analysis, confession was the outward evidence of an inner reorientation of the psyche. 'Screening' – the interrogation of detainees – was therefore rehabilitative work. Catherine Warren-Gash, the officer in charge of the women's prison at Kamiti, thought that confession was 'better than a course of beauty treatment.' Women arrived in camp 'sullen, sour, unpleasant and downright ugly,' but after confessing to their deeds, many became 'really pretty.'[122] 'There is no doubt whatsoever that these adherents of Mau Mau experience relief through getting the filth out of their systems,' a British officer averred. 'Their physical appearance and health improves, their eyes become clear, their address direct and confident, their skin begins to shine and their hair blackens.'[123]

---

[118] The violence of detention camps is discussed in Elkins, *Imperial Reckoning*, chapters 3 to 7; and in Anderson, *Histories of the Hanged*, chapter 7.

[119] KNA JZ 8/11: Secretary of Defence circular, 'Identification of Detainees,' 14 October 1954.

[120] James Breckenridge, *Forty Years in Kenya* (Great Britain, n.d.), 218.

[121] Louis Leakey, *Defeating Mau Mau* (London, 1954), 85–86.

[122] KNA AB 1/112: Warren-Gash in *Sunday Post*, 1 April 1956.

[123] KNA JZ 8/1: Tom Askwith, 'Medicine for Mau Mau,' n.d. (but 1956).

British officers' hopes for detainees' renewal overlapped with Christian revivalists' religious vocation. The transformation that British officers sought to achieve was formed in the likeness of a religious conversion. Detainees who confessed to their involvement in Mau Mau were labeled 'white' and released from confinement; detainees who refused to confess were labeled 'black' or 'grey.' They spent years in detention camps, undergoing a program of reeducation.[124] Tom Askwith, the British officer who devised the program of 'rehabilitation,' moved easily between secular and Christian descriptions of the process: he compared his work to an exorcism.[125] Revivalists' evangelistic vocation was most closely allied with the project of political reorientation at Athi River camp, which opened in March 1953 with 600 detainees. Its leading architect was Howard Church, the younger brother of the Revival evangelist Joe Church. Howard Church – formerly a missionary – was one of the Revival's first converts in Kenya and an advocate of Frank Buchman's Moral Re-Armament Movement.[126] He thought Athi River to be a field for evangelistic endeavor. 'Satan crouches over those compounds as clearly as he appears in the Bible story of the Garden of Eden,' Church wrote. 'It is terrifying and horrible.'[127] Church was sure that 'an evil ideology has gripped these people. If they are again to be useful citizens this ideology must be supplanted by a better and more powerful ideology.'[128] The authorities at Athi River employed a team of twelve revivalists, equipped with loudspeakers, to preach to recalcitrant detainees for several hours each day. Howard Church called them a 'Christian commando.' 'You have been fooled, you are lost and forgotten, your families, your women, your people despise you' was their refrain.[129] Detainees who were convinced of their sinfulness were obliged to appear before a camp official, where they made a confession, in writing, describing their 'own part and evil deeds in the Mau Mau.'[130]

Howard Church and his colleagues at Athi River were relieved of their duties early in 1956.[131] British officers thought them to be naïve: they trusted detainees' confessions too readily. Their efficacy notwithstanding, revivalist techniques had a critically important role to play in the program of Mau Mau rehabilitation. In 1955, Kenya's Protestant churches posted eight

---

[124] Described in Elkins, *Imperial Reckoning*, 108–10.

[125] KNA JZ 8/1: Tom Askwith, 'Medicine for Mau Mau,' n.d. (but 1956).

[126] HMC JEC 1/2: 'Lizzo' to Joe Church, 26 April 1937.

[127] RH Mss. Afr. s. 2257: Howard Church, 'The Athi Experiment,' n.d.

[128] RH Mss. Afr. s. 2257: No author, 'Athi River Detention and Rehabilitation Camp,' 4 April 1955.

[129] RH Mss. Afr. s. 2257: Howard Church, 'Memorandum on the Reorientation of Detainees,' 7 April 1953.

[130] RH Mss. Afr. s. 2257: No author, 'Athi River Detention and Rehabilitation Camp,' 4 April 1955.

[131] KNA ARC (MAA) 2/5/2221: Colin Munro to Commissioner for Community Development, 22 February 1955; KNA AB 1/85: Tom Askwith to James Breckenridge, 1 March 1956.

African clergymen, two British missionaries, and several African laypeople to work Kenya's camps.[132] For a time, Kenya's detention camps became a field where enterprising British university graduates went to live out their Christian vocation.[133] Gikuyu revivalists likewise considered detention camps to be a forum for evangelistic endeavor. The Presbyterian clergyman Wanyoike Kamawe regularly convened Revival meetings at a detention camp near his home. Detainees who confessed joined a Bible class.[134] Geoffrey Ngare, from Nyeri, was one of the loquacious converts who had offended Tumutumu's church elders during the 1940s (see Chapter 9). Ngare converted after hearing a preacher speak on Second Corinthians 13:5, which read 'Examine yourselves ... Don't you know that you will be found reprobate?'[135] By 1954, Ngare had come to see the evangelization of Mau Mau detention camps as his particular calling. 'I am fighting the Spiritual Warfare which should not be neglected if we wish to win,' he told a British officer.[136] He and other revivalists led Christian cleansing services in the detention camps, obliging penitent detainees to stand, individually, before an assembly, confess to their dark deeds, and ask for forgiveness.[137] In 1956, 493 female detainees at the Kamiti camp were 'cleansed' in this way.[138]

In cleansing ceremonies, in interrogation rooms, and in other venues, detainees were obliged to take account of the smallest of offences. They were compelled to sort through their memories, categorize their actions and their relationships, and find shreds of evidence that established their guilt. The confessions that Mau Mau detainees composed overlapped, procedurally and structurally, with the testimonies of Christian revivalism. In August 1955, for example, the Mau Mau detainee Wangenye Kiiru confessed to a laundry list of transactions: he told screeners at Manyani camp that he had bought a watch and a pair of trousers for a Mau Mau fighter; donated three pounds of meat to a neighbor sheltering Mau Mau partisans in his home; and given a raincoat, aspirin, castor oil, quinine, a tin of coffee, and two packets of cigarettes to another man, who had passed them on to the forest fighters.[139] Other detainees similarly confessed to a series of small exchanges:

[132] KNA MAA 9/930: Stanley Morrison, Christian Council of Kenya 'Bulletin #2,' 21 November 1955.

[133] SOAS CBMS A/T 2/6 Box 279, 'Miscellaneous, 1954–57': J. Pilgrim to Stanley Morrison, 6 July 1956. Among the applicants for work in Kenya's detention camps was George Delf, who would later write a biography of Jomo Kenyatta; and Richard Jolly, later Assistant Secretary General of the United Nations.

[134] E. N. Wanyoike, *An African Pastor: The Life and Work of Rev. Wanyoike Kamawe* (Nairobi, 1974), 214–17.

[135] Interview: Geoffrey Ngare, Nairobi, 27 May 1994.

[136] HMC JEC 5/4: Geoffrey Ngare to Provincial Education Officer, Nyeri, 19 July 1954.

[137] KNA AB 17/14: E. Martin to Tom Askwith, 13 September 1955.

[138] SOAS CBMS A/T 2/6 Box 279, 'Miss Martin' file: Betty Martin, circular letter, 7 May 1956. See Elkins, *Imperial Reckoning*, 231.

[139] KNA JZ 7/40: Confession report, AWC 898: Wangenye Kiiru, 4 August 1955.

one detainee told his interrogators that he had bought a packet of cigarettes, a box of matches, and three raincoats for Mau Mau.[140] Neither of these men had gone into the forest or taken up arms on Mau Mau's behalf. They were among the thousands of people who, out of a deep sense of human sympathy and civic duty, had supported the young forest fighters with their money, time, and talent. British officers saw the social work that these men had been engaged in as criminal activity. They compelled detainees to distinguish their work on behalf of Mau Mau from a whole swath of sociable human interactions, identifying their deeds as crimes to be confessed.

Faced with the evidence, some detainees converted. Mwaniki Mugweru wrote to his friend and colleague Gakaara wa Wanjau in 1954, announcing that he had confessed to taking the oath because 'it hinders my spiritual progress.'[141] Mugweru had come to see the Mau Mau oath as a religious problem, not simply a violation of the secular law. In his conversion, he put his sinful deeds in the past. When the detainee H. K. Njoroge converted in 1957, he wrote to his former employers to confess that he had taken a Mau Mau oath. 'I decided to change completely this afternoon,' he wrote, 'as a result of which I decided to CONFESS my connection with the Mau Mau.' Njoroge was sure that he had 'started a new life and new attitude.'[142] The confessions of converts like Njoroge and Mugweru were extensive. They cast a very wide net, reaching backward in time and confessing to deeds that had nothing to do with Mau Mau. One detainee wrote to several businessmen for whom he had once worked, listing the goods he had stolen from each of them. The list filled two pages of foolscap paper, with information on the date of the theft and the value of the stolen item.[143] Another detainee wrote to his schoolmaster, confessing that, as a student, he had stolen a fork from the school's kitchen and made a shirt out of a piece of stolen cloth.[144] These converts did not distinguish sin from illegality. They felt themselves encumbered by a list of deeds that made them guilty before God and before the British courts. Detainee Onesimus Gachoka reminded readers of the detention camp newspaper that 'each and every secret has been revealed,' quoting Luke 12:2–4 as evidence.[145] The text read 'Whatsoever ye heard spoken in darkness shall be heard in the light.' Gachoka was reminding detainees of a coming Christian epoch when their secrets would be revealed. Men like Gachoka did not distinguish between the pragmatic objectives of detention-camp screeners and the Christian project of conversion. Revivalists

---

[140] KNA JZ 7/40: Confession report, AWC 847: Muraguri Karia, 15 June 1955.
[141] GW 'Detention Correspondence' file: Mwaniki Mugweru to Gakaara wa Wanjau, 1 July 1954.
[142] Bristol Breckenridge papers, file 2002/218/002–074: H. K. Njoroge to Breckenridges, 9 April 1957.
[143] Described in K. N. Phillips, *From Mau Mau to Christ* (London, 1958), 56.
[144] Philips, *From Mau Mau to Christ*, 55.
[145] KNA AHC 9/58: Onesimus Gachoka Kamanu in *Atīrīrī* II (2) (12 September 1957).

and British rehabilitation officers together demanded that detainees should reveal their innermost secrets.

The program of 'rehabilitation' in central Kenya's detention camps was revivalism in a coercive mode. Detainees were compelled to parade their deeds before their companions and to incriminate other people. At detention camps in Fort Hall, the District Commissioner required those who wished to confess to stand on a soapbox in front of an assembled crowd. 'If that truth embarrassed the hearers they too knew we were on their trail,' he remembered.[146] Confessions had to be framed in the accusative. Detainees were required to share the names of the people who had given them the oath and to identify friends and neighbors who had supported the forest fighters. Ndegwa Gichohi, from Nyeri District, implicated no less than twenty-two other people when he confessed in 1955, describing each individual's particular deeds.[147] At Athi River and other camps, British officers took penitent detainees to their home villages to identify those men and women who had not yet confessed.[148] In 1956, Gakaara wa Wanjau attended a public meeting where detainees confessed their oaths. One man identified the men from whose hands he had taken three oaths. Another detainee confessed to killing his neighbors. In his Gikuyu-language diary, Gakaara described his surprise at the spectacle: he and his friends *twagegire*, were 'amazed, astounded, astonished' at the confessions they heard.[149]

What made these public confessions astonishing? In the view of many detainees, men who confessed were slanderers. Detention camp screeners were engaged in a smear campaign. In 1956, Reuben Emesi and three other detainees at Saiyusi Island camp accused fellow detainee Aram Ndirangu of slander.[150] They had been sitting quietly in their barracks when, over the loudspeaker, they heard Ndirangu say 'I hate Mau Mau, Jomo Kenyatta and in particular these bastards,' naming Reuben and his colleagues. 'You are Mau Mau leaders,' said Ndirangu, 'your souls will rot in hell.' Reuben Emesi and his colleagues urged British officials to stop loudmouthed detainees like Ndirangu from sullying other people's characters. In other camps, they wrote, a detainee was only allowed to use the loudspeaker 'to confess his own personal misdeeds.' It was 'never his business to go on the air and defame or scandalize other detainees' characters.' Straight-backed detainees thought each man should be responsible for his own actions. In 1954, Gakaara wa Wanjau composed a short statement revealing some of his work on behalf of Mau Mau organizers.[151] The following day, he learned that his

---

[146] Bristol 1996/86/B: W. Thompson, 'Only the Foothills,' n.d.
[147] KNA JZ 7/40: AWC 842, Ndegwa Gichohi, 5 August 1955.
[148] Breckenridge, *Forty Years in Kenya*, 228.
[149] Gakaara wa Wanjau, *Mwandĩki wa Mau Mau*, 147.
[150] KNA AH 9/37: Secretary for Legal Affairs to Secretary for Community Development, 30 October 1956.
[151] GW 'Detention Diary Ms.' file: entries for 20 and 22 March 1954.

confession was to be published in the *East African Standard*. In a panic, Gakaara rushed to protest to the camp commandant. He was horrified at the thought that his private dealings with other people would be opened to public examination.

Many detainees refused to confess because they would not agree to slander other people. Their chief criticism of the Kenya government's rehabilitation program was that it deprived detainees of their moral agency by loosening their tongues with physical abuse. In 1957, detainees at Aguthi camp urged the Commissioner of Prisons not to force men to confess. 'An ethical man should know how it is not worth[while] to force man since God moves darkly in men's brains using their passionate hearts as his tools,' they wrote.[152] Detainees at Athi River similarly criticized the British for forcing detainees to incriminate other people. 'We are always forced to say what one doesn't know ... so as to commit himself into some mistakes or crimes which to the fact he knows nothing,' they wrote in a 1957 petition. 'Pliers are applied to work as the apparatus of castrating the testicles, and also the ears ... All this is done so as to ... oblige them to agree to what has been alleged against some one whether [it] is true or not true.'[153] Detainees at Kandara Camp in Thika thought that it was a 'shabby state for [the] British empire' to force people to confess.[154] Forced confessions were objectionable because, against their will, detainees were being made into loudmouths. For similar reasons, detainees complained when Catholic priests turned the confessional against them. 'The priest would come with a tape recorder and would deceive you and later take you to court,' ex-detainee Elijah Kiruthi told me in an interview. 'He could cheat you and [you would] tell him the people you had killed or those people who had killed people.'[155]

Confronted with the power of rehabilitation camp screeners, many detainees kept their mouths closed. On arriving at Manyani camp early in 1957, one British officer found that 'Every time I got near a detainee I said [Hello], the reply I received [was] merely a stare, or downcast eyes.'[156] A Catholic priest who visited Mwana Camp interviewed 199 detainees, and found that all of them answered his queries in 'monosyllables or grunts.'[157] When the revivalist Geoffrey Ngare tried to give his testimony at Manyani camp, he found it hard to make himself heard. 'When I would come in,' he remembered, detainees 'looked for an empty tin or basin to bang on to make

[152] KNA JZ 7/4: Aguthi detainees to Commissioner of Prisons, March 1957.
[153] KNA JZ 7/4: Detainees at Athi River to Commissioner of Prisons, 10 January 1957. Elkins (*Imperial Reckoning*, 207) reads this petition as a complaint against physical abuse, and ignores the writers' wider point.
[154] KNA JZ 7/4: Detainees at Kandara Repatriation Camp to Legislative Council, 25 July 1957.
[155] Interview: Elijah Kiruthi, Mahiga, Nyeri, 15 June 1998.
[156] KNA AB 1/108: Wild to Minister of Community Development, 9 May 1957.
[157] KNA AB 17/14: Fthr. E. Colleton to Tom Askwith, 16 February 1955.

a racket, together with their loud yelling so no one could hear, until I got tired.'[158] Disciplined detainees kept hold over their tongues and were careful about what they listened to. The work of Mau Mau rehabilitation involved a struggle over what could be said in public. In August 1955, detainee Maina Nyama confessed that he had taken two Mau Mau oaths. But he would say nothing more: on 6 September, 29 September, and 20 October screeners at Manyani found him unwilling even to open his mouth.[159]

When detainees did agree to confess, they sought to avoid slandering other people. At Manyani camp, detainees incriminated fictitious people, telling British officers that they were given the oath by, for example, Muthariti wa Riigi, 'Door Handle Son of Door.'[160] Ngugi wa Kabiro, worried about his starving family and needing a job, went to confess at a screening center in Kiambu, but first he plotted out his confession with his neighbors. They agreed to name as culprits several dozen people who they knew to be dead.[161] Gakaara wa Wanjau similarly coordinated his confession with his wife. He wrote to her several weeks in advance of his confession, telling her that 'I will say that I myself took you … into the oath together with others … but the names you don't know them, because you don't know their matters.'[162] Many detainees were deliberately evasive during screening. Wanyakionge Thigui from Nyeri, for example, confessed that he had taken an oath in March 1952. But when pressed for details, Thigui professed ignorance. 'I was drunk. A man from Kiambu took me in a car but I did not recognize him. I was oathed by a man from the bush whom I did not recognize.'[163] Thigui's confession was framed in the passive voice. He left British screeners in the dark about the identity of the people who had given him the oath. When Mwangi Kamai confessed to taking the oath, he conjured up a cloudy scene, full of unrecognizable people.

One night about 11 pm I was met by some gangsters, whom I did not recognize, and taken to a place about 2 1/2 miles away. I did not know the name of the administrator … I did not recognize the owner of the house. The room was dark and we were oathed by the light of torches. I do not know if others also took the oath.[164]

Detainees like Thigui and Kamai were keeping their secrets and guarding other people's reputations.

British officials thought that men and women who confessed had 'broken' in their allegiance to Mau Mau. In fact it was their loyalty to their families,

[158] Murray papers: interview with Rev. Geoffrey Ngare, n.d.
[159] KNA JZ 7/40: Confession report, AWC 806: Maina Nyama, 20 August, 6 and 29 September, and 20 October 1955.
[160] Gakaara wa Wanjau, *Mau Mau Author*, 183.
[161] Ngugi wa Kabiro, *Man in the Middle*, 73–74.
[162] GW Detention file: Gakaara to wife and mother, 3 May 1956.
[163] KNA JZ 7/40: Confession report, AWC 815: Wanyakionge Thigui, n.d.
[164] KNA JZ 7/40: Confession report, AWC 820: Mwangi Kamai, 22 April 1955.

not their broken loyalty to Mau Mau, that led some detainees to confess and seek release from detention. In a letter urging his wife and mother to confess in 1956, Gakaara wa Wanjau wrote about his worries over their home:

There is no doubt that the war is over and it is a rotten person who will refuse to confess his Mau Mau oath so that we can return to our homes. Or look, mother and Wairire, our homes are in what condition? ... We have got a great trouble, and other people even now are going ahead, they have planted coffee and are cultivating the garden very well. If you think, you will remember that our children are eating troubles because of your refusal to confess the oath which are brought us all this trouble.[165]

Shifra Wairire, Gakaara's wife, was similarly worried about their children. She was detained at Kamiti prison until 1957, suspected of having fed and aided Mau Mau guerrillas. 'Do not think that it is the home people I have forgotten,' she wrote in reply to one of Gakaara's exhortatory letters. 'Every time I am remembering the home.'[166] After her release from Kamiti, Shifra dedicated herself to her children's welfare, building a six-room, grass-thatched house for them to live in. Male detainees likewise worked, within their limited means, to uphold their families. Kahinga Wachanga, locked away in Mweru camp, hid two shillings in his shoe; when his wife paid him a visit, he gave the money to her.[167] Gakaara wa Wanjau used the postal service to provision his family during his eight years in detention. He sent his first package home from Takwa camp in January 1956, enclosing a large piece of calico and a handkerchief, two exercise books, and an Oxford reader and fountain pen for Shifra.[168] From early 1957, Gakaara – making a regular wage as a member of staff at Athi River camp – contributed ten shillings each month to pay the wages of a house girl.[169]

The British officials who ran the Mau Mau detention camps knew that detainees were worried about their families. They consciously worked to heighten detainees' sense of domestic duty.[170] At Thiba Works Camp in Embu, the commandant brought in a truckload of women who encouraged their husbands to confess. 'When one man saw his wife, he ran away and hid himself in the huts,' an observer wrote. 'The brave wife followed him and pulled him out of the hut. She told him, "I have come to see you, why are you hiding?" He said, "I do not know you."'[171] British officers and African authorities brought detainees face to face with their responsibilities at home. In an open letter to detainees, Chief Wangombe from Nyeri described how

[165] GW 'Detention' file: Gakaara wa Wanjau to Shifra Wairire, 3 July 1956.
[166] GW 'Detention' file: Shifra Wairire to Gakaara wa Wanjau, 18 October 1956.
[167] Wachanga, *Swords of Kirinyaga*, 147.
[168] GW 'Detention' file: Gakaara wa Wanjau to Shifra Wairire, 26 January 1956.
[169] GW 'Detention' file: Gakaara wa Wanjau to Raheli Warigia, 8 July 1957.
[170] As argued in Elkins, *Imperial Reckoning*, 203–04.
[171] Bristol 2002/218/002–074: G. Mviti to the Breckenridges, 11 April 1957.

the wives of one detainee had addressed themselves to their husband: 'Let me put my tears into the letter,' said one wife. 'What prevents him from coming home to help us is only his refusal to repent and confess his connection with Mau Mau.'[172] In 1953, the government's radio service began to carry occasional talks from Gikuyu women, who described current events in their families and communities. The aim, according to the broadcasting officer, was to remind detainees of 'what they are now missing as a result of their criminal stupidity in respect to home life.'[173]

All of this propaganda was meant to spur detainees to confess and seek a quick release from confinement. It would not have been credible if it did not intersect with Gikuyu men and women's real, deeply-felt sense of duty. Many Gikuyu people argued that recalcitrant detainees were willfully lazy and neglectful of their obligations to their families.[174] They debated family values in the weekly newsletter *Atīrīrī*, published in 1956 and 1957 in Athi River and distributed in all of Kenya's detention camps. The newspaper's editor was Gakaara wa Wanjau who, after his confession, worked alongside the camp's staff. The newspaper featured serialized novels, reports on events at Athi River and other camps, and letters, cartoons, and jokes composed by detainees. One letter captured detainees' worst nightmare. 'You are bearing no children,' the correspondent told his readers. 'Your wife is not barren, but she is childless. Many of your wives have run away from home after facing difficulties.'[175] Learning from their remembered history of forest clearing, Gikuyu men knew that their reputations depended on the orderly character of their homes. This correspondent argued that detainees were being irresponsible to their progeny. Another correspondent castigated detainees for frittering their lives away. 'Who will inherit from your father if you waste your time in detention? Do you think you are growing young or old?'[176] Time was passing detainees by. They had work to do. In an editorial, a correspondent explained his decision to confess by saying 'I realized that a person in a detention camp is just like a sick person in hospital, for he cannot help his wife, children or parents.'[177] In this correspondent's view, detainees could not be moral agents: they had deserted their homes and left their wives and children to suffer. A detainee from Athi River warned other detainees about the consequences of their turpitude. 'Laziness can make you a *muhoi* ['tenant'], a *kionje* ['maimed, disabled person'] or even a *muguruki* ['madman'],' he warned. He was sure that if

[172] KNA AB 11/61: Gakaara wa Wanjau to Community Development officer, 27 July 1957.
[173] KNA JZ 8/10: Broadcasting Officer, African Information Services, to Provincial Information Officer, 21 October 1953.
[174] Branch, *Defeating Mau Mau*, 130–47.
[175] KNA AHC 9/58: Amos Kamuhu Ndegwa, 'Just Remember,' in *Atīrīrī* II (6) (9 November 1957).
[176] KNA AHC 9/58: Simeon Njiri in *Atīrīrī* II (4) (26 October 1957).
[177] KNA AB 11/61: Editorial in *Atīrīrī* II (8) (23 November 1957).

detainees used their gumption and exerted themselves, 'no doubt our country would be prosperous.'[178]

Gakaara wa Wanjau's play *Reke Acirithio na Mehia Make* ('Let Him be Judged by his Sins') sheds light on the moral dilemmas that detainees faced.[179] The play was composed and staged in Athi River camp in August 1956. Athi River's British commandant hoped that Gakaara's play would encourage detention camp audiences to confess. Theatrical performances were a way of 'making a joke of the whole thing,' wrote the commandant, a way to encourage detainees to make scornful judgments on their ridiculous pasts.[180] But Gakaara's script was more than a slapstick comedy. Gakaara's play stars a rich old man, Mariko, who is in a business partnership with another man, Laban. As the play opens, Mariko administers the Mau Mau oath to his two wives. Laban, the villain of the play, informs the police about Mariko's allegiance to Mau Mau, and Mariko is sent to a detention camp. In Mariko's absence Laban usurps their joint business, registering the property in his name. He also seduces Mariko's beautiful younger wife. At the detention camp, Mariko is warned by a visitor that his livelihood is in danger. Worried over his future, Mariko goes to the screening officer to confess his involvement with Mau Mau. The play does not actually show Mariko confessing. Instead, the screening officer and Mariko decorously conduct their business offstage, between scenes. In the play's last scene Mariko is released and reinstalled in his business; his double-faced wife returns to the marital fold; and Laban, Mariko's persecutor, falls down in a faint. The play ends with the entire cast reciting the Tenth Commandment, 'Thou shalt not covet.'

The playwright Gakaara was very proud of his work. He sent photographs of the performance home to his family.[181] British officers were less enthusiastic, finding Gakaara's play to be uncomfortably ambiguous in its message. The Staff Officer of Community Development and Rehabilitation, who saw the play during its first performance, thought *Reke Acirithio na Mehia Make* to be 'definitely immoral.' 'It shows an unbelievable depth of moral degradation,' he wrote. 'All the characters have taken the oath, they are all twisters, liars and scoundrels.'[182] This critic complained that none of the characters 'ever denounces Mau Mau as a bad thing in itself.' Gakaara's play encouraged detainees to confess for pragmatic reasons, so that they could return home and look after their property. The British critic wanted the play to be entirely restructured, with a straight character brought in to make the play into a definitely anti-Mau Mau statement.

---

[178] KNA AHC 9/58: Esau Chege, 'The Other Unknown Enemy,' in *Atĩrĩrĩ* II (6) (9 November 1957).

[179] GW 'Plays' file: Gakaara wa Wanjau, 'Let His Wickedness Judge Him,' 1956.

[180] Breckenridge, *Forty Years in Kenya*, 226–27.

[181] GW 'Detention' file: Gakaara wa Wanjau to Shifra Wairire, 15 November 1956.

[182] KNA AB 1/85: Staff Officer Education to Secretary of Community Development, 18 September 1956.

Whereas British officials looked for anti-Mau Mau propaganda, Gakaara wa Wanjau wrote a play that illuminated the quandaries that detainees confronted. Like the fictional character Mariko, Gakaara and other detainees worried that the substance of their lives was draining away as neighbors, relatives, business partners, and strangers helped themselves to their property. Like Mariko, they made choices to protect themselves and their families against dissolution. Gakaara's play shows us that the battle behind the wire was not fought over detainees' loyalty to a Mau Mau movement. Some detainees, offended by the verbal incontinence that detention camp screeners promoted, kept their mouths closed. The British labeled them 'black' or 'hard core.' Other detainees, committed to caring for their wives and children, followed Mariko's pragmatic path: they confessed and sought an early release. Everyone had their families in mind. Detainees did cultural work to bind their kin together, creating institutions that integrated disparate people and promoted harmony. Detention camps were engines for the composition of patriotic thought.

CONCLUSION

Mau Mau was largely a Gikuyu movement, and detention camps were therefore full of Gikuyu men. There were a few exceptions: at Saiyusi Island in Lake Victoria, fifty-six Luo and Luyia men were held alongside 600 Gikuyu detainees; while at Takwa camp there were eight Luo detainees.[183] But more generally, the conduct of the Mau Mau war set Gikuyu patriots at odds with Luo men. Leaders of the Luo Union convened a meeting in Nairobi in June 1954 to denounce Mau Mau. They expressed their disdain for Mau Mau's 'nefarious deeds, atrocious methods and all their written doctrines,' and claimed to be 'prepared at all times to assist the Government in preventing Mau Mau movements among the Luo community.'[184] The young men of the 'Luo Youths Conference' went even further. Its leaders complained that Mau Mau partisans robbed Luo traders, and that Luo leaders faced intimidation from Gikuyu hooligans.[185] Ambrose Ofafa, the treasurer of the Luo Union and a member of the Nairobi City Council, had been assassinated, presumably by Mau Mau partisans. Luo patriots wanted Gikuyu people to be expelled from Kisumu town, and they argued that Nairobi should be segregated along ethnic lines, because

---

[183] Bristol 2002/218/002–074: Gerald Marbay, Saiyusi camp, to Mrs. Breckenridge, 16 October 1956; KNA JZ 7/4: Officer in Charge, Takwa, to Commissioner of Prisons, 19 November 1955.

[184] KNA PC Nyanza 3/1/316: Ibrahim Were, Chairman, Luo Union Nairobi, memorandum, 6 June 1954.

[185] KNA PC Nyanza 3/1/332: James Ochwata to PC Kisumu, 28 April 1954.

Gikuyu 'inspired bad behaviour among the Luo people.' 'It is high time that we must be protected and our interests be safeguarded,' the president of the Luo Youths Conference wrote.[186]

Their political differences should not obscure how much Luo patriots shared with the moralists of central Kenya. Gikuyu and Luo conservatives were worried about the same things. Living as bachelors in Nairobi, Luo men were jockeying for leverage over their wives (see Chapter 6). Gikuyu men were likewise worried over women's indiscipline: their poverty in land made it difficult to establish secure households, throwing wives' loyalty into question. Luo men felt their property was in danger when local government in Nyanza began a program of land consolidation in 1957. Gikuyu men were likewise terrified by government surveyors. The Swynnerton Plan, inaugurated in central Kenya in 1954, made it urgent for Mau Mau detainees to find ways to protect their landholdings from greedy neighbors. Luo men and Gikuyu men shared the same nightmares. They created parallel institutions to uphold social order. The Ramogi African Welfare Association and the Luo Union were means by which Luo husbands civilized the city, compelling women to behave in accordance with tradition. Gikuyu patriots similarly fought against sexual indiscipline. Mau Mau was, among other things, a movement of moral reform to which Christians and other public-spirited people committed themselves. The men of the Luo Union and the moralists of central Kenya were together horrified by converts of the East African Revival, whose loquaciousness was a symptom of their irresponsibility. Luo and Gikuyu patriots alike sought to close converts' mouths, building up institutions that protected their people's integrity.

The history of Kenya's nationalisms needs a wide frame.[187] It is not enough to cast a larger net, to diversify the study of politics, to populate the story of Kenya's national independence with trade unionists, South Asians, women and other groups. Kenyans did not all fight for freedom.[188] Kenya's patriots were engaged in overlapping moral projects, projects that they shared by conservative reformers in northwestern Tanganyika, central Uganda, and elsewhere in eastern Africa. Living at a distance from their families, Luo and Gikuyu men created institutions that valorized tradition, celebrated patriarchy, and upheld a particular kind of social order. East Africa's patriotisms

---

[186] KNA (ARC) MAA 2/5/155: Shadrack Owuor Akach, Luo Youths Conference, Kisumu, 9 March 1954.

[187] Argued in Bethwell A. Ogot, 'Mau Mau and Nationhood: The Untold Story,' in *Mau Mau and Nationhood: Arms, Authority, and Narration*, eds. E. S. Atieno Odhiambo and John Lonsdale (Oxford, 2003), 8–36.

[188] *Contra* Jomo Kenyatta's speech on 20 October 1964, in which he famously averred that 'We all fought for freedom.' See Jomo Kenyatta, *Harambee! The Prime Minister of Kenya's Speeches, 1963–64* (Oxford, 1964), 2.

were conceived as moral projects, arising out of a crisis over land, marriage, and social discipline that had no regard for boundaries. Mau Mau detainees should not be canonized, and neither should other Kenyans be obliged to genuflect toward them. Detainees' heroism was part of a larger patriotic struggle against social disorder in which a great many East Africans participated.

11

Contests of Time in Western Uganda

Founded in 1962 by leaders of the Konzo ethnic minority, western Uganda's Rwenzururu kingdom was a product of history.[1] The kingdom's architects were homespun historians who had conducted research showing that Konzo people were autochthons, unjustly colonized by Uganda's government.[2] In their declaration of independence, they asked for 'the re-establishment of our power in Rwenzururu, we the natural owners of our land.'[3] With the evidence of history at hand, Rwenzururu's founders could argue that they were restoring an old order of cultural and political sovereignty. But in October 1970, after eight years of low-level guerrilla warfare, time ran out for Rwenzururu's patriots. The charismatic prophet Timosewo Bawalana announced that the old antagonisms and enmities had come to an end, that Rwenzururu stood at the edge of a new epoch, and that the kingdom of God had come to earth. 'The war is over for the [Konzo] revolutionary movement against our enemy,' he announced. 'Atrocities like killing and burning of houses and envy are now over.'[4] He instructed his supporters to 'repent and make an apology' to their former antagonists, citing Ecclesiastes 3:11–12, which read 'He hath made every thing beautiful in his time.' Hundreds of soldiers were convinced that they were actually living in God's time, and they buried their spears in pits that Bawalana prepared for them.

---

[1] The title of this chapter refers to John Lonsdale's 'Contests of Time: Kikuyu Historiography, Old and New,' in *A Place in the World: New Local Historiographies from Africa and South Asia*, ed. A. Harneit-Sievers (Leiden, 2002), 201–54.

[2] For 'homespun historians,' see Derek R. Peterson and Giacomo Macola, 'Introduction: Homespun Historiography and the Academic Profession,' in *Recasting the Past: History Writing and Political Work in Modern Africa*, eds. Peterson and Macola (Athens, OH, 2009).

[3] KabDA Box 21, 'Baamba/Bakonjo Secession Movement' file: Isaya Mukirane et al. to Milton Obote, 15 August 1962.

[4] KabDA Box 23, 'Baamba/Bakonjo Secession Movement: Rwenzururu' file: Timosewo Bawalana, circular letter addressed to Katwe church, 14 October 1970.

Within a year, though, indignant Rwenzururu partisans had driven Bawalana out of the kingdom. By 1972, the kingdom's leaders had rediscovered their historical vocation. 'Since 1830 our great grandfathers had never ceased to fight for our power,' wrote Rwenzururu's new Prime Minister. 'We are also fighting for the same cause.'[5]

East Africa's patriots – men like the founders of Rwenzururu – claimed to be heirs to ancient cultures. They composed inspirational history books that documented their forefathers' customs and traditions, celebrated their heroic struggle against their enemies, and highlighted the lessons they had to teach to their descendants. By positioning their people as legatees of their ancestors, entrepreneurs sought to create a *patria* to instruct, defend, and speak for. Visionaries like Timosewo Bawalana, by contrast, were living on the precipice of a new millennium, awaiting Christ's imminent return. All over eastern Africa, nonconformists like Bawalana were reframing chronology, upending patriotisms, and creating new politics. In their self-directed pilgrimages they challenged the political and discursive order that defined twentieth century eastern Africa.

Kwame Nkrumah once labeled the mid-twentieth century 'the decade of African independence,' and East Africa's historians have generally followed Nkrumah's directions. Scholarship on the political history of the 1950s and 1960s is framed by the 'search [for] a nation.'[6] But other polities besides the nation were coming to life during the era of African independence. In eastern Kenya, Arab, and Swahili advocates of the *Mwambao* (Swahili 'coastline') movement argued that a ten mile wide strip of land along the Indian Ocean coast belonged by historical precedent to the Sultan of Zanzibar, not to the government of independent Kenya.[7] *Mwambao*'s leaders sought to secede from Kenya, forming a 'State of Azania' whose citizenry would be limited to natives born within the ten-mile strip. In central Uganda, parliamentarians declared the kingdom of Buganda to be a sovereign, independent state. 'Buganda is an ancient Kingdom with a long history, and her dynasty exceeds thirty seven kings in an unbroken line,' they argued in 1959.[8] Their glorious pre-colonial history was proof that the kingdom could choose its own political future, separate from Uganda

---

[5] KabDA Box 20, 'Bakonzo/Baamba Secession Movement' file: Yolamu Mulima to 'All Rwenzururuians,' 9 June 1972.

[6] See Gregory Maddox and James Giblin, eds., *In Search of a Nation: Histories of Authority and Dissidence in Tanzania* (Oxford, 2006).

[7] A. Salim, 'The Movement for "Mwambao" or Coast Autonomy in Kenya, 1956–63,' in Bethwell Ogot, ed., *Hadith* 2 (Nairobi, 1970); James Brennan, 'Fighting for the Sultan's Flag: Sovereignty and Decolonization in Coastal Kenya, 1945–1964,' *Comparative Studies in Society and History* 50 (4) (2008), 831–61.

[8] RH Mss. Afr. s. 1483 (3): 'A Memorandum to Her Majesty Queen Elizabeth II Submitted by Members of the Lukiiko of the Kingdom of Buganda,' n.d. (1959). See Hugh Dinwiddy, 'The Search for Unity in Uganda: Early Days to 1966,' *African Affairs* 80 (1981), 501–18.

(see Chapter 4). In northwestern Tanganyika, politicians argued that Haya people shared a culture and a political trajectory with their Ganda neighbors. In 1960, they sought to secede, forming what one critic called the 'Katanga of Tanganyika.'[9]

In his seminal work *Imagined Communities*, Benedict Anderson highlighted the horizontality of the nationalist imagination, the sense of comradeship that citizens developed by reading the same newspapers, attending national memorials and museums, and traveling to capital cities.[10] It was the homogenizing, enfolding power of nationalist politics that terrified the organizers of Rwenzururu, *Mwambao*, and independent Buganda. In a scurrilous memorandum that circulated in Buganda in 1966, an author masquerading as Ugandan president Milton Obote described how he planned to squash Uganda's kings, outlaw Christianity, and introduce Communism. 'The population of Buganda will be reduced because they are beggars,' the memoirist wrote, 'I must keep them as slaves and I will never let them free.'[11] The memo captured Ganda patriots' worst nightmares. Nation building threw people together without discrimination, undermining the institutions that protected moral order and turning people into slaves. In Buganda and elsewhere in eastern Africa, worried patriots elaborated a discourse of ornamentalism as a defense against the deculturing, enslaving, unaccountable power of national governments.[12] They composed historiographies that highlighted their unique cultural properties, gilded their separatism with the veneer of authenticity, and positioned them outside the boundaries of majoritarian, national cultures. By identifying themselves as inheritors of antique civilizations, eastern Africa's separatists relativized the authority of national leaders. They practiced history because they needed to distinguish their polities from the flattened-out citizenries that national governments sought to create.

But even as patriotic historians composed their lessons about heritage, Africans were ever more open to new things. Today, Christians comprise 57 percent of the total population of sub-Saharan Africa. According to a recent survey, roughly half of them believe that Jesus will return within their lifetime. The numbers are higher in eastern Africa: at least 60 percent of

---

[9] Discussed in E. B. M. Barongo, *Mkiki Mkiki wa Siasa Tanganyika* (Nairobi, 1966), chapter 28. The Bukoba District Council felt obliged to respond to newspaper reportage by vowing that 'Buhaya is one within Tanganyika.' Rwamishenye archives: Bukoba District Council minutes, 31 October 1960.

[10] Benedict Anderson, *Imagined Communities: Reflections on the Origins and Spread of Nationalism* (London, 1983).

[11] CoU 1 Abp 157/11: Unknown author (given as Milton Obote), 'This is my Secret Plan,' n.d. (but 1966).

[12] David Canandine, *Ornamentalism: How the British Saw Their Empire* (New York, 2002); John Lonsdale, 'Ornamental Constitutionalism in Africa: Kenyatta and the Two Queens,' *Journal of Imperial and Commonwealth History* 34 (1) (2006), 87–103.

Christians in Uganda, Kenya, Tanzania, and Rwanda think that Christ's return is imminent.[13] Heritage is not the only framework in which Africans can think about history. Today as in the mid-twentieth century, many East Africans look forward to a moment when the steady progress of historical time will suddenly break, when former things will pass away, and when a new epoch will begin.

This chapter is about the politically destabilizing promise of the eschaton. It begins in the Toro kingdom, where elites in the 1940s and 1950s were engaged in the work of state-building. They needed to make a good impression in Uganda's political theater, where the stage was dominated by Buganda, colonial Uganda's most powerful polity. Toro's elites therefore decorated their monarchy with ancient trappings, inviting the kingdom's inhabitants to comport themselves as disciplined, dignified royalists. Not everyone would acknowledge Toro's monarchy as their own. In the 1950s, members of the Konzo ethnic minority conducted field research on the political history of the Rwenzori Mountains and found evidence of their distinctive language and history. In their heritage work, the organizers of the Rwenzururu movement positioned themselves within linear time, as the latter-day heirs of their forefathers. As legatees of a people who had once been sovereign, they set out to build a state, using the techniques of modern governance – census-taking, mapping, and bureaucracy – to make their independent polity visible, credible, and worthy of support. By this means, they lifted Rwenzururu out of Uganda, making it possible for international brokers – and Rwenzururu's own citizenry – to recognize an independent state.

Whereas the architects of ethnic patriotism sought to organize time as a forward march, radical visionaries like Timosewo Bawalana were following a different cadence. Bawalana and his followers would not agree to pursue their forefathers' antagonisms. Learning from East African revivalists, Bawalana urged Rwenzururu's people to lay down their weapons and confess their sins in anticipation of God's coming kingdom. Bawalana interrupted the heritage lessons that Rwenzururu's patriots conducted, opening up an experimental form of community. His brief and controversial career lets us see how, in Rwenzururu as in other of eastern Africa's fatherlands, the definition of political communities involved an argument over the form and direction of history.

CULTURE AND KINGSHIP IN TORO

The Toro kingdom was created in 1822, when the son of the king of Bunyoro rebelled against his father and carved out a territory just to the east of the Rwenzori Mountains. In the 1880s, Kabalega, the warlord king of a

---

[13] Pew Forum on Religion and Public Life, *Tolerance and Tension: Islam and Christianity in Sub-Saharan Africa* (Washington, D.C., 2010), 13.

resurgent Bunyoro, invaded Toro, again folding the kingdom into his growing empire. Only one prince of Toro – a young man named Kasagama – survived Kabalega's *reconquista*. He made an alliance with the British soldier
Frederick Lugard and, in 1891, Kasagama returned to Toro with Lugard's
military at his back. The kingdom that Lugard's army established stretched
from the flatland east of the Rwenzori Mountains to the Semliki River on
the west (see Map 1).[14] The kingdom's political elite were pastoralists, whose
cattle were pastured on the plains in the eastern part of the kingdom. The
kingdom's population also included a large minority of Konzo and Amba
peasants who lived in the Rwenzori Mountains.

King Kasagama's relationship with Frederick Lugard stood at the center
of twentieth century debates over the Toro kingdom's position in Uganda.
For British colonial administrators, the kingdom's history showed Toro to be
a British dependency, not an allied power worthy of respect. Administrators
made a point of treating Kasagama as a puppet whom Lugard had plucked
out of obscurity. In 1913, for example, Kasagama argued with the Provincial
Commissioner over the appointment of a new chief. Disgusted at Kasagama's
arrogance, the British Governor summoned him to Entebbe and read out a
memorandum reminding him 'When Captain Lugard found him hiding in
the bush he was a refugee in his own country ... He therefore has nothing
to be proud of as a warrior.'[15] Colonial officials were convinced that the
Toro kingdom owed its very existence to British power. The history of Toro,
wrote one official in 1928, 'shows that there was no settled and ordered
form of Government such as existed in Buganda.'[16] Toro's rulers therefore
had no grounds on which to claim the special treatment that Buganda's elite
received. In the British view, Toro's past was a mark of its dependency, not a
source of royalist prestige.

After the Second World War, a new generation of British officials found
even more reason to scorn Toro's elite. The pageantry of 'indirect rule'
seemed anachronistic, inappropriate in an age of developmentalism. All
over eastern Africa, British officers set about organizing local councils,
holding elections, and cultivating the rituals of representative government. In northwest Tanganyika, British officers made Haya kings subject
to election in 1952 (see Chapter 8). Officials in Uganda took notes on
Tanganyika's experiments with electoral procedure. The historian Sir Keith
Hancock, sent out to Uganda in 1954, was sure that 'the best remedy for an
introverted, feudalistic vanity is ... political and constitutional progress.'[17]

[14] This history is given in Edward Steinhart, *Conflict and Collaboration in the Kingdoms of
   Western Uganda* (Princeton, 1977), chapter 1; and in Kenneth Ingham, *The Kingdom of
   Toro in Uganda* (London, 1975), chapters 2, 3, and 4.
[15] UNA A 46/1112: Governor's minute to Daudi Kasagama, 31 July 1913.
[16] UNA A 46/2323: Land Office, Entebbe, to Chief Secretary, 19 March 1928.
[17] KabDA Box 145, 'Relationships with Rulers in Agreement Countries' file: Keith Hancock,
   'Brief Reflection on my Discussions in Ankole, Toro and Bunyoro,' 1 September 1954.

By 1955, Toro's District Commissioner was warning the kingdom's parliament that 'native government and its staff and chiefs must show themselves to be responsible and able to work hard and perform their duties properly.'[18] The new District Councils Ordinance set strict limits on the Toro government's authority: it was responsible for 'the control of drinking and brewing of beer,' the 'prevention of soil erosion,' the 'maintenance of tree nurseries,' and the 'control and disposal of refuse.'[19] Postwar British administrators treated Toro's rulers as low-level functionaries whose authority would only extend to the most mundane aspects of governmental work.

Confronted with colonial administrators' scorn, Toro's royalists portrayed themselves as allies of the British, not as their dependents. 'The word LOCAL GOVERNMENT for Toro Government should not be applied,' argued Toro's Prime Minister. 'The History of this country is one of a Kingdom about 2,000 years old.'[20] Toro elites emphasized their royalty's power and longevity in order to make their kingdom worthy of respect. Royalists laid on an impressive pageant when the British lawyer Dingle Foot visited the court. 'As in Buganda, no one stands in the presence of his sovereign,' Foot reported. 'There is a court Jester who welcomes visitors by leaping about with a spear, and both sunrise and sunset are heralded with the beating of drums.'[21] By 1958, Toro's parliamentarians were urging that their king should be given four motorcyclists, a white-uniformed chauffeur, and a brass band, all clad in blue, to accompany him during state functions. By this means, they sought to protect the 'dignity and conventional prerogatives' of Toro's throne.[22] Royalist pageantry gave Toro elites means to contrast their kingdom's order with the uncivil, disordered politics of their neighbors. 'All districts without a king should be persuaded to elect a hereditary king from among their noble families,' argued Toro parliamentarians. 'The Kikuyu people have no hereditary king ... If they had kings there would have been no Mau Mau.'[23] Toro state-builders had little respect for the agonized husbands and fathers of central Kenya (see Chapter 10). Kingship, they argued, was a bulwark against social disorder and a guarantee of political respectability.

---

[18] Muchwa archives, file with no cover: District Commissioner's address to the Toro Rukurato, 10 June 1955.

[19] Churchill DGFT 5/8: 'The District Administration Ordinance: The Rukurato of Toro Regulations,' 1955.

[20] KabDA Box 122, 'Petitions, Complaints and Enquiries' file: H. Nkojo to Governor, 20 August 1953.

[21] Churchill DGFT 5/8: Foot, editorial letter, 30 July 1956.

[22] KabDA Box 145, 'Relationship with Rulers in Agreement Countries' file: J. Babiiha to Katikiros of Toro, Bunyoro and Ankole, 19 July 1958. The District Commissioner marked this memorandum with the annotation 'Good God!'

[23] Churchill DGFT 5/8: 'Kingdom of Toro, Revised Proposals,' n.d. (1956).

PHOTO 6. The Toro king Edward Rukidi and Governor Walter Coutts signing the Toro Agreement in Fort Portal, 1961. Courtesy of Mr. Charles Komurasi.

Their defensive ornamentalism gave Toro's leaders traction in postwar Uganda's competitive political world. In the press and in their fiery orations, the Buganda kingdom's politicians were arguing that the Kabaka, their ruler, should take his place at the head of postcolonial Uganda's government. Toro's leaders replied to Buganda's arrogance by highlighting their distinctive political history. In 1957, the Toro parliament resolved that the name of the Uganda Protectorate should be changed to Kiira, the Toro name for the Nile River. 'Uganda,' they reasoned, sounded too much like 'Buganda.'[24] Toro's leaders sought to relativize the power of the Buganda kingdom. In 1958, Toro politicians proposed that postcolonial Uganda should be governed on a federal model, with Uganda's four kings acting as head of state on a rotating basis.[25] Each kingdom would have its own police force, educational system, courts, and national parks. As a precedent, they pointed to Switzerland, or sometimes to Zanzibar, whose sultan

[24] KabDA Box 115, 'District Councils' file: Special Branch to Commissioner of Police, 19 June 1957.
[25] Muchwa archives, 'Leg. Co.' file: J. Babiiha, constitutional proposals, n.d. (but 1958).

was, for a brief time, leader of an independent kingdom.[26] Toro leaders were not antiquarians. In archaic rituals, with brass bands and chauffeurs, and in the historical lessons they delivered to British officials, Toro's patriots established their kingdom's distinctive identity. By their ornamentalism they sought to marginalize their political competitors and make allies of their colonial rulers.

But historical precedent in itself would not earn Toro a favored place in Uganda. Toro patriots sought to live differently than their neighbors, to give evidence of their respectability and political maturity through their lifestyles. Their patriotic project obliged Toro royalists to engage in the work of moral reform. Conjugality in Toro had hitherto been a matter of negotiation, not a source of creditable masculine respectability. Anthropologist Melvin Perlman estimated that an astonishing 80 percent of the marital unions contracted in Toro during the 1950s were informal, without even the most basic ceremony to validate the union.[27] Most Toro fathers did not even bother to ask for brideprices from their daughters' suitors, fearing, Perlman explained, that 'they will have to repay it quickly when their daughters change partners.' Some 52 percent of the teenage girls that Perlman surveyed were unmarried. Many of these young women experimented with conjugality, entering informal liaisons with men, and then moving on to form other alliances. These independent Toro women were not sexual libertines. They made pragmatic, careful choices about their relationships, seeking out other partners when their husbands refused to support them. The wife of Edward Kayombya, for example, sued for a divorce once it was clear that her husband would not support her properly: she had received only three articles of clothing over the course of their eighteen year marriage.[28] Angry women like Kayombya's wife had considerable success in bringing the courts round to their point of view. The anthropologist Perlman found that, between 1940 and 1949, female litigants in the Toro kingdom's courts won 13 percent more cases than male litigants.[29] Supported by the courts, Toro's women made demands on their husbands, and when husbands did not fulfill their part of their conjugal bargains, wives struck up relationships with other men.

In the 1950s, Toro patriots came to see their negotiable married lives as a political liability. In northwestern Tanganyika, western Kenya, and

---

[26] For Zanzibar, see 'Q.C. Silent on Talks on Toro Constitution,' in *Uganda Argus* (8 February 1960). For Malaya or Switzerland, see Muchwa archives, file with no cover: Rukurato minutes, n.d. (but June 1957).

[27] Melvin Perlman, 'Law and the Status of Women in Uganda: A Systematic Comparison Between the Ganda and the Toro' (Amsterdam, Summer 1969). See also Brian Taylor, *Tropic Toro: A Ugandan Society* (Brighton, 1998), 26–27.

[28] KabDA Box 766, file with no cover: No author, appeal to District Magistrate, n.d. (but 1941).

[29] The statistics are given in Perlman, 'Law and the Status of Women'; and in SOAS PP Ms. 38: Melvin Perlman papers.

Gikuyuland, patriots were arguing that women's sexual and social independence was an embarrassment (see Chapters 6, 7, and 10). Toro men participated in this regional discourse over married life. They modeled their own programs of conjugal reform on the initiatives that men elsewhere in eastern Africa were pioneering. In 1955, members of the 'Kampala Batoro Association' wrote to the District Commissioner decrying the 'rapid migration of young men and women of teen age [years] into Kampala from the Toro District.' While some of the immigrants earned jobs in 'respectable offices,' many were obliged by their straightened circumstances to 'resort to evil means of living.' The Kampala Batoro Association warned that the kingdom's political standing was endangered by the immorality of its subjects. 'The reputation we Toros had enjoyed in the past has been dwindling by the ill reputation earned by such irresponsible young men and women in Kampala,' they complained.[30] Like the offended men of the Haya Union, Toro city-dwellers felt themselves engaged with other men in a competition for respectability. Their social position was compromised by the immoral decadence of young men and women.

The anxiety that city-dwelling Toro men felt helped to inspire conservative reform. By representing independent women as undisciplined, self-indulgent floozies, Toro husbands sought to make wives subject to legal oversight. They argued that the independent women who had captured the ear of the Toro judiciary were in fact deviants. In 1956, the Toro parliament formed a special committee to deal with the problem of prostitution. Its chairman was the Chief of Police.[31] Toro's Prime Minister corresponded with the government of the Buganda kingdom, asking for help in repatriating Toro prostitutes living in the city of Kampala.[32] Colonial Uganda's patriots could agree that delinquent women needed a firm hand to control them. But notwithstanding official outrage, it was commoners who actually conducted the anti-prostitution campaign. Patriotic men were seeking out Toro women living in Uganda's cities, inquiring into their sexual and social lives, and forcing them to marry. 'They simply come into your house during your absence,' wrote a complainant named Rushenyaya, and 'ask the women that "Is your husband a [Toro man] or not?"' If the answer was yes, then the woman was set at liberty; but if the answer was in the negative, the woman was taken away. A man who wished to obtain his lover's release was obliged to bring a letter from her chief and provide proof that he had paid bridewealth, in full. The complainant Rushenyaya was astounded at the hypocrisy of Kampala's moral crusaders. 'You can

[30] KabDA Box 123, 'Native Affairs: Repatriation of Africans' file: B. Bingaamo, S. Mugesa et al. to DC Fort Portal, 23 December 1955.
[31] Muchwa archives, Rukurato minute book: minutes for 17–21 February 1956.
[32] KabDA Box 123, 'Native Affairs: Repatriation of Africans' file: Katikiro of Toro to Katikiro of Buganda, 22 November 1955; Muchwa archives, Rukurato minute book: minutes for 4–7 January 1956.

find more than five thousand men in [the rural districts of Toro] who have never paid anything for their wives,' he argued, 'but they are not arrested.'[33] Rushenyaya argued that Kampala's moral crusaders were hypocritically imposing an impossible discipline on city-dwelling men and women. Toro patriots had no time for debate. By 1957, they had repatriated several dozen women from Kampala and a similar number from Mombasa, on Kenya's Indian Ocean coast.[34]

In religion, as in family life, Toro polity-builders made a point of behaving with creditable decorum. From the late nineteenth century onward, Toro's rulers cultivated a close alliance with the Anglican church. King Kasagama, baptized in March 1896, had named himself 'Daudi' after the Old Testament king of Israel. His mother, baptized a few months later, had taken the name Victoria; while his son and successor had the baptismal name George.[35] Their Anglicanism aligned Toro's elite with the British monarchy. In the 1940s, Toro elites forwarded their civilizing mission by adopting the disciplines of revivalism. The kingdom's first Revival convention took place in 1941. Leading the preaching was William Nagenda. Alongside Nagenda on the preaching platform in Toro was Daudi Ikuratire, a Kiga evangelist from southern Uganda.[36] From these evangelists, Toro people learned how to take account of their sins, and how to claim moral authority over other people. Dolosi Irumba, a schoolteacher, had run away from her conjugal home in the early 1930s, and in 1934 she was accused of practicing prostitution. She was drummed out of the teaching service as punishment.[37] Her disgraceful past put Irumba on the margins of polite society. But in the late 1930s, she heard Revival evangelists give their testimonies, and by converting, she took up a new position in the social world. In a series of letters and sermons, Irumba condemned Toro's clergy for baptizing the children of wealthy fornicators and adulterers. Clergymen were 'segregating between the rich and disowning the poor,' she argued, by 'ushering deceivers into church and making them the most trusted and ignoring those who tell the truth.'[38] She listed the names of children who Toro clergymen had illicitly baptized, and identified the wealthy divorcees for whom the clergy had arranged Christian weddings.[39] Irumba was particularly indignant about Aberi Balya, Toro's

---

[33] KabDA Box 123, 'Native Affairs: Repatriation of Africans' file: Rushenyaya to Governor Cohen, 21 March 1956.

[34] KabDA Box 123, 'Native Affairs: Repatriation of Africans' file: DC Mombasa, circular to Uganda District Commissioners, 4 October 1957; DC Toro to DC Mombasa, 24 October 1957.

[35] Steinhart, *Conflict and Collaboration*, 116.

[36] CoU 02 Bp 227/28: Joe Church to Bishop Stuart, 20 April 1941.

[37] CoU 02 Bp 19/1: Aberi Balya to Bishop Stuart, 8 May 1937.

[38] CoU 02 Bp 19/1: Dolosi Irumba and Evalina Irumba to Bishop Stuart, 21 May 1937.

[39] CoU 02 Bp 19/1: Dolosi Irumba to Bishop Stuart, 30 March 1937.

leading clergyman, who 'associated with sexually immoral women, and even baptized their children who were born in sin.'[40] When Rev. Balya banned her from communion for her refusal to respect church authority, Irumba refused to make an apology. 'I am like a person who has escaped from death,' she told the Anglican bishop, 'so asking me to go back is like asking me to be killed.'[41]

Some Toro leaders condemned revivalists as gossipmongers, willfully destroying other people's reputations for their own gain. The missionary in charge at Toro thought Irumba and her mother to be 'two idle women whose sole occupation … seems to be to make as much trouble as possible.'[42] Aberi Balya, the subject of many of their sermons, took the Irumbas more seriously. He scorned Dolosi and her mother as 'people of many words,' and reminded the bishop how Dolosi had once had an illegal abortion from the hands of her mother. More generally Toro church authorities condemned revivalists for their salacious testimonies. It 'is not good,' wrote a group of critics, for a convert to 'publicly show that he wronged or had sins, because in the church there are young children.'[43] These critics wanted the church's life to be decorous and respectable. They criticized revivalists for shouting during their long sermons. 'This brings shame to the church,' they wrote.

For a moment, the Revival seemed to pose a threat to the Anglican hierarchy that dominated the Toro kingdom's politics. But even as Dolosi Irumba composed her incendiary jeremiads against the corruption and nepotism of church authorities, Toro elites were finding the Revival to be a useful means of buttressing their kingdom's reputation for rectitude and civility. Ruth Komuntale converted in 1937, the same year that Dolosi Irumba first took up her pen. Komuntale was the *Rubuga*, the Toro king's chief sister. She made no distinction between her official role and her position as a convert. Komuntale insisted that the tenants who inhabited her private estate should comport themselves scrupulously, and she expelled tenants who sold or drank alcohol.[44] She traveled long distances to attend conventions organized by revivalists, using her brother's car, with the royal coat of arms emblazoned on the door, for transportation.[45] As she acted as an emissary for the Revival, Komuntale also reinforced Toro's political position. She toured the kingdom's schools, inviting teachers to join the newly formed Uganda National Congress, which was then pressing the British government to sign

[40] CoU 02 Bp 19/1: No author, 'Minutes of the Diocesan Meeting,' n.d. (but 1937).
[41] CoU 02 Bp 19/1: Dolosi Irumba to Bishop Stuart, 27 April 1937.
[42] CoU 02 Bp 19/1: Russell to Bishop Stuart, 31 May 1937.
[43] CoU 02 Bo 19/1: Pastor in charge, CMS Kabarole, to 'Class of the Church in Christ,' 6 June 1949.
[44] KabDA Box 16, 'Civil Appeal 32/55: R. Rubuga v. Melena Katyabiri.'
[45] HMC JEC 3/4: Joe Church, circular letter, 24 August 1940.

a more favorable agreement with the Toro kingdom.[46] When the British governor paid a short visit to Toro in 1957, it was Komuntale who handed him a petition, under the king's official seal, asking that the kingdom's prerogatives should be respected.[47] That same year, revivalists organized a large convention in Fort Portal. The theme was 'Seek ye first the kingdom of God.' Ruth Komuntale attended every session. Toro's king hosted the preaching team for an afternoon tea party at his palace, on the hill overlooking the Anglican cathedral.[48]

Ruth Komuntale and other Toro polity-builders moved fluidly between royalist nationalism and revivalist evangelicalism. For them, revivalism was a means by which to burnish the Toro kingdom's reputation, and a means by which to knit the kingdom's disparate people together. Komuntale and other Toro converts journeyed to the kingdom's most distant borders, to the Rwenzori Mountains and to Bwamba county in the northwest (see Map 1). Their evangelistic travels consolidated the Toro kingdom's cultural integrity. The most prominent revivalist in Bwamba county was Metusera Mujungu, who converted in 1950.[49] In 1957 and 1958, Mujungu worked as the local leader of the Uganda National Congress, the political party that was pressing British government to expand the Toro kingdom's powers.[50] In 1963, Mujungu was made the Toro government's county chief in Bwamba, the first locally born person to occupy the position.[51] In Bwamba county and in the remote Rwenzori Mountains, revivalism went hand in hand with the Toro kingdom's cultural hegemony. Mikaili Nturanke, an Anglican priest and a leading Revival evangelist in Bwamba, is said to have spoken Lutoro more fluently than the Toro aristocracy.[52] Hosea Nkojo was the Toro kingdom's Prime Minister in the 1950s and a leading member of the committee that was charged with standardizing the language of Toro.[53] Nkojo was also a leading revivalist, who played a prominent role in the 1957 convention. For Toro patriots like Nkojo, Mikaili Nturanke, Ruth Komuntale, and Metusera Mujungu, the kingdom of God shared a boundary and a mode of discipline with the Toro kingdom. In their evangelistic work, converts were drawing Toro's people together as Christians and as political subjects.

---

[46] KabDA Box 125, 'District Council' file: Assistant DC Toro to DC Toro, 15 April 1956.
[47] KabDA Box 261, 'HE, Presidents and VPs tours' file: Special Branch, Western Province to Commissioner of Police, 8 June 1957.
[48] HMC JEC 4/4: 'Short Report of the Toro Mission,' 5–18 March 1957.
[49] Interview: Metusera Mujungu, Kabutabule, Bubandi, Bundibugyo, 4 September 2007.
[50] KabDA Box 262, 'Touring Reports, Bwamba' file: Assistant DC Toro to DC Toro, 2 May 1958.
[51] For Mujungu's political career, see KabDA Box 803 'B/B Secessionist Movement' file: Mujungu to Administrator, 15 July 1964.
[52] Interview: Rev. Richard Baguma, Fort Portal, 16 August 2005.
[53] KabDA Box 44, 'Runyoro/Rutoro Orthography' file: Minutes of the Fifth Meeting of the Language and Literature Subcommittee, 3 July 1956.

Toro's revivalists found it possible to be patriots. Their culture-building work set them apart from their trouble-making contemporaries elsewhere in eastern Africa. In Kigezi and in Bugufi, revivalists behaved in antisocial ways, trembling, shaking, and noisily preaching about the fires of hell (see Chapters 3 and 5). In Nyanza, converts refused even to share food with their relatives (see Chapter 6), while converts in northwestern Tanganyika made a point of scorning Buhaya's polite society (see Chapter 8). Toro's converts, by contrast, cast themselves as agents of a kingdom that was both immanent and yet-to-come. Their discipline was impeccable. 'Traditionally,' the kingdom's leading historian writes, 'a Mutooro is not supposed to speak words or make any utterances that distort the mouth and make the person look undignified.'[54] Like the Luo 'big men' whose slowness of speech and generosity of manner established their social position (see Chapter 6), Toro elites ate slowly, walked with dignity, and comported themselves with reserve. Revivalists in the Toro kingdom behaved in accordance with this model of self-discipline. During the late 1970s, Richard Baguma traveled throughout the kingdom in the company of the king's sister, the revivalist Ruth Komuntale. He remembered the moderation and civility with which she preached. 'Here, you don't rush things,' he told me. 'You don't jump on every person and annoy him.'[55] Toro's revivalists were unique in their discretion. One of my interviewees described how, during her occasional visits to her sister's home in the kingdom of Ankole, she watched with embarrassment as Nkole revivalists confessed to adultery, stealing, and other sins. Toro converts, by contrast, behaved with commendable discretion. My interviewee remembered that her father, a leading Toro convert, reprimanded a party of evangelists from Buganda and Kigezi who were demanding that prospective converts should give a detailed testimony. 'Why do you force them to confess?' he asked them.[56] Toro's revivalists kept their mouths closed. Their self-discipline buttressed their vocation as culture-builders.

Toro's people had to be dignified, sober, and disciplined because they knew themselves to be involved in a politically consequential movement of moral reform. The men and women who converted to the Revival in the 1950s joined with anti-prostitution campaigners and other moralists working to overhaul the kingdom's social fiber. One of my interviewees, a woman named Dolosi Magabali, remembered how, as a younger woman, she admired her sister, who was a sex worker in Dar es Salaam.[57] Her sister encouraged Dolosi to join her in the business, and she seriously considered the invitation. But in 1948, Dolosi heard a preacher speak on Matthew

---

54 Richard Baguma, 'Emyenda ya Tooro [People of Tooro],' typescript in the author's possession, n.d.
55 Interview: Richard Baguma, Fort Portal, 16 August 2005.
56 Interview: Janet Kabuzi, Nyakasura, Kabarole, 30 August 2007.
57 Interview: Dolosi Magabali, Fort Portal, 11 August 2005.

11:28, 'Come unto me, all ye who labor and are heavy laden, and I will give you rest.' She followed the preacher to the palace of the Toro king, and there she publicly announced that 'I want to rest in Jesus' arms.' For Dolosi, as for eastern Africa's revivalists more generally, conversion was a movement passing from degradation to a new life. But in Toro, the pilgrims' progress led to the palace of the king.

It is not a coincidence that the 1957 Revival convention in Toro was organized around the theme 'Seek ye first the kingdom of God.' Toro's royalists worked for the kingdom from a variety of angles. Parliamentarians positioned their kingdom alongside Buganda and Great Britain as co-participants in the work of government. They wrote history, organized elaborate ceremonies, and made their monarchy look respectable. At the same time, Toro's patriots worked to reform their people's manners, naturalizing certain forms of creditable behavior. In married life, conservatives imposed a rigorous discipline on independent women. In religion, Toro's culture-builders sought to make converts and push out the borders of the kingdom of God. In their work, Toro's patriots burnished their kingdom's reputation and took up a respectable position in Uganda's competitive political theater.

A STATE OF MIND

This culture-building project left little space for the plurality of ethnic communities within the Toro kingdom's boundaries. In 1932, census takers in western Uganda counted a mere 123 Konzo and 395 Amba people living in the Toro kingdom. They managed to count 190,272 Toro people.[58] The District Commissioner was sure that the census takers' technique was flawed, and he ordered that the numbers should be discounted. The accuracy of the count notwithstanding, the 1932 census shows how difficult it was for minorities to claim a place within the Toro kingdom. Census takers could not see the Konzo and Amba minorities because Toro patriots – preachers like Ruth Komuntale and administrators like Metusera Mujungu – were actively making minorities subject to the kingdom's hegemony. When leaders of the Konzo and Amba minorities argued that they should enjoy equal rights under the Toro kingdom's new constitution, the Prime Minister put them off with the slogan 'We are all Batoro [Toro people].'[59]

Toro was not, in fact, a homogeneous polity. A 1961 census – conducted with more rigor than in 1932 – counted 183,000 Toro living in the kingdom. There were 103,000 Konzo, living mostly in Busongora on the slopes of the Rwenzori Mountains, and there were 32,000 Amba living on the

[58] KabDA Box 120, 'Census, 1931' file: PC Western Province to Chief Secretary, 7 October 1932.
[59] KabDA Box 123, 'Secret Reports' file: Special Branch to Commissioner of Police, 13 February 1962.

lowlands just to the north of the Rwenzoris.[60] The west was Toro's economic heartland, rich with coffee. In the late 1950s, 54 percent of the tax
revenue collected by the Toro government came from Konzo and Amba
farmers.[61] But government resources were distributed in favor of the Toro
lowlanders. Most of the kingdom's schools were built on the plains, where
the classrooms were full of Toro children. Mountaineers, by contrast, had
little opportunity to educate their children: in 1940 there were only two
schools in Busongora and Bwamba counties, the homeland of the Konzo
and Amba people.[62] In politics, too, the Amba and Konzo minorities were
disadvantaged. All the kingdom's county chiefs were Toro.[63]

In culture – as in education, politics, and economics – Toro elites lorded
over the kingdom's minorities. Toro royalists were engaged in a civilizing
mission, and like any colonial power, they contrasted their cultural attainments with their subjects' barbarity. The Toro chief in Bwamba county gave
his subordinate chiefs their marching orders in an essay on the 'Qualities of
Leadership.' 'Have confidence in yourself; be brave; be prudent,' he wrote.
'In body and in action meet any peril without retraction ... Work very
much but speak little.'[64] Toro's elites practiced the habits of command. They
scorned their subjects for their backwardness. A group of Konzo petitioners
complained that their Toro parish chief often called them 'idiots,' saying that
'dogs are better than we.'[65] At Nyahuka market in Bwamba, people who
wished to purchase goods from a Toro shopkeeper were made to kneel and
plead for his attention.[66] The Toro chief of Kyarumba nearly caused a riot
when he likened Konzo children to the 'small rats' that were often used to
feed kittens. In the same way, the chief said, Konzo babies would be used to
nourish Toro children.[67] Toro's cultural imperialism was brutally hierarchical. In a kingdom upheld by the discipline and rectitude of its elite, uncul-
tured minorities had to be made subject to Toro's guiding hand.

The insults they endured were not in themselves enough to mobilize
Konzo and Amba people against Toro overlordship. It took intellectual and
political work to create a radical state of mind among Toro's minorities. The

---

[60] KabDA Box 120, 'Relationships Commission' file: DC Kabarole, notes, 26 February 1951.
[61] Arthur Syahuka-Muhindo, *The Rwenzururu Movement and Democratic Struggle* (Kampala, 1991), 39.
[62] KabDA Box 40, 'Education, General' file: DC Toro, 'Notes on Education in Toro District,' 18 April 1940.
[63] 'Report of the Commission of Inquiry into the Recent Disturbances Amongst the Baamba and Bakonjo People of Toro' (Entebbe, 1962).
[64] KabDA Box 262, 'Touring, Bwamba' file: Saza Chief Bwamba to gombolola chiefs, 17 September 1953.
[65] KabDA Box 111, 'Petitions and complaints, Bunyangabu' file: Firipo Kumanda et al. to Omukama, 14 December 1955.
[66] KabDA Box 111, 'Petitions and Complaints, Bwamba' file: Anonymous to Katikiro of Toro, n.d. (but 1956).
[67] KabDA file with no cover: Assistant DC Toro to DC Toro, 15 November 1962.

'Bakonzo Life History Research Society' was founded in the early 1950s. Its members aimed to give a history, and a political direction, to the nameless people whom Toro's elite had scorned. The Society's moving spirit was Isaya Mukirane, a Konzo schoolteacher who lived in the Rwenzoris' northern foothills. Their aim, said the Society's constitution, was to 'instill patriotism among the Konzo people and have them unite together.'[68] Swalehe Musenene defined the central research questions in an open letter to the Society's chairman.[69] He began by asking about Konzo language. 'Why is it whenever you find a Konzo man he is always speaking a diluted Konzo language?' Musenene asked. 'How should we rejuvenate the purity of this language?' With this question in view, Musenene set out a research program for the Society to pursue.

> What are the equivalent Konzo names for West, North or South?
> What is the Konzo name for Rwenzori Mountains?
> What is the Konzo name for River Semliki?

There was more than academic interest behind these questions. For Musenene, research into language led directly to research on demography. 'Why is it that we are not aware of the total population of the Konzo people in Toro, Congo, the rest of Uganda, and the diaspora?' Musenene asked. He was inviting Society researchers to cast a wide net, to identify themselves with the Konzo-speaking people who lived in the Congo, across the international border. For Musenene, as for Society researchers more generally, research into Konzo history and language was politically creative: it made them a recognizable people.

With questions like Musenene's in view, members of the Bakonzo Life History Research Society set out to do fieldwork. Researchers were given a cyclostyled form on which a series of ethnographic, linguistic, and historical questions was printed. Each question had a space below it, where researchers wrote in the answers that interviewees provided. The questions were didactic and instructional. Konzo patriots had little time for objectivity. The first question was 'What was the origin of the Konzo people and the Amba people?' 'Who was the main chief of the Konzo people in ancient times?' went another question.[70] Researchers were identifying the Konzo as indigenes, possessing a social structure of their own. They focused on the history of the Toro government in the mountains, asking 'How did the Toro people, who came over from Bunyoro Kitara, enter the Rwenzori region?' 'How did the chiefs of the Toro come to dominate the subjects among the Konzo people?' asked another question. 'Did the chiefs beat them up?'[71]

[68] Kahigwa: Constitution, Bakonzo Life History Research, central office, 12 January 1959.
[69] Kahigwa: Swalehe Musenene, Lake Katwe, Busongora, to Chairman, Bakonzo Life History Research, Rwenzori, 21 January 1960.
[70] Interview: Yolamu Mulima, Kasese town, 29 May 2010.
[71] Interview: Yolamu Mulima, Kasese town, 11 September 2007.

A further set of questions inquired about the ownership of the mountain's natural resources. 'Who found the Kilembe mine, and who was the owner of it?' one question went.[72] The Society's researchers were carefully developing a body of evidence that could prove their ownership of the mountain's resources. Their work led to an inescapable conclusion. 'Now that the Toro have suppressed the Konzo,' went the questionnaire's final declaration, 'they should go.'[73]

Historical research was thrillingly consequential. Their field research gave Konzo historians the moral authority to speak as representatives of an oppressed Konzo collectivity. Isaya Mukirane was elected president of the Bakonzo Life History Research Society, and soon thereafter began to describe himself as president of the Konzo people.[74] One of my interviewees objected to this conceit: 'I told him that if you are going to be president of the Konzo people, it is they who will elect you,' he said. But Mukirane did not need an election to make himself a spokesman for the Konzo people. His authority was derived from the body of research material he was collecting. When a Norwegian anthropologist began to conduct research on Konzo ethnography in 1958, Mukirane wrote an angry letter telling him that 'the Bakonzo Life History members are not accepting you to write our history as they have already begun writing it by themselves.'[75] Mukirane was exerting authority over the Konzo past even as he claimed a political position in the contemporary world.

By 1960, the Society had collected enough material to publish a pamphlet.[76] Sadly, the research findings were never written up. Mukirane is said to have taken the reports, the cyclostyled forms and other research materials into the mountains in 1962, where they were destroyed during the long guerrilla war. The best indication of the Society's findings comes from the British journalist Tom Stacey, who visited Mukirane in his mountain-top hideaway. He described the origins of the Toro kingdom in this way:

The Batoro throne survived by virtue of Bakonjo courage and loyalty. When Kabarega swept down from the north with his Banyoro warriors seventy five years ago and ravaged Toro, the child king of the Batoro, Kasagama, and his mother sought refuge in the mountains with the Bakonjo, who hid the two refugees in the caves of Bwamba ... Bakonjo leaders then smuggled the boy via Ankole to Buganda, and brought him to [Captain Frederick] Lugard ... Thus Batoro and British alike owed an ancient debt of honor to the Bakonjo.[77]

---

[72] Interview: Yohana Masereka, Kisinga, 12 September 2007.

[73] Interview: Mundeke Ibrahim, Kakuka, Bundibugyo, 5 September 2007.

[74] Interview: George Kahigwa Bukombi, Harugali, Bundibugyo, 3 September 2007.

[75] KabDA Box 24, 'Miscellaneous, Anthropology' file: Mukirane to Axel Sommerfelt, 9 February 1958.

[76] KabDA Box 112, 'Miscellaneous' file: Cooperative Officer Manyindo to DC Toro, 17 August 1960.

[77] Tom Stacey, *Summons to Rwenzori* (London, 1965), 12.

The official account said nothing about Toro people's ancient debt of honor to the Konzo people. Toro's royal historians gilded their monarchy with the trappings of antiquity, representing themselves as allies of their British rulers. Researchers of the Bakonzo Life History Research Society, by contrast, treated the Toro aristocracy as the abject dependents of Konzo protectors. For Konzo activists, this account usefully illuminated Toro elites' hypocrisy. In February 1962, several members of the Society met with Uganda's Minister of Local Government. They used the occasion to present their research findings. When the king of Bunyoro invaded Toro, they said, Kasagama and the Toro elite escaped to the mountains 'in order to survive, and so the Bakonzo [Konzo people] could assist them to drive away the [Nyoro] army.'[78] Instead of being grateful to his Konzo protectors, the Toro king had secretly made a deal with the British, so that the whole of the Rwenzori Mountains was annexed to the Toro kingdom without reference to the Konzo or the Amba, 'the real inhabitants of the country.' The Toro had stolen the country from their Konzo protectors, reneging on their ancient debt of honor. The historian Isaya Mukirane thought it to be an open-and-shut case. In 1962, he told a commission of inquiry that 'I think any lowest judge in the world can see it clearly how unfair it was – Batoro who came from Bunyoro, grazing their cattle and made themselves over rulers in the country which was not theirs!'[79]

This was political history, meant to humble arrogant Toro aristocrats. It was also inspirational history, for in their research Konzo activists made a struggle for independence seem morally necessary. In the last months of 1961, the police reported on a 'subversive organization' that was working to free Bwamba County from the Toro kingdom's government. Its members were said to be manufacturing bows and arrows.[80] The police thought it to be an 'unsophisticated movement without a name,' though they did take note of its members' favorite hymn, which went 'When the time comes, we shall send off the Batoro.'[81] By 1962, the separatists had found themselves a name and a political community to fight for: Rwenzururu.[82] The name first appears as the return address on a letter sent by Isaya Mukirane to the government

[78] Documented in Lazaro Makoma, 'The Genesis of the Rwenzururu Freedom Movement, 1960,' handwritten ms. in possession of Cosmas Mukonzo, 1 January 1994. The minutes of the meeting are in KabDA Box 21, 'Bamba/Bakonjo Secession Movement' file: 'Record of a Meeting Held in Ministry of Local Government,' 17 February 1962.

[79] KabDA Box 21, 'Bwamba/Bakonjo Secession Movement' file: Mukirane to Chairman, Commission of Inquiry, 27 September 1962.

[80] KabDA Box 23, 'Security Reports' file: Special Branch, Western Province, to DC Fort Portal, 1 November 1961.

[81] KabDA Box 23, 'Security Reports' file: Special Branch, Western Province, to Commissioner of Police, Kampala, 13 February 1962.

[82] *Rwenzururu* was the Lukonzo name for the Rwenzori Mountains. See Randall Packard, *Cheifship and Cosmology: An Historical Study of Political Competition* (Bloomington, 1981), 69.

committee that was reviewing the Toro kingdom's constitution.[83] Mukirane argued that minority groups in Toro should enjoy equal rights, and that Konzo and Amba individuals should be allowed to stand for election as Prime Minister of the Toro kingdom. When Toro's leaders refused to accept this arrangement, Mukirane and eighteen other elected members of the Toro parliament marched out of the parliament building in protest. There were scattered attacks on Toro government chiefs in August 1962. This violence was not random. Rwenzururu activists used violence to differentiate their political community from Toro, to carve out a geographic and political space in which a distinct polity could be seen. In September 1962, two buildings containing the tombs of Toro's kings were burnt.[84] In November, a party of men shouting 'Rwenzururu' chased off builders constructing a bridge in Bwamba. The road was meant to link the highlands to the Toro kingdom's capital in Fort Portal.[85] The same group broke into the local government building, destroying all the books and files that it contained. By December 1962, Toro's authority in the mountains had effectively collapsed, as chiefs sought refuge in the lowlands. Most of the schools in the highlands were likewise closed.[86] In a circular letter, Rwenzururu's organizers proclaimed that 'We must show the central government that the Toro government has failed to administer the country.'[87] Government buildings vacated by Toro chiefs were occupied by Rwenzururu chiefs, and committees were set up to hear litigation in every parish.

The architects of Rwenzururu were setting their people apart from Toro, and from Uganda. On 15 August 1962, Isaya Mukirane and a group of colleagues wrote to Ugandan Prime Minister Milton Obote to announce their independence.[88] They began by summarizing the findings that the Bakonzo Life History Research Society had generated: how 'from time immemorial Bakonzo and Bamba were the true natives of what is now called Toro'; how, during Bunyoro's invasion, 'Rwenzururu clan leaders successfully defended [Kasagama] as a mere refugee against Kabalega'; and how the perfidious Kasagama had struck an iniquitous deal with Captain Lugard to enslave Konzo and Amba people. With their research findings in front of them, Mukirane and his colleagues could prove that 'We Bamba/Bakonjo

---

[83] Kahigwa: Isaya Mukirane to Toro Constitutional Special Committee, 12 January 1962.

[84] KabDA Box 21, 'Bwamba/Bakonjo Secession Movement' file: Telegram to Sec. Inpol., 5 September 1962.

[85] KabDA Box 21, 'Bwamba/Bakonjo Secession Movement' file: F. Kyamiza, 'Explanation Regarding the Damage of Bubukwanga Gombolola,' n.d.

[86] KabDA Box 21, 'Baamba/Bakonzo Secession Movement' file: District Education Officer to PC, 14 December 1962.

[87] KabDA Box 24, 'Baamba/Bakonjo, Reports from the Public' file: 'A Campaign will be Made at Katwe,' 6 January 1963.

[88] KabDA Box 21, 'Bwamba/Bakonjo Secession Movement' file: Isaya Mukirane, Yeremiah Kawamara, Petero Mupalya et al. to Obote, 15 August 1962.

are created different from Batooro in our build, appearance, traditions, languages, customs, marriage, native dances, circumcision, and mourning for our deceased relatives.' Their culture and biological make-up made their political independence seem essential. Mukirane and his colleagues described how, on 30 June 1962, Rwenzururu's founding fathers had celebrated their national independence: on the hills above Bwamba county, they wrote, they had lit a bonfire, hoisted a flag, and sung an anthem. It is not clear that these ceremonies actually took place, but on paper, at least, Rwenzururu's founders were claiming an inspirational political history. On 30 June 1960, the Belgian Congo had become the independent Republic of the Congo; and on 1 July 1962, the Belgian territories of Rwanda and Burundi had achieved their independence. Rwenzururu's independence day was carefully chosen: it positioned Rwenzururu as one of a consecutive series of polities claiming independence from central Africa's colonial rulers. It also gave Rwenzururu's founders precedence over Uganda's leaders, as the British protectorate of Uganda was not to get its independence until October 1962.[89]

Rwenzururu's founders were claiming an important place in political history, but independence ceremonies would not make Rwenzururu independent. Rwenzururu's founders had to work to make their polity distinct, visible, and worthy of attention. They had, that is, to manage their people's culture. Language was one arena in which Rwenzururu's founders sought to set themselves apart from their Toro overlords. They would not agree to speak the Toro lingua franca. In 1962, members of the Bakonzo Life History Society wrote to the Colonial Secretary, complaining that the Toro language was 'different from Rukonjo/Ruamba and we are forced to use it.'[90] In fact, the Konzo language shared a great deal with the Toro language: one estimate had it that two-thirds of Konzo words were identical with the Toro vocabulary.[91] Konzo patriots could not acknowledge a vocabularic overlap. They had to be essentialists about their language. By August 1962, Konzo-speaking crowds were shouting down speakers who addressed them in the Toro language.[92] In 1963, a petitioner wrote to the chair of the Uganda Language Board asking for recognition of the 'Lubwisi' language.[93] He had done extensive research, he wrote, and found in Bwamba 'strange syllables

---

[89] Rwenzururu's independence day, wrote Isaya Mukirane, 'had already been prepared for them by God and the authorities to be on 30th June 1962, before Uganda's independence.' KabDA Box 21, 'Bwamba/Bakonjo Secession Movement' file: Mukirane to Toro Prime Minister, 19 March 1962.

[90] KabDA Box 21, 'Bwamba/Bakonjo Secession Movement' file: S. Mutooro et al. to Colonial Secretary, 6 June 1962.

[91] Emin Pasha, *Emin Pasha: His Life and Work* (Westminster, 1898), 221–22.

[92] KabDA Box 21, 'Bwamba/Bakonjo Secession Movement' file: Assistant DC Toro to DC Toro, 29 August 1962.

[93] UNA Secretariat file 20381/1: J. Kintu to Uganda Language Board, 7 March 1963.

which do not exist in the [Toro] orthography.' He asked for the Board's help in the financing of Lubwisi language publications.[94] Rwenzururu partisans had as their national anthem a song that went 'Our language! Our olden language, where has it gone now? It has turned into [Toro].'[95] Rwenzururu's partisans were defining a national vernacular, free from the corruptions of cultural imperialism.

In ecclesiastical life, as in linguistics, Rwenzururu's creators worked to create a distinct, recognizable polity. The World Council of Churches convened the 'All-Africa Church Conference' in Kampala in April 1963. Some 420 church leaders attended, among them the Patriarch of Moscow and All Russia, who assured the congregation that 'We are exceedingly glad of the renewal of the existence of African nations, [and] of the development of their national independence and state sovereignty.'[96] The conference showed that church politics could attract attention and support from international power brokers. By early 1964, the 'Rwenzururu Kingdom Church Ministry' was ordering Anglican clergymen to pay Easter collections to Rwenzururu coffers. In a Konzo-language letter, the Anglican bishop of the Toro kingdom was 'stopped and warned from visiting and moving around churches in the Rwenzururu kingdom.'[97] Anglican clergymen working in Rwenzururu were put under house arrest in their parishes and ordered to absent themselves from the synodical meetings held in Toro's capital.[98] Rwenzururu leaders were constituting a national church, creating Konzo-speaking parishes worked by a native clergy. Josephat Kule, Rwenzururu's long-serving Minister of Churches, told me how he used to preach that 'The church should not remain in Toro, it should go to Mount Rwenzururu, like the ark of the Bible.'[99] Just as the Israelites had once traveled with the ark in their midst, so too, said Kule, did Rwenzururu's separatists bring the church with them as they left Toro.

Their separatist project was expressed spatially in the management of territory. The ethnographic and historical work conducted by the Bakonzo Life History Research Society showed Konzo and Amba people to be autochthons, natives who had inhabited the Rwenzori Mountains since ancient times. Rwenzururu's architects sought to exercise sovereignty over the terrain they identified as a fatherland. From the earliest years of their war, Rwenzururu's founders told their supporters to leave their homes on the

[94] The request was declined, as government officials feared the 'Lubwisi' would advance the cause of Rwenzururu separatism. UNA Secretariat file 20381/1: Secretary Language Board to Kintu, 3 July 1963.

[95] Stacey, *Summons*, 101.

[96] HMC Leech papers, file 9: 'All Africa Church Conference, Kampala Assembly,' 25 April 1963.

[97] CoU 1 Abp 51/4: Rwenzururu Kingdom Ministry of Security to Erica Sabiti, 7 May 1964.

[98] CoU 1 Abp 51/4: Rwenzururu Kingdom Ministry of Security to Erica Sabiti, 7 May 1964.

[99] Interview: Josephat Kule, Bwera town, 13 September 2007.

plains and to move uphill, into the Rwenzori Mountains.[100] Political sovereignty was organized topographically. Many people found it hard to live on ethnically divided terrain. Government officials reported that 5,000 refugees – most of them Toro people – were living in camps in the lowlands, having fled from their homes in the mountains.[101] Rwenzururu's founders could not afford to worry over this humanitarian problem. They needed to sort out a constituency. When Uganda's government planned to take a census in 1969, Rwenzururu's Prime Minister wrote to the census organizers warning that 'some of the Rwenzururu citizens are hidden in Uganda' and asking Uganda's government to 'chase all of them back to their country of Rwenzururu.'[102] As they worked to consolidate their citizenry, Rwenzururu's architects also sought to limit their movements. Rwenzururu's Minister of Security instructed supporters to destroy buses and other motor vehicles owned by Toro people.[103] Rwenzururu partisans sought to orient their constituents' loyalties by tying them securely to a particular, bounded homeland, and by limiting their ability to travel.

The organizational work of self-identification gave Rwenzururu's organizers the grounds on which to appeal to the international community for attention and support. By the 1960s, the United Nations had become a forum where African and Asian nation-builders could advance their argument for self-determination.[104] In November 1963, Isaya Mukirane sent a telegram to UN Secretary General U Thant, asking for protection against the 'Batoro officials, rifles, Companies and Foreign Visitors who are disturbing the Kingdom of Rwenzururu.'[105] When the journalist Tom Stacey sought to deliver a letter from Ugandan President Milton Obote to Mukirane, Mukirane refused to accept it. President Obote, he said, 'has no right to discuss with me privately. The matter is put into the hands of the U.N. Organization.'[106] Stacey thought Mukirane was delusional. But a clear political strategy drove Miukirane's internationalism. By framing their movement as a struggle for national self-determination, Rwenzururu's organizers lifted their polity out of Uganda. In February 1965, Mukirane's supporters gathered on a mountaintop to

[100] Interview: Mumbere Asanasiyo Mulokole, Kabatunda, Busongora, 10 September 2007; KabDA Box 22, 'Bakonjo/Baamba Secession Movement' file, vol. V: Rwenzururu Minister of Security, circular letter, 25 January 1968.

[101] KabDA Box 21, 'Bakonzo-Baamba Internal Refugees' file: Assistant DC Toro, 'Banyabindi and Banyagwaki,' n.d. (but 1964).

[102] KabDA Box 22, 'Bakonjo/Baamba Secession Movement' file: Samwiri Mukirane to Dr. Milton Obote, 24 May 1969.

[103] KabDA Box 21, 'Bakonzo/Baamba Secession Movement, vol. V' file: Rwenzururu Minister of Security, circular letter, 25 January 1968.

[104] For which, see Mark Mazower, *No Enchanted Palace: The End of Empire and the Ideological Origins of the United Nations* (Princeton, 2009).

[105] Stacey, *Summons*, 83; KabDA Box 20, 'Bamba-Bakonjo Secession Movement, vol. III' file: Isaya Mukirane to U Thant, 15 January 1964.

[106] Stacey, *Summons*, 178.

organize Rwenzururu's bureaucracy. The meeting appointed Ministers of Finance and Education, Immigration, Internal Affairs, and Health, and named permanent secretaries for each new ministry.[107] The meeting also appointed chiefs for each of the counties that Rwenzururu claimed. This bureaucratic machinery provincialized the Ugandan state. In 1967, the Rwenzururu Permanent Secretary for Natural Resources could write to the manager of Kilembe Mines, ordering him to stop 'spoiling and digging our copper from the Rwenzururu Kingdom soil.'[108] In 1973, Rwenzururu's king could write to Ugandan president Idi Amin, warning him that 'you are restricted and strongly proscribed … from taking intervention into Rwenzururu kingdom government affairs.'[109] By transforming a portion of Uganda into a distinct, sovereign polity, Rwenzururu's independent government put the agents of Milton Obote and Idi Amin at the margins.

Isaya Mukirane received no reply to the letters he addressed to the authorities in Kampala, New York, and Addis Ababa. That was not his purpose. There was a local audience for his letters. Rwenzururu typists had supplies of carbon paper close at hand, and the correspondence addressed to the United Nations, Milton Obote, and other power brokers were distributed in marketplaces or read aloud in public assemblies. In their locally-circulated correspondence with the international community, Rwenzururu's diplomats sought to make their low-level guerrilla struggle look like a war of independence. When Milton Obote announced his intention to reunite Rwenzururu forcibly with Uganda, Rwenzururu's Prime Minister wrote to 'All Rwenzururu citizens,' reminding them that 'Rwenzururu state gained her independence from Uganda protectorate on the 30th of June 1962,' and announcing that 'the government of Rwenzururu is making consultations with African states for recognition as a sovereign state.'[110] For Rwenzururu separatists, the archive itself – the body of correspondence they posted to international power brokers – was evidence that established their polity's sovereignty. When Rwenzururu's Prime Minister wrote to the Secretaries General of the Organization of African Unity and the United Nations, he opened up the archive catalogue for their inspection.

Referring to the letter dated 18th February 1962, which was written to the Governor of Uganda, and the Telegram no. 6, and that of 21st May 1962, which was addressed to the Prime Minister of Uganda government indicating that Rwenzururuians were

---

[107] KabDA Box 21, 'Bwamba/Bakonjo Secession Movement' file: Fenehasi Bwambale, case file, October 1965. See also Tom Stacey, *Tribe: The Hidden History of the Mountains of the Moon* (London, 2003), 297–98.

[108] KabDA Box 21, 'Bwamba/Bakonjo Secession Movement' file: Ndambireki to Manager, Kilembe Mines, 3 January 1967.

[109] KabDA Box 20, 'Bakonzo/Baamba Secession Movement' file: Wesley Mumbere to Idi Amin, 8 March 1973.

[110] KabDA Box 20, 'Bakonzo/Baamba Secession Movement' file: Samwiri Mukirane to 'All Rwenzururu Citizens,' 2 May 1969.

going to hoist the Rwenzururu National Flag on the 30th June 1962: after hoisting the Rwenzururu Kingdom National Flag, the Rwenzururuians began to collect and pay poll tax to a Government and [to] develop the Government.[111]

A skein of letters and telegrams – indexed and enumerated by date – was proof of Rwenzururu's independence. In 1969, the Uganda government appointed chiefs over the uphill parts of Bwamba county. The local people refused to recognize them, arguing that 'they have already an independent nation of their own in Africa without being included in the Uganda Republic.'[112] Rwenzururu's organizers used their correspondence, and the bureaucracy they created, to make their state look as though it was already sovereign. By this sleight of hand they sought to transform their ragtag followers into the founding fathers of a national community.

Rwenzururu activists aimed to make the mountains' cosmopolitan inhabitants into sons and daughters of the soil. In their historical research, they identified the cultural and political characteristics that set their people apart from their Toro overlords; and in their archived correspondence, they made themselves spokesmen for an oppressed people. As the legatees of an ancient, sovereign people, partisans could identify the injustices that the kings of Toro had done to them; and as legatees of their ancestors, Rwenzururu's architects could make their partisan guerrilla conflict look like a just war, fought to right the wrongs of the past. Rwenzururu's organizers needed to organize history in a linear fashion in order to establish a program of action and to orient their constituents' loyalties. The past was the forum wherein Rwenzururu's partisans established a political persona and identified a project to pursue.

BRINGING IN A NEW ERA

In 1970 and 1971, the charismatic prophet Timosewo Bawalana came to power in the Rwenzururu kingdom. He argued that a new era of peace and comity was at hand, that the epoch prophesied in Revelations was at the door. Learning from the forensic techniques that revivalists had pioneered, Bawalana induced Rwenzururu's partisans to make a break with the past, lay down their antagonisms, and forge a common purpose with Toro people. His new epoch disrupted the linear historical narrative that Rwenzururu's organizers had crafted.

---

[111] KabDA Box 21, 'Bakonzo/Baamba Secession Movement, vol. V' file: Samwiri Mukirane to Secretary Generals of the Organization of African Unity and the United Nations, the 'Chairman of the World Human Rights Council,' and 'The European, United Nations,' 1 September 1967.

[112] KabDA Box 21, 'Bakonzo/Baamba Secession Movement' file: Yosamu Muhindo to Omukumbya, Bwamba, 25 November 1969.

Christian revivalists were the Toro kingdom's most aggressive emissaries. In the view of most converts, the kingdom of God shared a border, and a form of personal discipline, with the kingdom of Toro. Metusera Mujungu – himself a member of the Amba minority – was both the Toro kingdom's chief and the leading revivalist in Bwamba county. Like other revivalists, Mujungu regarded his political position as an expression of his vocation as a revivalist. When Mujungu applied for the post of Bwamba county chief, he cited his self-discipline as evidence of his suitability for the job: his 'private work at home,' he wrote, was 'acclaimed in the whole of the Toro kingdom.'[113] Like Toro's converts more generally, Mujungu thought his rectitude to be politically consequential, a mark of fitness to govern. In May 1962, Mujungu agreed to testify on behalf of the prosecution against Isaya Mukirane, who was on trial for sedition in Kampala. After Mukirane and two of his colleagues were convicted, Mujungu's homestead was attacked by Rwenzururu partisans, and two of his buildings were burnt down. At a public meeting convened to discuss the growing violence, Mujungu was beaten by a group of five men.[114] Over the following months, Mujungu's crops were torn up and one of his adopted daughters was speared by a Rwenzururu soldier.[115]

Rwenzururu activists' war against Metusera Mujungu was an aspect of their larger effort to define and delimit a homeland. Rwenzururu's architects were engaged in a struggle over geography: in order to configure Rwenzururu as a sovereign polity, activists had to transform mobile, cosmopolitan people into natives. Revivalists' itineraries would not be confined by Rwenzururu's boundaries. One of Rwenzururu's leaders in Bwamba county petitioned Uganda's government to complain against 'vagrant religious parties whose leaders aimlessly leave Bwamba and go into other counties of Toro, calling themselves to be peace makers in pretence and deception to unite Baamba/Bakonzo with the Toro government.'[116] The revivalist Mikaeli Nturanke – famously fluent in the Toro language – was particularly to blame. Rwenzururu's Minister of Security warned him that 'It is understood that you are a traitor to your country by disguising yourself that you are a saved person.'[117] Nturanke was known to take Konzo converts to Fort Portal for Revival meetings in his car. On one occasion, he had testified

---

[113] Muchwa archives, 'Toro Public Service Commission' file: Metusera Mujuingu to Chairman, 24 March 1962.

[114] KabDA Box 21, 'Bwamba/Bakonjo Secession Movement' file: Assistant DC Toro to DC Toro, 29 August 1962.

[115] KabDA Box 22, 'B/B Emergency Area, General' file: Metusera Mujungu to Administrator, 25 July 1965.

[116] KabDA Box 21, 'Bwamba/Bakonjo Secession movement' file: Polycarp Ruchulera to Administrator, 11 October 1966.

[117] KabDA Box 21, 'Bwamba/Bakonjo Secession Movement' file: 'Rwenzururu' to Mikaeli Nturanke, 24 October 1966.

about his conversion at the grave of the late king of Toro. Rwenzururu's leaders ordered him to desist in his travels 'before we cut you to pieces.' Late in 1966, a gang of spearman attacked Nturanke's home, and he was forced to flee to the Toro capital for safety.[118]

Timosewo Bawalana borrowed techniques of self-presentation and a chronological framework from the revivalists who troubled Rwenzururu's organizers. Bawalana was the son of Obadiya Munakenya, a founding member of the Bakonzo Life History Research Society, one of the authors of Rwenzururu's partisan historiography. But Bawalana's authority did not derive from his mastery over history. His eye was fixed on the new era that he saw on the horizon. Bawalana enlisted in Rwenzururu in 1968, working as a clerk in a sub-county chief's office. He was horrified at the violence he witnessed. One man was speared in the back while fleeing from Rwenzururu tax collectors, and as he died, he lamented 'I am dying for nothing.' This and other violent episodes convinced Bawalana that he should 'fight for peace, trying to spare lives.'[119] By 1970, Bawalana had earned a reputation as a prophet. He sent letters to Rwenzururu's leaders, warning them that 'God is tired of the smell of blood on his handiwork.' On 3 October 1970, Bawalana was invited to preach at Rwenzururu's capital, in a remote part of the mountains called Buhikira. Isaya Mukirane had died in 1966, and his son and successor, Charles Wesley Kisembo, was a boy of only fourteen years. Wearing white robes, Bawalana addressed Rwenzururu's assembled government, telling them to 'Spear me, and forget spearing the people. I have come here to sacrifice myself.' He spent eighty minutes praying for peace. It was a convincing performance. Rwenzururu's leaders appointed a commission of inquiry to investigate Bawalana's credentials, and, after a day's deliberation, the commission determined that Bawalana's prophecies had been borne out by the evidence.[120]

Over the course of the following days, Bawalana established control over Rwenzururu's government. 'He would look for some verses in the Bible,' remembered one of his critics, and 'he would inform people at the headquarters that he had been directed by God that he should tell them those verses.'[121] In a handwritten letter condemning his political opponents, for example, Bawalana began by quoting Isaiah 1:10: 'Hear the word of the Lord, you rulers of Sodom! Listen to the law of our God, you people of Gomorrah!'[122] Bawalana was ventriloquizing God's voice, speaking to a people who – like the corrupted citizens of Sodom and Gomorrah – had incurred the righteous

---

[118] KabDA Box 21, 'Bwamba/Bakonjo Secession Movement' file: Notes for Administrator, n.d.

[119] Interview: Timosewo Munakenya Bawalana, Fort Portal, 28 May 2010.

[120] Interview: Yoweri Nziabake, Kasese town, 17 June 2010.

[121] Interview: Paulo Rweibende, Hima, Kasese, 11 September 2007.

[122] KabDA Box 21, 'Bakonjo/Baamba Secession Movement' file: Timosewo Bawalana to 'Comrade,' Katwe church, 18 November 1970.

anger of God. His exegetical practice gave Bawalana's words an overpowering force. His contemporaries remember how, with Bible in hand, he would read out a passage and command 'that minister so-and-so should be transferred, and so-and-so should be promoted.'[123] The Secretary of State and the army commander were summarily dismissed, and the Prime Minister was compulsorily retired. Bawalana took his place, forming a close alliance with the widow of Isaya Mukirane and building a house within the precincts of the palace.

On 15 October 1970, two weeks after his arrival at Rwenzururu's capital, Bawalana wrote to the District Commissioner in Fort Portal to announce that Rwenzururu's soldiers had unilaterally laid down their weapons.[124] They were inspired, he wrote, by Revelation 19:11–16. The passage describes a white-clad king, his eyes aflame, with the words 'King of Kings, and Lord of Lords' written on his thigh. Arrayed behind him is a heavenly army, clothed in white linen. The vision taught Bawalana and his followers that 'We should tell our people to stop enmity and bloodshed which had been practiced for a long time.' But that was not the only lesson that Bawalana drew from Revelation 19. The biblical text placed a king at the center of a peaceable army. And so, later that month, Bawalana crowned Charles Wesley Mumbere, Isaya Mukirane's teenaged son, as Rwenzururu's king, prophesying that the 'kingdom of Rwenzururu was going to last a long time.'[125] Bawalana placed Rwenzururu's king at the head of his people. He argued that the coronation marked a new era in Rwenzururu's history. 'The war is over for the Bakonzo Baamba revolutionary movement against our enemy,' he wrote in a cyclostyled letter.[126] 'Look, Mumbere Charles Wesley has been crowned as your king. Atrocities like killing and burning of houses and envy are now over.' Bawalana cited Isaiah 2:4–6 as guidance: 'They shall beat their swords into plowshares, and their spears into pruning hooks. Nation shall not lift up sword against nation, neither shall they learn war any more.' Bawalana buried a great number of spears. He remembered that Rwenzururu soldiers delivered hundreds of them into his hands.[127] Bawalana the king-maker was aligning Charles Mumbere's reign with biblical prophecies about the coming millennium. The era that the Old Testament prophets had once dreamt of, Bawalana argued, had at last arrived.

---

123 Interview: Yeremiya Byasalya, Katatinda, Kyabarungira, Busongora, 7 September 2007.
124 KabDA Box 20, 'Bakonjo/Baamba Secession Movement: Rwenzururu' file: Bawalana to DC Fort Portal, 15 October 1970.
125 Interview: Christine Mukirane, Kasese town, 12 September 2007; see Stacey, *Tribe*, 310–11.
126 KabDA Box 21, 'Bakonzo/Baamba Secession Movement' file: T. Bawalana, cyclostyled memorandum addressed to Katwe church, 14 October 1970.
127 Interview: Timosewo Munakenya Bawalana, Fort Portal, 28 May 2010.

Rwenzururu's architects had composed history in order to make their partisan war appear to be a morally necessary struggle for freedom. Bawalana, by contrast, made a clean break with the past. He configured time in a number of registers. Bawalana created a new army regiment, clad in red caps, which he called *Mwiherere*. The scarlet headgear, he told me, was meant to remind soldiers that 'the blood is on your heads. Do not shed more.' The regiment's name, *Mwiherere*, referred to the biblical book Joel, which is a contemplation on the changeable character of God's favor. 'Let the weak say, I am strong,' commands Joel the prophet.[128] One of my informants offered a further definition, calling *mwiherere* 'something that can happen instantly,' as when a goat dies without a cause, or a child perishes without falling sick.[129] The red-capped soldiers who enlisted in the regiment named *Mwiherere* were reminded about contingency, about the precariousness of human purposes, and about the changeability of fortune. Whereas Rwenzururu partisans derived righteous energy from their study of the past, Bawalana led his soldiers to question their vocation.

Bawalana's correspondence made the same point. From 1962 onward, Isaya Mukirane and his colleagues had fought on behalf of 'Rwenzururu.' Their correspondence, composed in the vernacular and carbon copied to partisans all over the mountains, helped constitute Rwenzururu as a political community. Bawalana's correspondence, by contrast, raised unanswerable questions. In 1970 and 1971, Bawalana listed the 'African Corner of Why?' as his return address, or sometimes *Coin de Quoi*, the 'Corner of What.' Bawalana told me that he hoped his readers would ask 'Where are we, and what am I doing, and what should I do next?'[130] Rwenzururu's partisans wrote in the name of a polity that was built on the foundation of culture, language, and history. Bawalana, by contrast, wrote as a provocateur, inviting his readers to ask questions about their direction. His circular of 14 October 1970 began with an invocation:

Swala Alahu – Lahuma inis Alfagira Omega ina Omnibus de l'Obusingha Rwenzururiene en Afrique.[131]

The sentence is a concoction of holy words. 'Swala Alahu' gestures toward the Arabic-language invocation that opened Islamic prayer services; while 'Alfagira' is perhaps 'Alfajiri,' the prayer with which Muslims open the day. From 'Alfajiri' Bawalana skips to 'Omega,' and so calls to mind Revelation, where God, seated on his throne, calls himself 'Alpha and Omega, the Beginning and the End.' Then comes a Latin word, 'Omnibus,' recognizable from the Catholic mass. The invocation ends with 'l'Obusingha Rwenzururiene en

---

[128] Joel 3:10.
[129] Interview: Yoweri Nziabake, Kasese town, 17 June 2010.
[130] Interview: Timosewo Munakenya Bawalana, Fort Portal, 28 May 2010.
[131] KabDA Box 21, 'Bakonzo/Baamba Secession Movement' file: Timosewo Bawalana, cyclostyled memorandum addressed to Katwe church, 14 October 1970.

Afrique,' a French translation of the phrase 'the Kingdom of Rwenzururu in Africa.' To everyone, whether or not they read the Konzo language, the phrase was nonsense. It was a jumble of holy words. It invited readers to skip between different sacred settings, different languages, and different holy books. Rwenzururu's patriots had always written in the vernacular. In their circulars, they addressed a people that had inherited a language, and an inspirational heritage, from their forebears. Bawalana's readers, by contrast, were invited to place themselves in a variety of settings, and to read in a variety of languages. His multilingual concoctions took Rwenzururu's constituents outside their vernacular homeland and into a cosmopolitan arena.

Bawalana was decoupling the Rwenzururu movement from the engine of nativism. After a break in time, neither history nor culture could determine human action. In this new epoch, physical aggression was revalued, transformed from a patriotic act to an offense against God and king. In his definitional work Bawalana found revivalist disciplines to be eminently useful. Testimonial practice was for Bawalana a means by which Rwenzururu's partisans could put distance between themselves and a violent past. 'It is good for anyone who committed a lot of atrocities during the war to make his confession,' Bawalana told Rwenzururu's fighters in a circular letter. 'It is good for such people to repent and make apology.'[132] On 30 October 1970, Bawalana convened a service of repentance at the Anglican church at Nsenyi. Letters of invitation were distributed widely, promising that Rwenzururu had 'left a system of killing anyone.' Some 5,000 people attended the service. The speakers stressed that killing people, burning houses, and theft had all been abolished.[133] Rwenzururu soldiers were ordered to stop using violence when collecting taxes, and prisoners slated for execution were pardoned and released from detention. Speakers exhorted their listeners to 'cooperate with non-Rwenzururu on the land as they were brothers.'[134] Bawalana drove the point home through his cyclostyled correspondence. 'It is declared by God that whomever committed sin against his people should immediately repent in order to save his soul,' he wrote.[135] Confession had long been a critically important revivalist discipline. Bawalana capitalized on the propulsive power of the testimonial genre. His followers were invited to make a break with the past, to categorize what had formerly been patriotic heroism as sin. Their testimonial practice pushed them into a new era in history.

[132] KabDA Box 21, 'Bakonzo/Baamba Secession Movement' file: Timosewo Bawalana, cyclostyled memorandum addressed to Katwe church, 14 October 1970.

[133] KabDA Box 21, 'Bakonzo/Baamba Secession Movement' file: Yustasi Mukirane to Secretary General, 6 November 1970.

[134] KabDA Box 102, 'Toro Intelligence Reports' file: Toro Intelligence and Security meeting, 11 November 1970.

[135] KabDA Box 21, 'Bakonzo/Baamba Secession Movement' file: Timosewo Bawalana to 'Comrade,' Katwe church, 18 November 1970.

Timosewo Bawalana was not a starry-eyed idealist. He needed hard evidence to show that a new order was, indeed, at hand. He therefore corresponded with officials in Uganda's government, encouraging them to follow the path of peace. In October 1970, Bawalana wrote to Uganda's local authorities offering guidance about good government. 'Did courageous leaders like Alexander the Great and Charles Magne succeed because of stealing goats and chickens?' he wrote. 'Of what use can one benefit from claiming to be a tyrant and yet he has no dignity among the people?'[136] He urged Uganda's officials to desist from drunkenness, and to make a proper assessment of taxpayers' wealth before collecting taxes. As Bawalana sought to reform the machinery of local government, he also conducted clandestine negotiations with the District Commissioner, insisting that the Uganda government's soldiers and police should match Rwenzururu's self-sacrificing commitment to peace. Uganda officials responded to his overtures: the District Commissioner ordered that 'this period of non-violence' should be used to open a dialogue with Rwenzururu's leaders.[137] When Toro's chiefs arrested a few Rwenzururu partisans in January 1971, Bawalana sent a stern letter – written in English – to the Uganda government. 'Since I started preaching, no human blood has ever been shed,' he noted, complaining that 'when I want to guide the people in the right channel, the [Ugandan] authorities around try to block the way.' In his diplomatic negotiations, Bawalana was working to keep violence at bay, and creating a body of evidence to show that a new epoch had arrived.

Not everyone welcomed Timosewo Bawalana's new era. Many partisans complained about his arbitrary dictates and about his self-promoting assumption of political power. Others suspected him of colluding with Uganda's government to undermine Rwenzururu's cause. In September 1971, Paulo Rwibende, Rwenzururu's 'Operations Commander,' mustered a force of seventy-five soldiers, secured the armory, and attacked the house in which Bawalana was living.[138] Bawalana's lightly-armed supporters were unable to defend him, and Bawalana ran away in fear. His critics gleefully remember how he 'was chased away even without clothes.'[139] By February 1972, Bawalana was in the custody of the Uganda police.[140] Within a few months of Bawalana's overthrow, Rwenzururu's partisans had rebuilt

---

[136] KabDA Box 21, 'Bakonzo/Baamba Secession Movement' file: Timosewo Bawalana, cyclostyled letter, 14 October 1970.

[137] KabDA Box 263, 'Touring Reports, Bukonjo' file: Touring Report, Bukonjo, 25 January 1971.

[138] Interview: Paulo Rwibende, Hima, Kasese, 11 September 2007; KabDA Box 102, 'Toro Intelligence Reports' file: Toro District Intelligence Committee minutes, 9 November 1971.

[139] Interview: Josephat Kule, Bwera town, 13 September 2007.

[140] KabDA Box 20, 'Bakonzo/Baamba Secession Movement' file: Regional Police Headquarters, minutes for 8 February 1972.

their archive and recaptured their historically determined sense of direction. In June 1972, Prime Minister Yolamu Mulima, newly installed after
Bawalana's ouster, made a point of reminding Rwenzururu partisans that
'foreign intruders, namely the Batoro, the British, and the Congo Republic,
even though they seized power of our land, they met strong resistance from
our great grandfathers.' Their forefathers' sacrifices set out an agenda for
Rwenzururu partisans to pursue. 'We have not been fighting for small parts
or counties,' Mulima wrote, but 'to return the full powers of our Kingdom
to ourselves.'[141]

Men like Paulo Rwibende and Yolamu Mulima could not afford to
acknowledge Timosewo Bawalana's radically new epoch. In their historical
research, members of the Bakonzo Life History Research Society had identified their people as indigenes, illuminating the crimes that Toro interlopers
had committed in their grandfathers' time. Rwenzururu's partisans fought
to right the wrongs of the past. Their linear view of time made partisans see
themselves as co-sharers of a distinct culture, inherited from their distant
ancestors. At the same time, their linear view of history gave partisans a
common purpose, as latter-day legatees of a people against whom injustices
had once been done. It was history that constituted Rwenzururu's consti-
uency and gave it a shared purpose. Their nativism set Rwenzururu's patriots against Timosewo Bawalana, whose epoch-making prophesy sapped
Rwenzururu of its purpose and direction. Whereas Rwenzururu's partisans
knew themselves to be the products of history, Bawalana was making a
break with the past. It was as patriots that Paulo Rwibende and others took
up their weapons and drove Bawalana from their kingdom. They had no
time for a new epoch.

CONCLUSION

Rwenzururu never earned international recognition, and its Toro critics
thought Rwenzururu's organizers were delusional. In September 1962, on the
eve of Uganda's national independence, an editorialist wrote to the *Uganda
Argus* newspaper arguing that 'It was never heard that there existed in history, written or traditional, a kingdom or district known as Rwenzururu.
There is not a single sign which shows the boundaries of that district or
kingdom.'[142] Whereas Rwenzururu organizers were busily identifying their
distinct cultural inheritance, Toro's kingdom-builders were folding minorities into a homogeneous population. When Toro's Prime Minister toured
the Rwenzori Mountains in 1965, he urged Rwenzururu partisans to 'come

---

[141] KabDA Box 20, 'Bakonzo/Baamba Secession Movement' file: Yolamu Mulima to 'All
Rwenzururuians,' 9 June 1972.
[142] K. Kasore, editorial letter in *Uganda Argus*, 6 September 1962.

forward and forget the past.'[143] Toro's culture-builders asked minorities to ignore the lessons of history.

Rwenzururu broke into postcolonial Uganda's political theater by creating a standardized language, nationalizing the church, outfitting a bureaucracy, and creating a government. Whereas Toro's culture-builders worked to make minorities into biddable subjects, the homespun historians of the Bakonzo Life History Research Society emphasized their long struggle against Toro overlordship. The state they helped to build was a construct meant to draw attention from international power-brokers. But Rwenzururu's government was also real: it limited citizens' movements, redirected their tax revenues, reoriented their tongues, and reshaped their religion. By these means, Rwenzururu organizers sought to anchor people in place, both spatially and culturally, as sons and daughters of a homeland.

In a war that was a production of history, epochal time upset entrenched antagonisms and opened novel forms of political community. Patriots in Rwenzururu and elsewhere in eastern Africa thought of history as a foundation for morality. Prophets like Timesewo Bawalana regarded the past as a time of ruin and degradation. Rwenzururu's patriotic founders thought themselves to be the lineal heirs to ancient cultures, and comported themselves in accordance with the will of their forefathers. Time-breakers like Bawalana would not take on their fathers' projects. They invited people to live in expectation of a new millennium, to act as radicals, not as patriots. In his brief but momentous career Timosewo Bawalana helps us glimpse a time when the immanent frame breaks apart, when the curriculum of heritage is torn asunder and new forms of agency become possible.

[143] KabDA Box 105, 'Annual Reports' file: Toro Kingdom Annual Report, 31 December 1965.

12

Conclusion

Pilgrims and Patriots in Contemporary East Africa

In this book, I have looked at the history of mid-twentieth century eastern Africa from a different angle. The engine driving political innovation was not the anti-colonial struggle for democratic rights and national independence. Scholars have focused too much on the debate between African nationalists and European colonists, ignoring the moral arguments that Africans conducted in their vernacular languages. The engine that drove political innovation was men's anxiety over independent women and delinquent children. In postwar eastern Africa, men were thrown together in military barracks, in urban slums, in labor lines, and in wire-ringed detention camps. They were obliged to compete with other men for moral authority, and in this competitive world they elaborated patriotic theory. Patriotism was a philosophy that configured political community as a hierarchically organized family. As patriots, Haya, Luo, Gikuyu, Ganda, and Toro reformers claimed responsibility for policing the conduct of independent women. In the name of a fatherland, they composed inspirational history lessons, codified customary law, invented traditions, and called deviants to order. It was through this disciplinary work that eastern Africa's civil societies were composed. The postwar crisis of gender relations was at the core of eastern Africa's political history.

Territorial nationalism – the movement for independence in Kenya, Uganda, or Tanganyika – played a role in this story, but not in the way that liberal political scientists expect. The 1950s and 1960s were not marked by the steady expansion of rights, by the creation of vibrant electoral democracies, or by the elimination of discriminatory social hierarchies. Instead, the era of African independence was marked by increasing intolerance of minorities, by the solidification of unequal gender roles, and by the multiplication of nativisms. Seen through patriots' eyes, national independence was not an occasion to experiment with freedom and liberty. 'I take "Freedom" … to mean that men, women, girls and boys are free to roam about towns and country sides spreading their evil doings to the many decent tribesmen, the upkeepers of family life,' wrote the chair of the Ramogi African Welfare Association in 1951. 'Surely, people would be more free without such practices, and roguery would diminish.'[1] East Africa's patriots knew themselves to be under examination as husbands and fathers whose ability to organize their homes testified to their political responsibility. They needed to keep independent women under wraps, chasten their behavior, reform their morals, and create a public whose civility was social capital.

East Africans today live in a world that patriots made. In October 2009, Uganda's parliament was asked to consider a new piece of legislation, the 'Anti-Homosexuality Bill.'[2] The bill would make homosexual practices – and same-sex marriage – punishable with imprisonment for life. 'Aggravated homosexuality' – defined as homosexual sex with a minor, or with a disabled person – is to be punishable with death. The bill's drafter, Hon. David Bahati, argues that the legislation would 'protect the cherished culture of the people of Uganda,' safeguarding their 'legal, religious and traditional family values' against the 'attempts of sexual rights activists seeking to impose their values of sexual promiscuity' on Uganda's people. International human rights organizations condemned the proposed legislation. Press analysis focused on the role that American evangelicals had played in formulating the legislation: the *New York Times*, for example, suggested that Uganda had become 'a far-flung front line in the American culture wars.'[3] Scholars have similarly emphasized European and American outsiders' role in prompting Africans' antipathy toward homosexuality. In his book *Heterosexual Africa?*, historian Marc Epprecht traces how 'Western authors across a range of professional discourses contributed to the notion of an African sexuality that was almost exclusively determined by or structured around reproduction and family.'[4] In successive chapters, Epprecht focuses on the European anthropologists, psychiatrists, and scientists whose research concealed the presence of homosexual practices in African societies. Epprecht argues that homophobia in contemporary Africa is derived from this body of pseudo-scientific literature. There is a 'fairly direct intellectual path,' he writes, from the European scholars of colonial Africa to modern-day demagogues like Hon. David Bahati.[5]

In their haste to lay the blame for anti-homosexual demagoguery at the door of European missionaries and scientists, critics have ignored the home-grown genealogy of ethnic patriotism. The gender politics of contemporary East Africa were forged, together with its patriotisms, in the crucible of the postwar crisis over marriage and prostitution. In his 1945 complaint against

[1] KNA PC Nyanza 3/1/376: Ramogi Association secretary to PC Nyanza, 11 January 1946.
[2] 'The Anti-Homosexuality Bill, 2009,' *Uganda Gazette* CII (47) (25 September 2009).
[3] 'Americans' Role Seen in Uganda Anti-Gay Push,' *New York Times* (3 January 2010).
[4] Marc Epprecht, *Heterosexual Africa? The History of an Idea from the Age of Exploration to the Age of AIDS* (Athens, OH, 2008), 131.
[5] Epprecht, *Heterosexual Africa?*, 132.

Haya prostitutes in Nairobi (see Chapter 7), Corporal Arbor Godfred argued that, if Haya women were forcibly removed from Nairobi, he and his compatriots would be able to

learn, without any disturbances, any defaming remark, any behind pushing talk, how to live in community, how to become good citizens, how to deal with other tribes, and lastly to copy from other countries good ways, customs, and civilization which is very often made an uncivilization by Haya harlots.[6]

Corporal Godfred had not read the founding texts of liberal political theory. But like John Locke and Jean-Jacques Rousseau, he thought citizenship to be a managerial test for householders to meet. In her book *The Disorder of Women*, the political philosopher Carole Pateman illuminates the gendered logic that upheld the first contract theorists' models of civil society.[7] For the architects of democratic politics in early modern Europe, it was men who possessed the capacity to sublimate their passions, develop a sense of justice, and pursue the common good. Women were thought to be unable to transcend their bodily natures and sexual desires. Contract theorists therefore brought women into the new political order as inhabitants of the private sphere, as part of civil society yet separated from the public world of freedom and equality. The public sphere was constituted as a 'fraternal social contract,' Pateman writes, in which women posed a permanent threat to civil order.[8] Like Locke and Rousseau, Corporal Godfred knew the public sphere to be an arena of moral judgment, a place where men were making scornful evaluations of their competitors' conduct and manners. Husbands and fathers needed first to organize their family lives before they could act effectively in the political world. As the historian John Lonsdale has argued, the question 'Why am I fit to rule?' is hard to face, for it is an audit of personal integrity.[9] Only when troublemaking women and other embarrassing spectacles had been pushed out of the public view could patriotic men hope to refute the 'defaming remarks' and 'behind pushing talk' and take their place in eastern Africa's public sphere. The prospect of national independence thereby made the work of moral reform more urgent. New freedoms entailed new prisoners.[10]

---

[6] Rwamishenye archives, Box 18, 'Rwamishenye' file: Corporal Godfred to District Commissioner, Bukoba, 12 November 1945.

[7] Carole Pateman, *The Disorder of Women: Feminism and Political Theory* (Stanford, 1989).

[8] The same theorists also positioned religious belief in the private realm, constituting secularism as the only valid grounds for political action. For which, see Talal Asad, *Formations of the Secular: Christianity, Islam, Modernity* (Stanford, 2003); and Derek R. Peterson and Darren Walhof, eds., *The Invention of Religion: Rethinking Belief in Politics and History* (New Brunswick, NJ, 2002).

[9] In John Lonsdale, 'Writing Competitive Patriotisms in Eastern Africa,' in *Recasting the Past: History Writing and Political Work in Modern Africa* (Athens, OH, 2009), 251–67.

[10] Harri Englund, *Prisoners of Freedom: Human Rights and the African Poor* (Berkeley, 2006), 4.

Some of the patriotisms that East Africans conceived were avowedly republican in character. Rwanda's 1959 revolution set the tone: it was fought by Hutu activists who cast themselves as an indigenous majority, ruled by an autocratic Tutsi minority.[11] Rwanda's violent revolution shaped politics in the kingdom of Ankole, in southern Uganda, where the Hima elite exercised political power over the Iru majority. Iru activists positioned themselves as indigenes, contrasting their vigorous self-discipline with the tyranny of their Hima overlords. 'How long shall we, the native [people of Ankole], be living under such a ruling of a foreign tribe and tyrannous race of the [Hima] people?' wrote one of their advocates in 1944.[12] He compared the Hima to the 'Egyptians' who, in the Old Testament story of the Exodus, had oppressed God's own people.[13] Iru activists cast themselves as an oppressed people, held down by foreign despots. In other parts of eastern Africa, by contrast, patriotic activists were decidedly enamored with the glitter and pomp of royalism. The mannered royalists of Toro and Buganda used kingship to make their self-interested struggle for resources and political power appear to be a restoration of an old order of cultural and political sovereignty (see Chapters 4 and 11). All of eastern Africa's patriots – republicans and royalists alike – were sure that they were indigenes, natives in a country they had inherited from their forefathers. By identifying themselves as autochthons, patriots could push their competitors to the margins and establish their rights over land and other resources.[14] As autochthons, patriots could identify their native homeland and contrast their forefathers' discipline with the degradation of their contemporary world.

Royalists and republicans shared a fervent regard for the lessons of history. They also shared a firm conviction that patriarchy was the surest foundation for political community. It is for this reason that the African-run governments of independent Kenya, Uganda, and Tanzania set out to reform marriages, control urban women, and organize family life. In Tanzania, Julius Nyerere and the architects of *ujamaa* – Tanzanian socialism – borrowed both a method and a discourse from the anti-prostitution campaigners of Bukoba (see Chapter 7). 'We have to stop [prostitutes'] shameful business of selling their bodies which disgraces our respected free nation of Tanganyika,' wrote a Haya activist living in Nairobi in 1963.[15] *Ujamaa* harnessed governmental

[11] The genealogy of Hutu patriotism is given in Catharine Newbury, *The Cohesion of Oppression: Clientship and Ethnicity in Rwanda, 1860–1960* (New York, 1988) and in Mahmood Mamdani, *When Victims Become Killers: Colonialism, Nativism, and the Genocide in Rwanda* (Princeton, 2001).

[12] CoU 02 Bp 2/1: Eriya Bitaruho to D. Robertson, 19 October 1944.

[13] CoU 02 Bp 2/1: Eriya Bitaruho to Charles Kafureka, 10 February 1948.

[14] See Peter Geschiere, *The Perils of Belonging: Autochthony, Citizenship, and Exclusion in Africa and Europe* (Chicago, 2009).

[15] Mwanza archives, Bukoba acc., L5/II/B: Sospeter Matolu Matovu to Secretary, Tanganyika African Club, 10 January 1963.

power to rework gender relations, establishing patriarchal domesticity as the authorized lifestyle of Tanzania's citizenry. Uganda's government similarly engaged in the essential work of conjugal reform. In 1964, Ugandan president Milton Obote appointed a commission to consider the laws regulating marriage and divorce. The six commissioners – all save one of them men – were charged to establish laws that were 'appropriate to the position of Uganda as an independent nation.'[16] Uganda's state-builders knew that their political status as a self-governing people obligated them to organize their married lives decorously. The churchmen called to testify before the commission argued that all marriages should be registered by the state, because 'registration would help give more stability to the home.'[17] When the commission issued its report in 1965, it recommended that even 'irregular marriage' – a union formed when man and woman lived together for the period of a year – should be put on a statutory basis.[18] Eastern Africa's state-builders were using the instruments of government bureaucracy to coordinate conjugal life, solidify shaky marriages, and bind husbands and wives together in legally validated relationships.

Even as married life came under government supervision, African culture was also bureaucratized and made into a foundation for creditable moral discipline. The Gikuyu intellectual Gakaara wa Wanjau – whose biography is discussed in Chapter 10 – was one of the architects of contemporary Kenya's cultural order. Gakaara emerged from his long incarceration in Mau Mau detention camps with a considerable body of material ready for publication. By 1960, he had prepared manuscripts on 'How Kikuyu Governed Themselves Before the Whiteman Came,' 'Brideprice and Marriage,' and several other subjects.[19] After Kenya's independence, Gakaara transformed this body of writing into a textbook for Gikuyu traditionalism. With financial backing from Mwai Kibaki, Kenya's vice president, Gakaara purchased a printing press and opened a publishing house. One of his first publications was *Mīhīrīga ya Agīkūyū* ('Clans of the Gikuyu'), the book he had composed out of his ethnographic research with Mau Mau detainees.[20] This and several others of Gakaara's books were put on the syllabus in postcolonial Kenya's schools, once Gakaara

---

[16] Described in H. F. Morris, 'Uganda: Report of the Commission on Marriage, Divorce and the Status of Women,' *Journal of African Law* 10 (1) (Spring 1966), 3–7; and in Sylvia Tamale, 'Law Reform and Women's Rights in Uganda,' *East African Journal of Peace and Human Rights* 1 (2) (1993), 164–94.

[17] CoU 1 Abp. 45/3: 'Report of the Committee on the Revision of the Marriage Laws,' 10 September 1962; CoU 1 Abp. 45/3: Catholic Church of Uganda, 'Memorandum on Uganda Marriage Ordinance,' 29 April 1964.

[18] Morris, 'Uganda.'

[19] GW 'Correspondence, 1959–70' file: Gakaara wa Wanjau to Director of Trade and Supplies, 27 July 1960.

[20] Gakaara wa Wanjau, *Mīhīrīga ya Agīkūyū* (Karatina, 1998 [1960]).

had assured the Minister of Education that his writings would 'play an important part in teaching [young people] ... our customs and traditions.'[21] In the early 1970s, Gakaara founded the 'Kikuyu Welfare Association,' an organization that aimed to 'promote family relations within the Kikuyu speaking people,' 'encourage self-help projects,' and 'combat juvenile delinquency.'[22] Like other East African political thinkers, he regarded political independence as a test of household management. 'If an impoverished home owner has to beg for charity from wealthy strangers in order to run his home,' Gakaara wrote in an indictment of Kenya's reliance on foreign donor money, 'he should consider himself a home owner only in name.'[23] In his textual work, Gakaara sought to impose a straight-backed order on family life, instruct the young about their traditions, and guide contemporary morality. By this means, he worked to teach Kenyans the discipline necessary for self-government.

Contemporary East Africa's gender politics have been formed by this long-running work of moral and conjugal reform. When Hon. David Bahati and other campaigners seek to use government bureaucracy to control homosexuality, they are carrying forward a project that patriotic activists like Gakaara wa Wanjau conceived. It was not by coincidence that in the same month – October 2009 – that Hon. Bahati submitted his bill, Uganda's government formally recognized the Rwenzururu kingdom as one of several neo-traditional 'cultural institutions.' Uganda's royalists have been involved in a flurry of patriotic culture-building. The kingdoms of colonial Uganda were legally abolished in 1967, as Milton Obote consolidated political power in his dictatorial hands. By the early 1990s, the tide had turned, and, in 1993, Uganda's parliament adopted the 'Restoration of Traditional Rulers' act. Several kingdoms – first Buganda, then Toro, Busoga and Bunyoro, and most recently Rwenzururu – have been recognized under the law. The Uganda government's embrace of neo-traditionalism owes much to political expediency, but it is also a response to commoners' advocacy.[24] In Buganda, the early 1990s were marked by crisis in social relations, widespread panic over witchcraft, and a spate of child abductions. Ganda patriots argued that the restoration of the kingship would buttress social order. 'The Baganda have a special unity, which is what makes them a mature nation,' wrote an

[21] GW 'Correspondence, 1959–70' file: Gakaara wa Wanjau to Secretary of the Education Minister, 18 September 1960.

[22] GW 'Correspondence, 1970–80' file: 'Constitution of the Kikuyu Welfare Association,' n.d. (but circa 1970).

[23] Gakaara wa Wanjau, *Mau Mau Author in Detention* (Nairobi: Heinemann, 1988), viii.

[24] Argued in Mikael Karlström, 'Modern and its Aspirants: Moral Community and Developmental Eutopianism in Buganda,' *Current Anthropology* 45 (5) (December 2004), 595–619. See also Martin Doornbos, *The Ankole Kingship Controversy: Regalia Galore Revisited* (Kampala, 2001), chapter 7.

editorialist in 1993. 'This unity has relied upon the knot, the umbilicus. This knot is the king.'[25] Calls for the restoration of Buganda's kingship were also calls for the rehabilitation of sociable relationships. Rwenzururu's advocates are similarly sure that their kingship will underpin social solidarity. The Konzo king, wrote a partisan in 2005, is a 'symbol of dignity of the people,' inspiring their 'sense of unity, peace, tranquility, joy, happiness and the guaranteed continuity of the generations yet to come.'[26]

Uganda's kingdoms have been conceptualized as guardians of morality, institutions that can define and defend traditional social relations. The instructive texts of an earlier age are being republished and repackaged for a contemporary readership. Paulo Ngologoza's *Kigezi and Its People*, composed as an answer to undisciplined revivalists (see Chapter 3), was recently reprinted, as was John Nyakatura's 1947 book on the kings of Bunyoro, and a 1955 book on the kings of Ankole.[27] New research is being conducted. The past few years have seen the publication of texts on 'The Ways of our Ancestors' in the Toro kingdom, on 'The Bakonzo/Banande and Their Culture,' on the 'History and Culture' of the kingdom of Ankole, and on 'The People and the Rulers' of the kingdom of Bunyoro.[28] Uganda's kingdoms have used the Internet to expand the audience for their heritage lessons. The Bunyoro kingdom's website, for example, welcomes viewers with a photograph of the king, resplendent in a gold-trimmed robe. It invites readers to 'Get an insight into the Kingdom's inspiring history, its rich culture, development projects and what the King ... and the Royal family are up to lately.'[29] The Buganda kingdom likewise has a website, at <www.buganda.or.ug>, and the Rwenzururu kingdom has both a website and a Facebook page.[30]

The cultural and intellectual world in which eastern Africans live today is structured by ethnic patriots' creative work. In the publishing industry, in government, and in legal discourse, the texts and institutions that patriotic

---

[25] Editorial letter in *Ngabo*, 13 August 1993; quoted in Karlström, 'Modernity and Its Aspirants.'
[26] Swaleh Tibawenda Basikania, 'Chronological Appraisal on the Bakonzo/Bamba Traditional Leadership' (Kampala, 25 May 2005).
[27] Paulo Ngologoza, *Kigezi and Its People* (Kampala, 1998 [1968]); J. W. Nyakatura, *Abakama of Bunyoro-Kitara* (Kisubi, 1998 [1947]); Joshua Kamugungunu, *Abagabe b'Ankole* (Kampala, 2005 [1955]).
[28] L. T. Rubongoya, *Naaho Nubo: The Ways of our Ancestors* (Köln, 2003); M. W. Magezi, T. E. Nyakango, and M. K. Aganatia, *The People of the Rwenzoris: The Bayira (Bakonzo/Bananade) and Their Culture* (Köln, 2004); G. N. P. Kirindi, *History and Culture of the Kingdom of Ankole* (Kampala, 2008); David Kihumuro-Apuli, *A Thousand Years of Bunyoro-Kitara Kingdom: The People and the Rulers* (Kampala, 1994).
[29] At http://www.bunyoro-kitara.com. Accessed on 17 August 2011.
[30] Website at http://www.rwenzururu.org; Facebook page at http://www.facebook.com/pages/Rwenzururu-Kingdom/128514997228678. Accessed on 17 August 2011.

thinkers composed in the 1940s and 1950s are now enjoying a new life. In Kenya, the loudest advocate of Gikuyu neo-traditionalism is *Mungiki*, a cultural movement-cum-street gang that since the early 1990s has menaced the urban residents of Nairobi.[31] Like the ethnic welfare associations of an earlier time, *Mungiki*'s members regard the campaign against independent women as their duty. They break up inter-ethnic marriages, force Gikuyu girls to have circumcisions, and attack women who wear miniskirts and other revealing clothing. One of their earliest advocates was Gakaara wa Wanjau, who in the twilight of his life thought *Mungiki* to be a reincarnation of Mau Mau.[32] In western Kenya, the discourse of Luo 'tradition' is being fed by stream of new publications. Paul Mboya's 1938 compendium of Luo customs (see Chapter 6) was republished in English translation in 2001.'[33] There is a website, <www.jaluo.com>, where Luo people can discuss their customs and traditions, and a radio call-in show regularly features Luo elders who offer advice about marriage, burial, and other matters.[34] Like the ethnic patriots of an earlier time, today's advocates of neo-traditionalism use the most contemporary technologies to advance conservative reforms (see Chapter 1).

But now, as in the mid-twentieth century, there is more than one scale on which East Africans can live. Many people have converted to Pentecostal Christianity, which has grown dramatically since the 1980s.[35] Revivalists greeted the first Pentecostals with scorn. 'They have brought a lot of confusion and difficulty into salvation.' a leading Ugandan revivalist complained. 'They lay emphasis on healing miracles, being filled with the Spirit, tongues, fasting etc., but repentance, restitution, being cleansed with the Blood, walking in the light – they don't emphasize at all.'[36] This convert was defending revivalists' particular discipline of self-accounting: whereas revivalists became converts through a rigorous work of self-examination, Pentecostals were seduced by superficial displays of charisma. Notwithstanding their tendentious relationship, Pentecostals borrowed both vocabulary and a model of historical time from their revivalist contemporaries. Uganda's Pentecostals call themselves *balokole*, the 'saved ones,' the same name by

---

[31] See David M. Anderson, 'Vigilantes, Violence and the Politics of Public Order in Kenya,' *African Affairs* 101 (4) (2002), 531–55; Grace Nyatugah Wamue, 'Revisiting our Indigenous Shrines through Mungiki,' *African Affairs* 100 (4) (2001), 453–67.

[32] GW 'Theological writing' file: Gakaara wa Wanjau, 'Mungiki and the *Matigari ma Njirungi*,' n.d. (but 1990s).

[33] Jane Achieng, ed. and trans., *Paul Mboya's Luo Kitgi gi Timbegi* (Nairobi, 2001).

[34] Described in Ruth Prince, 'Salvation and Tradition: Configurations of Faith in a Time of Death,' *Journal of Religion in Africa* 37 (1) (2007), 84–115.

[35] Pentecostals currently comprise 16 percent of all Christians in Kenya; 8 percent in Uganda; and 10 percent in Tanzania. Pew Forum on Religion and Public Life, *Tolerance and Tension: Islam and Christianity in Sub-Saharan Africa* (Washington, DC, 2010), 23.

[36] HMC JEC 15/2: Peter Kigozi to Malcolm and Barbara, 20 February 1985.

which the revivalists of the 1930s and 1940s were known.[37] Like an earlier generation of revivalists, Pentecostals position themselves as agents of a new social order. They commonly compare themselves with the biblical character Joseph, who refused to succumb to the overtures of his Egyptian master's oversexed wife.[38] Like Joseph, Pentecostals police their lifestyles carefully and cast scorn on culturally validated hierarchies. In western Kenya, Pentecostals disagree with Luo traditionalists over the etiology of AIDS.[39] Traditionalists contend that AIDS is a consequence of people's failure to follow the rules of kinship. Pentecostals argue that the customary practices of kinship – widow inheritance and polygamy in particular – are unhealthy and immoral. Like an earlier generation of Luo revivalists (see Chapter 6), Pentecostals refuse to honor their obligations to their relatives, turning their backs on the customs that uphold healthy communities. Today, as in former times, converts pose a challenge to the discursive and political order of tradition.

In post-genocide Rwanda, revivalist techniques are structuring the work of political reconciliation. There are courts in 9,000 communities around Rwanda, charged with trying the perpetrators of the 1994 genocide. These *gacaca* courts are headed by elected panels of lay judges, and local citizens are obliged to attend the weekly sessions. 'It is essential,' reads the law that established the courts, 'that all Rwandans participate on the ground level in producing evidence, categorizing the perpetrators of the offences by taking into consideration the role they played, and establishing their punishments.'[40] This is proper police procedure, a means of collecting evidence. But Rwanda's *gacaca* courts are also theaters of autobiographical production, where witnesses sort through their memories, make apologies, plead for forgiveness, and put distance between themselves and the past. The forensic work of testimony at *gacaca* courts parallels the autobiographical work at Revival meetings. Like converts, witnesses at *gacaca* courts are obliged to conform to the conventions of the genre. That is what Janvier Munyaneza, a witness to the genocide, seems to have meant when he told a visiting journalist that

I can feel that my memory is sorting out my memories as it pleases, without my being able to affect this. There are certain episodes which are very often retold, so

[37] Amos Kasibante, 'The Challenge of the New Pentecostal Churches to the East African Revival: The Confluence of the Two Movements in My Life,' in *The East African Revival: History and Legacies*, eds. Kevin Ward and Emma Wild-Wood (Kampala, 2010), 90–104.

[38] Alessandro Gusman, 'HIV/AIDS, Pentecostal Churches, and the "Joseph Generation" in Uganda,' *Africa Today* 56 (1) (2009), 67–86.

[39] Ruth Prince, 'Salvation and Tradition: Configurations of Faith in a Time of Death,' *Journal of Religion in Africa* 37 (2007), 84–115. See also Paul Wenzel Geissler and Ruth Jane Prince, *The Land is Dying: Contingency, Creativity and Conflict in Western Kenya* (Oxford, 2010).

[40] Quoted in William Schabas, 'Post-Genocide Justice in Rwanda: A Spectrum of Options,' in *After Genocide: Transitional Justice, Post-Conflict Reconstruction and Reconciliation in Rwanda and Beyond*, eds. Phil Clark and Zachary Kaufman (New York, 2009), 207–27.

they grow thanks to all the additions one person or another brings to them ... Other episodes are left behind and they grow obscure as in a dream.[41]

Like any credible convert, Munyaneza and other witnesses are obliged to stand back from the whole fabric of their lives, classify their deeds and actions, and conform their autobiographies to a standard template. Like the audiences at Revival conventions, the lay judges of *gacaca* courts make strict evaluations of witnesses' sincerity. At one locality in southern Rwanda, nearly 40 percent of witnesses are judged to have offered an incomplete confession.[42] According to the law, people who wish to confess are obliged to make a full disclosure of the crimes they committed, name their accomplices, and offer an apology to those they harmed.[43] Like converts, penitent witnesses have to confront the hard evidence of their guilt. When two people at Ruhengenge confessed to the murder of several children in March 2003, the president of the court ordered the victims' bodies exhumed. At the next *gacaca* session their bones and clothing were displayed before a horrified audience.[44]

There is a procedural and discursive overlap between revivalists' auto-biographies and testimonies delivered at *gacaca* courts. *Gacaca* testimonies share a narrative arc with conversion stories. Some of these testimonies – carefully edited and dramatically presented – have found their way into print, and there is now a growing Christian literature about the Rwanda genocide. *Faith Under Fire*, for example, contains 'testimonies of Christian bravery' that describe how Christians protected their neighbors from the *genocidaires*, while *God Sleeps in Rwanda* narrates the author's spiritual 'journey of transformation'.[45] Many Rwandans feel constrained by the pre-determined roles that *gacaca* courts oblige them to play. Hutus must always describe themselves as perpetrators; survivors must always forgive their persecutors.[46] The testimonies delivered at *gacaca* courts are shaped by the

---

[41] Quoted in Jean Hatzfeld, *Into the Quick of Life: The Rwandan Genocide: The Survivors Speak* (London, 2005 [2000]), 37.

[42] Max Rettig, 'Gacaca: Truth, Justice, and Reconciliation in Postconflict Rwanda,' *African Studies Review* 51 (3) (December 2008), 39.

[43] Rettig, 'Gacaca,' 25–50.

[44] Phil Clark, 'The Rules (and Politics) of Engagement: The *Gacaca* Courts and Post-Genocide Justice, Healing and Reconciliation in Rwanda,' in *After Genocide*, eds. Clark and Kaufman, 297–319.

[45] Antoine Rutayisire, *Faith Under Fire: Testimonies of Christian Bravery* (Essex, 1995); Joseph Sebarenzi with Laura Ann Mullane, *God Sleeps in Rwanda: A Journey of Transformation* (New York, 2009). See also Alexis Bilindabagabo with Alan Nichols, *Rescued by Angels: The Story of Miracles during the Rwandan Genocide* (Brunswick, Australia, 2001); Jean Hatzfeld, *Into the Quick of Life: The Rwandan Genocide: The Survivors Speak* (London, 2005); and Meg Guillebaud, *Rwanda: The Land God Forgot? Revival, Genocide and Hope* (London, 2002).

[46] Susan Thomson, 'The Darker Side of Transitional Justice: The Power Dynamics Behind Rwanda's *Gacaca* Courts,' *Africa* 81 (3) (August 2011), 373–90.

political ideology of the ruling Rwandan Patriotic Front, which uses the progress of reconciliation as evidence to legitimate its government.[47] But the testimonies nonetheless do real social work. The narrative form leads the teller from a former life of hatred, fear, and sin toward a new life of forgiveness and peace. In *As We Forgive*, for example, Rwandan autobiographers describe the painful process by which they laid down their hatred for their neighbors; while the autobiography of Immaculée Ilibagiza documents the author's difficult effort to recover a sense of moral vocation after the horror of the genocide.[48]

Comparing the testimonies produced in Rwanda's *gacaca* courts with revivalists' conversion narratives makes it possible to understand the work of 'peacemaking' in a different light. Scholars and human rights activists generally study the *gacaca* courts as a traditional alternative to punitive, Western-style justice.[49] We might, instead, see *gacaca* courts as extensions of the disciplines and practices that revivalists established. Revivalism has always had a close relationship with legal procedure (see Chapter 8). In Rwanda, the conversion narrative has wound its way from the Revival convention back to the courtroom, where it structures the testimonies that witnesses give.[50] This is not the first time that revivalists' forensic techniques have been harnessed to serve the purposes of political reorientation. In Mau Mau detention camps during the 1950s, the work of 'rehabilitation' was patterned on the model of conversion (see Chapter 10). Mau Mau detainees were compelled to create narratives about themselves, categorize their formerly uncontroversial deeds as sin, confess, and enter a new life. I have termed the program of Mau Mau rehabilitation 'revivalism in a coercive mode.' But in fact, revivalism has never been free of coercion. Africans' testimonies of conversion were always structured by generic conventions. Their autobiographies had to conform to a template, and a critical audience judged their validity. Rwanda's *gacaca* courts overlap, discursively and organizationally, with the wire-ringed theaters where Mau Mau detainees made their confessions and with the wooden platforms where revivalists addressed their audiences. These theaters are machines that generate autobiography, structure judgment, and produce penitence, forgiveness, and new life.

---

[47] Argued in Filip Reyntjens, 'Constructing the Truth, Dealing with Dissent, Domesticating the World: Governance in Post-Genocide Rwanda,' *African Affairs* 110 (438) (2011), 1–34.

[48] Catherine Claire Larson, *As We Forgive: Stories of Reconciliation from Rwanda* (Grand Rapids, MI, 2009); Immaculée Ilibagiza with Steve Erwin, *Left to Tell: Discovering God Amidst the Rwandan Holocaust* (Carlsbad, CA, 2006). Less moralistic testimonies can be found in Jean Hatzfeld, *Machete Season: The Killers in Rwanda Speak* (New York, 2005).

[49] See, e.g., Phil Clark, *Justice Without Lawyers: Peace, Justice and Reconciliation in Rwanda* (Cambridge, 2010); Ariel Meyerstein, 'Between Law and Culture: Rwanda's *Gacaca* and Postcolonial Legality,' *Law and Social Inquiry* 32 (2) (2007), 467–508.

[50] Argued in Nick Godfrey, 'Anglican Revivalists and the Rwandan Genocide: Survivors' Narratives of Divine Intervention,' in *The East African Revival: History and Legacies*, eds. Kevin Ward and Emma Wild-Wood (Kampala, 2010), 249–67.

Muthoni Likimani's 1974 novel *They Shall be Chastised* is a cuttingly critical portrait of revivalists and their self-advancing testimonies.[51] Set in a fictionalized locale in colonial Kenya, the story features a convert named Jocabed, who testifies before a large audience about the adulterous acts he had committed with his friends' wives.

Jocabed talked too much. He said things which were very embarrassing, mentioning the women's names, the children whom he had fathered, incidents which could create real problems leading possibly to divorces. He spoke out loud and clear, and some half-converted people left the group in disgust; others, particularly the young girls and boys, buried their faces, hiding them with shyness, and tried to walk away unnoticed.

The novelist Likimani first heard revivalists preach in the mid-1940s, while she was attending an Anglican girls' school in central Kenya. Her father, the Rev. Livai Gachanja, was a friend of Charles Muhoro Kareri (see Chapter 8) and one of the Revival's leading critics. He once stormed out of a Revival meeting, complaining that converts 'have no manners.'[52] The fictional preacher Jocabed is a figure drawn straight from her father's nightmares. But the novelist Likimani is uncommonly aware that revivalists, even in their unmannered denunciations of other people, were also prisoners of literary form. In her novel she describes how

The outpouring of consciences went on. They were all trying desperately to purge themselves of their sins ... They had to have something with which to compare the life before and after. There were those after stopping alcoholic drinks and ending their profligate lives with women who would count what they were able to purchase with the money saved. For the first time they had peace at home and happiness in their families.[53]

Revivalists did not set themselves at liberty through their conversions. As the novelist Likimani recognizes, converts were bound by the rules of the genre, compelled to produce evidence that could dramatize their passage to a new life. Converts were constituted through the compression of life-as-lived into an arc that led from sin to redemption. In their forensic self-examinations they propelled themselves forward, but offended against traditional standards of comportment and propriety. Likimani spends two full chapters – titled 'Confusion,' Part One and Part Two – describing how revivalists ruined parties, broke marriages, and destroyed reputations with their never-ending confessions.

They Shall be Chastised returns us to the argument that has oriented this book. As an advocate of decency and civility, Muthoni Likimani is like Paulo Ngologoza, the Kiga chief whose historical work instructed refractory

---

[51] Muthoni Likimani, *They Shall be Chastised* (Nairobi, 1974), 51.
[52] Muthoni Likimani, *Fighting Without Ceasing* (Nairobi, 2005), 41.
[53] Likimani, They Shall be Chastised, 53.

Kiga converts about propriety and obedience. She is like the men of the Haya Union, who harnessed bureaucratic techniques to suppress the embarrassment of prostitution. She is like Chief Paulo Mboya and the founders of the Luo Union, who found in tradition a means by which to guide their contemporaries' conduct. She is like Gakaara wa Wanjau, whose writing showed Gikuyu men how to master themselves. These and other ethnic patriots worked to establish normative standards of conduct, authenticated by history. They were unabashed inventors of tradition and energetic creators of tribalism. They sought to channel the flow of time in order to direct people's actions in the here-and-now. They sometimes worked in concert with nation-builders, but more often the architects of eastern Africa's patriotisms thought territorial nationalism to be a mortal challenge. Nation-building threw people together without discrimination, severing the young from the instruction that history could provide. Patriots entered the public sphere as spokesmen for an honorable, disciplined people. That is why, in the decade of African independence, so much work was being done to refurbish traditions and codify customs. Ethnic patriots were not out of step with their times. To the contrary: they involved in the very contemporary work of constructing a moral order.

The *patria* was not the only home that east Africans conceived during the 1940s and 1950s. Revivalists used the novel infrastructure of communication – the post office, the newspaper, and the bicycle – and conceived themselves in relation to a cosmopolitan, multilingual world. They composed their life stories in dialogue with a large ecumene, with fellow travelers who they knew through the post, through the media, or through their peripatetic travels to conventions. Their cosmopolitanism, I have argued, was intrinsically part of their self-understanding: converts thought of themselves as pilgrims, wending their way toward the gates of heaven. Their propulsive testimonies and their carefully edited lifestyles set them at odds with the patriotic organizers of their time. It is good to hear converts' testimonies again, not as sanitized morality tales, nor as endearing Christian literature, but as subversive work, challenging the order of tradition. Revivalists would not inherit their fathers' antagonisms. Their conversion was cultural criticism, a work of dissenting politics. Through it, they unbuckled the consolidating power of patriotism and opened a new horizon of possibility.

Bibliography

Archives in Uganda

Uganda National Archives, Entebbe (UNA)

The following deposits were consulted:

A 46	Correspondence and reports, Chief Secretary
A 13	Unyoro and Western province
A 14	Toro correspondence
A 22	CMS, 1900–1906
A 42–45	Toro district, reports
R	Secretariat
S	Secretariat

Kabarole District Archives, Fort Portal (KabDA)

This collection has recently been moved from the derelict attic of the Kabarole District headquarters to Mountains of the Moon University in Fort Portal, where the papers are currently being cleaned, preserved, and re-boxed. I have used the original box numbers in this book's notes. A catalogue is currently being prepared, and the old box numbers will be cross-referenced with the new numbering system. The boxes are now organized under the following topical headings:

Boxes 1–17	Judicial
Boxes 20–24	Rwenzururu
Boxes 26–37	Statistics and Census
Boxes 38–39	Chiefs
Boxes 40–49	Education
Boxes 50–56	Veterinary and Agriculture
Boxes 58–62	Information
Boxes 65–70	Development
Boxes 75–83	Sports and Leisure
Boxes 84–85	Water
Boxes 87–89	Elections

Box 91	Religion
Boxes 100–148	Local government, administration
Boxes 160–169	Labor
Boxes 190–196, 198	Trade
Boxes 197, 199	Agriculture
Boxes 200–252	Finance
Boxes 260–268	Tours and Visits
Boxes 270–274	Transport
Boxes 280–282	Soldiers
Boxes 283–290	Arms and Ammunition
Boxes 294–298	Medical
Boxes 300–318	Personnel
Boxes 320–329	Land
Boxes 330–343	Building and Housing
Boxes 344–345	Forestry
Boxes 347–351	Roads
Boxes 352–353	Building and Housing

Toro Government archives, Fort Portal (Muchwa)

This collection of files and loose papers is kept in a cellar below the Toro kingdom's parliament chambers. The covers of a great number of files have been torn away. It is hoped that these papers will soon be added to the new archival repository at Mountains of the Moon University. The following files were consulted:

Agricultural Productivity (Policy)
Annual Reports
Chiefs: Appointments, Transfers, Dismissals
Control of Drinking
Ebaruaziga Omulimo omu Government
Honours
Kabarole Hospital
Kaboyo School
Kyebambe Girls School
Leg. Co.
Markets
Misc. Minor Works
No cover (Police)
No cover (Rukurato minutes)
Programme of Rukirabasiaja
Provincial Team
Roads, Bridges
St Leo's College
Toro Government Policy
Toro Native Government Tax
Toro Public Service Commission
Uganda Prime Ministers' Conference
Visit of Uganda Africans to UK

Catholic Diocese of Fort Portal archives, Virika Cathedral,
Fort Portal (Virika)

The following boxes were consulted:

260 Bible Society of Uganda
276 Kasese Diocese
413 Ordinary marriage
822 Fort Portal municipal government
807 Constitutional commissions

Church of Uganda Provincial Archives, Uganda Christian University,
Mukono (CoU)

This archive has been reorganized in the course of a microfilming project organized by the Yale Divinity School. My reference numbers refer to the system in use prior to the reorganization. A cross-reference catalogue is available. The following deposits were consulted:

02 Bp Bishop's papers
1 Abp Archbishop's papers
CMS   CMS papers
MU   Mothers Union papers

Kigezi District Archives, Kabale (KigDA)

This archive is held in the attic above the offices of the Regional District Commissioner in Kabale. The materials are organized in numbered bundles, bound with twine. The following files were consulted, numbered by bundle:

15 Appointment and Dismissal of Chiefs, 1939–47
20 Church Missionary Society
    Labour, General
    Labour Inspection Reports, 1949
23 Safaris, Rukiga County
    Resettlement in Ankole
26 No cover (wartime correspondence)
27 Native Affairs
    RC Mission Plots
    Consolidated Resettlement Return
45 Native Affairs, Relations with Ankole
49 Immigration and Emigration
56 File 178: Miscellaneous (Native Courts)
    Native Affairs, Chiefs' Appointments and Dismissals
60 Blue Book Returns
62 Secret
72 Marriage, General
    Agriculture
78 Native Affairs, Diseases and Sickness
88 Roman Catholic Mission

96	Criminal Courts, 1931–35
118	Native Affairs, Presents to Chiefs
	Medical, Sleeping Sickness
122	Native Affairs, Chiefs' Appointments
130	Reports on Native Administration, 1936
132	Famine
146	File 160: Judicial, Native Courts
149	File 2433: Askaris Serving, Family Matters
158	Native Labour
171	Rhona Ross and Cyril Sofer, 'Survey of the Banyaruanda Complex,' 22 May 1950.
195	Correspondence with Ruanda
218	File 1295: Judicial
258	Native Affairs
	Native Administration, General
249	File 62: No cover
	Return of Lunacy Cases, 1939
250	Relations with Belgian Ruanda
251	Land, Mission, General policy
	Luwalo Inspectorate
659	Land and Survey
	File 217: Land and Survey
	File 1414: Land Policy, Natives in Kigezi
	Forestry, General
661	File 58: Native Affairs: Political Disturbances
	File 406: Nyakishenyi: Rebels and Disturbances
	File 165: Fugitive Offenders
	File 202: Native Affairs, Chiefs Labor and Tribute
	File 542: Veterinary: Relations with Belgian Territory
	Native Affairs, Belgian Congo
662	Native Affairs, Repatriation of Banyaruanda
	File 280: Political Deportees
	File 39: Reports and Returns
	Native Affairs, Correspondence with Biumba
	File 810: Famine Reports
	File 914: Kigezi Resettlement

Ankole District Archives, Mbarara (Mbarara)

This archive is held at the office of the Chief Administrative Officer in Mbarara. The following files were consulted:

61	Tsetse
	Resettlement in Ankole

Archdiocese of Kampala archives, Rubaga Cathedral, Kampala (Rubaga)

This archive contains the papers and correspondence of the priests and lay workers of the White Fathers Mission in Uganda. The following files were consulted:

D.19 folio 1	Bishop Forbes' Correspondence
D.20 folio 1	Streicher's Correspondence
D.20 folio 2	Streicher's Correspondence
D.20 folio 3	Correspondence with Government
D.21 folio 4	No title
D.22 folio 3	Luganda Orthography
D.31 folio 6	Protectorate Government, 1933–34
D.32 folios 5 & 6	Marriage
D.34 folio 1	Correspondence with Government
D.39 folio 5	Bishop Michaud, Criticisms and Complaints, 1935–1946
D.39 folio 9	No title
D.47 folio 5	Various
D.47 folio 2	Correspondence with Missions/Parishes
D.48 folio 4	Annual Parish Reports, 1944–1960
D.84 folio 2	Hancock Commission
D.94 folio 9	No title
D.99 folio 1	No title
D.99 folio 2	Buganda Government, 1932–35
D.99 folio 5	Bulungi bwa nsi Schools Troubles, 1947–1948
D.99 folio 7	Disturbances, 1949

Kasese District Archives, Kasese (KasDA)

This archive is kept in the offices of the Chief Administrative Officer. The following files were consulted:

Research Projects and Archives
Mr. Bonne Baluku-Nyondo

Hoima District Archives, Hoima (HDA)

This collection is kept on the premises of the Chief Administrative Officer. The following files were consulted:

Ankole District Report, 1960
Annual Report 1938
Annual Report 1951
Annual Report 1957
Bujenje Saza, Touring
Bugahya Touring Book
Bujenje Touring Book
Bunyoro District Book
Census, 1948
Clubs and Other Societies
CMS
Courts: Civil Cases
District Council
District Team
Empire Day

Excessive Drinking
Honours
Language, Orthography
Local Government Policy: Lost Counties
Maps, Places, Historical Notes
Missions, Land
Mukama and Saza Chiefs
Native Courts
No cover (courts) (two files)
No cover (standing committees)
No cover (veterinary)
Personal Records, Chiefs, Masindi
Petitions and Complaints
Petitions and Complaints, Bujenje
Petitions, Complaints and Enquiries, General
Political Parties
Queen Elizabeth's Coronation
RA the Mukama
Records of Chiefs and Officers, Bunyoro
Relationships Commission
Rukurato Speeches
Tombs of the Bakama in Mubende District
Uganda Independence Celebrations
Visits of Uganda Africans to Other Territories

Makerere University Library archives, Kampala (Makerere)

The following deposits were consulted:

AR N 3	Native Anglican Church, Archbishop's papers
MS 276	Papers concerning the African Orthodox Church
AR J 3	B. L. Jacobs papers
AR L 1	Ladbury papers
K I 9	Apollo Kivebulaya papers
AR KA 43	S. Kadumukasa papers, 1927–1947
No number	Yusufu Bamu'ta papers

George Kahigwa papers, Harugali, Bundibugyo (Kahigwa)

These are papers relating to the Bakonzo Life History Research Society, in the possession of the late Mr. George Kahigwa, who kindly allowed me to view them.

Diocese of Kabarole archives, St. John's Cathedral, Fort Portal (KabDio)

This is a loose collection of papers and files kept at the diocesan offices in Kabarole. I consulted the Minute Book of the church council and a correspondence file without a cover.

Diocese of Kigezi archives, St. Peter's Cathedral, Kabale (St. Peter's)

This collection consists of baptism registers, minute books and some scant correspondence. The following files were consulted:

Ababatiziibwe, 1922 to 1927
Abasoma Okubatizibwa, 1929–39
Abasoma Okubatizibwa, 1939–45
Abasoma Okubatizibwa, 1945–1953
Cash Book, 1932–37
Enkiiko za Kanisa, 1950s
Ekyababatize, Ndorwa and Rukiga Counties, July 1933 to December 1938
Olukiko lweisaza Ndorwa, 1943-
Olukiko lwe Twale, 1954

Archives in Kenya

Kenya National Archives, Nairobi (KNA)

The following deposits were consulted:

AB	Ministry of Community Development
AH	Ministry of Defence
AHC	Ministry of Information and Broadcasting
PC Nyanza	Provincial Commissioner, Nyanza
PC Central	Provincial Commissioner, Central Province
HB	Provincial Commissioner, Western
DC Central Nyanza	District Commissioner, Central Nyanza
DC Kisumu	District Commissioner, Kisumu
DC Kakamega	District Commissioner, Kakamega
DC Mombasa	District Commissioner, Mombasa
DC North Nyanza	District Commissioner, North Nyanza
DX	District Commissioner, Kakamega
HT	District Commissioner, Central Nyanza
JZ	Prisons and Police
MAA	Ministry of African Affairs
ARC/MAA	Ministry of African Affairs
MSS 61	Church Missionary Society special collection
MSS 129	Christian Council of Kenya

Presbyterian Church of East Africa archives, Nairobi (PCEA)

This collection is kept in the tower above St. Andrew's church in Nairobi. I have referenced material from this archive by listing the series number, followed by the topical category and the box number. Topical categories are as follows:

A	General Correspondence
B	Annual Reports
C	Tumutumu Papers

D   Thogoto Papers
E   Education
F   Land
G   Publications
H   Finance
J   Medical
K   Kikuyu Language Committee
L   Literature
M   Contracts and Testimonials for Mission Apprentices
Y   Minutes
Z   Log Books; Dictionaries; Bible Translations

Tumutumu Church archives, Karatina (TT)

The following files were consulted:

Conference Reports
Constitutions
Correspondence with Chogoria
Correspondence with Kikuyu
DC and Forest Officer, June 1935 to December 1939
DOs and Chiefs, 1950s
Domestic Science
Education Misc., 1939–63
Estimates
Finance
Fort Hall Supervisor
General and Miscellaneous
Government Exams
Hospital Board: Correspondence
Kiama gia Coci ya Tumutumu, 1930–1946
Kiamwangi Kirk Session, 1936–42
Kirk Session ya Tumutumu, 1936–58
Language: Kikuyu Orthography
Ministers, to 1955
Ministers, 1956
Minutes cia Presbytery
Marua Makonii Synod
Nyeri District Law Panel minutes, 1950s
Presbytery Business, Minutes etc. to 1932
Presbytery of Kenya, Tumutumu, 1933-
Presbytery of Tumutumu: Marua Makonii Kirk Session o na kana Members Acio
Presbytery ya Tumutumu: Committee ya Presbytery, 1938–50
Presbytery ya Tumutumu: Letters
Presbytery ya Tumutumu: Maciira Maria Mangi
Property
Religious Instruction for Teachers in Training, 1930s-50s
Rev. C.M. Kareri
Statistics

Teachers Detained, Court Cases, 1954
Teachers Training
Tumutumu Parish
Women's Guild

Anglican Church of Kenya archives, Nairobi (ACK)

The following files were consulted:

ACSO/CPN/1   North Nyanza Rural Deanery, 1951–52
Nyanza Chaplaincy, Central and South Nyanza, 1948–51
Nyanza Chaplaincy, Kisumu and South Nyanza Rural Deanery
   Council, 1947–52
Bishop of Mombasa, North Nyanza Ruridecanal Council,
   1951–52
Ruridecanal Council, Ng'iya, Nyanza Chaplaincy, 1935–42
Kavirondo archdeaconry, 1939–1952
Nyanza Chaplaincy, 1942–51
Nyanza Chaplaincy, 1951–53
Nyanza Chaplaincy, 1954–60
ACSO/CPN/2   Nyanza Chaplaincy, Nyanza Conventions, 1951–55
South Nyanza Rural Deanery, April 1951 to December 1958
North Nyanza Rural Deanery, December 1952- December
   1960
CMO/EARM/1   Revival Movement, 1953–56
CMO/BSK/3   Luyia Translation, 1938–1946
No number   Mau Mau I
North Highlands Rural Deanery

Kenya National Archives, Kakamega Provincial Records Centre (Kakamega)

This archive, which is kept in an unmarked warehouse at the District Commissioner's headquarters in Kakamega, contains material of comparatively recent provenance. The following deposits were consulted:

ATW   District Officer, Sirisia
DA   Provincial Commissioner, Nyanza
DF   District Commissioner, Bungoma
DG   District Agricultural Office, Bungoma
DX   District Commissioner, North Nyanza
NE   Provincial Education Office, Nyanza
YC   District Commissioner, South Nyanza

Kenya National Archives, Kisumu Provincial Records Centre (Kisumu)

This archive is kept in an office in the children's prison in Kisumu. It contains material of recent provenance. The following deposits were consulted:

DA   Provincial Commissioner, Nyanza
DAC   District Land Office, Kisumu
HT   District Commissioner, Kisumu

Africa Inland Mission archives, Nairobi (AIM)

The following files were consulted:

Papers on 'Isms'
Problems, Dowry etc., 1920s-30s
Sects, Dangers etc.

Papers of the Kikuyu Traders Association, Othaya (KTA)

This is a collection of registers, log books, minutes, and correspondence concerning the Kikuyu Traders Association of Othaya division. The materials are in the possession of Mr. Kariuki Kiboi of Othaya town, who kindly allowed me to view them.

National Museum of Kenya, Nairobi (NMK)

The following deposits were consulted:

Den/A	Gordon Dennis papers
Den/G	Gordon Dennis photographic collection
GSBB	Gladys Beecher papers
Not indexed	Leonard Beecher papers

Archives in Tanzania

Tanzania National Archives, Dar es Salaam (TNA)

The following deposits were consulted:

Acc. 59	Bukoba District, Courts
Acc. 64	Bukoba Regional Office
Acc. 71	Bukoba District
Acc. 197	Ngara District Office
Acc. 201	Biharamulo
Acc. 215	Annual Reports
Acc. 217	Ngara
Acc. 227	Ngara District, courts
Acc. 239	District Agricultural Office, Ngara
Acc. 268	Ngara District
Acc. 289	District Agricultural Office, Bukoba
Acc. 318	Bukoba District
Acc. 435	Medical and Sanitary
Acc. 450	Medical and Sanitary
Acc. 529	Bukoba District
Acc. 530	Ngara District
Acc. 571	Papers of Mzee Hassan Suleiman
Acc. 602	Shabaan Robert papers
S	Secretariat papers

Tanzania National archives, Mwanza Regional Records Centre (Mwanza)

This rich collection is exceptionally well maintained by the archivist, Mr. Herman Rwechungura. The archive is kept in Kirumba stadium in Mwanza town. Accession 1 (Mwanza) and Accession 9 (Bukoba) were consulted.

Bukoba District Archives, Bukoba (Rwamishenye)

This collection is housed at the local council's administrative center in Rwamishenye, outside Bukoba town. There is a rough catalogue. The following files were consulted:

Box 2	Local Councils
Box 7	Football Association
Box 12	Chief of Missenye
Box 17	Bahaya Union School, Rubare
Box 18	Rwamishenye
Box 21	Church of the Holy Spirit
Box 26	Mukama Lutinwa
Box 30	Ex-Askaris
Box 31	Native Authority Dressers
Box 32	Destitute Persons
Box 33	Omukama of Kianja
Box 35	Communicable Diseases
Box 36	Maternity Services
	War Graves
Box 43	Photography
	Leprosy
	Bukoba District Council minute book

Hans Cory papers, East Africana Collection, University of Dar es Salaam (Cory)

This collection contains the papers, correspondence, and notes of Hans Cory, Tanganyika's government sociologist during the 1950s and early 1960s.

White Fathers Mission (Société des Missionnaires d'Afrique) archives, Dar es Salaam (WFM)

This is a collection of logbooks from several White Fathers Mission stations in Tanganyika, kept at Atiman House in Dar es Salaam. The following materials were consulted:

Buhororo Mission diary, 1932–1949
Rubya (Ihangiro) Mission diary, 1904–1961
Katoke Mission diaries
Herman Schleiber, 'Kihaya proverbs,' n.d.
Kashozi Mission diary, 1909–1928
Kashozi Council book, 1909–1947
Kagondo Mission diary

Diocese of Central Tanganyika archives, Dodoma, Tanzania (DCT)

This small collection is kept in the diocesan offices at MacKay House in Dodoma. The following files were consulted:

Diocesan Council Minutes, 1953–60
Diocesan Newsletters, 1928–56
Diocesan Council Minutes, 20 May 1933 to 4 November 1950
Gogo dictionaries and grammar books
Minute Book of the Central Church Council of the Tanganyika Mission
Missionaries' Annual Letters, 1951
Msingi, Maelezo, Sheria na Kanuni za Uaskofu wa Central Tanganyika
No title, labeled 'Mrs. Dyson'

Evangelical Lutheran Church of Tanzania, Northwest
Diocese archives, Bukoba (ELCT)

This collection is kept in the ELCT's diocesan headquarters. Much of the correspondence is written in Swedish, especially after the Second World War when the work of the Lutheran mission in Tanzania was taken on by the Church of Sweden. There is no catalogue. The following boxes were consulted:

Box A II b:2
Box A IV:1
Box A X:1
Box B II:1
Box B II:2
Box E I a:1
Box E I a:2
Box E I b:1
Box E I b:3
Box E I b:6
Box E I b:12
Box E II f:1
Box E IV b.3
Box E IV b:4
Box E IV b:5
Box E VI b:2
Box E VI b:3
Box E VI b:4
Box F
Box F II c:1
Box WCI 6:N
Logbook: Kashasha Girls' School, 1937–58

Diocese of Ngara archives, Murugwanza, Ngara (Murugwanza)

The following materials were consulted:

Baptismal Register, August 1932–
Marriage Register, October 1936–
Record of Habari Cards, 1928–

Archives in the United Kingdom

Cambridge University Library

The following deposits were consulted:

Add. 7916   Derrick Stenning papers
BSA   British and Foreign Bible Society archives

Church Missionary Society archives, University of Birmingham Library (CMS)

The following accessions were consulted:

Acc. 392   Records of Maseno Mission, 1959–1966
Acc. 83   Papers of Archdeacon Owen, 1909–1945
G3 A7   Uganda Mission papers
G3 A11   Ruanda Mission papers
G3 A8   Tanganyika Mission papers
G3 A5   East Africa Mission papers
M   Medical Department

Church Missionary Society archives, Oxford (CMS Oxford)

The papers of Rwanda missionary Dora Skipper were consulted.

Churchill College archives, Cambridge (Churchill)

The papers of British parliamentarian Fenner Brockway (FEBR) and advocate Dingle Foot (DGFT) were consulted.

Edinburgh University Library, Edinburgh (EUL)

The following deposits were consulted:

Gen. 1785/1–10   A. R. Barlow, Kikuyu language notes
Gen. 1786/1–11   A. R. Barlow, correspondence, papers, photographs and recordings

Entebbe Secretariat Archives, notes in the possession of Prof. John Lonsdale (JML)

Prof. Lonsdale conducted research at the Entebbe Secretariat Archives (now the Uganda National Archives) in the 1960s, where he took notes on files that are now no longer available in Uganda. I have referenced these materials by listing the original file number, as noted by Prof. Lonsdale.

Henry Martyn Centre, Cambridge (HMC)

The Joe Church collection came to the Henry Martyn Centre in 2007. There were eight footlockers and eleven box files of material, all carefully organized by Dr. Church himself. The material has now been placed in archive boxes and a catalogue has been created. The Church collection is referenced with the abbreviation JEC.

Imperial and Commonwealth Museum, Bristol (Bristol)

The following deposits were consulted:

Mss. 2002   James Breckenridge papers
Mss. 2000   Robin Wainwright papers
Mss. 1996   W.H. Thompson papers

London School of Economics archives, London (LSE)

The papers of anthropologist Audrey Richards were consulted.

Mid-Africa Ministry archives, University of Birmingham (MAM)

The following subject classifications were consulted:

A   Administrative Correspondence and Papers, 1926–49
C   Minutes of the Ruanda Council, 1926–40
E   Education
Y   Correspondence

National Library of Scotland, Edinburgh (NLS)

The following deposits were consulted:

ACC 7548   Church of Scotland Mission, Kenya papers
MS 7605–08   Church of Scotland Mission, Kenya papers

National Archives of Britain, Public Records Office, Kew (NAB)

The following deposits were consulted:

CO 691   Correspondence, Tanganyika Territory
CO 533   Correspondence, Kenya
CO 536 & 682 Correspondence, Uganda
CO 822   Correspondence, East Africa

Rhodes House Library, University of Oxford (RH)

The following deposits were consulted:

Mss. Afr. 592   Ralph Leech papers
Mss. Afr. 622   George MacLean papers
Mss. Afr. 642   Peter Bostock papers
Mss. Afr. 951   Boyd papers
Mss. Afr. 1047   Vickers-Haviland papers
Mss. Afr. 1352   Herbert Carr papers
Mss. Afr. 1384   James Elliot papers
Mss. Afr. 1475   T. Cashmore, interview
Mss. Afr. 1478   M. Moller papers
Mss. Afr. 1483   Papers regarding Buganda
Mss. Afr. 1534   Mau Mau papers, misc.
Mss. Afr. 1579   Sidney Fazan, interview

Mss. Afr. 2114   Richard Stone, interview
Mss. Afr. 2257   Howard Church papers

School of Oriental and African Studies archives, London (SOAS)

The following deposits were consulted:

PP Ms 38   Melvin Perlman papers
MCF   Movement for Colonial Freedom
CBMS   Council of British Mission Societies
IMC   International Missionary Council

Jocelyn Murray papers, London Mennonite Centre (Murray papers)

This un-catalogued collection consists of the papers of church historian Jocelyn Murray. The following files were consulted:

Revival: Secondary Literature
Revival: Replies to Questionnaire
Correspondence with ex-missionaries
Kabare, Embu, Meru
Revival: Analysis
Box of notebooks

Archives in the United States

Gakaara wa Wanjau papers, Yale University Library, New Haven, CT (GW)

The papers of the late Gakaara wa Wanjau are kept at his home in Karatina. At the invitation of his wife, Shifra Wairire, several thousand pages were photocopied by Ann Biersteker and Dorothy Woodson. The photocopies were deposited in the Yale University Library, where I catalogued them. The material has now been microfilmed and will be deposited at the Kenya National Archives.

Interviews

I conducted oral interviews in Bukoba and Ngara districts (northwestern Tanzania); Kigezi District (southern Uganda); Hoima, Kabarole, Kasese, and Bundibugyo districts (western Uganda); Buganda (central Uganda); Nyanza Province (western Kenya); and Nyeri District (central Kenya). I worked alongside a very generous cadre of colleagues and translators: in Ngara, Canon Fareth Sendegeya; in Hoima, Rev. David Kato; in Fort Portal, Rev. Richard Baguma; in Kigezi, Canon John Basingwire and Mr. Wilson Mbabazi; in Nyanza, Mr. Henry Adera; and in Kasese and Bundibugyo, Mr. Ezron Muhumuza.

Western Kenya

Truphena Obisa Abayo, Masogo, West Kano, Nyanza, 20 November 2007
Habakuk Onyang'o Abongo, Kisumu, 20 November 2007
Fanuel Aguoko Agong'a, Rabuor, Nyanza, 21 November 2007

Baraka Amumi Agwengo, Rafael Akobi Arua, Harun Oguma, Kesia Odela, Doris Achola Nyawara, Wilikista Goro Otieno, Lois Achieng' Juma, and Pilista Olanga, Tieng're, Nyanza, 22 November 2007
Matthew Ajuoga, Kisumu town, 24 November 2007
Joshua Aluoch Gawo, Maseno, 23 November 2007
Julia Okumu Mubiri, Helen Anyang'o, Preska Sewe, Preska Wajewa, Kisumu town, 24 November 2007
Eusto Ndege, Masogo, West Kano, Nyanza, 20 November 2007
Nathaniel Gaya Ogado, Ndira, Central Nyanza, 23 November 2007
Naomi Olweny, Nyayiera, Siaya, Nyanza, 23 November 2007
Okello Pande, Helena Onyango, and Seleina Onyango, Gobei, Asembo, Nyanza, 23 November 2007

Central Kenya

Liliani Gachigua, Kiamariga, Nyeri, 9 and 10 August 1998
Daudi Gachonde, Tumutumu, Nyeri, 22 February 1998
Arthur Kihumba, Othaya town, Nyeri, 7 July and 16 September 1998
Gerard Gachau King'ori, Gitugi, Nyeri, 19 June and 8 July 1998
Jedidah Kirigu, Magutu, Nyeri, 12 August 1998
Elijah Kiruthi, Mahiga, Nyeri, 15 June and 16 September 1998
Muriuki Kiuria, Magutu, Nyeri, 13 May 1998
Peterson Muchangi, Tumutumu, Nyeri, 15 September 1998
Cecilia Muthoni Mugaki, Tumutumu, Nyeri, 25 July 1996 and 16 September 1998
Peter Munene, Iruri, Nyeri, 12 May and 9 August 1998
John Muriuki, Ngorano, Nyeri, 14 May and 6 August 1998
William Mwangi, Ruare, Nyeri, 3 April 1998
Geoffrey Ngare, Nairobi, 27 May 1994
Ngunu wa Huthu, Magutu, Nyeri, 12 August 1998
Timothy Gathu Njoroge, Kangema, 29 June 1994

Northwestern Tanzania

Dario Bakundukize, Raymond Kagero, and Mary Kagero, Mugisagala, Ngara, 18 August 2006
Philemon Uwitijije Bashigwari, Dar es Salaam, 28 March 2007
Anord Biyoboke and Lameck Bitemba, Mukarehe, Kagera, Ngara, 18 August 2006
Richard Bugwoya, Mubinyanganya, Ngara, 18 August 2006
Samuel Habimana, Bukoba town, 22 August 2006
Jafeth Kabyemera, Bukoba town, 8 August 2006
Herman and Dorothy Kataraia, Bukoba town, 11 August 2006
Martha Kibira, Kibeeta, Bukoba, 22 August 2006
Erasto and Elina Kigabogabo, Murugina, Kagera, 19 August 2006
Christian Komulaga, Kashai B, Bukoba town, 14 August 2006
Wilson Lugakingira, Bukoba town, 12 August 2006
Ernest Lutashobya, Dar es Salaam, 25 August 2006
Philemon Majoro, Nyamiaga, 20 August 2006

Samuel Masoko, Biharamulo town, 16 August 2006
William Migembe, Mugisagala, Ngara, 18 August 2006
Eustace Mujoauzi, Bukoba town, 22 August 2006
Christian Mushumbuzi, Kibeeta, Bukoba, 11 August 2006
Eliabu Ndimugwanko, Murutabo, Ngara, 17 August 2006
Urias Ntamalengelo, Mabawe, Ngara, 19 August 2006
Nathan Nzisehere, Salmon Nzikobanyanka, Dani Nyanana, Elias Bitambikwa,
    Danieli Sempiga, Muruvyagila, Ngara, 17 August 2006
Wilson Nzobakenga and Mathayo Mutabazi, Mubuhenge, Ngara, 17 August
    2006
Apolonia Rugina, Mumahoro, Ngara, 19 August 2006
Johanssen Rutabingwa, Bukoba town, 14 August 2006
Paulina Sendegeya and Anastasia Sendegeya, Murugina, Mabawe, Ngara, 19 August
    2006
Juliana Shogotera, Mabawe, Ngara, 20 August 2006

Southern Uganda

Amos Bakeine, Kabale town, 21 August 2005
Amos Betungura, Ruharo, Ankole, 7 July 2004
Nasani Biryabarema, Kabale town, 19 August 2005
Kezia Bwegye, Kabale town, 21 August 2005
Rwamangye Eliezar, Kabale town, 20 August 2005
Ida Marere Ezina, Kabale town, 20 August 2005
Ibrahim Kagungule, Anna and Joy Kagungule, and Nasani Ndasarorera, Rugarama,
    Kabale town, Kigezi, 4 July 2004
Azaliya Kamara, Kabale town, 20 August 2005
Eldad Kanje, Kamwezi, Kigezi, 5 July 2004
George William Kasigairi, Kabale town, 19 August 2005
Festo Karwemera, Kabale town, 28 June and 1 July 2004
Alfred Katebalirwe, Kabale town, 20 August 2005
Wilson Komunda, Bukinda, Rukiga, Kigezi, 25 June 2004
Kosiya Kyamabara, Kabale town, 19 August 2005
Enoch Lugimbirwa, Ruharo, Ankole, 8 July 2004
Ezra Mahega, Bubare, Ndorwa, Kigezi, 26 June 2004
Zebedee Masereka, Kabale town, 21 August 2005
Stanley Matheka, Bukinda, Rukiga, Kigezi, 25 June 2004
Amos Mbitama, Kagarama, Ndorwa, Kigezi, 27 June 2004
Julaina Mufuko, Kandago, Bukinda, Kigezi, 25 June 2004
Phinhas Nyenda, Ruharo, Ankole, 7 July 2004
Gersamu Ruhindi, Kabale town, 21 August 2005
Enoch Rukare, Ruharo, Ankole, 7 July 2004
Robin Rwaminyonyo, Georgina Kajagyi, and Gershom Kashaje, Kabale town, 18
    August 2005
Asanasio Rwandare, Rwenyunza, Rukiga, Kigezi, 26 June 2004 and 21 August
    2005
David John Ziine, Rugarama, Kabale town, 1 July 2004

Central Uganda

Zeb Kabaza, Kasanga, Kampala, 10 July 2004
Peter Kigozi, Ntinda, Kampala, 13 July 2004
Yowasi Musajakaawa, Kampala, 12 July 2004

Western Uganda

Hezironi Acurubwe and Seremasi Baseka, Kisanja, Masindi, 1 September 2005
Agabus Baguma, Fort Portal, 28 August 2007
Richard Baguma, Fort Portal, 16 August 2005
Joram Bahwere, Harugale, Bundibugyo, 3 September 2007
Timosewo Munakenya Bawalana, Fort Portal, 28 May 2010 and 15 July 2011
Erina Bira, Buganikere, Bundibugyo, 6 September 2007
Isaac Bitanihirwe, Fort Portal, 16 August 2005
James Bizarwenda, Nyakasura, Kabarole, 30 August 2007
Hezekiah Bukombi, Bundibugyo town, 3 September 2007
Yeremiya Byasalya, Kabatinda, Busongora, 10 September 2007
Michael Gafabusa, Kyambogo, Kabarole, 1 September 2007
Mundeke Ibrahim, Kakuka, Bundibugyo, 5 September 2007
Yonia Irumba, Duhaga, Hoima, 30 August 2005
Jotham and Janet Kabuzi, Nyakasura, Kabarole, 30 August 2007
Erasto Kakongolo and Rachel Kakongolo, Kigama, Hoima, 1 September 2005
Irene Kamanyire, Fort Portal, 12 August 2005
Eustace Kamanyire, Fort Portal, 14 August 2005
Augustine Kayonga, Fort Portal, 27 August 2007
Benezeri Kisembo, Fort Portal, 28 August 2007
Edison Kithamuliko, Kabatunde, Busongora, Kasese, 10 September 2007
Charles Komurasi, Fort Portal, 27 August 2007
Buusu Koronen, Kasindi, Bubandi, Bundibugyo, 7 September 2007
Josephat Kule, Bwera town, Kasese, 13 September 2007
Yona Kule, Kisinga, Kasese, 12 September 2007
James Murumba Kwirabosa, Kisonko, Galilaya, Nduguto, Bundiguyo, 12 June 2010
Erinesti Kyambyo, Tombwe I, Bubandi, Bundibugyo, 7 September 2007
Daudi Lhubibi, Mutiti, Bundibugyo, 5 September 2007
Yofesi Maasa, Kirabaho, Busongora, Kasese, 10 September 2007
Shemu Maate, Buganikere, Bundibugyo, 6 September 2007
Yonia Maate, Buganikere, Bundibugyo, 6 September 2007
Dolosi Magabali, Fort Portal, 11 August 2005
Celili Makoma, Kisinga, Kasese, 12 September 2007
Paulo Makwera, Nyahuka, Bundibugyo, 4 September 2007
Yeremiya Maliba, Kayenze, Busaru, Bundibugyo, 12 June 2010
Atenasi Masereka, Kasese, 4 June 2010
Yohana Masereka, Kisinga, Kasese, 12 September 2007
Zebedee Masereka, Kasese town, 11 September 2007
Yowasi Mateso, Kanyampura, Burahya, Kabarole, 9 June 2010
Shemu Matte, Kasanzi, Buganikere, Bundibugyo, 6 September 2007

Edison Mujuku, Bubandi, Bundibugyo, 4 September 2007
Grace Mujuku, Bubandi, Bundibugyo, 4 September 2007
Metusera Mujungu, Kabutabula, Bubandi, Bundibugyo, 4 September 2007
Christine Mukirane, Kasese town, 12 September 2007 and 29 May 2010
Yustasi Mukirane, Bwera town, Kasese, 13 September 2007
Edrana Kabugho Mukirania, Kitsutsu, Munkunyu, Kasese, 30 May 2010
Cosmas Mukonzo, Karambi, Bwera, 13 September 2007
Yolamu Mulima, Kasese town, 11 September 2007 and 29 May 2010
Mumbere Asanasiyo Mulokole, Kabatunde, Busongora, Kasese, 10 September 2007
Asumani Mumbere, Kasese town, 12 September 2007
Charles Wesley Mumbere, Kasese town, 4 June 2010
Petero Kaamba Mupalya, Fort Portal, 15 August 2005 and 28 August 2007
Kaheru Mutusera and Kezia Kaheru, Bulindi, Hoima, 31 August 2005
Sam Mweisigya, Hoima town, 29 August 2005
Tito Ndorotyo, Duhaga, Hoima, 1 September 2005
Eriya Ngobi, Nabwina, Rwimi, Bunyangabu, Kabarole, 8 June 2010
Paul Mutabali Nyamwesa, Bunyangari, Bundibugyo, 5 September 2007
Georgina Nyaruboona, Bulindi, Hoima, 31 August 2005
Yoweri Nziabake, Kasese town, 17 June 2010
Mary Nzura, Kakuka, Bundibugyo, 5 September 2007
Jotham Rugomboora, Nyakasura, Kabarole, 30 August 2007
Edward Rugumayo, Fort Portal, 1 September 2007
Julaina Ruhukya, Hoima town, 31 August 2005
George Kahigwa Rukambi, Harugali, Bundibugyo, 3 September 2007
Erinesti Rupunjura, Butama III, Bundibugyo, 7 September 2007
Sylvester Rutaara and Agabus Baguma, Fort Portal, 10 August 2005
Shem Rutaare, Fort Portal, 17 August 2005
James Rwabwoni, Fort Portal, 28 August 2007
Dinah Rwakaikara, Bulindi, Hoima, 31 August 2005
Paulo Rwibende, Hima, Kasese, 11 September 2007 and 29 May 2010
Amon Seruboyo, Nyahuka, Bundibugyo, 6 September 2007
Eliezar Sirabwa, Mutiti, Bundibugyo, 5 September 2007
Wanza Stanley, Kakuka, Bundibugyo, 5 September 2007
Muhindo Yusuf, Kakuka, Bundibugyo, 6 September 2007

Books, Articles, and Manuscripts

Achieng, Jane. *Paul Mboya's Luo Kitgi gi Timbegi.* Nairobi: Atai Joint, 2001.

Ahimbisibwe-Katebaka, John. 'The Revival Movement and its Impact on the Church of Uganda in West Ankole Diocese, with Particular Reference to Kabwohe Archdeaconry, 1935–1995.' Dip. Theo. thesis, Bishop Tucker Theological College, 1997.

Ahmed, Ali, ed. *The Invention of Somalia.* Lawrenceville, NJ: Red Sea Press, 1995.

Akita, J. M. 'The Development of the National Archives and the National Documentation Centre.' Paris: UNESCO, 1979.

Allman, Jean M. *The Quills of the Porcupine: Asante Nationalism in an Emergent Ghana.* Madison: University of Wisconsin Press, 1993.

ed. *Fashioning Africa: Power and the Politics of Dress.* Bloomington, IN: Indiana University Press, 2004.

'Americans' Role Seen in Uganda Anti-Gay Push.' *New York Times* (3 January 2010).

Anderson, Benedict. *Imagined Communities: Reflections on the Origins and Spread of Nationalism.* London: Verso, 1983.

Anderson, David M. 'Depression, Dust Bowl, Demography, and Drought: The Colonial State and Soil Conservation in East Africa during the 1930s.' *African Affairs* 83, no. 332 (1984), 321–43.

'Vigilantes, Violence and the Politics of Public Order in Kenya.' *African Affairs* 101, no. 4 (2002), 531–55.

Histories of the Hanged: The Dirty War in Kenya and the End of Empire. New York: Norton, 2005.

'"Yours in the Struggle for Majimbo": Nationalism and the Party Politics of Decolonization in Kenya, 1955–64.' *Journal of Contemporary History* 40, no. 3 (2005), 547–64.

'The Anti-Homosexuality Bill, 2009.' *Uganda Gazette* CII, no. 47 (25 September, 2009).

Appiah, Kwame Anthony. *Cosmopolitanism: Ethics in a World of Strangers.* New York: W.W. Norton, 2007.

Apter, David. *The Political Kingdom in Uganda: A Study in Bureaucratic Nationalism.* Princeton: Princeton University Press, 1961.

Asad, Talal. *Formations of the Secular: Christianity, Islam, Modernity.* Stanford: Stanford University Press, 2003.

Askew, Kelly. *Performing the Nation: Swahili Music and Cultural Politics in Tanzania.* Chicago: University of Chicago Press, 2002.

Austen, Ralph. *Northwest Tanzania under German and British Rule: Colonial Policy and Tribal Politics, 1889–1939.* New Haven: Yale University Press, 1968.

Ayany, Samuel. *Kar Charuok Mar Luo.* Nairobi: East African Literature Bureau, 1952.

Barber, Karin, ed. *Africa's Hidden Histories: Everyday Literacy and Making the Self.* Bloomington, IN: Indiana University Press, 2006.

The Anthropology of Texts, Persons, and Publics: Oral and Written Culture in Africa and Beyond. Cambridge, 2007.

Barongo, Edward. *Mkiki Mkiki wa Siasa Tanganyika.* Nairobi: East African Literature Bureau, 1966.

Barra, G. *1000 Kikuyu Proverbs.* Nairobi: Kenya Literature Bureau, 1994 [1939].

Basikania, Swaleh Tibawenda. 'Chronological Appraisal on the Bakonzo/Bamba Traditional Leadership.' Kampala: Office of the Crown Prince, 25 May 2005.

Bayart, Jean-François. *The State in Africa: The Politics of the Belly.* London: Longman, 1993.

Beck, Ulrich. *The Cosmopolitan Vision.* Cambridge: Polity Press, 2006.

Beecher, Leonard and Gladys. 'A Kikuyu-English Dictionary.' Nairobi: CMS Bookshop, 1938.

Bender, Thomas. *The Anti-Slavery Debate: Capitalism and Abolitionism as a Problem in Historical Interpretation.* Berkeley: University of California Press, 1992.

Benhabib, Seyla. *Another Cosmopolitanism.* Oxford: Oxford University Press, 2006.

Bennett, George. *Kenya, A Political History: The Colonial Period.* London: Oxford University Press, 1963.

Benson, T. G. *Kikuyu-English Dictionary.* Oxford: Clarendon Press, 1964.

Bernstein, Henry. 'Notes on State and the Peasantry: The Tanzanian Case.' *Review of African Political Economy* 8, no. 21 (1981), 44–62.

Bessell, M. J. 'Nyabingi.' *Uganda Journal* 2, no. 2 (1938), 73–86.

Bilindabagabo, Alexis with Alan Nichols. *Rescued by Angels: The Story of Miracles during the Rwandan Genocide.* Brunswick East, Australia: Acorn, 2001.

Bjorklund, Diane. *Interpreting the Self: Two Hundred Years of American Autobiography.* Chicago: University of Chicago Press, 1998.

Blount, Ben G. 'Aspects of Luo Socialization.' *Language in Society* 1, no. 2 (October 1972), 235–48.

Boesen, Jannik, Birgit Madsen, and Tony Moody. *Ujamaa: Socialism from Above.* Uppsala: Scandinavian Institute of Development Studies, 1977.

Branch, Daniel. *Defeating Mau Mau, Creating Kenya: Counterinsurgency, Civil War, and Decolonization.* Cambridge: Cambridge University Press, 2009.

Branch, Daniel, Nic Cheeseman, and Leigh Gardner, eds. *Our Turn to Eat: Politics in Kenya Since 1950.* Berlin: LitVerlag, 2010.

Brazier, F. S. 'The Nyabingi Cult: Religion and Political Scale in Kigezi, 1900–1930.' Kampala: East African Institute for Social Research, 1968.

Breckenridge, James. *Forty Years in Kenya.* Great Britain: Creeds, n.d.

Breckenridge, Keith. 'Verwoerd's Bureau of Proof: Total Information in the Making of Apartheid.' *History Workshop Journal* 59, no. 1 (2005), 83–108.

Brennan, James. 'Realizing Civilization through Patrilineal Descent: The Intellectual Making of an African Racial Nationalism in Tanzania, 1920–50.' *Social Identities* 12, no. 4 (2006), 405–23.

'Blood Enemies: Exploitation and Urban Citizenship in the Nationalist Political Thought of Tanzania, 1958–75.' *Journal of African History* 47, no. 4 (2006), 389–413.

'Fighting for the Sultan's Flag: Sovereignty and Decolonization in Coastal Kenya, 1945–1964.' *Comparative Studies in Society and History* 50, no. 4 (2008), 831–61.

Brennan, James, Andrew Burton, and Yusuf Lawi, eds. *Dar es Salaam: Histories from an Emerging Metropolis.* Dar es Salaam: Mkuki na Nyota, 2007.

Brounéus, Karen. 'The Trauma of Truth Telling: Effects of Witnessing in the Rwandan Gacaca Courts on Psychological Health.' *Journal of Conflict Resolution* 54, no. 3 (2010), 408–37.

Brownlie, Ian. *African Boundaries: A Legal and Diplomatic Dictionary.* London: Hurst and Co., 1979.

Bunyan, John. *The Pilgrim's Progress from This World to That Which is to Come.* Uhrichsville, Ohio: Barbour and Co., n.d. [1678].

Butler, Bill. *Hill Ablaze.* London: Hodder and Stoughton, 1976.

Calamy, Edmund, ed. *Abridgement of Mr. Baxter's History of His Life and Times.* London: John Lawrence, 1713 [1702].

Canandine, David. *Ornamentalism: How the British Saw Their Empire.* New York: Oxford University Press, 2002.

Carotenuto, Matthew. 'Cultivating an African Community: The Luo Union in 20th Century East Africa.' Ph.D. dissertation, Indiana University, 2006.

'*Riwruok E Teko*: Cultivating Identity in Colonial and Postcolonial Kenya.' *African Affairs* 53, no. 2 (2006), 53–73.

Carotenuto, Matthew and Katherine Luongo. 'Navigating the Kenya National Archives: Research and its Role in Kenyan Society.' *History in Africa* 32 (2005), 445–55.

Carswell, Grace. *Cultivating Success in Uganda: Kigezi Farmers and Colonial Policies*. Oxford: James Currey, 2007.

Chanock, Martin. *Law, Custom, and Social Order: The Colonial Experience in Malawi and Zambia*. Portsmouth, N.H.: Heinemann, 1998.

Chatterjee, Partha. *The Nation and its Fragments: Colonial and Postcolonial Histories*. Princeton: Princeton University Press, 1993.

Chidester, David. *Savage Systems: Colonialism and Comparative Religion in Southern Africa*. Charlottesville: University Press of Virginia, 1996.

Chrétien, Jean-Pierre. *The Great Lakes of Africa: Two Thousand Years of History*. New York: Zone Books, 2003.

Church, Joe. *Awake, Uganda! The Story of Blasio Kigozi and His Vision of Revival*. Kampala: Uganda Bookshop, 1957 [1936].

Forgive Them: The Story of an African Martyr. London: Hodder and Stoughton, 1966.

William Nagenda: A Great Lover of Jesus. London: Ruanda Mission, 1974.

Quest for the Highest: An Autobiographical Account of the East African Revival. Exeter: Paternoster, 1981.

Churchill, Winston. *My African Journey*. London: Hodder and Stoughton, 1908.

Clark, Phil. *Justice Without Lawyers: Peace, Justice and Reconciliation in Rwanda*. Cambridge: Cambridge University Press, 2010.

Clark, Phil and Zachary Kaufman, eds. *After Genocide: Transitional Justice, Post-Conflict Reconstruction and Reconciliation in Rwanda and Beyond*. New York: Columbia University Press, 2009.

Clough, Marshall. *Mau Mau Memoirs: History, Memory, and Politics*. Boulder, CO: Lynne Rienner, 1998.

Cohen, David William and E. S. Atieno Odhiambo. *Siaya: The Historical Anthropology of an African Landscape*. London: James Currey, 1989.

Burying S.M.: The Politics of Knowledge and the Sociology of Power in Africa. Portsmouth: Heinemann, 1992.

Cole, Henry. 'Notes on the Wagogo of German East Africa.' *Journal of the Anthropological Institute of Great Britain and Ireland* 32 (July–December 1902), 305–38.

Coleman, James S. 'Nationalism in Tropical Africa.' *American Political Science Review* 48, no. 2 (1954), 404–26.

Comaroff, John and Jean Comaroff. *Of Revelation and Revolution, vol. I: Christianity, Colonialism, and Consciousness in South Africa*. Chicago: University of Chicago Press, 1991.

Of Revelation and Revolution, vol. II: The Dialectics of Modernity on a South African Frontier. Chicago: University of Chicago Press, 1997.

Cook, Albert. *A Medical Dictionary and Phrase Book in Luganda*. Kampala: Uganda Book Shop, 1921.

Cory, Hans and M. M. Hartnoll. *Customary Law of the Haya Tribe, Tanganyika Territory*. London: International African Institute, 1945.

Creary, Nicholas. *Domesticating a Religious Import: The Jesuits and the Inculturation of the Catholic Church in Zimbabwe, 1879–1980*. New York: Fordham University Press, 2011.

Dann, Frances. 'The Work of an Australian CMS Missionary in the Late Colonial Period in Tanganyika, 1929–1945.' B. Theo. thesis, Yarra Theological Union, 2002.

Davidson, Basil. *The Black Man's Burden: Africa and the Curse of the Nation-State*. New York: Three Rivers Press, 1993.

Davis, David Brion. *The Problem of Slavery in Western Culture*. Ithaca: Cornell University Press, 1966.

Denoon, Donald, ed. *A History of Kigezi in South-West Uganda*. Kampala: The National Trust, 1972.

des Forges, Alison. *Defeat is the Only Bad News: Rwanda Under Musinga, 1896–1931*, edited by David Newbury. Madison: University of Wisconsin Press, 2011.

Dinwiddy, Hugh. 'The Search for Unity in Uganda: Early Days to 1966.' *African Affairs* 80, no. 321 (1981), 501–18.

Dobson, Andrew. 'Thick Cosmopolitanism.' *Political Studies* 54, no. 1 (2006), 165–84.

Doornbos, Martin. *The Ankole Kingship Controversy: Regalia Galore Revisited*. Kampala: Fountain Publishers, 2001.

Doyle, Shane. *Crisis and Decline in Bunyoro: Population and Environment in Western Uganda, 1860–1955*. Oxford: James Currey, 2006.

'"The Child of Death": Personal Names and Parental Attitudes Towards Mortality in Bunyoro, Western Uganda.' *Journal of African History* 49, no. 3 (2008), 361–82.

'Immigrants and Indigenes: The Lost Counties Dispute and the Evolution of Ethnic Identity in Colonial Buganda.' *Journal of Eastern African Studies* 3, no. 2 (2009), 284–302.

Before HIV: Sexuality, Fertility and Mortality in East Africa, 1900–1980. London: Oxford University Press, forthcoming.

Eakin, John Paul. *How Our Lives Become Stories: Making Selves*. Ithaca: Cornell University Press, 1999.

Eckert, Andreas. 'Useful Instruments of Participation? Local Government and Co-operative Societies in Tanzania, 1940s to 1970s.' *International Journal of African Historical Studies* 40, no. 1 (2007), 97–118.

Edel, May. *The Chiga of Uganda*. New Brunswick: Transaction Publishers, 1996 [1957].

Elkins, Caroline. 'Detention, Rehabilitation, and the Destruction of Kikuyu Society.' In *Mau Mau and Nationhood: Arms, Authority, and Narration*, edited by John Lonsdale and Atieno Odhiambo, 191–226. London: James Currey, 2003.

Imperial Reckoning: The Untold Story of Britain's Gulag in Kenya. New York: Henry Holt, 2005.

Ellerbek, Finn Allan. *Karagwe Diocese: A Lutheran Church History, As Seen and Studied by a Missionary*. Copenhagen: Academic Press, 1992.

Ellis, Stephen and Gerrie ter Haar. *Worlds of Power: Religious Thought and Political Practice in Africa*. London: Hurst and Co., 2004.

English, Patrick. 'Archives of Uganda.' *American Archivist* 18, no. 3 (July 1955), 224–30.

Englund, Harri. *Prisoners of Freedom: Human Rights and the African Poor.* Berkeley: University of California Press, 2006.

Epprecht, Marc. *Heterosexual Africa? The History of an Idea from the Age of Exploration to the Age of AIDS.* Athens, OH: Ohio University Press, 2008.

Fallers, Lloyd. *The King's Men: Leadership and Status on the Eve of Independence.* London: Oxford University Press, 1964.

Feierman, Steven. *Peasant Intellectuals: Anthropology and History in Tanzania.* Madison: University of Wisconsin Press, 1990.

'Colonizers, Scholars, and the Creation of Invisible Histories.' In *Beyond the Cultural Turn: New Directions in the Study of Society and Culture*, edited by Victoria Bonnell and Lynn Hunt, 182–216. Berkeley: University of California Press, 1999.

Fields, Karen. *Revival and Rebellion in Colonial Central Africa.* Princeton: Princeton University Press, 1985.

Fisher, Humphrey. 'Conversion Reconsidered.' *Africa: Journal of the International African Institute* 43, no. 1 (1973), 27–40.

Frazer, J. G. *The Golden Bough.* London: MacMillan, 1890.

'Questions on the Manners, Customs, Religion, Superstitions &c. of Uncivilized or Semi-Civilized Peoples.' *Journal of the Royal Anthropological Institute* 18 (1889), 431–40.

Freedman, Jim. 'Ritual and History: The Case of Nyabingi.' *Cahiers d'Etudes Africaines* 14, no. 53 (1974), 170–80.

'Three Muraris, Three Gahayas and the Four Phases of Nyabingi.' In *Chronology, Migration, and Drought in Interlacustrine Africa*, edited by J. B. Webster, 175–87. Thetford: Longman, 1979.

Nyabingi: The Social History of an African Divinity. Tervuren: Annales du Musee Royal de l'Afrique Centrale, 1984.

Furedi, Frank. *The Mau Mau War in Perspective.* Nairobi: Heinemann, 1989.

Gathigira, Stanley. *Mĩikarĩre ya Agĩkũyũ.* Nairobi: Scholars Publications, 1986 [1933].

Gatu, John. *Joyfully Christian, Truly African.* Nairobi: Acton Publishers, 2006.

Geiger, Susan. *TANU Women: Gender and Culture in the Making of Tanganyikan Nationalism.* Portsmouth: Heinemann, 1997.

Geissler, Paul Wenzel and Ruth Jane Prince. *The Land is Dying: Contingency, Creativity and Conflict in Western Kenya.* Oxford: Berghahn Books, 2010.

Geschiere, Peter. *The Perils of Belonging: Autochthony, Citizenship, and Exclusion in Africa and Europe.* Chicago: University of Chicago Press, 2009.

Giblin, James. *A History of the Excluded: Making Family a Refuge from State in Twentieth Century Tanzania.* Oxford: James Currey, 2005.

Gifford, Paul. *Ghana's New Christianity: Pentecostalism in a Globalizing African Economy.* Bloomington: Indiana University Press, 2005.

Christianity, Politics, and Public Life in Kenya. London: Hurst, 2009.

Gikoyo, Gucu wa. *We Fought for Freedom.* Nairobi: East African Publishing House, 1979.

Gilroy, Paul. *Postcolonial Melancholia.* New York: Columbia University Press, 2006.

Godfrey, Nick. 'Understanding Genocide: The Experience of Anglicans in Rwanda.' Ph.D. dissertation, University of Cambridge, 2008.

'Anglican Revivalists and the Rwandan Genocide: Survivors' Narratives of Divine Intervention.' In *The East African Revival: History and Legacies*, edited by Kevin Ward and Emma Wild-Wood, 249–67. Kampala: Fountain Publishers, 2010.

Goodwin, James. *Autobiography: The Self Made Text.* New York: Twayne Publishers, 1993.

Grant, James A. *A Walk Across Africa, or, Domestic Scenes from my Nile Journal.* Edinburgh: Blackwood, 1864.

Green, Ian. *Print and Protestantism in Early Modern England.* New York: Oxford University Press, 2000.

Grillo, Ralph D. *African Railwaymen: Solidarity and Opposition in an East African Labour Force.* Cambridge: Cambridge University Press, 1973.

Guillebaud, Meg. *Rwanda: The Land God Forgot? Revival, Genocide and Hope.* London: Mill Hill Books, 2002.

Gusman, Alessandro. 'HIV/AIDS, Pentecostal Churches, and the "Joseph Generation" in Uganda.' *Africa Today* 56, no. 1 (2009), 67–86.

Hall, R. de Z. 'A Study of Native Court Records as a Method of Ethnological Enquiry.' *Africa: Journal of the International African Institute* 11, no. 4 (1938), 412–27.

Hanson, Holly. *Landed Obligation: The Practice of Power in Buganda.* Portsmouth, NH: Heinemann, 2003.

Harneit-Sievers, Axel, ed. *A Place in the World: New Local Historiographies from Africa and South Asia.* Leiden: Brill Publishers, 2002.

Harries, Patrick. *Butterflies and Barbarians: Swiss Missionaries and Systems of Knowledge in South-East Africa.* Oxford: James Currey, 2007.

Harris, Tim. *Donkey's Gratitude: Twenty Two Years in the Growth of a New African Nation—Tanzania.* Edinburgh: Pentland Press, 1992.

Haskell, Thomas. 'Capitalism and the Origins of Humanitarian Sensibility.' *American Historical Review* 90, no. 2 (1985), 547–66.

Hastings, Adrian. *The Church in Africa, 1450–1950.* Oxford: Oxford University Press, 1994.

Hatzfield, Jean. *Into the Quick of Life: The Rwandan Genocide: The Survivors Speak.* London: Serpent's Tail, 2005 [2000].

Machete Season: The Killers in Rwanda Speak. New York: Picador, 2005.

Hawkins, Sean. *Writing and Colonialism in Northern Ghana: The Encounter between the LoDagaa and 'the World on Paper.'* Toronto: University of Toronto Press, 2002.

Hindmarsh, D. Bruce. *The Evangelical Conversion Narrative: Spiritual Autobiography in Early Modern England.* Oxford: Oxford University Press, 2005.

Hobley, C. *Eastern Uganda: An Ethnological Survey.* London: Anthropological Institute of Great Britain and Ireland, 1902.

Hobsbawn, Eric and Terence Ranger, eds. *The Invention of Tradition.* Cambridge: Cambridge University Press, 1983.

Hodgson, Dorothy L. *The Church of Women: Gendered Encounters Between Maasai and Missionaries.* Bloomington: Indiana University Press, 2005.

Being Maasai, Becoming Indigenous: Postcolonial Politics in a Neoliberal World. Bloomington, IN: Indiana University Press, 2011.

Hofmeyr, Isabel. *The Portable Bunyan: A Transnational History of* The Pilgrim's Progress. Princeton: Princeton University Press, 2004.

Hollis, Patricia. 'Anti-Slavery and British Working Class Radicalism in the Years of Reform.' In *Anti-slavery, Religion, and Reform: Essays in Memory of Roger Anstey*, edited by Christine Bolt and Seymour Drescher, 294–315. Folkestone: Wm. Dawson, 1980.

Hopkins, Elizabeth. 'The Nyabingi Cult of Southwestern Uganda.' In *Protest and Power in Black Africa*, edited by Robert Rotberg and Ali A. Mazrui, 258–336. New York: Oxford University Press, 1970.

Horton, Robin. 'African Conversion.' *Africa: Journal of the International African Institute* 41, no. 2 (1971), 85–108.

'On the Rationality of Conversion, Part I.' *Africa: Journal of the International African Institute* 45, no. 3 (1975), 219–35.

Huemer, A. A. *The Invention of 'Race': the Columbian Turn in Modern Consciousness.* Lander, WY: Agathon, 1998.

Hyam, Ronald. *The Labour Government and the End of Empire, Part I.* London: Institute of Commonwealth Studies, 1992.

Hyden, Goran. *Political Development in Rural Tanzania: A West Lake Study.* Nairobi: East Africa Publishing House, 1969.

Beyond Ujamaa in Tanzania: Underdevelopment and the Uncaptured Peasantry. Berkeley: University of California Press, 1980.

Ibingira, Grace. *The Forging of an African Nation: The Political and Constitutional Evolution of Uganda from Colonial Rule to Independence, 1894–1962.* New York: Viking Press, 1972.

Idowu, E. Bolaji. *Olodumare: God in Yoruba Belief.* London: Longmans, 1962.

African Traditional Religion: A Definition. London: SCM Press, 1973.

Ilibagiza, Immaculée with Steve Erwin. *Left to Tell: Discovering God Amidst the Rwandan Holocaust.* Carlsbad, CA: Hay House, 2006.

Iliffe, John. *A Modern History of Tanganyika.* Cambridge: Cambridge University Press, 1979.

Honour in African History. Cambridge: Cambridge University Press, 2005.

Africans: A History of a Continent. Cambridge: Cambridge University Press, 2007.

Ingham, Kenneth. *The Making of Modern Uganda.* London: Allen and Unwin, 1958.

The Kingdom of Toro in Uganda. London: Methuen, 1975.

Isichei, Elizabeth. *A History of Christianity in Africa: From Antiquity to the Present.* Grand Rapids, MI: Eerdmans, 1995.

Itote, Waruhiu. *'Mau Mau' General.* Nairobi: East African Publishing House, 1967.

Ivaska, Andrew. *Cultured States: Youth, Gender, and Modern Style in 1960s Dar es Salaam.* Durham, NC: Duke University Press, 2011.

Jackson, William. 'Poor Men and Loose Women: Colonial Kenya's Other Whites.' Ph.D. dissertation, University of Leeds, 2010.

James, William. *Varieties of Religious Experience.* New York: Barnes and Noble, 2004 [1902].

Jeater, Diana. *Marriage, Perversion, and Power: The Construction of Moral Discourse in Southern Rhodesia, 1894–1930.* Oxford: Clarendon Press, 1993.

Jennings, Michael. '"A Very Real War": Popular Participation in Development in Tanzania During the 1950s and 1960s.' *International Journal of African Historical Studies* 40, no. 1 (2007), 71–95.

Joshi, Sanjay. *Fractured Modernity: The Making of a Middle Class in Colonial North India*. New Delhi: Oxford University Press, 2001.

Kabiro, Ngugi. *Man in the Middle*. Richmond, British Columbia: LSM Information Center, 1973.

Kaborooga, Mariire Edward. 'The Impact of the Bakiga Immigration on the Religion of the Banyabutumbi of North Kigezi Diocese.' Dip. Theo. thesis, Makerere University, 1994.

Kafureeka, George. 'The Impact of the Revival Movement on the Church in East Ankole Diocese, with Particular Reference to Rushere Archdeaconry, Mbarara District, Uganda, 1965–75.' Dip. Theo. thesis, Uganda Christian University, 1999.

Kaggia, Bildad. *Roots of Freedom, 1921–1963: The Autobiography of Bildad Kaggia*. Nairobi: East African Publishing House, 1975.

Kagwa, Apolo. *Ekitabo kye Basekabaka be Buganda*. Kampala: Uganda Bookshop, 1901.

Kalu, Ogbu. *African Christianity: An African Story*. Pretoria: University of Pretoria, 2005.

Kamugungunu, Joshua. *Abagabe b'Ankole*. Kampala: Wava Books, 2005.

Kanogo, Tabitha. *Squatters and the Roots of Mau Mau, 1905–63*. Nairobi: East African Educational Publishers, 1987.

Dedan Kimathi: A Biography. Nairobi: East Africa Educational Publishers, 1992.

Karanja, John. *Founding an African Faith: Kikuyu Anglican Christianity, 1900–1945*. Nairobi: Uzima Press, 1999.

Kareri, Charles Muhoro. *The Autobiography of Charles Muhoro*, edited by Derek R. Peterson, translated by Joseph Kariuki Muriithi. Madison, WI: University of Wisconsin African Studies Center, 2000.

Kariuki, J. M. *'Mau Mau' Detainee: The Account by a Kenya African of His Experiences in Detention Camps, 1953–1960*. Nairobi: Oxford University Press, 1963.

Kariuki, Obadiah. *A Bishop Facing Mount Kenya: An Autobiography, 1902–1978*. Nairobi: Uzima Press, 1985.

Karlström, Mikael. 'On the Aesthetics and Dialogics of Power in the Postcolony.' *Africa* 73, no. 1 (2003), 57–76.

'Modern and Its Aspirants: Moral Community and Developmental Eutopianism in Buganda.' *Current Anthropology* 45, no. 5 (December 2004), 595–619.

Karwemera, A. 'Christianity comes to Nyakishenyi (1925–1935).' In *Occasional Research Papers*, vol. 31, edited by Tom Tuma. Kampala: Department of Religious Studies and Philosophy, Makerere University, 1975.

Kasore, K. Editorial letter. In *Uganda Argus* (6 September 1962).

Katarikawe, James and John Wilson. 'The East African Revival Movement.' Masters of Theology and Missiology thesis, Fuller Theological Seminary, 1975.

Katoke, Israel. *The Making of the Karagwe Kingdom*. Dar es Salaam: East African Publishing House, 1970.

Kenya Colony and Protectorate, *Kenya African Agricultural Sample Census, 1960–61*. Nairobi: Government Printer, 1961.

Kenyatta, Jomo. *Harambee! The Prime Minister of Kenya's Speeches, 1963–64.* Oxford: Oxford University Press, 1964.

Kershaw, Greet. *Mau Mau from Below.* Oxford: James Currey, 1997.

Kibira, Josiah M. *Church, Clan and the World.* Uppsala: Almqvist and Wisell, 1974.

Kihumuro-Apuli, David. *A Thousand Years of Bunyoro-Kitara Kingdom: The People and the Rulers.* Kampala: Fountain Publishers, 1994.

Kingdom of Buganda, *The Native Laws of Buganda.* Kampala: Uganda Argus, 1947.

Kirindi, G. N. P. *History and Culture of the Kingdom of Ankole.* Kampala: Fountain Publishers, 2008.

Kitching, Gavin. *Class and Economic Change in Kenya.* New Haven: Yale University Press, 1980.

Kivengere, Festo, with Dorothy Smoker. *Revolutionary Love.* Fort Washington, PA: Christian Literature Crusade, 1983.

Kodesh, Neil. 'Renovating Tradition: The Discourse of Succession in Colonial Buganda.' *International Journal of African Historical Studies* **34**, no. 3 (2001), 511–41.

    'Networks of Knowledge: Clanship and Collective Well-being in Buganda,' *Journal of African History* **49** (2008), 197–216.

    Beyond the Royal Gaze: Clanship and Public Healing in Buganda. Charlottesville and London: University of Virginia Press, 2010.

Kyle, Keith. *The Politics of Independence in Kenya.* New York: Palgrave MacMillan, 1999.

Kyomuhendo Grace Bantebya and Marjorie Kenitson McIntosh. *Women, Work and Domestic Virtue in Uganda, 1900–2003.* Kampala: Fountain Publishers, 2006.

Kyomukama, James. 'The Impact of the Balokole Movement on the Anglican Church in North Kigezi Diocese, with Particular Reference to Rubirizi Archdeaconry, Rukungiri District.' Dip. Theo. thesis, Bishop Tucker Theological College, 1995.

Landau, Paul. '"Religion" and Christian Conversion in African History: A New Model.' *The Journal of Religious History* **23**, no. 1 (February 2), 8–30.

    Popular Politics in the History of South Africa, 1400–1948. Cambridge: Cambridge University Press, 2010.

Larson, Catherine Claire. *As We Forgive: Stories of Reconciliation from Rwanda.* Grand Rapids, MI: Zondervan, 2009.

Larsson, Birgitta. *Conversion to Greater Freedom? Women, Church and Social Change in North-Western Tanzania under Colonial Rule.* Stockholm: Almquist and Wiksell, 1991.

Leakey, Louis. *Defeating Mau Mau.* London: Methuen, 1954.

    The Southern Kikuyu before 1903. London: Academic Press, 1977.

Lejeune, Philippe. 'The Autobiographical Pact.' In *On Autobiography*, by Philippe Lejeune, 3–30. Minneapolis: University of Minnesota Press, 1989.

Leo, Christopher. *Land and Class in Kenya.* Toronto: University of Toronto Press, 1984.

Levine, Philippa. *Prostitution, Race and Politics: Policing Venereal Disease in the British Empire.* New York: Routledge, 2003.

Lewis, Joanna. *Empire State-Building: War and Welfare in Kenya, 1925–52.* Oxford: James Currey, 2000.

Lichtheim, Mariam. *Ancient Egyptian Autobiographies Chiefly of the Middle Kingdom: A Study and an Anthology.* Göttingen: Vandenhoeck & Ruprecht, 1988.

Lihamba, Amandina, Fulata L. Moyo, M. M. Mulokozi, Naomi L. Shitemi, and Saida Yahya-Othman, eds. *Women Writing Africa: The Eastern Region.* New York: The Feminist Press, 2007.

Likimani, Muthoni. *They Shall be Chastised.* Nairobi: Kenya Literature Bureau, 1974.

Fighting Without Ceasing. Nairobi: Noni's Publicity, 2005.

Lohrmann, Ulrich. *Voices from Tanganyika: Great Britain, the United Nations, and the Decolonization of a Trust Territory, 1946–1961.* Berlin: Lit Verlag, 2007.

Lonsdale, John. 'The Prayers of Waiyaki: Political Uses of the Kikuyu Past.' In *Revealing Prophets: Prophecy in Eastern African History,* edited by David M. Anderson and Douglas H. Johnson, 240–91. London: James Currey, 1995.

'KAU's Cultures: Imaginations of Community and Constructions of Leadership in Kenya after the Second World War.' *Journal of African Cultural Studies* 13, no. 1 (2000), 107–24.

'Contests of Time: Kikuyu Historiography, Old and New.' In *A Place in the World: New Local Historiographies from Africa and South Asia,* edited by Axel Harneit-Sievers, 201–54. Leiden: Brill Publishers, 2002.

'Moral and Political Argument in Kenya.' In *Ethnicity and Democracy in Africa,* edited by Bruce Berman, Dickson Eyoh, and Will Kymlicka, 73–95. Oxford: James Currey, 2004.

'Ornamental Constitutionalism in Africa: Kenyatta and the Two Queens.' *Journal of Imperial and Commonwealth History* 34, no. 1 (2006), 87–103.

'Writing Competitive Patriotisms in Eastern Africa,' In *Recasting the Past: History Writing and Political Work in Modern Africa,* edited by Derek R. Peterson and Giacomo Macola, 251–67. Athens, OH: Ohio University Press, 2009.

'Kenya: Home Country and African Frontier.' In *Settlers and Expatriates: Britons over the Seas,* edited by Robert Bickers, 74–111. Oxford: Oxford University Press, 2010.

Lonsdale, John and Bruce Berman. *Unhappy Valley: Conflict in Kenya and Africa.* London: James Currey, 1992.

Lonsdale, John and Caroline Elkins. 'Memories of Mau Mau in Kenya.' Unpublished conference paper, n.d.

Lott, Tommy. *The Invention of Race: Black Culture and the Politics of Representation.* Malden, MA: Wiley-Blackwell, 1999.

Low, David A. *The Mind of Buganda.* London: Heinemann, 1971.

Buganda in Modern History. London: Weidenfeld and Nicolson, 1971.

Lumley, E. K. *Forgotten Mandate: a British District Officer in Tanganyika.* London: Archon Books, 1976.

Lynch, Gabrielle. *I Say to You: Ethnic Politics and the Kalenjin of Kenya.* Chicago: University of Chicago Press, 2011.

Maack, Pamela. '"We Don't Want Terraces!" Protest and Identity Under the Uluguru Land Usage Scheme.' In *Custodians of the Land: Ecology and Culture in the*

History of Tanzania, edited by Gregory Maddox, James Giblin, and Isaria Kimambo, 152–69. London: James Currey, 1996.

Maari, E. 'The Balokole Movement in Nyabushozi County of Ankole.' In *Occasional Research Papers in African Religions and Philosophies*, vol. 22, edited by A. Byaruhanga-Akiiki. Kampala: Makerere University, 1974.

Maathai, Wangari, *Unbowed: A Memoir*. London: Heinemann, 2007.

MacArthur, Julie. 'Mapping Political Community among the Luyia of Western Kenya, 1930–63.' PhD dissertation, University of Cambridge, 2010.

MacGuire, G. *Toward 'Uhuru' in Tanzania: The Politics of Participation*. Cambridge: Cambridge University Press, 1969.

Maddox, Gregory H. and James L. Giblin, eds. *In Search of a Nation: Histories of Authority and Dissidence in Tanzania*. Oxford: James Currey, 2006.

Mafune. 'The Concept of Illness and Death in the Kiga Traditional Society.' In *Occasional Research Papers*, vol. 12, edited by A. Byaruhanga Akiiki. Kampala: Dept. of Religious Studies and Philosophy, Makerere University, 1973.

Magambo, N. 'The Balokole Movement in Mitooma Parish.' Dip. Theo. thesis, Makerere University, 1974.

Magezi, M. W., T. E. Nyakango, and M. K. Aganatia. *The People of the Rwenzoris: The Bayira (Bakonzo/Bananade) and Their Culture*. Köln: Rüdiger Köppe Verlag, 2004.

Mair, Lucy. *An African People in the Twentieth Century*. London: George Routledge, 1934.

Malo, Shadrack. *Dhoudi mar Central Nyanza*. Nairobi: Eagle Press, 1953.

Maloba, Wunyabari. 'Christianity in Colonial Kenya.' *Journal of African History* 45, no. 2 (July 2004), 343–44.

Mamdani, Mahmood. *Citizen and Subject: Contemporary Africa and the Legacy of Late Colonialism*. Princeton: Princeton University Press, 1996.

When Victims Become Killers: Colonialism, Nativism, and the Genocide in Rwanda. Princeton: Princeton University Press, 2001.

Marshall, Ruth. *Political Spiritualities: The Pentecostal Revolution in Nigeria*. Chicago: University of Chicago Press, 2009.

Mascuch, Michael. *Origins of the Individualist Self: Autobiography and Self-Identity in England, 1591–1791*. Cambridge: Polity Press, 1997.

Masuzawa, Tomoko. *The Invention of World Religions*. Chicago: University of Chicago Press, 2005.

Mathu, Mohammed. *The Urban Guerilla: The Story of Mohammed Mathu*. Richmond, British Columbia: Liberation Support Movement, 1974.

Matiba, Kenneth. *Aiming High: The Story of my Life*. Nairobi: People Ltd., 2000.

Mazower, Mark. *No Enchanted Palace: The End of Empire and the Ideological Origins of the United Nations*. Princeton: Princeton University Press, 2009.

Mbembe, Achille. *On the Postcolony*. Berkeley: University of California Press, 2001.

'The Power of the Archive and its Limits.' In *Refiguring the Archive*, edited by Carolyn Hamilton, Verne Harris, Jane Taylor, Michele Pickover, Graeme Reid, and Razia Saleh, 19–26. Cape Town: David Philip, 2002.

Mbiti, John. *African Religions and Philosophy*. New York: Praeger, 1969.

Introduction to African Religion. Portsmouth, NH: Heinemann, 1975.

Mboya, Paul. *Luo Kitgi gi Timbegi*. Kisumu: Anyange Press, 1983 [1938].

Richo ema Kelo Chira. Nairobi: Equatorial Publishers, 1978.

Mboya, Tom. *Freedom and After*. Nairobi: Heinemann, 1986 [1963].

McMaster, D. N. 'Change of Regional Balance in the Bukoba District of Tanganyika.' *Geographical Review* 50, no. 1 (1960), 73–88.

Meyer, Birgit. *Translating the Devil: Religion and Modernity among the Ewe in Ghana*. Trenton, NJ: Africa World Press, 1999.

Meyerstein, Ariel. 'Between Law and Culture: Rwanda's *Gacaca* and Postcolonial Legality.' *Law and Social Inquiry* 32, no. 2 (2007), 467–508.

Mill Hill Fathers. *Vocabulary Nilotic-English*. Nyeri: Catholic Mission Press, n.d.

Milne, G. 'Bukoba: High and Low Fertility on a Laterized Soil.' *East African Agricultural Journal* 4 (1938), 13–24.

Miti, James Kibuka. 'Buganda, 1875–1900: A Centenary Contribution.' Unpublished manuscript, n.d. [1946].

Mjama, Nathan. 'Archives and Records Management in Kenya: Problems and Prospects.' *Records Management Journal* 13, no. 2 (2003), 91–101.

Morris, H. F. 'Uganda: Report of the Commission on Marriage, Divorce and the Status of Women.' *Journal of African Law* 10, no. 1 (Spring 1966), 3–7.

Msafiri: Kitabu Hiki Kimefasirika Katika Kitabu cha Kiingreza Kiitwacho 'Pilgrim's Progress.' London: Religious Tract Society for the Universities' Mission, 1888.

Mudimbe, V. Y. *The Invention of Africa: Gnosis, Philosophy, and the Order of Knowledge*. Bloomington: Indiana University Press, 1988.

Mugambi, J. N. K. *African Heritage and Contemporary Christianity*. Nairobi: Longman, 1989.

Mugarura, B. 'The Nyabingi Cult in South Kigezi with Particular Reference to Ndorwa.' In *Occasional Research Papers in African Religions and Philosophies*, vol. 188, edited by A. Byaruhanga Akiiki. Kampala: Dept. of Religious Studies and Philosophy, Makerere University, 1974.

Muhanguzi, John. 'The Spread of the Revival Movement at Burunga in Nyabushozi County, East Ankole, Uganda.' Dip. Theo. thesis, Makerere University, 1985.

Muoria, Henry. *Writing for Kenya: The Life and Works of Henry Muoria*, edited by Wangari Muoria-Sal, Bodil Folke Frederiksen, John Lonsdale, and Derek R. Peterson. Leiden: Brill, 2009.

Muriithi, Kiboi. *War in the Forest*. Nairobi: East African Publishing House, 1971.

Mutabaha, G. *Portrait of a Nationalist: the Life of Ali Migeyo*. Nairobi: East African Publishing House, 1969.

Murphy, John D. *Luganda-English Dictionary*. Washington, D.C.: Consortium Press, 1972.

Musisi, Nakanyike. 'A Personal Journey into Custom, Identity, Power and Politics: Researching and Writing the Life and Times of Buganda's Queen Mother, Irene Drusilla Namaganda (1896–1957).' *History in Africa* 23 (1996), 369–85.

'Morality as Identity: the Missionary Moral Agenda in Buganda, 1877–1945.' *Journal of Religious History* 23, no. 1 (February 1999), 51–74.

Mutembei, Richard. *Kristo au Wamara? Historia ya Dayosisi ya Kaskazini Magharibi ya Kanisa la Kiinjili la Kilutheri Tanzania, 1890–1985*. Mwanza: North Western Publishers, 1993.

Mutesa, Edward. *The Desecration of my Kingdom*. London: Constable, 1967.

Mutibwa, Phares. *The Buganda Factor in Uganda Politics*. Kampala: Fountain Publishers, 2008.

Mutongi, Kenda. *Worries of the Heart: Widows, Family, and Community in Kenya*. Chicago: University of Chicago Press, 2007.

Ndahiro, Samuel. 'The Impact of the Abalokole Revival on the Church of Uganda with Particular Reference to the Diocese of Namirembe from 1940–1992.' BA thesis, Association of Theological Institutions in Eastern Africa, 1992.

Ndege, Peter. *Olonana Ole Mbatian*. Nairobi: East African Educational Publishers, 2003.

Nestor, Hellen Byera. *500 Haya Proverbs*. Mwanza: Northwestern Publishers, 1978.

Neubauer, Carol. 'One Voice Speaking for Many: The Mau Mau Movement and Kenyan Autobiography.' *Journal of Modern African Studies* 21, no. 1 (1983), 113–31.

Newbury, Catherine. *The Cohesion of Oppression: Clientship and Ethnicity in Rwanda, 1860–1960*. New York: Columbia University Press, 1988.

Newbury, David. 'Precolonial Burundi and Rwanda: Loyal Loyalties, Regional Loyalties.' *International Journal of African Historical Studies* 34, no. 2 (2001), 255–314.

Ngologoza, Paul. *Kigezi and its People*. Kampala: Fountain Publishers, 1998 [1967].

Njagi, David. *The Last Mau Mau Field Marshals*. Meru: Ngwataniro Self Help Group, 1993.

Njama, Karai and Donald Barnett. *Mau Mau from Within: An Analysis of Kenya's Peasant Revolt*. New York: Monthly Review Press, 1966.

Noll, Mark. *The New Shape of World Christianity: How American Experience Reflects Global Faith*. Downers Grove, IL: IVP Academic, 2007.

Noll, Mark and Carolyn Nystrom. *Clouds of Witnesses: Christian Voices from Africa and Asia*. Downer's Grove, IL: InterVarsity Press, 2011.

Nyakatura, John. *Abakama of Bunyoro-Kitara*. Kisubi: Marianum Press, 1998.

Nyerere, Julius. *Freedom and Unity*. London: Oxford University Press, 1967.

Ujamaa: Essays on Socialism. Nairobi: Oxford University Press, 1968.

The Arusha Declaration, Ten Years Later. Dar es Salaam: Government Printer, 1977.

Nyong'o, Peter Anyang'. 'State and Society in Kenya: The Disintegration of the Nationalist Coalition and the Rise of Presidential Authoritarianism, 1963–78.' *African Affairs* 88, no. 351 (1989), 229–51.

Obote, Apollo Milton. *The Common Man's Charter*. Entebbe: Government Printer, 1969.

Odaga, Asenath Bole. *Dholuo-English Dictionary*. Kisumu: Lake Publishers, 2005.

Odhiambo, E. S. Atieno. 'Luo Perspectives on Knowledge and Development: Samuel G. Ayany and Paul Mbuya.' In *African Philosophy as Cultural Inquiry*, edited by Ivan Karp and D. A. Masolo, 244–58. Bloomington: Indiana University Press, 2000.

Odinga, Oginga. *Not Yet Uhuru: An Autobiography*. Nairobi: Heinemann, 1967.

Ogot, Bethwell A. 'Mau Mau and Nationhood: The Untold Story.' In *Mau Mau and Nationhood: Arms, Authority, and Narration*, edited by E. S. Atieno Odhiambo and John Lonsdale, 8–36. Oxford: James Currey, 2003.

Ogot, Bethwell A. and W. R. Ochieng', eds. *Decolonization and Independence in Kenya, 1940–1963*. London: James Currey, 1995.

Olang', Festo. *Festo Olang': An Autobiography*. Nairobi: Uzima, 1991.

Olney, James. *Tell Me Africa: An Approach to African Literature*. Princeton: Princeton University Press, 1973.

ed. *Autobiography: Essays Theoretical and Critical*. Princeton: Princeton University Press, 1980.

Olupona, Jacob K. and Sulayman S. Nyang, eds. *Religious Plurality in Africa: Essays in Honour of John S. Mbiti*. Berlin: Mouton de Gruyter, 1993.

Omutambuze. London: Religious Tract Society, 1900.

Omutambuze. Kampala: Uganda Bookshop, 1927.

Orme, Rev. William, ed., *Practical Works of the Rev. Richard Baxter*, vols. 1 to 23. London: James Duncan, 1830.

Osborn, Herbert. *Revival: A Precious Heritage*. Eastbourne: Apologia, 1995.

Revival: God's Spotlight. Crowborough, East Sussex: Highland Books, 1996.

Pioneers in the East African Revival. Eastbourne: Apologia, 2000.

The Living Legacy of the East African Revival. Eastbourne: Apologia, 2006.

Otieno, Wambui. *Mau Mau's Daughter: A Life History*. Boulder, CO: Lynne Rienner, 1998.

Packard, Randall. *Cheifship and Cosmology: An Historical Study of Political Competition*. Bloomington: Indiana University Press, 1981.

'Cheifship and the History of Nyavingi Possession among the Bashu of Eastern Zaire.' *Africa* 52, no. 4 (1982), 67–90.

Parikh, Shanti. 'Going Public: Modern Wives, Men's Infidelity, and Marriage in East-Central Uganda.' In *The Secret: Love, Marriage, and HIV*, by Jennifer S. Hirsch, Holly Wardlow, Daniel Jordan Smith, Harriet M. Phinney, Shanti Parikh, and Constance A. Nathanson, 168–96. Nashville: Vanderbilt University Press, 2009.

Parkin, David. *The Cultural Definition of Political Response: Lineal Destiny Among the Luo*. London: Academic Press, 1978.

Parsons, Timothy. *The African Rank-and-File: Social Implications of Colonial Military Service in the King's African Rifles*. Portsmouth, NH: Heinemann, 1999.

Pasha, Emin. *Emin Pasha: His Life and Work*, vol. II. Westminster: Archibald Constable and Co., 1898.

Pateman, Carole. *The Disorder of Women: Feminism and Political Theory*. Stanford: Stanford University Press, 1989.

p'Bitek, Okot. *African Religions in Western Scholarship*. Nairobi: Kenya Literature Bureau, 1971.

Peace, Ndambuki. 'The Impact of the 1935–1937 Revival Movement on the Church of Uganda with Particular Reference to Kihanga Archdeaconry in Kigezi Diocese.' Dip. Theo. thesis, Makerere University, 1990.

Peel, J. D. Y. 'Conversion and Tradition in Two African Societies: Ijebu and Buganda.' *Past and Present* 77 (November 1977), 108–41.

'For Who Hath Despised the Day of Small Things? Missionary Narratives and Historical Anthropology.' *Comparative Studies in Society and History* 37, no. 3 (July 1995), 581–607.

Religious Encounter and the Making of the Yoruba. Bloomington, IN: Indiana University Press, 2000.

Pels, Peter. *A Politics of Presence: Contacts Between Missionaries and Waluguru in Late Colonial Tanganyika*. Amsterdam: Harwood Academic Publishers, 1999.

Pennacini, Cecilia. 'Religious Mobility and Body Language in Kubandwa Possession Cults.' *Journal of Eastern African Studies* 3, no. 2 (2009), 333–49.

Percox, David. *Britain, Kenya and the Cold War: Imperial Defence, Colonial Security and Decolonisation*. London: Tauris, 2004.

Perlman, Melvin. 'Law and the Status of Women in Uganda: A Systematic Comparison Between the Ganda and the Toro.' Amsterdam: Yearbook of the Department of Anthropology of the Royal Tropical Institute, Summer 1969.

Peterson, Derek R. *Creative Writing: Translation, Bookkeeping, and the Work of Imagination in Colonial Kenya*. Portsmouth, N.H.: Heinemann, 2004.

'"Be Like Firm Soldiers to Develop the Country": Political Imagination and the Geography of Gikuyuland.' *International Journal of African Historical Studies* 37, no. 1 (2004), 71–101.

'Language Work and Colonial Politics in Eastern Africa: the Making of Standard Swahili and "School Kikuyu".' In *The Politics of Language Study*, edited by David Hoyt and Karen Oslund, 181–210. Maryland: Rowman and Littlefield, 2006.

'Abolitionism and Political Thought in Britain and Africa.' In *Abolitionism and Imperialism in Britain, Africa and the Atlantic*, ed. Derek R. Peterson, 1–37. Athens, OH: Ohio University Press, 2010.

Peterson, Derek R. and Darren Walhof, eds. *The Invention of Religion: Rethinking Belief in Politics and History*. New Brunswick, NJ: Rutgers University Press, 2002.

Peterson, Derek R. and Giacomo Macola, eds. *Recasting the Past: History Writing and Political Work in Modern Africa*. Athens, OH: Ohio University Press, 2009.

Pew Forum on Religion and Public Life, *Tolerance and Tension: Islam and Christianity in Sub-Saharan Africa*. Washington, D.C.: Pew Research Center, 2010.

Philipps, J. E. T. 'Mufumbiro: The Birunga Volcanoes of Kigezi-Ruanda-Kivu.' *The Geographical Journal* 61, no. 4 (1923), 233–53.

Phillips, K. N. *From Mau Mau to Christ*. London: Africa Inland Mission, 1958.

Pick, Vittorio Merlo. *Ndaĩ na Gĩcaandĩ: Kikuyu Enigmas*. Bologna: E.M.I., 1973.

Pickens, George F. *African Christian God-Talk: Matthew Ajuoga's Johera Narrative*. Dallas: University Press of America, 2004.

Portal, Sir Gerald. *The British Mission to Uganda in 1893*. London: E. Arnold, 1894.

Porter, Andrew. 'Cambridge, Keswick, and Late-Nineteenth-Century Attitudes to Africa.' *Journal of Imperial and Commonwealth History* 5, no. 1 (1976), 5–34.

Prince, Ruth. 'Salvation and Tradition: Configurations of Faith in a Time of Death.' *Journal of Religion in Africa* 37, no. 1 (2007), 84–115.

Proud, Edward. *The Postal History of Tanganyika, 1915–1961*. Heathfield, East Sussex: Proud-Bailey Co. Ltd., 1989.

The Postal History of Uganda and Zanzibar. Heathfield, East Sussex: Postal History Publications Co., 1993.

Pugliese, Cristiana. *Author, Publisher and Gikuyu Nationalist: The Life and Writings of Gakaara wa Wanjau*. Bayreuth: African Studies Series, 1995.

Rathbone, Richard. *Nkrumah and the Chiefs: The Politics of Chieftaincy in Ghana, 1951–1960*. Athens, OH: Ohio University Press, 2000.

Ray, Benjamin. *African Religions: Symbol, Ritual, and Community*. Upper Saddle River, NJ: Prentice Hall, 2000.

Read, James S. 'A Milestone in the Integration of Personal Laws: The New Law of Marriage and Divorce in Tanzania.' *Journal of African Law* 16, no. 1 (1972), 19–39.

Reed, Colin. *Walking in the Light: Reflections on the East African Revival and its link to Australia*. Victoria: Acorn Press, 2007.

Reining, Priscilla. 'Haya Land Tenure: Landholding and Tenancy.' *Anthropological Quarterly* 35, no. 2 (1962), 58–73.

'Report of the Commission of Inquiry into the Recent Disturbances Amongst the Baamba and Bakonjo People of Toro.' Entebbe: Government of Uganda, 1962.

Rettig, Max. 'Gacaca: Truth, Justice, and Reconciliation in Postconflict Rwanda.' *African Studies Review* 51, no. 3 (December 2008), 25–50.

Reyntjens, Filip. 'Constructing the Truth, Dealing with Dissent, Domesticating the World: Governance in Post-Genocide Rwanda.' *African Affairs* 110, no. 438 (2011), 1–34.

Richards, Audrey, ed. *Economic Development and Tribal Change: a Study of Immigrant Labour in Buganda*. Cambridge: Heffer and Sons, 1954.

Robbins, Catherine. '*Tukutendereza*: A Study of Social Change and Sectarian Withdrawal in the *Balokole* Revival of Uganda.' PhD dissertation, Columbia University, 1975.

Robbins, Joel. 'Continuity Thinking and the Problem of Christian Culture: Belief, Time, and the Anthropology of Christianity.' *Current Anthropology* 48, no. 1 (February 2007), 5–38.

Roberts, A. D. 'The Sub-Imperialism of the Baganda,' *Journal of African History* 3, no. 3 (1962), 435–50

Robertson, Clare. *Trouble Showed the Way: Women, Men and Trade in the Nairobi Area, 1890–1990*. Bloomington: Indiana University Press, 1997.

Rodegem, F. M. *Anthologie Rundi*. Paris: A. Colin, 1973.

Rosberg, Carl G. and John Nottingham. *The Myth of Mau Mau: Nationalism in Kenya*. Stanford, CA: Stanford University Press, 1966.

Routledge, W. Scoresby and Katherine Routledge. *With a Prehistoric People*. London: Edward Arnold, 1968.

Rowe, John. 'Myth, Memoir, and Moral Admonition: Luganda Historical Writing, 1893–1969.' *Uganda Journal* 33, no. 1 (1969), 17–40, 217–19.

Rubongoya, L. T. *Naaho Nubo: The Ways of our Ancestors*. Köln: Rüdiger Köppe Verlag, 2003.

Ruddock, E. Harris. *The Homeopathic Vade Mecum of Modern Medicine and Surgery*. London: Homeopathic Publishing Co., 1879 [9th edition].

Rutabajuka, Simon. 'Migrant Labour in Masaka District, 1900–62: the Case of Coffee Shamba Labourers.' In *Uganda: Studies in Labour*, edited by Mahmood Mamdani, 11–52. Dakar: Codesria, 1996.

Rutanga, Murindwa. 'People's Anti-colonial Struggles in Kigezi Under the Nyabingi Movement, 1910–1930.' In *Uganda: Studies in Living Conditions, Population Movements, and Constitutionalism*, edited by Mahmood Mamdani and Joe Oloka-Onyango, 229–71. Vienna: Austrian Journal of Development Studies, 1994.

Politics, Religion and Power in the Great Lakes Region. Kampala: Fountain Publishers, 2011.

Rutayisire, Antoine. *Faith Under Fire: Testimonies of Christian Bravery.* Essex: African Enterprise, 1995.

Said, Edward. *Orientalism.* New York: Vintage Books, 1978.

Culture and Imperialism. New York: Vintage, 1994.

Salim, A. 'The Movement for "Mwambao" or Coast Autonomy in Kenya, 1956–63.' In *Hadith 2*, edited by Bethwell Ogot, 212–28. Nairobi: East Africa Publishing House, 1970.

Sanneh, Lamin. *Translating the Message: The Missionary Impact on Culture.* Maryknoll, NY: Orbis, 1989.

Schmidt, Elizabeth. *Peasants, Traders and Wives: Shona Women in the History of Zimbabwe, 1870–1939.* Portsmouth, N.H.: Heinemann, 1992.

Schmidt, Peter. 'Archaeological Views on a History of Landscape Change in East Africa.' *Journal of African History* 38, no. 3 (1997), 393–421.

Schneider, Leander. 'The Tanzania National Archives.' *History in Africa* 30 (2003), 447–54.

'Freedom and Unfreedom in Rural Development: Julius Nyerere, Ujamaa Vijijini, and Villagization.' *Canadian Journal of African Studies* 38, no. 2 (2004), 344–92.

'Colonial Legacies and Postcolonial Authoritarianism in Tanzania: Connects and Disconnects.' *African Studies Review* 49, no. 1 (2006), 93–118.

Schoenbrun, David. *A Green Place, a Good Place: the Social History of the Great Lakes Region, Earliest Times to the Fifteenth Century.* Portsmouth: Heinemann, 1997.

Scott, Mrs. Henry. *A Saint in Kenya: A Life of Marion Scott Stevenson.* London: Hodder and Stoughton, 1932.

Scott, James. *Seeing like a State: How Certain Schemes to Improve the Human Condition Have Failed.* New Haven: Yale University Press, 1998.

Sebarenzi, Joseph and Laura Ann Mullane. *God Sleeps in Rwanda: A Journey of Transformation.* New York: Atria, 2009.

Seitel, Peter. 'Blocking the Wind: a Haya Folktale and an Interpretation.' *Western Folklore* 26, no. 3 (1977), 189–207.

Shadle, Brett. '"Changing Traditions to Meet Current Altering Conditions": Customary Law, African Courts, and the Rejection of Codification in Kenya, 1930–60.' *Journal of African History* 40, no. 3 (1999), 422–23.

Shannon, Dr. 'The Changing Face of Kenya.' *Kikuyu News* 210 (October 1955).

Shaw, Rosalind. 'The Invention of "African Traditional Religion".' *Religion* 20 (1990), 339–53.

Shipton, Parker. 'The Kenyan Land Tenure Reform: Misunderstandings in the Public Creation of Private Property.' In *Land and Society in Contemporary Africa*, edited by R. E. Downs and S. P. Reyna, 91–135. Hanover, N.H.: University of New Hampshire Press, 1988.

The Nature of Entrustment: Intimacy, Exchange, and the Sacred in Africa. New Haven: Yale University Press, 2007.

Mortgaging the Ancestors: Ideologies of Attachment in Africa. New Haven: Yale University Press, 2009.

Shumway, Nicolas. *The Invention of Argentina.* Berkeley: University of California Press, 1991.

Skaria, Ajay. 'Writing, Orality and Power in the Dangs, Western India, 1800s-1920s.' In *Subaltern Studies IX: Writings on South Asian History and Society*, edited by Shahid Amin and Dipesh Chakrabarty, 13–58. Delhi: Oxford University Press, 1996.

Smith, Sidonie, and Julia Watson, eds. *Getting a Life: Everyday Uses of Autobiography*. Minneapolis: University of Minnesota Press, 1996.

Smoker, Dorothy. *Ambushed by Love: God's Triumph in Kenya's Terror*. Fort Washington, PA: Christian Literature Crusade, 1993.

Snowden, J. D. 'A Study of Altitudinal Zonation in South Kigezi and on Mounts Muhavura and Mgahinga, Uganda.' *The Journal of Ecology* 21, no. 1 (1933), 7–27.

Sorrenson, M. P. K. *Land Reform in the Kikuyu Country*. London: Oxford University Press, 1967.

Southall, A. W. and P. Gutkind. *Townsmen in the Making: Kampala and its Suburbs*. Kampala: East African Institute of Social Research, 1957.

Spear, Thomas. 'Neo-Traditionalism and the Limits of Invention in British Colonial Africa.' *Journal of African History* 44, no. 1 (2003), 3–27.

Spencer, John. *KAU: The Kenya African Union*. London: KPI, 1985.

Stacey, Tom. *Summons to Rwenzori*. London: Secker and Warburg, 1965.

Tribe: The Hidden History of the Mountains of the Moon. London: Stacey International, 2003.

Stanley-Smith, A. *Road to Revival: The Story of the Ruanda Mission*. London: Church Missionary Society, 1946.

Steinhart, Edward. *Conflict and Collaboration in the Kingdoms of Western Uganda*. Princeton: Princeton University Press, 1977.

Stenning, Derrick. 'Preliminary Observations on the Balokoli Movement, Particularly Among Bahima in Ankole District.' Kampala: East African Institute of Social Research, 1957.

'Persistence of Cult Elements in an East African Population.' Cambridge: British Psychological Society annual meeting, April 1959.

Stevenson, Marion. 'Widening Horizons.' *Kikuyu News* 21 (July 1910).

St. John, Patricia. *Breath of Life: The Story of the Ruanda Mission*. London: Norfolk Press, 1971.

Stoler, Ann Laura. *Along the Archival Grain: Epistemic Anxieties and Colonial Common Sense*. Princeton: Princeton University Press, 2009.

Carnal Knowledge and Imperial Power: Race and the Intimate in Colonial Rule. Berkeley: University of California Press, 2010 (2002).

Straight, Bilinda. *Miracles and Extraordinary Experience in Northern Kenya*. Philadelphia: University of Pennsylvania Press, 2007.

Stultiens, Andrea, Kaddu Wasswa John, and Arthur C. Kisitu. *The Kaddu Wasswa Archive: A Visual Biography*. Rotterdam: Post Editions, 2010.

Summers, Carol. 'Grandfathers, Grandsons, Morality, and Radical Politics in Late Colonial Buganda.' *International Journal of African Historical Studies* 38, no. 3 (2005), 427–47.

'Radical Rudeness: Ugandan Social Critiques in the 1940s.' *Journal of Social History* 39, no. 3 (2006), 741–70.

Sundkler, Bengt. *Bara Bukoba: Church and Community in Tanzania*. London: C. Hurst, 1980.

Swantz, Marja Lisa. *Beyond the Forest Line: the Life and Letters of Bengt Sundkler*. Herefordshire: Gracewing, 2002.

Swynnerton, J. 'Kenya's Agricultural Planning.' *African Affairs* 56, no. 224 (1957), 209–15.

Syahuka-Muhindo, Arthur. *The Rwenzururu Movement and Democratic Struggle*. Kampala: Centre for Basic Research, 1991.

Tamale, Sylvia. 'Law Reform and Women's Rights in Uganda.' *East African Journal of Peace and Human Rights* 1, no. 2 (1993), 164–94.

Taylor, Brian. *Tropic Toro: A Ugandan Society*. Brighton: Pennington Beach, 1998.

Taylor, John. *The Growth of the Church in Buganda: An Attempt at Understanding*. London: SCM Press, 1958.

Thomson, Joseph. *Through Masai Land*. London: Sampson Low, Marston & Co., 1895 [1885].

Thomson, Susan. 'The Darker Side of Transitional Justice: The Power Dynamics Behind Rwanda's *Gacaca* Courts.' *Africa* 81, no. 3 (August 2011), 373–90.

Throup, David. *Economic and Social Origins of Mau Mau*. London: James Currey, 1988.

Thuku, Harry. *An Autobiography*. Nairobi: Oxford University Press, 1970.

Tomonari, Noboru. *Constructing Subjectivities: Autobiographies in Modern Japan*. Plymouth, U.K.: Lexington Books, 2008.

Trochu, F. *The Cure D'Ars: St. Jean-Marie-Baptiste Vianney*. Rockford, IL: Tan Books, 1977.

Tumusiime, Gershom. 'Impact of Bachwezi Bashomi on Christians: a Case Study of Kwamakanda Church in Uganda, Archdeaconry North-Kigezi Diocese.' Dip. Theo. thesis, Makerere University, 1990.

Turyahikayo-Rugyema, Benoni. 'The Impact of Christianity on the Bakiga of Southwest Uganda: The Revival Movement.' In *Occasional Research Papers*, v. 31, edited by Tom Tuma. Kampala: Department of Religious Studies and Philosophy, Makerere University, 1975.

Twaddle, Michael. 'On Ganda Historiography.' *History in Africa* 1 (1974), 85–100.

Uzoigwe, G. N., ed. *Uganda: The Dilemma of Nationhood*. New York: NOK Publishers, 1982.

'Uganda and Parliamentary Government.' *Journal of Modern African Studies* 21, no. 2 (June 1983), 253–71.

Vail, Leroy, ed. *The Creation of Tribalism in Southern Africa*. Berkeley: University of California Press, 1989.

Vansina, Jan. *Antecedents to Modern Rwanda: The Nyiginya Kingdom*. Madison: University of Wisconsin Press, 2004.

Vaughan, Megan. 'Mr. Mdala Writes to the Governor: Negotiating Colonial Rule in Nyasaland.' *History Workshop Journal* 60, no. 1 (2005), 171–88.

Viswanathan, Gauri. *Outside the Fold: Conversion, Modernity, and Belief*. Princeton: Princeton University Press, 1998.

Vokes, Richard. *Ghosts of Kanungu: Fertility, Secrecy, and Exchange in the Great Lakes of East Africa*. Rochester, NY: James Currey, 2009.

Wachanga, Kahinga. *The Swords of Kirinyaga: the Fight for Land and Freedom*. Nairobi: Kenya Literature Bureau, 1975.

Wairimu, Teresia with Anne Jackson. *A Cactus in the Desert: An Autobiography*. Nairobi: Faith Evangelistic Ministry, 2011.

Walls, Andrew. *The Missionary Movement in Christian History*. Maryknoll, NY: Orbis, 1996.

Walser, Ferdinand. *Luganda Proverbs*. Berlin: Reimer, 1982.

Wamue, Grace Nyatugah. 'Revisiting Our Indigenous Shrines Through Mungiki.' *African Affairs* 100, no. 4 (2001), 453–67.

Wamwere, Koigi wa. *I Refuse to Die: My Journey for Freedom*. New York: Seven Stories Press, 2002.

Wandiiba, Simiyu. *Masinde Muliro: A Biography*. Nairobi: East African Educational Publishers, 1996.

Wanjau, Gakaara wa. *Mĩhĩrĩga ya Agĩkũyũ*. Karatina: Gakaara Press, 1998 [1960].
Mwandĩki wa Mau Mau Ithamĩrio-inĩ. Nairobi: East African Educational Publishers, 1983.
Mau Mau Author in Detention. Nairobi: Heinemann, 1988.

Wanyande, Peter. *Joseph Daniel Otiende*. Nairobi: East African Educational Publishers, 2002.

Wanyoike, E. N. *An African Pastor: The Life and Work of the Rev. Wanyoike Kamawe, 1888–1970*. Nairobi: East African Publishing House, 1974.

Ward, Kevin. 'Obedient Rebels: The Relationship Between the Early "Balokole" and the Church of Uganda: The Mukono Crisis of 1941.' *Journal of Religion in Africa* 19, no. 3 (1989), 194–227.

Ward, Kevin and Emma Wild-Wood, eds. *The East African Revival: History and Legacies*. Kampala: Fountain Publishers, 2010.

Weiss, Brad. *The Making and Unmaking of the Haya Lived World: Consumption, Commodification, and Everyday Practice*. Durham: Duke University Press, 1996.

Welbourn, F. B. *East African Rebels: A Study of Some Independent Churches*. London: SCM Press, 1961.

Welbourn, F. B. and B. A. Ogot. *A Place to Feel at Home: a Study of Two Independent Churches in Western Kenya*. London: Oxford University Press, 1966.

Westgate, T. 'The Home of the Wagogo.' *Church Missionary Gleaner* **XXXCI** (1909).

Whisson, Michael. 'The Journeys of the JoRamogi.' Kampala: East African Institute for Social Research, July 1962.

White, Luise. *The Comforts of Home: Prostitution in Colonial Nairobi*. Chicago: University of Chicago Press, 1990.
Speaking with Vampires: Rumor and History in Colonial Africa. Berkeley: University of California Press, 2000.
'Matrimony and Rebellion: Masculinity in Mau Mau.' In *Men and Masculinities in Modern Africa*, edited by Lisa Lindsay and Stephan Miescher, 177–91. Portsmouth, NH: Heinemann, 2003.

Willis, Justin. '"A Model of its Kind": Representation and Performance in the Sudan Self-Government Election of 1953.' *Journal of Imperial and Commonwealth History* 35, no. 3 (2007), 485–502.

Wilson, Gordon. *Luo Customary Law and Marriage Customs*. Nairobi: Republic of Kenya, 1968.

Wiseman, Edith. *Kikuyu Martyrs*. London: Highway Press, 1958.

Woodson, Dorothy and Derek R. Peterson. 'A Guide to the Yale University Microfilm Collection of the Gakaara wa Wanjau Papers.' Unpublished manuscript, 2007.

Wordsworth, Christopher. *The New Testament of our Lord and Saviour Jesus Christ: In the Original Greek*. London: Rivingtons, 1857.

Wrong, Michela. *It's Our Turn to Eat: The Story of a Kenyan Whistle-Blower*. New York: HarperCollins, 2009.

Wu, Pei-Yu. *The Confucian's Progress: Autobiographical Writings in Traditional China*. Princeton: Princeton University Press, 1990.

Wuodh Jawuoth. Nairobi: Society for the Promotion of Christian Knowledge, 1943.

Index

Books in This Series